Thanos Zartaloudis' *The Birth of Nomos* renovates entirely our understanding of a fundamental term in the history of Western culture. From
this unprecedented book, it becomes clear that we will need to rethink
all of the themes that our ethical and political tradition has gathered
around the word 'Law'.

Giorgio Agamben

Generosity is not a word Zartaloudis explicitly deploys in this remarkable investigation – a veritable *cosmonomy*, to invoke the author's erudite
terminology. And yet, what better way to describe what he does in
The Birth of Nomos, as he genially apportions and distributes, scrupu-
lously gives and grants, deftly dispensing and setting apart the multiple
sources and resources that have nourished, or been fed by, the word
nomos (differentially accented) and its 'family of words'? Throughout,
Zartaloudis reads and roams, disposes, arranges and orders anew
centuries of use, fields of practice and thought (poetry and prophecy, tragedy and philosophy, shepherding and *mousikē*, to name just
a few), engrossing traditions of reading, of performance and conduct,
as well as persistent issues and concepts of manifest currency – and
intense urgency. The outer edges of law (that most common translation of *nomos* from which Zartaloudis knowingly seeks to guard us,
'the danger', he says, 'is, as ever, to miss the point') are traversed and
carefully circumvented, revealed for their still unchartered expanses,
the multifarious forms of life and worlds they are and have been. A
masterful and exemplary, truly creative and generous work.

Gil Anidjar, Columbia University

Writing in the grand tradition of humanistic legal research, *The Birth of
Nomos* proffers an extraordinarily sophisticated and extremely precise
tracking of the European roots of the legal tradition. Contemporary
legal theory defines *nomos* and norm as law and rule. In a meticulously
erudite work of philological and philosophical investigation, *The Birth
of Nomos* patiently and decisively evidences the paucity and inaccuracy
of such designations. Zartaloudis in this scintillatingly original study
traces the plural roots and multiple forms of *nomos* and in doing so
redraws the boundaries of jurisprudence.

Peter Goodrich, Cardozo Law School

Like no one else before, Thanos Zartaloudis has broken through the
complexities of the concept of *nomos* with a tour de force. As incisive
and imaginative as one wants intellectual work to be, *The Birth of Nomos*
bursts even more with stunning philological prowess, poetic invention,
and philosophical ingenuity – a real gem to behold and a treasure to
mine over and over.

Stathis Gourgouris, Columbia University

ENCOUNTERS IN LAW AND PHILOSOPHY
SERIES EDITORS: Thanos Zartaloudis and Anton Schütz

This series interrogates, historically and theoretically, the encounters between philosophy and law. Each volume published takes a unique approach and challenges traditional systemic approaches to law and philosophy. The series is designed to expand the environment for law and thought.

Titles available in the series

STASIS: Civil War as a Political Paradigm
Giorgio Agamben

On the Idea of Potency: Juridical and Theological Roots of the Western Cultural Tradition
Emanuele Castrucci

Political Theology: Demystifying the Universal
Marinos Diamantides and Anton Schütz

The Birth of Nomos
Thanos Zartaloudis

General Advisor
Giorgio Agamben

Advisory Board
Clemens Pornschlegel, Institut für Germanistik, Universität München, Germany
Emmanuele Coccia, École des Hautes Études en Sciences Sociales, France
Jessica Whyte, University of Western Sydney, School of Humanities and Communication Arts, Australia
Peter Goodrich, Cardozo Law School, Yeshiva University, New York, USA
Alain Pottage, London School of Economics, Law School, UK
Justin Clemens, University of Melbourne, Faculty of Arts, Australia
Robert Young, NYU, English, USA
Nathan Moore, Birkbeck College, Law School, University of London, UK
Alexander Murray, English, Queen's University Belfast, UK
Piyel Haldar, Birkbeck College, Law School, University of London, UK
Anne Bottomley, Law School, University of Kent, UK
Oren Ben-Dor, Law School, University of Southampton, UK

edinburghuniversitypress.com/series/enlp

THE BIRTH OF NOMOS

Thanos Zartaloudis

EDINBURGH
University Press

Edinburgh University Press is one of the leading university presses in the UK. We publish academic books and journals in our selected subject areas across the humanities and social sciences, combining cutting-edge scholarship with high editorial and production values to produce academic works of lasting importance. For more information visit our website: edinburghuniversitypress.com

Edinburgh University Press Ltd
The Tun – Holyrood Road
12 (2f) Jackson's Entry
Edinburgh EH8 8PJ

Typeset in 11/13 Palatino by
Servis Filmsetting Ltd, Stockport, Cheshire,
and printed and bound in Great Britain

A CIP record for this book is available from the British Library

ISBN 978 1 4744 4200 8 (hardback)
ISBN 978 1 4744 4202 2 (webready PDF)
ISBN 978 1 4744 4203 9 (epub)

Contents

Contents

Contents

Abbreviations

adesp.	*adespota*
Ael.	Aelianus
V.H.	*Varia Historia*
Ael. Arist.	Aelius Aristides
Or.	*Orationes*
Aes.	Aeschylus
Ag.	*Agamemnon*
Choe.	*Choephoroi*
Eum.	*Eumenides*
Per.	*Persae*
Sept.	*Septem contra Thebas* (*Seven against Thebes*)
Sup.	*Supplices*
Alcm.	Alcman
Andoc.	Andocides
Anth. Pal.	*Anthologia Palatina*
Apol. Rhod.	Apollonius Rhodius
Argo.	*Argonautica*
Arist.	Aristotle
Ath.	*Atheniensium Respublica* (Athenian Constitution)
Eth. Nic.	*Ethica Nicomachea*
GA	*De Generatione Animalium*
Metaph.	*Metaphysics*
Phys.	*Physica*
Per. Lal.	*The Polity of the Lakedaimonians*
Poet.	*Poetics*
Pol.	*Politeia*
Prob.	*Problemata*
Rhet.	*Rhetorica*
Aristoph.	Aristophanes
Av.	*Aves*

Abbreviations

Eq.	*Equites*
Thes.	*Thesmophoriazusae*
Ath.	Athenaeus
Ath. [Bohn]	Athenaeus (1854)
BCH	*Bulletin de Correspondance Hellénique*
Cic.	Cicero
N.D.	*De Natura Deorum*
Clem. Alex.	Clemens Alexandrinus
Strom.	*Stromateis*
Dem.	Demosthenes
Din.	Dinarchus
Diod. Sic.	Diodorus Siculus
Diog. Laert.	Diogenes Laertius
Vit.	*Vitae*
Eur.	Euripides
Alc.	*Alcestis*
Ba.	*Bacchae*
Cycl.	*Cyclops*
El.	*Electra*
He.	*Helena*
Hec.	*Hecuba*
Her.	*Heracles*
IA	*Iphigenia Aulidensis*
IT	*Iphigenia Taurica*
Phoen.	*Phoenissae*
Rh.	*Rhesus*
Eust.	Eustathius
Il.	*Ad Iliadem*
Ex.	*Exodus*
FGrHist.	Jacoby's *Fragmente Der Greichischen Historiker*
fr.	fragment
Hdt.	Herodotus
Her.	Heraclitus
Heraclid. Pont.	Heraclides Ponticus
Protr.	*Protrepticus*
Hes.	Hesiod
Th.	*Theogony*
W.D.	*Works and Days*
Hippocrates	
Art.	*De articulis*

Dent.	*De dentione*
Fract.	*De fracturis*
Moch.	*Mochlicum*
Prorrh.	*Prorrheticus*
Ulc.	*De ulciberus*
Hom.	Homer
Il.	*Iliad*
Od.	*Odyssey*
Hsch.	Hesychius
Hym. to Ap.	*Hymn to Apollo*
Hym. to Aphro.	*Hymn to Aphrodite*
Hym. to Dem.	*Hymn to Demeter*
Hym. to Herm.	*Hymn to Hermes*
Hym. to Ven.	*Hymn to Venus*
Iambl.	Iamblichus
Vit. Pyth.	*Vita Pythagorae*
In de interpr.	*De Interpetatione* (Ammonius)
Inst.	*Institutes* (of Marcian)
Lat.	Latin
Lyc.	Lycurgus
Leoc.	*Against Leocrates*
Matt.	*Matthew*
P. Oxy.	*Oxyrhynchus Papyri*
Parm.	Parmenides
Paus.	Pausanias
PCelt.	Proto-Celtic
PGM	*Greek Magical Papyri*
Phot.	Photius
Bibl.	*Bibliotheca*
Pind.	Pindar
Isthm.	*Isthmean Odes*
N.	*Nemean Odes*
O.	*Olympian Odes*
P.	*Pythian Odes*
Pae.	*Paeanes*
Pl.	Plato
Crat.	*Cratylus*
Criti.	*Critias*
L.	*Laws*
Ph.	*Phaedrus*
Phileb.	*Philebus*

Prot.	*Protagoras*
Rep.	*Republic*
Sym.	*Symposion*
Tht.	*Theaetetus*
Tim.	*Timaeus*
Plut.	Plutarch
Adv. Col.	*Adversus Coloten*
De Pyth.	*De Pythiae Oraculis*
Lyc.	*Lycurgus*
Mor.	*Moralia*
Num.	*Numa*
Phoc.	*Phocion*
Quaes. Conv.	*Quaestiones convivales*
Quaes. Graec.	*Quaestiones Graecae*
Poll. Onom.	*Pollux Onomasticon* (*Thesaurus of Greek terms*)
Porph.	Porphyrius
De abstin.	*De Abstinentia*
Vit. Pyth.	*Vita Pythagorae*
Procl.	Proclus
Chre. Ap.	*Chrestomathia suppleta ex Apollod*
Ps.	pseudo
Ps. Aesch	Pseudo Aeschylus
P.V.	*Prometheus Vinctus*
Ps. Arist.	Pseudo Artistotle
Ps. Plut	Pseudo Plutarch
Mus.	*De Musica*
Schol.	scholiast or *scholia*
Skt.	Sanskrit
Sol.	Solon
Soph.	Sophocles
Aj.	*Ajax*
Ant.	*Antigone*
El.	*Electra*
Ich.	*Ichneutae*
OC	*Oedipus at Colonus*
OT	*Oedipus Tyrant*
Phil.	*Philoctetes*
Stes.	Stesichorus
Stob.	Stobaeus
Ecl.	*Eclogues*
Flor.	*Florilegium*

Strab.	Strabo
Geog.	*Geographica*
s.v.	*sub verbo*
Terp. *test.*	Terpander Testimonies [Gostoli]
Thgn.	Theognis
Thuc.	Thucydides
Xen.	Xenophon
Hell.	*Hellenica*
HG	*Historia Graeca*

Preface
Anthroponomikos

1. The *idea* of *nomos*

At the opening of (Ps.) Plato's *Minos* at 313a, in his dialogue with an unnamed Athenian companion-student (*hetairos*), Socrates asks: ὁ νόμος ἡμῖν τί ἐστιν; ('What, for us, is *nomos*?').[1] The companion responds by asking in turn: τί οὖν ἄλλο νόμος εἴη ἄν, ὦ Σώκρατες, ἀλλ᾽ ἢ τὰ νομιζόμενα; ('What else is *nomos*, Socrates, but the *nomizomena* [νομιζόμενα])?' The *nomizomena*, at this point, may imply whatever is 'recognised' as such, 'believed to be', 'habitually' used, or 'accepted' as *nomos* (and, possibly, what is 'prescribed by *nomos*'; 313b), hence, arguably, indicating a multiplicity of *nómoi* (plural of *nómos*). An issue, at first sight, with the companion's preliminary answer in the form of a question is its self-referential character. Socrates responds by telling him that, if that is the case, then (for the companion) '*logos*' must analogically be 'what is said', 'sight' must be 'what is seen' and 'hearing' 'what is heard'; and then he asks: 'or is it that *logos* is distinct from what is said, sight from what is seen and hearing from what is heard?' (313b–c). A related issue that is implied in the dialogue is the uncertain sense of the *nomizomena* and, by extension, of *nómos* itself, given that *nómos* can range widely from, for instance, a sense of habit, use and opinion through to custom, norm or 'law', among more besides – as

---

[1] Later in the dialogue, the oldest (divine) *nómoi* are named as those practised in Crete, which the Greeks, in general, are said to use. In addition, the oldest law-giver king is named and praised: Minos. The authorship of the dialogue remains disputed; on Ps. Plato's *Minos*, see, indicatively: Strauss (1987); Cobb (1998); Rowe (2000); Lewis (2006); and Lindberg (2007).

will be seen later. What may appear as an early (too early) self-referential juridical inquiry and, for the companion, with particular emphasis on a *nómos* that is 'posited', is, instead, for Socrates, at least in part, a focusing of attention on the multiplicity that characterises the uses of the word *nómos* and its family of words (i.e. the *nomizomena*). Indeed, it is this multiplicity of uses that Socrates appears to presume in order to evoke his eventual definition of *nómos*.

In this study, I examine in some detail the uses of the term *nómos*, as well as those of the *nomizomena* (from the verb νομίζω, *nomizō*), but it is worth noting provisionally that the *nomizomena* can refer to a 'traditional or accepted way or view' (of living or doing something), in which sense there is some proximity to – though non-identification with – *ēthos* ('habit or custom'). Equally, the wide range of uses that *nómos* can refer to is, in fact, indicated by Socrates when he later mentions medical, agricultural, gardening, cooking and political (administration) *nómoi* (316c–b) along with 'the *nómoi* of *mousikē*', the '*nómoi* of the gymnast' and those of 'the shepherd' (317e–18a). All of which could be said to be related, more or less, to an act of 'distribution-sharing' or 'arrangement' (for example, the way a gymnast 'distributes' the parts of the body).[2] Crucially, the act of 'distribution' is not metaphoric in these examples, and we therefore need to listen to occurrences of these archaic (and classical) uses in their everyday – concrete – sense(s).

It could be that, at the start of the dialogue, there is already discernible an etymological inquiry into the word *nómos*. However, there is more to it than etymology (or, rather, there is more to etymology than we commonly appreciate).[3] For Socrates, *nómos* and the *nomizomena* are quite distinct, even if in some sense also related. It could be said that their relation-

---

[2] Such width may also be implied by the fact that the word ἄνομος (*a-nomos*), which signifies, to some extent, the opposite of *nomos*, or, better, its lack (in the sense of 'inhumanness', 'disregard of sacred social norms/customs'), is only encountered once in Hesiod (*Th.* 307) and can then be observed from the fifth century BC onwards. For a survey of its uses, see Orrù (1985).

[3] See the discussion in Cobb (1988: 203, n. 4). See also, crucially, the rethinking of 'etymology' in Pl. *Crat.*

ship is, in fact, a dynamic (*dunamis*) one.[4] In what sense is this so? Later in the dialogue, Socrates states that the question that needs to be asked is: in what way does *nómos* become known? Is it an experience akin to the way in which an *epistēmē* 'discovers' things (or the way medical practice 'discerns' what is 'healthy' and what is not) or, alternatively, is it similar to what the seer 'determines' as regards what the gods 'think', given that each *technē* (if *nómos* is one)[5] aims at the εὕρεσίς (*heuresis*, 'discovery') of what is true (314b)?

Socrates' companion responds to this by stating that, for him, *nómos* is, in fact, the ψηφίσματα (*psēphismata*) and the δόγματα (*dogmata*) of the polis; effectively defining *nómos* as the *doxa* and the *dogma* of the polis (314b–c). Socrates, however, challenges this definition and claims that *nómos* is not ultimately a matter of *doxa*, or the *dogma* of the polis, but that, instead, its *dunamis* lies in the 'revelation' of the true (ἀληθής, *alēthēs*) and good *doxa*; the 'highest' *doxa* that it is, in fact, preferable to 'use' (χρηστή; *chrēstē*; 314e). Thus, Socrates defines *nómos* as follows: ὁ νόμος ἄρα βούλεται τοῦ ὄντος εἶναι ἐξεύρεσις ('*nómos* desires to be the revelation/discovery of what is', namely 'the truth of being'; 315a).[6]

It is important to note that the word used to describe what one does with a *nómos* is the verb to 'use' (*chrēsis*).[7] It is in the use of a *nómos* that a *nómos* is revealed to be good or not good in the first place. Thus, in this sense, it could be said that 'use' is the experiential plateau in which what is ('the truth of being') can be revealed or found. In this manner, the *idea* (ἰδέα from ἰδεῖν, *idein*: 'to see'; εἶδος, *eidos*: 'form') of *nómos* is the experience of its use(s). It is possible therefore to speculate from the outset that the experiential 'form' of a *nómos* is

---

[4] See Cobb (1988: 203, n. 5), who describes this as a 'function' or 'capacity'. It is worth noting that all the examples of *nómos* that the companion refers to in the dialogue are related to 'rituals' (i.e. sacrifices, burials, and so forth).

[5] It is not clear whether this is a proximate reference to a *technē*, such as the *technē nomothetikē* defined in Arist. *Eth. Nic.* 1180bff.

[6] The emphatic ἐξ-εύρεσις [*ex-heuresis*], 'out of invention' or 'discovery' but also 'finding', is a classical use, prevalent in Plato. See also the distinction with διάθεσις (*diathesis*) in *Ph.* 236a.

[7] On the most compelling philosophical genealogy of *chrēsis* that I presuppose here, see Agamben (2016a).

a *dunamis* (power) as distinct from what is 'held' (actualised) as a *nómos* (the *nomizomena*) in each instance. 'Transcendent' to the actuality of this or that *nómos*, however, is only the *dunamis* (or potentiality) of *nómos*, which does not lie outside of its actuality, but rather is immanent in its use(s).[8] In the dialogues, this peculiar 'desiring' *nómos* is, in part, personified in Socrates' definition, since *nómos* lies within the very uses of the mortals. Its form, in this manner, is inseparable from 'living' or 'using'. It is in this sense that I refer to it as the *idea* or experience of the *anthroponomikos*.

Nómos is, in a philosophical sense, simultaneously the unpresupposable (ἀνυπόθετον; *anhupotheton*) of the *Republic* (510b): that is, the *idea* (even though in the *Minos* the *idea* is never mentioned as such). What is revealed in and by a *nómos* is the appearance of 'what is', and this 'searching out' or 'discovery' (ἐξ-εύρεσις, *ex-heuresis*) takes place each time according to the *dunamis* of *nómos* to indicate the intelligibility or potentiality (the *idea*) of 'what is'. In this reading, the *idea* is, crucially, not another intelligibility or reality, but the potency (the experience of intelligibility) of 'what is' – 'truth' or the 'good', the 'arrangement', and in this sense 'distribution', or use of things. The Platonic *anamnēsis*, in this way, does not turn towards a 'transcendent' past or to a separate world of the *Ideas* in order to locate 'true being', but to the appearance (the power of 'arrangement' or 'distribution') of what appears – *its idea, which is its nómos.*[9]

2. *Pré-droit*

With regard to the classical period, Karl-Joachim Hölkeskamp writes:

> The general framework of notions and concepts applied to the history of early Greek law is to a great extent extrapolated from the sophisticated classical (and modem) ideas on law, justice and their origins, which are themselves the

---

[8] On potentiality and the reading of Aristotle's *dunamis* that I presuppose here, see Agamben (1999a: part III).

[9] I borrow this particular philosophical understanding of the *'Idea'* from Agamben (1995).

result of a long historical process. Consequently, such a framework cannot provide a satisfactory instrument to conceptualize and explain the specific 'pre-' and 'proto-legal' conditions and the concrete social, institutional and intellectual impulses which set the process in motion in the first place and determined its direction – the process in the course of which, in a long series of small steps, a differentiated set of legislative institutions and procedures of law-making and also a sophisticated idea of law as the basic principle of life in the polis came into being and eventually evolved into later, more complex forms. (1992a: 59–60)

Without directly being concerned with 'sophisticated Greek law' in this study, or, in fact, with the classical period, Hölkeskamp's critique applies to the way in which archaic 'foundations' for/of Greek 'law'[10] are identified, as well as, more generally, to how the word '*nómos*' is to be understood in the midst of its polyvalent forms and uses, which, in fact, do not lend themselves to universal definitions, or presuppositions of some self-evident sense of 'law'; an 'idea of law' into which frequently, as in Hölkeskamp, *nómos* is presumed to 'eventually' or 'naturally' 'evolve'. Instead of examining the particular and relatively well-known developments during the classical age and the specific reforms with regard to 'law-making', in this study I focus on the polyvalent duality of *nómos and nomós* (two words and their families) in the preceding centuries. The intelligibility of such an inevitably (in part) speculative cognition of what

---

[10] On Greek law(s) in its/their various forms and periods of 'development' the literature is constantly proliferating, as well as renewing its methodologies and interdisciplinary approaches. See, for instance, Gernet (1917; 1938; [1955] 1979; [1968] 1982; in English in 1981); Wolff (1946); Jaeger ([1947] 1960); Jones (1956); MacDowell (1978); Cantarella (1979; 1994); Biscardi (1982; 1999); Garner (1987); Cohen (1989; 1995); Todd (1992); Foxhall and Lewis (1996); Thomas (1996); Thür (1996; 2003); Hölkeskamp (1999); Hunter and Edmondson (2001); Papakonstantinou (2002; 2004; 2008); Harris and Rubinstein (2004); Gagarin and Cohen (2005); Martini (2005); Harris (2006); Lanni (2006); Stolfi (2006); and Lewis (2007). On writing and law, see, indicatively, Hölkeskamp (1992a; 1992b; 1999; 2002); Camassa (1988; 1996; 2011b); Thomas (1996); Faraguna (2007); Gagarin (2008); and Hawke (2011).

can be called 'the uses of *nomos*' during the archaic period becomes ever more difficult to discern when the language of many interpreters itself appears to be already 'juridified'.[11] In the Western (juridical) modality of cognition, it seems that 'always-already' the terms used to describe what predates the so-called juridical forms and actions are those of the juridical (or, rather, fictional or magical) *dis/juncture* between word and action and, more widely, the perennial juridico-philosophical enigma of the *dis/juncture* between 'language' and 'reality'.[12]

In *Droit et société dans la Grèce ancienne*, the seminal philologist and sociologist Louis Gernet (1882–1962) defines *pré-droit* (pre-law) in relation to archaic 'law' as follows:

> Before coming to constitute an independent technique, law is pre-moulded in certain traditional procedures in which gestures and *verba* have a force that one cannot yet call juridical, as they lack specialization of time and space, personnel, and means of operation. Their meaning and effects, however, are analogous to those that would make themselves in actual law. ([1955] 1979: 2)[13]

Hence, the Homeric 'pre-juridical' milieu is characterised by a certain binding reciprocity, intense ritualisation, the sacred process of the oath and a collective or 'public' nature of 'pre-juridical' action, all of which are marked by a certain effective

---

[11] For engaging introductions to the history of the archaic age, see, for instance, Snodgrass (1980); Murray (1993); Hall (2006); and Osborne ([1996] 2009).

[12] In this regard, the work of the one of the most important legal historians and thinkers, Yan Thomas, in particular relation to the Roman tradition, remains paradigmatic. See, for instance, Thomas (2011; 2015). However, archaic (or classical) Greek 'law' should not be read through the lens of the Roman tradition.

[13] It is worth noting that Gernet presumes, to an extent, that the 'meaning and effects' of the 'pre-law' means are analogous to 'legal' ones ([1948–9] 1951: 21–119); this should be read in conjunction with *Le temps dans les formes archaïques du droit* (1956: 379–406); see, further, Gernet (1917) and, handily, the later anthology ([1968] 1982) that contains reprints of the earlier-mentioned works. Finally, for a brief introduction to Gernet's work in English, see Humphreys (1971) and Taddei (2000; 2001).

performativity (ultimately of 'law').[14] Above all, the archaic period is characterised, for Gernet, in this regard, by the indiscernibility of 'religion-magic' and 'law'. Thus, in *Droit et pré-droit en Grèce ancienne*, Gernet writes:

> The symbols of pre-law are essentially effective: the hand that gives or receives; the staff that asserts power or relinquishes it or confers it; the imprecatory speech, the gesture or posture equivalent to imprecation ... everything that acts immediately and in virtue of its own *dunamis* [power]. ([1948–9] 1951: 104)

In Gernet there persists, however, a liminal sense of a process of transformation from 'pre-legal' rites to more 'abstract' or elaborate forms of (legal) action and decision; a pre-legal ritual-language (different means) that transforms into a legal language (same effects). The difficulty of such 'translation' lies in the inherent deposition and transposition of any language by the language that performs its description as such. In a different context but to similar effect, the Polish anthropologist Bronislaw Malinowski, who founded the 'anthropology of law', wrote in the early 1920s: 'In looking for "law" and legal forces, we shall try merely to discover and analyse all the rules conceived and acted upon as binding forces, and to classify the rules according to the manner in which they are made valid' (1926: 15). A similar intention, but still predetermining the process of discovery or translation of the 'pre-legal' on 'rules', can be observed in the 'binding forces' and the process of 'validating' them; a self-evidently, even if sensitively, juridical model of cognition. It is, of course, undeniably complex to write of ancient cultures and practices, but the attempt is rendered ever more cumbersome when what is said to precede the 'legal' is already marked by it, which could be called – recalling Lucien Lévy-Bruhl's term ([1910] 1960) – the subjection to the 'frontier' *of* law.

Michel Foucault, in turn, seems to take for granted Gernet's notion of 'pre-law' in, for instance, the *Leçons sur la volonté de savoir* ([1970–1] 2011), in which he adopts Gernet's

---

[14] See Cantarella (1979; 1987; 1994).

'pre-juridical' description of the Homeric oral tradition in order to develop, among other matters, a genealogy of judgment and *krisis* (ibid. 171). Foucault is concerned only in part with the late archaic and mostly with the classical period as to the 'democratisation' of the so-called 'legal process', with particular regard to the ritualisations of 'popular religions' (such as, crucially, for him, the cult of Dionysus; ibid. 163–6).[15] Proximate to Foucault's work, Giorgio Agamben in *The Signature of All Things – On Method* (2009) turns to Gernet's distinction between the 'pre-legal' and the 'legal', in order to highlight the caution required in the drawing of such a distinction in the first place. Agamben proposes that when such a distinction is made, using the terms 'law' and 'religion' (even while considering them to be indistinct), and in order to describe what pre-dates 'law' and/or 'religion', it is best to avoid the antecedent terms and instead explicitly mark what lies 'before' as an 'unknown X': 'In such cases, one must take care not merely to project upon the presupposed "primordial instinct" [Prodi 1992] the characteristics defining the religious and political spheres known to us, which are precisely the outcome of the split [e.g. between 'law and religion']' (2009: 5; my comments). What lies before the 'law', as we (re)cognise it,[16] is not a 'more ancient law'; similarly, what lies before 'religion' is not some 'more primitive religion' (ibid.). When, instead, we proceed according to the presumption of an 'unknown X', our archaeological markers must suspend the pre-emptive marking of predicates that 'we commonly ascribe to religion and law' (ibid.). It would, thus, be misleading, for my purposes, to consider this 'transformation' or 'development' as, for example, some kind of progressive movement from a so-called *nomocracy* to a *democracy*, or from *physiocracy* to *nomothesis*. It would be equally misplaced to suppose that the Greeks at some point lifted the veil of 'religious' rites and found underneath it the autonomous and liberating 'secular' law-giving of the polis or, lastly, to presume the 'developmental' transposition of cognition from

---

[15] See also Foucault ([1970–1] 2011: 143–60; 2014, Lectures: 10–11) for the developments with regard to *nomos* and *nomisma*.
[16] Although 'our' own (re)cognition of 'law' is anything but simple or universal.

the obscurity of (oral) poems to the lucidity of (written) law and prose (including that of Plato's 'philosopher-king').

3. Preliminary linguistic aspects

Consequently, it is important to observe in some detail the uses of the verb *nemein* and its family of words (including *nómos*) in the extant literary evidence amidst the poets and the early philosophers during the (late geometric and) archaic age (c. 900–480 BC; notably, with some reference to earlier elements and some retrospective references to archaic uses as met in the classical age, 480–323 BC). To do so, I shall juxtapose untranslated all the key terms as I attempt to pinpoint their interpreted uses as tightly as possible, as well as pointing out the indistinguishability of commonly understood separable domains – for instance, 'religion', 'law', 'culture' and 'poetry'. The aim is to allow the singularity and complexity of the rich literary material to evoke an affirmatively inconclusive line of questioning.

This study is, in one sense, about two words, or rather a family (or two) of words. By its nature, it is inevitably a fragmented juxtaposition (rather than a mapping) of the uses of the words *nómos* and *nomós* and the family of words to which they belong, subject to a number of evidentiary and other limitations. In another respect, this study is about the *idea* of the words *nómos/nomós*: that is, about their uses, which cannot be separated from the word(s) and vice versa. We can call this method, if it is one, a genealogy, if we agree that words do not have 'core' meanings, but rather uses (and that these uses cannot be distinguished from the existence in which they are experienced). At least for us, in contrast perhaps to the experience of the ancients, some of the uses of the word(s) that will be examined in this study may be, at first, surprising (at least to non-specialists), and some will have to remain so, given that it is not possible to establish some kind of 'historical causation' among them with any certainty. Yet we can at least hold to one premise: the words *nómos and nomós*, in their numerous uses, are (among other places) prevalent in the normalcy-setting and *ēthos*-transmitting Greek poetry and thought from at least Hesiod onwards, while their experiential milieux stretch, presumably, much further back.

The second hypothesis is that in the most ancient literary sources the words *nómos and nomós* mean many things other than 'law' (and for the most part they do not mean 'law' at all). As is quite well-known, there were many words to signify 'norms' or 'rules' in ancient Greece, but prior to the classical period there is no word (let alone 'concept') that signifies what we generally appear to understand in the modern sense(s) of 'law'. It is, thus, highly problematic, as will be seen, to even refer to what precedes this 'law' with equally modern (legal) terms such as 'customary law', 'natural law', 'divine law' and so forth. It is doubtful that we will ever come to a conclusion as to how a few hundreds of years of use of the families of the words in question, through no apparent linear 'development' or 'progress', 'led' to (also) a sense of 'law' that would simply be added to *nomos*, before it also came to denote specifically 'written law', more explicitly during the classical period. It can be noted, for instance, that written 'laws' or 'norms' had already appeared by the mid-seventh century BC (Thomas 1996), but we have no evidence of the term *nómos* being used to describe them (Hölkeskamp 1992b).[17] My approach is not that of a search for a strict definition or justification, in any case. I shall, instead, note the persistent, overlapping and renewed uses of the words in question in what forms a broad spectrum of experiences on the basis of the extant literary (and predominantly poetic) sources that act as relative evidence in the absence of other indications, while situating these uses to the extent possible within the social milieux in which they occur.

Notably, while some are more exuberant than others in their compositions (for example, Pindar), the poets, as much as the early philosophers, express themselves, to a significant extent, in the everyday language of their audience, thus providing some relative insight into their use(s) of vocabulary in the archaic polis, and perhaps beyond. The most extensive study of the linguistic history of the uses of *nomos* and its family of words remains that of Emmanuel Laroche (1914–91), who was director of studies at the *École Pratique des Hautes Études* between 1954 and 1982 and whose work

---

[17] See Faraguna (2007).

forms a seminal starting point for this study. For this reason, it is useful to summarise some of the parameters that Laroche elaborates for the study of the words in question in his *Histoire de la racine νεμ- en grec ancien* (1949). Laroche analyses the root *nem-* across linguistic levels (Homeric, post-Homeric), epochs ('primitive', archaic, classic, Hellenistic) and dialects (Attic, *koinē*, Ionian), without losing sight of the predominantly oral transmission of tradition(s), as well as the later, arguably significant, impact of writing and of an increasingly complex formation and re-formation of the polis.[18]

From a morphological perspective, Laroche examines the Indo-European root **nem* and identifies three relatively distinct series that characterise the structure of the root, which is for him 'the degree zero': the Homeric νεμ- (*nem-*), νεμε- (*neme-*) and νεμη- (*nemē-*) (1949: 53). It is worth noting that grammarians have indicated two Indo-European roots: **nem1* and **nem2*. First, there is the root **nem1* from which, in Greek, we derive the verb νέμω (*nemō*) meaning 'to assign', or 'to allot' (Laroche: 'to distribute'), but not 'to take' (**nim*), or 'to divide'. At this point it is worth stressing that the verb *nemein* entails such a wide semantic variation that the question of its root cannot be definitively clarified (Frisk 2: 302). Second, the root **nem2* appears to be unrelated to *nemein* in that it is understood to signify 'to bend' and, for some, appears to be linked to **nemos* ('wooded pasture, glade, grove'). The latter is an unclear hypothesis (later rejected, for instance, by Émile Benveniste) which is largely determined through non-Greek sources (Sanskrit *námati* 'bow, bend'; Proto-Celtic **nem-eto-* 'sacred grove, sanctuary'; and Lat. *nemus*, 'sacred grove' or 'holy wood').[19]

More importantly, according to linguists, from the root **nem*, in Greek there derive two verbs. For Laroche, the most ancient and persistent meaning of the verb *nemein* (νέμω, *nemō*) and νωμάω (*nōmaō*), along with a wide family of words, is that of a certain kind of 'distribution': that is, the concrete act of 'distributing', in the sense of 'allotting' parts or 'dealing

---

[18] See, for instance, Nieddu (1982); Havelock (1986); Harris (1989); Powell (1989: 321–50); Wachter (1989); Thomas (1992; 1995b); and Svenbro (1993).

[19] I return to this in Chapter Three.

out'. As is evident in the Homeric uses that I examine in some detail, a most prevalent use of *nemein* (in the active mode) is the concrete action of a 'ritual' distribution-sharing of food to guests at a feast following a 'sacrifice'.[20] In this case, we can test a key hypothesis that a/the primary milieu within which the verb's uses are expressed is that of 'ritual' worship (or, as it is often described in the literature, anachronistically, while for modern convenience, 'religion'),[21] and this may be markedly so if such a 'ritual distribution-sharing' can be said to remain constant in Greek antiquity. While, with good reason, Laroche holds to this semantic line, it remains hard, if not impossible, to establish with absolute certainty which particular sense or use among many is primary (chronologically, morphologically and semantically). In addition, while the uses under examination are intimately linked to concrete actions, this does not mean that rich metaphoric, and in some sense 'abstract', uses are not coexistent subject to poetic invention and popular use and frequency. In fact, this is so to such an extent that the sense of the distribution of μοῖρα (*moira*, 'fate', 'portion', 'destiny'), as will be seen later, as well as the uses of νέμεσις (*nemesis*), all relate, to one extent or another, to the intimate family of words and uses of *nemein*.[22]

Along with the above-mentioned senses, we also meet a variety of 'pastoral' uses of νέμω (*nemō*), whether directly or proximately. For Laroche, some of these uses are secondary (for example, in relation to *nemesis*), but one (pastoral) sense of the verb is indicated already in the passive mode of the ancient νέμομαι (*nemomai*). Whether there are, in fact, not one but two separate semantic branches (*nem-* and *nom-*) remains in dispute (Beekes 1885), but the connections are close enough to indicate a relative (though distinct to some extent) development of the uses. While Laroche is critical of pastoral derivations in the sense of an 'allotment' or 'distribution of *moirai*' (plural μοῖραι), or 'lots' of land, the varied uses may be relatively close semantically, as well as historically. That the 'pastoral' sense of *nemō* is located within the passive

---

[20] I examine these in more detail in Chapter One.
[21] *Nomos* as a personified deity can be seen in the Orphic *Hymn to Nomos*, as 'worshipped and sung'; see Athanassakis and Wolkow (2013).
[22] See Chapter Five.

mode *nemomai* may be in itself instructive, since it later attains the signification of a certain sense of 'enjoyment', 'holding', 'possessing' in the wider, but concrete, plateau of 'living, inhabiting and occupying'. For my purposes, however, it is not a question of strictly separating 'domains' of different uses, or unfeasibly insisting on strict distinctions between the concrete and the more 'abstract'.

The whole history of the uses in question is, from the start, subject to multiplication, extension, 'abstraction' or metaphoric – and more generally, predominantly, poetic – uses. Indeed, this is also the case for Laroche who maintains that the 'centre of gravity' is that of the act of 'distribution' or 'dealing out', while admitting that there remains constant alteration amidst the relevant uses and, in particular, within a language (in its numerous dialects) that is particularly dynamic, localised and fluid. We shall see how the verb *nemō* will acquire the sense of 'to dominate', 'to be a master', in the poets in particular, and how a seed for a sense of 'government' ('management, administration') becomes available quite early on, before it becomes popular with the orators and the philosophers of the classical period. As with the function of *nomaō* (i.e. 'to handle'), *nemō* comes to signify 'power' ('possessing', 'being the master of') which is linked to the milieu of worship. Yet when so used, it is still the power of a certain act of distribution (in agreement with Laroche) that is implied and, even in later times, the ancient sense is hardly eclipsed. It is in the classical and Hellenistic usage(s) that the notion of 'administration' or 'management' will become more pronounced and will also take the forms of common composites (such as the *oikonomos* and *oikonomia*). Yet whatever the case, as we shall see, these uses will be prevalent in poetry and beyond, and thus not limited, for instance, to a 'juridico-political' domain (I observe this in particular in relation to Pindar and some of the tragedians – especially, Aeschylus).

In addition, it is hard to know whether the pastoral senses of 'to graze', 'to live' and 'to inhabit' develop as early as some of the other uses that are more directly linked to the acts of different kinds of 'ritual distribution-sharing', or not. Yet some relationship between them appears plausible on many occasions, and this may be further due to the complex derivations that take place in the transition from the active to the passive mode (or in fact the elimination, in some instances, of the passive mode entirely, as in the Attic). After all, some related proximate sense of 'living' or 'inhabiting' is already present in Homer. The different, but linked, uses need to be noted further, in relation to how – in different regions and amidst different dialects – certain uses prevail over others. For instance, in the Attic, as Laroche showed, a sense of ritual distribution-sharing remains evident in later references to the earlier Homeric uses; meanwhile, other uses are not as frequent in the presence of new practices of administration, such as the development of uniform practices of 'inheritance' and so forth (1949: 25).

Next to the act of 'distribution-sharing', we also meet a varied 'pastoral' use, as in 'to graze' (in the active) and 'grazing' (i.e. animals, in the passive, though with metaphoric uses also as to humans). The two are perhaps separable while clearly remaining in some proximity (or at least, enough so for the poets to articulate it). Furthermore, the extension of the particular pastoral sense to mean 'to devour' will also be evident in the use by Hippocrates in medical practice (and perhaps earlier too). In addition, early on, some degree of 'abstraction' extends the uses of the *nemō* family of words to a certain sense of 'opinion', 'recognition', 'belief', 'classification', 'ordering', 'thinking' and so forth (notably with regard to the uses of *nomizō*). Later, though it seems not before the fifth century BC, it may also be linked to *nomisma* ('currency', in a political sense).[23]

The 'development' of the said uses is not, as I have already noted, linear or progressive. For example, some of these uses will be viewed as archaisms during the classical period, while others may flourish further. Nor are the uses restricted within the verbal forms and their immediate derivations. A rich range of composites evidences a complex extension of uses to signify, for instance, 'association', 'adaptation', 'observation' and so forth. Philosophers will play a significant role in the varied uses in question, starting, as far we know, with

---

[23] See Arist. *Pol.* 1257 b11 and *Eth. Nic.* 1133a30; Laroche (1949: 234–8); and Seaford (2004).

Heraclitus;[24] but also including later philosophers – to whom I will refer occasionally, such as in relation to the remarkable fact that Aristotle will define 'justice' (*dikaiosunē*) as a 'distributive disposition' (for example, in *Eth. Nic.* 1130b30), and Plato, who links a 'distributive' sense between mathematics, music and the polis, as well as coupling νωμῶ (*nōmō*) to σκοπῶ (*skopō*, one of the 'visual senses') in the *Cratylus* (at 411d), which in fact connects, henceforth, the *nemein* family with σκέψις (*skepsis*) and φρόνησις (*phronēsis*).

For Laroche, the dual semantic roots of the family of words in question are summarised in the act of distribution-sharing and the sense of the pastoral. While this may indeed indicate an isolated group with a different root (*nom*-; Beekes 1885), Laroche accepts that they are both early and linked, while – in time – they are reinterpreted, whether towards semantic limitation or expansion. In this regard, the most famous of the *nemein* family of words is precisely a key matter of interest: *nómos*. In fact, while some legal historians (and not only them) are often misled when they simply consider *nómos* as in the sense of *nómos*-'law', the starting point towards a preliminary clarification, in the field of (ancient) legal history, is the archaic coexistence of not one but two *nomos* words (later differentiated by accent – oxytone and paroxytone – and uses).[25] As Laroche has shown (1949: 116–17), it is likely that it is the oxytone *nomós* (νομός) that was 'primary', indicating at its root pasturage in an unlimited space (i.e. in undivided land), thus not falling under the semantic root of an act of 'distribution-sharing', or at least not directly in the sense of 'parts' or 'shares'. In addition, the symbiotic word νομή (*nomē*) may be a good illustration of the way in which *nomē* is part of 'habitable land' (with a local emphasis) and

---

[24] See Chapter Seven.

[25] The terms used by the Greeks for these accents are ὀξύς (*hoxus*, sharp, rising) and βαρύς (*barus*, 'heavy, falling'); these are different in kind, but the Greeks did not necessarily consider words marked by either as opposites. The marking of the accent, the τάσις (*tasis*, 'stretching'), is musical (see Pl. *Rep.* 349e); and see, further, the analysis by Davis (2006). The accentuation I use here to mark them is: *nómos* and *nomós*. It is worthwhile noting that the early Greeks did not use diacritics. It should finally be noted that in the rendering of the phonetic transliteration of the ancient Greek texts I have omitted the indication of the other accents.

only much later an 'administrative province' (a sense, in fact, that can still be met with in modern Greek). It is, however, presumed that, early on, *nomós* does not designate anything other than a pasture for animals, or a habitat without limits for human beings (Laroche 1949: 119, n. 18).

In the later 'juridico-political' sense(s), it is perhaps possible that the earlier senses get mixed up in their uses by philosophers and orators, in particular, although possibly the earliest sense, for Laroche, remains that of an act of distribution (without a sense of formal appropriation or a 'juridical', or other, sense of uniform or equal 'division'). The particular function of the Νόμιος (*Nomios*), already so in Homer as we shall see, is pastoral-worship-related and not 'juridical', like that of the νομεύς (*nomeus*, shepherd). It is much later, in the poets and the philosophers, that these will be likened to the *basileus*, or tyrant, as in the iconic expression of the 'shepherd of the people', arguably fusing the two senses of 'to graze' and 'to distribute' ('power'; 1949: 119).[26] When we encounter, furthermore, the late derivation in Plato's *Politeia* (266e) of the ἀνθρωπονομικός (*anthrōponomikos*), it contains a connotation of a 'right' and 'just' partition, in the sense of 'distribution-sharing', that yet still links with the ancient uses, even though it has by the fourth and fifth centuries BC become a philosophical and poetic extension that is not met in the long history of the uses examined in this study. Νομός, νομή, νομεύς [*nomós, nomē, nomeus*], then, but also νομάς (*nomas*; including a sense of the 'nomad'), share a (perhaps pastoral) sense in common from early on, and it is only in the later Attic that a semantic and rhetorical relation to the family of *nemō* (in the sense of 'distribution', 'dealing out') is explicitly expressed. These two key senses of the verb *nemō*, arguably, coexist. However, I shall question the extent to which they are proximate in their use(s) when observing how the early Greeks raised this question themselves. If some speculation can be afforded, a working hypothesis would be that it appears that there is a wide variety of uses wherein the family of the *nemein* words relates in some sense to an allocated way of life or being, a way of acting properly and enjoying or using things or 'oneself'.

---

[26] Perhaps this is where a trace of the later shift from 'being a power' (*dunamis*) to 'having a power' takes place, too.

Now, for Laroche, the sense of the paroxytone *nómos*-'law' (νόμος) is secondary, though significant in the classical period in particular. The suggestion that *nómos*-'law' is directly derived from the sense of 'distribution' is not necessarily convincing or specific enough in terms of the complex historical, morphological and semantic 'evolution' of the word it presumes (1949: 164). Yet it may be possible to articulate and speculate some such link. Nonetheless, it is important first to distinguish this use of *nómos*-'law' (whatever sense of 'law' is meant in such uses) from the other much earlier attested uses and related 'legal' words that belong to a certain 'worship–political' milieu.[27] One such is *rhētra* (ῥήτρα; the 'pronouncement aloud'), which signifies a verbal convention that is associated with 'law-making'. Another is *thesmos* (θεσμός), arguably from the root τίθημι (*tithēmi*, 'what is set'), with wide variation in the Dorian, Locrian and Boeotian τεθμός (*tethmos*), Locrian τετθμός (*tet-thmos*) and Tegean θεθμός (*thethmos*). This is the name that, for example, the 'laws' of two famous early 'law-givers', Dracon and Solon, will take, while at the same time the term has a complex history that exceeds the archaic period. Yet another is the orally transmitted customary and divinely ordained pronouncement of Θέμις (*Themis*) (Vos 1956). *Themis*, already found in Homer (and prevalent later among the tragedians), can be interpreted as indicating 'divine ordinances', a 'ritualised' social function, setting 'rules or conventions' among mortals (Giraudeau 1984: 40–1).[28] *Themis* and *themistes* are broad terms, in any case, that encompass 'customs, norms, formal authorisations' and so forth. In addition, with the word *dikē* the early Greeks arguably eventually thought of a practice of 'justice' or 'judgment' (Gagarin 1974; Havelock 1978),[29] though this is a complex notion that deserves its own study with regard to its complex ancient uses. Suffice to say that *dikē*, in the archaic period, remains a 'divine function',

---

[27] See Hirzel (1907); Latte (1946); and Gehrke (2000: 145–6).

[28] A separate work will be devoted to the long history of the term *themis*, with special regard to its Homeric and pre-Homeric past. The complex *nomos–themis–dikē* needs to be re-examined as an indiscernible theophysic experience.

[29] See the recent study by Pelloso (2012b).

though it can also signify 'convention', a 'usage' without, however, a necessarily 'universal normative value' attached to it.[30]

Irrespective of the above, it would be misleading to suggest that we have clear evidence as to exactly how all these words (and more) were used and how they related to each other to the extent that they may have done so (a situation not assisted perhaps by the telling fact that among the poets these terms are often used without much distinction: for example, *thesmia, nómoi* and *nomima* appear often as related or inter-changeable). Nor do we have – at least not yet – an absolutely convincing explanation as to how, in prose in particular, and in political practice, *nómos*, as it is commonly argued, 'takes

---

[30] It is important to note that in the archaic age, which most concerns this study, there is neither lack of 'law', in the sense of 'formal' and 'informal' ways in which norms are set and are considered binding, nor 'processes' through which disputes are settled. Yet my position regarding the earlier uses of *nómos* and the *nemein* family is similar to that regarding other archaic terms employed in polyvalent ways. While it is understandable that scholars will use modern legal terms to translate or situate the archaic uses, more often than not it is misleading to do so. It is considered apt to refer to these terms with regard to a relatively flexible sense of 'norms, social perceptions and practices, ordering paradigms, enunciations of authority' and so forth, rather than 'laws' or 'legal systems'. This is not to suggest, however, that my hesitation is here in alignment with that of Gagarin (1986), who adopts a largely formalist understanding of 'law' and instead generally hesitates to recognise 'legalities' or, in my terms, 'norms' at any time before the 'fully "legal" stage of development' (ibid. 8–10; for a critique of Gagarin's thesis, see Thomas 1992; 1995b; 2005). In any event, it could be agreed that, early on, the milieux within which norms were set and challenged were, above all, a highly contested social field that was the polis itself, and some of this polyvalence and 'adaptability' continues all the way into the classical period and beyond. For a recent general introduction, see Papakonstantinou (2008), who, it should be noted, opts for the term 'legal narratives' instead of the more open-ended 'norms' that I adopt in this study; in addition, his understanding of such 'narratives' is based, though with some calibration, on the paradigms in cultural legal studies of 'legality' or 'legal consciousness', akin to that of 'legalities' among legal pluralists (ibid. 143–4, n. 50). Papakonstantinou provides, further, a good summary of the emergence of written enactments of norms or 'laws' during the archaic period and of communal 'courts', 'magistrates', 'judges', 'legal records' and 'civic officers'; see especially chs 3 and 4. For an early, schematic, though incomplete, outline of the uses of the words *nomos*, see McCullagh (1939).

the place' of *thesmos* during the classical period (for example, in Hdt. 3.31, although this question cannot be explored in any substantial sense in this study).

Finally, I should note the sense of the term 'ordering' as it is used in this work to suggest, at times, an affinity with *nómos* and *nomós* and their families of words, which is particularly difficult to specify. Unless otherwise indicated, I use it in the sense of a practical arrangement without a necessarily strict framework. This is especially crucial in the context of the two key words that signify some kind of 'order' and 'ordering' at different periods: the late Attic word τάξις (*taxis*), which one meets famously in Aristotle; and the older and more, or at least equally, complex sense of 'ordering' in the Homeric κόσμος, κοσμέω (*kosmos, kosmeō*). Before it is associated with the 'command' of an ordering, or, in fact, with *taxis* (since it is later seen as synonymous), *kosmos* appears within a wide spectrum of uses, which, early on, are adjacent to the sense of an 'arrangement' in what I call a *cosmopoietic* sense. At first, it is not 'political', 'aesthetic' or 'moral', but experiential or 'practical'. This sense is, in fact, sometimes linked to *nomos* with regard to the word *eunomia/-ēn* (εὐνομίην).[31] As will be seen, understanding what *eunomia* means is, itself, not straightforward. Linked to aristocratic politics, a sense that survives all the way to Pindar and beyond, it is later affiliated with democracy (as well as oligarchy) and often referred to along with the classical *isonomia* (Ehrenberg 1940; [1946] 1965), though it should not be confused with it.[32] Early on, it is a social notion, a 'value' as to the ordering of the polis, but its etymology (and use) remains unclear.[33] Laroche, for instance, notes that the etymology linking *eunomia* to εὖ νέμειν (*eu nemein*) and εὖ νέμεσθαι (*eu nemesthai*; with a sense of 'management, ordering or government') is a later derivation from the sixth century BC, while others, in contrast, find its early Homeric usage to be evidence of the 'earliest' reference to a *nómos*-'law' when there may, in fact, be no such sense to its

---

[31] On *eunomia*, see Andrewes (1938); Ehrenberg ([1946] 1965); and Ostwald (1969: 62ff).

[32] See Vlastos (1953).

[33] See Cartledge (1998); Finkelberg (1998a); and the earlier comprehensive study by Kerschensteiner (1962).

uses. The paroxytone *nómos* is most probably, as I observe below, not met with in Homer, yet is met with in Hesiod. The question remains: in what sense(s) is this so? While concrete actions are at the heart of the earlier uses, it may be admissible that the breadth of such a variety of uses provided a fertile ground for some kind of non-diacritic differentiation (for example, from 'a way to doing something' to a 'song'). In light of the available evidence, there may be sufficient ground to suggest that *nemō* as a pastoral verb, that signifies the 'ritual' act of distribution-sharing, is pre-Homeric (or, at least, Homeric), while the more 'abstract' uses may, indeed, be post-Homeric.

According to Felix Heinimann's seminal study, there are two key transitive meanings: 'to distribute', 'to allocate' and 'to graze' ([1945] 1965/1972: 60), which, from early on, do not have any distinct 'political or juridical' sense(s) attached to them. For instance, it remains possible that the deviant sense of a fire 'distributing' itself, expressed early on with *nemō*, or later the 'distribution' of an 'encroaching' ulcer may indicate the lack of a strict normative sense, but instead point to a descriptive-factual sense, at least in the majority of relevant uses. It may also be the case that in the passive use of the word (and its family) it no longer signifies the action of the verb, but the separable 'result' of the action; as, for example, in the oxytone *nomós*, the 'result' being the allocated living space (Heinimann [1945] 1965/1972: 61). For Heinimann (but also for others, including most emphatically Benveniste), there is a certain 'binding' value to the use of *nemein* at all times. Yet how are we to think of such a sense of 'binding authority'? For Heinimann, one thing is clear: such an 'authority' is not 'external' ([1945] 1965/1972: 65). Further clues towards an answer to this question will be forthcoming in this study.

As Laroche argues, from a 'historical perspective' the three words νομός, νομή and νόμος [*nomós, nomē, nómos*] may have the same root in common, while in the early ancient texts they are fairly autonomous semantic units. Max Pohlenz, who (in contrast to Laroche) supports to an extent the 'evolutionary perspective', has shown that the different formations of the (concrete) oxytone and paroxytone *nomos* are generally accepted ([1948] 1965: 139) along the lines of similar formations in the comparable couples τροχός/τρόχος (*trochós/tróchos*), φόρος/φορός (*phóros/phorós*), τρόπος/τροπός (*trópos/tropós*), ὅλκος/ὁλκός (*ólkos/olkós*). Yet as he observes, it is 'rare that the Greek forms two distinctly emphasized verbal substances of the same root' (ibid.), while at the same time a certain line of uses leads from one word to the other (ibid. 140). The rich and complex uses of the Greek by the poets and the early philosophers perhaps gives rise to the expansion of the uses of the relevant words, including at times uses that are in direct or implicit reflection of their more ancient derivations. But this is not a linear, let alone a self-evident, 'succession or progression'. Even in music (in the particular sense of *mousikē*) where *nómos* – as will be seen in Chapter Ten – finds a remarkable use, the sense of a 'formal rule' is, in fact, later and in some uses highlighted as 'technical'. While a relation to the 'juridical-political' sense can be ventured, it is not present, early on, in the emphatic terms in which, for example, Plato will famously render *nómos* in the classical period.

A further complexity concerns the senses of 'tradition' and 'convention' – or, more commonly, 'custom' (though as Laroche indicates, care is needed as to how 'custom' is to be understood; 1949: 172). This concern relates initially to 'ritual' acts and later to more 'abstract' principles of arrangement and allocation along with extensive 'moral' and 'political' connotations that appear to be quite prevalent in the most ancient sources.[34] For many scholars, in fact, the 'originary' sense is that of 'customary uses or practices'. For instance, for Heinimann, binding *nómoi*-customs ([1945] 1965/1972: 67) as well as, later on (post-Hesiod), non-mandatory customs are ubiquitous (ibid. 72). It is, then, worth questioning in what sense the term 'custom' is designated in such observations and with particular regard to the nature of its supposed 'binding character'. 'Law', even in modernity, does not have the monopoly of an obligatory-binding sense, nor is the

---

[34] It is particularly problematic to separate 'custom' from the so-called 'legal' uses of *nómos* early on, whether through an 'evolutionary' or a related perspective. Herodotus remains the richest source for the variety of the uses of *nómos* in relation to customs or ways of living, but this merits a dedicated work. All of the key uses, however, are largely engaged with in this study, to one extent or another, on the basis of earlier sources.

'legal norm' the only norm-setting power (even if the former remains quite distinctively formed). Thus, it is, perhaps, possible to understand early 'custom' as to what was 'used' in an empirical sense (and one undifferentiated from the doxastic-local sense).

It is not until the classical period that a pronounced differentiation between the doxastic and the physiological will become the subject of the well-known contrast between *nómos* and *phūsis* (with interest also as to the way in which the related word *nomizō* will be transformed to declare a 'subjective opinion/human artifice', in some contrast to earlier uses; Heinimann [1945] 1965/1972: 76). For Ulrich von Wilamowitz-Moellendorff (1962: 96), *nómos*-custom implies a certain sense of 'ordering'; and Werner Jaeger ([1947] 1960) agrees with the sense of *nómos*-custom as the 'oldest sense'. It is worth asking how much an anachronistic sense of 'custom' is prevalent in some of these interpretations, especially to the extent that this sense is held as a presupposition for the completion of a 'long process' that 'leads to law' (well expressed in Shipp 1978: 6).[35] An evident barrier to such evolutionary approaches, whether admitted or implied, remains the coexistence of many different uses, as they will be gradually encountered in this study. For instance, *nómos*-custom, whether wider or localised, continues to be prevalent in Herodotus' later 'ethnographic' account (Giraudeau 1984). The only constant may be the polymorphous concern of the Greeks over the 'arrangement' of associative living, long before, say, the *nómos basileus* ('*nómos* king') of Pindar and the *nómos despotēs* ('rule of law') of Demaratus (Hdt. 7.104.4–5).

Martin Ostwald (1969), in his classic and still essential study, arrives at relatively similar conclusions to Laroche by following, however, a semantic (rather than an etymological) method of analysis. I will therefore examine to what extent

---

[35] For an introduction to the 'development' of early Greek law, see Gagarin (2005; 2008); though note, once more, that Gagarin's parameters for what counts as 'law' are quite narrow (1986: 7). In addition, his speculation remains that there was far more widespread 'legislation' during the archaic period than is commonly accepted; compare Hirzel (1907); Ehrenberg (1921); Heinimann ([1945] 1965/1972); Ostwald (1969); de Romilly (1971); Giraudeau (1984); and Hölkeskamp (2000).

the sense of 'distribution' in question, as Ostwald suggests, concerns a distribution that is being made each time 'in an authoritative fashion': that is, in a way that is considered/ accepted as 'valid' (i.e. a norm). This is, in fact, the point of criticism that Ostwald raises as to the largely etymological analysis of Benveniste, who, according to Ostwald, disregards the 'fact' that the distribution is done not from the point of view of 'the agent', but from that of the 'accepted norm' (1969: 10). It seems that Ostwald may miss, however, a key point of Benveniste's analysis in *Le Vocabulaire des institutions indo-européennes, 1: Économie, parenté, société*, which is not to disregard that 'fact', but rather to examine its fundamental component: that is, the ritual (for Benveniste) performance of the act of 'distribution', an act which, in this sense, establishes a norm as such. According to Benveniste, etymologically the *nemein* family signifies 'legal'/'regular distribution' or 'sharing out' (in contrast to Laroche's emphasis on distribution as such); a 'sharing out' that is not enacted by arbitrary decision, but by 'law' or 'custom'.[36] He also explains, in this way, the oxytone *nomós* as a 'sharing out of pasture land' according to customary 'law'. Thus, *nemō* does not mean 'to take', but 'to distribute according to law', a 'legal apportionment'. In the light of my study, it may be the case that Benveniste summons the family of words to the 'law' too early and too widely, forming a premature 'self-sufficient circuit'. But the question remains: was this how the uses of these words were experienced early on?

Ostwald confirms that there is no precursor to *nomos* in the pre-archaic Linear B. For him, the word *nómos*, from the start, is characterised as an order of some kind: that is, a norm that is valid in a given situation (1969: 20). I would add that this, in a general sense, appears to be evident, if by a 'norm' we understand not a formal normativity (of law), but what I call an *ethological* ordering that is valid in (and only because of) a particular situation or milieu. Ostwald, in his study, presents at least thirteen different uses of *nomos*, ranging from an 'order or way of life' to 'a way in which something is to

---

[36] Benveniste stresses this point further in *Noms d'agent et noms d'action en indo-européen*: 'partager légalement, faire une attribution régulière' ([1948/1975] 1993: 79).

be done', 'a belief or custom', a 'ritual process' or the 'mores of a group' and, of course, certainly in the classical period, some kind of 'law', although, in any case, without *nómos* ever meaning exclusively 'law' (ibid. 20–54). While very useful in one sense, any such listing may also mislead one to expect a rather abstract or schematised range of uses that are ahistorically available (of which Ostwald is, of course, aware). Hence, it is necessary to attempt, to the extent possible, an intimate situating of the uses in their milieux of experience while letting the multiplicity of uses and their intersections speak, in a sense, for themselves.

For the exceptional linguist Pierre Chantraine (1899–1974) (director of Greek Philology studies at the *École Pratique des Hautes Études* in Paris), the semantic range is first concrete and later more abstract, while the root of *nemō* is ambivalent, ranging from 'to make a regular allocation' to 'to assign', 'to deal out' and 'to allot portions' (1968–2009).[37] For Chantraine, the earliest milieu for the uses of the verb *nemō* is, in fact, agriculture and food, where the dealing out of portions is performed according to custom or rite. An appropriate distribution of pastures for breeding and the sense of 'inhabitation' are also noted as already prevalent early on. Yet when *nómos* begins to have a slightly clearer sense of a 'rule', it may be in the musical sense of a certain kind of *nómos* that precedes the so-called legal sense in the seventh century BC (a hypothesis which I examine in more detail in the last chapter of this study).

The British archaeologist John L. Myres, incidentally, argued similarly, though he denied the presence of the use of 'custom/norm' in the Homeric period ([1927] 1969: 151). The question of the so-called 'norm or ordering principle' is, perhaps, a rather intransigent notion to 'apply' to the early Greek context in a time when, as Myres noted, the so-called norm or order of human life coheres with the order of *phusis* and, in turn, with that of the divinely protected order of the whole (ibid. 154). The 'source' is divine *phusis*, in a sense, albeit clearly through an understanding of *phusis* that is not yet that of the famous antithesis between *nómos* and *phusis*

[37] See Vincenti (2007).

in the classical period.[38] Early on, the way of life ('custom', *ēthos*) is not separable from *phusis* or the divine, similarly to the way in which *ēthos* initially is associated with the concrete acts of living in one's haunts, long before it will be thought of as entailing principles of wider application (as in a modern understanding of 'ethics'; Havelock 1963: 62–3). However, 'ethics' perhaps finds implicitly its root in the way in which, for instance, Aristotle confirms (in the *Eth. Nic.* 11, 1152a30f) that habit or *ēthos* is 'unnatural' (*ou kata phusin*), but a 'secondary nature', that is, a 'human artifice', while earlier *ethēa* (abode) and *ēthos* (local way of life, habit) do not have a wider 'moral' or 'psychological' content (Arist. *De Mundo* 398b32).[39]

According to the invaluable study of the German classical scholar Rudolf Hirzel (who at some point cohabited with Gottlob Frege) at the start of the twentieth century, in contrast to Laroche, the sense of *nómos*-custom is quite prevalent prior to the fifth century BC. For him, the starting point is 'tradition' or 'convention' (of a certain kind), which is not far from the sense of *ēthos* and habit – a way of living or of doing things, though in a quite concrete sense. In the 'beginning', for Hirzel, there was 'custom' (and a sense of 'customary law'; 1907: 365–6). But, as he notes, this 'law' is not exactly a 'law' at all for it describes the 'divine ordinances' of the *themistes*, who are initially 'judges', and also the *thesmoi* that were prevalent in the sixth and seventh centuries BC. It does not relate to a regulatory sense, but rather is a way of acting, a way of behaviour, or living, more generally. This sense is always expressed in the particular milieu in which it applies and remains self-explanatory: that it is, in other words, in the '*phusis*' of this or that to be in this way (*nómos*) or that (ibid. 367). That is to say, it is the *nómos* of the 'thing' or the milieu, not the *nómos* of the subject, that 'commands or rules'. A power that *is*; not a power that is 'had'. When we meet the first 'commands', in this sense, they are not of the 'individual subject', but of the gods or of the common situation (which, in any case, cannot be easily distinguished).

---

[38] On the *nómos–phusis* contrast, see, indicatively, Heinimann ([1945] 1965/1972); Guthrie (1969); McKirahan (1994: ch. 19); and Hoffmann (1997). On *phusis*, see Naddaf (2006).

[39] On *ethēa* and *ēthos*, see Schwartz (1951).

For this reason too, it will once more be necessary to extricate the uses of not one but two words (*nómos* and *nomós*). It is only much later that *nómos* will entail, conceivably, the sense of a coercive 'command', as seen in Plato and Aristotle (*Sym.* 182b and *Eth. Nic.* 10, 1180a21, respectively). When *nómos*-'law' emerges most vividly in the classical period, but perhaps in some sense earlier too, it will tellingly interrupt, at least to an extent, the old 'customs or habits',[40] not so dissimilarly, perhaps, to the way in which the old 'customs' or *nómoi* will, in Hesiod, be emphatically opposed to 'violence' (*bia*). In other words, some sense of 'custom', or, better, 'forms of life or ways of life', is present in the sense of 'distribution-sharing or arrangement' which the crucial family of *nemein* appears to have expressed from early on in a variety of ways. Initially, the concrete sense may be that of the use (*chrēsis*)[41] of a 'rule', rather than one of the 'application of an external authority or principle' or some kind of 'law'.[42] The early *nómos* is, perhaps, in a modern sense, an 'objective' rule or ordering, but it is not separable from the life to which it applies. It is not a form that can be distinguished from the living that it 'commands'. So impossible is it to separate life from its 'rule' that the 'rule' is believed to have pre-existed the polis or more widely the *kosmos*, or to have been immanent in it from 'time immemorial'.[43] Such, then, is the problem with approaching the untranslatable.

The early Greeks were neither 'naturalists' nor 'positivists', neither 'religious' nor 'secular'. If, earlier on, *nómos* meant 'law' in any sense, then it was in the sense, perhaps, of a 'binding norm' in a quite general manner, which for centuries remained oral, divine and only later was associated with the [ἄγραφα] *agraphos nómos* that would be thought of as common to peoples outside of one's local milieu (as Antigone most famously refers to it).[44] Thus, it remains misleading to say that 'originally' 'law' simply means 'distribution', 'appro-

---

[40] See Hirzel (1907: 371); as regards the classical period see, for example, the discussion in Por. *De asbstin.* 4, 22.

[41] See, generally, Agamben (2016a).

[42] On the latter, see Ehrenberg (1921).

[43] See Pelloso (2012a: 60, n. 175).

[44] See Pl. *Nom.* 3.680a; and Arist. *Rhet.* 1373b4–6.

priation', 'division' and so on, and equally so to say that *nómos* is 'originally' 'political', 'juridical', 'religious' and so forth. As already noted, most probably the ancients did not call their 'laws' *nómoi* before the fifth century BC (Hölkeskamp 1999: 44–59; Avilés 2010) and, when they did so, what they meant is subject to ongoing debate.[45] Nor should one call this *nómos* a somewhat philosophical 'Law of law' (as, in some sense, Carl Schmitt does by implication), using the very term that does not apply to *nómos* in order to simultaneously explain it as if it were its 'outside' (as he does in *Der Nomos der Erde* [*The Nomos of the Earth*], 1974). There was no evolution from 'custom' to 'law' (Camassa 2011a: 471), but there was neither 'law from the start' (Shipp 1978) nor law from 'early on' (Camassa 2011a; 2011b). Perhaps the use is present in the sixth century BC, as Giorgio Camassa argues, but is the right term for it the quite modern monolithic and unifying term 'law'? The use(s) of *nomos*-'law' may have taken place as a result of a political-economic situation, which probably had to do (though this remains speculative) with the complex events that connect the long period of the expansion of the territory of the Greek polis (between the earlier extensive

[45] Ostwald advances the thesis, since then widely repeated, that the term *nómos* signifies 'law', most evidently late in the sixth or fifth century BC, when it 'replaces' *thesmos*. Yet the 'break' that he seems to advocate is not without doubt. While I will not examine this question in this work, a key point that the literature makes clear and that I shall maintain is that the ancients were fully aware of the multiplicity of the uses in question, as well as of the intersections between them; see Borecký (1971). Furthermore, Quass (1971) suggested that *nómos* may not be the earliest term to replace *thesmos*, but rather *psēphisma*. See also the valuable study by Jones (1956). As Humphreys has noted, the earliest inscription to use *nómos* in relation to a (written) 'law', crucially perhaps with regard to a 'religious' matter, is a decree dated 418/7 BC (*IG* I³, 84.25) (1988: 217). For Humphreys, with good reason, *nómos* appears to indicate – throughout the centuries – something that has long been held to be so within a particular milieu, and that cannot be reformed easily (ibid.). Papakonstantinou offers, in his way, an adjustment to Ostwald's view as to the 'replacement', when he writes (2008: 135): 'Overall, it is far more probable that any changes in legal terminology, and especially in the use of *thesmos* and *nomos*, in archaic and classical Athens were effected over long periods of usage and emerged as a result of, and not in conjunction with, pivotal moments of legislative and constitutional change (e.g. Solon and Cleisthenes).'

'colonisation' and the so-called 'radical democracy' of the fourth century BC). Camassa is partly inspired for his view by the earlier expression of dissent by George Pelham Shipp, for whom *nemein* and its family entail a sense of 'division', with particular regard to the arrangement and settlement of 'colonial' lands (Shipp even compares it to the common-law notion of 'radical title'; 1978: 5). In this manner, *nómos* becomes, in a juridical sense, the 'measure' that 'divides the land' (ibid. 12). Yet Shipp's view of a *nómos* that is completely and rather suddenly redefined during the 'colonial' experience (i.e. in *Magna Grecia*), in a way which remains juridical and 'entirely secular', appears perhaps a bit far-fetched, if not insufficiently supported (ibid. 17). It should be further noted that, for Shipp, *nómos* already means 'written law' in the eighth or seventh century BC. In some contrast, in this study, I hold as an equal, if not earlier, possible contender for the supposed 'earliest' milieu of *nemein-nómos* that of 'sacrificial (feast) ritual', rather than 'land distribution/division' (following the earliest, so far as I know, use of the term *nómos*, in Hesiod's fr. 322 [MW]).

In the classical period, *nómos* will convey the idea, among other uses, of both the 'custom' that is based on a convention (or the gods) and, eventually, the *nómos*-'law' that is established by a formal decision creating an obligatory norm (Pohlenz [1948] 1965), but this will take place through a polymorphous conflict with the old that will transform, if not generate, the use of *nómos* as the *dogma* of the polis (δόγμα πόλεως; Pl. *Minos* 314c, 415b), yet without eliminating other uses. Before then, *nomos* appears more proximate to the practices of a particular way of life, a proto-regular form of life (Pohlenz [1948] 1965: 138), a particular 'movement' in doing things, rather than a 'state' or a 'law'. A partly speculative sense, then, of a way of doing something, a living-rule, a certain ordering, can, at least to an extent, be derived from one of the most ancient literary sources in the act of distributing-sharing, allotting or arranging. I shall maintain then that it is particularly reductionist (and in some respects anachronistic) to consider *nómos* to be semantically or etymologically derived from, or leading to, an exclusive or linear sense of 'law'. In addition, what is designated as 'law' (including, crucially, what 'precedes' it), in itself broadly conceived, calls attention to the complexity and multi-threadedness of the uses of the family of words in question (as well as to the multiplicity of other words that designate aspects of 'custom', 'ordering', 'rule' and 'law-making' which already coexist in a rather complex manner during the archaic period). Ultimately, we can, perhaps, project that the experiential senses of the word, the *nómos*-'ritual' act (way, rule of action, rite) and the pastoral uses, as well as the relatively 'abstract', or, better, wider sense of ordering (convention, custom, arrangement, way of rule and political administration, 'law' or government), are genuinely 'Greek' experiences of *nómos* that coexist and co-depend on each other (allowing for contradiction, as much as contingent, or otherwise, tuning).

It is significant too, for my purposes, that the Greek 'ordering' (earlier: *kosmos*) is, in a sense, practical, situational *and* holistic (Hölkeskamp 2000: 76). For Hölkeskamp, the ordering co-ordinates two senses of the term – a 'factual' and a 'normative' one – but, in any case, the crucial aspect is their interrelatedness or inseparability. This will become further evident in this study, given that the different levels of practices indicated with the *nemein* family of words are coexisting uses, and this will also be seen to be so as to the uses of *nómos* (ibid. 77). It is crucial to appreciate, then, that 'fact' and 'right' are not separable here, or at least not in the way in which we are accustomed to discern them. Perhaps later, when the new – albeit even then not to be assimilated to the modern – sense of 'law' is added to *nómos*, *nómos* institutes a new form for the 'relation', or better, arrangement in the life of 'norms'. Still, this new, relatively 'technical', significance (more 'political' than 'juridical', which in any case were also not rigidly separated) would remain one among multiple coeval uses of the words in question.

To Emilie and Rémi

Part One

Homeric Nomos

One

The Nomos of Feasts and 'Sacrifices'

οὐδ' ὑμῖν ποταμός περ ἐΰρροος ἀργυροδίνης
ἀρκέσει, ᾧ δὴ δηθὰ πολέας ἱερεύετε ταύρους.
Hom. Il. 21.130–2[1]

ἀλλ' ἄγε δὴ καὶ νῶϊ μεδώμεθα, δῖε γεραιέ,
σίτου·
Hom. Il. 24.619–20[2]

1. Distribution-sharing

In Plato's *Protagoras*, Protagoras, in response to Socrates, recounts through a fable the creation of mortal creatures and their 'distribution' (utilising the verb *nemein*) of power (*dunamis*) by Prometheus and Epimetheus:[3]

προσέταξαν Προμηθεῖ καὶ Ἐπιμηθεῖ κοσμῆσαί τε καὶ νεῖμαι δυνάμεις ἑκάστοις ὡς πρέπει. Προμηθέα δὲ παραιτεῖται Ἐπιμηθεὺς αὐτὸς νεῖμαι, 'νείμαντος δέ μου',

[1] 'Not even your silver-whirling, mighty-tiding river I can save you, not for all the bulls you have "sacrificed" to it for years.' I would like to thank the anonymous reviewers, Dimitris Karabelas, Gil Anidjar, Stathis Gourgouris, Evi Gorogianni, Nick Piška, Peter Fitzpatrick, William Watkin, Jan-Patrick Oppermann, Evangelos Kyriakidis, Peter Goodrich, Eleonora Rocconi, Poulheria Kyriakou and, especially, Anton Schütz and Giorgio Agamben for their friendliness and their encouraging reading of the whole or parts of the study in earlier drafts. I would also like to thank Giorgio Camassa, Eleonora Rocconi, Poulheria Kyriakou and Krystyna Bartol for kindly sharing their work with me. Finally, I would like to thank the editors Marie Selwood, Eddie Clark and Michael Ayton for the generous advice and patient corrections.
[2] 'Come then, we too, old king, we must think of food.'
[3] See *Prot.* 320c–d.

Homeric Nomos

ἔφη, 'ἐπίσκεψαι': καὶ οὕτω πείσας νέμει. νέμων δὲ τοῖς
μὲν ἰσχὺν ἄνευ τάχους προσῆπτεν, τοὺς δ᾽ ἀσθενεστέρους
τάχει ἐκόσμει: τοὺς δὲ ὥπλιζε, τοῖς δ᾽ ἄοπλον διδοὺς
φύσιν ἄλλην τιν᾽ αὐτοῖς ἐμηχανᾶτο δύναμιν εἰς σωτηρίαν.
ἃ μὲν γὰρ αὐτῶν σμικρότητι ἤμπισχεν, πτηνὸν φυγὴν ἢ
κατάγειον οἴκησιν ἔνεμεν: ἃ δὲ ηὖξε μεγέθει, τῷδε αὐτῷ
αὐτὰ ἔσῳζεν: καὶ τἆλλα οὕτως ἐπανισῶν ἔνεμεν.

In translation, the passage can be rendered as follows:

> They [the gods] charged Prometheus and Epimetheus
> to allot [*neimai*] to each their proper *dunameis* [powers].
> Epimetheus besought Prometheus that he undertake the
> allotment [*neimai*] himself; 'And when I have assigned'
> [*neimantos*], he said, 'you shall examine' and having per-
> suaded him so, he allotted. In allotting [*nemōn*] he attached
> strength without speed to some, while the weaker ones he
> provided with speed; and some he armed, while granting
> to others who were unarmed, another *dunamis* for their
> preservation. To those which he invested with smallness
> he allotted [*enemen*] a winged escape or a habitat under the
> earth; and those which he increased in size he preserved
> by this very means; and he dealt all other [*dunameis*]
> according to symmetry.[4]

In the literary evidence (in this case, in Homer), long before
this use of the verb to describe the distribution of powers, one
of the earliest, if not the earliest, uses of the verb appears to
have entailed the essential matter of the 'ritual'[5] distribution-
sharing of meat (often at a feast).[6] No occasion was said to be
more enjoyable than a feast (*Od.* 9.5–11). A feast was, among
other things, an occasion when collective decisions were made
among distinguished chiefs and social status was formed or

---

[4] Throughout this study all translations are mine unless otherwise
indicated.
[5] On the caution needed in using the term 'ritual' in the archaic context,
see, for instance, Hitch (2009: chs 1 and 2).
[6] It should be noted that the consumption of meat for the Greeks is neither
frequent nor daily.

'negotiated'.[7] Thus, the verb νέμω (*nemō*; to 'distribute', 'dispense', 'deal out') is used regularly in the epics to indicate the act of distribution-sharing (namely, of bread, wine, a 'sacrificial' victim's hair and so forth) among participants in predominantly 'ritualised' feasts as well as in equally joyous sacrifices.[8] Thus, the fabled distributor, Prometheus, in a famous scene in Hesiod's *Theogony* (507–616), is described as distributing meat and attempting to deceive Zeus by granting him the thigh bones wrapped in fat, behaviour which was considered to be inappropriate.[9]

I turn then to examine, below, the milieu within which the verb *nemō* and its family of words, as well as other related words, are often utilised in this regard. It is useful, first, to summarise from the outset the particular uses of *nemō* and its cognates in this sphere of action. *Nemō* in the particular milieu of feasts and sacrifices appears to have a fairly standard use regarding the manner of 'distributing', 'dealing out', 'dispensing' food, wine and sacrificial parts in shared, 'ritualised' practices. Hence, in the common manner of such distribution-sharing, *nemō* can be observed in the following main uses:

1. In the distribution-sharing, giving out, of bread or barley, as in, for instance, *Od.* 14.449: σῖτον δέ σφιν ἔνειμε [*eneime*] Μεσαύλιος.

2. In the distribution-sharing of wine and drinking vessels with an implicit or explicit sense of receiving or assigning one's portion, in, for instance, *Od.* 8.470, where the

---

[7] In the Homeric epics 'sacrifices' are at times described as collective actions, for instance, in *Od.* 3.5–9.

[8] The distinction between a feast and a 'sacrifice' is not to be collapsed (Dietrich 1988: 36; and, generally, 1965). Neither, however, should the distinction be maintained in (for the ancients) meaningless terms of (e.g.) 'secular' and 'religious' purposes. Feasts can take place, thus, with some 'ritual' elements present while not being a 'sacrifice', and some killings/'sacrifices' can take place that are not followed by a feast. On 'sacrifices' and feasts, see Säflund (1980); Rudhardt and Reverdin (1981); Burkert ([1972] 1983); Dietrich 1988; Schmitt-Pantel (1990, 1992); Kitts (2002); Hermary et al. (2004); and Hägg and Alroth (2005). The most recent detailed study on Homeric 'sacrifices' is by Hitch (2009); for a comparison with the classical period, see, for instance, Rosivach (1994).

[9] See Meuli (1975: 907–1021); Vernant (1989).

wine is dealt out or dispensed: οἱ δ' ἤδη μοίρας τ' ἔνεμον [*enemon*] κερόωντό τε οἶνον; or, similarly, in *Od.* 7.179 and 13.50, where wine is distributed to all the participants: Ποντόνοε, κρητῆρα κερασσάμενος μέθυ νεῖμον [*neimon*] πᾶσιν ἀνὰ μέγαρον, ἵνα καὶ Διὶ τερπικεραύνῳ. Drinking vessels are distributed among the participants in a feast, for example, in *Od.* 10.357: ἡδὺν ἐν ἀργυρέῳ, νέμε [*neme*] δὲ χρύσεια κύπελλα; and in *Il.* 1.471: νώμησαν [*nōmēsan*] δ' ἄρα πᾶσιν ἐπαρξάμενοι δεπάεσσιν. The particular importance of vessels, κύπελλα (*kupella*) or δέπα (*depa*), can be shown by the fact that they are ritual elements as such within a feast or sacrifice and are also customarily provided as gifts to a guest, someone who is being honoured, or a friend (for example, *Il.* 6.220; 23.741–8).

3. In the distribution-sharing of meat, which, as we shall see, is of central importance in feasts and sacrificial rituals and which is often described as a 'dealing out', a 'giving' or 'offering' to the participants. For example, *Od.* 14.436: Θῆκεν ἐπευξάμενος, τὰς δ' ἄλλας νεῖμεν [*neimen*] ἑκάστῳ. In this verse, it is worth noting that the act of distribution is quickly followed in the next verse by the division and sharing out that is expressed by the term διηνεκέεσσι (*diēnekeessi*; 437); while in two verses prior to 436 one can also observe the similar use of διεμοιρᾶτο δαΐζων (*diemoirato daizōn*; *dais*; 434) to signify a division or distribution.[10] The acts of division and distribution are of course practically connected. However, while they intersect in the particular acts in question (and beyond, as we shall see later in this study, as, for instance, with regard to the particular uses of *dais*, as well as of *moira*), they remain semantically separate and so the verb *nemō* should not be confused with the act of dividing. Another characteristic example of meat distribution within a 'ritual' context is found in *Il.* 9.217: καλοῖς ἐν κανέοισιν, ἀτὰρ κρέα νεῖμεν [*neimen*] Ἀχιλλεύς (and similarly in *Il.* 24.626). The special case of the dealing out of the inward parts of the sacrificial or slaughtered animal, for the purposes of a feast, is encountered in *Od.* 20.252–3: σπλάγχνα δ' ἄρ' ὀπτήσαντες

---

[10] On *dais* and the distribution of meat, see Donlan (1993: 163–4); and Schmitt-Pantel (1990: 22; and, generally, 1992).

ἐνώμων [enōmōn], ἐν δέ τε οἶνον | κρητῆρσιν κερόωντο· κύπελλα δὲ νεῖμε [neime] συβώτης. Here, the handing out of the innards (σπλάγχνα, *splagchna*) is followed by the distribution of drinking vessels and wine. As will be observed later, the dealing out of the innards (namely, the heart, lungs, liver, kidneys, and so on) served a distinguished component of the 'ritual' in Homeric sacrifices, since these parts were reserved to be eaten by the participants at the start of the feast that followed.[11]

4. In the distribution of the hair of a sacrificial animal between the Achaian and the Trojan elites, as described in *Il.* 3.274: κήρυκες Τρώων καὶ Ἀχαιῶν νεῖμαν [neiman] ἀρίστοις.

5. We also find the composite form of ἐπινέμω (ἐπι-νέμω, *epi-nemō*) that is used with the same sense of 'to distribute' or 'deal out' among a company. Bread is distributed in this manner in *Il.* 9.216: Πάτροκλος μὲν σῖτον ἑλὼν ἐπένειμε [epeneime] τραπέζῃ (where Patroclus brings bread and distributes it to the table). Comparably, in *Od.* 20.254: σῖτον δέ σφ᾽ ἐπένειμε [epeneime] Φιλοίτιος, ὄρχαμος ἀνδρῶν.

6. In the practice of distributing equal portions in feasts, which is frequently noted in the poems. For instance, in *Od.* 11.185, at the shared tables (of portions/feasts): Τηλέμαχος τεμένεα νέμεται [nemetai] καὶ δαῖτας ἐΐσας.

7. We also meet the use of the verb νωμάω [nōmaō] in equivalent uses with regard to 'serving out', 'handing out' and actions akin to these in ritualised practices, as is evident in the following formulaic expressions: in *Il.* 9.176: νώμησαν [nōmēsan] δ᾽ ἄρα πᾶσιν ἐπαρξάμενοι δεπάεσσιν; in *Od.* 3.340: νώμησαν [nōmēsan] δ᾽ ἄρα πᾶσιν ἐπαρξάμενοι δεπάεσσι (and, similarly, in *Od.* 7.183–4; 13.54; 18.425; 21.272). This use is also observed in the famous 'handling' of the two-eared cup of gold by Odysseus in *Od.* 22.10, χρύσεον ἄμφωτον, καὶ δὴ μετὰ χερσὶν ἐνώμα [enōma],

---

[11] The *splagchna* are, for instance, consumed by the suitors, though improperly, in *Od.* 20.252; see, further, Seaford (1994: 30). On the 'distribution/division' of animal parts, more generally, see Hermary (2004: 118–20). On the parts reserved for the gods, see van Straten (1988; 1995); on the relation to social structuring, see van Wees (1995).

7

where a sense of 'enjoyment' or 'possession' may also be implied.

8. Lastly, we encounter (only once) the verb *nemō* in the middle voice form of νεμέθω [*nemethō*], in the sense of 'to distribute among themselves', and with an implication of 'holding or possessing' one's assigned portion or share, in *Il.* 11.635, with particular reference to birds eating their food: πελειάδες νεμέθοντο [*nemethonto*].

In these key exemplary instances, the sense of distribution or dispensing and, in this manner, of a 'sharing out', in the concrete practice of feasts in particular, appears to be both commonplace and, at least in part, 'ritualised'.

2. Feasts

In more ways than one, the *Odyssey* is, for some, the most significant archaic 'critique' of violence (in the form of a 'woven' song of songs that was probably composed in its later surviving form during the seventh century BC): ordering, it could be said, necessitates an all too human tragic violence, at least in the sense that human acts are necessarily exposed to their own rootlessness.[12] The order of the *oikos* causes the epic hero to act in the most illegitimate of ways and indeed, now, to do so within his *oikos*. Iliadic war continues in the *oikos* of Odysseus, by the same means. Odysseus stands under the sign of Heracles as he crosses the threshold of 'ritualised' killing.[13] Indeed, to a reader of the epics, it should not go unnoticed that it is the slaughter and consumption of the sacred cattle of the Sun that will subject Odysseus to his ten years of wandering (as well as his crew's death), and also that the socially forbidden consumption of the absent hero's cattle 'will mark the suitors for destruction' (McInerney 2010: 80). And this is directly resonant with the marked trepidation of Odysseus (*Od.* 24.358–62) over his violent actions (of 'purification') that questions the 'slaughter' of the suitors (who,

---

[12] A certain tradition has Homer being blind, which is highly unlikely, but a certain 'symbolic' mythologeme, in the sense implied here, cannot be entirely excluded.

[13] See the discussion in Nagler (1990).

in fact, sit on the hides of cattle) with regard to whether it would be acceptable to the gods since, while the suitors have brought pollution to his *oikos*, Odysseus is not free of pollution himself (ibid.).

Feasting (and 'sacrifice' or 'slaughter') is central to the Homeric world and the poem's structure. Indeed, feasting in the poems is a very frequent activity and it is at times so central to the narrative that it can occupy almost an entire book (for example, *Od.* 1.104–424).[14] The feast is, to an extent, a 'ritualised' activity that often follows the sequence of a 'sacrifice'. Homeric feasts tend to take place in the *megaron* (a hall which forms the most prestigious site of a wealthy residence) made of stone and timber, with weapons, armour and precious artefacts for decoration, high chairs and footstools, and with an open hearth for cooking.[15] Feasts involve predominantly meat, cereal and wine (*Od.* 1.147; 17.343); and the meat is derived from domestic cattle, sheep, goats and pigs and, occasionally, hunted game (for example, mountain goats in *Od.* 9.155 or deer in 10.156–77). Furthermore, feasts are of different types and purposes, ranging from large-scale feasts within or among communities to military feasts during battle and funeral feasts, as well as divine feasts among the gods.[16] Susan Sherratt schematises two general types of feast: those whose purpose is to propitiate gods (for example, Nestor's sacrifice in *Od.* 3) and those where the 'ritual' is implied, or reduced to a minimum (2004: 182). Yet while this is a helpful indication, there probably cannot be a precise dividing line between the two.

It is worth noting that the manner of 'feasts' can also be differentiated through the variety of terms used to describe a meal. For example, a nutritive meal can be described as ἄριστον (*ariston*; used twice in *Il.* 24.124; *Od.* 16.2) and δειελιήσας (*deieliēsas*, for example, *Od.* 17.599). Such a meal takes place early in the morning, in the middle of the day or at evening. Another form of a nutritive meal is the δεῖπνον (*deipnon*; for example, *Il.* 2.383), or the δόρπον (*dorpon*; for

---

[14] On the later significance of the *sumposion* as a form of social organisation, see Murray (1983). On feasts in general, see Schmitt-Pantel (1992).

[15] Van Wees (1995: 148–54).

[16] Gods can be seen feasting in *Il.* 11.534–5; see, further, Węcowski (2002).

example, *Od.* 2.20), a late meal. The *deipnon* occurs more frequently than other terms to indicate a particularly satisfactory meal (interestingly so, for human as well as other animals) and it can take place at various moments of the day or evening. Thus, in *Od.* 5.95 it is said that a *deipnon* satisfies the θυμός (*thumos*): αὐτὰρ ἐπεὶ δείπνησε καὶ ἤραρε θυμὸν ἐδωδῇ. It should be noted that *thumos*, linked earlier to smoke and later to the seat of the soul as well as of anger, may derive from the same root as *thusia* (one of the later standard words for a 'sacrifice'). It is notable, too, that it is also associated with the capacity to fight and with the courage required in battle (for example, *Il.* 19.167–92), or the strength that is necessary in manual labour (for example, *Il.* 11.86; 23.158; *Od.* 9.311).

The central elements to a feast are described in telling detail in *Il.* 7.313–22:

οἳ δ᾽ ὅτε δὴ κλισίῃσιν ἐν Ἀτρεΐδαο γένοντο,
τοῖσι δὲ βοῦν ἱέρευσεν ἄναξ ἀνδρῶν Ἀγαμέμνων
ἄρσενα πενταέτηρον ὑπερμενέϊ Κρονίωνι.
τὸν δέρον ἀμφί θ᾽ ἕπον, καί μιν διέχευαν ἅπαντα,
μίστυλλόν τ᾽ ἄρ᾽ ἐπισταμένως πεῖράν τ᾽ ὀβελοῖσιν,
ὄπτησάν τε περιφραδέως, ἐρύσαντό τε πάντα.
αὐτὰρ ἐπεὶ παύσαντο πόνου τετύκοντό τε δαῖτα,
δαίνυντ᾽, οὐδέ τι θυμὸς ἐδεύετο δαιτὸς [*daitos*] ἐΐσης·
νώτοισιν δ᾽ Αἴαντα διηνεκέεσσι γέραιρεν
ἥρως Ἀτρεΐδης εὐρὺ κρείων Ἀγαμέμνων.

Which can be rendered as:

When they came into the shed of the son of Atreus,
Agamemnon, the *basileus* of men, slew a bull for them,
a five-year-old male, and to the son of Kronos, Zeus, the mightiest.
They then flayed it, prepared and butchered the carcass.
And they cut and pierced the meat with spits,
they very carefully roasted it, then they drew all of the portions.
When they ceased from the labour and had prepared the feast,
they took their shares and feasted, no one lacking a fair portion.

Finally, the heroic son of Atreus, wide-ruling
   Agamemnon,
rewarded Ajax with the unbroken chine.

It is worth turning to these elements in some more detail in order to appreciate the practice of distribution and its milieu. Feasts can be seen to involve certain patterns.[17] For instance, the consumption is quite formulaic in descriptions as to the use of the hands (as in οἱ δ' ἐπ' ὀνείαθ' ἑτοῖμα προκείμενα χεῖρας ἴαλλον; *Il.* 9.221); in the equality of the portions at the meal (as in δαίνυντ', οὐδέ τι θυμὸς ἐδεύετο δαιτὸς ἐΐσης [*daitos eisēs*]; *Il.* 1.468); and in the indication of the end of a feast, with expressions akin to the dissipation of the desire to eat and drink (as in αὐτὰρ ἐπεὶ πόσιος καὶ ἐδητύος ἐξ ἔρον ἕντο; *Od.* 3.67). Such formulaic expressions are indicative of the commonality, as well as the value, of a feast as an activity of great significance. This can be seen, ever more emphatically, when a proper feast is contrasted to impropriety, as in the savage practices of the Cyclopes whose social deficiency is marked in this particular regard.[18] In addition, with regard to the equal portions in the sense of δαιτὸς ἐΐσης [*daitos eisēs*], the significance appears particularly marked in Homer (Nagy 1979: 128) by a certain sense of 'political' or 'social' merit.[19]

The value of a feast is, further, accentuated by its presence on Achilles' famous shield. In the Iliadic microcosm, as depicted on the very middle of the shield, we find the king standing with his sceptre (σκῆπτρον, *skēptron*) next to the swath cut through the grain.[20] At a distance, heralds (κήρυκες, *kērukes*), who hold some kind of 'religious' role, are preparing a feast (δαῖτα, *daita*) under an oak and around a large slaughtered ox.[21] Meanwhile, women are depicted preparing white barley for the meal (δεῖπνον, *deipnon*) of the labourers (*Il.* 18.550–60):

---

[17] On the terms used to describe different types of feast, see Saïd (1979: 14–17); and Rundin (1996: 185–6).

[18] See *Od.* 9.

[19] See Seaford (2004: 52f).

[20] On the sceptre, see Carlier (1984: 193 and 202–3).

[21] On heralds and their relation to 'religion', see Berthiaume (1982).

ἀσπερχὲς πάρεχον· βασιλεὺς δ᾽ ἐν τοῖσι σιωπῇ
σκῆπτρον ἔχων ἑστήκει ἐπ᾽ ὄγμου γηθόσυνος κῆρ.
κήρυκες δ᾽ ἀπάνευθεν ὑπὸ δρυΐ δαῖτα πένοντο,
βοῦν δ᾽ ἱερεύσαντες μέγαν ἄμφεπον· αἱ δὲ γυναῖκες
δεῖπνον ἐρίθοισιν λεύκ᾽ ἄλφιτα πολλὰ πάλυνον.

In this scene, John Rundin observes: 'This image encodes something about the political and economic organisation of the Homeric world. The workmen gather in wealth – here, the harvest – for the king, the centre of power. He in turn redistributes from his own wealth food for the workmen' (1996: 181). As will be seen later, the centrality of a distributive power, among the elites, is key to the (to an extent) stratified social divisions of Homeric society[22] and related practices, though the degree of redistribution in which this is so remains subject to question. Feasts, as is the case with 'sacrifices', are in any case central 'social-worship' events.

That a 'sacrifice' was a significant social act is already evident in the fact that joining the feast entailed obligations for mortals (*Il.* 4.343–6; 18.546) and the gods (*Il.* 4.45–6), as well as requiring a particular status.[23] It is possible that, at least in principle, anyone could participate (*Od.* 15.373–9), though, in practice, it seems this was not so. Arguably, the embedded collective values in such practices are, in fact, generally common among feasts and 'sacrifices': companionship, commensality, a certain sense of equality in sharing, reciprocity and obligations of hospitality, and, to an extent, inclusivity.[24] As will be seen in relation to 'sacrificial rituals' in particular, these values are of grave importance to the founding of social bonds. For example, in the so-called commensal sacrifices (one among many types of sacrifice), the 'binding/bonding' of participants can take place through a cementing of hospitality expectations, disturbance of which can even be a

[22] Whether Homeric societies were stratified or in transition towards being stratified (from earlier chiefdoms) remains an interesting question, but here I use the term 'stratified' in a non-strict sense in order to indicate the unequal access to sources of subsistence (see also Raaflaub 1997).

[23] See Sherratt (2004: 184); note the close link between feasts and singing (of tales), *Od.* 4.15–18; 9.5–10; 13.26–8; and dancing *Od.* 1.144–55; 8.99; 17.269–71, etc.

[24] Sherratt (2004: 184).

cause of war. Similarly, in the epic feasts 'several encounters – Diomedes and Glaucos, Achilles and Lycaon – remind us that dining together, ancestrally or personally, is expected to ensure an enduring bond' (Kitts 2005: 237) – a 'bonding', however, that takes place predominantly among an elite group of feasting men (or the gods).[25] Women and animals, it seems, were generally excluded from participating in feasts.[26] Some animals are present, while female servants are not entirely excluded, yet their role remains at all times minor. One exception appears to be a woman who is the mistress of the host, who appears to be expected to be present, but who cannot engage in all of the feast's activities, as she does not have the required status (for instance, *Il.* 18.496), other than in perhaps initiating conversation with guests.[27] Furthermore, women appear not to be permitted to participate in the preparation of meat, nor are they allowed to drink, although these may be to an extent poetic idealisations.[28]

3. 'Sacrifice'

The term 'sacrifice' is imbued with Roman and Christian perceptions that do not assist its understanding in archaic (and classical) Greece; and the same caution is needed with regard to the terms 'religion' and 'ritual'.[29] Some, in fact, hold with good reason that there is no such thing as ancient Greek

---

[25] See Vernant (1981; 1989), who emphasises that the feasts shared by mortal 'sacrificers' should not be read as an anachronistic device of communion with the gods.

[26] See Murray (2009: 513); on animals, Hesiod's famous distinction in *W.D.* 276–9, where animals eat each other, lacking the *dikē* that humans have been granted by Zeus; also see Rundin (1996: 188–9), and Vernant (1989: 21–86); indicatively, on the participation of women, see Keuls (1985: 210–15) and van Wees (1995: 154–63). On female servants, see *Od.* 1.147; 7.175; on the related gods, Patton (2009) and Thomsen (2011).

[27] Van Wees (1995: 158–9).

[28] See van Wees (1995: 159). This may be a Homeric root to the type of feasting that women, in particular, are in contrast associated with later, which has been characterised as a 'vegetarian feast' and attested in the *Thesmophoria*; see Détienne and Vernant (1989: 190–1) and Palaima (2004: 218, n. 14).

[29] See Hitch (2009: chs 1 and 2).

'religion' (Gould 2001: 203).[30] In addition, another reason for caution is the oral nature of the traditions in question and the fact that the literary evidence is often late or, crucially and for the most part exclusively, poetic.[31] There seem to be two terms that approximate the act of 'sacrifice' in the Homeric epics. The term ἱέρευσεν (*hiereusen*), possibly earlier attested in Linear B (*Tn* 316), which in the classical period will be used to mean 'sacrifice', is present in the Homeric poems (for example, *Od.* 14.74), but, in the latter, it probably means 'to slaughter' (as in *Od.* 14.28).[32] Sarah Hitch comments that the ambiguous use of the verb ἱέρευειν (*hiereuein*) is most evident when it is used on nine occasions in the *Odyssey* with reference to the improper slaughter (and consumption) of Odysseus' livestock by the suitors (2009: ch. 1, n. 180; for example, *Od.* 2.56). Yet the hypothesis that this word was used in relation to both 'ritual' and 'non-ritual' acts remains plausible. Similarly, the other equally ancient and common term in the Homeric poems, which is met with in 'sacrificial' practices, is the verb σφάζειν (*sphazein*; for example, *Od.* 14.426), which probably signifies the act of killing (of an animal), which may or may not be followed by a 'sacrifice' (Heinrichs 2000: 180; Hitch 2009: ch. 1, nn. 185 and 186).

'Sacrifices' are often the preceding event to a feast, and they, like feasts, follow particular patterns.[33] Homer describes

---

[30] On Greek religious culture, ritual authority and inscription, see, for instance, Heinrichs (2003).

[31] On the terms, see Bremmer (1998 and 2007). I do not attempt here to interpret the practice of 'sacrifice', which in any case remains particularly cumbersome to appreciate without substantial anachronisms. Burkert's ([1972] 1983) well-known seminal interpretation of slaughter-sacrifice is largely based on classical sources and is centred on psychological factors that at times seem all too modern. In turn, Détienne and Vernant (1989), to mention only one other well-known attempt, tend to be largely Freudian in their approach. That the archaic Greeks had a particular concern over the propriety of 'ritual' killing remains the case, while its manner attains transformations in the classical period that I cannot engage with here.

[32] See Hitch (2009: chs 1 and 3) for a detailed discussion.

[33] For example, in *Od.* 3.418–62; 14.418–52; *Il.* 1.458–66; 2.419–29. Feasting and 'sacrificing' may have been similarly linked in the earlier Mycenaean period (Wright 2004). The Linear B tablets indicate commensal feasting of significant size, particularly ceremonial patterns and paraphernalia (see Killen 1992; 1994; Halstead and Barrett 2004; Fox 2012). Feasts involved

them, for instance, in *Il.* 1.446–74 and *Od.* 14.414–45.[34] In particular, in the *Iliad* (1.458–66), we read:

αὐτὰρ ἐπεί ῥ 'εὔξαντο καὶ οὐλοχύτας προβάλοντο,
αὐέρυσαν μὲν πρῶτα καὶ ἔσφαξαν καὶ ἔδειραν,
μηρούς τ 'ἐξέταμον κατά τε κνίση ἐκάλυψαν
δίπτυχα ποιήσαντες, ἐπ 'αὐτῶν δ 'ὠμοθέτησαν:
καῖε δ 'ἐπὶ σχίζης ὁ γέρων, ἐπὶ δ 'αἴθοπα οἶνον
λεῖβε: νέοι δὲ παρ 'αὐτὸν ἔχον πεμπώβολα χερσίν.
αὐτὰρ ἐπεὶ κατὰ μῆρε κάη καὶ σπλάγχνα πάσαντο,
μίστυλλόν τ 'ἄρα τἆλλα καὶ ἀμφ 'ὀβελοῖσιν ἔπειραν,
ὤπτησάν τε περιφραδέως, ἐρύσαντό τε πάντα.

In translation:

When all had made the prayers and flung down the
   barley,
they drew back the victims' heads, and then slaughtered
   and skinned them.

---

honey, wheat, wine, cheese, oil, sheepskin, spelt and at least two kinds of 'sacrificial' animal. The individuals who appear to be in charge of proceedings are collectively named as *o-wi-de-ta* (sheep-flayers) and the animals destined for ritual slaughter are designated as *sa-pa-ke-te-ri-ja*. The link to deities is also occasionally evident in the tablets. The size of feasts and ceremonies could vary from very large (*P Un* 2) to local-ised ceremonies of a smaller scale (*Tn* 316). On these, see Palaima (2004: 217–46). McInerney has suggested that the feast should be understood as one part of a wider system of food distribution, a central social institution that included dedication, ceremonies and 'sacrifice' (2010: 61). Not unlike the Homeric practices, McInerney argues that Mycenaean 'sacrifices' and feasts affirmed, or reaffirmed, the social status of the elite, as much as of subordinate dependent parties (2010: 63). The cosmological signifi-cance of such practices in conferring powers should also be noted (see Hamilakis and Konsolaki 2004: 147; McInerney 2010: 81). While in the proto-geometric and later geometric periods distinct evidence of *sympo-sia* as a common practice have been noted (see Mazarakis-Ainian 1997: 287–305, 369–72), Halstead provides penetrating diachronic, though not assimilatory, analysis as to commensality in the Neolithic and Bronze Ages, as well as the link between the two (2012: 29–51; see also Pullen 2011: 190–2).

[34] See Détienne (1977); Burkert ([1972] 1983); Vidal-Naquet (1986); Grottanelli and Parese (1988); Vernant (1989); Gebauer (2002). For a com-parative analysis, see Dietler and Hayden (2001).

They then proceeded to cut away the meat from the
thighs
and they wrapped them in fat, in a double fold,
as well as laid shreds of flesh upon them.
The old man burnt these on the skewers while pouring
the wine over,
and meanwhile the young men with forks in their hands
awaited nearby.
When the thigh pieces had burnt, they tasted the vitals,
before they cut all the remainder into pieces and spitted
them,
roasting it all carefully and taking off the pieces.[35]

The most detailed description occurs in the *Odyssey* (at 3.430–
63), and it is worth reading the passage in full:

ὣς ἔφαθ᾽, οἱ δ᾽ ἄρα πάντες ἐποίπνυον. ἦλθε μὲν ἄρ βοῦς
ἐκ πεδίου, ἦλθον δὲ θοῆς παρὰ νηὸς ἐίσης
Τηλεμάχου ἕταροι μεγαλήτορος, ἦλθε δὲ χαλκεὺς
ὅπλ᾽ ἐν χερσὶν ἔχων χαλκήια, πείρατα τέχνης,
ἄκμονά τε σφῦραν τ᾽ ἐυποίητόν τε πυράγρην,
οἷσίν τε χρυσὸν εἰργάζετο: ἦλθε δ᾽ Ἀθήνη
ἱρῶν ἀντιόωσα. γέρων δ᾽ ἱππηλάτα Νέστωρ
χρυσὸν ἔδωχ᾽: ὁ δ᾽ ἔπειτα βοὸς κέρασιν περίχευεν
ἀσκήσας, ἵν᾽ ἄγαλμα θεὰ κεχάροιτο ἰδοῦσα.
βοῦν δ᾽ ἀγέτην κεράων Στρατίος καὶ δῖος Ἐχέφρων.
χέρνιβα δέ σφ᾽ Ἄρητος ἐν ἀνθεμόεντι λέβητι
ἤλυθεν ἐκ θαλάμοιο φέρων, ἑτέρῃ δ᾽ ἔχεν οὐλὰς
ἐν κανέῳ πέλεκυν δὲ μενεπτόλεμος Θρασυμήδης
ὀξὺν ἔχων ἐν χειρὶ παρίστατο βοῦν ἐπικόψων.
Περσεὺς δ᾽ ἀμνίον εἶχε: γέρων δ᾽ ἱππηλάτα Νέστωρ
χέρνιβά τ᾽ οὐλοχύτας τε κατήρχετο, πολλὰ δ᾽ Ἀθήνη
εὔχετ᾽ ἀπαρχόμενος, κεφαλῆς τρίχας ἐν πυρὶ βάλλων.
αὐτὰρ ἐπεί ῥ᾽ εὔξαντο καὶ οὐλοχύτας προβάλοντο,
αὐτίκα Νέστορος υἱὸς ὑπέρθυμος Θρασυμήδης
ἤλασεν ἄγχι στάς: πέλεκυς δ᾽ ἀπέκοψε τένοντας

---

[35] Translation by Murray (1924). The importance of burning well the portions dedicated to a deity relates to the need to produce smoke (*knise*) that
would satisfy the deity's nose; this could have been the character of *thusia*
in the first place and the derivative origin of the *thumos*.

αὐχενίους, λῦσεν δὲ βοὸς μένος. αἱ δ᾽ ὀλόλυξαν
θυγατέρες τε νυοί τε καὶ αἰδοίη παράκοιτις
Νέστορος, Εὐρυδίκη, πρέσβα Κλυμένοιο θυγατρῶν.
οἱ μὲν ἔπειτ᾽ ἀνελόντες ἀπὸ χθονὸς εὐρυοδείης
ἔσχον: ἀτὰρ σφάξεν Πεισίστρατος, ὄρχαμος ἀνδρῶν.
τῆς δ᾽ ἐπεὶ ἐκ μέλαν αἷμα ῥύη, λίπε δ᾽ ὀστέα θυμός,
αἶψ᾽ ἄρα μιν διέχευαν, ἄφαρ δ᾽ ἐκ μηρία τάμνον
πάντα κατὰ μοῖραν, κατά τε κνίσῃ ἐκάλυψαν
δίπτυχα ποιήσαντες, ἐπ᾽ αὐτῶν δ᾽ ὠμοθέτησαν.
καῖε δ᾽ ἐπὶ σχίζῃς ὁ γέρων, ἐπὶ δ᾽ αἴθοπα οἶνον
λεῖβε: νέοι δὲ παρ᾽ αὐτὸν ἔχον πεμπώβολα χερσίν.
αὐτὰρ ἐπεὶ κατὰ μῆρ᾽ ἐκάη καὶ σπλάγχνα πάσαντο,
μίστυλλόν τ᾽ ἄρα τἆλλα καὶ ἀμφ᾽ ὀβελοῖσιν ἔπειραν,
ὤπτων δ᾽ ἀκροπόρους ὀβελοὺς ἐν χερσὶν ἔχοντες.

In translation:

So he spoke, and they all set busily to work.
The heifer came from the plain and from the swift,
shapely ship came the comrades of great-hearted
    Telemachus;
the smith came, bearing in his hands his tools of bronze,
the implements of his craft, anvil and hammer
and well-made tongs, wherewith he wrought the gold;
and Athena came to accept the sacrifice.
Then the old man, Nestor, the driver of chariots, gave
    gold,
and the smith prepared it, and overlaid therewith the
    horns of the heifer,
that the goddess might rejoice when she beheld the
    offering.
And Stratius and goodly Echephron led the heifer by the
    horns,
and Aretus came from the chamber, bringing them water
for the hands in a basin embossed with flowers,
and in the other hand he held barley grains in a basket;
and Thrasymedes, steadfast in fight, stood by,
holding in his hands a sharp axe, to fell the heifer;
and Perseus held the bowl for the blood.
Then the old man, Nestor, driver of chariots,
began the opening rite of hand-washing and sprinkling

with barley grains, and earnestly he prayed to Athena,
cutting off as first offering the hair from the head, and
    casting it into the fire.
Now when they had prayed, and had strewn the barley
    grains,
straightway the son of Nestor, Thrasymedes, high of
    heart,
came near and dealt the blow;
and the axe cut through the sinews of the neck,
and loosened the strength of the heifer.
Then the women raised the sacred cry, the daughters and
    the sons' wives
and the revered wife of Nestor, Eurydice, the eldest of the
    daughters of Clymenus,
and the men raised the heifer's head from the broad-
    wayed earth and held it,
and Peisistratus, leader of men, cut the throat.
And when the black blood had flowed from her
and the life had left the bones, at once they cut up the
    body
and straightway cut out the thigh-pieces all in due order,
and covered them with a double layer of fat,
and laid raw flesh upon them.
Then the old man burned them on billets of wood,
and poured over them sparkling wine, and beside him
    the young men
held in their hands the five-pronged forks.
But when the thigh-pieces were wholly burned,
and they had tasted the inner parts, they cut up the rest
    and
spitted and roasted it, holding the pointed spits in their
    hands.[36]

As with different types of feast, multiple kinds of 'sacrifice' are described in the epics.[37] Margo Kitts has observed that 'commensal sacrifice' scenes are distinctly patterned in *Iliad* 1, 2, 7, 9 and 24; while the patterning in the particular type of

[36] Translation by Murray (1919).
[37] See Grottanelli (1988). It should also be noted that, in Homer, there are also unconsumed 'sacrifices' (*sphagia*); see, further, Rosivach (1994).

'oath-sacrifice' scenes is 'conspicuous' in 3 and 19 (2005, especially ch. 3). It is worth noting that a key difference between oath and commensal 'sacrifices' is, apart from the practices involved, the greater emphasis on generating pleasure and, perhaps, a degree of dread, respectively.[38]

A 'sacrifice' was a patterned act that was not to be confused with improper practices of it (for example, *Od.* 10.516–40, 571–2; 11.16.47).[39] At the same time a 'sacrifice', which is often indicated in Homer by the verb ἱερεύω (*hiereuō*, to make holy, to separate, but also to slaughter), was a joyous act of high importance and it was often, as has already been seen, closely identified with feasting.[40] In the Mycenaean context Chadwick translated the verb *i-je-to-qe*, in the famous sacrificial Linear B tablet from Pylos (*Tn* 316), as 'sacrifice'. Caution, however, is necessary when the word 'sacrifice' is used in the Homeric context, since not only is there not one single type of 'sacrifice' (or, equally, of 'feast'), but also, more importantly, the modern understanding of a 'sacred' act in the name of a deity does not fit the experiences evidenced in the Homeric poems. Indeed, the line that separates 'mere' eating from a 'sacrifice' appears to be very thin, though the two are not necessarily confused. Arguably, one of the best-known words used to describe some instances of animal sacrifice is θύειν (*thuein*), which does not mean 'sacrifice' in the poems, but burning or the producing of smoke.[41] Fritz Graf has, in fact, argued that 'animal sacrifice has a practical aim, the provision of edible meat' (2002: 120), though this remains subject to scholarly contention.

Jan Bremmer, among others, has suggested that the

---

[38] On oath-sacrifices, see Kitts 2005; on patterns, see Kitts (2011) and Arend (1933).

[39] See Vidal-Naquet (1981: 20). On proper/improper 'sacrifice', see *Od.* 12.357, 362–3. On 'sacrifice' more generally, see indicatively: Casabona (1966); Burkert ([1972] 1983); Georgoudi et al. (2005); Mehl and Brulé (2008); Georgoudi (2010: 92–105); and Mikalson (2016: 56–83).

[40] See the use of ἱέρευσεν (*hiereusen*) in *Od.* 14.74. In classical times, it seems that this verb is used to signify a 'sacrifice' at most times. On some exceptions in relation to feasting, see *Il.* 19.190; 19.250–68.

[41] See Benveniste and Lallot (1973: 486–7): 'Its origin is certain: *thúô* goes back to a present tense **dhu-yô*, the root of which properly means "to produce smoke"' (486).

'sacrificial ritual' could be schematically described as taking place in 'stages'.[42] A preliminary stage usually entailed hand-washing and the laying out of cereal goods by predominantly female servants. For instance, in *Od.* 1.136–40 we read:

χέρνιβα δ᾽ ἀμφίπολος προχόῳ ἐπέχευε φέρουσα
καλῇ χρυσείῃ, ὑπὲρ ἀργυρέοιο λέβητος,
νίψασθαι· παρὰ δὲ ξεστὴν ἐτάνυσσε τράπεζαν.
σῖτον δ᾽ αἰδοίη ταμίη παρέθηκε φέρουσα,
εἴδατα πόλλ᾽ ἐπιθεῖσα, χαριζομένη παρεόντων.

In translation:

A handmaid brought water for washing
in a fine golden pitcher and poured it above a silver basin
so they could wash, then pulled a polished table beside
   them.
And a venerable housekeeper brought bread and set it
   before them
placing many foods on it, pleasing them from her stores.[43]

This is followed by the 'stage' of skinning the victim and then the carving of the meat.[44] Invariably, the overall handling of the meat appears to be exclusively performed my men.[45] For instance, the central role of the carver is indicated in *Od.* 1.141–3:

δαιτρὸς δὲ κρειῶν πίνακας παρέθηκεν ἀείρας παντοίων,
παρὰ δέ σφι τίθει χρύσεια κύπελλα·
κῆρυξ δ᾽ αὐτοῖσιν θάμ᾽ ἐπῴχετο οἰνοχοεύων.

A carver, here, raised and placed platters of meats of all kinds before the participants, and placed golden cups beside them. A 'herald' came frequently and poured wine for them. If the partly speculative analysis of Hans van Wees is correct,

---

[42] On different interpretations of the so-called 'stages', compare Rudhardt (1958); Graf (2002); and Bremmer (1994).
[43] Translation by Murray (1919).
[44] See Ekroth (2008).
[45] See *Od.* 15.140–1; Fiddes (1991).

the male-dominated act of distributing the meat as such extends the already mentioned social division further, by suggesting that the distribution of meat may be the exclusive privilege of 'free-men' (1995: 158, n. 23), though in most cases high-ranking men.[46] Bremmer writes of the patterned treatment of meat as follows:

> After the two thigh-bones had been taken out and all meat removed from them, they were wrapped in a fold of fat, small pieces 'from all the limbs' were placed on top, and the whole was burned as an offering to the gods . . . Homer interpreted the small pieces on top as a first-fruit offering (*Od*. 14.428), but historical and anthropological comparison shows that these acts reproduce age-old customs of hunters. By gathering the bones the sacrificers symbolically returned the animal to the god(s) to ensure future success in the hunt . . . In addition to the thigh-bones, the gods also received some other parts, such as the gall bladder and the tail. (2007: 137 and see, generally, 132–44)

The separation of special parts dedicated to the gods is a crucial part of the ritual and these were distinct from the roughly equal parts to be distributed later to the participants.[47] It can be noted, as briefly indicated earlier, that in later times the gods receive a share of the innards ($\sigma\pi\lambda\acute{\alpha}\gamma\chi\nu\alpha$, *splagchna*):[48] namely, the spleen, kidneys, liver and, probably, the heart and lungs. Instead, in Homer, the innards were consumed by the participants at the start of a 'sacrificial' feast. We see, for example, Nestor's son offer a share of the entrails to Telemachus and Athena on their arrival in Pylos, followed by a traditional libation of mixed wine (*Od*. 3.40–4).[49] Lastly, with regard specifically to an 'oath-sacrifice' (a distinctive type of sacrificial act which is of great importance in the *Iliad*), Kitts (2005: 138) notes that the cutting is particularly

---

[46] See Burkert ([1972] 1983: 37).
[47] See Ekroth (2008: 265). The honorary portions were the better and larger parts, chief among which appears to be the back of an animal (for instance, in *Od*. 14.437–8).
[48] For example, in *Il*. 2.426; *Od*. 3.461.
[49] See Lissarrague (1995: 126–44).

emphasised, though in this case it was not the cutting of meat (since no meal takes place), but of the victim's hair, performed with a 'ritual' knife, the μάχαιρα (*machaira*; 3.273–4, 19.254).[50] Interestingly, Kitts, draws on the cognate words of *machaira*, μάχομαι (*machomai*, 'to fight'), μηχανάομαι (*mēchanaomai*, 'craft') and μῆχος (*mēchos*, 'a means of healing or carrying out one's wishes'), in order to suggest that a 'ritual sacrifice' and an act of 'healing' (or, in a wider sense, 'communication') were highly proximate acts.[51]

Finally, it is worth noting a type of feast that demonstrates, in exemplary fashion, the close tie with a 'sacrifice'. The practice of the εἰλαπίνη (*eilapinē*), which is a form of 'sacrificial' feast (δαίς, *dais*), was offered by a single donor to a civic audience (for example, *Od.* 1.224–9). Thus, as Ian Tewksbury describes, in Book 23 after Achilles propitiates the gods, 'Iris rushes to the winds to fulfil his prayer. When she arrives, she is invited to share in the εἰλαπίνη of the winds: *Il.* 23.200–7.' And he continues: 'There also appears to be an association between the winds and feasting, preserved in the depiction of Aeolus' perpetual feasting (*Od.* 10.8–11, 10.61)' (2015: 33). In addition, Tewksbury links this, tentatively, to the time in which mortals 'feasted with the gods' (ibid. 33 and 34–7).[52] On the basis of this, Tewksbury lastly adduces that perhaps the feast's particular 'ritual' character lies in the distribution of honour (the heroic κλέος, *kleos*; ibid. 37–9).

4. Meat

The function of the distribution-sharing of meat, in particular, is key to my study. Bremmer writes: 'After these preliminary acts, the actual carving of the victim was continued. This was a complicated affair . . . After the carving, the meat had to be boiled before it was distributed' (2007: 137–8).[53] Meat could,

---

[50] For instance, Agamemnon's *machaira* is mentioned in *Il.* 3.271–2.
[51] For an example of the use of a *machaira* in a healing ritual, see *Il.* 11.844. On the 'theology of sacrifice', Osborne (2016: 233–48).
[52] Compare Apollon. 1.12–14; see, further, the discussion in Tewksbury (2015: 35–7).
[53] On cooking descriptions, see *Il.* 19.316–17; *Od.* 15.321.

however, have been distributed raw as well.[54] Since not all pieces of meat[55] were of equal quality or quantity, this probably generated some complexity. But this problem can be resolved, if it is appreciated that in the (to a degree) stratified Homeric society, meat was distributed in accordance with the rank and status of the guests. In *Od.* 17.331–2, the carver (δαιτρός, *daitros*) divides up (δαιόμενος, *daiomenos*) the meat at the feast (δαινυμένοισι, *dainumenoisi*) of the suitors in the grand hall (similarly so in *Od.* 3.65–6). We can note, in a preliminary manner at this point, the particular use of the *dais* and its family of words. When Achilles hosts Odysseus, Ajax and Phoenix, as well as when he hosts Priam, the importance of meat distribution is made clear when the poet states that Achilles, and not his servants, distributes the meat (*Il.* 9.217; 24.626).[56] Further, the humble and honest swineherd Eumaios supplies us with strong confirmation of the practice of distribution that marks a feast. When Eumaios entertains Odysseus at his hut, upon his slaughtering a pig, his distribution of the meat is typical in this regard. Eumaios offers a special part (the chine, νῶτος; *nōtos*) of the pig to Odysseus (14.437: νώτοισιν δ᾽ Ὀδυσῆα διηνεκέεσσι γέραιρεν).[57]

This distribution pattern is of central significance. For now, it is worth merely noting that it is only after the distribution has been observed properly that the meal could begin. Anticipating some of the broader implications I shall draw upon below, Bremmer writes:

> The importance of the distribution also appears in a different way. The names of the most important gods of fate, *Moira* and *Aisa* (related to Oscan *aeteis*, 'part'), are also words meaning 'portion'. The name of *Kēr*, 'Death',

[54] Ekroth (2008: 274).
[55] See Nagy (1985: 45–52); on the special portions, see *Il.* 7.321–2; and *Od.* 14.437–8.
[56] See Sherratt (2004: 184–6).
[57] On the Eumaios scene, see Kadletz (1984). The gods are never described as consuming the meat, except by implication in *Od.* 14.435–6, where one portion is left for Hermes and the nymphs. Different ways of slaughtering depended on the animal, as indicated, for example, in *Od.* 3.437–8. On the centrality of meat consumption in Homer, see, generally, Bakker (2013).

the god connected with man's definitive fate, is probably related to *keiro*, 'to cut', and the Greeks usually blamed a *daimon*, literally 'distributor', for sudden and malevolent interference. The Greeks apparently derived their ideas about fate from sacrifice, the occasion in life where portions were cut and distributed. Even the later Greek word for 'law, order', *n[ó]mos*, literally means 'dispensation'; originally, it may have meant the right order of sacrificial distribution. (2007: 138)

With this in mind, it becomes perhaps clearer that feasts may function as the plateau in which a guest's social status could be affirmed, honoured or negotiated through the use of distribution practices and diacritics. For instance, at a feast the seating order itself may be an indication of 'social status' (ἐξείης [*hexeiēs*]; for example, in *Od.* 9.7–8; *Il.* 12.310–21).[58] The type of vessels from which participants drank wine may also function accordingly.[59] Finally, the act of distribution, the affirmation or negotiation of one's honour and a certain sense of 'equality' may be interrelated.

One of the most frequently used nouns (with over eighty occurrences, not to mention its cognates and variants) to describe such a division/distribution is, as mentioned earlier, δαίς (*dais*).[60] For example, in *Od.* 9.551, one reads: μήλων δαιομένων δόσαν ἔξοχα: τὸν δ᾽ ἐπὶ θινὶ ('[the ram my well-greaved comrades gave to me alone,] when the flocks were divided [*daio-menōn*], as a gift apart').[61] Δαίς (*dais*) may be, in fact, both a type of feast/'sacrifice' and also one of the words used to indicate a 'portion' or 'share' (closely related to δαιτρεύειν, *daitreuein*; δαΐζω, *daizō*: 'to divide, to cut, to destroy'). This is attested in relation to the cutting, or 'division', that momentarily precedes a distribution (of meat; possibly of land, and so on), but the act can also indicate a distribution as such (for instance, in *Od.* 6.10, or *Il.* 9.333).

In fact, all the verbs derived from the root *dā̃(i)-* mean

---

[58] On the ordering of seating, see Clay (1994: 36–9).
[59] See Griffin (1980: 14–15); van Wees (1995); and Rundin (1996: 188).
[60] See Rundin (1996: 186).
[61] Translation by Murray (1919).

'to distribute' or 'to apportion'.[62] *Nemō* appears to be used more sharply in the sense of 'to distribute', yet often in close connection with δατέομαι [*dateomai*].[63] In fact, most probably the meaning of the two verbs was not strictly demarcated. Sherratt (2004: 189) noted that a feast and a 'share' become, within such ambiguity, indistinguishable (for example, *Il.* 4.48–9; *Od.* 16.479 and *Il.* 1.468; 2004). The common root of *dais* and its variants lies, as Pierre Chantraine has shown, in the verb δαίομαι (*daiomai*), meaning 'to divide' and, in a sense, 'to distribute' (1968–2009). In the active voice, δαίνυμι (*dainumi*) is used to mean 'to give a feast'. Moreover, within the family of *dais* we also meet δαιτρός (*daitros*, the apportioner, or carver; διανέμων, *dianemōn*), δαίνυνται (*dainuntai*, to divide up, meaning to give a feast), δαιτρόν (*daitron*, a portion). This is also the case with δαίνυσθαι (*dainusthai*, the middle voice of δαίνυμι, *dainumi*: to participate in a feast), and δαῖτα (*daita*) meaning 'to share a feast' (for example, in *Il.* 9.70; *Od.* 3.66).[64] Furthermore, Sherratt indicates a possible semantic association with the Linear B word *e-pi-de-da-to*, ἐπιδέδασται (*epidedastoi*; ibid.).[65] In Linear B texts we also meet the related δασμός (*dasmos*: 'share, portion'; Palmer 1994: 79), though it occurs only once in the epics with regard to the division of booty (*Il.* 1.166).[66] It is also worth noting that, in the context of a feast, *dais* is used in contradistinction to a *deipnon* in a way that perhaps indicates a certain differentiation of types of commensality. In the *Iliad* (2.398–433), for instance, we read of the milieu in which the *dais* family of words is utilised in a remarkably vivid manner:

Ἀνστάντες δ᾽ ὀρέοντο κεδασθέντες κατὰ νῆας,
κάπνισσάν τε κατὰ κλισίας, καὶ δεῖπνον ἕλοντο.
Ἄλλος δ᾽ ἄλλῳ ἔρεζε θεῶν αἰειγενετάων

---

[62] See Boisacq (1923), s. vv. δαίομαι, δατέομαι.

[63] See Laroche (1949: 7).

[64] See Cunliffe ([1924] 2012), s.v. δαῖτα; Autenrieth ([1877] 1960), s.v. δαῖτα.

[65] Note the pre-Homeric verb δατέομαι, meaning division or apportionment among members of a group, for example, *Od.* 6.10; 14.208; 17.80; *Il.* 18.511; 20.394.

[66] See Ventris and Chadwick (1973: 178). On the distribution and redistribution of booty, see Ready (2007). For Seaford (2004: 40), the distributions of meat and booty are considered proximate.

εὐχόμενος θάνατόν τε φυγεῖν καὶ μῶλον Ἄρηος.
Αὐτὰρ ὃ βοῦν ἱέρευσε ἄναξ ἀνδρῶν Ἀγαμέμνων
πίονα πενταέτηρον ὑπερμενέϊ Κρονίωνι,
κίκλησκεν δὲ γέροντας ἀριστῆας Παναχαιῶν,
Νέστορα μὲν πρώτιστα καὶ Ἰδομενῆα ἄνακτα,
αὐτὰρ ἔπειτ᾽ Αἴαντε δύω καὶ Τυδέος υἱόν,
ἕκτον δ᾽ αὖτ᾽ Ὀδυσῆα Διὶ μῆτιν ἀτάλαντον.
Αὐτόματος δέ οἱ ἦλθε βοὴν ἀγαθὸς Μενέλαος·
ᾔδεε γὰρ κατὰ θυμὸν ἀδελφεὸν ὡς ἐπονεῖτο.
Βοῦν δὲ περιστήσαντο καὶ οὐλοχύτας ἀνέλοντο
τοῖσιν δ᾽ εὐχόμενος μετέφη κρείων Ἀγαμέμνων·
Ζεῦ κύδιστε μέγιστε κελαινεφὲς αἰθέρι ναίων
μὴ πρὶν ἐπ᾽ ἠέλιον δῦναι καὶ ἐπὶ κνέφας ἐλθεῖν
πρίν με κατὰ πρηνὲς βαλέειν Πριάμοιο μέλαθρον
αἰθαλόεν, πρῆσαι δὲ πυρὸς δηΐοιο θύρετρα,
Ἑκτόρεον δὲ χιτῶνα περὶ στήθεσσι δαΐξαι
χαλκῷ ῥωγαλέον· πολέες δ᾽ ἀμφ᾽ αὐτὸν ἑταῖροι
πρηνέες ἐν κονίῃσιν ὀδὰξ λαζοίατο γαῖαν.
Ὣς ἔφατ᾽, οὐδ᾽ ἄρα πώ οἱ ἐπεκραίαινε Κρονίων,
ἀλλ᾽ ὅ γε δέκτο μὲν ἱρά, πόνον δ᾽ ἀμέγαρτον ὄφελλεν.
Αὐτὰρ ἐπεί ῥ᾽ εὔξαντο καὶ οὐλοχύτας προβάλοντο,
αὐέρυσαν μὲν πρῶτα καὶ ἔσφαξαν καὶ ἔδειραν,
μηρούς τ᾽ ἐξέταμον κατά τε κνίσῃ ἐκάλυψαν
δίπτυχα ποιήσαντες, ἐπ᾽ αὐτῶν δ᾽ ὠμοθέτησαν.
Καὶ τὰ μὲν ἂρ σχίζῃσιν ἀφύλλοισιν κατέκαιον,
σπλάγχνα δ᾽ ἄρ᾽ ἀμπείραντες ὑπείρεχον Ἡφαίστοιο.
Αὐτὰρ ἐπεὶ κατὰ μῆρε κάη καὶ σπλάγχνα πάσαντο,
μίστυλλόν τ᾽ ἄρα τἆλλα καὶ ἀμφ᾽ ὀβελοῖσιν ἔπειραν,
ὤπτησάν τε περιφραδέως, ἐρύσαντό τε πάντα.
Αὐτὰρ ἐπεὶ παύσαντο πόνου τετύκοντό τε δαῖτα
δαίνυντ᾽, οὐδέ τι θυμὸς ἐδεύετο δαιτὸς ἐΐσης.

In translation:

> And they arose and hasted to scatter among the ships,
> and made fires in the huts, and took their meal [*deipnon*].
> And they made sacrifice one to one of the gods that
> are for ever, and one to another, with the prayer that they
>   might
> escape from death and the toil of war.
> But Agamemnon, king of men, slew a fat bull of five years

to the son of Cronos, supreme in might, and let call the
    elders,
the chieftains of the Achaean host, Nestor, first of all, and
    king Idomeneus,
and thereafter the twain Aiantes and the son of Tydeus,
and as the sixth Odysseus, the peer of Zeus in counsel.
And unbidden came to him Menelaus, good at the
    war-cry,
for he knew in his heart wherewith his brother was
    busied.
About the bull they stood and took up the barley grains,
and in prayer lord Agamemnon spoke among them,
    saying.
'Zeus, most glorious, most great, lord of the dark clouds,
that dwellest in the heaven, grant that the sun set not,
neither darkness come upon us, until I have cast down in
headlong ruin the hall of Priam, blackened with smoke,
and have burned with consuming fire the portals thereof,
and cloven about the breast of Hector his tunic, rent with
    the bronze;
and in throngs may his comrades round about him fall
headlong in the dust, and bite the earth.'
So spoke he; but not as yet would the son of Cronos grant
    him fulfilment;
nay, he accepted the sacrifice, but toil he made to wax
    unceasingly.
Then, when they had prayed and had sprinkled the
    barley grains,
they first drew back the victims' heads and cut their
    throats, and flayed them;
and they cut out the thigh-pieces and covered them
with a double layer of fat, and laid raw flesh thereon.
These they burned on billets of wood stripped of leaves,
and the inner parts they pierced with spits,
and held them over the flame of Hephaestus.
But when the thigh-pieces were wholly burned
and they had tasted of the inner parts,
they cut up the rest and spitted it, and roasted it carefully,
    and drew all off the spits.
Then, when they had ceased from their labour and had
    made ready the meal [*daita*],

they feasted [*dainunt'*], nor did their hearts lack aught of the equal feast [*daitos*].[67]

It should be emphasised that, in Homer, *dais* relates to a feast or food. It has been argued that *dais* has a more general use in the epics beyond the practice of feasts (for example, *Od.* 3.309; 5.61), such as in the distribution of 'possessions' and land.[68] In fact, Borivoj Borecký (1963: 44–50) has suggested that the verb *daiein* may indicate the distribution of common property by a collective, whereas *nemein* signifies the distribution of property by an individual, linking them both with an earlier origin in primitive tribal life. Borecký (1963: 49, n. 8) notes that we find the verb νέμω (*nemō*) 'without application to a particular person' only once (at *Od.* 8.470). Interestingly, the word δατέομαι (*dateomai*) has, at least later, in Hesiod, the meaning of distribution by a collective, as much as by a single source.[69] Whether through *nemein* or *dais*, then, in the manners of feasts, the feast is shown to be rooted in a practice of distribution (perhaps, for some, with a certain character of 'redistribution' among a collective) with some equality or share-dealing between participants.[70] Lastly, it could be noted that the god of the underworld, Pluto, is later described as Ἰσοδαίτης (*Isodaitēs*), a divider of equal portions or shares,[71] while, it is worth adding that the word *dēmos* (Doric *damos*) may be itself etymologically related to *daiein* (Frisk [1954] 1960: 380–1).[72]

To refer to some indicative examples, it could be observed that in the *Odyssey* (9.39–42), when Odysseus and his group of men sack the city of Cicones, they 'distribute or deal out' (δασσάμεθ', *dassameth'*) the possessions of the Cicones among themselves in an equal manner (ἴσης, *isēs*), while Odysseus, their leader, performs the distribution:

---

[67] Translation by Murray (1924).
[68] For instance, *Od.* 3.316; 6.10. I return to this in Chapter Three.
[69] Borecký (1963: 75–7), who also notes that in Homer we find the verb in relation to the distribution of *moirai* three times in the form of δάσσασθαι (*Od.* 3.66; 19.423; and 20.280); note also the use of κατὰ μοῖραν (*kata moiran*) in *Od.* 9.352 and 14.509. I turn to this in Chapter 2.
[70] See Saïd (1979: 14–23).
[71] See Seaford (2004: 51).
[72] See Donlan (1970).

Ἰλιόθεν με φέρων ἄνεμος Κικόνεσσι πέλασσεν,
Ἰσμάρῳ. ἔνθα δ' ἐγὼ πόλιν ἔπραθον, ὤλεσα δ' αὐτούς·
ἐκ πόλιος δ' ἀλόχους καὶ κτήματα πολλὰ λαβόντες
δασσάμεθ', ὡς μή τίς μοι ἀτεμβόμενος κίοι ἴσης.

In translation:

From Ilios the wind bore me and brought me to the
    Cicones,
to Ismarus. There I sacked the city and slew the men;
and from the city we took their wives and great store of
    treasure,
and divided them among us, that so far as lay in me no
    man might go defrauded of an [equal share.[73]

Another notable instance is met when the *dēmos* of Pylos divides equally (δαιτρεύειν, *daitreuein*) the booty (horses, sheep and goats) stolen by Nestor from the Epeians (*Il.* 11.670–761); as well as when, soon after, the *basileus* performs the distribution upon reserving a special portion for himself (*Il.* 11.703–5):

τῶν ὃ γέρων ἐπέων κεχολωμένος ἠδὲ καὶ ἔργων
ἐξέλετ' ἄσπετα πολλά· τὰ δ' ἄλλ' ἐς δῆμον ἔδωκε
δαιτρεύειν, μή τίς οἱ ἀτεμβόμενος κίοι ἴσης.

In translation:

[By reason of these things], both deeds and words, was
    the old man wroth
and chose him recompense past telling; and the rest he
    gave to the *dēmos*
to divide, that so far as in him lay no man might go
    defrauded of an equal share.[74]

Finally, in an iconic passage of the *Odyssey* (14.427–41) which demonstrates the use of multiple, though closely related, terms used for the acts of distribution in a feast, we read:

[73] Translation by Murray (1919).
[74] Translation by Murray (1924).

αἶψα δέ μιν διέχευαν· ὁ δ᾽ ὠμοθετεῖτο συβώτης,
πάντων ἀρχόμενος μελέων, ἐς πίονα δημόν,
καὶ τὰ μὲν ἐν πυρὶ βάλλε, παλύνας ἀλφίτου ἀκτῇ,
μίστυλλόν τ᾽ ἄρα τἆλλα καὶ ἀμφ᾽ ὀβελοῖσιν ἔπειραν,
ὤπτησάν τε περιφραδέως ἐρύσαντό τε πάντα,
βάλλον δ᾽ εἰν ἐλεοῖσιν ἀολλέα· ἂν δὲ συβώτης
ἵστατο δαιτρεύσων· περὶ γὰρ φρεσὶν αἴσιμα ᾔδη.
καὶ τὰ μὲν ἕπταχα πάντα διεμοιρᾶτο δαΐζων·
τὴν μὲν ἴαν νύμφῃσι καὶ Ἑρμῇ, Μαιάδος υἱεῖ,
θῆκεν ἐπευξάμενος, τὰς δ᾽ ἄλλας νεῖμεν ἑκάστῳ·
νώτοισιν δ᾽ Ὀδυσῆα διηνεκέεσσι γέραιρεν
ἀργιόδοντος ὑός, κύδαινε δὲ θυμὸν ἄνακτος·
καί μιν φωνήσας προσέφη πολύμητις Ὀδυσσεύς·
αἴθ᾽ οὕτως, Εὔμαιε, φίλος Διὶ πατρὶ γένοιο

In this scene, the swine herder is doing the carving (δαιτρεύσων, *daitreusōn*), since he had exceptional knowledge of things which are of due measure (αἴσιμα ᾔδη, *aisima hēdē*). In carving (δαΐζων, *daizōn*), he allotted/divided (διεμοιρᾶτο, *diemoirato*) seven portions: he separated out one for the nymphs and Hermes, while the rest of the portions he distributed (νεῖμεν, *neimen*) to each man. He then honoured (γέραιρεν, *gerairen*) Odysseus with the long back of the white-tusked pig. At this point, if we follow Borecký's analysis to its partly speculative conclusion, we meet the older verb δαίομαι (*daiomai*) adjacent to the relatively newer use of *nemō*, whereby gradually we could say we are witnessing already in Homer the clarification of the act of distribution through the use of *nemō* that will eventually come to relate to a certain sense of 'equality'. That is, an emerging relationship between equal portions among the elite, in (a not necessarily evolutionary) transition from an (arguably) older sense of tribal (possibly more communal) sharing. It is later, in classical times, that *nemō* will come to denote also, in one sense at least, a 'giving' related to a sense of 'having' or 'enjoying' that could be said to approximate an early sense of 'possession'.

5. Commensality

Some emphasis on 'equality' is particularly present in these exemplary verses. The *daita* are usually praised for their equality: a proper feast is, in this sense, an equal feast (δαίς ἐΐση; *Il.* 2.431), between men or gods.[75] Chantraine had earlier summarised the consensus of scholars on the etymology of ἐΐση (*eisē*) – which had, in fact, already been attempted by Athenaeus (1.12c) – as a by-form of ἴσος (*isos*; 1968–2009). Meanwhile, John Rundin has illustrated that the limitation of this particular 'egalitarianism' is that it takes place at feasts among the top rank of a hierarchy of men (1996). This is closely associated with the indication of a necessary 'propriety' or merit, a degree of 'entitlement', as a key part of this type of commensality.[76] In turn, Rundin has observed the use of the word *isos* across the epics and has shown that Homer's particular use of *isos* in contexts where 'a lower ranking individual tries to attain equal status to that of a higher individual' reveals that it is, in fact, used to indicate or confirm a higher status: that is, rendering a certain equality among those with high ('equal') status (for instance, *Il.* 5.440–1). Thus, Rundin writes: 'Accordingly, the equal feast instantiates the relations of equal and balanced reciprocity that characterize exchange among those of high status who are, in some sense, not subordinate to one another' (1996: 195).

Such feasts among 'equals' may provoke, to an unaccustomed modern eye, the complaint that they are not, in fact, equal 'proper'.[77] The point of reference, in this regard, lies with the giving of γέρας (*geras*), namely, a disproportionate (in terms of quantity and perceived quality) portion of meat to one of the elite participants, usually a guest of honour or a *basileus*. For example, in the *Iliad* (7.319–23) we read:

αὐτὰρ ἐπεὶ παύσαντο πόνου τετύκοντό τε δαῖτα,
δαίνυντ᾽, οὐδέ τι θυμὸς ἐδεύετο δαιτὸς ἐΐσης·
νώτοισιν δ᾽ Αἴαντα διηνεκέεσσι γέραιρεν
ἥρως Ἀτρεΐδης εὐρὺ κρείων Ἀγαμέμνων.

---

75 On *dais eisē*, see *Il.* 2.421–31; 9.205–25; 23.53–6; *Od.* 11.185; 19.418–27; see, also, Saïd (1979: 17–19); and Ando (2004: 89–90).
76 Contrast with the improper feasts of the suitors; Saïd (1979: 9–49). On Homeric commensality, see Bruns (1970); Rundin (1996: 179–215); van Wees (1995: 147–82); and Sherratt (2004: 181–217).
77 See Ostwald (1996: 56–7); also Arnheim (1977); and Morris (1996).

In translation:

> But when they had ceased from their labour and had
>   made ready the meal,
> they feasted, nor did their hearts lack aught of the equal
>   feast.
> And unto Aias for his honour was the long chine given
> by the warrior son of Atreus, wide-ruling Agamemnon.[78]

Another characteristic example is met when Eumaios honours (*gerairen*) Odysseus with a special portion of meat (*Od.* 14.437): νώτοισιν δ᾽ Ὀδυσῆα διηνεκέεσσι γέραιρεν ('Odysseus he honoured with the long chine of the white-tusked boar').[79] Rundin suggests that *geras* 'may have meant privilege of old age' (1996: 196), while noting, however, that the use of the word is significantly too wide for any certainty as to its derivation to be affirmed. Richard Cunliffe defined *geras* as meaning: (a) 'a meed of honour, a special prize, or portion from the general division of spoils' (for instance, *Il.* 1.118); (b) 'something given by way of showing honour to a person (for example, *Od.* 4.66); (c) 'an honour paid' (for example, *Il.* 4.49); (d) 'a privilege' (*Il.* 4.323); (e) 'the dignity or honours of a king' (for example, *Od.* 15.522); and (f) 'a gratuity' (for example, *Od.* 20.297) ([1924] 2012: 77). Nonetheless, Rundin has emphasised, somewhat abstractly, that the political significance of the term is proximate to the indication of an 'office' (1996: 196). The political significance, or, in any case less emphatically, the formal value of the practice of giving *geras*, can also be indicated by the fact that it had to be granted appropriately. Hence, a guest neither assigns *geras* nor determines the initial apportioning of meat (*Od.* 8.474). This has to be done, instead, by the host. Nor can *geras* be given to a person who does not enjoy adequate status (for example, *Od.* 20.292–8; 1996: 197), usually, as already noted, a *basileus*. Furthermore, the importance of one's part or portion can be emphasised with reference to the deprivation of one's *geras*. Thus, such a deprivation threatens to render Achilles in his dispute with Agamemnon

---

[78] Translation by Murray (1924).
[79] Translation by Murray (1919).

in Book 1 of the *Iliad* into a *metanastēs*; that is, a vagrant wanderer.

Hugh Lloyd-Jones has noted that this is a concern with one's part, not so much as a matter of 'property', but as one of *timē* (honour in one's *ēthos*; 1971: 11). Early on, the equality of feasts, as has already been suggested, is an 'equality' of corresponding worth in terms of honour, rather than necessarily an equality in terms of quantity. To appreciate this form of 'equality' between participants at a feast, and even more so in relation to those who are excluded from participation, Rundin suggests that one has to imagine a network of exchanges ('within which a dominant element is feasting') and an archaic social-political reciprocity in such exchanges, whereby, for example, the receiver of a special honour offers, in return, some benefit 'to the whole community' (such as military services; 1996: 201–3).[80] A degree of reciprocation may have softened a sense of 'inequality', though in any case this cannot be transposed on to a modern set of values (the latter remaining often self-contradictory per se). Tension there may be, but this is not its locus. Instead in the epics the main differentiation may be depicted in the marked negotiation of a heroic 'individualism' in relation to the earlier *ēthos* of a speculative degree of some kind of communal distribution-sharing.[81]

6. Sympotic distribution-sharing

A few additional words should suffice as to wine sharing and drinking in this context.[82] Drinking and feasts are intimately related social acts.[83] A similar, if not in some respects identical, pattern of honour and attribution takes place in the sympotic practices during feasts. The scene of the *Iliad* (4.257–64) where Idomeneus is honoured by a special quantity of wine is perhaps exemplary:[84]

---

[80] See Donlan (1982b).
[81] See Seaford (2004: 45–7).
[82] On wine in Mycenaean society and economy, see Palmer (1992; 1994).
[83] See Węcowski (2002: 625–37); Ando (2004: 87–99); and Papakonstantinou (2009: 1–24).
[84] See Sherratt (2004: 307–8); Papakonstantinou (2009: 15–16).

Ἰδομενεῦ περὶ μέν σε τίω Δαναῶν ταχυπώλων
ἠμὲν ἐνὶ πτολέμῳ ἠδ᾽ ἀλλοίῳ ἐπὶ ἔργῳ
ἠδ᾽ ἐν δαίθ᾽, ὅτε πέρ τε γερούσιον αἴθοπα οἶνον
Ἀργείων οἱ ἄριστοι ἐνὶ κρητῆρι κέρωνται.
Εἴ περ γάρ τ᾽ ἄλλοι γε κάρη κομόωντες Ἀχαιοὶ
δαιτρὸν πίνωσιν, σὸν δὲ πλεῖον δέπας αἰεὶ
ἕστηχ᾽, ὥς περ ἐμοί, πιέειν ὅτε θυμὸς ἀνώγοι.
Ἀλλ᾽ ὄρσευ πόλεμον δ᾽ οἷος πάρος εὔχεαι εἶναι.

In translation:

> I honour you, Idomeneus, beyond the Danaans,
> both in battle, and in any other action,
> whether it be at the feast, when the great men of
> the Argives blend in the mixing bowl the gleaming wine
>   of the princes.
> Even though all the rest of the long-haired Achaians
> drink their allotted portion [*daitron*], still your cup stands
>   forever
> filled like mine, for you to drink when the pleasure takes
>   you.
> Rise up then to battle, be such as you claimed in time past.

The sympotic event, then, has similar characteristics to that of the eating part of a feast, in that it is hierarchical, while commensal, exclusive and once more gendered,[85] but above all a quite regulated (in both senses) affair. The quantity of mixed wine, as well as the vessels used to drink from, signified a particularly observed ranking of honour, and thus the distribution of wine can be appreciated as a common act of interaction and status formation.[86]

7. A distributive *ēthos*?

The extent to which distribution (and redistribution) are observed in the Homeric poems may suggest the social-worship significance of the act of distribution among mortals,

---

[85] On a few exceptions, see *Od.* 6.75–8; 13.53–62; 20.66–9; discussion in Papakonstantinou (2009: 7–8, n. 23).

[86] On vessels, see *Od.*1.142; 3.472; 8.121; and *Il.* 11.629–43; 24.234–5.

as well as between mortals and gods and, indeed, between the gods themselves.[87] In fact, with regard to the latter, Chantraine has suggested that the word δαίμων (*daimōn*) may be itself etymologically related to *daiomai* (1968–2009). Thus, for Francis M. Cornford, a *daimōn* is a 'partitioner' ([1912] 1957: 95–110). Zeus, himself (as will be explored in more detail when I turn to the notion of *moira*: see Chapter Two) is in more than one sense the distributor of 'prosperity' (as in *Od.* 6.188; and the prevalence of this notion in Hesiod will be noted, later on, too: see Chapter Six). The distribution of 'patrimony', the spoils of war, land, food, wine and so forth appears to comprise a (not necessarily uniform) paradigm of social-*oikonomic* apportionment (of honour). Further, the variety of words used in the epics to describe such an act of apportionment (namely, in the uses of *daiomai, dais, diemoirato, nemein, aisima* and so forth) in itself suggests the importance of the act(s) in the Homeric world. The particular apportionment of meat, in this regard, could be speculatively said to project, or to 'ritually' reflect, the archaic socio-worship ordering of a valued *ēthos*, a way of life; and perhaps, in time, the act of apportionment surpasses concrete ritualised regulation and 'functional' differences between, say, meat distribution in a sacrifice and the distribution of booty or land.

Distribution, then, appears to be a particularly vital act across a number of different early patterned practices. Gerhard Baudy has, not without reason, suggested that the origin of 'civilisation' may be grounded in the ordered distribution of food (1983: 131–74); alternatively, if animal 'sacrifices' and feasts were to be understood as articulations of social worth and community, then the act of distribution would be, by definition, at least a powerful and power-forming act of status affirmation and negotiation.[88] In particular, *nemein*'s early connection with food and drink in their distribution has been clearly noted. Some scholars have, further, ventured to suggest that, as a result, *nómos* originates from the 'fundamental' practice of meat distribution (Baudy 1983: 157–61). In his exhaustive study, Guy Berthiaume has shown that meat distribution was always,

---

[87] See Rose (1992).
[88] See Schmitt-Pantel (1992).

or almost always, derived from a 'sacrificial' practice (1982: 62–70 and 79–93). Thus, distribution may be symbolic of a wider experience with regard to subsistence or living, while indistinguishably being an experience within a 'socio-worship' sphere (though without, here, a strictly necessary reference to divinity). Furthermore, Gunnel Ekroth has argued, following Berthiaume's conclusions, that the Greek terms *thusia* and *thuein* may have signified a certain early sense of a 'sacrifice', 'but also the consumption and handling of meat in a ritual context' (2007: 271), hence inviting an understanding of 'sacrifice' in a far wider and less certain – though entirely concrete – sense than our comprehension may tend to expect.

We have seen, with the aid of Borecký's analysis, that the verb *nemein* is used for the sense of 'to distribute-share' more generally, while, in the particular case of a patterned distribution-sharing (of land, booty, inheritance and food), we also noted the related use of the possibly more ancient *daiesthai* and its cognates. If Borecký's hypothesis is correct – that *daiesthai*, as well as *moira*, relates to an earlier phase of some kind of collective distribution/redistribution (immanent in the collective), to whatever degree, as opposed to a more centrifuged distribution by an elite host or *basileus* – it may be that the practice of distribution-sharing is a significant marker of an earlier, perhaps, tribal *ēthos* (1963: 41–60; 1965; Seaford 2004: 50–1), which is 'remembered', to an extent, in its transformation during Homer's time. It should be noted in this regard that the portions of meat, too, were often themselves designated as *moira* or *meris* (and *moira* as 'share' is arguably attested already in the Linear B tablets).[89] In this way, Richard Seaford notes, Plutarch, later on, may be reporting on such a long-held tradition/transmission (which is always also a betrayal) when he says that meals were once apportioned by *Moira* and *Lachesis* in an equal manner (*Mor.* 644a; 2004: 52). Plutarch's own anachronism and/or reinvention may indeed be at work here, but, given the antiquity of the feast practices, there is sufficient room for speculation. In

---

[89] In the *Iliad*, the portion for the gods consists of the *meria* (thigh bones).

any event, we do know that the nature of the particular 'equality' depicted in the Homeric poems (but also
earlier) is that one received what one was due (which,
in turn, marked a pronounced, though common, social
differentiation).[90]

---

[90] See Ekroth (2011: 15–41).

Two

Nomos Moirēgenēs

μοῖράν τ' ἀμμορίην τε καταθνητῶν ἀνθρώπων
Hom. *Od.* 20.76[1]

Ζεὺς δ' αὐτὸς νέμει ὄλβον Ὀλύμπιος ἀνθρώποισιν
Hom. *Od.* 6.188[2]

... ὁ μέγας δὲ κίνδυνος ἄναλκιν οὐ φῶτα λαμβάνει.
θανεῖν δ 'οἶσιν ἀνάγκα, τί κέ τις ἀνώνυμον
γῆρας ἐν σκότω καθήμενος ἕψοι μάταν,
ἁπάντων καλῶν ἄμμορος ...
Pind. *O.* 1–81–3[3]

1. *Moira*

In Homer, as already noted in Chapter One, we meet the word νέμω (*nemō*) and its cognates and composites in a wide variety of uses. Here I turn to examine the relation between *nemein* and what is held to be its ancient line of use as a 'distribution-sharing', a 'dispensing of one's portion', or a 'lot'. In the sense of an 'allotment of portions', we meet *nemein* used, on occasion in close proximity to, though not identically with, μοίρα (*moira*). This occurs, for instance, in *Od.* 14.436, θῆκεν ἐπευξάμενος, τὰς δ' ἄλλας νεῖμεν [*neimen*] ἑκάστῳ· where the act of distributing portions of meat in a feast is, a

---

[1] 'What is and what is not *moira* of mortals.'
[2] 'Zeus distributes or dispenses good fortune to mortals.' On Zeus and cosmic order, see Gernet and Boulanger (1932).
[3] 'It is not to the weak that great risks will yield. We all have to die down here. Why sit scared in the shade? Why stew away old age in obscurity, of all *moira* (good fortune, happiness) devoid?'

few verses earlier, preceded by the use of the terms to divide/
share, διηνεκέεσσι (*diēnekeessi*, 437) and διεμοιρᾶτο δαΐζων
(*diemoirato daizōn*, 434). What is the relation between *nomos*
and *moira*? Emmanuel Laroche has suggested that *moira* is
essentially a 'division', while *nomos* in its primary Homeric
sense is a 'distribution', proposing that, while the two terms
are connected in the sphere of such acts, they are of separate
semantic lines (1949: 8). Yet the notion that a sense of 'distribution' remains closely associated with *moira* is a contention
that merits further investigation. An early or late (depending
on the dating of the *Orphic Hymns*) attestation of the possible
relation is provided in the *Hymn to Moirai* [Kern] where, at 10,
the *Moirai* are linked to the ancient *nómos* (νόμου ὠγυγίου), as
well as to *eunomia* (εὐ νόμου ἀρχῆς, *eu nómou archēs*).

According to the inspired approach by Francis M. Cornford
([1912] 1957) *nomos* was, in fact, 'prefigured' in archaic thought
in the impersonal power of μοίρα (*moira*), and it is still worth
engaging with this hypothesis in some more detail. Homeric
moira is not 'fate', nor is she blind, senseless and 'absolute'.
Neither is Homeric *moira* the (perhaps more familiar) *moira*
met in 'heaven' in Plato's *Republic* whereby a compulsive
Ἀνάγκη (*Anangkē*), with spindle and distaff, determines the
lots of life along with the help of the famous sisters – *Lachesis*[4]

---

[4] In Homer, we do not meet *Lachesis*, though the verb λαγχάνω [*laghanō*] is
used to describe, inter alia, 'to receive' or 'get one's assigned lot or portion'
(for example, in *Il.* 4.49; 24.70), as well as through a 'lot' (for example, *Il.*
15.190, 191; 23.356, 357, 862). In this sense, *lachos* is synonymous with *klēros*,
a 'lot', or 'holding of land', originally signifying the piece of wood used for
casting lots. *Moira*, especially in the plural, will later be used to also signify
the 'distribution-sharing/division' of land (as, for instance, in Pindar), but
we shall see in this chapter too its use as such in Homer to indicate an original allotment of land or *dasmos*. The so-called *archaia moira* of the Spartans,
or as Hodkinson called it 'the enigmatic ancient portions' (1986: 404–5),
has been a question for scholars for over a century. It is seen in Plutarch,
for instance, with regard to a *diatetagmenēs moiras* ('divided/allotted' *moirai*;
Mor. 21–2, 238e), but the famous later reference is found in Aristotle, who
probably quotes Herakleides of Lembos (Arist. fr. 611, 12 [Rose (1886)]).
While I cannot engage with this debate here, it is worth observing that
irrespective of perspective some link of the ancient *moira* to land was most
probably prevalent in Sparta (and possibly elsewhere), as I note further
in Chapter Three. Lupi has recently suggested, with good reason, that the
ancient *moira* of the Spartans possibly referred to the 'inalienable land' of
the father which his heirs would receive upon his death, and which was

(the allocator; the 'past'), *Atropos* (who cannot be turned, rigid; the 'future') and *Klōthō* (the spinner; the 'present').[5] In the epics it is worth noting that the verb κλώθω (*klōthō*) is never used as an act of *moira* or *aisa*, but only in the description of the gods' act of spinning, which I examine in more detail below. In the Homeric epics, *Moira* or *aisa* (perhaps more 'abstract' in its use than *moira*)[6] appears hardly ever to be personified as a single entity, nor does she appear in the plural (*moirai*), a modality in which we meet the so-called Sisters or Fates in later literature.[7] So the following questions could be asked. Is *Moira* a goddess in the poems? Is she a 'power' of sorts, a 'normative principle' or a 'divine imperative'? The answer may prove more elusive than might be expected. However, the working hypothesis can be stated from the outset: if *moira* is, among other things, indicating something more ancient in Homer than a notion of 'fate', then it could be 'a part' (and, in this sense, a 'life').

It should be noted that, perhaps closely associated with this sense of 'distribution', though more directly evident in the post-Homeric world, the words ἰσομοιρία (*isomoiria*) and ἰσομοιρέω (*isomoireō*), in, for instance, Isocrates and Thucydides, signify a sense of 'equality' as an equality of shares and are even used as synonyms for ἰσονομία (*isonomia*).[8] In Homer, we do meet the word in its variation as ἰσόμορος (*isomoros*), as we shall see below. Borijov Borecký has, in fact, argued that in Homer the words μοῖρα (*moira*),

probably the subject of radical reform in the later part of the classical period (2003; see, further, the studies of Hodkinson 1986; Link 1991; and Lazenby 1995).

[5] Pl. *Rep.* 10.616b–d. In the Homeric epics, *moira* in the plural form (*moirai*) makes only one appearance, in Apollo's speech where he berates the gods for enabling Achilles to abuse Hector's body: τλητὸν γὰρ Μοῖραι θυμὸν [*thumon*] θέσαν ἀνθρώποισιν [*thesan anthrōpoisin*] ('there is a limit to mourning that is endured by the patience allotted by the *moirai*'; *Il.* 24.49).

[6] *Aisa*, in Homer, but also in Hesiod and beyond, tends to be assimilated to the usage of *moira* and so their use can be quite interchangeable. *Aisa* is etymologically linked to Oscan *aeteis*; see Giannakis (1998: 4).

[7] See, for differing approaches, Meuss (1889: 468–75); Cornford ([1912] 1957: 1–72); Berry (1940); Greene ([1944] 1948); Buriks (1948); Anwander (1949–50: 48–54, 128–35); Bianchi (1953: especially 61–71); Onians (1954); Pötscher (1960: 5–39); Adkins (1960); and Dietrich (1965).

[8] See Borecký (1963: 43).

αἶσα (*aisa*), δαίομαι (*daiomai*) and λαγχάνω (*lagchanō*) 'are closely related to the primitive custom of division of common property among members of the collective' (1963: 47). Thus, perhaps the experiences of 'sacrifice' as well as that of the allotment of land were closely associated. As George Thomson argued inspiringly in the 1940s, the idea of *moira* may have 'originated as a symbol of the economic and social functions characteristic of the primitive tribe – the sharing of food, the sharing of booty, the sharing of land, and the division of labour between the clans' (1946: 50).

Moira is etymologically derived from the root **(s)mer* (μόρος, *moros*; μέρος, *meros*; Lat. *mereo*) meaning 'part', 'allotment', 'apportionment' (for example, *Il.* 16.68). *Moira* is, let us say in a preliminary manner, the allotment that one is assigned at birth, in fact at the very moment of birth, as we shall see below, and it is one that invariably runs its course towards death, a course later conceived as equal among mortals. In one example from the *Iliad*, we see Andromache stating that Hector has had his end spun by *Moira* at birth with her thread: τῷ δ᾽ ὥς ποθι Μοῖρα κραταιὴ γιγνομένῳ ἐπένησε λίνῳ, ὅτε μιν τέκον αὐτή (*Il.* 24.209); in another, Achilles' *moira* is described as having been spun at his birth – αἶσα γιγνομένῳ ἐπένησε λίνῳ ὅτε μιν τέκε μήτηρ (*Il.* 20.127). To this spinning act itself I will return shortly, but for now it is worth noting the genesis-setting of *moira* as spinning *at birth*. Certainly, in Homer, *moira* is most often associated with death in one way or another, but it would be misleading to simply identify *moira* with mortality or the event of death early on. Undeniably, θάνατος (*thanatos*, death) and *moira* often occur in the poems together.[9] Hence, in the *Iliad*, in its most frequent use, *moira* signifies death itself. It is death that is indicated in most of the utilisations of the expression μοῖρα ἐστί (*moira esti*, 'it is *moira*') in the *Iliad*,[10] although one can also find its opposite there as well ('it is not *moira* to die' (*Il.* 20.302), or 'to kill' (*Il.* 5.674)), suggesting an association between *moira* and death, rather than an identification.[11] It is

[9] For example, *Il.* 3.101; 5.83; and *Od.* 17.326; 21.24.
[10] For the use of this expression, see, for example, *Il.* 7.52; 16.434; 17.421; 18.119; 23.80; and *Od.* 5.41, 114; 9.532.
[11] See Yamagata (1994: 108).

also the case that the word μόρος (*moros*), from the same root (the verb μείρομαι, *meiromai*)[12] as *moira*, means death in both the *Odyssey* and the *Iliad*: a 'bad death' (κακὸν μόρον, *kakon moron*; *Il.* 21.133), the coming of death, a premature death, and so on.[13] The same fatal sense is expressed by *moira* in poetic expressions such as 'the darkness of death that envelops one' (μοῖρα δυσώνυμος ἀμφεκάλυψεν; *Il.* 12.116). It is on the 'opposite shore' to that of death, however, that we need to look to understand the experience that *moira* describes in the epics.

What takes place at birth? If the Muses delve in the birth of poetry, *moira* is weaved (ὑφαίνω, *hyphainō*) at the birth of life (Dietrich 1962: 94). It is possible that in early cults a deity or deities of birth were associated with this birth-blessing act to a greater or lesser degree (perhaps in the worship of Eileithyia, Artemis or the Nymphs)[14] and that an ancient tradition of magical practices was also linked to this. Bernard C. Dietrich refers to descriptions of the magical strength of 'the act of spinning and the material spun at the moment of birth' (1962: 89). Wool was widely used in rites in Greece in both raw and spun form, closely connected to apotropaic, expiatory and fertility purposes (ibid. 91). Linen threads of flax or, later, wool were used for medicinal purposes to cure female ailments and, especially, infertility (ibid. 92).[15]

---

[12] See, for example, *Il.* 1.616 and *Od.* 5.335. On the etymology, see Krause (1936: 146–7; Boisacq (1950: s.v. μοῖρα, μείρομαι), Chantraine (1968–2009: s.v. μείρομαι), and Frisk ([1954] 1960: s.v. μοῖρα, μείρομαι). For the linguistic evidence in Homer, see Ramat (1960).

[13] See *Od.* 9.61; *Il.* 18.465; 22.280; 24.85. One meets in the poems the impersonal μόρος ἐστι (*moros esti*), for example, *Od.* 6.357; 21.133; and in *Il.* 18.465; 19.42. One further encounters compounds that emphatically accentuate the meaning, as with αἰνομόροισιν [*ainomoroisin*] in *Od.* 24.169; δύσμορον [*dusmoron*] in *Il.* 22.60, etc.; and with ὠκύμορος [*ōkumoros*] in *Il.* 417, etc. See, further, Duffy (1947: 144–9). Finally, note another common near-synonymous expression, θέσφατόν ἐστι [*thesphaton esti*], for example, *Od.* 4.561; 10.473.

[14] See Eliade (1949: 163).

[15] See references in the Greek magical papyri, for example in *PGM* II.71; reference to Κλωθώ [*Klōthō*] in *PGM* IV 2249 and 2280. Κλῶθες [*Klōthes*] are met with in Homer once, though no mention of a triad is found, *Od.* 7.197. It is Hesiod who renders *moira* in the triadic form for the first time, in *Th.* 238. In Hesiod's *Theogony*, the sisters are introduced as

Dietrich goes on to suggest that the Homeric linking of *moira* with birth (and fertility) indicates a 'syncretism of popular belief and epic thought', rather than a mere poetic invention (ibid. 100; contra Wilamowitz-Moellendorff 1931: 358–62). The essential function of *moira* at birth appears to be, according to Dietrich, the act of marking someone's death, rather than 'fate' in general. Yet it can be intimated that this may be to misplace an emphasis of *moira* towards death, as opposed to its birth-given life. Curiously, returning to the association with wool or cloth, such fabrics lie unworked on the knees of cloth-worker gods and, thus, have a potency of their own (*Il.* 17.514; *Od.* 1.267). This implies a new question: is *moira* a potency, that is, a life? Is *moira* potent in itself, or is it, in fact, the spinning powers of the gods that are so instead?

2. *Klothology*: weaving a life

Moira is often described in relation to an act of 'weaving' (ὑφαίνειν, *huphainein*), 'sewing' (ῥάπτω, *rhaptō*), 'spinning', and/or 'binding', though, it needs to be noted, never as a spinner herself.[16] *Huphainein* in Homer signifies 'to weave' as well as to 'piece together in the mind, contrive, devise, and develop' (Cunliffe [1942] 2012).[17] The latter meaning is clear in, for example, *Il.* 7.324 and *Od.* 5.336. It can even be

---

Klōthō ('the Spinner'), *Lachesis* ('the allocator of lots') and *Atropos* ('the one who cannot be turned'), their father being Zeus, though, in a blurring of different traditions, they are described, on separate occasions, as having two different mothers (Night and *Themis*). Between Homer and Hesiod there is some poetic continuity though I do not examine this in this work, yet Hesiod's personified *Moira* is of an essentially different modality that centres *Moira* on the cosmic order overseen by an almighty Zeus's divine *dunamis*/'power': *Moira* is effectively divine action and Zeus is an active, living god at a more 'cosmic' level than in Homer (Mackowiak 2010: 39–49). The sense of allotment or dispensing remains, though in the sense of a more just attribution between gods and mortals (*Th.* 544). On *moira* (and *aisa*) as the *dunamis* of Zeus, see Tsagarakis (1977: 117–34). It could be said that this is the 'background' to the granting of *dikē* by Zeus to humans, on which see Chapter Six.

[16] See Giannakis (1998: 4), who, however, categorises *moira* as 'fate'; in later literature it is also described as 'an act of singing', see Leitzke (1930); and Dietrich (1962: 89, n. 15). On singing, see Chapter Ten.

[17] See Wace and Stubbings (1962: 531–2).

likened to the very composition of songs or poetry (Tuck 2006; 2009). It has been speculated that *humnos* (hymn) and *huphainō* may have a common origin (Nosch 2014a, 91) and that, more generally, weaving is closely linked to singing and by metaphorical extension to 'intellectual' activities in a wider sense.[18] The other word used in Homer that relates to the craft is, as noted above, the verb ῥάπτειν (*rhaptein*, 'sewing, stitching'), which can also attain the sense of 'devising or plotting' (Cunliffe [1942] 2012; for example, *Il*. 18.367), or 'singing' (as in ῥαψῳδός, *rhapsōdos*, rhapsody). Βουστροφηδόν (*boustrophēdon*: the technical term for a text running from left to right and then from right to left on the following line), Marie-Louise Nosch notes, is the same as the 'pattern made by the plowing ox in the fields going back and forth' (2014a: 93) and 'it is the same route as the weft threads (πήνη, *pēnē*) going into the warp system from left to right and from right to left, a *πηνοστροφηδόν [*pēnostrophēdon*] of a fabric' (ibid.).

Nosch adds a further connection of weaving to playing a musical instrument, as evident in the use of the verb κρέκειν (*krekein*), which means both (2014a: 94). Nosch notes that the 'acoustical landscape' of the household included the sound of the looms and weaving, the impact of loom weights and so forth, and, she adds, remarkably that 'the weaver orchestrates' (ibid.). The weaver is, it seems, always a woman in Homer (and beyond). Weavers, in Homer, are in fact central characters, such as Circe, who sings while weaving (for example, *Od*. 10.220–3), Helen (*Il*. 3.125), Calypso, who is also depicted weaving while singing, the Nymphs and, of course, Penelope (for example, *Od*. 2.94, 104; 5.517).[19] Women can even be said to 'speak' by weaving (Nosch 2014a: 96).[20] Their voices may be vividly heard, later, in Sophocles' vivid verse ἡ τῆς κερκίδος φωνή [*phōnē*] (the voice of the shuttle),[21] while the *grammata* (what is drawn or written), Nosch crucially notes, were also 'figurative ornamentation', 'designs' (ibid. 96).

---

[18] See Patzer (1952: 322–3); Snyder (1989: 193–6); Nagy (2002); and Beekes (2010: 1531).

[19] See Nosch (2014a: 92–3; 2003).

[20] See Bergren (2008: 15).

[21] Aris. *Poet*. 1454b, quoting Sophocles; see also Nosch (2014a: 93–6).

Logically, binding takes place after weaving or spinning. The act of spinning is consistently expressed in a formulaic fashion, suggesting a popular sense to it, whether as a matter of poetic invention, a reflection of social practice, or as a way of inheriting or adapting a much earlier tradition.[22] One is drawn, in any case, to imagine an everyday image of a group of spinners hard at work, an image that is confirmed by the centrality of wool production during the Bronze Age in particular, but also later.[23] Textile production forms the subject of approximately half of the Linear B tablets, mostly from the perspective of an administrative register. Yet Nosch has shown that it would be misleading to ignore the cosmological and mythological experience of weaving as a craft (2014a: 91). Nor are the terms used to describe the relevant acts, she notes, products of mere technical administration. A wider and central social experience can be presumed as widespread in myth and tradition, from Jason's search for the Golden Fleece, to the *Hersephoria* (weaving) festival in Athens.

In the few verses where Homer arguably personifies *moira* or *aisa*, he depicts them as spinning the *moira* of a person.[24] This appears linked to an arguable early cult personification that is rendered in the following verses (to which I also referred earlier): τῷ δ᾽ ὥς ποθι Μοῖρα [*Moira*] κραταιή

---

[22] The relation to a common and crucial (female) occupation is obvious. Speculation about an earlier 'Spinner' in European and Eastern popular religions as an 'absolute' power is offered in Krausse (1936: 151–2), perhaps a 'nature goddess' akin to Artemis or the Thracian Bendis (see *Il.* 16.183; 20.70; and *Od.* 4.122), Artemis' spindle is, perhaps, described. This is critically discussed by Dietrich (1962: 88–9) so far as the Greek evidence is concerned, while he also speculates, within reason, that spinning was perhaps attributed to *moira* at a later time, possibly by the poets themselves. In any case, an earlier (possibly even matriarchal) tradition prior to later archaic religious development cannot be discounted. In the Mycenaean tablets, lastly, we can note the word *a-ra-ka-te-ja*, 'spinners'; see Ventris and Chadwick (1973: 533).

[23] On the centrality of wool production, see Burke (1999); Nosch (2014b; 2014c); and Militello (2007). I return to this in Chapter Four.

[24] The personification is disputed. In any case, it is one without qualities or parentage, which perhaps confirms once more the precedence of the Homeric epics over the Hesiodic (where the fates, in fact, receive not one, but two genealogies). On personification in more general terms, see Webster (1994); and Northrup (1976).

| γιγνομένῳ ἐπένησε λίνῳ [*linō*] (*Il.* 24.209); possibly also: αἶσα | γιγνομένῳ ἐπένησε λίνῳ [*linō*] ὅτε μιν τέκε μήτηρ (*Il.* 20.127); and in αἶσα κατὰ κλῶθές [*klōthes*] τε βαρεῖαι | γιγνομένῳ νήσαντο λίνῳ, ὅτε μιν τέκε μήτηρ (*Od.* 7.196–7). In the latter verses, the addition of the, arguably, personified plural *klōthes* is most probably a poetic development, rather than an indication of independent figures in popular belief, while it may still be just a poetic plural. The only passage, however, where *moira* appears personified (*Moira*) with any accepted certainly is that of *Il.* 19.87: ἀλλὰ Ζεὺς καὶ Μοῖρα καὶ ἠεροφοῖτις Ἐρινύς; this is, in fact, perhaps the only time when *Moira* is described as an active agent, equal to Zeus and Erinys.[25]

In Homer, we also meet such spinning of *moira* as an act of the gods on many occasions, such as in ὄλβον ἐπικλώσῃ [*epiklōsē*] γαμέοντί τε γεινομένῳ τε (in this case by Zeus; *Od.* 4.208); or in relation to how an old man's misery is 'a lot spun by the gods': ὥς γὰρ ἐπεκλώσαντο [*epeklōsanto*] θεοὶ δειλοῖσι βροτοῖσι (*Il.* 24.525); or, indeed, with regard to how the gods have woven a web for Nestor: ἀλλ᾽ οὔ μοι τοιοῦτον ἐπέκλωσαν [*epeklōsan*] θεοὶ ὄλβον (*Od.* 3.208).[26] It is worth noticing the evocative descriptions of a 'thread spun as laid upon or around' (περιθεῖεν, *peritheien*) individuals, as in the instance when Telemachos says: . . . θεοὶ δύναμιν περιθεῖεν, . . . ἀλλ᾽ οὔ μοι τοιοῦτον ἐπέκλωσαν [*epeklōsan*] θεοὶ ὄλβον (*Od.* 3.205–8).[27] There is also a description of Odysseus' *moira* as a thread spun by an unspecified *daimon* in ὥς γὰρ οἱ ἐπέκλωσεν [*epeklōsen*] τά γε δαίμων (*Od.* 16.64).[28] It is pertinent here to note that in all these cases the gods' spinning is described by others.

In the case of the spinning of *moira* by the gods, most of the relevant verses have the verb in the past tense, perhaps 'implying that the spinning by the gods was anterior in time

[25] See Yamagata (1994), who observes likewise at 109–10; see also Hedén (1912: 148–9); and Otto ([1955] 1961: 268–9).
[26] See, inter alia, *Il.* 10.71; *Od.* 11.139; and 1.17 (τῷ οἱ ἐπεκλώσαντο [*epeklōsanto*] θεοὶ οἴκόνδε νέεσθαι).
[27] See *Il.* 24.515; *Od.* 8.579; 16.64; and 20.196.
[28] Perhaps an inspiration, even if critically appropriated, later on for Heraclitus in fr. 119: ἦθος ἀνθρώπῳ δαίμων [*ēthos anthrōpō daimōn*].

to the actualisation in life' (Onians 1954: 335). Richard B. Onians writes:

> The essential fact is that the spinning was thought of not as simultaneous with but as anterior to the fortunes spun. Something more was required for actualisation. We might expect that something to be one of the processes which naturally follow spinning among men, since there too spinning is but a preliminary. What is spun has still to be used. What are the normal uses of thread or cord? To bind and to weave. Binding is the fundamental purpose, the ἔργον [ergon], which gives a cord its significance, and to binding weaving itself and still more obviously the kindred process of net-making may be reduced or analysed. It was exactly this process, binding, which for the gods in Homer does, as we have seen, follow spinning. (1954: 335)

In this sense, *moira* could be conceived in one verse as a potential bond that is placed or allotted to mortals (*Od.* 3.269) and even more vividly so in ἐκπάγλως ἤχθηρε, τεῖν δ᾽ ἐπὶ μοῖραν ἔθηκεν [*moiran ethēken*] (from τίθημι, τιθέω; *tithēmi, titheō*) (*Od.* 11.560).[29] For Onians, this is the key meaning of *moira*: 'At birth the gods or fate(s) spin the strands of weal or woe which a man must endure in the course of his life, strands conceived quite literally as λίνον [*linon*], as threads . . . Later they bind them upon him no less literally as bonds, πείρατα [*peirata*]' (1954: 336, my edit).[30] Yet this binding or limit-setting (*peras*) is an *ex*-perience (Lat. *experiri*) that takes place in life, as life's acts (*erga*) that spin (i.e. that are potent). While a well-known sense is encountered in the later *Atropos* (meaning the one who cannot turn), here the sense in question is akin to *tropos*, way, and στροφεύς (*stropheus*), the spinner that 'turns'. It is worth noting that πείρατα (*peirata*), πεῖραρ (*peirar*), πέρας (*peras*), as a limit or bond is of cosmological significance in the archaic experience.[31] This is how

---

[29] See *Il.* 4.517; 22.5. The instances of the gods 'binding' *moira* are numerous: for example, in *Il.* 1.18; 3.309; and *Od.* 9.52; 15.523.

[30] On the use of λινόν [*linon*], see *Il.* 20.127; 24.210; and *Od.* 7.197.

[31] This 'bond or binding' is characteristically placed next to μοῖρα in

Odysseus' binding on the mast of the ship – standing with his hands and feet tied by a rope – is described while he hears the song of the Sirens: ὀρθὸν ἐν ἱστοπέδῃ, ἐκ δ' αὐτοῦ πείρατ' [*peirat'*] ἀνήφθω (*Od.* 12.51).[32] Incidentally, the link between a binding and limit-setting as a magical force is also evident in acts of speech that bind (spells, etc.), but also songs that 'bind', δέσμιος (*desmios*), ὕμνος (*humnos*), a binding song, and ἐπῳδή (*epōdē*), a song sung over the dead.[33]

Theorising further, it could be said that *Moira* is the potency, the infancy, that needs to be actualised through binding, that is, through an experience of and within the limit (a *peras*, namely, a 'lot of life'). Dietrich offers well-placed caution in noticing subtly that when the gods spin in Homer, and they do so on far more occasions than *moira* (or *aisa*) does: they spin (at times, prolonged) 'events' (rather than a 'whole' path of life, though this is also the case, in fact, for *moira* and *aisa*). To expect to find a linear fateful (as much as fatal) line, however, at a time when 'time' is neither 'a sequence of nows' nor a time divided between 'past, present and future' would be an anachronism. Furthermore, the gods are said to spin such 'events', while they could grant them in far simpler terms, to the point that it may be that in Homer such descriptions of divine spinning-acts are reflecting their (otherwise ordinary) potent functions, but in a more poetic or emphatic fashion (Dietrich 1962: 99). If *moira* and *aisa*, as such, spin the end-marking of death, rather than a particular life, the gods are seen to spin a much wider range of experience. Yet as Dietrich maintains, in the *Iliad* in particular, but also more generally, *moira* indicates traces of an earlier popular idea of 'fate' as equal to the giving of death, in the sense of 'the share of death' (Dietrich 1965: 90) or 'the limited portion' (Burkert [1977] 1985: 129–30, 270ff), the limit of any lot in life. The origin of *moira* can be speculated, in this sense, as being chthonic, but, in any case, as being a limited 'part' (a 'life').

Homer through the use of the word πεδάω [*pedaō*], 'bind with fetters'; for example, in *Il.* 4.517: ἔνθ' Ἀμαρυγκεΐδην Διώρεα μοῖρα πέδησεν [*pedēsen*]; *Il.* 10.5; *Od.* 3.269.

[32] See, for example, *Od.* 7.402; 22.174; and *Il.* 12.79; 13.358–60.

[33] See Giannakis (1999: 107, n. 36).

Nomos Moirēgenēs

3. Apportionment

Moira in the Homeric poems is utilised in more ways than one, far beyond her arguable personified appearances, or the 'apportionment' of a limit/death. One of the most frequent and characteristic employments regards the indication or assignment of a portion, a share or a part of something in a large variety of situations, for instance: a 'part of honour' (*Il.* 9.318); the 'third part of the night' (τῶν δύο μοιράων, τριτάτη δ᾽ ἔτι μοῖρα λέλειπται; *Il.* 10.253);[34] a portion of food;[35] on one occasion 'a parcel of land' (*Il.* 16.68); or a part of a 'property' (δώμασι, *dōmasi*; *Od.* 4.97; *Od.* 5.41 and *Il.* 9.318: ἴση μοῖρα [*isē moira*]); *Il.* 16.68: ἐκλίαται, χώρης ὀλίγην ἔτι μοῖραν, of sleep (and *Od.* 19.592); and a 'share of the spoil' (*Od.* 5.41 and *Il.* 9.318: ἴση μοῖρα [*isē moira*]; *Il.* 16.68: ἐκλίαται, χώρης ὀλίγην ἔτι μοῖραν ἔχοντες [*moiran echontes*] – and see differentiation as to γέρας [*geras*] in *Od.* 11.534); an 'allotted share' (καὶ κρατερός περ ἐὼν μενέτω τριτάτη ἐνὶ μοίρῃ [*moirē*], *Il.* 15.195); or, with regard to meat, the σπλάγχνων μοίρας [*splagchnōn moiras*] (the interior parts, *Od.* 3.40; 20.260); or the wine, as in οἱ δ᾽ ἤδη μοίρας τ᾽ ἔνεμον [*enemon*] κερόωντό τε οἶνον (*Od.* 8.470); the 'placed' (θέσαν, *thesan*) moira of Odysseus (*Od.* 20.281); the 'divisions of *moira*' in μοίρας δασσάμενοι [*moiras dassamenoi*] δαίνυντ᾽ ἐρικυδέα δαῖτα (*Od.* 3.66); and an 'allotted', divinely ordained, marriage (*Od.* 21.162). While these 'situations' can be semantically differentiated, their intersection is also evident.

Within such a range, the apportionment of a lot in life, one's *moira* as allotted appears as one of many, yet it is a common one, for example: in that it is 'not yet one's time to die' in οὐ γάρ πώ τοι μοῖρα θανεῖν (*Il.* 7.52); in 'if *moira*

---

[34] In the Homeric *Hym. to Dem.* (446) *moira* is the third part of the year; while in the *Hym. to Ap.* (229–38), the *moira* of Poseidon is his sacred *temenos*, a portion of land where his worship takes place.

[35] See, for example, *Od.* 3.40, 66; 14.448; 15.140; 17.258; 20.260, 280, 281, 293. A meal as such was a δαίς [*dais*] (from δαίομαι [*daiomai*], 'to apportion'; from the Indo-European root *dāi-, 'to divide'): *Od.* 3.66; 20.280; a sense of 'equality of shares' is understood as being according to one's worth or honour: *Od.* 20.279–83, 292–300. In the Homeric *Hym. to Herm.*, 128–9, the portions of meat offered to the gods are associated with their *moira* and their *timē*; see Finkelberg (1998b: 14–28).

49

wishes our death', ὦ φίλοι, εἰ καὶ μοῖρα παρ' ἀνέρι τῷδε δαμῆναι (*Il.* 17.421); or as to 'a lot ordained' in καὶ δὲ σοὶ αὐτῷ μοῖρα, θεοῖς ἐπιείκελ' Ἀχιλλεῦ (*Il.* 23.80); and in 'fleeing from one's allotted *moira*', as in γαίης Φαιήκων, ὅθι τοι μοῖρ' ἐστὶν ἀλύξαι (*Od.* 5.345).[36] This shows, once more, that if one must insist on a 'core' semantic of *moira* it is that of a part or portion with regard to a wide array of situational allotments without an exclusively positive or negative connotation. If *moira* points to fatal events in the *Iliad* in a more predominant sense than in, perhaps, the *Odyssey*, in the latter we find her describing Odysseus' return to Ithaca, or an inability to flee a scene, or the act of being led to insult someone, or the division of spoils, as much as the fitting of oars. The significance of this apportionment is also illustrated by its link to honour (*timē*) and one's worth (see, for example, *Il.* 1.278; *Od.* 5.335),[37] and especially so in situations where it is lacking. The value of such assignation is illustrated, thus, when one suffers the fate of a homeless wanderer without a lot or portion, that is, when one is ἀμμορίη (*ammoriē*, without *mōros* or *moira*; *Od.* 20.76; *Il.* 6.408).[38]

4. Binding

It is quite commonplace to conceptualise 'fate' as somewhat akin to anachronistic predestination (or a 'sovereign norm') and (monotheistic) divine intervention: that is, as a matter of the exercise of a 'divine sovereignty' (whether of an older goddess-spinner, or of the Olympian gods, or, as some argue, of the will of Zeus as an absolute sovereign).[39] Yet this is misguided when alleged as a point of 'origin'. It is certain that the gods are not creators of the universe, and also that, at least, in Homer's poems, which possibly speak of an amalgam of periods and traditions, there is a transitional poetic intersection at stake as to both the powers of gods and those of mortals and, crucially, as to the relationship between them. To take one of the underlying issues in this matter, let

[36] See *Il.* 15.117; 16.434; 18.120; and *Od.* 4.475; 5.41, 114; 9.532; 19.592; 20.171.
[37] See Dietrich (1965: 225).
[38] See *Od.* 5.275; and *Il.* 18.489.
[39] See Farnell (1896–1909: 79); and Duffy (1947: 477–85).

us consider for a moment the question of whether the gods are 'subject' to *moira*. Whatever point of view one takes in this long-standing debate,[40] it should be noted from the start that one thing is rarely disputed – the widespread understanding of the apportionment of 'fate' as such: so much so that even Achilles' horse, empowered by Hera, can speak and indicate his master's death in μόρσιμόν ἐστι θεῷ τε καὶ ἀνέρι (*Il.* 19.417). That *moira* is potent and forceful is expressed in a myriad of ways, including, as we have seen, when spun by the gods, as in ἀλλὰ θεοὶ δυόωσι πολυπλάγκτους ἀνθρώπους | ὁππότε καὶ βασιλεῦσιν ἐπικλώσωνται ὀϊζύν ('yet it is true; the much-wandering men are those whom the gods hold | in despite, when they spin misery even for βασιλεῖς' [*basileis*]; *Od.* 20.195–6). That the gods are subordinate, in one sense, to *moira* is a view that was strongly expressed by, for example, Cornford ([1912] 1957), while it was equally strongly rejected by James Duffy (1947). Yet Duffy seems to underappreciate that Cornford refers speculatively to an older *moira* (one that is perhaps only implied in Homer), an ancient goddess to whom the gods were subject as much as the mortals. Without necessarily resorting to this archaeology of *moira*, which will probably remain inconclusive, we can turn to the poems themselves for clues as to an answer.[41] There we can find, amidst the Homeric universe, a *moira* that will 'dispense' one's lot in the predominantly aristocratic *Iliad*, or be 'co-dispensed', to one degree or another, among the gods, and Zeus in particular. Yet above all, we will still sense a *moira* that *is* herself the potency of apportionment (μοιρηγενής, *moirēgenēs*, *Il.* 3.182), a life.

Moira, as apportioned by the gods as their 'apparatus' for the exercise of their power (or that of Zeus in particular) can be interpreted, at least to a degree, from a variety of key passages in the poems, though this is something that is

---

[40] Yamagata summarises the four main strands in this debate as follows, referring to *moira*, however, as 'fate': '(1) fate is identical to the will of the gods or of Zeus; (2) the gods are only the instruments of fate; (3) the gods and fate belong to two separate spheres of religious principles, which the poet failed to coordinate into a coherent system; (4) fate is only the poet's plan or what the legend says, i.e. the plot of the poem' (1994: 105); see, further, Ehnmark (1935: 74); and Leitzke (1930: 65–7).

[41] See, generally, Dietrich (1962; 1965).

mostly later developed in Hesiod. It is worth starting our brief engagement with the following extensive passage (*Il.* 15.185–95):

ὢ πόποι ἦ ῥ᾽ ἀγαθός περ ἐὼν ὑπέροπλον ἔειπεν
εἴ μ᾽ ὁμότιμον [*homotimon*] ἐόντα βίη ἀέκοντα καθέξει.
τρεῖς γάρ τ᾽ ἐκ Κρόνου εἰμὲν ἀδελφεοὶ οὓς τέκετο Ῥέα
Ζεὺς καὶ ἐγώ, τρίτατος δ᾽ Ἀΐδης ἐνέροισιν ἀνάσσων.
τριχθὰ δὲ πάντα δέδασται [*dedastai*], ἕκαστος δ᾽ ἔμμορε
    τιμῆς [*emmore timēs*]·
ἤτοι ἐγὼν ἔλαχον [*elachon*] πολιὴν ἅλα ναιέμεν αἰεὶ
παλλομένων, Ἀΐδης δ᾽ ἔλαχε [*elache*] ζόφον ἠερόεντα,
Ζεὺς δ᾽ ἔλαχ᾽ οὐρανὸν εὐρὺν ἐν αἰθέρι καὶ νεφέλῃσι·
γαῖα δ᾽ ἔτι ξυνὴ πάντων καὶ μακρὸς Ὄλυμπος.
τώ ῥα καὶ οὔ τι Διὸς βέομαι φρεσίν, ἀλλὰ ἕκηλος
καὶ κρατερός περ ἐὼν μενέτω τριτάτῃ ἐνὶ μοίρῃ [*moirē*].

Richard Lattimore (1967) translates:

> No, no. Great though he is, this that he has said is too
>   much,
> if he will force me against my will, me, who am his equal
> in rank. Since we are three brothers born by Rheia to
>   Kronos,
> Zeus, and I, and the third is Hades, lord of the dead men.
> All was divided among us three ways, each given his
>   domain.
> I when the lots were shaken drew the grey sea to live in
> forever; Hades drew the lot of the mists and the darkness,
> and Zeus was allotted the wide sky, in the cloud and the
>   bright air.
> But earth and high Olympos are common to all three.
>   Therefore
> I am no part of the mind of Zeus. Let him in tranquillity
> and powerful as he is stay satisfied with his third share.

In this episode Poseidon, as we shall see below, will state that the three sons of Kronos, himself, Zeus and Ades, enjoy *isomoira* (equal portions of *moira*; at 209), but first he refers to the allotted territories or regions as reflecting that they are *homotimoi* (of 'equal honour or worth'; 185–6). Poseidon has the lot (*elakhon*) of the sea, Ades the darkness and Zeus the sky, while the earth and Olympus are common to all of them (*xunē pantōn*). Poseidon will crucially add that, while Zeus is powerful in his allotted portion of the universe (the sky), he cannot interfere with Poseidon's portion.[42] Iris, who responds to Poseidon (200–4), suggests caution to him, since Zeus remains the eldest-born among the brothers (204) and far superior in strength and force (κρατερόν; βίη πολὺ φέρτερος εἶναι, as described earlier at 181):

τὸν δ᾽ ἠμείβετ᾽ ἔπειτα ποδήνεμος ὠκέα Ἶρις·
οὕτω γὰρ δή τοι γαιήοχε κυανοχαῖτα
τόνδε φέρω Διὶ μῦθον ἀπηνέα τε κρατερόν τε,
ἦ τι μεταστρέψεις; στρεπταὶ μέν τε φρένες ἐσθλῶν.
οἶσθ᾽ ὡς πρεσβυτέροισιν Ἐρινύες αἰὲν ἕπονται.

Lattimore (1967) translates:

Then in turn swift wind-footed Iris answered him:
'Am I then to carry, o dark-haired, earth-encircler,
this word, which is strong and steep, back to Zeus from
   you?
Or will you change a little? The hearts of the great can be
   changed. You know the Furies, how they forever side
   with the elder.'

Poseidon replies to her (206–9) and states that, while she speaks well, he will be enraged if any one, among equals (ἰσόμορον, isomoron; ὁμῇ πεπρωμένον αἴσῃ, homē peprōmenon aisē), attempts to reproach another:

Ἶρι θεὰ μάλα τοῦτο ἔπος κατὰ μοῖραν ἔειπες·
ἐσθλὸν καὶ τὸ τέτυκται ὅτ᾽ ἄγγελος αἴσιμα εἰδῇ.
ἀλλὰ τόδ᾽ αἰνὸν ἄχος κραδίην καὶ θυμὸν ἱκάνει
ὁππότ᾽ ἂν ἰσόμορον καὶ ὁμῇ πεπρωμένον αἴσῃ

---

[42] Poseidon is portrayed here as presenting his own genealogy whereby the earth and heaven are parents to all the gods and hence common; see Cornford ([1912] 1957: 16, n. 2). On a different division of the earth, the sea and the sky in particular, consider *Il.* 18.483, where Hephaistos makes the Shield; see also *Od.* 12.315.

Lattimore's (1967) translation, with additional modifications, can be rendered as:

> Now this, divine Iris, was a word spoken *kata moiran*.
> It is a fine thing when a messenger is conscious of 'justice'.
> But this comes as a bitter sorrow to my heart and my *thumos*,
> when [Zeus tries] in words of anger to reprimand one who is his equal in *moira*, and *aisē*.

Poseidon is suffering because he feels that his *isomoria/isomoiria* is being infringed. Boundaries should not be crossed; the gods cannot and should not encroach on each other's portion or *moira*. It can be noted, further, that the word πεπρωμένος (*peprōmenos*) is possibly etymologically related to the Latin *pars*, *portio* (portion).[43] The expression of the territories as ἔμμορε τιμῆς (*emmore timēs*, at 189) underlines the complaint of Poseidon in a 'spatial or territorial' sense.[44] In this scene, the gods are seen to have received their apportionment by a lot through an act of their own. Yet it is easy to miss in Iris's response that this apportionment remains *kata moiran*, that is, according to the order of things that *moira* itself is, and as guarded by the Erinyes (the 'darker' *moirai*).[45] That the gods decide among themselves as to their domains therefore needs to be measured by the fact that this is done by a lot (*moira*'s domain) and that ultimately what their apportionment met with was *moira*, as the order of the cosmos. The gods' apportionment could be said to be immanent in their *moira*. This is a fundamental episode for Cornford, who argues on this basis that the gods are 'subordinate' to an older pre-Homeric *moira* (as a representation of 'natural facticity'), which in the epics the gods (and Homer) can be seen to gradually attempt to overthrow ([1912] 1957: 16–17).

---

[43] See Borecký (1963: 44).

[44] See *Od.* 5.335, where Leukothea's portion or domain is described in a similar manner, though the terms 'spatial' and 'territorial' should be understood merely as loose indicators.

[45] See Dietrich (1965: 205–12, 223–30) for the social and juridical senses of *moira*; also, on 'order' and *moira*, see Pötscher (1960: 5–39).

Zeus, in a well-known verse, is described as stronger than all other immortals and as able to increase or diminish a mortal's *aretē* (worth; for example, *Il.* 20.241–2: Ζεὺς δ᾽ ἀρετὴν [*aretēn*] ἄνδρεσσιν ὀφέλλει τε μινύθει τε | ὅππως κεν ἐθέλησιν· ὃ γὰρ κάρτιστος ἁπάντων). It is in this manner that he is perhaps depicted also as the 'dispenser of fate' (*Il.* 24.527–30). In this manner, he is the spinner of a specific *moira* on several occasions, where *moira*, in fact, is stated as μοῖρα Διός (*moira Dios*) by Ares in *Il.* 15.117, as well as by Odysseus in *Od.* 11.560. Yet similar instances can be found regarding Apollo (for example, *Il.* 19.410), or Hera (*Il.* 18.119), or the gods collectively (as in *Od.* 22.413). In the latter instance, it is worth noting that the suitors are said to be killed by μοῖρα θεῶν (*moira theōn*) and by their own σχέτλια ἔργα (*schetlia erga*, 'their own deeds'). Yet it seems to me that it would be rather anachronistic to find here, and more generally, a notion of 'omnipotence', or a divine sovereign will.[46] No doubt, Naoko Yamagata points out, 'clearly men believe that at least some μοῖραι come from the gods' (1994: 109). This can be illustrated in the scene where Melampus is the prisoner of a divine *moira* (θεοῦ μοῖρα, *theou moira*; *Od.* 11.292),[47] or in the statements, so Yamagata notes, of Ares (*Il.* 15.117) and Xanthus (*Il.* 19.410). Zeus is also described as 'knowing (οἶδα, *oida*) all the apportioned *moira* of mortals', or lack of it: ὃ γάρ τ᾽ εὖ οἶδεν ἅπαντα, | μοῖράν τ᾽ ἀμμορίην τε καταθνητῶν ἀνθρώπων (*Od.* 20.76). While it can be said that Zeus here is able to see, or to know, the *moira* of mortals, he is not described as 'the author of it'.[48] The universe's power or *moira*, its ordering, is not divided according to a strict separation of powers, and often *moira* and the gods can be seen to share a part in the poetic causality of events (which, however, does not mean that these parts collapse into a single one).

We can also note, briefly, what happens when Zeus wishes to intervene as to a mortal's *moira*, in particular. In the well-known passage in the *Iliad*'s Book 16, where Zeus is confronted with the fate of his son Sarpedon, who is doomed to die, he states (431–8):

---

[46] For instance, Duffy (1947); and Lloyd-Jones (1971).
[47] See, generally, Berry (1940).
[48] See Yamagata (1994: 109).

τοὺς δὲ ἰδὼν ἐλέησε Κρόνου πάϊς ἀγκυλομήτεω,
Ἥρην δὲ προσέειπε κασιγνήτην ἄλοχόν τε·
ὤ μοι ἐγών, ὅ τέ μοι Σαρπηδόνα φίλτατον ἀνδρῶν
μοῖρ᾽ ὑπὸ Πατρόκλοιο Μενοιτιάδαο δαμῆναι.
διχθὰ δέ μοι κραδίη μέμονε φρεσὶν ὁρμαίνοντι,
ἤ μιν ζωὸν ἐόντα μάχης ἄπο δακρυοέσσης
θείω ἀναρπάξας Λυκίης ἐν πίονι δήμω,
ἦ ἤδη ὑπὸ χερσὶ Μενοιτιάδαο δαμάσσω.

Lattimore (1967) translates:

> And watching them the son of devious-devising Kronos
> was pitiful, and spoke to Hera, his wife and his sister:
> 'Ah me, that it is destined that the dearest of men,
>   Sarpedon, must go down under the hands of Menoitios'
>   son Patroklos.
> The heart in my breast is balanced between two ways
>   as I ponder, whether I should snatch him out of the
>   sorrowful battle
> and set him down still alive in the rich country of Lykia,
> or beat him under at the hands of the son of Menoitios.'

While Zeus accepts that it is his son's portion (*moira*) to die by
Patroclus' hand, his heart is torn and he considers removing
Sarpedon from the battle and placing him in Lykea. However,
Hera, who is angered by Sarpedon's *moira*, responds (439–47)
by stating:

τὸν δ᾽ ἠμείβετ᾽ ἔπειτα βοῶπις πότνια Ἥρη·
αἰνότατε Κρονίδη ποῖον τὸν μῦθον ἔειπες.
ἄνδρα θνητὸν ἐόντα πάλαι πεπρωμένον αἴση
ἂψ ἐθέλεις θανάτοιο δυσηχέος ἐξαναλῦσαι;
ἔρδ᾽· ἀτὰρ οὔ τοι πάντες ἐπαινέομεν θεοὶ ἄλλοι.
ἄλλο δέ τοι ἐρέω, σὺ δ᾽ ἐνὶ φρεσὶ βάλλεο σῆσιν·
αἴ κε ζὼν πέμψῃς Σαρπηδόνα ὃν δὲ δόμον δέ,
φράζεο μή τις ἔπειτα θεῶν ἐθέλησι καὶ ἄλλος
πέμπειν ὃν φίλον υἱὸν ἀπὸ κρατερῆς ὑσμίνης·

Lattimore (1967) translates:

> In turn the lady Hera of the ox eyes answered him:

'Majesty, son of Kronos, what sort of thing have you
   spoken?
Do you wish to bring back a man who is mortal, one long
   since doomed by his destiny,
from ill-sounding death and release him?
Do it, then; but not all the rest of us gods shall approve
   you.
And put away in your thoughts this other thing I tell you;
If you bring Sarpedon back to his home, still living,
think how then some other one of the gods might also
wish to carry his own son out of the strong encounter . . .

In these verses, Hera is alerting Zeus to what his act of intervention in saving his son from certain death could mean.
Sarpedon's fate is, however, bound to death by *moira* and
it could not be unbound by Zeus (Hera seems to clearly
imply so at 441), even if it were to be temporarily delayed.
Furthermore, she adds, if Zeus were to take this action, this
would set a precedent that could be taken advantage of by
other gods. Zeus refrains from action in the end and his son
falls. Order needs to be maintained; *moira* cannot be undone
or unbound by divine intervention. *Moira* is a fact of the
cosmos, as much as of mortal manners (or, better, of their
indistinctness). When Poseidon considers intervening (in *Il.*
20.335–6), just before Aeneas is about to face Achilles, he
does so, but this is not against the bond of *moira*, since it was
ordained (μόριμον, *morimon*) that Aeneas would survive the
war (*Il.* 20.302). In a somewhat similar episode to that of Zeus
above, involving the mortal Hector – who was also bound
to die by *moira* when he faced Achilles outside the walls of
Troy in what is described as an unequal battle (*Il.* 22.5) – his
parents are seen to beg him to retreat behind the walls and to
avoid his fate, but Hector says that his *dunamis* (his power)
is not sufficient against his *moira* (at 20).[49] If a break or intervention was ever possible for Hector, it was never actualised
(and so is the case with all such contemplations to contravene
moira in the poems). More than anything else, the ultimate
fate of all mortals cannot be altered (*Od.* 3.236–8).

[49] Similarly, in *Od.* 11.292–3; and *Il.* 4.517.

5. Weighing the scales

Zeus' capacity to intervene or to alter *moira* is captured in three well-known passages that we need to consider. In the first passage (*Il.* 8.68–74),[50] Zeus is described to Priam by Achilles as balancing his scales, wherein are placed the death-lots of the Trojans and the Achaeans. In this scene, the dispenser of ill and good holds the scales and lifts them, as a result of which the Achaeans' *moira* sank down and that of the Trojans was raised to the sky:

ἦμος δ᾽ Ἠέλιος μέσον οὐρανὸν ἀμφιβεβήκει,
καὶ τότε δὴ χρύσεια πατὴρ ἐτίταινε τάλαντα·
ἐν δ᾽ ἐτίθει δύο κῆρε τανηλεγέος θανάτοιο
Τρώων θ᾽ ἱπποδάμων καὶ Ἀχαιῶν χαλκοχιτώνων,
ἕλκε δὲ μέσσα λαβών·ῥέπε δ᾽ αἴσιμον ἦμαρ Ἀχαιῶν.
αἱ μὲν Ἀχαιῶν κῆρες ἐπὶ χθονὶ πουλυβοτείρῃ
ἑζέσθην, Τρώων δὲ πρὸς οὐρανὸν εὐρὺν ἄερθεν

Lattimore (1967) translates:

But when the sun god stood bestriding the middle
 heaven,
then the father balanced his golden scales, and in them
he set two fateful portions of death, which lays men
 prostrate,
for Trojans, breakers of horses, and bronze-armoured
 Achaians,
and balanced it by the middle. The Achaians' death-day
 was heaviest.
There the fates of the Achaians settled down toward the
 bountiful earth,
while those of the Trojans were lifted into the wide sky
 . . .

The second passage (*Il.* 19.223–4)[51] is where Zeus inclines his scales towards war, dispenser of destruction that he is (ταμίης πολέμοιο, *tamiēs polemoio*), and is described as:

[50] See *Il.* 16.658.
[51] Compare *Il.* 22.209.

ἄμητος δ᾽ ὀλίγιστος, ἐπὴν κλίνῃσι τάλαντα | Ζεύς, ὅς τ᾽ ἀνθρώπων ταμίης πολέμοιο τέτυκται.

The final passage is from rhapsody 22, where Zeus is depicted by Odysseus as weighing up the two κῆρες (kēres) of Achilles and Hector, and it is Hector's that sinks to Hades (Il. 22.209–13):

καὶ τότε δὴ χρύσεια πατὴρ ἐτίταινε τάλαντα,
ἐν δ᾽ ἐτίθει δύο κῆρε τανηλεγέος θανάτοιο,
τὴν μὲν Ἀχιλλῆος, τὴν δ᾽ Ἕκτορος ἱπποδάμοιο,
ἕλκε δὲ μέσσα λαβών· ῥέπε δ᾽ Ἕκτορος αἴσιμον ἦμαρ,
ᾤχετο δ᾽ εἰς Ἀΐδαο, λίπεν δέ ἑ Φοῖβος Ἀπόλλων

Lattimore (1967) translates:

> then the Father balanced his golden scales, and in them
> he set two fateful portions of death, which lays men
> prostrate,
> one for Achilleus, and one for Hektor, breaker of horses,
> and balanced it by the middle; and Hektor's death-day
> was heavier
> and dragged downward toward death, and Phoibos
> Apollo forsook him.

To these three depictions of 'the scales of Zeus' we can add one minor reference to them in rhapsody 16 (at 658) of the *Iliad* where Hector flees because, as he says, γνῶ γὰρ Διὸς ἱρὰ τάλαντα ('he has known the scales of Zeus').

In the first passage (rhapsody 8), but more generally too, it is easy to forget, given the imagery, that it is *moira* that the Trojan war takes place, and it is *moira* that Zeus executes his plan through the war (as do the other gods with their own interventions in it).[52] The immortals exercise their divine powers through mortal manners, which marks Homer's own 'balancing' in the poem as analogous to an everyday activity of mortals.[53] The gods' immortal hand, their divine potency, is

---

[52] See Yamagata (1994: 98).

[53] In another scene, such a metaphor of balancing is instead an everyday activity in the balancing of the wool by a widow (*Il.* 12.433) to determine the amount of wool to spin in one day, although the wool-worker is

moira, the cosmic allotment or ordering. This is most evident, as we saw earlier, when the gods act against their own feelings. It is not their 'sovereignty' or 'moral imperatives' that the gods 'exercise', but instead their frustrations *and* compliance with their *moira*, as well as that of mortals. The gods do not need to 'submit' to an impersonal *moira*, because they are or they 'have' their own *moira*. *Moira* is not, at least in the Homeric epics, superior to the gods (or vice versa), but coexistent, even if in the Homeric poems it is, perhaps, possible to see a transition taking place, incoherently as much as incompletely, towards the rising predominance of the Olympians.[54] Above all, in any case, in the passages of rhapsodies 8 and 22, Zeus' balancing has nothing to do with any kind of 'fate'.[55]

In both cases, tellingly, the outcome was already known before Zeus' balancing of the scales. It is easy to suggest that, instead of Zeus dispensing *moira* here, the scales are merely held by Zeus, yet operate as scales do. But what is it that the scales actually do in the passages that concern us? In the two passages of Books 8 and 22, the lots are expressed with the word κήρ (*kēr*, plural κήρες, *kēres*).[56] Κήρ (*kēr*), κηρός (*kēros*, from κείρω, *keirō*, 'cut'), which in a secondary sense can mean 'death' (as in *Il.* 8.68–74, κήρ θανάτοιο, *kēr thanatoio*),[57] as

balancing equal weights (used metaphorically also in *Il.* 12.437); while in the scene in Book 22 there is no equalisation of the two weights, see Dietrich (1964: 102). On the poignant and related metaphor of balancing on Nestor's edge of a razor, see *Il.* 10.173. More generally, it can be noted that metaphors drawn from everyday activities are often used (as seen with regard to weaving and spinning), and especially creative acts, to describe key scenes, indicating that the poet(s) draw(s) from familiar everyday scenes more often than not. A famous scene of this kind is Penelope weaving the great web, in *Od.* 2.105. For further examples, see *Il.* 6.187; 10.19; *Od.* 4.678; 20.11.

54 The tension is evident in the at first sight directly conflicting descriptions of the gods as subject to *moira* (for example, *Od.* 3.236–8; 9.528–35; and *Il.* 16.439–50), as well as appealing to *moira* (for example, *Il.* 17.321; *Od.* 5.345); see Eidinow (2011: 30–5).

55 See Dietrich (1964: 99).

56 One can note also the homophone κῆρ [*kēr*], namely, the heart, the seat of the passions or life; see, for example, *Il.* 1.491; 7.309; 10.504; and usage as one's character or disposition in *Od.* 23.167.

57 See, inter alia, *Il.* 1.228; 2.352; 5.22; and *Od.* 2.165, 283.

can *daimōn*,[58] is the weight[59] that is put in the scales, typifying it as a *kērostasia*; at times also personified as the agent of death (*moira*),[60] or, indeed, in the sense of mortals, as agents of death.[61] Like *moira*, κῆρες (*kēres*), as death spirits, can, in some instances, but mostly in an impersonal fashion, be delayed or enabled to act more quickly (*Od.* 11.397; and *Il.* 12.402, etc.), but what they are (or are agents of) is not ultimately avoided. Again, to indicate the more general point, it is by *moira* 'that the gods are immortal and men mortal, and the abyss between them must not be bridged' (Yamagata 1994: 97). The predominant sense of *moira* is, in fact, 'spatial' in this sense.[62] But, as Dietrich has convincingly shown, the *kēres* do not represent 'fate(s)' (1964).

The *kēres* assumed a function most associated with *moira*, as in *Od.* 14.207, where they are bearing the victim off to Hades, or in *Il.* 23.78, where the *kēr* is a 'lot at birth', invariably 'death', not so much as fate but as a 'fact of life'.[63] Yet crucially, *moira* is never imagined as 'weighing' anyone's fate.[64] The classicist D. J. N. Lee disputed, with some good reason, the etymology from *Kērā, κεραΐζω (keraizō)* as signifying primarily 'death', 'destruction' or a 'death-goddess' (1960/1961: 193). Death ('fate of death') appears secondary, while fate/destiny in the sense of *moira* appears more primary: that is, as a lot (ibid. 194). Thus, *kēr* is from the Indo-European root **(s)qer*, meaning primarily 'part', 'allotment', 'lot', whereby κείρω, *keirō* means 'cut', 'allot'. Lee has noted that Hesychius equated *kēr* with *moira*, early on, and that Plato clearly thought of *kēres* as 'lots' (ibid. 192).[65] *Moira, kēr*

---

[58] See *Il.* 8.166 and 18.155
[59] See *Il.* 10.210.
[60] See, inter alia, *Od.* 2.316, 352; 4.512; 23.332; and *Il.* 4.11; 13.283; 18.535; 21.565.
[61] See *Il.* 2.353; or regarding an animal, *Il.* 3.6; see, further, Dietrich (1964: 103–4).
[62] In direct contradiction to our temporal sense of 'fate' ('power' as well as 'space'). The 'spatial' here has nothing to do with modern trepidations concerning the scission between 'time and space'.
[63] See Dietrich (1964: 104–5); and *Il.* 12.326.
[64] See Dietrich (1964: 109).
[65] Pl. *Rep.* 2.379d, reading *Il.* 24.528: κηρῶν ἔμπλειοι, ὁ μὲν ἐσθλῶν, αὐτὰρ ὁ δειλῶν.

and *aisa* are, in this sense, closely related in meaning as they
are interchangeable in usage (ibid. 196–7). Finally, it is worth
noting that in the negative ἀκήρατος (*akēratos*), its meaning
entails being 'intact, undivided', possibly also 'unpastured',
'uneaten' (ibid. 203).[66] In this manner, 'death' can be conceived, as Martin P. Nilsson suggested, as 'the last and inevitable portion' (1949: 169).

With regard to Zeus' use of the scales in Homer, Dietrich
has observed:

> No real balance is implied here . . . the essential point in
> this image – whenever Zeus makes use of his scales – that
> a death or, in a developed form, a defeat is at hand. It is
> only in this way that we can comprehend the seemingly
> perverse fact . . . that the heavier side of the scales is also
> the less desirable one. (1964: 107)

Dietrich demonstrates in some detail that we may have here
traits (most likely 'religious' and with some foreign influence) of what will later become a famous depiction of justice
(in *dikē, dikaiosunē,* but also in the Lat. *aequitas, justitia*) as
an art of balance, though at this point we are not meeting
with justice in this later sense (1964). The use of scales is a
common experience (already so in Mycenaean times), and
as one with 'religious' significance it is expressed in Homer
in a slightly awkward manner (given that in his use, nothing
actually ever happens that is not already known), suggesting
that this may be a long-standing tradition that 'finds itself
at the end' (Dietrich 1964: 113).[67] Dietrich, in fact, points out
that what lies in the traditional background of the *stasis* of
the *kēres* in Homer is a transition from a certain form of judgment, a 'proto-judicial' function, though one that is immersed
in an everyday 'religious' practice, long before the Greeks
have any formal notion of judgment with strong moral and
legal implications. Its early milieu, it remains thus possible

---

[66] On the pastoral, see Chapter Four.
[67] Dietrich brilliantly points to the lost epic of the Epic Cycle, preceding the
Iliad and the *Odyssey,* the *Aethiopis,* as the source of the more complete
form of the *kērostasia;* see, also, Harrison (1955: 43–4); and the earlier
study by Hedén (1912: 101–3).

to speculate, is not in 'judgment' but in the distributed 'cut or part' of life, the cut that the Greeks most probably derived from the practices of 'sacrifice' (Bremmer 2007: 138).

6. *Dunamis*

What can be avoided, if anything, when it comes to *moira*? Mortals cannot challenge what is beyond them in a wider sense; hence they cannot challenge the immortal gods (as this is not their *moira*; for example, *Il.* 22.8–13). *Moira* indicates an abyss between the mortal and the immortal planes. Can the gods challenge other gods? In a prevalent modality of strife or difference between the gods, the Homeric epics bring the narrative alive far too frequently to enlist here. Yamagata points at two occasions that are worthy of mention at this point. In the first, Poseidon intervenes against Odysseus' return to Ithaca (*Od.* 2.175–6), but, in any case, it remains Odysseus' *moira*, even if delayed, to eventually return home. In the second, Athena plots excessively against the suitors in Odysseus' favour, but ultimately it is *moira* to avoid further bloodshed (*Od.* 24.544; 1994: 98). Yamagata, in fact, sees here, with good reason, not a morality play, but an orientation as to *moira*; what can be interpreted by mortals as a 'punishment' of the gods, or as a misfortune, is instead what *moira*'s 'order' dispenses (ibid. 99–100). Nestor contemplates that the reason Klytemnestra changed her mind to betray her husband was a divine *moira* (*Od.* 3.269), while, in contrast, Zeus insists on his opposition to any kind of involvement, in this case, by the gods (*Od.* 1.32).[68] What mortals suffer is down to their own power and *moira*. *Moira* (or *aisa*) is not an overpowering force, but rather is a life subject to the ordering of the cosmos (at a time when 'nature' and 'culture', *phūsis* and *nomos* or *ēthos* are not distinguished).[69]

Mortals can, in fact, act and suffer ὑπὲρ μόρον (*huper*

---

[68] Yamagata (1994: 109), who discusses the observation.

[69] In the same way that it is anachronistic and misleading to describe the exercise of the gods' power as an expression of their will, it is misplaced to understand the acts of mortals as acts that are divided between those that are fated and predetermined and those that are willed and free.

moron),[70] ὑπὲρ μοῖραν (*huper moiran*)[71] ('beyond *moira* or their share') or ὑπὲρ αἶσαν (*huper aisan*)[72] ('beyond one's measure').[73] The potency to exceed one's portion or *moira* is ever present, but overstepping the limit is ill advised, for both mortals and gods, since it tends towards cruelty. The ordering of the cosmos is a 'civilising' ordering. While possible, such transgression does not in reality take place, even if it has to be diverted through intervention by another mortal or immortal.[74] Nowhere in the epics does anything actually occur contrary to *moira* or *aisa*. But this should not be understood in the sense of an overwhelming imperative, a despotic principle, a *cosmos basileus*. Instead, we need to view it in light of an ancient juncture between what we separate as 'necessity' and 'normativity', as 'the must' and 'the ought'.

The ordering of the cosmos, the *moira*, is dynamic. *Moira* is the threshold, in contemporary terms, between necessity and normativity, between the must and the ought, between nature and right (or rather their indistinctness). In the epics, when someone strays beyond *moira* or *aisa*, that person is going beyond the bounds of their ethical limit, allotted portion, or fair share, that is, their way of life (*ēthos*). The only 'causality' that can be determined in this manner lies in the interim of the ethical ordering side of things, not in the realm of an absolute necessity. In Homer, then, we could say that there is no 'fate'. There is in this sense, too, nothing absolutely impossible in Homer (even death can, potentially, be overcome upon the granting of eternal life by a god). To venture a philosophical remark: there is only

---

[70] See, for example, *Il*. 2.155; 20.30; 21.517; and *Od*. 5.436.

[71] See, for example, *Il*. 20.335–6; *Od*. 1.35.

[72] See *Il*. 2.155; 16.779; 17.319; 20.30 and 335; a certain sense of moderation is implied here by staying within one's measure in social terms; as regards the gods' *aisa*, see *Il*. 24.33.

[73] This, as we saw earlier by implication, possibly applies to the gods also; *Od*. 3.236. See also ὑπὲρ κῆρας [*huper kēras*], which is used synonymously, for example, *Il*. 13.234.

[74] For example, *Od*. 1.16–7. The gods can delay someone's time of death but cannot avert death. Similarly, they can bring the sunset forward (*Il*. 18.239–40) or delay it (*Od*. 23.241–6), but they cannot stop the sunset from happening, as Yamagata (1994: 116) notes.

the ethical im/potentiality (*dunamis–adunamia*, to remember Aristotle's formulation, here in the sense of weakness or cruelty, or rather a passivity with regard to a limitation)[75] of one's power (*dunamis*), though conceived as entailing the experience of a limit that should not be crossed as a matter of honour (*timē*).[76] The Homeric allotment of *moira* is, perhaps, the distant predecessor of the ethical self of the classical period.

7. One cannot go permanently without sleep

What takes place κατὰ μοῖραν (*kata moiran*) or ἐν μοίρῃ (*en moirē*, negated in the forms of οὐ κατὰ μοῖραν, *ou kata moiran*, or παρὰ μοῖραν, *para moiran*) is an expression used in a wide variety of contexts to indicate that something is done 'properly', or in 'due order'. This will only be 'properly' expressed in Homer in a somewhat parallel sense as κατὰ κόσμον (*kata kosmon*, the 'arrangement of parts'),[77] and with perhaps some echo in the cosmic significance in Anaximander's famous κατὰ τὸ χρεών (*kata to chreōn*). But maybe we can already see here a Homeric prefiguration of the cosmic significance of *moira* as taking place in the order (and ordinariness) of one's life as a part, a limited domain.[78] The contexts in question vary widely, from the milking of goats (*Od.* 9.245, 342), to the distribution of portions of food (*Od.* 15.140), to being killed as one's due portion (*Od.* 22.54). In each case, it is the taking place of one's life in its *ēthos*,

---

[75] Though not so much, or not exclusively, with regard to physical possibility or impossibility; a limitation, *moira*. See Arist. *Met.* 1050b10; I have in mind here Agamben's rethinking of potentiality (*dunamis*) throughout his writings; see, for example, Agamben (1999a).

[76] On *timē*, see Gernet (1917: 290); Riedinger (1976: 254–5); see also Finkelberg (1998b: 16), who writes of the formulaic expression ἔμμορε τιμῆς [*emmore timēs*] as follows: 'The formula and its modifications appear in the Homeric corpus, in Hesiod, and in elegy; its dispersion and productivity show that the idea of the allotment of *timē*, rather than gaining it in fair competition, was deeply rooted in the epic tradition. This seems to indicate that *timē* should be regarded not as a competitive, but rather as what can be called a "distributive value".'

[77] See, for example, *Od.* 4.783; 8.54; 9.245, 309, 342, 352; 16.385; *Il.* 16.367; 19.256; 23.626.

[78] Also in δασμός (*dasmos*), *Il.* 1.166.

that is, in the due order of one's deeds, social status, worth, honour and virtue.[79] One is expected to act in accordance with the due order of one's portion, which always relates to a prescribed conduct or custom (Dietrich 1965: 21). As one's life is a potency, so is one's *moira* (in the sense of a 'course of living').

Yet as we have seen, while one can act beyond one's position or social expectations, one should not. Measure or 'moderation' is preferable to excess, the crossing of boundaries, in what we can perhaps describe as an 'ethical' sense in the poems, though one that is not subscribed to any kind of moralism other than the ethological sense of respecting limitations and not committing *hubris*. *Hubris* is not the 'having' of power, or the overpowering of others.[80] The self-centred assertion of *hubris* is, at base, essentially the failure to pay respect where respect or honour is due according to one's lot. *Hubris* offends the distribution (the *eunomiē*). What the measure of appropriateness or moderation is or should be is determined by what is apportioned (which is, as cosmic is by definition, fair) and what is common (*xunon*; for example, *Il.* 19.172–6). The order of the cosmos is not political; it is *ethological*.

One's portion is what it is and it is also always in the middle (the *meson*, the common, the *xunon*). This, according to a fundamental tradition of early Greek ethology, may find its Homeric seed here: a portion is a 'just' portion – it is *moira*. The manner of gods and mortals in Homer is *ethological*. It accepts the possibility of transgressions, but it also prescribes that mortals (and possibly gods) admit that, when overstepping, the responsibility lies entirely within their own (common) powers; and as such this accords with their cosmic *moira*. One can attempt to transgress one's boundaries, or rise up to defend the transgression against another's, but this is

---

[79] See *Il.* 9.59: Ἀργείων βασιλῆας, ἐπεὶ κατὰ μοῖραν ἔειπες; *Il.* 15.206: κατὰ μοῖραν ἔειπες; *Od.* 3.331: εἰ πλεόνεσσι μάχοιτο· σὺ δ' οὐ κατὰ μοῖραν ἔειπες; *Od.* 17.580: μυθεῖται κατὰ μοῖραν, ἅ πέρ κ' οἴοιτο καὶ ἄλλος; and *Od.* 3.457: πάντα κατὰ μοῖραν; with further examples in *Od.* 12.35; 13.48, 385; 15.170; 22.486. On the particular negation of κατὰ μοῖραν, in the case of the Cyclops, see *Od.* 9.357.

[80] See Fisher (1979).

66

precisely what is *moira* in Homer. It is the *moira* of mortals to not commit *hubris*, to not overstep, but this is not because they fear the 'punishment' of the gods. Rather, it is because it is what *moira* territorialises within and between mortals' powers in the polis, as their limitation within the share of existence that is their own part, as much as it is their 'ever-common' (*xunon*). In its most ordinary, yet equally telling poetic sense (as Homer has it in *Od.* 19.591–3), one cannot go permanently without sleep:

ἀλλ᾽ οὐ γάρ πως ἔστιν ἀΰπνους ἔμμεναι αἰεὶ
ἀνθρώπους· ἐπὶ γάρ τοι ἑκάστῳ μοῖραν ἔθηκαν
ἀθάνατοι θνητοῖσιν ἐπὶ ζείδωρον ἄρουραν.

Which can be translated as:

but mortals cannot go permanently without sleep,
this is the divinely allotted *moira*
for dwellers on the life-gifting earth.

Moira delimits things (and, in this sense, determines them in her ordering) as a distribution of parts that are bound to their boundaries. The bond is the singularity and limit of a life as experienced in events and *erga*, 'acts' (actualisations), that take place in the middle of the *xunon*. *Moira* in its 'original' form is indeterminate, undifferentiated. It is a potentiality – what there is in the *xunon*. The experience of the limit (*peras*) as *moira* fastens and binds the indeterminacy of existence, of the *xunon* into actuality. To be left without a *moira* (ἀμμορίης, ἄμμορος, ἄμοιρος; *ammoriēs, ammoros, amoiros*) means philosophically, in this sense, to be left in a state of indeterminacy, a state of permanent potentiality, without a share, outside, without (an articulated) voice – though earlier the primary sense was most probably that of the part (*moira*) of the meat that was to be distributed as one's own and most common.

8. *Meropes anthrōpoi*

We can now briefly examine an enigmatic description in the Homeric formula of μέροπες ἄνθρωποι (*meropes anthrōpoi*) as in, for instance, *Il*.18.288[81] and 18.490: ποίησε πόλεις μερόπων ἀνθρώπων [*poleis meropōn anthrōpōn*]. The earlier forms of the expression, which appear formulaic, are in the sense of tying mortals to the *polis/poleis* or the *genos* (*genus*). In what precise manner, however, remains a question, since the etymology of the word *meropes* is unclear. Andreas Willi (2014) has convincingly shown that the earliest form, found only in poetic language, is probably that of the tying of certain mortals to the polis. Karel Oštir, in the previous century, proposed a wild etymological derivation of *anthrōpos* from this formula: με-(θ)ρōπ- in μέροπες + *ἀ-μ[ε]θρωπ- = ἄνθρωπος' (1929: 293). This is no longer supported.[82] Other Greek or non-Greek etymologies have linked *meropes* to mortal, terrestrial appearance, or consideration/concern/remembrance, a share (*moros*) of 'fate' (Chantraine 1936: 124–7; but Willi 2014: 51–73). *Meropes* have also been linked to the peoples of a particular geographical location (possibly Kos) or a more general designation of various non-Greek heroes (Willi 2014: 57). An earlier, perhaps specific, designation was probably already forgotten in Homeric times resulting in a more general stereotyped use, namely to indicate those who are somehow connected to the polis as 'free' residents who follow a 'leader' (Koller 1968; Willi 2014: 58–60). As Willi (2014) suggests, it was largely only when this designation itself was forgotten that connection to *meros* and *moira* could be speculatively drawn to designate a general human characteristic or condition.

If we presume here, for our purposes, the later speculative derivation from *μεῖρος [meiros] < *(s)merjo- (as opposed to *meros*), this could be to the effect that the formulaic phrase refers to those who distribute (rather than articulate) a voice, *phōnē* (ὄψ, *ops*; ὀπός, *opos*; Lat. *vox*). The latter, notably, was even posited as the second part of the composite *anthrōpos*

[81] See also *Il*. 1.250–2; 3.399–402; 9.340–3; 11.26–8; 18.339–42, 490–1; and 20.215–17; in the *Od*. 20.49–51, 131–3; also, in the Homeric *Hym. to Ap.*, at 29–42. This formula is also used in Hesiod to describe his five γένη (*genē*) of mortals (*genos meropōn anthrōpōn*), in Hes. *W.D.* 109–10, 143–4, 180–1; see also Hes. fr. 204.96–100; see Willi (2014) for a recent re-examination.
[82] See Chantraine (1968–2009), s.v. μείρομαι [*meiromai*], and the analysis in Willi (2014: 51–73), with extensive references to the key early and recent literature; Willi argues instead for a possible early derivation from 'subject of/to' a (military) settlement/*polis*.

as well, as seen in Ammonius, *In de interpr.* 38.13: ἄνθρωπος κατὰ τὸ δαιρθροῦν τὴν ὄπα; and also in Eust. *Il.* 1.53.2, among others (Lebedev 1994). According to the late scholiast (as we shall see below), in contrast to other animals, humans divide/distribute/transmit (*memerismenēn*) a voice. This scission/distribution is at the same time what unites humanity in its common experience of speech as a power (potency). Only later, as the scholiast perhaps has it, could the speculation be understood with regard to those who can and have to 'distribute a voice' (φωνή, *phōnē*) in the sense of 'articulate speech'; a speech that is, in one sense, bound to articulation, actualisation (*erga*). But how are we to appreciate this general supposition that is evident in Homer, too, when he refers to μερόπεσσι βροτοῖσιν (*meropessi brotoisin*, *Il.* 2.285), whereby such a condition or distribution is the core characteristic of mortals? This expression may, in fact, be in a certain sense a key description of the *moira* of mortals that we have engaged with here.

This is by implication perhaps poignantly described with regard to mortal life in the Hesiod fragment (Hes. fr. 276) in which the formula appears in one of its forms, and which is transmitted by the scholiast on Lycophron, *Alexandra* 682[83] in the following:

Ζεῦ πάτερ, εἴθε μοι εἴθ᾽ ἥσσω μ᾽ αἰῶνα βίοιο
ὤφελλες δοῦναι καὶ ἴσα φρεσὶ μήδεα ἴδμεν
θνητοῖς ἀνθρώποις· νῦν δ᾽ οὐδέ με τυτθὸν ἔτισας,
ὃς μακρόν γέ μ᾽ ἔθηκας ἔχειν αἰῶνα βίοιο
ἑπτά τ᾽ ἐπὶ ζώειν γενεὰς μερόπων ἀνθρώπων

Father Zeus, would that you had granted me an equal span of life (sc. as you have granted to other mortals) and (that you had granted me) to know the same thoughts in my mind as the (other) mortal men; instead you have not honored me in the least, since you forced me to have a long period of life and live for seven generations [*geneas*] of [*meropōn anthrōpon*].[84]

---

[83] Merkelbach and West (1967); see Scheer (1908: 225).

[84] Trans. by Vergados (2013: 9), with my comments in brackets; and see, further, for discussion, Vergados's rendering of 'articulate' for *meropōn*, though this is perhaps far-fetched.

Here the blinded seer (possibly Teiresias) complains of Zeus' 'gift' to him of an extraordinarily long life (*bios*; that is, seven generations long, with seer abilities), instead of a life (*bios*) that would be equal to the life-span (*zōein*) of mortal men. Zeus' gift has left Teiresias with a life that is neither immortal nor mortal, but suspended somewhere in between, as opposed to the *moira* that is specifically due to mortals (as opposed to other animals), which the scholiast interprets as μεμερισμένην [*memerismenēn*] τὴν φωνὴν [*phōnēn*] ἐχόντων (Hsch. *Sch.* 11.1.250). The seer has a prophetic voice but neither an immortal nor a mortal form of life. Μέροπες is perhaps derived from μέροψ (*merops*, a possibly metrical adaptation of μείρομαι, *meiromai*; and note that the Mycenaean *mo-ro-pa* means the possessor of a portion)[85] and is used as a later stereotyped epithet of mortals to signify mortality, arguably, in the sense of a distribution (share, *[s]mer-*) of, initially, food; then of a certain civic membership; and only later, speculatively (as in the scholiast), of voice, or the endowment of (for some, articulate) speech. Yet it should be noted that voice and speech are not the same thing for human animals, who are themselves suspended somewhere between animal voice and human speech (Agamben 1991).

What mortals receive is the ordering, the distribution, of voice (a non-articulate voice that is characteristic of human beings, *anthrōpoi*), which they then have to articulate or actualise. It is with this in mind that *nomos* can be understood, as we shall see later on, as a dispensation of provinces or forms of life, that is, as the order of things: the condition (initiation, institution) of constitution. Cornford ([1912] 1957), in this general sense, may, then, be accurate in his early admirable speculation: *moira* is a social-cosmic *nomos*, an apportionment of powers (*dunameis*), a binding of a potency; and, one could add, an *ēthos*, that is, a way of life (and, later, a primary, conditional, equality among mortals denoted by their common path towards death). The *moirai*, after all, are now the experiences of a potency that have to be articulated or actualised, but early on perhaps they were not exhausted in their fated articulation (the act).

---

[85] See Dietrich (1965: 206, n. 4); and Seaford (2004: 51, n. 27).

What were the Κλῶθες (*Klōthes*) or *moira* weaving at birth? Was it (the distribution of) forms of life, figures/patterns/clothes (potencies) for the new-born? *Moira*, in this speculative philosophical sense, may be the muse of potency or power, whose actualisation in life is conditioned on the continuously active enactment of one's lot or portion. A portion once spun cannot be unspun, though Penelope, it should be noted, cunningly did so (yet this was, after all, her *moira* or potency). *Moira* in its *klothology*[86] generates life as a spun thread which, in its dizzying spinning, *composes* a line of life; a life that is eventually designated as 'human' and which has to be 'human' (if it is to avoid *hubris*).

It should be noted in this regard, too, that *moira* (or later a plurality of *moirai*) does not appear to be associated with other animals. Furthermore, in Homer we find *moira* depicted as both a 'natural share' and as 'allotted' by Zeus, or another figure of authority, which may also indicate a social transition between a (to some extent) collective, indistinct, previous state and the formation of a new social *ēthos*. Earlier, the line of life spun was magically instituted, perhaps, as one's intimacy with life, one's clothing as a mortal classification, one's distinctive (non-Homeric: *gnōrisma*) 'form' of life inseparable from its *phusis* (vital force or potency). In Homer, it was woven, already, in the web-song of the word as to the mortal, common part (*meros*).

> Στησαμένη μέγαν ἱστὸν ἐνὶ μεγάροισιν ὕφαινε
> Hom. *Od.* 2.94[87]

---

[86] I thank Anton Schütz for coining this term and for our inspiring discussions.

[87] 'She set up in her halls a great web, and fell to weaving.'

Three
The Nomos of the Land

γαῖαν παμμήτειραν ἀείσομαι, ἠυθέμεθλον,
πρεσβίστην, ἣ φέρβει ἐπὶ χθονὶ πάνθ᾽ ὁπόσ᾽ ἐστίν,
ἠμὲν ὅσα χθόνα δῖαν ἐπέρχεται ἠδ᾽ ὅσα πόντον
ἠδ᾽ ὅσα πωτῶνται, τάδε φέρβεται ἐκ σέθεν ὄλβου.
ἐκ σέο δ᾽ εὔπαιδές τε καὶ εὔκαρποι τελέθουσι,
πότνια, σεῦ δ᾽ ἔχεται δοῦναι βίον ἠδ᾽ ἀφελέσθαι
θνητοῖς ἀνθρώποισιν
Hom. *Hym. to Gaia*, 1–7[1]

1. *Nemō*-land

With regard to land 'holding' and the 'apportionment' of land we encounter the νέμω (*nemō*) family of words in various uses closely attached to a sense of 'possession-use' or 'holding' (as well as indissociably attached to 'enjoying', 'dwelling', 'inhabiting', 'using', and, to an extent perhaps, implicating a wider sense of *ēthos* or 'way of being'). Once more, I suggest, what we do not meet, at least explicitly, is a 'juridico-political' sense. For instance, in *Od.* 11.185 we read Τηλέμαχος τεμένεα νέμεται (*temenea nemetai*), where Telemachos is said to possess or 'hold' a 'divided/distributed' or 'separated' *temenos*.[2] In a related sense, in *Il.* 12.313 we find καὶ τέμενος νεμόμεσθα μέγα Ξάνθοιο παρ᾽ ὄχθας ('we

---

[1] 'I will sing of well-founded Earth, mother of all, eldest of all beings. She feeds all creatures that are in the world, all that go upon the goodly land, and all that are in the paths of the seas, and all that fly: all these are fed of her store. [5] Through you, O queen, men are blessed in their children and blessed in their harvests, and to you it belongs to give means of life to mortal men and to take it away'; translation by White (1914).

[2] On *temenos*, see the final section of this chapter. The *temenos* would later become a 'sacred precinct'.

have received a *temenos,* a substantial piece of land . . .'). With particular regard to land, in what is a frequent use, we read, for instance, in *Od.* 20.336: ὄφρα σὺ μὲν χαίρων πατρώϊα πάντα νέμηαι; whereby Telemachus and Penelope are told to enjoy the πατρώϊα (*patrōia*), the paternal, 'inherited' land. Further, in the sense of being given one's lot or portion for the purposes of a dwelling, we meet, for example, in *Od.* 14.210: αὐτὰρ ἐμοὶ μάλα παῦρα δόσαν καὶ οἰκί' ἔνειμαν [*eneiman*] ('a small portion was given to me and I was allotted a dwelling'). The sense of 'occupying', 'dwelling in', or 'enjoying' can be observed quite directly in *Il.* 6.195: καλὸν φυταλιῆς καὶ ἀρούρης, ὄφρα νέμοιτο [*nemoito*]; here, the Lyceans are said to be 'distributing-sharing', but more so perhaps 'enjoying or occupying', a 'fertile parcel of land'; and, further, in *Il.* 20.8: οὔτ' ἄρα νυμφάων αἵ τ' ἄλσεα καλὰ νέμονται [*nemontai*]; where the nymphs are said to 'dwell' the forests.[3] Emmanuel Laroche has noted, in this regard, that in the Homeric epics and hymns νέμομαι (*nemomai*) indicates 'to live/inhabit' twice as many times as οἰκῶ (*oikō*), οἰκέω (*oikeō*); 'to live', 'to dwell', 'to abide' (1949: 23). It is also worth noting, incidentally, that the servant who most closely serves Penelope and the *oikos* in the *Odyssey,* while Odysseus is away, is named – Εὐρυνόμη (*Eurynomē*).

In the middle voice, we find the same sense of νέμω [*nemō*] in, for example, *Od.* 2.167: οἳ νεμόμεσθ' [*nemomesth'*] Ἰθάκην εὐδείελον ('us who dwell in Ithaca'). In this verse, the sense of 'having an allotted place' or 'dwelling' takes the more generalised sense of the dwelling of a community, rather than a single person or an *oikos* (family). Similarly, we see, in *Od.* 7.26, ἀνθρώπων, οἳ τήνδε πόλιν καὶ ἔργα νέμονται [*nemontai*], where 'the inhabitants or possessors' of the city and the fields are said to be unknown to Odysseus, the stranger, when he speaks to Athena.[4] This use can be generalised further to indicate the occupiers of a place, or a country at large, thus indicating a people's origin or region, for instance, in *Il.* 2.496: οἵ θ' Ὑρίην ἐνέμοντο [*enemonto*] καὶ Αὐλίδα πετρήεσσαν (in the sense of those who have been 'sent – allotted – by Aulis and Iria'); or in *Il.* 2.531: οἳ Κῦνόν τ' ἐνέμοντ' Ὀπόεντά τε

[3] See Homer, *Hymn to Aphro.* 97.
[4] Note, though, the possible alternative verse ending καὶ γαῖαν ἔχουσιν.

Καλλίαρόν τε ('those who came from . . .'). Here, ἐνέμοντ' (*enemont'*) may indicate both the act of movement and the sense of those who come from and/or are settled in the land of a particular region. Thus, 'holding', 'dwelling in' and 'inhabiting' or 'living' on a particular piece of land appear to intersect in the use of νέμω, νέμομαι [*nemō, nemontai*]. This is also the case with the related ἀμφινέμω (*amphinemō*; 'to have one's lot, to dwell'), which is usually associated with particular place names, as in the many occurrences of it in Book 2 of the *Iliad*. Hence, in verse 2: 521 we find οἵ τ' Ἀνεμώρειαν καὶ Ὑάμπολιν ἀμφενέμοντο [*amphenemonto*],[5] where the 'dwelling about', 'wandering in', 'holding' of a particular plot of land seem intermixed. Lastly, it is worth noting that, in this context, we encounter reference to a νέμος (*nemos*) in *Il*. 11.480: ἐν νέμεϊ [*nemei*] σκιερῷ· ἐπί τε λῖν ἤγαγε δαίμων ('ravening jackals rend him amid the mountains in a shadowy grove').[6] Francis M. Cornford earlier associated *nemos* (which he understood as a wooded pasture or glade) with the Latin *nemus* (a forest, wood, with open glades and grazing land, as deriving from the same Indo-European *nem-* root, that is, what is 'distributed-shared'). Yet he also noted, with a possible connection with *nemesis* in mind, that

> the word has no etymological connection with trees, and to account for it we must suppose that it did not at first mean simply a natural stretch of woodland. There is reason to believe that a *nemos* was at first rather a sacred enclosure or clearing in a wood, perhaps a clearing round a sacred tree. ([1912] 1957: 31)

However, as I noted earlier in the Preface, linguistically at least, this is a disputed hypothesis.

2. Mycenaean land-'holding'

In 1957, Moses Finley famously expressed the view that in the Homeric poems 'the property regime', as he called it, was 'already fully stabilized' (1957: 136). As ever with Homer the

---

[5] See also, further examples such as: *Il*. 2.574, 585, 634, 649, 655, 835, 853.
[6] Translation by Murray (1924).

question is, 'When'? The more 'primitive' divisions of land that formed the early settlement in and use of the land are, according to Finley, 'scarcely visible' in the poems (ibid.). Despite the inevitable questioning of the use of the terms 'primitive', 'private' or 'ownership'[7] to describe relations to land (but not only land) in the epics, Finley held that what we do find in the epics is an established 'regime of private ownership', though one that is radically different from the 'conditional' holding of 'private' property in Mycenaean times (1600–1100 BC), as well as the (then) common holding of 'open fields' (ibid. 138):

> It is enough to indicate that there was free, untrammelled right to dispose of all movable wealth – a right vested in a *filius familias* as well as in a *pater familias*; that the continuous circulation of wealth, chiefly by gift, was one of the major topics of the society; and that the transmission of a man's estate by inheritance, the movables and immovables together, was taken for granted as the normal procedure upon his death. These rights might be disturbed on any given occasion, but that was always because of some defect in the sanctions, specifically in the capacity of the holder of the right to exercise it; never because the existence of such rights was questioned. Even Antinoos conceded that both the estate and the kingship of Odysseus were Telemachus' 'patrimony by birth'. (*Od.* 1.387; 1957: 138)

Furthermore, as Jados Sarkady argues similarly, to an extent, in the earlier Mycenaean period '[t]he original communities had already grown over into agricultural communities, characterized by strongly individualistic use and ownership of land with a complex inner articulation, partly already anticipating the antique form' (1981: 310). Aside from the

---

[7] In the epics, but also far beyond, we do not find any term that denotes 'ownership', 'land-owner' or land 'appropriation'; see MacDowell (1978: 133). It is perhaps no accident, as we shall see, that a certain sense of 'land-holding' or 'possession' is commonly indicated with the word *klēros* and later with words that place *klēro-* as a prefix (as in *klēronomos* 'inheritor or distributor' of land lots). If there was a 'proprietor', Burford notes, that was the polis (1993: 16ff), and she includes overseas settlements in that, though still not in a narrow sense.

question of such 'survivals', the strength of this 'individualism' will need to be measured with reference to evidence
of collective landholding and administration, but also with
the particular sense in which land was 'held', especially by
the *oikoi*. For our purposes, we need to relativise some of
these presumptions. In general terms, to what extent can we
speak of 'ownership' or 'individual/private property'? We
will not reach a definite view in this work, and perhaps more
generally, but, in any case, it is to be noted that perhaps the
use of the terms 'ownership', 'private', and so forth, while a
useful shorthand to the reader and widely used in the interdisciplinary literature, are not as helpful as they might at
first seem. I shall maintain a schematic sense of 'possession'
when writing 'ownership', then, and note that a generalised
sense of 'individual ownership/possession' may be, in one
sense, the exception rather than the norm so far as land is
concerned. Thus, I turn to examine some of these aspects in
order to consider the manners in which relations to land were
experienced as 'held', on the concrete basis of the particular
ways through which land was used, inhabited, divided and
distributed-shared in a continuous social relation. I propose
that it is possible to understand the 'social-economic' experience, with reference to the Mycenaean as well as the Homeric
land-holding, as encompassing the political, cultural, administrative and worship elements, which are not yet functionally
differentiated, while equally, at the same time, not conceiving
them as a neat totality.

Thus, before I turn to the Homeric pluriverse once more, it
is helpful to briefly engage with the Mycenaean period in this
regard.[8] Of the so-called 'pre-history' to the Homeric age(s)

---

[8] One vastly debated matter remains, which period's society or societies
do the Homeric epics depict? Without entering this debate in this work,
and while being alert to the density of the question, it is worth noting
that there are indisputable Mycenaean elements within the epics that
were transmitted through collective oral tradition, for some even possibly from the late dark ages, though this may be too far-fetched (Whitley
1991), while more recent scholarship determines the chronological
period as that of the mid- to late ninth century to the early to mid-seventh
century BC. Most likely the epics entail a mixture of earlier elements and,
crucially, more 'contemporary' elements. See, indicatively, Ulf (1990);
Raaflaub (1997); Raaflaub and van Wees (2009); Crielaard (1995; 2002);

we know increasingly more through the work of archaeologists and linguists. In particular, as regards the Mycenaean era, we have benefited greatly from the decipherment of Linear B and this thriving field of study since the 1950s. It is worth examining, even if superficially for my limited purposes, what we can learn from the decipherment of certain groups of Linear B texts as to land 'holding' and land 'rights' as they are observed in the remarkably salvaged Pylian tablets.[9] The most precious of the tablets, in this respect, are those in the *Pylian E* series, which is a 'land-register' of some land holdings in Pylos that laconically records the allotments, the contributions expected and the grains required (though not their locations and boundaries).[10] In this series, as Alexander Uchitel's analysis has shown, we have, for instance, a land survey of the key area of *Pa-ki-ja-ne*, one of the administrative units of the hither provinces of the Pylian kingdom, near Pylos (2005: 473–4), where the city's most important sanctuary was located.[11] Uchitel writes: 'The heading of *Eq 213* confirms the conclusion that this is the only existing Pylian "cadastre" [though not a 'cadastre' that would form the basis of 'arbitration', it should be noted, despite Uchitel's liberal use of the term here]: *o-wi-de A-ko-so-ta to-ro-qe-jo-me-no a-ro-u-ra a2-ri-sa* ("thus saw *A-ko-so-ta* inspecting the *a2-ri-sa–fields*")' (ibid. 479: my insertion). It needs to be noted that

and Osborne (2004a). A related question, further, that has to be at least noted concerns the composition of the epics, a question that remains and probably will continue to remain largely uncertain (a current prevalent view is that the epics were written down under Peisistratos in the mid-sixth century BC and completed by the Alexandrian philologists, but this is still disputed by many scholars). It should also be noted that, apart from the *Iliad* and the *Odyssey*, we know also of the so-called *Epic Cycle*; that is, a series of epics that begin with the creation of the *kosmos* and end with the death of Odysseus.

[9] Compare Duhoux (1976: 7–27); and Lejeune (1972: 135–54).

[10] See Bennett (1956). It is perhaps incisive in itself that we never observe records of territories and boundaries in the tablets.

[11] In *Pakijane* or *Pakijana* (*Σφαγιᾶνες* or *Σφαγιᾶνα*) most of the land was held by 'religious' personnel; see Lupack (2008: 44ff). Arguably, the name is from the Greek root σφαγ-, linked to the verb σφάζω (*sphazō*) meaning to slay or 'sacrifice', rendering plausible a designation of *Pa-ki-ja-ne* as 'the place of slaughter'; see Palaima (1995: 119–39); and Lupack (2008: 45).

such written records are not an indication of the supposedly lessened importance of a wider complex system of administration which was largely oral.[12] The Pylian state was divided between the western hither and the eastern further provinces, comprising numerous settlements and district centres. One of the striking features of the land-holding administration in this region, but also perhaps more generally so in this period, is the fact that land can be 'held' by individuals, as well as by communities (i.e. the *damos*, *da-mo*).

Land 'owners', as becomes evident from the tablets, had to pay contributions and 'taxes' (unless exempted) to the palace/*wanax*, which could often take the form of products (i.e. a portion of the crop). But while scholars have suggested that because of such 'dependencies' the Pylian kingdom, and possibly by extension the Mycenaean economy more generally (though with notable differentiation), is characterised by a predominantly '(re)distributive' economy (rather than a 'market' or 'money-based' economy), recent scholarship has provided good reasons to believe that this is a rather monocular, if not in part misleading, view.[13] In fact, it has been suggested that instead of a merely 'palace-dominated' economy (and by extension social life more generally), there were three highly significant coeval sources of 'powers': notably, the palace, the sanctuary and the *damo(s)*.[14] A 'distributive' (and 'redistributive' to an extent, at least) economy it may have been, but the administrators of the distribution, as well as the 'ownership' of land, were not necessarily centralised, or exclusive to the palace/*wanax* (Halstead 1992: 72–3), unless

---

[12] See Bendall (2007).

[13] On 'redistribution', see, for example, Killen (1985: 241–2); Morris (1986: 109–10); Nakassis et al. (2011); on the Mycenaean palace/*wanax*, see Thomas (1976: 93–116; 1995: 63–80); Palaima (2006: 53–71); Shelmerdine (2006: 73–86); Wright (2006: 7–52); and Kyriakidis (2010). *Wanax*, it should be noted, is not a Greek word. It should also be stressed that the (to an extent misleading) image of an omnipotent or centrifugal ruler is further challenged by possible reinterpretations of the role of the *lawagetas* (*ra-wa-ke-ta*), the 'prince' or 'leader of the people' who perhaps oversees the internal administration of the palace and its lands, while the *wanax* is the warrior-king; see also Bendall (2013). I thank Evangelos Kyriakidis for pointing out this possibility to me.

[14] See Sarkady (1981); Earle (2011); contrast with Killen (2008: 180); and, especially, Lupack (2011).

the land in question was adjacent to the palace (as is perhaps evident in the *E* series of the tablets).

Thus, for instance, Evangelos Kyriakidis has shown convincingly that, in addition, a potential fourth party to the above-mentioned triad of 'powers' may have been the 'aristocratic collectors', who, he argues, were 'owners' rather than 'beneficiaries', which, if so, challenges the image of the primacy of the *wanax* further and offers us a view into the Mycenaean world (and economy) that may suggest, inter alia, that (some of) the lands and other 'properties' of the 'collectors' were, at times at least, simultaneously 'property' of the palace/*wanax* as well.[15] These elite 'collectors' 'comprised' the palace as its 'stakeholders', as much as holding 'property' in their own capacity (2010: 164–6). Hence, not everything belongs to the *wanax* or the 'state', Kyriakidis concludes, and this may be the earliest example (in the region) of 'a separation of the ruler(s) from the state' (ibid. 169; though, it can be noted, we would need to learn more about such an arguable early 'separation' of 'powers'). The bureaucratic administrative operation is perhaps singular, while the 'owners' are plural and intersecting in their interests.[16] Perhaps it is of use, to a degree, to speak instead, then, of an increasingly centralised administrative system in the palatial era (along with coexisting sub-administrators) over variously dispersed land-'holdings' and uses.

Two particular forms of 'holding' are observable in the tablets. The *En* tablets (74, 467, 609, 659) record the *ki-ti-me-na* 'private' holdings of the palace and/or high-status officials (the *te-re-ta*/*telestai* in charge of the land when leased) or the 'religious' personnel, who can and do 'sublease' (*o-na-to*, a more adequate term than 'leasehold', though still not entirely accurate; the sense is, most likely, that of a 'bestowal of a benefit') them to other parties. *Te-re-ta* is a technical term always associated with 'holding' land, designating an official

---

[15] Kyriakidis usefully notes that the name 'collectors' was given to these elites by Chadwick, who was influenced by the collector operatives of the British empire in the Indian provinces (2010: 165, n. 70). On the 'collectors', see Bennet (1992); Carlier (1992); Godart (1992); and Rougemont (2001; 2009).

[16] See Kyriakidis (2010: 169, n. 85).

thought to be in the service of the palace, but it is worth noting that this appears to be often linked to a *te-le-sta* (initiation priest or official) under whose care lay perhaps not only 'sacral' functions, but also land supervision and 'holding' (Dietrich 1974: 256). Sigrid Deger-Jalkotzy has speculated that most likely initially such *ki-ti-me-na* land was not dissociable from communal *ke-ke-me-na* land and that the growing power of the *wanax* in Pylos resulted in some of it being 'held' otherwise (1983: 109).

In turn, the *Ep* tablets (212, 301, 539, 704, 705) record the *ke-ke-me-na* collective holdings, which are often 'leases' (*onato*) 'granted' (*pa-ro da-mo*, 'by the *damo*'; indicating possibly some kind of demotic 'authority' or 'autonomy' to do so, the nature of which, however, remains unclear)[17] to the various parties detailed in the records (Killen 2008: 164). Interestingly, D. J. Norris Lee has interpreted *ke-ke-me-na* (the land held in common by the *damos*) as etymologically derived from κείρω (*keirō*), which means 'allotting', 'distributing' (and not 'splitting'; 1960/1: 199). Killen has further argued that the *ke-ke-me-na* lands are collectively held by the *damos* of, for example, the particular district of *Pa-ki-ja-ni-ja* (*Pa-ki-ja-na* or *Pa-ki-ja-ne*) in a variety of different types of plots (2008: 164), indicating widespread operations. But who were the *damos*?

They were certainly a local collective, and they possibly comprised either landowning families or administrator-representatives, or both. In any case, the key to understanding the *damos* at this time lies in the act of using-possessing, distributing (and managing) land (that is, land that is actually or potentially communally apportioned).[18] Yet we should already note that the *temenos*, to which I turn below in more detail, was a part of land that was separated from the rest and was, in one sense, excepted from 'distribution-sharing'. It is worth noting, too, that, of the relevant words that we meet much later in Homer, only two appear to have already existed in the Linear B tablets: τέμενος (*temenos*) and ἄρουρα

---

[17] If the palace collected 'taxes' from such lands this was not necessarily due to 'ownership' of such lands; see Lupack (2008: 67).

[18] See Lejeune (1972: 146); Palaima (2004: 231); and Nikoloudis (2006: 67), who narrows the meaning of the *damos* to land-owning families and local representative administrators, rather than the wider community.

(*aroura*; field), the latter being the same word, Uchitel notes, which we encounter in the cadastres of Hellenistic Egypt (2005: 479).[19]

Scholars have generally accepted that the Mycenaean land 'tenure' system entailed two 'types of land': the *ki-ti-me-na* plots which could be understood as in some sense 'private', and the *ke-ke-me-na* plots which, in turn, are to be understood as 'common'. In this sense, the distribution of land (or relations to land) could have taken place as, for example, both a 'distribution-use-sharing' of *ki-ti-me-na* land by the palace/ *wanax* and as a distribution of land by the *damos*. Common land, it should also be noted, was given out but not 'subleased' (Nikoloudis 2006: 70; while some plots were not given out, *anono*). Yet these 'two types of land holding', as Stavroula Nikoloudis shows, need to be understood as complementary, rather than as sharply or 'juridically' opposed (ibid. 69, n. 18).

John Chadwick identified in the tablets (in particular in the *Ea* 28–*Eq* 146 series) these two types of land as follows. First is the *ko-to-na ki-ti-me-na* (*ktoina ktimena*), which he defined as land 'held' or 'resided' on by major land-owners (and partly by tenants; though in these tablets no source is mentioned) in some sense of 'private-use' land. Second is the *ko-to-na ke-ke-me-na* (*ktoina ke-ke-me-na*), which he defined as abandoned land ('left out of distribution') and which he contrasted to 'private' land, labelling it instead 'public' land held by the *damos* (*Ep* series) and given over (*o-na-to, onato,* 'leased') to individual holders, possibly for the servicing of an obligation of a 'religious' nature (1958: 113).[20] The *damos* (*da-ma-te,* δάμαρτες, 'family units' or 'households') could possibly still be perceived in a sense as the local community in its totality with the power to administer significant parts of the land, but it is crucial to note that the *damos* is indissociably also the land.[21] Crucially, whether the *ki-ti-me-na* were in fact held by the *damos* rather than the palace remains subject to continuing debate, though in any case, as Nikoloudis argues, at least the interest of the palace in recording the landholdings

---

[19] See also Snodgrass (1971); Donlan (1989b: 5–29).

[20] See tablets *Ep* 212, 539, 705, 617 and 301, in particular; on *da-mo,* see Lejeune (1972: 35–154); and Chadwick (1979).

[21] See Killen (1998: 20); Palaima (2004: 231); and Nikoloudis (2006: 224).

is certainly clear, and especially so if seen in the frame of palatial interests overlapping with local interests during its earlier rise and development.[22] Meanwhile, Michel Lejeune speculates that 'uncut' or 'undistributed' land was possibly coexistent with the system of 'landholding' in general and with the land held by the *damos* in particular (1972: 141–5).

Was the 'common' land commonly held before it was 'distributed'? It would be misleading to understand this landholding as 'public' land or 'common' land in a rigid technical sense, especially if understood retrospectively with the still-dominant sense we continue to derive for these terms from Roman law categories (which are, it should be noted, anything but self-evident in themselves).[23] It is considered here as land held by the *damos*, *damos*-land, and, in this sense, as common to a particular collective. It is land that is distributed-shared as such, rather than as subject to a process. How 'common' was *damos*-land? *Damos*-land is land distributed among the local *damos* and held (*pa-ro da-mo*) (or 'leased')[24] as such, while some land was left 'uncut' or 'undistributed'; the latter could either be land available as 'undivided' for pastures, or land reserved for future distribution. What is common among the *damos* is the portions/shares in *damos*-land. As Arnaud Macé has put it in a different context, this is not the type of 'common' that is placed, so to say, in the equidistant 'middle', but one that arises, most interestingly, 'from the consideration of a relation between the individual parts' (2014: 48). It may be at this point that a further sense of 'possession'/'use' 'holding' rather than 'ownership' may be more helpful to the understanding of such landholding, and perhaps of 'holding' land more generally, in that what may be emphasised instead is the practice of use(s) of land and its indissociable relation to the *damo* or later the *oikos*, rather than some sense of holding in a formal juridical sense.

In general, then, it is probably safer to presume that the palace is not at this point an absolute centralised owner, or

---

[22] See Palmer (1963: 85–7); Nikoloudis (2006: 224); contrast with Carlier (1987: 68–9).

[23] See Thomas (2002); for a comparison, see Macé (2014: 659–88).

[24] In contrast, *ki-ti-me-na* land is 'leased' from a *te-re-ta*; see Lupack (2008: 57).

the singular, exclusive source for the distribution of land (Palmer 2002: 227–8). Indeed, when it is appreciated that the *damos* was itself highly organised as an administrative body (which included 'head administrators', *ko-to-no-o-ko*, and 'officials', *te-re-ta*) which had the power to dispute holdings of land as a collective (Susan Lupack notes that perhaps the priestess of a sanctuary had such power too; 2011: 213), or act on behalf of the community in other areas,[25] and which held a substantial amount of land (perhaps even more than previously thought),[26] then it becomes more and more evident why the image of a centralised political-economic sphere in Mycenaean society has been disintegrating in recent scholarship, with good reason. Arguably, as Lupack suggests, it may be that before the *wanax* became more and more powerful over time, so overshadowing, at least to an extent, the earlier independence of the *damos* (but also perhaps later on concurrently with the greater concentration of power by the *wanax*), the *damos* was led and represented by its own *damos*-officials (2011: 214) and land was indissociably 'common land' subject to different uses and 'possessions'.[27]

Ruth Palmer provides a lucid image of the 'landholding' practices in question, as follows:

> The village communities own their land collectively but rights to the land are divided up among extended families (οἰκίαι [*oikiai*]). The members of the village community pay taxes and/or labour service to the state. The state/ royal sector also owns land, with a dependent labour force to work it. Royal land could be granted to individuals of different statuses, in return for service; the type of service depended upon the profession of the individual. 'Private' non-community landholding develops through the purchase of community land by the wealthy who were not part of the village community; such people tend to be connected to the ruler. (2002: 241)

---

[25] See Lupack (2011: 214); compare Sarkady (1981).

[26] See Lupack (2011: 213), who refers to de Fidio (1977: 114–18, 145–61; 1987: 142–7).

[27] With reference to Shelmerdine (2008: 134).

Palmer derives from this practice the beginning of a kind of 'private' property in the sense that once a piece of common land is assigned to a chief shepherd and so forth (the association of occupations with particular lands is common in the tablets), it becomes arable by particular persons (in any case, possibly, common people) who, in time, become 'owners' of the lands, though this remains hard to verify. Irrespectively, land is evidently held/distributed in multiple manners, for instance: lands called *ko-to-na* (*ktoina*), meaning, perhaps, apportioned or divided 'common' land; or the *ka-ma* type of land, meaning 'field' (*agros*) with its particular *ka-ma* holders. Neither *kekemena* or *ktimena* are met with in classical Greek, but it is accepted, as it has already been seen, that *ktoina kekemena* arguably refers to 'common land', 'holdings-uses', and that *koina ktimena* refers to some kind of 'private land', or perhaps better, particular 'holding-uses' (notably and invariably assigned to 'occupational' holders/users as varied as a bee-keeper, a swine-herder, a cattle-herder and so forth).[28] It is of interest, as Nikoloudis has noted, that etymologically *ki-ti-me-na* could be understood, in general terms, as settled land ('from **κτεῖμια* [**kteimia*] from the root **ktei->kti-* "settle, inhabit"'; 2006: 224). *Ki-ti-me-na* would then be the present medio-passive participle of the verb *kteimi* with the sense of 'occupation or inhabitation', possibly linked to cultivation, though (in Mycenanean times) that remains uncertain (Lupack 2008: 57). Whereas for the *ke-ke-me-na*, a perfect medio-passive participle, Nikoloudis derives the (still debated) etymology 'from the root **kei-* "lie" or "cut" from *κεάζω* (*keazō*) from the root **kei-* "cut, split"' (ibid.), or 'distributed-divided'.[29] Robert L. Palmer has, in fact, argued that, more generally, many if not most 'land terms' are derived in the Indo-European by verbs meaning 'to cut' (1963: 86–7). In this manner, the common 'uncut' lands,[30] *ke-ke-me-na*, or unsettled ('undistributed' perhaps) lands, were possibly located in the *eskhatiē* (rocky or wooded upland districts), though perhaps not exclusively so.[31] What was their purpose?

---

[28] See Brown (1956).
[29] See also Lejeune (1972: 142–5); Lupack (2008: 58).
[30] Palmer (1998–9: 230).
[31] Carpenter (1983: 88); see also Lejeune (1972: 145).

As set aside, abandoned lands, or at least uncultivated lands
(*a-ki-ti-to*), their use may instead have been for pasture, or
possibly, as not yet under cultivation, as a reservoir of a kind.
While the etymological derivations are of value, they cannot
over-determine the continuing research into the meaning and
uses of the two terms. That said, nor can these two terms be
over-juridicised in a strict manner.[32]

It is worth considering briefly at this point the 'holding'
of land by religious personnel.[33] We meet in the tablets, at
times, as mentioned earlier, the use of the word *te-re-ta*,
which possibly means to 'sacredly guard' (a land or plot).[34]
The word *te-re-ta*, if derived from τηρέω (*tēreō*), meaning 'to
observe or guard', could be practically linked in use to οὖρος
(*ouros*), which, at least in the archaic period, relates to the
guarding of 'boundaries' (as well as 'norms', oaths, etc.).[35]
Parenthetically, the lasting close relation of land use and
holding with myth as well as religion, as Anthony Snodgrass
has observed, can also be shown through the rediscovery
of Mycenaean or iron age tombs during the eighth century
BC, around which, spatially, the development and spread of
arable farming can be archaeologically attested (1980: 39).
Further, the spatial proximity of the palace to the sanctuary
in what seems to be a planning pattern indicates, perhaps,
that the relationship between the two was one of an intersection (as well as, possibly, conflict) of interests. Above all,
the intersection between 'production' and worship practices renders entirely plausible an image of coexistence (and
potential conflict) between parallel forms of 'authority' and
land distributions, possessions and uses.[36]

Furthermore, recent scholarship has suggested that the
sanctuary, and more generally the importance of 'religion'
to the Mycenaeans, would be misunderstood if sanctuaries were perceived as (merely) dependent on the palace.
While the palace is recorded to be collecting and offering

[32] For both the 'juridical' and the 'anti-juridical' approaches, see the discussion in Lupack (2008: 58–72), with further references.
[33] See the most recent illuminating study by Lupack (2008).
[34] See tablets *PY Eb* 149 and *PY Ep* 613, 1131.4.
[35] See Kazanskiene (1995: 605–7); and Bendall (2001; 2007).
[36] See Shelmerdine (1999: 23–4).

large amounts of goods for a religious festival (*PY Un* 718), the sanctuary may be seen to enjoy significant power (as in initiation ceremonies, for example, *PY Un* 2), as well as 'economic' influence.[37] As noted earlier, we should perhaps think indeed of a triad of spheres of influence, as Lupack suggests, between the palace, the sanctuary and the *damos* (2011).[38] In the remarkable 'disputes' between the *damos* and a priestess recorded in the tablets, we possibly have evidence of the conflict of power between the *damos*, the sanctuary and the palace. One example can be seen in tablet *PY* 218.1–6. Under the heading *odaa2 anakee operote* ('and the following are due to draw the boundary furrows') five men are recorded: 'a priest whose qualification has probably been lost, another priest and land-divider (*da-i-ja-ke-re-u* = δαϊαγρεύς, *daiagreus*), and three counts (*e-qe-ta*; important officials of the "court") who are no doubt acting on behalf of the *wanax*)' (Ruipérez 1957: 175). It is probably safe to assume that the lands in question in such 'leases' are linked to the needs of a sanctuary in some relation, partly or wholly, to mutual palatial interests (the latter of which would become increasingly centralised in time); yet it is likely that the (relative) independence and power of the sanctuary also remains significant. Marie-Louise Nosch has noted in parallel that, possibly, while the 'collectors' enjoy their own set of administrative practices (with their own scribes and separate storage noted in the tablets), the Potnian (*po-ti-ni-ja-we-jo*) part of the administration seems 'much more embedded into the general administration' (2008: 603). Perhaps this is reflective of the earlier origins of the role and practices of the sanctuary and the development of cult-worship as 'an in-house activity which has followed the development of palace systems' while 'collectors' are a later phenomenon 'which developed in the period when Mycenaean administration expanded and became more complex' (ibid.). Yet we know now that 'religious personnel' enjoyed much more independence for this to have necessarily been the norm (Lupack 2008). It goes

---

[37] See Lupack (2011: 208–12), from whom I draw; on the sanctuary, see Palmer (1963); on *PY Un* 2, see Palmer (1963: 44–9).

[38] On the role of the 'religious sector', see Lupack (1999; 2008), and (2010) on Mycenaean 'religion' more generally.

without saying that perhaps our rigid categorisations are not apt to the task of approximating an understanding of ancient cultures and practices.

Another example is met with in tablet *PY Ep* 704.5–6, where there is an astonishing record of a 'dispute' with regard to the holding and use of a large piece of land. Lupack writes:

> the root cause of the dispute between the priestess *e-ri-ta* and the *damos* was that the *wanax* had taken a portion of the *damos* land (on most likely a 'lease') and presented it as a religious offering to Potnia and the sanctuary at *pa-ki-ja-ne*. *E-to-ni-jo* land, then, could simply refer to land that the *wanax* had classified as free of taxes and had given as a gift to someone ... The *damos'* protest may indicate why [we have few indications of such land reclassifications] stepping on the *damos'* collective toes may not have been without consequence even where the *wanax* was concerned. (2011: 214–15: my insertion)

The priestess appears to have some 'autonomy' as a 'lease-holder' of land ultimately held by the *damos*. In *PY Eb* 297 we read: 'This the priestess holds, and declares that the god has the true ownership, but that the plot-holders have the leases of the plots in which it is laid out' (Ventris 1954: 20).[39] The priestess effectively argues that the land ought to be exempt or that it was already exempt from the regular form of lease-holding and the related taxation. Whether such fields were held in common under the sacral guardianship of a god/goddess remains a question. Suffice it to note that in a highly developed system of land organisation such as the Mycenaean, complex land relations, disputes and some 'regulation', as well as gifts and exemptions, are often noted, or can be presumed. And the same is perhaps true, generally, with regard to land that is either held or managed by the *damos* as such. No matter what exact relation the *damos* had with the palace, their role as communal holders of land and, crucially for our purposes, as 'distributors' is quite obvious in the tablets, and, evidently so, in the dispute

---

[39] '*i-je-re-ja, e-ke-qe , e-u-ke-to-qe , e-to-ni-jo , e-ke-e , te-o | ko-to-no-o-ko-de , ko-to-na-o , ke-ke me-na-o , o-na-ta , e-ke-e.*'

in question, since the priestess addresses the *damos* who object to her.[40]

It is worth elaborating a bit further on the *damos* at this point. As Nikoloudis notes, the etymology of *damos* appears itself to lie at the root **deh2-*, meaning to 'divide, distribute' (2006: 233).[41] It is worth noting, too, that perhaps the act of distribution is still 'remembered', as well as practised, in the Homeric epics where *dēmos* (*damos*) often means, in a wider sense, 'land' or 'territory' (for example, *Od.* 1.237; 3.220; 24.31). As far as the tablets are concerned, we have sufficient evidence of land held 'in common' by the *damos*. Such holding is not 'legal ownership' in an anachronistically rigid sense, since it was more likely experienced in the sense of a 'having' (*e-ke*), or 'holding' that perhaps entails a sense of guardianship or a degree of a protective inter-relation with other 'parties' (including the palace). It was, however, a 'holding' that, as suggested earlier, could have been derived from an early religious-social sense, or at least a sense whereby the 'juridical', the 'religious' and the 'social-economic' are not yet functionally distinguished.

It appears quite plausible that the *damos* enjoyed economic and possibly political independence to a significant degree. In this regard, Nikoloudis summarises three of the key interpretations as to the landholding of the *damos* as follows:

(1) according to Killen, all the land was owned by the palace and the *da-mo* was simply a local administrative body working for the palace; (2) de Fidio and Carlier regard both *ki-ti-me-na* and *ke-ke-me-na* as belonging to the *da-mo*, but see the palace as having ultimate control; (3) in Deger-Jalkotzy's view, *ke-ke-me-na* land was owned by the *da-mo*, but *ki-ti-me-na* was palace property. (2006: 77)[42]

Recent scholarship, as mentioned above, has increasingly recognised that the earlier palace-centred view of the eco-

---

[40] For a number of readings of this dispute and further analysis, see Lupack (2008: 65–7).

[41] See Watkins (2000: 14).

[42] See Palmer (2002: 243–3), with further references; Nikoloudis (2006: 78, n. 43).

nomic-political context of Mycenaean society may have been exaggerated, marred possibly also by anachronisms of later Western conceptions of 'sovereignty', as well as 'property ownership'. This may be another reason why it may be better to speak of land possessions/uses rather than 'ownership', and, in fact, such that is 'held' simultaneously to one degree or another by parties who possibly intersected and interacted in a variety of ways.

As was noted at the beginning of this chapter, Finley underlined that in the tablets we find strong evidence that a certain form of 'tenure' was frequently, if not always, conditioned towards the satisfaction of palatial needs, on the basis of which he further adduced the significant differentiation, as we shall see below, with Homeric land possession considered as being entirely opposite to such conditionality (1957: 139–40). The extent of such 'conditions' is not entirely clear, but, in any event, such 'conditions', or, better, relations, are coeval (though not undisputed). This is now an intensified concern in the scholarship since, as Lupack writes, 'it is now recognized that the general population did not acquire its staple goods through a palace-governed system of redistribution' (2011: 210). A triadic sphere of influence and power renders the interest in the act of 'distribution-sharing' ever more intriguing.

3. Homeric land-'holding'

Let us now turn to the Homeric epics. By the ninth century BC all significant trace of the earlier Mycenaean civilisation had disappeared, including its elaborate system of landholding (Snodgrass 1980: 15). As a result, in Homer we perhaps find traces of the Mycenaean kingdoms as reminiscences, as well as, arguably, some indications of a tribal form of social organisation reflecting the interim period of the 'dark ages' (ninth–eighth centuries BC) and, of course, predominantly elements of Homer's 'own time', a characteristic component being that of the later growth of the polis in a time of relative stability.

What remains observable as, in a sense, common is that the land was apportioned/divided/shared and used in one way or another. In this act of 'division', it is perhaps worth noting a certain relation in use between the terms ἄρουρα (*aroura*) and οὗρος (*o[u]ros*). Ἄρουρα, in the poems, is frequently met with, and signifies arable land (not a portion of a single furrow or the headlands).[43] In *Il.* 12.314 we read καλὸν φυταλιῆς καὶ ἀρούρης πυροφόροιο (indicating a field); while in *Il.* 20.185 we note καλὸν φυταλιῆς καὶ ἀρούρης, ὄφρα νέμηαι, where Aeneas is asked whether he has been promised an 'apportioned' (νέμηαι, *nemēai*) 'plot of arable land' by the Trojans.[44] It is of interest, perhaps, that the word may appear adjacent to the term ὄρος (*oros*), or the inflection οὖρον (*ouron*), as in *Il.* 21.405, οὖρον ἀρούρης (*ouron aourēs*), suggesting an etymological, or at least a poetic, link. Furthermore, the importance of boundary formation for the purposes of the delineation and security of land division appears central and it could be semantically linked to the Homeric οὖρον (*ouron*), meaning a 'limit' or 'boundary' (or indeed 'boundary-stone'). It is worth adding that the compound δαϊαγρεύς (*daiagreus*) from δαί-ζω (*dai-zō*) and ἀγρός (*agros*), meaning the land-divider, is noticeable in its spatial relation to the earlier Mycenaean term *a-ro-u-ra* (*aroura*, 'field'), which is a word we also meet in Homer, meaning generally 'earth' or 'a measure of land' (in one instance, for example, in reference to Egyptian practice). In this light, we can reread the iconic passage in the *Iliad* where two men are depicted quarrelling over boundaries,[45] with their measuring rods at hand, and then contending in a small space of common land divided between potentially equal plots (12.421–3):

ἀλλ᾽ ὥς τ᾽ ἀμφ᾽ οὔροισι δύ᾽ ἀνέρε δηριάασθον
μέτρ᾽ ἐν χερσὶν ἔχοντες ἐπιξύνω ἐν ἀρούρη [*arourē*],
ὥ τ᾽ ὀλίγω ἐνὶ χώρω ἐρίζητον περὶ ἴσης,

Which can be translated as follows:

---

[43] See Ridgeway (1885: 321); he also marks the connection with ἐν ἀρούρη (*en arourē*): οὖρον (*ouron*) and the Ionic ὄρος (*oros*). He describes the οὖρα (*oura*) in the Homeric fields as 'formed of stones' (see *Il.* 21.405), and as akin to 'the balks of green turf in English common fields' (ibid. 322).

[44] The references are numerous; for example, *Il.* 3.115 ('ground', 'space'); 3.246 ('soil'); 12.422; 14.122; 23.599; *Od.* 5.10; and the generalisation in *Od.* 1.407 as to 'country'; for a full list, see Cunliffe ([1924] 2012; 56).

[45] On boundary disputes, see Chaniotis (1988: 21–39).

But just as two men contend over boundary-stones
in a common field holding measuring rods
fighting over an equal portion in the land.

Ὅρος (*oros*) can mean 'limit' or 'range', but also primarily 'boundary stone' and, perhaps later on, a 'boundary' itself.[46] In Homer, it also means, as Richard J. Cunliffe notes, 'the distance between the side limits of an area ploughed by such and such an animal in a given time, the length of the furrow being regarded as constant' ([1924] 2012: 306).[47] In the above-quoted verses, Martin S. Ruipérez interestingly reads a 'reminiscence of the Mycenaean open-fields system' (1957: 174–206); or, similarly, in *Il.* 18.541, a 'simultaneous tillage, [as] one of the most outstanding features of the open fields' (ibid.). This action of marking and dividing as taking place in the (open) fields is particularly vivid in the poems.[48] Homer depicts the ploughers driving their yokes, in *Il.* 18.541, or the 'wheat-bearing plain' around Troy (*Il.* 21.602), where before the war men had placed the boundary stones that marked and delimited their fields, or strips of (arable) land, and the *oikos*. Further, as Hugh E. Seebohm noted, it is 'One of these [stones that] Athena uses to hurl against Ares, who, falling where he stood, covers seven of the *pelethra* that the stones were used to divide' (1895: 104).[49] We have later evidence of inscribed *horoi*, too, as *horos temenos* or *horos* followed by the name of a deity indicating 'sacred land' (for example, the inscriptions at the Artemision in Lemnos).[50] Seebohm adds:

> Easily dislodged as these landmarks were, they were specially protected by a curse against their removal, and were with the Greeks under the awful shadow of a special deity of boundaries [referring to Pl. *L.* 842e]. They seem however to have been liable to considerable violation. The ass, according to Homer, being driven along the field-way, if his skin was thick enough, easily disregarded the

---

[46] Apol. Rhod. *Argo.* 2.795; see, further, Horster (2010: 440–2).
[47] See *Od.* 8.124; also of a discus, *Il.* 23.431, as noted in Cunliffe ([1924] 2012).
[48] On boundaries, see Rocchi (2007: 87–105); and Horster (2010: 435–58).
[49] A *pelethron* is a measure of about nine square metres.
[50] See Horster (2010: 441).

expostulations of his attendants, and made free with the growing crop. [referring to *Il.* 11.558] (1895: 105)[51] (my insertions)

In Homer, in a period of relative stability after the mass migrations of the previous era, land was divided in two main ways in particular: into κλῆροι (pl. *klēroi/s, klēros*) and into τέμενη (plural *temenē/s, temenos*). Let us examine these in turn.

Cultivated land derived from within the portion of the *dēmos* called the πεδίον (*pedion*; 'nucleus', 'plain'),[52] or the ἀγρός (*agros*; 'field') (for example, *Il.* 23.832; *Od.* 1.190). On the other hand, we have uncultivated land (at the ἐσχατιή, *eskhatiē*, in the periphery or margins, for example, *Od.* 4.517; 5.358, 489) or land not worth cultivating which was primarily used for pasturing flocks and herds and was possibly dominated by the flocks of the rich βασιλεῖς (*basileis*; though not exclusively), especially on plains and valley bottoms (for example, *Od.* 14.104; 24.150).[53] The allocation by way of κλῆρος (*klēros*) lay perhaps with the *dēmos* (the local community). It should be observed that the *klēros* will only much later become, in Attic law, the object of a formal assignation, usually a plot of land, as well as the object of an 'inheritance', and it is indeed from this word that we derive the further, telling, later composite κληρονόμος (*klēronomos*; the 'inheritor').

4. *Klēros*

In the epics, the word κλῆρος (*klēros*) entertains three meanings amidst numerous occurrences.[54] The first is a concrete object used in an appeal to the gods with regard to 'chance'. This was possibly its primary sense. For example, in *Il.* 3.315–16 and 324–5, Zeus is appealed to in order to determine the result of lots placed within a bronze helmet as to who would be the first to throw a spear. In addition, this use is

---

[51] See also Ridgeway (1885: 319–39).
[52] See *Il.* 3.263; 6.393; 11.167, etc; *Od.* 3.241; 15.183, etc; the intensity of agricultural work is well depicted in *Od.* 14.366–81.
[53] See Donlan (1989a: 136).
[54] See Cunliffe ([1924] 2012).

encountered with regard to who will fight Hector (*Il.* 7.171, 182), or as to who will pierce the Cyclops' eye (*Od.* 9.331).[55] Moreover, as already implied, the *klēros* is commonly met as 'the lot', as in πρῶτος κλήρῳ λάχεν (*prōtos klērō lachen*; *Il.* 23.862 or 24.400). Lastly, as Cunliffe indicates, it signifies an actual plot of land that has been permanently allotted to someone (as in οἶκόν τε κλῆρόν τε; *oikon te klēron te*; *Il.* 14.64 and 15.498), though this remains speculative as it can more generally mean portion (akin to *moira*) given that a necessary or exclusive link to land as such remains open.[56] It can also be noted, in some regards, that the term *geōmoroi* signifies 'sharers of land' and the elite land-holders in Samos and Syracuse in particular.[57] It is of interest, then, to note that while *klēros* is found in the epics in eighteen instances, only two of these have the signification of or a relation to 'land'. On this basis, Lee has proposed that *klēros* 'suggests a new type of social organisation, perhaps a band of settlers in Asia Minor, with no *wanax* and no old community organisation, taking land by force of arms, and sharing it out among themselves by the simple egalitarian process of drawing lots', and he speculates that '*νόμος* [*nómos*], not in Homer, could belong to the same social conditions' (1960/1: 206). Lee speculatively notes that the expression κλῆρος ἀκήρατος (*klēros akēratos*) may be a 'modernisation' of an original '*ktoina ke-ke-me-na*' (that is, signifying perhaps a land that is unallotted, undivided; ibid. 207).

In a combination of the last two uses ('portion' and, in some sense, 'land') we find the word utilised to describe the iconic claim of Poseidon as to the way in which the universe has been allotted (indicated by the use of the verb λαγχάνω, *lagchanō*) to the three gods (himself, Zeus and Hades; on which see further Chapter Two). While each of the gods received their portion, we are told, the earth and Olympus were not part of this distribution (τὰ δέδασται, *ta dedastai*)

---

[55] Some contrast between a landed productive polis as opposed to a 'barbaric' pastoralist community is implied in the encounter of Odysseus with the Cyclopes, see *Od.* 9.106–12. See, further, the discussion in Burford (1993: 5ff).

[56] See Finley (1957: 148).

[57] Plut. *Quaes. Graec.* 303e–4c.

and they remained undivided and, in this sense, 'common' (the earth is described as ξυνή, *xunē*). Equality among the three gods is ensured, in Poseidon's eyes, by an equality in the apportionment of lots/shares, as much as, by implication perhaps, by their undivided sharing of the non-apportioned 'common', the earth.

How are we to understand the type of 'common land' that is referred to then in an apportionment by *klēros*? The land that perhaps *could* be apportioned by *klēros*, in Homer, is most probably 'common' land, as in *Il.* 15.495–8, where Hector promises that the *oikos* and the *klēros* of each fallen warrior will be secured for his family (or elsewhere with regard to how the portions of spoils will be given to members of raiding parties). *Klēros*, then, we can surmise, is most often a valued portion of a kind that serves the central purpose of subsistence. That the *klēros* was a sign of wealth, too, is clear when we read in Homer of 'men with many κλῆροι' (pl. *klēroi*; πολυκλήρων ἀνθρώπων, *poluklērōn anthrōpōn*; *Od.* 14.211), which may signify an early instance of 'over-accumulation'. We encounter also the negative term of ἄκληρος (*aklēros*) in *Od.* 11.489–90. The *aklēros* was presumably either a person of poverty or a person with no land, effectively an outsider or outcast. Such outcasts would most probably settle in the wastelands or margins of the community.[58] What remains clear is that the history of the custom of the *klēros* is largely unknown.

It is worth diverting our attention momentarily to the implied notion of 'property' or 'ownership' in this regard.[59] Whether land, especially 'common land', was held in any comparable sense of 'property/ownership' remains a rather abstract anachronistic notion, especially if by 'common land' we refer (also) to unallotted land, namely land that was available largely for pasture. It is also worth noting that pasture land is not mentioned as a matter of 'possession' in the epics. To risk an extensive speculation, we could suggest that such land, but perhaps also land more generally (except, for instance, land that was *geras* and *temenos*), was designated for possession/use, rather than 'exclusive ownership'. The

---

[58] See Ridgeway (1885: 333).
[59] On 'ownership' in ancient Greek law, see, for instance, Kränzlein (1963).

94

development of a type of 'private property' in at least one vague sense (i.e. in *temenos*), as will be seen below, indicates that in this context 'ownership' may be the exception at this time, rather than the rule.[60] For the Marxist classicist George D. Thomson, writing speculatively in the 1940s, this forms a key 'trace' of tribal 'distribution practices' in Homer. In fact, Thomson proceeds even to distinguish the antiquity of these practices of allotment or distribution between the oldest tradition as that of the distribution of food, followed by the distribution of booty ('chattels and inanimate movables acquired through warfare') and, finally, the later distribution or division of land (for 'the purposes of agriculture') (1946: 43). Apart from such speculation, one thing remains clear in this regard: the indistinction of the land and its people. If the *demos* had 'proprietorship', it was a 'common proprietorship'. Equally, that an *oikos* held land permanently is clearly evident in Homer, but also, significantly, so it was long before Homer's era. That it could not be 'lost' is a signature not of 'property ownership', but of a different possibly communal relation to land.

It is worth noting, in contrast, that some of the proximate characteristics of 'property' were approximated, not with regard to land, but with regard to 'slaves' (*dmōes, dmōai, douloi*, essentially, of the *oikos*). 'Slaves' in the poems are disposable at will and can be bought and sold, while, as Herbert A. Applebaum notes, 'there was no manumission nor slavery for debt' (1992: 6). Possession of 'slaves' was in one sense 'exclusive' (for example, *Il.* 1.161–2) for the duration of the master's life (and they could possibly be 'inherited', *Il.* 19.330–3). In addition, the claim to punish 'slaves' was as well established, as was, in turn, the slaves' claim to be protected by their master (for example, *Od.* 22.25–41). Achilles is, thus, depicted killing his captured 'slaves' in *Il.* 18.336–7. The children of 'slaves', their 'fruits', as Edward Harris observes, could be subject to the claims ('rights') of a master (for example, *Od.* 17.212).[61] At the same time, slaves belong to the *oikos* and in a sense to the family-plateau of the noble or king (with which, it should be noted, Homer

---

[60] See the outdated, but still valuable, work by Thomson (1946: 109–12).
[61] See, further, Harris (2012: 10f).

is most concerned), who is said to have cared for them in a rather patriarchal manner (*Od.* 16.14–18). Slaves, thus, are depicted seated at the same dinner table of the *oikos* in *Od.* 24.411.[62] In addition, a *klēros* in 'common land' could still be bestowed on a loyal slave (*Od.* 14.62–5; Ridgeway 1885: 332). In any event, without doubt, the devaluation of one's worth in becoming or being a slave is quite evident in the epics.[63] Similarly, and more generally, increasing instances of poverty across 'classes' would arguably lead to a formalisation of relations to land, leading to the famous legislative reforms of the classical period.

To divert our attention for just a little longer, it is worth noting at this point that the vexed question – which has not ceased to be raised since the nineteenth century, if not since the archaic period – as to whether land was 'inalienable' or not remains so still to an extent.[64] The classic point of reference relates to the alleged Spartan practice of considering it shameful to sell land as 'it is illegal to sell the ancient portion (*archaia moira*)', as Herakleides (Lembos) reports in the second century BC in fr. 12 [Dilts].[65] The 'ancient portion' is held, by some, to relate to the part of land that was considered 'common' (*politikē chōra*), whereas other forms of 'alienation' were perhaps possible.[66] By extension, for William Ridgeway, property in land is foreign to the Homeric epics (1885: 327). It is pertinent to emphasise that the verb κτάομαι (*ktaomai*) is never used for the 'acquisition' of land, though it is used (in a sense approximating to 'chattel') with regard to slaves (*Od.* 14.3, 460), or a wife (*Od.* 24.193), and an *oikos* (*Od.* 20.265). Yet despite the non-use of this verb in relation to the 'acquisition' of land, the view as to a general 'inalienability' is today

---

[62] See Applebaum (1992: 6). One 'slave' in *Od.* 20.222 is depicted as considering leaving Odysseus in search of a new master.

[63] See, for example, Mele (1968); Rihll (1996: 89–111); Cartledge (2002: 156–66); and Osborne (2004a).

[64] See, for example, Guiraud (1893: 46–63); and Fine (1951: 177–82).

[65] See Arist. *Lak. Pol.* fr. 611.12 [Rose] = Herakleides (Lembos) 373.12, which is considered to be its source. Hodkinson disputes the reliability and the conclusions of studies based on this (1986: 378–406) and, in fact, suggests that the peculiarity of the Spartan land tenure was probably an invention of later moralists and critics of democratic politics.

[66] See Finley (1977: 156).

largely rejected, since it is suggested that the forbidding of the
'selling' of land is a measure that would only be considered
possible in a situation akin to an emergency.[67] Overall, in the
epics, the loss of one's 'property-possession' is reflected upon
particularly negatively (for example, *Il.* 18.288–92).

5. *Apoikia*

Now we can return to the *klēroi* anew, from another angle.
We can perhaps learn more about the way in which the *klēros*
operated as a 'process' or, better, as an *ēthos* if we attach
to our brief engagement material that is derived from the
(stories of) practices of founding an (independent from
the motherland)[68] ἀποικία (*ap-oikia*; I use this term instead
of the anachronistic 'colony').[69] Already from the eleventh
century BC, but more so for our purposes between the ninth
and mid-sixth centuries BC[70] in particular, the Greeks settled
in *apoikiai* with or without violence, settlements in Sicily and
what later became conventionally known as *Magna Grecia*
(i.e. the coastline of southern Italy) being probably the earliest (from the first half of the eighth century BC). The reasons
for such settlements were probably multiple (need for land,
resources, crisis in the motherland, etc.).

The settlement of an *apoikia* in the archaic period is barely
noticeable in the poems in any implicit or explicit ways.[71]
Irad Malkin (1998; 2009) and Carol Dougherty (2001), taking
slightly different approaches, suggest that Odysseus can
be read as the founding father of Ithaca who must return
in order to inaugurate a new beginning. More directly, in
Od. 6.9–10 the resettlement of the Phaeacians in Scheria is
described as follows:

---

[67] See Thomson (1946); and Richter (1968a; 1968b); and contrast De
Coulanges (1903); Finley (1957; 1973); and Cassola (1964).
[68] See Finley (1976: 173–4).
[69] In agreement with Osborne (1997: 253).
[70] These dates are subject to continuous updating on the basis of archaeological discoveries.
[71] See Schaefer (1960: 77); on the Greek *apoikiai*, see Casevitz (1985); Malkin
(1987; 1998; 2009); Boardman (1999); Dougherty (2001); Tsetskhladze
(2006); and Domínguez (2011).

Homeric Nomos

εἶσεν δὲ Σχερίῃ, ἑκὰς ἀνδρῶν ἀλφηστάων,
ἀμφὶ δὲ τεῖχος ἔλασσε πόλει, καὶ ἐδείματο οἴκους,
καὶ νηοὺς ποίησε θεῶν, καὶ ἐδάσσατ' ἀρούρας.⁷²

Homer depicts here a wall surrounding the city and the building of houses and temples followed by the 'division' of the fields. The land of the *apoikia* was to be 'divided equally' among the small number of settlers exemplifying the vital importance and 'sacrality' of the prime (and arguably sought-after) resource of arable land. This required some accuracy and technical measurement, with plots assigned both within and outside the walled area of the new settlement.⁷³ Such was the task of the γεωνόμος (*geōnomos*, γεωνόμης, *geōnomēs*), later illustrated comically in Aristophanes' *Birds*, in which one 'wishes to survey the sky and divide it up in fields', but ultimately proceeds to plan a polis (995–6). Later, too, we find a reference in a decree concerning the colonists in Brea (446/5 BC): (γεονόμοι, *geonomoi*) δὲ νεμάντ[ον τὲν γῆν], referring to officials assigned the specific task of 'distributing-sharing' (*nemanton*) the land among the settlers.⁷⁴ Who actually did the allocation remains, however, a question.

For Ridgeway, the notion that early on an often noble chief (later on a more formalised *oikist*) allocated the lands is not implied in *Od*. 6.9–10. An *oikist*, he writes,

> directs all the important details of the founding of the settlement, and amongst these not the least would have been the selecting of those portions of the newly acquired territory suitable for tillage, and marking out into equal portions, which in all probability were distributed by lot amongst the settlers, whether they were to be held absolutely or in common. (1885: 330)

I will return to the role of the *oikist* briefly below, but first some more general remarks about the process of the foundation of an *apoikia* that may assist the approach. Despite the mostly late derivation of relevant literary evidence (some

⁷² See also *Od*. 6.4–5; and Osborne (2004b; 31).
⁷³ See Malkin (1987: 135ff).
⁷⁴ *IG* I² 45.7–8.

98

late archaic inscriptions, but chiefly evidence occurring in the fifth century BC and in much later authors)[75] that such an inquiry is inevitably reliant upon, David Asheri, in his extensive study, proposes that the primary agrarian partition in a territory was to be retained as 'legally indivisible', and this operation was denoted by terms such as δάσμος (*dasmos*; Il. 1.166; which signifies 'distribution'), κληρουχία (*klērouchia*) (with κατακληρουχέω, *kataklēroucheō*, or διανέμω, *dianemō*), νομή (*nomē*), πρώτη (*prōtē*, the first or initial), νέμησις (*nemēsis*), μερισμός (*merismos*) and ἀναδασμός (*anadasmos*), in a 'distributory' sense (for example, *Od.* 4.10) (1966: 5). Thus, the act of the institution or foundation of the *apoikia* via the distribution-sharing of the territory was to be best exemplified in relation to virgin or uninhabited lands (ἔρημος χώρα, *erēmos chōra*);[76] or, as Asheri notes, in relation to the post-war division of a δορίκτητος γῆ (*doriktētos gē*, 'land won by the spear'; ibid. 6). Unrelated to the *apoikiai*, we also find a similar practice in relation to the assignation of reserved common or 'sacred' land. For Asheri, thus, the division was in any case an act of a collective nature via the hand of an appointed representative, or 'chief' (later on a designated *oikist*), to the point that the term *apoikia* becomes synonymous with the term *klērouchia*, the 'distribution of lots'.

The *apoikia* would be composed of *oikoi* and their total number would be equal to the number of *klēroi* (lots) (Asheri 1966: 8–9). Asheri mentions such technical division as taking place under the guidance, or instruction, of the γεωμέτραι (*geōmetrai*; those who 'measure the land') or the ὁρισταί (*oristai*; 'boundary-setters').[77] The main 'division' to take place first would be that between the nucleus (πεδίον, *pedion*; τῶν ἰδιωτῶν χώρα, *tōn idiōtōn chōra*) and the periphery (ἐσχατιά, *eskchatia*). The former would be further distinguished into types such as arable land (γῆ ἀρόσιμος, *gē arosimos*), ἀρίστη (*aristē*) or ἐξαίρετος χώρα (*exhairetos chōra*); while the latter would be distinguished between γῆ (*gē*) ψιλή (*psilē*), ἀγροική (*agroikē*) and δασεῖα (*daseia*), along with inferior parts (ἡ

---

[75] See Graham (1964; 1982) and Malkin (1994; 1998).
[76] Diod. Sic. 5.53.1 (*erēmon*); 5.53.3 (*erēmos*); 5.81.2 (*erēmon tēn men chōran*) and 5.81.5 (*chōran erēmon*); Strab. 9.5.12 (*chōras teleōs erēmōmenēs*).
[77] See Hdt. 1.66.

χείρων, ē *cheirōn*; ἡ ἄλλη χώρα, ē *allē chōra*). Finally, the land near or 'adjacent' to the polis would be described as ἡ προς τῇ πόλει (ē *pros tē polei*), ἡ συνεγγύς τῇ πόλει χώρα (ē *syneggus tē polei chōra*; ibid. 9–10). Asheri, further, suggests that in the initial period of the foundation of the *apoikia*, the periphery zones were not included in this primary-foundational division/distribution: instead they were used commonly (as undivided, κοινή χώρα [*koinē chōra*]; γῆ ἀδιαίρετος [*gē adiairetos*]), until perhaps they were designated in a future distribution among later groups of *apoikoi* ('settlers') (ibid. 10). *Temenē*, notably, would also be distinguished and dedicated to, for instance, the gods, but to this I turn later.

Hence, the primary division/distribution would take place through the determination of the first lots (πρῶτοι [*prōtoi*] or παλαιοί [*palaioi*] κλῆροι [*klēroi*], ἀρχαῖα μοῖρα [*arhaia moira*]) by the γεονόμοι (*geonomoi*; Asheri 1966: 11).[78] Asheri emphasises that the lots in the *apoikiai* were equal (ἰσομοιρία, *isomoiria*) and possibly mirrored the divine division of the *klēros* (as in Pl. *L.* at 5.741: ὁ νείμας [*neimas*] Κλῆρος [*Klēros*], ὧν Θεός [*ōn theos*]; ibid. 12). We find references to this potential 'equality' in Homer, too, in the form of an ἴση μοῖρα (*isē moira*), κλῆρος ἐπ᾽ ἴσης (*klēros ep' isēs*) as in *Il.* 1.166, although we do know that the societies he describes were not really based on 'equality'.[79] For Asheri, however, this is a significant early conception of landholding 'equality' that, crucially, precedes 'democratic developments' (ibid. 14), while we have seen earlier that such 'equality' probably signifies a form of parity of portions/lots over 'plots' of differing quality and as an equalising means which were gradually transforming in Homer's time (*Il.* 12.421–3) to the point that a *klēros* (as attested in classical times) may have also become a particular form of

---

[78] See Arist. *Pol.* 1266B21, 1319A12; later also found as γεωμόρος (*geōmoros*), Dion. Hal. 9.52.2 [LS]; note also: *IG* 12.10.3; οἱ γεωνόμοι νειμάντων τὴν γῆν (*oi geōnomoi neimantōn tēn gēn*); ibid. 45.7. The class of, most likely, oligarchs in the settlement of Syracuse, named γαμόροι (*gamoroi*), may or may not be linked to this sense of the allotment of land; see Hdt. 7.155.

[79] See also *Il.* 2.226; 4.40–2, 138; 12.421–3; Diod. Sic. 12.2.2, 14.7.4; and Callim. *Hymn Apoll.* 63–4, to which Asheri also refers. In contrast to Asheri, Hüttl disputes the supposed equality (*isomoiria*) among initial settlers (with reference to the establishment of Syracuse; 1929). Aristotle notes in *Pol.* 1290b12–15 that in (some) settlements oligarchies were created.

'measuring'.[80] Lastly, Asheri offers an interesting theory as to the so-called 'inalienability' of the primary lots/lands, which I have already mentioned,[81] as a practice that developed into a kind of necessity, owing to a particular need to sustain the service of the *hoplites* (the warriors) and their families (ibid. 17–18); and, in this sense, he points to the distinction between a *klēros* that is 'hereditary' and 'inalienable' and the αὐτόκτιτα (*autoktita*; 'private' acquisitions) that were, in contrast, at least in one sense, 'alienable' (ibid. 21).[82] In the classical period, and in Plato famously so, the apportioned land was to be allotted but remain ultimately common (*L.* 740a).

Once more, the 'religious'-social nature of this practice of division/distribution needs to be further emphasised. The act of founding the *apoikia* was in itself fundamentally a sacred act (later possibly testified by oath, *horkos*). As Alexander J. Graham writes, in addition, later on it was 'sacred enough to be performed by a god', or in co-operation with a god (most frequently Apollo, Hera, Poseidon and Zeus, along with the establishment of sanctuaries and cults of respective worship); he adds that, 'apart from the cities of Greece proper, like Athens, many colonies claimed Apollo as their *oikist*' (1964: 26).[83] Equally, such performance could be carried out by a godlike character, such as Nausithous in the resettlement of Scheria, described by Homer in *Od.* 4.7–11 as we saw earlier, who was upon his death worshipped as a hero (Graham 1964: 28).[84] While much has been written about the role of the *oikist* (founder) of an *apoikia*, it is quite credible to suppose that this *oikist*-foundation model is probably a later normalisation of a practice that originally was probably more heterogeneous.[85] What we find in the Homeric poems are elements of

---

[80] See *SIG*[3] 141.8–9.

[81] Compare the classical locus in Arist. *Pol.* 1319a8. On alienation see, more generally, Fine (1951: 195); Finley (1975); Finley (1952: 270, n. 46) notes that there is no word for 'seller of land'. Land was not 'commodified'.

[82] See Graham (1964: 59) and Asheri (1966: 13–15).

[83] The instances are collected in Lampros (1873: 8–20).

[84] See Malkin (1987: 198ff). *Oikists* possibly functioned as 'law-givers' (see ibid. 5). For the worship of an *oikist* as a hero with the offering of a sacrifice, see Hdt. 6.38.1.

[85] See Mele (2007); on the *oikist* in later settlements, see Graham (1964: 29–39); and Dougherty (2001: 128–9).

precisely such a more disparate practice, though the evidence is limited. As Alfonso Mele observes, for instance, we see the 'preconditions' for the establishment of a 'colony' in the scene where the Goat Island, opposite the Cyclopes' land, is described as

> a wooded, uninhabited island, showing no sign of the presence of humans – no hunters, or shepherds, or plough-ers – but grazing land for a multitude of goats. The island shows a good potential: its land is suitable for grazing and for growing vines and cereals. It has a safe harbor and water resources. But it has remained uninhabited because the Cyclops are not sailors and do not build ships to travel to other people's cities nor carry out the typical activities which men undertake when they cross the seas and meet with other men. (2007: 3–4)[86]

In need of arable land and new sources of subsistence (rather than, initially at least, 'wealth'), such an expedition would possibly be led by a military leader who would head the process from start to finish, and, who, in Mele's speculative sense, attempts to restore his own lost prestige and the set-tlers' lost land back in the motherland (2007). The *oikist* (such as Nausithous) would presumably have been the trusted 'founder' for the planning and the building of a settlement, within which some function of distribution or allotment would have been necessary and potentially typical.

6. *Oikos*

Before we turn to the *temenos*, which was a particular practice of land apportionment, we need to clarify the particular role of the οἶκος (*oikos*). The *oikos* is the settlement-kinship unit (possi-bly from the Indo-European root **wik-*, settlement, house, clan) that most likely grew out of larger families or clans into the relatively smaller-scale and independent units that we meet in the epics.[87] In the Homeric epics, the *oikos* is central to the tran-sitional social transformation of the earlier 'tribal elements'

[86] See also, *Od.* 9.116–41.
[87] See Benveniste (1973: 165–7 and 176; 239–61); and Donlan (1989b: 23).

and the palatial era into an aristocratic, male-dominated, territorial and administrative unit that forms a self-sufficient (to
an extent) though often idealised institution (never, however,
independent from its wider community as such).[88] Earlier
in the pre-polis era the *oikos* arguably was, in fact, more self-
sufficient than in Homer's and Hesiod's time (i.e. mid-eighth
century BC).[89] Indeed, the *oikos* is the unit, continuously central
from the so-called dark ages to the archaic era, that eventually
served as the model for the foundation of the polis-state or a
sunoikism (Demand 1990), possibly in embryonic form from
1050 BC onwards.[90] Homer, of course, is mostly concerned with
the dominant elites in the epics, while the 'commoners' are
described as the πλῆθος (*plēthos*, 'multitude'; *Il.* 11.299–309).
The *plēthos* of the 'commoners', one may presume, were free
peasants and herders for the most part, though we also meet in
the epics the rise of the new group, the *dēmiourgoi*, described as
part-time 'prophets, healers of ills, workers of wood, wonderful singers and heralds' who serve the community.[91] The land
is already in the hands of the dominant elite forming their *oikoi*,
who forbid 'upward mobility'.[92] Gifts, reciprocal exchanges
and crucially (monogamous) marriages would preserve the
domination of the nobles among their *oikos*-land.[93]

In the poems, the word *oikos* indicates 'a house or abode'
of a nuclear family, which crucially includes the building
and its contents, the curtilage, and all its inhabitants including the unfree and hired labour force, as well as a circle of
free non-kin attendants.[94] The important thing to appreciate
is that the (aristocratic, but not only so) *oikos* includes the
family (and its home), but crucially the (moveable and

---

[88] Though it needs to be noted that the notion of an aristocracy in this
period is not to be understood in the strong sense of a sharp division
between an elite and the poor *dēmos* of the rural areas; see Glotz ([1926]
1965); Duplouy (2006).

[89] See Donlan (1989b: 7–13).

[90] See the discussion in Donlan (1989b: 20ff).

[91] See Applebaum (1992: 7), who also notes intermediate strata between the
two main social groups.

[92] See Applebaum (1992: 5–7).

[93] On gifts in Homer, see Scheid-Tissinier (1994).

[94] See, for example, *Il.* 1.30; 3.233; 24.471; *Od.* 1.248, 258; and 5.9. On houses
in the *Odyssey*, see Gray (1955: 1–7); and Burford (1977).

unmoveable) 'wealth' that it possesses, and especially the land that it holds. The Homeric *oikos*, as a predominantly social subsistence unit, was inseparable from the land.[95] For instance, Odysseus' large *oikos* (*Od.* 14.93–108) can serve as paradigmatic here; analogically, so can Nestor's farmland as it is described in *Od.* 4.600–4, or that of Alkinoos in *Od.* 7.114–31. Further, the vivid description of Laertes' *oikos* (in *Od.* 24.205–12, 220–7) includes the house with quarters for the slaves, fields, stables, orchards and vineyards; and the importance of farm work is depicted furthermore in the farmland on Achilles' shield (*Il.* 18.541–89). Around the *oikos* we see a mainly agricultural and bucolic agrarian life taking place, but also the focal point of the most significant part of the social and worship practices of the early archaic polis. The 'agrarian renaissance' of the period after the so-called dark ages, as Maria Vania Cavalli identifies it, is characterised by three key elements: 'the occupation of previously free and uncultivated land, intensification of land exploitation and diversification in the type of crops' (2008–9: 73). While, simultaneously, it is important to appreciate that this was an *ēthos* of a predominantly divine-worship character, the typicality of the valorisation of the *oikos* from its earlier form is perhaps depicted also, in that Zeus has his own *oikos* and is said to have to keep it in order. The *oikos* is, in this manner, a remarkably long-surviving social unit, vitalised anew by an *ēthos*, central within which would be hard physical agrarian work and adherence to the attached worship-tradition of one's *moira*.

The entire household worked, however, not only in order to secure its subsistence, but also in order to satisfy a certain kinship with the 'natural world' (the proto-ground of the famous Promethean act), as well as the gods, in an essentially worship-oriented social milieu. One can note that *kairos*, in this respect, which has been reinterpreted as a radical, and part-utopian, political concept in late modernity,[96] had its origins in 'a moment' that is seized by the worker, if work were to be successful.[97] Applebaum comments:

---

[95] See Finley (1968; [1954] 1977/1988); and Lacey (1968).

[96] See Negri (2003).

[97] See Pl. *Rep.* 370b–4c; Applebaum (1992: 10).

In the Homeric poems, work on the land was not viewed as acting upon nature in order to transform it, but rather participation in a natural and divine order that is superior to man. There is little evidence of the commercial aspect of work. The fruits of the earth are consumed in the household. Consumption and the giving of gifts is set in opposition to commerce and trading. The worse insult that could be hurled at Odysseus was the accusation that he was some type of trader. (*Od.* 8.145–64; 1992: 17)

One works (πρακτῆρα τε ἔργων; *praktēra te ergōn*) in the satellite fields and administers the household in direct personal contact with nature and the gods. In this sense, the apportionment and possession of land that concerns us here has to be understood in this context as the ground through and on which 'virtue' is to be accomplished. Such a virtuous existence would not be possible if the apportionment of land, its cultivation and use more generally were not stabilised, to a significant extent, through a sense of possession that would have the capacity to be somehow 'held' and 'inherited'.

The headship of the *oikos*, in this sense, is characterised by a patriarchal *ēthos* that requires marriage and a large family, so that the original apportionment can be preserved in posterity and so crucially maximise its labour and fighting power. In a scene that is already familiar, Eumaios, the swineherd, says that Odysseus would have given him a possession-property (κτῆσις, *ktēsis*),[98] including an οἶκος (*oikos*), a κλῆρος (*klēros*) and a wife (*Od.* 14.62).[99] This may explain better, now, the speculation as to a certain sense of 'inalienability' in the so-called 'private property' of the *oikos*. That is, the sense in which both the 'religious' motivation for the virtuous possession of an *oikos* and the use of the land for the purposes of subsistence, as well as the continuation of the possession and 'work' through the line of the (noble) family, in early times rendered necessary a relatively stable pattern of patrilineal inheritance for *oikonomic*, 'religious' and military reasons. The *oikos* was an *ēthos*, a whole way of life indissociably tied to the land.

---

[98] See, for example, *Il.* 5.158; 15.66; *Od.* 4.687; 7.225; 15.62.
[99] See Seebohm (1895: ch. 5).

We can observe an interesting example of an 'inheritance' taking place at the death of a father (Castor) among several legitimate sons in *Od.* 14.207–10, whereby, in fact, a *klēros* is used to distribute-share the land presumably equally (in terms of 'value' measured according to a hierarchy of nobility). Thus, the less nobly-born son, in this case, will receive a smaller portion of land than the others. If the earlier concept of the use of a lot eventually lost its meaning of actually 'receiving by lot', it later still retains the general sense of 'receiving' a portion or part. To return anew to one of my earlier concerns, in this light, then, I could say that, if not 'inalienability' in the strict sense, a predominant practice of securing subsistence and lineage appears prevalent and plain enough, while, as the population grew accordingly alongside economic activity (as much as poverty), 'wealth acquisition' and 'hereditary' transfer of 'possession' and 'use' could have become gradually distinguished.[100] In other words, 'ownership' could be understood as 'common', in perhaps this sense: as 'inalienable' within the lineage or for a particular social group's possession-use, where the *oikos* and the community at large were differentiated, but not dissociated.[101] A good example of such emphatic communal experience and of an *ēthos* of reciprocity is offered in the case of the gift of a *temenos*, which I address next.

7. Temenos

I turn finally to idea of the τέμενος (*temenos*).[102] A *temenos*, as noted earlier, is the only, arguably common, 'landholding' term between the remnants of Linear B and the Homeric poems, though the 'holdings' of land in Homer and the Mycenaean tablets are separated by a yawning chasm (of time and differentiation, as well as evidence). The Pylos tablets provide the earliest written evidence of *temenos* in the *Er* series. In fact, two different types of 'landholding' are described: the first is that of the 'private land-holding', *wa-na-*

---

[100] See Quale (1988).
[101] See Della Volpe (2004).
[102] See Hahn (1977: 299–316); Donlan (1989a: 129–45); and Guizzi (2010: 86–91).

ka of an ἄναξ (*anax*, 'king') and of a military chief (*ra-we-ke-ta*), followed by a grain sign.[103] The other is that of a 'sacred' *temenos* devoted to a god. Angela Della Volpe (2004), summarising the interesting etymological inquiry, notes the following.[104] First, it remains unclear whether the word *temenos* is of an Indo-European origin (possibly Akkadian, Sumerian), but it is most likely to be so (*tem-H-no-s* and the root *tem*, 'to cut') – in Greek: τέμει (*temei*), 'cut', (τέμνειν, *temnein*) and τομή, (*tomē*) 'slice or fragment' (for example, *Il.* 13.707). Della Volpe, thus, proposes 'that which is cut', the result of an action performed by an agent (2004: 121).[105] Second, the primary sense of such a cut may be, to use anachronistic terms, the approximate separation of a 'sacred' from a 'profane' space/land. The early practice of the Greeks of worshipping in groves may lie at the root of this; and it should be noted that a temple or altar was usually adjacent to, or lay within, a *temenos* (ibid. 123). But it is neither necessary nor likely that the *temenos* was a portion of land cut from 'common land' initially for worship purposes. What was necessary was a certain delimitation of the perimeter and an altar for the performance of rites.[106]

The word *temenos* occurs several times in Homer. Walter Donlan reports thirteen such occurrences and singles out four *temenoi* that are dedicated to gods with an altar for 'sacrifice' (*Il.* 2.696; 8.48, 363; 23.148), while the rest are held by men of high status (1989a: 129ff). As Donlan explains: 'Since all the holders (or potential holders) are identified as βασιλεῖς [*basileis*], or as sons of βασιλεῖς, it has been generally assumed, with reason, that a τέμενος was granted only to men of chiefly status' (ibid. 130).[107] In the epics, the *temenos* is of substantial size and has the essential characteristic of being fertile agricultural land.[108] The *temenos* is a gift to a significant individual, which in the Homeric epics does not seem to

---

[103] 152 = Er 01 [312]; see Palmer (1963); and Della Volpe (2004).
[104] See further Della Volpe (2004) with extensive references.
[105] See also Manessy-Guilton (1966: 14–38); and Della Volpe (1994).
[106] See Bergquist (1967: 6–7), who stresses that the *temenos* is the whole of its constitutive elements and finds its proper sense as an 'estate belonging to a god' (ibid. 5).
[107] See Latte (1934: 435–7); and Bergquist (1967).
[108] See *Il.* 9.578; 20.391; *Od.* 6.291; 17.299; see, further, Donlan (1989a: 130).

give rise to any 'obligations' or 'conditions'.[109] Primarily, the *temenos* signifies, perhaps, 'god's land' and its more general sense is probably that of a 'dedication', a separated portion of land. In a Homeric exercise in poetic etymology, too, we meet the expression τέμενος τέμνειν (*temenos temnein*), as a separated land/area (*Il.* 4.194 and 20.184).

Seebohm, early on, understood the *temenos* to be the differentiated holding of land by the βασιλεύς (*basileus*), while 'the swarms of tribesmen are allotted their κλῆροι [*kleroi*] in the open field, their share in the common pasture, and depend on each other for help in the vintage and harvest' (1895: 102). Such was, for him, the *oikos* of Odysseus, whose wealth was incomparable with his dozens of servants, twelve herds of cows, flocks of sheep, droves of swine and herds of goats with shepherds and others pasturing on his land. Odysseus is in fact depicted enjoying more than one *temenos* (*Od.* 11.184–5). A key example that Seebohm drew upon is that of Bellerophon's grand allotment by the Lykians to honour his bravery (*Il.* 4.574). Seebohm writes:

> Such allotments of land seem only to have been made to princes and gods, but when once allotted, remained as far as can be seen the property of their descendants. It was a common fancy of the Homeric prince that he was worshipped as a god, and they often mistook each other for some deity. The godlike Sarpedon asks his cousin Glaukos, wherefore are they two honoured in Lykia as gods, with flesh and full cups and a great τέμενος. (*Il.*12.313; 1895: 101)

The key verses of Sarpedon's speech are as follows (12.310–21):

Γλαῦκε τί ἢ δὴ νῶϊ τετιμήμεσθα μάλιστα
ἕδρῃ τε κρέασίν τε ἰδὲ πλείοις δεπάεσσιν
ἐν Λυκίῃ, πάντες δὲ θεοὺς ὡς εἰσορόωσι,
καὶ τέμενος νεμόμεσθα μέγα Ξάνθοιο παρ᾽ ὄχθας
καλὸν φυταλιῆς καὶ ἀρούρης πυροφόροιο;
τῶ νῦν χρὴ Λυκίοισι μέτα πρώτοισιν ἐόντας

---

[109] See Richter (1968b; 1988a); and Hahn (1977).

ἑστάμεν ἠδὲ μάχης καυστείρης ἀντιβολῆσαι,
ὄφρά τις ὧδ᾽εἴπῃ Λυκίων πύκα θωρηκτάων:
'οὐ μὰν ἀκλεέες Λυκίην κάτα κοιρανέουσιν
ἡμέτεροι βασιλῆες, ἔδουσί τε πίονα μῆλα
οἶνόν τ᾽ἔξαιτον μελιηδέα: ἀλλ᾽ἄρα καὶ ἲς
ἐσθλή, ἐπεὶ Λυκίοισι μέτα πρώτοισι μάχονται.'

In translation:

'Glaucus, wherefore is it that we twain are held in honour
above all with seats, and messes, and full cups
in Ly[k]ia, and all men gaze upon us as on gods?
Aye, and we possess a great demesne by the banks of
    Xanthus,
a fair tract of orchard and of wheat-bearing plough-land.
Therefore now it behoveth us to take our stand
amid the foremost Ly[k]ians, and confront
the blazing battle that many a one of the mail-clad Ly[k]
    ians may say:
"Verily no inglorious men be these that rule in Lycia,
even our kings, they that eat fat sheep and drink choice
    wine,
honey-sweet: nay, but their might too is goodly,
seeing they fight amid the foremost Ly[k]ians."'[110]

Here, the *basileus' kleos* (κλέος; 'glory and ruleship') is, in one
sense, identified with the honourable granting of special portions of food and land in reciprocity perhaps to the military
services offered to the community – depicting a relatively
equitable distribution, or reciprocity in a more general sense,
central to the Homeric *ēthos* (emphatically pronounced in the
epics, at least, among the elites). Hence, the *temenos* will be
termed the apportionment of the πατρώιον (*patrōion*), one's
'patrimony' (or, we could say, *patrinomē*) handed down from
one's ancestors (*Il.* 2.46, 101–8; *Od.* 1.407: πατρὶς ἄρουρα,
patris aroura). The verb used to describe this allotment is,
again, *nemein*: as in *Od.* 11.185, where Telemachos νέμεται
τεμένεα (*nemetai temenea*; 'holds the land [of Odysseus]'); and

---

[110] Translation by Murray (1924).

in Od. 20.336: πατρώια πάντα νέμηαι (*patrōia panta nemēai*). Donlan, perhaps, overstates the 'legal nature' of such apportionment at this time as a type of 'legal acquisition' (1989a: 130 n. 5). Instead, it is suggested that, in verses like *Il.* 6.194–5, 12.313–14 and 20.184–5, the most likely sense of νέμομαι (*nemomai*) is that of 'possession'.

It is, indeed, with reference to the practices associated with the τέμενος βασιλήϊον (*temenos basilēion*), that Ridgeway identified his own version of an early formation of 'private property' as gradually supplanting the older order:

> A chieftain who had capital, i.e. oxen and slaves, more than sufficient to cultivate the τέμενος, might take possession of a piece of waste land remote from the town and from the divided lands of the community. His slaves would till it for him, and protect it against marauders. It would become his undisputed property, and at his death would naturally pass to his heirs, whilst the royal τέμενος would revert to the community to be bestowed on the next chieftain. (1885: 334)

The *temenē* would, incidentally, be cultivated by slaves or labourers (ἔριθοι, *erithoi*; in *Il.* 12.310–14). Ridgeway suggested, as an example of this gradual transformation, Odysseus' famous holding (*Od.* 11.184–5; ibid.). Yet the long-standing question is not so much why a *temenos* was granted, but rather how.

As we have seen, the *temenos* is, like γέρας (*geras*), an honorary piece of land due to someone for reasons of recognition, as a gift or compensation for highly valued services to the community.[111] Hence, the difficulty lies with the how, or to be more precise: whose land was 'cut' to give a *temenos*? Donlan analyses the complexity of this question and notes that scholarship in the nineteenth century, 'heavily influenced by [then] contemporary sociological theory', suggested that land was generally held under 'an ancient common field system that would be periodically redistributed' (1989a: 132).[112] The *temenos* was a grant of land, a royal domain, given to the king

---

[111] See, for example, *Il.* 20.176.
[112] Influencing later work, for example Thomson (1949: 317–18).

by the people out of land signified as 'common'. As this part of the 'common' land would be cut out it would, perhaps, become a progenitor to a prototype of 'private property' (as Ridgeway suggested).

Finley, in the late 1950s, challenged this and eventually rejected it, with most scholars now agreeing with his conclusion (1957).[113] Yet Donlan (1989a: 133) sustains the question by reasonably asking if, as has been suggested, there was no 'common' landholding (at least) in Homeric times, then would new *temenē* have to be taken out of 'private' land? While Finley (1957; and Dieter Hennig more recently: 1980) proposed that the honoured recipient would receive privately-held land of his choice, Donlan considers that the implications of such a 'cut' would be a considerable loss for a family and, thus, by implication, perhaps socially unsustainable (1989a: 133; Hennig 1980). While in the epics there is no such implication, there is a much later one in Herodotus as to the finest *klēroi* of Apollonia being freely chosen by Euenios (Hdt. 9.94), and, significantly, what we do have evidence for in the epics is possibly only an implied manner of 'compensation' for such loss, lying in the hands of chiefly power (i.e. *Od.* 13.13–15).

With this in mind, Donlan proposed a different theory: since we are told that the giver of *temenē* in the epics was the *dēmos*, they must be giving out their 'own' land (1989a: 134).[114] Which land did they have available to them? Donlan suggests that 'New τεμένη were cut out of uncultivated (i.e. unowned) arable land and not, as traditionally assumed, from land already being farmed'. This surplus arable, he maintains, was '*ager publicus*' and its distribution resided in 'community power' (ibid. 134; though, inevitably, the anachronism of an *ager publicus* here needs to be noted). The *dēmos*, which was identified with the ancestral land and the polis, did enjoy a clear corporate unity (i.e. the *dēmos* could 'owe' a debt 'in common', *Od.* 21.17; or give *geras* to its leaders, an act that was by definition communal, as in *Od.* 7.150).[115] To

---

[113] See, for example, Starr (1977: 150–1); and Donlan (1989a: 151).

[114] See Donlan (1985: 298–302).

[115] See Donlan (1989b: 14); on *geras*, see *Il.* 1.123, 161, 276, 392; 2.228; 20.182; *Od.* 1.117; 7.150; 9.160; 11.175, 184; 23.357–8. Similarly, on *timē*, see *Il.*

my knowledge, we do not have definitive evidence of this possibility, and, to the extent that uncultivated land would lie in the ἐσχατιή (*eskhatiē*), this remains a fragile possibility at least with regard to some of the Homeric references, since we are often told in the epics that the land of the *temenē* was particularly fertile (whereas the *eskhatiē* were not so), unless there was uncultivated cultivable and thus prosperous land fitting for a gift, which remains entirely possible.

Della Volpe's (2004) alternative suggestion may also be considered. The setting aside, or 'cutting', of a piece of land is designated in the epics as a cutting or separation from 'common use', which could suggest that the use of the *klēros* was feasible at least in one modality of granting *temenē*: but 'common' to whom? It appears, in this line of speculation, more reliable to suggest that a *temenos* could be drawn from the land of a particularly wealthy and powerful *basileus*, since, after all, *temenos* may usually mean 'royal land', at least in some parts of the Achaean and Trojan lands, which had earlier been received, possibly, by the *dēmos*.[116] In a practice that most likely derived from much earlier times, agnatic and patrilocal lineages acted as groups, as Della Volpe notes, so that each kinsman would acquire a 'right' 'that the kin supply them with the standard holding needed to uphold their status as head of a lineage' (2004: 125–6). It may be that the *temenos* was the land required to uphold or appease the head of the *oikos*:

> His kin had a duty to provide him with the standard holding. If they did not, it represented loss of status to the entire lineage. The *temenos*, then, might well have been the unit of land which bound together in one coherent system the lineage and the hierarchy of status. (2004: 126)

In any case, as we have seen, 'private alienation' of land is not really mentioned in the epics, other than in the form of gifts. In the same way, for instance, as in a 'sacrificial feast' a portion would be separated and devoted to the gods or a god,

---

9.616; *Od.* 11.495, etc. The distribution of land appears, in some respect, akin to the act of distribution of *geras*; see Donlan (1998: 62).

[116] See Finley (1957: 149).

the *temenos* could be the select portion allocated to the head
of the *oikos* as recognition of his status and service. Similarly,
in the case of 'inheritance' upon the death of the father of the
oikos, the *temenos* may also have been a share reserved from
the general allotment that would be 'awarded to the son who
was designated as the new head of the *oikos*' (ibid. 127). We
can only note here yet another element of the indissociably
'religious' nature of the *oikos* in that the *temenos*, a relative
portion, would become of great value as a 'sacred' space as
well as an administrative unit of the *oikos* that was, we are
told, part arable, part orchard (*Il.* 9.577–80).[117]

Therefore, in this transitional rationale, among the chiefdoms of Homeric times, and in the absence of any other more
powerful agent, the only 'corporate agency' to administer
oikos-family 'property' (possessions) was the lineage of the
oikos itself, and it was they who held ($\nu\varepsilon\mu\delta\mu\varepsilon\sigma\theta\alpha$, *nemomestha*)
'(an apportionment) in common' under the headship of the
father or his heir. With the stabilisation of the city-state,
perhaps then the *dēmos* would be able to formalise and gen-
eralise this practice of the *oikos* and the low-level chiefdom
under a more centralised *basileus* under whom the *dēmos*
would unify, while still vividly remembering their roots as
farmer-warriors and the distributive authority's frailty as
much as flexibility towards what was 'due' in terms of reciprocity.[118] In this sense, we can perhaps accept Macé's observation that in the Homeric poems, and perhaps also earlier,
the practices of 'distribution' (of 'land', but also more generally) also inevitably emphasise the importance of what is not
distributed or set apart (2014: 16). The act of distribution-
sharing establishes not only 'individual' (singled-out) portions, but also, crucially, a relation in and between them.[119] It
perhaps defined the very prototypical 'political' foundation
of the relation between each *oikos* and the polis. It may be
that, since among the uses of *nomos* lay the ordinary sense of
a certain distribution-sharing, when issues arose such as the
need for arable land – perhaps intensely so in the experience

---

[117] On the Homeric *temenos*, see Vlachos (1985: 251–2, n. 103).
[118] On Homeric 'economic' reciprocity, see Donlan (1982a: 137–75; 1999:
304–11); and Seaford (2004).
[119] See the discussion in Macé (2014: 659–88).

of the *apokiai*, but also more so in the later growth of the *poleis* – *nomos* could have been perceived as a particularly fitting word to use for the designation of a kind of 'distribution-by-"law"'.[120] With this in mind we can turn next to the pastures, which early on remained 'common' or undivided through their distributive-sharing uses, but which already, in Homer, may have been more distinctly reserved (Glotz [1926] 1965: 34–5) – a distribution-sharing, through which, in turn, *nomos* may have acquired one of its earliest senses of an apportionment without shares, a 'common' use.

8. The word that wasn't there

The proem of the *Odyssey* famously opens with the following verses (1.1–3):

> ἄνδρα μοι ἔννεπε, μοῦσα, πολύτροπον, ὃς μάλα πολλὰ
> πλάγχθη, ἐπεὶ Τροίης ἱερὸν πτολίεθρον ἔπερσε·
> πολλῶν δ᾽ ἀνθρώπων ἴδεν ἄστεα καὶ νόον ἔγνω[,].

Which can be rendered in translation as:

> Tell me, O Muse, of the cunning man, who time and again
> wandered off course in many ways, after he sacked the
>   sacred city of Troy.
> Many were the men whose cities he saw and whose *noon*
>   he learned[,]

Among these remarkable opening verses of the *Odyssey*, just after the invocation of the Muse and the announcement of the epic themes, lies the source of a peculiar controversy of interpretation that has been sustained for over a century among scholars of different disciplines – though more recently with less interest, it seems. The controversy concerns the

---

[120] See Camassa (2011b: 91–5 and 265). Camassa notes that in the *Magna Grecia* colonies the act of distributing or dividing the land was described through the verb *nemein*, but he also confirms that the epigraphic evidence does not confirm a relation of *nomos* to this act. Hence, the presumption that the experience of the new settlements led to a 'new' use of *nomos*-as-'law' remains largely speculative and significantly uncertain.

third verse in its conventionally accepted form (πολλῶν δ᾽ ἀνθρώπων ἴδεν ἄστεα καὶ νόον [noon] ἔγνω), and in particular the presence (or absence) of the word *nómon* in the place of *noon*. The verse can be translated as stating that Odysseus visited the cities of many different peoples and encountered/ learned of their different 'ways' or 'minds'.[121] The supposed controversy, in fact, had already taken root in ancient times, when Zenodotus (*c.* 284 BC), the first superintendent of the library of Alexandria and probably the first editor of Homer's epics, replaced *noon* with νόμον (*nómon*);[122] a replacement that was criticised by the grammarian Aristarchus of Samothrace (*c.* 217–45 BC), the later chief librarian in Alexandria.

This replacement has led to two equally controversial, and in my view misleading, suggestions. On the one hand, and from early on, we find the strong view (at times even advancing the view of a 'primitive Homer'), as variably expressed by Josephus (*Contra Apion*, 2.16.155), as well as a myriad of modern scholars including Jean Bodin, that the 'law' (i.e. *nomos*-as-'law') was entirely unknown in the Homeric epics. The late lexicographer Hesychius of Alexandria (*c.* fifth–sixth century AD), in turn, suggested that the notion of 'law' itself is entirely lacking in Homer. It is, of course, one thing to suggest that any sense of 'law' as such is unknown to the Homeric world and another to suggest that *nómos* (in the sense of 'law') was unknown during the Homeric age (or the arguably polyvalent traditions that the poet describes).

On the other hand, we find the view that Homer did in fact originally refer to *nómos* in the third verse, and that on this basis the paroxytone *nómos* was already used in his time in the sense of 'law'.[123] Further, one could also dispute the

---

[121] Such a link between wandering and knowing is also found later in Parmenides (28B 1.2–3 [DK]). *Noos* is quite close, in fact, to ἦθος (*ēthos*), a way of living or being; and the verb νοεῖν (*noein*) is especially proximate to a sense of seeing. See also *Il.* 15.80–1, where a traveller who is said to have visited many lands envisages in his νόος (*noos*) the different places he has seen (ὡς δ᾽ ὅτ᾽ ἂν ἀΐξῃ νόος ἀνέρος, ὅς τ᾽ ἐπὶ πολλὴν | γαῖαν ἐληλουθὼς φρεσὶ πευκαλίμῃσι νοήσῃ).

[122] Schol. M on *Od.* 1.3: Ζηνόδοτος νόμον ἔγνω φησίν [*Zēnodotos nómon egnō phēsin*]; see also Aristarch. 2.150ff, 216ff.

[123] For the view that *nómos* is, in fact, the better or 'right' reading, see Hirzel (1907: 367, n. 1); Hirzel writes also that one of the reasons for

possibility of *nómos* in the said verse on the basis of grammatical issues, or affirm it on the basis, for instance, of Herodotus' (later, but still relatively) early quotations of the Homeric epic. One could say, as Rudolf Hirzel (1907) did, that *nómos* 'fits' the epic best, but then one could easily counter this claim with the 'fittingness' of *noos*, too. For instance, if the verse is to be read as meaning that Odysseus wandered among different people who had different νόοι (*nooi*), meaning, in a sense, different ways of perceiving and living, then it appears to me to be quite coherent. We do, indeed, meet such 'different people' in the poem who are described accordingly: for example, the Phaeakians with their νόος θεουδής (*noos theoudēs*; *Od.* 4.121), the Cyclopes with their lack of a 'god-respecting' νόος (*noos*; *Od.* 4.176), or, indeed, Aias and Achilles with their νόος ἀπηνής (*noos apēnēs*; *Il.* 14.35; 23.484; *Od.* 18.381). The following verses, in fact, from Book 8 could be said to respond directly to the proem's verse (*Od.* 8.572–6):

> ἀλλ' ἄγε μοι τόδε εἰπὲ καὶ ἀτρεκέως κατάλεξον,
> ὅππη ἀπεπλάγχθης τε καὶ ἅς τινας ἵκεο χώρας
> ἀνθρώπων, αὐτούς τε πόλιάς τ' ἐῢ ναιεταούσας,
> ἠμὲν ὅσοι χαλεποί τε καὶ ἄγριοι οὐδὲ δίκαιοι,
> οἵ τε φιλόξεινοι καί σφιν νόος ἐστὶ θεουδής.

Which can be translated as:

> But now tell me this and give me an account, unswerving,
> In what ways were you drawn off course, and what
>   human lands you did you reach,
> themselves and their cities well-built,
> both those who are hard to deal with, and savages,
>   without *dikē*,
> and those who are hospitable to strangers, and who have
>   a *noos* that fears the gods.

this view is that *noos* is a generally divine prerogative, not a mortal one, but he is reading Hesiod *Th.* 367 and 373ff; Hirzel (1907: 367); Dittrich (1926: vol. I, 23, n. 40); Nestle ([1942] 1975: 43ff); Shipp (1972). I agree more with Laroche (1949: 124–5), Heinimann ([1945] 1965/1972: 61, n. 11) and Pohlenz ([1948] 1965: 139), who hold the opposite view, though by divergent paths.

It is worth noting too that *noos* in Homer is not yet the more advanced *noein* of the so-called pre-Socratic philosophers, or the *nous* of the classical period. *Noos*, in fact, is quite common in Homer, while no longer so in later authors.[124] Thus, it seems to me that, for more than one reason, this 'controversy' remains a relatively futile (while admittedly tantalising) concern.

In Homer, it is the case that we do not have (sufficient) evidence of '*nómos*-law', though we meet ample elements of what one could describe as an early *ethological pluriverse* based on 'customs and traditions' (i.e. *themis* and *dikē*). Perhaps it can be also said, in a preliminary manner, that, whatever 'law' there was, it was, in a general sense, accustomed to the wider tradition of a way of life in a particular community. While this cannot be absolutely conclusive in itself, it is certainly worth noting that we do not meet *nomos* in its paroxytone form (*nómos*) in any other of Homer's verses. Even if we did, however, it seems quite certain that *nómos* in Homer's pluriverse would not yet mean 'law', since Homer remains far removed from the later Attic and relatively 'abstract' conception of *nómos*-law. The lack of uses of *nómos*-law in Homer's time renders Zenodotus' replacement an early anachronism. In fact, whether Odysseus met with different *nómoi* or *nooi*, depending on which theory one prefers, what remains the case is that he encountered different ways of doing and seeing things.

What we do meet in the Homeric pluriverse is, in fact, far more interesting than the concern with whether the word *nómos* could be identified with some sense of 'law' early on, especially amidst evidence of the existence of not one but two differently (though anachronistically) accented words (νόμος, *nómos* and voμός, *nomós*) that would eventually coexist, while entailing different and numerous uses. The variety of coexistent uses and senses of the *nemein* family of words does necessitate an approach that is premised on more conservative, while open-minded, speculation.

It is quite well known that Carl Schmitt grounds his understanding of *nomos* (and of his '*nomos* of the earth')

---

[124] See von Fritz (1943: 79–93); also *Il.* 4.307: τόνδε νόον και θυμόν.

through what he perceives to be its rootedness in the act of 'appropriating and dividing the land' (and 'the earth' more generally; while he perceives, it has to be said, the key processes of 'appropriation', 'distribution' and 'production' in their interrelation).[125] Yet Schmitt relies on a misleading reconstruction of the third verse. It seems that Schmitt's disdain for the work of philologists leads him to employ his own philological deductions, as Katerina Stergiopoulou has shown in some detail (2014: 95–122). That Schmitt's philology was obsessively marked, in this particular regard, is evident when one visits his grave at the Catholic Cemetery in Plettenberg-Eiringhausen, where the tombstone has the inscription '*KAI NOMON EΓNΩ*'.[126] Schmitt disregards, too, the differentiation (at least on the basis of the extant literary evidence) between the two words νόμος (*nómos*) and νομός (*nomós*), as well as the fact that *nomós* does not mean 'law' (which Schmitt indeed accepts), but neither does *nómos* entail predominantly the sense of a 'division/distribution of land' in the epics (which Schmitt seems to maintain). The earlier form of *nomós* has no 'legal' (or 'political') sense to it, but equally the later νόμος may have no distinct sense of distribution to it. Schmitt seems to disregard the fact that only *nomós* relates expressly to land allotted (for pasture). It is worth asking very briefly, then, what kind of *nomos* Schmitt has in mind.

Schmitt emphatically distinguishes *nomos* from *Gesetz* ('law') and *Recht*. He famously argues for a *nomos* that is 'immediate, concrete': a *nomos* that is not law but Law, 'the stuff' from which law is made, whereby it is 'the total concept of right that precedes and makes possible all laws' (Stergiopoulou 2014: 95), comprising 'a concrete order and community' (Schmitt 2006: 20). Schmitt defines *nomos*, for his

---

[125] Schmitt locates three strata of the noun *nomos* in the German *nehmen* ('to take' or 'appropriate'), *teilen* ('to divide' or 'distribute') and *weiden* ('pasturage' or 'productive work'), with the first considered as primary (1993: 54–5).

[126] In addition, Christian Meier has reported that cloth napkins in Schmitt's possession were embroidered with a Homeric verse 'in which the word [*nomos*] had not once been recorded with certainty' (*einen Homervers, in dem das Wort nicht einmal sicher überliefert ist*) (1988: 553); see, further, the note in Stergiopoulou (2014: 121, n. 72), who suggests that this may indicate the 'intensity of investment' of Schmitt in that particular verse.

purposes, as: 'the measure by which the land in a particular order is divided and situated; it is also the form of political, social and religious order determined by this process. Here, measure, order, and form, constitute a spatially concrete entity' (a constitutive historical event; ibid. 70). Ultimately, for Schmitt *nomos* is an 'order' and decisively not a 'law'. Schmitt needed to insist on the sense of division/distribution (regarding land in particular), but he arbitrarily to a significant extent collapses the extant rich and polyvalent literary evidence to a supposed primary, or even original, spatial sense. A sense of ordering is plausible enough within the Homeric milieu and beyond it more so, without, however, there being a necessary reference to a sense of 'law', or a primordial 'division/distribution' of land or 'spatial appropriation'. Indeed, as we shall see, perhaps the 'stuff' from which 'law' is made is, in part, rooted here. For Schmitt, this is an ordering that, nonetheless, and among others, orders *semantically* too (i.e. the word's various uses towards one univocal Greco-German meaning).

Schmitt has to insist on an original act of spatial-semantic ordering (especially in the sense of a 'division/distribution' of land; 2006: 78) with a particular emphasis on 'appropriation', in a manner akin to his act of philological reduction or diversion. As has already been seen, *nemein* and its family of words do relate, in complex ways, to a sense of 'allotment' or 'distribution-sharing'[127] (though not in any determinate 'original' sense as to 'land' or 'earth', let alone one of 'law'). *Nomós*, further, may relate to a certain later sense of 'possession', but in a socially bound sense, rather than as the primary act of an appropriating 'sovereign'. In addition, *nómos*, much later than in Homer, entails some direct sense of a 'juridical-political ordering' character to it (as Schmitt observes). Yet early on, this could only be understood in the sense of an *ēthos*, a way of life, a part of a 'ritualised' nexus,

---

[127] Centuries later, Cicero in *De Legibus* (1.6) writes that in Greek law the word *nomos* signifies the distribution of *a suum cuique tribuendo* ('what is due to someone'); see also Plut. *Quaes. Conv.* 644c; Simonides *PMG* 642 *apud* Pl. *Rep.* 331e. Of interest is also the expression in Pl. *L*, where *nómos* is defined as the νοῦ διανομήν (*nou dianomēn*; 714a), a 'distribution' of *nous*.

rather than a separable 'originary or primordial act' forming the ground of social order. It remains the case that the earliest extant instance of the word in question is that of *nomós*, not *nómos*.[128] The *nemein* family, as well as other related words, appear frequently in Homer's poems, and their wide coexistent uses and socio-worship *milieux* point to a multi-threaded understanding. In the archaic period, we are confronted with something far richer and more complex than a 'primordial' act of 'sovereign' semantics, or the equally 'sovereign' constitutive disputations of politico-theological legal dogmatics.

---

[128] For the earliest possible reference to *nomos* see Porphyrius, *De abstinetia* 2.18, who reports on the Hesiodic fr. 322 [MW] on how the ancient *nómos* over how a polis performs a 'sacrifice' is the best; see the recent discussion of this, in direct relation to Schmitt's thesis, in Pelloso (2012a: 55–6, n. 169).

Four
Pastoral Nomos

γλῶσσα ποιμαίνειν ἐθέλει
Pind. O. 11.9[1]

1. Pastoral *oikonomia*

On the mountains, among other pre-Olympian gods – and especially Hermes – lived young Artemis, the girl hunter with thundering feet, bow and arrows, protector of the nymphs and nubile girls.[2] In the Homeric cosmos of the late seventh to eighth century BC the gods were still closely associated with cattle: Zeus, for instance, famously transforms into a bull, Hermes is a cattle-thief, Apollo a cowherd, and so forth.[3] In the Homeric *Hymn to Hermes*, Hermes' song as to how the divine allotment took place is interrupted (at 436–8) by Apollo, who addresses him in the following manner: βουφόνε, μηχανιῶτα, πονεύμενε, δαιτὸς ἑταῖρε. Apostolos N. Athanassakis (2004) translates vividly as follows: 'scheming cattle slayer, industrious comrade of the feast [*daitos*]'. While there is a certain consensus as to the dating of the epic poems within the range of the late seventh to eighth centuries BC, it remains of use to briefly refer to related elements of the pastoral practices during preceding periods (in particular, the Minoan of c. 2700–1450 BC, the Mycenaean of c. 1600–1100

---

[1] 'my tongue wants to feed'; my trans. I would like to thank Evi Gorogianni for reading an earlier draft of this chapter and for her constructive comments.

[2] See, for Homeric examples, *Il.* 21.514; 24.470; *Od.* 6.102–9; see also the Homeric *Hym. to Art.*

[3] See McInerney (2010: 122–4). The cults of Zeus, Hera and Poseidon were closely associated with cattle.

BC and the so-called 'dark ages' of c. 1100–800 BC, namely the interim period that followed the palatial collapse). In fact, scholars have speculated, with caution, as to the peculiar nature of certain elements met in the Homeric epics by comparing possible similarities and differences in relation to earlier ages. After all, the part of the 'economy' that is 'pastoral' appears to enjoy some continuity of general practice across the ages, yet with varied intensity and significance.

While a commonplace assumption, it is misleading to suppose that, for instance, the earlier period of the bronze age Aegean was an example of 'primitive pastoralism', since 'pastoralism' was already highly administered and efficient. Marie-Louise B. Nosch writes:

> The Bronze Age Aegean witnessed the emergence of a highly particular system of wool economy, beginning with the Minoan and followed by the Mycenaean centralized palace economies with strict administration of flocks, herders, wool, and textile production by thousands of women and children. This system monitored annual wool production targets and breeding strategies ensuring that the palaces' needs were met. Wool textile production was the largest sector of the palace economy and employed the highest number of people, organized according to a strict division of labor. (2014b: 1)[4]

Further, in Knossos, Crete, the economy appears to be highly centralised. For instance, Nosch writes:

> The Knossos palace monitored 100,000 sheep, primarily wethers for optimal wool production since castration provides more homogeneous fleeces. Other flocks of sheep grouped female animals and their lambs. Some 700 shepherds tended these flocks throughout central and western Crete. In the villages, and around the palace of Knossos, ca. 1000 women and children were occupied with a wide range of tasks related to textile production, primarily wool. (2014b: 2)

---

[4] On different aspects of the pastoral economy, see Sherratt (1983: 90–104); Cherry (1988); and Halstead and Isaakidou (2011: 67–8).

In three distant locations, the evidence of palatial pastoral practices is significant. In Knossos (Crete), there are records of, predominantly, sheep but also goats and pigs, while in Pylos (Messenia) there is evidence of, at the least, ten thousand sheep (Rougemont 2004: 20), with the palace monitoring at least a 'few thousand head' (Halstead 1996: 32).[5] Further, the *o-pa* tablets, from Thebes, demonstrate that 'pigs, goats, sheep, and cattle were brought from as far away as Karystos and Amarynthos on the island of Euboia' (McInerney 2010: 64; Palaima 2004: 106). Despite the chronological distance, Homer refers to such practices when he writes that the herds of Odysseus have been sent to graze on the mainland and on Kephallonia (Hom. *Od.* 14.110–20; 20.234–44; McInerney 2010: 64). That said, by Homer's time (*c.* late seventh to eighth centuries BC) this kind of movement is probably less extensive: 'The difference between the Bronze Age practice shown on the frescoes [i.e. the miniature frescoes from the West house of Akrotiri; Morris 1989] and the recollection of it in epic poetry is that by Homer's day . . . cattle were no longer a critical part of the intricate exchange networks that connected different districts' (McInerney 2010: 54).

We learn of the size of herds also through the collection of hides as 'tax' in the Pylos tablets. Jeremy McInerney writes:

Although the numbers involved are not large, averaging just over eleven hides per village, they imply considerably larger herds if, as the records suggest, the communities were expected to fill the same quotas every year. Hide taxes were collected from all corners of the kingdom, so it follows that herds were also found in every territory under Pylian control. Each of these herds was owned by a community, the *damo* mentioned in a number of tablets, and were no doubt grazed on communally owned land, *ke-ke-me-na*, which seems to have been distinguished from the land allocated to the *wanax* and *lawagetas*. (2010: 64)

At the same time, many animals came from herds described as *a-ko-ra* (*agora*), 'collections' under the holding of 'collectors',

---

[5] See Killen (1993).

but herds were not restricted to the elite in, for instance, Pylos (for example, *PY Un* 138). It should be noted that the function of the 'collectors' appears to be a typical Mycenaean administrative category. Around 30 per cent of the *ta-ra-si-ja* [ταλασία] system of textile production and Cretan sheep is recorded as under the collectors.[6] In this regard, it is worth observing too that the flocks are divided in the records according to who 'possesses/manages' them.[7]

Economic and worship practices were interwoven. The role of herders and shepherds is thus crucial to the worship and economic practices of the late bronze age (1500–1100 BC). For instance, in Minoan Crete towards the end of the bronze age, there appears to have taken place a certain 'transformation' whereby ceremonial functions became quite dominant. McInerney writes: 'critical to this transformation was a new emphasis on the slaughter of bulls at sacrifice and two correlated practices: feasting and the distribution of meat' (2010: 49). Indeed, the recorded number of shepherds in the tablets is substantial. The recorded personal names (which are in the hundreds) may refer to actual shepherds, or to those who were to supervise the herding. There may have been a network of shepherds and 'under-shepherds', while it is of interest, too, that shepherds may have also been 'multifunctional' (Enegren 2004: 16). Incidentally, in the Knossian tablet *Am* 821, there is mention of a '*i-je-re-u po-me*', who could be a 'priest-shepherd'. Françoise Rougemont suggests that this remains uncertain and it could, instead, refer to 'a priest called Shepherd or a shepherd called Priest' (2004: 20). John Killen, instead, translates it as a priest 'who is also a shepherd' and probably a person of some consequence (2015: II, 577).

With regard to the 'dark ages', McInerney writes (with reference to John Bintliff's work on the bronze age):

[Bintliff] has observed that the cyclical fluctuations in population suggested by recent surveys is consistent with

---

[6] See Olivier (1967: 71–93); and Killen (2015: vol. I, 360–1).

[7] At Knossos, for instance, Scribe 117 records separate totals for the collectors' flocks (*Dn* 2016) and non-collector flocks (recorded as place names, in, for example, *Dn* 1093).

a shift from the intensive land use of the Bronze Age to a new period in which small communities controlled the fields close to their villages but left the outfields in the hands of the 'big men' who could make 'more effective use of the outfield (perhaps notably with stock)'. (2010: 69)[8]

Thus, the low population density and the frequency of conflicts in the dark ages suggest a localised and moderate use of cultivated land, allowing for significant open plains as grazing areas for local and migratory flocks. This seems to be confirmed by the excavations at Nichoria in Messenia (McInerney 2010: 69; see also McDonald et al. 1983: 323). But the shift to stock breeding, rather than arable farming, should not be exaggerated. Paul Halstead has suggested that it is plausible that pastoralism was, to a degree, combined with small-scale farming (1996). It is probably best to consider later pastoralism, more generally, as a flexible activity that could be fairly large (though not frequently so), while more often of smaller scale. At the same time, it is worth noting that in the period after the palatial collapse herding probably became the most practical survival strategy, given the wide availability of land and the shortage of labour. McInerney states: 'The world of the palaces would give way to the world of the *oikos*, yet in both societies cattle retained their status as the single most valuable commodity' (2010: 73). Claudia Chang and Harold Koster have described how they imagine earlier palatial herds 'competing' for pasture with 'privately owned' flocks; however, when the palatial structure collapsed herds were no longer centrally controlled, which freed land for pasture (1986).

Meanwhile, as noted earlier, to what precise extent the Homeric epics refer to differing past traditions and practices we cannot know with certainty, but we can still learn, at least to an extent, from earlier practices given that the geography and basic subsistence needs were not dissimilar to these of the Homeric world(s). In any case, it certainly seems to be the case that the Homeric economy was simpler and poorer than that of the palatial eras. In this brief account, I have drawn a

---

[8] See Bintliff (1982: 107).

few particular elements from both the Mycenaean period and the Homeric epics, while allowing for a degree of – it is to be hoped constructive – comparative speculation.

Some scholars have generally perceived Homeric descriptions (possibly poetically drawn from thinly transmitted or, equally probably, imagined elements of the tenth to eighth centuries BC) as based on a pastoral economy up to about 850 BC and centred on flocks that were predominantly possessed by the wealthy elites (the 'collectors'). Anthony Snodgrass has proposed that the evidence up to the eighth century BC continues to suggest a loose structure of 'tribalism' that was characterised by an economy of stock raising, whereby herds formed the predominant medium of wealth (1980: 35). Snodgrass writes:

> A severely diminished population, unable to cultivate all the available land, can effectively occupy and use it by pastoral methods. Even such a paradox as the survival of place-names for deserted sites can be easily explained by the hypothesis of grazing herds. (1980: 35)

Yet this coexisted, in Homer, with a layer of arable farming (Donlan 1997: 654–7), since the switch to more sedentary farming had already started during the ninth century BC. Stock raising, as Walter Donlan notes, is the key class-divider, as surmised by Homer's social-economic observations (ibid. 656), and, as a result, this necessitated a large number of shepherds (for example, Odysseus' 960 pigs are described to be tended by five swineherds; *Od.* 14.21–6; Donlan 1997: 656). Eventually, land 'distribution' became anew an issue of great importance from at least the eighth century BC, and the 'colonisation' movements could have been partly triggered by the need for new arable land. By 700 BC, Donlan suggests, the economy was mainly agrarian (ibid.). Homer's world, schematically, appears to have the hallmarks of a stock-raising society combined with farming. In the *Odyssey* (24.150) we read: ἀγροῦ ἐπ᾽ ἐσχατιήν, ὅθι δώματα ναῖε συβώτης. The swineherd here 'dwelt by the border' (or borderland of the settlement), the ἐσχατιήν (*eskhatiēn*). It remains plausible that, while grazing could take place on 'private' land, the majority of pasture was probably delimited away from cultivated or cultivable land. Such a place was the *eskhatiēn*, on the mountain slopes or generally hilly land located between agricultural land and upland. Large flocks of sheep and/or goats were probably not maintained in or near settlements. While one can part-speculate this far along with some evidential corroboration, we still do not know enough regarding the detail of the practices of herding and transhumance. Nonetheless, earlier age evidence may provide tentative indications. Paul Halstead writes:

> The Knossos records ... provide circumstantial support for long-distance seasonal movements: the largest flocks are located in the agriculturally rich Mesara plain of central Crete [see Olivier 1967: 86] and this, by analogy with the recent past, suggests the grazing of fallow fields in winter [see Halstead 1992] and so potential for extensive use of upland pasture in summer. (1996: 32)[9]

We can also, perhaps, retrospectively extrapolate that specific lands were designated for specific uses, with 'common' lands remaining as unlimited pasture lands. In even later times, this territorialisation remains evident, though in a more restricted sense in, for instance, a *lex sacra* regarding the sanctuary of Zeus *Diktaios* in East Crete, which, as Angelos Chaniotis has described, forbade 'the use of sacred land for economic purposes list[ing] the most important forms of land use on Crete: grazing (ἐννέμειν, [*en-nemein*]), keeping of livestock ... arable cultivation ... and cutting wood ...' (1995: 42).[10] It is possible that uncultivated sacred land was later used for grazing (and potentially other) purposes, although we have no evidence of *epinomia*, that is, honorific granted 'uses/rights' of grazing to, especially, non-citizens.[11]

We do know that in the earlier palatial eras herding was an organised, closely administered, specialist 'profession'. In Mycenaean times, a shepherd was distinctly called a *po-me/*

---

[9] See, further, Godart (1977: 31–42); and Killen (1993: 209–18).

[10] Citing reference *I. Cret.* III.iv 9 II 81–2 [112 BC]; on sacred 'laws', see Parker (2004: 57–90); and Lupu (2005: 9–112).

[11] As to the later periods, see Rousset (2002: 85–108); Horster (2010: 452–3); and Forbes (1995: 329–31).

poimēn. While we do not know with certainty if this was initially the name of the 'profession' or the name of a person, it occurs amidst an already highly specialist vocabulary. The word ποιμήν (*poimēn*) is derived from the Indo-European root **pō(i)*: feeding and caring for animals. Other terms to note, as Nosch adds, are: 'the goat herd is *a3-ki-pa-ta/*aigipástās*, the swineherd *su-qo-ta/subotās* and the cowherd *qo-u-ko-ro/boukolos*' (2014b: 2).[12] Further, the two common Mycenaean words that relate to herding are *qo-u-ko-ro* (which Nosch referred to above) and *qo-qo-ta-o*,[13] which are interpreted as βουκόλος (*boukolos*) and βουβότας (*boubotas*) respectively. Meanwhile, Dimitri Nakassis cautions:

> We should not conclude from the probable prosopographical identification of *ke-ro-wo* that all individuals in the *Cn* texts would have been termed ποιμένες [*poimenes*], however . . . since of the four individuals at Pylos identified as *poimenes*, only *ke-ro-wo* appears in the *Cn* texts . . . Other *poimenes* are *ko-do*, *mo-ro-qo-ro*, and *ti-qa-jo*. (2013: 105–6, n. 96; with reference to Lindgren 1973)[14]

We do know, also, that in the post-Homeric period and, in particular, in the classical, the term *poimēn* 'continues in use but as a more general designation for someone herding animals of all kinds' (Nosch 2014b: 2). Rougemont has shown that these possibly professional terms appear to be connected to land and the taking care of oxen and their fodder and hence are possibly specialised terms of herding (2004). The archaeologist Louis Godart has suggested, further, some hierarchical differentiation between the terms, yet without sufficient certainty (1977: 47–9). It may be the case that, as H. Landenius Enegren has argued, there was a differentiation of some kind between overseers of flocks 'who administer' and actual shepherds 'who tend' the animals (2008: ch. 4). To this I return below, but for now it is worth noting that the *boukolos* (cowherd) also appears in the Homeric poems

---

[12] See, for example, *PY Nn* 831.5; and *PY An* 18.9.
[13] See, for example, *PY Ea* 270.
[14] See Lindgren (1973: 2, 119–21).

with particular reference to cattle.[15] In addition, as Kathryn Gützwiller analyses, in Homer the term appears to have lost its 'exclusive reference' to cattle and was used to mean simply 'graze' or 'pasture', and now in fact with regard to a variety of animals. She also suggests that in Homer we meet a parallel use of the word as 'to tend or guard', which much later will be linked directly to the sense of 'to govern or manage'.[16]

The Linear B tablets from southern Greece provide us with most of the invaluable information we have so far on the practices of herding, animal management and administration during the Mycenaean period. The records are not indicated chronologically, yet the consensus seems to be that they refer to the last year of the palace before it was destroyed by fire. Each clay tablet usually relates to a particular district and follows a standard pattern of recording. The record is detailed in the order of: toponym; shepherd's name; ideogram (with, occasionally, animal descriptors); figures; and in one third of the surviving instances, the collector's name (Rougemont 2004: 20). It is worth noting that, on the Pylian tablet *Cn* 655, a word that possibly describes the function of herding is, as referred to earlier, *a-ko-ra* (*agora*).[17] Evangelos Kyriakidis elaborates on this as follows:

> Its classical Greek equivalent ἀγορά means 'gathering', 'collection' (from basic form *ə2ger- with an o-grade root) [Watkins 2000, 27]. I prefer the translation 'gathering' as the word is more often used, especially in classical times, to refer to live beings as opposed to lifeless things. The reconstructed Proto-Indo-European (*PIE*) form *ə2ger- appears most interestingly in the Latin *grex* (stem *greg-* from the reduplicated form *gre-g*) which simply means 'flock', 'herd' . . . This casts ample light on how the meanings 'gathering' and 'flock' can be interrelated, but also on how it is possible to have an earlier meaning of 'flock as gathering of animals' with a semantic expansion progressively with time to 'a gathering of people'. (2010: 142, n. 8)

---

[15] *Il.* 21.448; Hom. *Hym. to Ven.* 55; *Od.* 10.85; see, further, Gützwiller (2006b: 382).

[16] See Hom. *Hym. to Herm.* 167; see, further, Gützwiller (2006b: 382).

[17] See Kyriakidis (2010: 142, n. 8).

In Homer the gathering of people can be indicated by an *agora* (gathering or 'flock') (for example, *Il.* 2.664; 4.337; 16.129; *Od.* 3.140, etc.), while in *Iliad* 11.687–8 one can observe the gathering of the Pylian elite, who are described as *sun-agro-menoi* as still linked to the origin of the 'collectors'.[18]

With regard to the earlier practices involved, as Nosch has shown, it can be said that '[t]here are several important strategies of herding management of flocks of sheep, and these are clearly employed in the Late Bronze Age Aegean as we can read in the Linear B tablets from Knossos' (2014b: 2). Summarising Nosch's account (Nosch 2014b: 3–4), it is worth listing what these included:

1. *castration*: 'male sheep are castrated and gathered in flocks for wethers only';[19]
2. *isolation*: 'female sheep – ewes – and their lambs are isolated . . . They could then be joined with rams of the right properties in order to monitor reproduction';
3. *separation of genders*: 'probably soon after birth';
4. *division into age groups*: 'the shepherds and the scribes group the animals according to their age and classify them as lambs (*ki*), yearlings (*WE*) and adult animals (*OVIS*)'; and, finally,
5. *homogeneity of flocks*: in domestic settings and smaller societies a variety of different domestic animals live together. In the Mycenaean palaces this seems not to be the case. Sheep are kept in flocks alone, without goats (although in Pylos, sheep and goats are recorded together); oxen, horses and pigs also seem to be herded in mono-species flocks.

From this, Nosch adduces a high degree of specialisation and knowledge accumulation while she speculates, with good reason, as I have already noted, that the function and role of shepherds would have experienced a significant rise in importance during the late bronze age (ibid. 4).[20] In addi-

---

[18] See also Lupack (2008: 86–7); and Killen (2015: I, 200–1).
[19] Wethers are castrated rams.
[20] See Chang and Koster (1986: 97–148); Halstead (1987: 77–87); and Cherry (1988: 6–34).

tion, the two main purposes of herding flocks appear to be wool production and reproduction. It can be observed – in the Knossos records – that flocks are separated into breeding ewes and wool-producing wethers (Halstead 1996: 32).[21] Halstead also notes that at Pylos flocks of old sheep 'presumably destined for slaughter were distinguished from flocks drafted in to replace them' (1996: 32).[22] The primacy of wool production is evident in the tablets on the basis of the fact that the majority of the flocks are wethers, as they produce wool of higher quality (Killen 1964: 1–15).[23] Thus, Nosch considers that the Mycenaean flocks provided 'ca. 50–75 tons of raw wool per year, which, after cleaning . . . amounted to 25–40 tons for textile production' (2014b: 2), estimating an annual yield of raw wool of anywhere 'between 2500 and 25,000 textiles' (ibid.). Some scholars, including Nosch, have suggested that on the basis of this record it is possible to characterise the bronze age as the time of 'a shift' towards wool production.[24] The centrality of the shepherding 'profession', if so, could hardly be over-emphasised.

The particular palatial interest (and 'possession/ ownership') is recorded with relative accuracy in the tablets (as in *Cn* 131 and 655).[25] For instance, the *Cn* tablets record the number and type of animals in flocks monitored by the palace, setting targets (as well as deficits listed in the Cretan tablets)[26] that appear uniform and closely observed. Yet no explicit hierarchy or 'contractual' agreement is ever mentioned between the shepherds and the palace (Rougemont 2004: 21). Furthermore, the shepherds (whether as 'holders' or 'managers') are distinguished in the tablets from the 'collectors' (Ventris and Chadwick 1973: 200–1).[27] Collectors

---

[21] See, generally, Killen (1964; 1993).

[22] See Godart (1977); and Killen (1993).

[23] See also Rougemont (2004: 20).

[24] See Halstead (1981; 1987); Sherratt (1981; 1983); Cherry (1988); McCorriston (1997); Isaakidou (2006); Breniquet and Michel (2014); and Nosch (2014b: 2f).

[25] On the extent and nature of the palatial interest see, for example, Lupack (2008: 86–96).

[26] See Halstead (2001: 43); and the essential Ventris and Chadwick (1973: 199–208).

[27] On the 'collectors', see Killen (1976: 117–25; 1995: 213–24); Bennet (1992:

held, inter alia, sheep in significant quantities. Evangelos Kyriakidis offers a vivid example of the largest owner of animals in Pylos, named *A-ke-o*, described as follows:

> He has at least 1650 animals in 28 flocks . . . in both districts. His sheep are more widely spread than [those of others], especially in the further province, where he has flocks in three different districts. In the hither province, he has 17 flocks and 1107 animals all in *Pi-*82*, while in the further province he has 483 animals in total; one flock in *A-si-ja-ti-ja* . . . 231 animals in 4 flocks in *Ra-wa-ra-ti-ja* and another 222 animals in 3 flocks in *Ti-mi-to-a-ke-e*. Moreover, he has 30 animals in *Me-ta-pa*, a possible place-name of the further province and another 2 flocks with 60 animals in a district not preserved, possibly of the hither province. (2010: 160–1)

Where no 'collector' name is mentioned, however, it is plausible to assume that shepherds were possessor-'owners' of equal measure to the 'collectors' in other instances (Kyriakidis 2010: 144). The herders of flocks frequently appear in the tablets to be of low status (Nakassis 2013: 102–3). Yet Kyriakidis (2010: 145) has demonstrated that shepherds were indeed, at times, also possessor-'owners'. The fact that in the tablets we find separate records for collector and non-collector flocks seems to indicate this further (and the same applies to separate 'targets' set for them respectively; ibid. 167). This indicates that it is highly plausible that not all flocks were 'owned' by the palace. Kyriakidis observes evidence of even a possible separation of 'representation' ('state') functions and 'collector' capacities with regard to own interests: 'the ruling class [i.e. collectors] separately totalled (and perhaps managed) the property belonging to them as individuals from the property they managed otherwise as a state' (ibid. 169; I would note, however, that this is a 'separation' that was practical/ administrative rather than 'abstract or juridical').

Flocks could, therefore, be owned by the palace, by collectors and shepherds, while the latter could also 'manage'

65–101); Carlier (1992: 159–66); Driessen (1992: 197–214); Godart (1992: 257–83); and Rougemont (2001: 129–38).

palatial or collector flocks. Once more, some caution is needed with the use of the notion of 'ownership'; the distinction between 'possession' and 'ownership' was not pronounced in a strict juridical manner. In addition, Johannes Haubold has argued that in the epic things are already perhaps different since the shepherds are not described as 'owners' of the flocks, whereby the ἄναξ (*anax*) and the ποιμήν (*poimēn*) or νομεύς (*nomeus*) are 'clearly distinguished' (for example, *Il.* 20.219–22; *Od.* 4.87; 14.102; 15.503–5; 16.25–8; 2000: 18, n. 20). Haubold notes: 'Young warriors are often seen herding flocks, but they do so only until they grow up and become cattle-owners themselves' (ibid.), while, furthermore and later on, Homeric shepherds are never described as 'acting in their own interest' (ibid. 22). To what extent this applied universally to shepherds remains unclear.

On the basis of the Linear B evidence from Knossos, Halstead has suggested that, earlier, reciprocal exchange with individual herders is plausible: for the production of wool the palace could provide sheep (2001: 43). One of the interpretative matters of great interest relates to the observation that a number of shepherds' names 'are repeated in the same or in different tablets' (Kyriakidis 2008: 456–7). It is worth following Kyriakidis' analysis at this point as to the complications that arise in the tablets in this regard:

> In tablet *Cn* (4) 285 above the name *a-we-ke-se-u* is recorded both in lines .5 and .6. This name beyond doubt refers to the same shepherd as otherwise we would be talking about two individuals in the same place and recorded in the same tablet next to each other . . . This deviation from standard scribal practice must be because *a-we-ke-se-u* is the same person in both cases. (Kyriakidis 2008: 457)

On this basis, as Kyriakidis shows, we can establish that shepherds can 'have' more than one flock and, more crucially, that shepherds do not have an isolated 'professional function'. He explains:

> it is likely that we are not simply talking about single persons but rather representatives, or presidents, or seniors of groups, like clans, co-ops, work-groups, families

etc. . . . So shepherds would work together with cheese
and butter makers, distributors, weavers, dye manufac-
turers etc. These people often form distinctive groups
(our equivalent of co-ops) that often have the tendency to
correspond to pre-existing socio-economic groups such as
clans. So a co-op like that may be a smaller subgroup of a
large clan. (2008: 458)

The shepherds could be chiefs of clans (or 'big men'), or of
'co-ops', who manage the flocks, rather than necessarily herd
them: 'These men may then either "sub-contract" the sheep
to other people, or may just have asked other people to look
after them (not recorded in the tablets)' (ibid.).[28] The 'owners'
and/or administrators of a flock may be other than the shepherds at least in some cases, while, as suggested earlier,
'shepherds-owners/possessors' cannot be excluded.

2. Homeric shepherds

I return now to the Homeric poems to examine what evidence
can be adduced as to the life and practice of shepherds, in
order to elucidate the so-called pastoral uses of the verb $\nu\acute{\epsilon}\mu\omega$
(*nemō*) and the oxytonic $\nu o\mu\acute{o}\varsigma$ (*nomós*). The importance of
cattle farming, sheep and goat herding in the epics is clearly
evident. At the same time, shepherds are depicted as surviving 'on the margins of the inhabited world' (Haubold 2000:
18). Haubold notes that shepherds are described as 'lacking a
home' (for example, *Il.* 4279) and as living by the mountains,
or on riverbanks (for example, *Il.* 13.57; and *Od.* 9.182–92),
while they work for payment (for example, *Il.* 21.44; Haubold
2000: 18). In the *Iliad*, herders are not characters central to
the narrative, but they do appear, and, crucially, they appear
twice on Achilles' famous shield (at 18.525–9 and 577–86).
Lastly, as will be seen below, they are employed in metaphoric usage also.[29]

In Homer's description of Achilles' shield, we find the
image of a flock of sheep grazing and four herdsmen herding

---

[28] My emphasis on 'sub-contract'.
[29] See *Od.* 4.82; 10.82; and *Il.* 3.11; 4.455; 5.137; 8.559; 12.451; 13.493; 16.354;
18.162; 23.835.

cattle, when two lions attack a bull (*Il.* 18.483–608). The term
ποιμήν (*poimēn*) is, indeed, attested in Homer, for example
in the description of the land of the Laistrygonians, where
herdsmen move with cattle and sheep under diurnal and noc-
turnal rhythms (*Od.* 10.81–6: ποιμένα ποιμὴν, *poimena poimēn*,
at 10.82).[30] In Homer, as seen earlier, the verb βουκολέω
(*boukoleō*) is used to mean graze or pasture and is applied to
horses pasturing themselves (*Il.* 20.221),[31] as well as in the
sense of 'to tend' (Hom. *Hymn. to Herm.* 167). Shepherds are
depicted calming animals by playing the syrinx (*Il.* 18.526:
τερπόμενοι σύριγξι, *terpomenoi surigksi*) and the herdsmen are
called νομῆες (*nomēes*). The scene is, incidentally, immediately
followed by a cattle raid and the slaughter of the herders.

The paramount importance of the protection of a flock is
shown through scenes of theft or potential theft (as in *Il.*
3.10–11). Achilles, it may be remembered, considered an
attempt on his flocks a reason to join the Trojan war (*Il.* 1.153;
Haubold 2000: 18). Raiding is, in fact, more broadly 'cata-
lytic' in the epics. As McInerney notes (2010: 98), the scenes
where a raid is taking place or is avoided through the killing
of a raider are several. In fact, raiding became more 'commonplace', having increasingly lost its earlier mythic stature
(2010: 100).[32] Furthermore, Odysseus himself is a raider who
amasses splendid wealth as a result. Indeed, the emergence
of the 'hero', if between 1000 and 800 BC, could be derived
from within a largely pastoral tradition. McInerney, hence,
writes:

> The hero would steal cattle by raiding, would sacrifice
> them to show reverence to the gods, would swear mighty
> oaths over their dismembered carcasses, and would use
> feasts to entertain guests and strangers. He offers them as
> prizes in competition and pays them over as compensation
> for his wrongdoings. From these practices (and their oppo-
> sites) would emerge very clear notions of piety, generosity,
> and self-restraint. (2010: 74)

[30] See Huxley (2000: 5–9).
[31] See *Il.* 5.313; *Od.* 10.85.
[32] On raids, see: *Il.* 6.421–4; 20.89–93; *Od.* 9.42–63, 459–70; 10.95–101;
12.362–77.

McInerney goes even so far as to suggest that the Greek 'ideology' of this period is that of 'stock breeders'. Gützwiller, in turn, reads the *Odyssey* as essentially a 'poem about the reestablishment of economic order', since, as she adds: 'In Odysseus' absence the orderly structures that lead to fertility and economic well-being have dwindled to the point that they are found only in the upland pastures where the herdsman still controls' (1991: 26). For example, Eumaeus, the 'good shepherd' in *Od.* 14.5–20, can be contrasted with Melantheus, the 'inattentive' one in *Od.* 17.212. Indeed, the Homeric shepherd is described, in some instances, as ill-prepared to fulfil his pastoral function (for example, *Il.* 10.485–6; 15.630–6). Haubold locates, in fact, a paradox in the depiction of the shepherd in the epic: on the one hand, the social order depends on the shepherd, while on the other, the shepherd is, as a matter of poetic rule, depicted as ill-equipped and mostly failing to fulfil his pastoral function (for example, *Od.* 17.426: αὐτὰρ μῆλα κακοὶ φθείρουσι νομῆες [*nomēes*]; 2000: 18–20), whether owing to a force of nature, inattentiveness, or raids.

The general term νομεύς (*nomeus*), at times utilised in the Homeric epic, reflects perhaps an early sense of a kind of 'orderly distribution' (Gützwiller 2006a: 5). The terms *poimēn* and *nomeus* are essentially synonymous in the epic. But, in this regard, it should be noted that νομός (*nomós*) indicates itself 'a place of pasture'; and in Homer, εὐνομία (*eunomia*) is not, crucially, the political *eunomia* of the classical period, but an *ēthos* closely associated with the direct experience of the shepherds (*Od.* 17.487). We can sense perhaps how the gradual 'political' derivation could arise, nascent as it were in instances such as when Agamemnon distributes the booty unfairly and, as a result, is likened to a bad shepherd and king (δημοβόρος βασιλεύς [*dēmoboros basileus*], *Il.* 1.231; Gützwiller 2006a: 5). It is worth noting that, even in its later opposition to *hubris*, *eunomia* is also utilised with reference to plants and animals in a similarly suggestive manner – 'It refers to overly exuberant and so sterile growth in plants and to unruly behaviour on the part of animals'[33] – indicating, perhaps by implication, an orderly and efficient growth in

---

[33] Gützwiller (1991: 24, n. 14, and 25).

plants, as much as in pastures for animals and eventually, perhaps, in a wider political sense.

Metaphoric uses are frequent too, such as in Homer's comparison of Proteus, the seaman 'who tends a herd of seals' (*Od.* 4.351–575), with a shepherd (4.413). Another metaphor of the herdsman is linked, by analogy, to a seer as the one who knows or is observant. Gützwiller has underlined the importance of the names of the characters in this particular scene: for instance, Proteus meaning 'first' or 'primeval' and his daughter's name being Eidothea (meaning 'goddess of seeing and knowing') (1991: 34). This renders possible a sense that Proteus as a shepherd is someone who, in his normal role, is observant and on guard, and in this capacity 'remembers and knows' (ibid.). These are akin to the abilities of a seer,[34] reminding one of the suggestion that the original seers as the 'guardians of truth' in the archaic world may have been herdsmen.[35]

3. Pastoral *ēthos*

A pastoral *ēthos* is indicated in two further Homeric senses. In one instance, heroes are likened to herdsmen (*Il.* 2.474–6):

Τοὺς δ' ὥς τ' αἰπόλια πλατέ' αἰγῶν αἰπόλοι ἄνδρες
ῥεῖα διακρίνωσιν ἐπεί κε νομῷ μιγέωσιν,
ὣς τοὺς ἡγεμόνες διεκόσμεον ἔνθα καὶ ἔνθα

Διεκόσμεον (*diekosmeon*, δια-κοσμέω, *dia-kosmeō*) is posited in parallel here with διακρίνω (*diakrinō*), which is used 'for both the activities of the herdsman and those of the King'[36] – for example, Polyphemus dividing his animals according to age (in *Od.* 9.220) in the sense of an orderly 'distribution/division'. Κοσμέω (*kosmeō*), in Homer, is used to indicate a 'preparation', an 'order', or a 'drawing up', as well as 'a being in charge' (*Il.* 2.554, 704; 3.1). In addition, it is met with as having a sense of 'division': as in 'to divide into communities' (*Il.* 2.655), or the 'distribution/division' of the flocks and

---

[34] See also Vergil's *Georgic* 4.401–4 and 425–36.
[35] Ibid. 35; see the Melampus episode, *Od.* 11.287–97; 15.225–42.
[36] Ibid. 24.

their return to their 'possessors/owners' at the end of the day. Such a 'distribution/division' is expressed most clearly in *Il.* 1.16 with regard to the κοσμήτορε λαῶν (*kosmētore laōn*, the 'marshaller of the people'). This expression is likened to the more common expression ποιμένα (*poimena*) or ποιμένι λαῶν (*poimeni laōn*), the 'shepherd of the people', as kings and chiefs,[37] along with these coeval expressions: ὄρχαμε λαῶν (*orchame laōn*, for example, *Il.* 14.102); κοίρανε λαῶν (*koirane laōn*, for example, *Il.* 9644); and ἡγήτορα λαῶν (*hēgētora laōn*, for example, *Il.* 20.383).[38] Thus, in the verses quoted at the start of this section, the hero-king is marshalling his warriors on the battlefield in the way herdsmen 'organise', 'divide' (or 'apportion') and 'order' their grazing field. The sense of 'order' with an emphasis on a certain 'straightness' may not be far here from the understanding of *dikē* as entailing the need for a straight 'judgment', which is encountered in Homer. Warriors are also likened to shepherds. For example, the protectors of Patroclus' body are described as shepherds protecting a carcass from a ravenous lion (*Il.* 18.161–4).[39] A further key such instance is the description of Agamemnon and the warrior chiefs as chief herders or shepherd leaders (*Il.* 2.513–21). But what kind of 'order' or 'distribution' can we understand to be implied at this point?

Here, it is worth noting Michel Foucault's interest in his genealogy of 'pastoral power' and, in particular, his reference to the Homeric instances of the metaphor, as well as to Plato's later use and analysis of it in the *Politikos* (*Statesman*), where he refers to gods (as 'distributors of order', 271d–e)[40]

---

[37] For example, Agamemnon in *Il.* 2.243, 254, 772; 11.187, 202; Menelaus in *Il.* 5.566, 570; Aeneas in *Il.* 5513; Achilles in *Il.* 16.2; and, of course, Odysseus in *Od.* 18.70 and 20.106, on whom see, further, Johnson (1941: 273–4); see, also Cunliffe, who lists them (1963: 334); and Haubold who records fifty-six instances in Homer (2000: 17). The expression is found more frequently in the *Iliad* than in the *Odyssey*, while it diminishes radically in its frequency after Homer and Hesiod, to resurface in the fourth century BC in predominantly philosophical literature; see the discussion in Brock (2013: 44–8).

[38] See Haubold (2000: 197).

[39] Brock, in fact, suggests that the milieu of the expression may in fact be rooted in the military experience of 'ordering a crowd' (2013: 43–4).

[40] Plato often writes of the distribution of parts, and of lands in particular, between the gods, see *Criti.* 109b1–2; 120d6, and *L.* 747d1ff.

and to the philosopher-king as a 'legislator' who 'distributes' the 'just' (*dikaiotaton*; 297b). Foucault, in *Security Territory Population*, draws upon these, among others, for his key suggestion that the 'shepherd's power is not exercised over a territory but by definition over the flock in its movement from one place to another' (2007: 125). Leaving aside Plato's later use(s), as well as the characteristic references in the Christian tradition,[41] over the complex matter of pastoralism in the politico-theological use of the term, I restrict this brief note to the early archaic centrality of a 'good distribution' (*eunomia*); an 'order' of considerable value, though one that may seem, at first, paradoxical, if opposed to the particular and overall positive Judaeo-Christian image of the shepherd. In the epic, instead, it appears to be in an embryonic form, or better, a threshold order-image, that is not 'political' – between the bucolic care for the flock and the wider social milieu (with possible early roots in military uses). The sense, in any case, of a political authority, however, that remains resonant to modern ears in the expression 'shepherd of the people' is a much later understanding during the classical period (especially in the fourth and third centuries BC).

A sense of (military) order and *ēthos* is indicated, as Gützwiller has shown, in the passages where 'a number of Trojan noblemen display an intriguing propensity to herd their own animals' (1991: 27); that is, where Homer remarks that Priam's immediate family is dissociated from herding (there are many instances akin to this: *Il.* 6.21–6; but also 11.101–6, 15.547–5, 20.188–9 and 20.237–8). Gützwiller comments: 'Allusions to the pastoral economy of the defenders serves [*sic*], then, to enhance the contrast between the peace-loving Trojans, who are struggling to protect ordered life in the city, and the aggressive Greeks, who seek to dismantle their society' (1991: 27). The reverse use of the analogy, in one sense, is shown in the epic titled *Cypria*, referred to as background in the *Iliad* (24.28–30), and in the myth of Paris, who in a sense caused the Trojan war with his abduction of the Spartan queen Helen and who was raised by and was himself a herdsman (a piece of information which is used, in the epic,

---

[41] For example, *Matt.* 25: 32–3; *Ex.* 14: 11–12.

to hint at his – in this case – cowardly behaviour, his dress sense and lustful character) before he discovered that he was a Trojan prince.[42] Homer exploits the sharp social antithesis between the class of shepherds and that of the aristocratic warrior class. The class of herdsmen is considered inferior, and this, for Gützwiller (2006a), is shown further by reference to the way in which Homer portrays a typical trait of the herdsman, that is, the propensity for sexual pleasure or lust. It is in this regard that Homer describes the sexual encounters of the two herdsmen Bucolion and Enops with nymphs, while they are pasturing their flocks (at *Il.* 6.21–6; 14.444–5).

4. *Nemein*

With these parameters in mind, I turn now to examine the words that relate to pasture and herding within the family of *nemein/nemesthai* with regard to a sense of a certain 'ordering or distribution/sharing'. One of the common uses, as noted earlier, of the verb *nemō* is 'to allocate to a flock the place of pasture for grazing'. The herdsman is often a νομεύς (*nomeus*), while animals and flocks are said to be νέμονται (*nemontai*, pastured). For Emmanuel Laroche, this is a key sense of the archaic use of the word. Laroche, in fact, disputed the semantic primacy and root of *nomos*-'law' that afforded only a secondary sense to the 'pastoral' uses. In contrast, for Laroche, the pastoral uses formed an important early milieu for the most ancient Greek sources, while nomos-'law' is most probably the result of a later reinterpretation during the fifth century BC with particular regard to the 'distribution and partition of land' (1949: 9 and 115).[43] As was seen in Chapter Three, in the Homeric uses, when *nomós* relates to the 'distribution-sharing' of land, and especially so when in proximity to the polis, it indicates only 'an expanse of habitable land around a city before being an administrative province' (1949, 117). Thus, in the archaic use, the word *nomeus* indicates a wandering shepherd (without an *oikos*) and/or a flock or herd animal that roams freely across a (crucially) unlimited land (ibid. 122).

---

[42] See Gützwiller (1991: 27).
[43] Duchemin (1960), in some contrast, has argued for the primacy of the pastoral sense, as well as the pastoral origins of poetry as such.

Pastoral Nomos

Another French philosopher, Gilles Deleuze, in *Différence et répétition* (*Difference and Repetition*) refers to the pastoral sense of *nemō* in the sense of 'to pasture' in order to differentiate the sense of an 'allocation' from the sense of a 'distribution'. Deleuze writes:

> Homeric society had neither enclosures nor property in pastures: it was not a question of distributing the land among the beasts, but, on the contrary, of distributing the beasts themselves and dividing them up here and there across an unlimited space, forest or mountainside. The nomos designated first of all an occupied space, but one without precise limits (for example, the expanse around a town) – whence, too, the theme of the 'nomad'. ([1968] 1994: 309, n. 6)

For Deleuze's speculative purposes, this forms a sense through which he conceives the so-called nomadic distribution of being as an 'irreducible multiplicity': 'a nomadic distribution' that 'is no longer a division of that which is distributed but rather a division among those who distribute themselves in an open space – a space that is unlimited, or at least without precise limits' ([1968] 1994: 36).[44] This other 'space', the nomadic, is a 'distribution' without enclosure, measure or ownership.[45] It should be noted, since it is not made clear in the text, that Deleuze could only be referring here to νομός (*nomós*), rather than νόμος (*nómos*) – he does not specify the difference between the two, despite his reliance on Laroche.[46] It is worth noting, once more, that, for Laroche, the formation of the pastoral *nomós*, *nomeus* and *nemō* in this regard is indirect and possibly subject to 'an illusion of the

---

[44] See also Deleuze and Guattari 1981: 472.
[45] '[T]out autre est une distribution qu'il faut appeler nomadique, un nomos nomade, sans propriété, enclos ni mesure ... Rien ne revient ni n'appartient à personne, mais toutes les personnes sont disposées çà et là de manière à couvrir le plus d'espace possible' ('Every other is a distribution that must be called nomadic, a nomad *nomos*, without ownership [property], enclosure or measure ... Nothing comes back or belongs to anyone, instead all people are arranged here and there so as to cover as much space as possible') ([1968] 1994: 54).
[46] See Deleuze and Guattari (1981: 472, n. 44).

141

ancient grammarians' (1949: 115), while he further points to a possibly different or isolated -νομ [-*nom*] group. Nonetheless, it is worth observing briefly Deleuze's remarkable philosophical distinction, while on partly speculative grounds, between a distribution (of land) in the sense of a 'juridical' allocation and another type of distribution (of pasture). In the latter sense, Deleuze (with Félix Guattari) states in *Mille plateaux* (*A Thousand Plateaus*) that *nomos* (*sic*) does not designate 'the law' (*la loi*; or *logos*), but a mode of distribution (*mode de distribution*) (Deleuze and Guattari 1981: 472): in fact, a special type of 'distribution' without division (*partage*) that opposes the 'law' (or the settled polis as such) – a hinterland (*un arrière-pays*), the side of a mountain (*un flanc de montagne*) (ibid.).

Distribution-sharing here is not a juridical act, but one that is akin to a dispersal, somewhat orderly, in the sense of a power, the *puissance* of the flock, as practised by a shepherd and/with his flock. It is a power/potency that takes 'place' in an unlimited or random (nomadic) assignment of pastureland, wherein the herd is distributed on land that is not allocated-apportioned (i.e. juridico-economically limited). It is a potency that is 'creative' and, in this sense, for Deleuze and Guattari 'revolutionary' (a 'war machine-smooth space'), as opposed to the striated 'space' (though not strictly 'spatial') that is instituted by the state, the polis or law (1981: 474). The two, for Deleuze and Guattari, take place de facto at the same time through a constant transversality, while *de jure* they remain distinguished (ibid. 474–5). In such a 'distribution', one cannot speak of 'representation', 'ownership', or juridical or static settlement. It is a distribution-sharing where the distributory experience does not delimit, but 'plays', to use a term that Deleuze at times borrows from the philosopher Kostas Axelos.[47] In this smooth 'space' one finds only 'traits', rather than 'fences' (Deleuze and Guattari 1981: 472–3).[48]

In Homeric use, the driving of a flock for the purpose of

---

[47] See Axelos (1969).
[48] This philosophical bipolarity serves well Deleuze and Guattari's thought, while remaining in part problematic both because of its idealisation of the 'nomadic' and its sharp opposition to 'the settled', but also because of its arguable historical imprecision.

pasture-grazing and its return is expressed in, for instance: ἥμενοι, εἷος ἐπῆλθε νέμων [*nemōn*]. φέρε δ' ὄβριμον ἄχθος (*Od.* 9.233).[49] In the middle voice it is frequently met in the sense of feeding on/grazing, for instance in the *Odyssey* – δήεις τόν γε σύεσσι παρήμενον· αἱ δὲ νέμονται (*nemontai*; to feed on) (*Od.* 13.407); καὶ τοὺς μέν ῥ' εἴασε καθ' ἔρκεα καλὰ νέμεσθαι (*nemesthai*; grazing) (*Od.* 20.164) – and, in the *Iliad*, in relation to grazing by rivers: αἵ ῥά τ' ἐν εἰαμενῇ ἕλεος μεγάλοιο νέμονται (*nemontai*; *Il.* 15.631). It can be also expressed, by implication, in the sense of 'to cut/dispense the flowers' (i.e. to feed on them): ἀλλὰ πολὺ πρῶτος νέμεαι [*nemeai*] τέρεν' ἄνθεα ποίης (*Od.* 9.449). Furthermore, it is found in the form of νεμέθω (*nemethō*) in the middle voice, describing doves feeding: πελειάδες νεμέθοντο (*nemethonto*) (*Il.* 11.635). In the sense of 'feeding on', it is also met in the 'metaphoric' sense of something (for example, a polis) being consumed by fire: ὡς εἴ τε πυρὶ χθὼν νέμοιτο (*nemoito*) (*Il.* 2.780).[50] Here, too, the sense of an unlimited and destructive wandering/spreading of fire confirms, perhaps, the earlier sense as to a flock roaming in undivided land: a contingent ordering.

[49] Νεμέθοντο [*nemethonto*], in the middle voice, is used only once in *Il.* 11.635.

[50] See Heinimann (1945: 59); and *Il.* 23.177: πυρὸς μένος ἧκε, ὄφρα νέμοιτο [*nemoito*]; the verb *nemomai* is here used to describe the funeral pyre that devours the body of Patroklos; see also Aes. *Choe.* 325; Hdt. 5.101 (fire), 6.33 (ulcer). In medical uses, the *nemēsis* is used in a parallel sense with regard to a devouring disease that 'grazes and consumes' with great force. The verb *nemesthai* in the passive is used to describe a gnawing ulcer, feeding while spreading (Jouanna 2012: 90–3; with references to Aretaeus and Hippocrates). In the Hippocratic Corpus, whose *nómos* one swore by oath, we find references using *nomē* (*Prorrh.* 2.12; 2.13; *Ulc.* 2.18, and *Dent.* 2.20). Jouanna traces this to Galen, *De simplicium medicamentorum temperamentis ac facultatibus* 8.4, 12.179, 6 [Kühn] (Jouanna 2012: 92). The extension of a vessel (along the spine) is described also by Hippocrates as *nemomenē* (*Oss.* 13 [9.184.14, L.]; Jouanna 2012: 93); and the spreading of a disease is described using the verb *epinemomai* (*Epid.* 3.4.7). In Hippocrates, it is worth noting also that ways of 'treatment' or 'rules' are named *nómoi* (as in *Fract.* 7.26; *Art.* 18.17, 87.6; *Moch.* 6.5 and 38.1; see Jones and Withington (1923–31). Lastly, it is also worth observing that for the early Greeks 'health' was often defined as an *isonomia* or *isomoiria* of the *dunameis* (powers) or of portions, respectively (for example, Alcmaeon, fr. B4 [DK]).

Νομεύς (*nomeus*), meaning a herdsman or shepherd, is one of the two most common terms used in the Homeric poems. In one of the instances where *nomeus* is not used, we find the use βώτωρ, -ορες (*bōtōr, -ores*; for example, in *Od.* 14.102; it should be noted that the later νομάς [*nomas*] is not encountered in Homer). The instances of *nomeus* are numerous, for example, in the *Odyssey* (4.413): λέξεται ἐν μέσσῃσι, νομεὺς [*nomeus*] ὣς πώεσι μήλων, with regard to a shepherd of sheep; or, also in the *Odyssey* (21.19), νηυσὶ πολυκλήϊσι τριηκόσι' ἠδὲ νομῆας (*nomēas*; shepherds). Herdsmen are also indicated in the *Iliad* in the same manner (as in 18.577): χρύσειοι δὲ νομῆες [*nomēes*] ἅμ' ἐστιχόωντο βόεσσι (shepherds).[51] The verb νομεύω (*nomeuō*), at the root of *nomeus*, meaning 'to tend' or 'drive' the flock(s), is encountered in, for instance, the *Odyssey*: εὕρομεν, ἀλλ' ἐνόμευε νομὸν κάτα πίονα μῆλα (*enomeue nomón*; 'pasturing the flock') (*Od.* 9.217); ἑσπέριος δ' ἦλθεν καλλίτριχα μῆλα νομεύων· (*nomeuōn*; 'herding his flocks') (*Od.* 9.336); and, in a similar sense: τὸν μὲν βουκολέων (*boukoleōn*; 'herding cattle'), τὸν δ' ἄργυφα μῆλα νομεύων· (*nomeuōn*; 'pasturing sheep') (*Od.* 10.85). As discussed earlier, for Laroche the root of *nomeuō/nomeus* is not entirely clear, and he does point out that, if linked to a sense of 'distribution' (in the sense of 'a share', an 'allotment') via *nemō*, it could be misleading, since pasture was not an 'allotment of shares' as such. Pasturage was, generally, an unlimited 'space' (1949: 116, n. 4). This is the sense that Deleuze noticed. A *'nomos'* in the manner of an *ēthos*, a 'distribution or rule' that cannot be separated from its experience or life and vice versa.[52] For Laroche, still, the likely derivation of this is from *nomós*, though in what particular sense is the issue that I turn to next.

5. *Nomós*

Νομός (*-οῦ, -ό; nomós, -ou, -o*) indicates primarily a pasture or grazing-ground. Hence, in the *Iliad* (2.475), ῥεῖα διακρίνωσιν

---

[51] See *Od.* 16.3, 27; 17.214, 246; 20.175; *Il.* 11.697; 15.632; 17.65; 18.525, 583.
[52] To use a modality of Agamben's thought, see, for instance, 2016a. It can be noted that this modality is not too different from what, in fact, Luhmann understands as a 'system' (see, for instance, 1986 and 1995).

ἐπεί κε νομῷ [*nomō*] μιγέωσιν, where grazing is indicated; or, also in the *Iliad* (6.511), ῥίμφά ἑ γοῦνα φέρει μετά τ' ἤθεα καὶ νομὸν [*nomón*] ἵππων· (indicating grazing grounds); and, further, in the manner of grazing by the river, in the *Odyssey* (10.159), ἧκεν· ὁ μὲν ποταμόνδε κατήϊεν ἐκ νομοῦ [*nomou*] ὕλης. The same sense is met with in the *Iliad* (18.587): Ἐν δὲ νομὸν [*nomón*] ποίησε περικλυτὸς ἀμφιγυήεις; the grazing ground, where the famed god wrought (ποίησε; *poiēse*) a pasture (*nomón*). Finally, in the *Odyssey* (9.217): εὕρομεν, ἀλλ' ἐνόμευε νομὸν κάτα πίονα μῆλα; the shepherd drives afield (ἐνόμευε νομόν, *enomeue nomón*) the flock of sheep to pasture. In the middle voice, meaning 'to pasture oneself or graze', the use of *nomós* indicates its close link to *nemō* (in the sense of 'to pasture'), as has already been noted.[53] For Laroche, it is clear that *nomós* does not designate anything other than a pasture for animals, or a 'habitat' without delimitation in the case of human beings (1949: 117, n. 18). Gustave Glotz writes:

> In the *Iliad* the shepherds, be they kings or peasants, lead their flocks where they will, in full liberty, for the pastures, especially in the mountains are usually collective properties. When the poet enumerates the possessions of an individual he never includes pasture-land, although he is most careful to count all the cattle. ([1926] 1965: 34–5; noting, however, that such lands are perhaps already becoming 'appropriated' in the *Odyssey*, as in the *eskhatiē* of each suitor and Odysseus).

Finally, the use of νομόνδε (*nomonde*) can be also observed, indicating a pastoral sense, for instance, in the *Odyssey* (9.438),[54] while it is also worth adding the related metaphoric uses in Homer. Aeneas states, in the *Odyssey* (20.249), παντοῖοι, ἐπέων δὲ πολὺς νομὸς ἔνθα καὶ ἔνθα, indicating 'much room [*nomós*] to roam hither and thither, wide scope'. Aeneas' speech, in fact, indicates 'a great *nomós* of words', referring to 'variety of speech' that can be imagined as roaming, unlimited. There is a similar metaphoric use as

---

[53] See *Il.* 6.195; 20.8; *Od.* 11.185; 20.336. The 'etymological' phrasing νομεύω νομόν [*nomeuō nomón*] is also found in the *Hym. to Herm.* 492.

[54] See *Il.* 2.475; 6.511; 18.575, 587; and the *Hym. to Aphro.*78.

to a meadow of song in the Homeric *Hymn to Apollo* (19–21), where at verse 20 we read: πάντῃ γάρ τοι, Φοῖβε, νόμοι [plural *nómoi*] βεβλήατ᾽ ἀοιδῆς (the 'range' of Apollo's song has been extended or is extensive).[55] The depiction of language/song as 'an extended field' of pasture appears to be not a mere poetic metaphor, but perhaps a common expression.

6. *Nomios*

In a partly related sense, it is interesting to note the use of the epithet Νόμιος (*Nomios*) with regard to the god Apollo and elsewhere. It is worth observing that the word *Nomios*, as an adjective from *nomós*, is encountered in Homer in a singular instance as a proper name, in the *Iliad* (2.871): Νάστης Ἀμφίμαχός τε Νομίονος [*Nomionos*] ἀγλαὰ τέκνα. *Nomionos* here could be read with an implied pastoral sense.[56] The god Apollo is often named *Nomios* (and so is his son Aristaios; for example, Pind. *P.* 9.64–5). This is derived from varied traditions that seem to intersect in the divine power of the oracle, the ordering and protection of flocks (Hes. fr. 129), his divine instrument, the lyre that renders him god of music and song (*Il.* 9.186–91), as well as 'social ordering' in general (Dowden 2007: 50).[57] The pastoral significance is notable in more than one respect. Mythologically, he is said to have tended the flocks of King Admetus, as well as being a god of vegetation (Farnell 1896–1909: IV.123–4 and ch. 4). The tradition seems to emanate from Arcadia, and it is reported as both pastoral (in earlier sources)[58] and linked to 'social order' and *nómos* (in later sources).[59] Others report the intersection of (bucolic) song and the pasturing of flocks.[60] Arcadia, a largely pastoral economy (Roy 1999: 328–36), is, of course, the land of the god Pan, who was himself called, among other titles, the

---

[55] See Ford (1981); I turn in some detail to the musical uses of *nómos* in Chapter Ten.

[56] See Laroche (1949: 118, n. 21).

[57] See also Pl. *L.* 624: 'giver of *nómos*'; see, further, Otto (1954: 77).

[58] Farnell mentions an inscription from Epidauros (1896–1909: IV.360, n. 8a).

[59] Cic. *N.D.* 3.57; see Farnell (1896–1909: IV.360, n. 8b).

[60] Servius on the proem to Vergil's *Eclogues*; see Farnell (1896–1909: IV.360, n. 8b).

prokathēgétēs ('conductor [of flocks]'; *IG* v.2, 93; Jost 2007: 265). Interestingly, Pausanias writes that the *Nomian* mountains are so-called from the pasturages [*nomais*] of Pan (8.38.11).[61]

Pindar, in *P.* 9.63–5, describes Apollo as a hunter and calls him *Nomios*, following the tradition that connects Apollo to herds (Graf 2008: 99).[62] The other source for Apollo's pastoral derivation is his relation to goats and wolves (Farnell 1896–1909: IV.114). Karl Kerényi noted that Apollo is presented as a wolf-god, *Lukaios* (perhaps an earlier Arcadian deity), as well as a goat-god (1983).[63] The possible, though disputed, early link between cult and purification rites in Andania [Messene] (*Lukos* grove), as well as in Athens (the *lukeion* where, perhaps, the outcasts [*lukoi*] were purified), and Apollo's possibly apotropaic power (Apollo *Lukeios*) is possibly 'pastoral' (protector of the shepherds), at least in part, as attested in Pausanias (4.1.6). Notably, Arcadia's mythical first king was named *Lukaon* (Hes. fr. 163 MW). Furthermore, one of Apollo's possible sons is named Αὐτόλυκος (*Autolukos*; *schol.* Hom. *Od.* 14.432), although he might be the son of Hermes and the grandfather of Odysseus, a noble thief (*Od.* 19.395–6).[64] Finally, one of the etymological derivations of the mythical law-giver Lycurgus may indicate a 'self-wolf' (possibly werewolf) with a link to Arcadia, too, indicating the god of the shepherds (Chroust 1947: 47–53). As Alexandra Pappas argues, the marked liminality of the wolf for the Greeks (and others) arguably renders Apollo *Lukeios* in ever closer association 'with the initiation of young men who have come of age into the society of men' (2008: 108).[65]

Hermes was also called *Nomios* ('god of herds and flocks';

---

[61] See the discussion in Jost (2007: 265).

[62] See Farnell (1896–1909: IV.360, n. 9); see also Callimachus (*Hym. to Ap.*, 47–9), who does not, however, describe Apollo as a herder.

[63] See Gershenson (1991).

[64] See Pappas (2008: 107); Burkert links Odysseus to the liminal state of the werewolf ([1972] 1983: 133).

[65] With reference to Burkert ([1972] 1983: 145); see also Eckels (1937: 49–60); and the extensive study on the wolf in ancient Greece by Mainoldi (1984). The link to 'law' is unlikely, even though *Lukeios* appears in an oath in Eresos (IG xii, 2, 526b, 27–31, from c. 306 BC). The link to 'initiation' was earlier made by Harrison (1912: 439–41).

Lurker 1984: 80), possibly before Apollo.[66] The cult of Hermes
was probably recognised in most Greek communities, but it
appears to be more firmly established in Arcadia (Avagianou
2002: 65–112). Early on, as Lewis Richard Farnell noted,
Hermes was 'regarded as the father of Pan' (1896–1909: V.4)
and, he adds, 'it was probably in Arcadia that the close companionship between Hermes and the incoming Apollo arose'
(ibid.).[67] Burkert ([1972] 1983: 156) has proposed an etymology from ἔρμα (*herma*; 1985), while Herter (1976: 193–241)
and, earlier, Nilsson (1955: 503–5) are in agreement (contrast,
though, Hsch. s.v. ἔρμα; Diod. Sic. 5.70). The *herma* (*hermaia*,
hermata) is the pile of stones that marks the limits of a territory and crossroads (Strab. 8, 343).[68] According to Farnell, his
pastoral characterisation is probably the earliest manner in
which Hermes appeared whereby 'he is the lord of the herds
ἐπιμήλιος [*epimēlios*] and κριοφόρος [*kriophoros*], who leads
them to the sweet waters and bears the tired ram or lamb on
his shoulders, and assists them with the shepherd's crook,
the Kerykeion' (1896–1909: V.9–10).[69] In this manner, Hermes
is also associated with the nymphs, the natural protectors of
shepherds (ibid. 10). The cult festivals confirm the intensity
of the pastoral experience further. In the Tanagran festival,
when a young boy bore a ram round the walls to magically
avert a plague, he would do so in imitation of Hermes (Paus.
9.22.2; 1896–1909: V.10). Interestingly, Athenaeus writes of
the festival called the Ἕρμαια (*Hermaia*) where 'the slaves
and the masters changed their parts, the slaves making merry
and the masters waiting upon them' (ibid. 8–9). Further,

---

[66] See also Aristoph. *Thes.* 977 and on Hermes' ambiguous identity (L. Kahn
1979).

[67] Tsagrakis mentions that in a Linear B tablet the name Ἑρμῆς (*Hermēs*;
Ἑρμαhας, *E-ma-a2*) can be read, and he locates the deity in Arcadia also
(2015); he further notes that in Crete and in particular in Knossos Hermes
is named as a herder (*KN* D 411+511; *KN* X 9669), and notes the ancient
tradition that considers Hermes to be the father of Pan.

[68] On Hermes, see Curtius (1903); Eitrem (1909); Harris (1929); Kerényi
(1944); Brown (1947); Windekens (1961; 1962); Wrede (1986); and Rückert
(1988). Burkert considers that Hermes is also the inventor of 'sacrifice'
([1972] 1983: 165).

[69] See the descriptions in Hom. *Il.* 14.490; Hes. *Th.* 444; Hom. *Hym. to Herm.*
567.

Plutarch writes of a custom in Samos, where, upon sacrifice to Hermes χαριδότης (*charidotēs*, 'granting grace'), 'everyone who wishes has leave to steal and to pick pockets' (ibid. 24–5). Farnell suggests, in fact, that this was most probably linked to a carnival-day custom associated with the harvest, in that *charidotēs* tends to indicate (as when applied to Bacchus and Zeus) 'the giver of fruits of the earth' (ibid. 25).

It is perhaps in this light that Homer depicts Hermes as the god of shifty thieves and tricksters in the *Odyssey*. Farnell supposes that there is sufficient ground to suggest that in the earliest period of worship his physical functions were not limited to the role of the protecting *daimōn* of pastures and flocks; but that he was once conceived to be of a larger nature: 'one of the Chthonians or earth-divinities of vegetation and the underground world' (ibid. 11). Farnell adds that, importantly, in Arcadia Hermes was perceived as a 'god of ways' (ἀγήτωρ, *agētōr*; Paus. 8.31.7), in the sense, perhaps, both of ways of life and death (ψυχοπόμπος, *psuchopombos*; Diod. Sic. 1.96; Diog. Laert. 8.1.31.) and in the concrete sense of taking charge of roads (he is also called *hodios*) with a particular role in overseeing crossroads, a matter of particular superstition for the early Greeks (1896–1909: V.17). This is possibly a source for the early custom of heaping up stones along the way as sacred markers (and perhaps boundaries, *horoi*; as well as of important tombs), but also for the tradition that has Hermes linked to the *agora*, as the one who marks or distributes the *agora* (ἀγορανομήσας, *agoranomēsas*; Sikinos' dedication, *CIG* add. 2447ᵈ), as well as the manner of enunciation by heralds.

7. A nomad *nomós*

McInerney depicts a dual quality to the value of cattle in Homer, whereby they can connote the deeds of heroes, as well as the mundane 'hard work of farmers' (2010: 85). Furthermore, McInerney writes:

> While they listened to songs that repeatedly depicted a world in which cattle were sacrificed and consumed in epic quantities, they themselves will have been more occupied with tending herds, ploughing with yokes of oxen,

and protecting their cattle from raids. At times the distance between the heroic and the mundane contracts entirely: Andromache laments the loss of her seven brothers, all shepherds and cowherds killed by Achilles. (2010: 85)

And he continues: 'It is the possession of cattle that marks a man as prosperous. It is their sacrifice that shows that a hero is pious. It is the consumption of meat that reinforces social bonds, and it is the invitation to a stranger to share this that connotes proper behaviour' (ibid. 245). The pastoral uses, as well as the early milieux of the *nemein* family of words in Homer, are indeed better imagined in the interweaving of some of the most highly valued 'institutions' (*xenia*, feasting, and 'sacrifice').

Given the central importance of herding and the pastoral economy over, in part, largely open land in the Homeric world, it seems plausible to suggest that the pastoral senses are significant in the early archaic uses of *nemō/nomós*. The pastoral uses of both (among many for the verb *nemō* and near-predominantly so for *nomós*) suggest a possible affinity in use, as well as the precedence of *nomós* over the later *nómos*. One may not be able to suggest with absolute certainty which of the *nemō* uses was the 'original' one amidst such a wide variety of interweaved uses, but it appears fairly evident that the pastoral sense was one of the earliest uses of the word, in its wider, though concrete, milieu, along with the intimately related distribution-sharing of food in feasts and 'sacrifices'.

> φοιτᾷ δ᾽ ἔνθα καὶ ἔνθα διὰ ῥωπήια πυκνά,
> ἄλλοτε μὲν ῥείθροισιν ἐφελκόμενος μαλακοῖσιν,
> ἄλλοτε δ᾽ αὖ πέτρῃσιν ἐν ἠλιβάτοισι διοιχνεῖ,
> ἀκροτάτην κορυφὴν μηλοσκόπον εἰσαναβαίνων.
> Hom. *Hym. to Pan* 8–11[70]

---

[70] 'He [Pan] wanders all over the thick brushwood, | Now drawn to gently flowing streams, | Now again making his way through to steep crags | And climbing to the topmost peak overlooking the flocks'; translation by Athanassakis (2004).

Five

Nemesis

> die Gewalt jenes unheimlichen Princips,
> das in den früheren Religionen herrschte.
> Schelling (1857)[1]

> She subdues immoderate hopes and fiercely menaces the
>   proud;
> it was given to her to crush the arrogant minds of men
>   and
> to rout their successes and their ambitious plans.
> The ancients called her *Nemesis*, born of the silent night to
>   Ocean, her father.
> . . . Exchanging high and low, she orders and confounds
>   our actions by turns,
> and she is borne hither and thither by the whirling force
>   of the winds.
>   Poliziano, *Manto* ([1482] 2004: 7. 4–13)[2]

---

[1] 'The power of that uncanny principle [that violence reigns], which had dominated earlier religions' (my translation and comment; I thank Anton Schütz for discussing the translation with me); Friedrich Schelling understands *Nemesis* as a power before the 'law' (*nómos*) and before 'justice'. At the same time, it is possible to read him as reinterpreting *Nemesis* so that *Nemesis* is the strange, worrying, principle that exposes the fact that every law is itself 'unjust'.

[2] Translation by Charles Fantazzi, with some modifications. Amgelo (Ambrogini) Poliziano (or Politianus) (1454–94), a student of Marsilio Ficino and John Argyropoulos, was a poet and a leading figure in the circle of Lorenzo de' Medici 'il Magnifico' in Florence. He wrote *Manto* (the name, also, of the daughter of Tiresias) in Latin hexameters.

1. Indignation

There is an – at first sight peculiar – 'sentiment' that marks the *Odyssey* from the start, and that culminates, in fact, at its ending with regard to the suitors of Penelope, who receive intense νέμεσις (*nemesis*) from members of Odysseus' family and the community. Yet the suitors did not mend their ways (*Od.* 2.135–7; 22.39–40). We are accustomed to perceive *nemesis* as a personification, an abstraction of 'vengeance', a 'just retribution', or even a 'divine jealousy' (the latter is most pronounced in its later Latin form, which would eventually have *Nemesis* closely associated with the emperor).[3] However, *nemesis* is not met in this form in Homer. It is, thus, worth examining the word *nemesis* and its occurrences in Homer, and more so in order to elucidate its relation to *nemein*.

Nemesis, derived from *nemein*, is widely accepted as constituted according to verbal formations similar, for instance, to λάχεσις (*lachesis*; of λαχεῖν, *lachein*), and σχέσις (*schesis*; of σχεῖν, *schein*).[4] Furthermore, *nemesis* morphologically conforms to other words ending in -ις, which designate 'sentiments' or 'attitudes' (for example, *hubris, eris, charis, metis, themis*). Émile Benveniste, like Emmanuel Laroche, derives *nemesis* from the root **nem-*. Benveniste ([1948/1975] 1993) locates its meaning in terms of a 'proclamation', or 'presumption', of a 'fair distribution' that is commonly determined through the expression νέμεσίς ἐστί (*nemesis esti*) and its negation: οὐ νέμεσίς ἐστι (*ou nemesis esti*). These indicate circumstances (and consequences) where such a 'distribution' is performed or not (arguably pointing to a 'sacrificial' milieu).[5]

Moreover, Laroche derives *nemesis* from the ancient

---

[3] For its later, ancient and modern, imagination, see Stimilli (2003: 99–112); for its Roman history, see Hornum (1993).

[4] See Benveniste ([1948/1975] 1993: 75–86); also, Kretschmer and Locker (1944: 305); and Turpin (1980: 352–67).

[5] In addition, Benveniste links *nemesis* to αἰδώς (*aidōs*), to which I turn below ([1948/1975] 1993: 79–80). See also the use of the expressions μὴ νεμήσα (*mē nemēsa*) or ου νεμεσσητόν (*ou nemessēton*; '[feel] no *nemesis*'), for example, *Il.* 10.145. Hesychius reports on the later practice of the 'distribution' of protagonists among actors by lot; *Suda*, Phot., s.v. νεμήσεις ὑποκριτῶν (*nemēseis hupokritōn*).

Nemesis

νεμετις (*nemetis*) and notes that, in Homer, *nemesis* is generally an 'action attributed to someone, imputation'.[6] This attribution is said to be closely linked with an early sense of 'indignation' (though perhaps, as will be seen below, not necessarily 'originally' so) and as such it appears to be the key use of *nemesis* in the poems. It needs to be stressed that *nemein* is never an 'accusation' in the sense of a 'judgment'. Nowhere in Homer does *nemesis* signify 'retribution' or 'divine jealousy', as is commonly suggested.[7] Nor is Homeric *nemesis* ever deified (in contrast to Hesiod).[8] *Nemesis* (or *νεμέσσι*,

---

[6] See 1949: 89–11; Laroche relies on Ebeling ([1880–5] 1963: s.v. *νέμεσις*).

[7] On the morphological analysis, see Laroche (1949: 94). Fisher (1992) translates *nemesis* as 'anger or indignation', rather than 'vengeance' (358, n. 81). Incidentally, Laroche notes '*rancune, vengeance, jalousie, répartitrice, destinée*' (1949: 256), but he does not include the Homeric use under 'vengeance' or 'jealousy'. Laroche comments, in fact, that it is 'the jurists' who tend to deduce a vengeance, retribution or jealousy, in particular, while neglecting *nemesis*'s presence in myth, cult and worship, as well as its overall wide and varied use traversing antiquity.

[8] *Nemesis*'s oldest cults appear to have been Ionic: evident at the Attic *dēmos* of Rhamnus on the Attica coast (sixth century BC; Paus. 1.33.2–8) and Smyrna where she was later worshipped as two *Nemeseis* (Paus. 7.5.3). For the speculative early origins, see Cornford ([1912] 1957: 31–5). Consider, in this regard, the cult of a personified *Nemesis* at Rhamnus in Attica that links her to the lady of 'wild places' and 'wild things', akin to *Diana* and *Artemis Argotera* 'the lady of the wastes'. Myres writes: 'In this aspect *Nemesis* not only "assigns" to each of her fosterlings its "portion", but resents and repels encroachment. So, too, in early Italy, the source of fertility, Priapus, is also guardian of rural boundaries; and in Attica his counterpart, Hermes sanctions both possession and productivity in the ordinary course of things, and blesses also the "windfall" of unforeseen but no less providential events – good harvest, treasure-trove, unearned increment of every sort and kind' (1969: 152). What link Lady *Nemesis* at Rhamnus may have to later forms such as the Roman legend of *Numa* is not clear, but as legend has it 'the first "law-man", *Numa*, [was brought] to the Lady of the Grove for confirmation of his code of behaviour; or that men whom that "way of life" was designed to bring together into normal relations of give-and-take, of assignment and mutual respect, were themselves congregated fugitives from the crooked dealings of their own people, in that asylum or outland sanctuary which, as Livy described it later, was "the place which is now fenced off as you go down the slope between the two groves" (Livy, I. 8 *locus, qui nunc saeptus Descendentibus inter duo lucos est, asylum, aperuit*; Dionysius of Halicarnassus 2. 15 calls it *μεθόριον δυοῖν δρυμῶν* [*methorion duoin drumōn*], a boundary-space between two oak-woods)' (ibid. 152–3). Laroche, it should be noted,

nemessi) is encountered first in the *Iliad* (at 24.335): οὔ τοι ἐγὼ Τρώων τόσσον χόλῳ οὐδὲ νεμέσσι [*nemessi*] (expressing here a sentiment that is to an extent proximate to some degree to 'anger or vexation', though not exactly so). *Nemesis* is also encountered in close relation to αἰδῶς (*aidōs*), in αἰδῶ καὶ νέμεσιν· δὴ γὰρ μέγα νεῖκος ὄρωρεν (*Il.* 13.122; commonly translated as signifying the feeling of 'indignation', 'vexation' or 'reproach' of others). In the *Odyssey*, too, we read: νέμεσις δέ μοι ἐξ ἀνθρώπων (to fear the 'indignation' of others; at 2.136). At the opposite end, we find in Homer the sense of not being subject to indignation with the use of the negative οὐ νέμεσις (*ou nemesis*; for example, *Il.* 3.156; 14.80). It is useful to note that here, 'anger is related to exterior irritations'.[9] In contrast, *nemesis* is a predominantly reflective tension due to someone's extraordinary action, an action that is, or appears to be, 'out of place'.

Richard Cunliffe summarises the senses of *nemesis*, then, as follows: (a) 'righteous indignation or vexation' (but also 'reproach', 'censure', proximate perhaps to 'blame' to some extent)[10] whether feared or actual; and (b) something 'worthy of righteous indignation' or 'reproach, censure'.[11] While the sense of 'blame' is probably an ethic posterior to Homer, the acts that are frequently subject to *nemesis* often relate to one's affected 'honour' (τιμή, *timē*), as in the use of inappropriate talk, the

---

considers this pastoral sense of *nemō* in relation to *nemesis* as the arguable patron of animal and plant life, a type of hypostasis of the Asiatic great mother (1949: 89–90), but eventually disputes it both because the pastoral sense, he argues, is not from νομ- [*nom-*] and also because '*Nemesis* is never identified with/related to animals or plants in mythology' (ibid. 90; my translation).

[9] See Laroche (1949: 91; my translation).

[10] See Laroche (1949), who sees in *nemesis* 'a sense of fault in the Homeric sentiment' (91; my translation), yet he adds that '*nemesis* however is not a sentiment of culpability, but an introduction of a kind of a moral judgement, an appreciation of the act involved. *Nemesis – ou nemesis* (parallel to *themis, ou themis*.) . . . The concrete notion of it is secondary, the abstraction is instead primary. Before being a sentiment, *nemesis* is a judgement of value' (93). Yet it would be excessive to suggest a strong sense of moral judgement, especially since *nemein*, crucially, does not entertain a sense of judgement at all, as Laroche notes himself. In Homer, the sense perhaps is that of an *ethological* 'proper' of human life.

[11] See Cunliffe ([1924] 2012: s.v. νέμεσις).

lack of bravery, giving offence to one's hosts and the breach of obligations that relate to customary hospitality, the failure to observe *themis*, or other social conventions. Note, in particular, the wide range – from respect for funeral rites (*Od.* 2.101) to not approaching a virgin in 'public' (*Od.* 6.286–8).[12] The 'righteous' character of *nemesis*, then, as some form of 'indignation' is perhaps derived from this distinction between appropriateness and inappropriateness in action, possibly experienced earlier on in the sense of a wider duty not to transgress.

2. Visibilities

In Homer, we meet *nemesis* in other forms, too, such as νεμεσάω, νεμεσσάω (*nemesaō, nemessaō*), whereby to be 'indignant' can be felt, expressed or conceived at various levels (including in the extreme sense of being entirely overtaken by it, as in *Il.* 2.223; 13.119; 15.103; or in the reverse sense of a 'repressed' *nemesis* as in *Il.* 15.227).[13] In each case, note the expression of νεμεσσήθητε θυμῷ (*nemessēthēte thumō; Il.* 16.544), that is, of 'indignation' towards the act of another; or the feeling, imagining, of what others will feel towards you (for example, *Il.* 3.156, 410; 9.523). *Nemesis* is also expressed as a certain capacity, in the form of νεμεσητός (or νεμεσσητός; *nemesētos, nemessētos*): that is, as an 'inclination', or as 'being prone to an approximation of vexation' (for example, *Il.* 5.872; *Od.* 22.489). In the middle voice of νεμεσίζομαι (*nemesizomai*), we see the most expressive form of *nemesis* in relation to one's self, as in letting the thought of something sting you (*Il.* 16.254), or in arousing the wrath of the gods (*Od.* 1.263): ἐπεί ῥα θεοὺς νεμεσίζετο [*nemesizeto*] αἰὲν ἐόντας. Divine 'indignation', in turn, is poetically expressed towards either other gods or mortals; though in terms of frequency, *nemesis* is mostly a mortal expression (see, for example, *Od.* 2.130–7 and 22.39–40, where the two are posed in contrast).[14]

---

[12] See Yamagata (1994: 151–6). Telemachus feels indignant that a ξεῖνος, *xeinos* (i.e. goddess Athena disguised as Mentes) has been left standing and ignored (*Od.* 1.88–92).
[13] The occurrences are numerous; for further examples, see *Il.* 2.223; 8.198; 15.103, 227; 16.22; and *Od.* 2.101; 4.195; and 23.213.
[14] See discussion in Yamagata (1994: 149–50).

On many occasions, a sense of domain-infringement is expressed, as in Poseidon's famous *nemesis* towards Zeus for acting over-dominantly (*Il.* 15.211). Acting 'inappropriately' means acting in a non-ordinary way. It is worth observing the observer of *nemesis* for a moment at this point, for *nemesis* appears to engage a sort of evaluative criterion (though not, again, in the strong sense of a 'judgment'). This, instead, may be proximate to an experience of visibility: namely, being seen and disapproved of, or in observing oneself acting (or considering to act) 'inappropriately' (that is, beyond one's lot or *moira*, though the direct association with *moira* remains unclear). Observing the observer, in this context, is precisely what often takes place. You can be 'indignant' yourself towards others, but at the same time others can be 'indignant' towards you. In a characteristic example, Helen feels indignation towards Achilles (for not engaging in battle honourably), while Achilles feels indignation, in turn, towards the Trojans, who also feel indignation towards him (*Il.* 6.326, 439–51). In this sense, *nemesis* is a kind of social medium that acts as a type of restraint or ordering. It incorporates perhaps a sense of 'appropriateness', where acting within one's *moira*, or way of being (*ēthos*), is revered;[15] or where not offending one's *timē* is a fundamental virtue. In fact, the visibility of one's act, whether actual or prospective, needs to be understood in its early archaic context within the reality that one is, in a sense, visible at most times. The natural elements that surround one are full of *theoi* (gods), *daimones* and *Kēres* – all of whom are observers. Gilbert Murray beautifully notes what an early unidentified poet makes of this ever-present visibility: 'the air is so crowded full of them that there is no room to put in the spike of an ear of corn without touching one'.[16]

---

[15] See Telemachus justifying the bard's choice of theme for song, as is customary for bards to do (*Od.* 1.340–2). Not what is necessarily 'enjoyable', but what is 'appropriate' is shown to be at the core of this, as with a mother's 'fair reproach' (*Od.* 18.227).

[16] [Bergk] Fr. *adesp.* 2B: ἀμφὶ δὲ κῆρες | εἰλεῦνται, κενεὴ δ'εἰσδυσις οὐδ' αἰθέρι. Though this should not be taken for an instance of the 'all-seeing god(s)' in an anachronistic sense.

3. *Aidōs*

Naoko Yamagata has suggested, with good reason, that *nemesis* is not 'absolute'. Once someone finds an act undesirable, while another declares it not to be *nemesis* (οὐ νέμεσις), the unhappy party

> cannot push the matter very far to give their interest priority. In this sense, οὐ νέμεσις is a manifestation of social tolerance and a cooperative attitude which yields to interests of others, however undesirable to oneself, provided the values of the society as a whole allow the act. (1994: 156)

Nemesis' social character can be affirmed further as a form of 'public' reprobation (or non-reprobation), which implies a certain awareness or knowledge of what is or could be *nemesis* in a conventional sense. However, when some act that would otherwise receive *nemesis* takes place obscurely or in secret, it does not necessarily lead to the arousal of *nemesis*.[17] This perhaps suggests, in part, why it would be a mistake to hold *nemesis* as proximate to a notion of moral 'guilt' or a sense of 'judgment'. *Nemesis* is a 'sentiment' that has to be justifiable/observed in broad view, though not in a moralistic sense. Instead, its social sense is already implicit in *nemesis* being a part of a custom or way of being, while, at the same time, it is a 'sentiment' that appears to be adaptable to a rather wide array of situations. *Nemesis* is a πῆμα (*pēma*), a woe, for mortals in the sense of an infringement of the allotted *moira*. In fact, John L. Myres sees in Homeric *nemesis* a verbal substantive that means 'assignment' or 'assessment' of shares, but one that is already, in Homer, specialised as 'the estimate formed by a bystander about a breach of normal behaviour' ([1927] 1969: 151). *Nemesis* is observed in the action of another who acts 'improperly' or 'unusually'. When someone 'receives' *nemesis* from another, it is primarily because there is something out of line with that person's way of acting or being (*ēthos*).

Perhaps a correlative to *nemesis* is αἰδώς (*aidōs*). For Nick

---

[17] Yamagata (1994: 153–4).

Fisher, *nemesis* frequently indicates an offence or breach of a social custom or norm, 'when the agents were not restrained by *aidōs* from committing' them (1992: 181, n. 115). Thus Apollo, expressing the feelings of the gods, states that they may feel *nemesis* ('indignation') towards Achilles, who has no *aidōs* with regard to the treatment of Hector's corpse (*Il.* 24.39–54). That it is *aidōs*, and not *hubris*, that *nemesis* is opposed to is quite significant. It is also notable that, later, *aidōs* will be personified and expressed along with *Nemesis* in Hesiod (*W.D.* 197–201).[18] Fisher (1992), in his extensive study on *hubris*, points out that there is no necessary connection between *nemesis* and *hubris*: only that some acts that invite feelings of *nemesis* or resentment happen to be *hubris*.[19] Similarly, when Laroche explores what he calls the 'moral content' of *nemesis*, he suggests that the opposition to *aidōs* is most instructive (1949: 119–20). *Aidōs* is an individual sentiment, akin to honour (*timē*), which can be received as well as given. As Laroche writes, it can be understood as 'a reflection of conscience, whereas *nemesis* is a social manifestation, a public reprobation' (ibid. n. 17). 'Conscience', of course, needs to perceived lightly, since, like *nemesis*, *aidōs* is not a rigid 'order', but largely depends on 'the emotional sensitivity of the individual and on one's concept of due order'; and this, of course, at a time when no recognisable notion of conscience can be observed.[20]

It may not be so much a matter of stark opposition between the two, but of relation. Cunliffe derived four significations of *aidōs* as follows:

[18] See Schultz (1910); von Erffa (1937); Ferguson (1958: 12); Riedinger (1980: 69–74).

[19] Acts with a connection to *nemesis* are described in, for example, *Od.* 1.223 and 14.284, while others bear no connection: *Il.* 12.293; 18.198. Fisher, further, underlines that *hubris*, not a predominantly 'religious' notion, indicates 'specific acts or general behaviour against others' which cause 'the serious assault on the honour of another, which is likely [in turn] to cause shame, and lead to anger and attempts at revenge' (1992: 1 and 142–8). Contrast with Cairns (1996: 1–32); and Turpin (1980).

[20] Scott (1980: 26–7). Indeed, this lack of rigidity can be seen also with regard to *themis* and *dikē*, but there is also a degree of customary appropriateness in social terms that cannot be disregarded; see Yamagata (1994: 151–2, n.15); Verdenius (1944: 49–50); compare Murray (1934: 84).

1. 'regard or respect' (for example, *Il.* 24.111);
2. 'sensitiveness towards the opinion of others' (for example, *Il.* 24.44);
3. 'a sense of shame' (for example, *Il.* 5.787; esp. regarding sexual acts and parts); and
4. 'a sense of propriety or modesty' (for example, *Od.* 8.324); later related to *sophrosunē* (1963: 10).

Aidōs, a passion with a significant relation to sex, is proximate to 'shame, respect, propriety or modesty', though it is not identical to them as a restraining force on individual acts. Douglas L. Cairns (1993) noted, for instance, that *aidōs* is not 'shame' in any strong sense; it is rather a concern with one's 'honour', as well as with one's own 'visibility'. Indeed, *aidōs* is often described as something visible as such (Arist. *Rhet.* 1384a); *aidōs* is something apparent in the eyes. It is associated with one's visibility before an audience or oneself. *Aidōs* is, in a sense, like a 'virtue': highly valued for the preservation of 'propriety' in reciprocal arrangements, wherein one's own honour is bound to one's obligations (yet unlike a 'virtue', it remains a sentiment, not a characteristic).[21]

Aidōs is experienced in the *thumos*, the seat of 'impulses, passions and feelings' (for example, *Il.* 15.661–2). *Aidōs* is a sentiment which can be assimilated to a feeling of *nemesis* only when it is felt towards the public;[22] but more than that, the major difference remains that *aidōs*, in Homer, can only be felt by oneself.[23] Yamagata notes that no matter how much public pressure you impose on someone who is incapable of feeling *aidōs*, no effect would result other than the absence of *aidōs* in that person (1994: 156; citing the famous example of Penelope's suitors). Often *aidōs* and *nemesis* are closely

---

[21] An implied distinction between 'shame' and 'guilt' (or their relation) remains a long-standing debate among classicists and others who have suggested, borrowing from anthropological accounts, a distinction between a 'shame culture' and a 'guilt culture'; see Dodds (1951: 17–18 and ch. 2); Adkins (1960); and Lloyd-Jones (1971). However, this distinction remains structured on the anachronism of *external* sanctions for virtuous behaviour ('shame culture') and *internalised* self-sanction ('guilt culture').

[22] See *Od.* 16.75.

[23] See Yamagata (1994: 156).

related, or even appear together,[24] yet a differentiation remains.[25] Patroclus describes Achilles as αἰδοῖος νεμεσητός (*aidoios nemesētos*, *Il.* 11.649), a person who 'arouses αἰδώς and νέμεσις in front of him' (Yamagata 1994: 158). In Homer, in fact, people are often described as αἰδοῖος (*aidoios*), in other words those before whom one feels *aidōs*. Cairns, further, distinguishes between three such categories of people in the masculine: 'those before whom one feels inferior, who fill one with a sense of awe; those with whom one has a tie of φιλότης (*philotēs*); and those who are helpless or who throw themselves on one's mercy' (1996, 87). When expressed, Cairns adds, in the feminine, it relates, in particular, to 'any respectable woman' (ibid. 87).[26]

An early sense of 'propriety or moderation' is central to the epics more widely. *Aidōs* as inhibiting 'excess' appears, in fact, crucial (for example, in *Od.* 20.169–71; *Il.* 24.40); and the gods themselves are said to prefer 'moderation' (for example, in *Od.* 14.83–4; 22.413–15). 'Excess' is better understood, however, in the sense of overstepping one's limits or boundaries. James Thomas Hooker argues, in this sense, that the original meaning of the *aidōs* family of words is not, in fact, the potentially misleading notion of 'shame', but rather a type of 'religious awe', which in the epics is notably already dissipating (for example, *Il.* 24.44; some kind of 'shame' is a later specialised development; 1987: 121–5; for example, *Il.* 4.402). Yet an over-zealous distinction between 'awe' and some sense of 'shame', in this manner, is not necessarily justified. Such 'awe' is, perhaps, similarly felt by someone who acts beyond their lot, *moira*. Pindar states that the *Moirai*, for instance, condemn strife among kin to 'prevent' *aidōs* (αἰδῶ καλύψαι; Pind. *P.* 145–6).[27] In fact, Yamagata points out, further, that only inanimate objects and beggars are allowed to live without *aidōs* and even so only to a certain extent, since the beggars' needs for survival

---

[24] See *Il.* 13. 121–2; *Od.* 2.64–7.
[25] See *Il.* 1.787; 13.95; 15.561–3, 657; and *Od.* 2.64, 135–7; on the relation to *nemesis*, see von Erffa (1937); Redfield (1975); Riedinger (1980); and Scott (1980).
[26] For example, see *Od.* 9.270; 11.360; 17.188–9; and *Il.* 1.22–3.
[27] See Burton (1962: 159).

in less than human conditions temporarily supersede their sense of *aidōs*.[28]

Aidōs is felt, calculatively or spontaneously, through the awareness of one's existence as limited; and its lack is usually because of exceptional need or, at the opposite end of the spectrum, might. *Aidōs*, then, is a somewhat 'internal' restraint, at least in this sense, which, when anticipated or felt, can keep mortals from committing acts beyond their apportioned domain (and, crucially, such restraint is common, *xunon*): one acts 'shamefully' when one acts in a way that encroaches on the way of being, or lot, of another. *Nemesis* is, then, the consequence of such 'shameful' attributed acts (towards the perpetrator). *Nemesis* is what is attributed to improper acts as a fair or reciprocal consequence of the surpassing of one's share and the potential encroachment on another's. *Klothology is an ethology.*

4. *Huperdikon Nemesin*

Within this juxtaposition, we can now perhaps see the relation to *nemein*, as it is generally implied, in the exemplary case of Poseidon's statement that he will be enraged whenever the lot of another (their portion) is infringed (*Il.* 15.208–10). In both *aidōs* and *nemesis* there is reliance on the particularity of a common understanding as to the 'propriety or impropriety' of one's actions. *Nemesis* and *aidōs* (by implication) acknowledge a regular (in the sense of a mortal type of rule) social *ēthos*, a customary behaviour or mode of living that is particular as well as *xunon* (common).[29]

In Hesiod's *Theogony* both *Nemesis*, a child of the Night and sister of the Fates (*Th.* 211–25), and *Aidōs* leave the earth, anthropomorphised, at the end of the age of iron.[30] Their 'darkness' (as Hesiod perceives it) would, however, dispense a human-all-too-human shining shadow over the new age. It is in this sense, perhaps, that *nemesis* is characterised as ὑπέρδικον (*huperdikon*; in Pind. *P.* 10.44: ὑπέρδικον Νέμεσιν),

---

[28] See 1994: 172, for example, on objects (*Il.* 4.521; 13.139) and beggars (*Od.* 17.347).

[29] See Benveniste ([1948/1975] 1993: 79–80).

[30] On the genealogy of *Nemesis* in particular, see Duchemin (1980).

or, as Friedrich Wilhelm Joseph Schelling philosophically writes, a 'world-law',[31] namely the 'law' that presides over mortals and immortals, as the dispensing messenger of a human-all-too-human imperfect or failing 'justice', forcing mortals to affirm their *natura anceps*, that is, what lies 'before the law'.[32] Such 'justice' is the irreparable exposure of the mortals to their *natura anceps*, and its ambivalence is a boundary, worryingly marked by *nemesis*,[33] that at the same time is a threshold, the 'seat' of the *thumos*, the vital power, a finite heart (καρδία; *kardia*), which one hopes will not waver, though it will.

---

[31] '*Nemesis ist nichts anderes als die Macht eben jenes höchsten, alles in Bewegung bringenden Weltgesetztes, das nicht will, daß irgend etwas verborgen bleibe, das alles Verborgen zum Hervortreten antreibt und gleichsam moralisch zwingt sich zu zeigen*'; Schelling (1857: 11.2, 146–7). This can be contrasted, to some extent, with Carl Schmitt's attempt to recover a 'primordial' *nomos*, as seen in Chapter Three.

[32] See the analysis by Stimilli (2003).

[33] Pindar writes, in this sense, of a Νέμεσιν διχόβουλον (*Nemesin dichoboulon*), a 'worrying or wavering' *nemesis*, at *O.* 8.86; an early root of the scission, perhaps, between *ēthos* and *pathos* (*of boulēsis*).

Part Two

Post-Homeric Nomos

Six

The Nomos *of the Post-Homeric Poets*

Γίγνωσκε δ᾽ οἷος ῥυσμὸς ἀνθρώπους ἔχει.
Archilochus, 67a D. = 128 [West]¹

1. Hesiod's cosmonomy

Hesiod's two most famous surviving poems, the *Works and Days* and the *Theogony*, are dated from the late eighth to the early seventh century BC. Thus, they are either nearly contemporary with the Homeric epics (in the form that we have generally come to know them) or, more likely, proximate by fifty to one hundred years.² It was seen earlier that in the Homeric verses the words of the *nemō* family (and other related words) were used, to one degree or another, within the complex milieux of feasting-'sacrificial' distribution/sharing, but also apportionment of land and grazing practices, perceived here as immanent in socio-economic-worship practices in an economy that relied heavily on herding (as well as farming). In particular, in the Hesiodic tradition, this complexity coexists with an economy that is described as significantly agricultural. In Hesiod's *Works and Days*, we are

---

¹ 'Just know the kind of rhythm that possesses human beings' (my translation; meaning, possibly by extension, that all things human are unstable and transforming). Note here the word ῥυσμός (*rhusmos*), which is not met with in Homer; on the enigmatic derivation of this key word see, for example, Schröder (1918: 324–9); Plüss (1920: 18–23); Leemans (1948: 403–12); Treu (1955: 198); Wolf (1955: 99–119); and Renehman (1963: 36–8). See also Chapter Ten on *nómos* and *mousikē*.
² See, for example, Solmsen (1949); Heitsch (1966); Blusch (1970); Janko (1982: 94–8); Clay (1988; 1992); Caldwell (1989); Osborne ([1996] 2009: 152); Montanari et al. (2009); and Ulf (2009: 92–8).

evocatively no longer in the land of heroes.[3] The heroes had perished in war (*W.D.* 156–65) amidst wider social and economic changes. This is a harsher era, we are told, in which hard manual work dominates and individual farmers must struggle for subsistence, although Hesiod in part is probably idealising the conditions of his time.

The grain-giving goddess Demeter is ever watchful (*W.D.* 299f) during a period that is said to be largely farming-based by necessity.[4] Askra, Hesiod's south-western Boeotian village,[5] is most likely a pre-state polis, a fortified village comprising modest *oikoi* supporting a society that is to a significant extent agrarian. Hesiod himself tells us that he is a shepherd (*Th.* 23) and farmer, as well as a poet. He is said to have been pasturing his sheep on a (most likely) bright summer's day on Mount Helicon, when the Muses gave him a rod, a branch of flowering laurel, and breathed into him a divine voice (*Th.* 30–2) which, he tells us, inspired the *Theogony*. Similarly, in the *Work and Days*, the poet is guarding sheep and working the farm while composing and reciting poetry. Hesiod, like most small-scale farmers of his time, must have possessed and farmed a small parcel of land, as well as maintaining a flock of (probably) sheep and goats.[6] Honest farming work is largely depicted as the *nomos* of the earth for mortals, a part-idealised but harsh way of being.[7]

The 'kings' (*basileis*) of Hesiod's time are described as major landowners who predominate and preside as 'administrators' and 'judges' over the assemblies in the *agora*. They are often said to be petty and dishonest. There do not seem to be references to any kind of written laws in the poems, so it is likely that decisions were made on the basis of an oral tradition (*themistes*) and fairly patterned social conventions, norms and customs. It appears that land is scarce for the average farmer, and Hesiod's characteristic dispute with

---

[3] I consulted: Hes. *W.D.* [Sinclair] 1932; Schwartz (1960); West (1966; 1978); Verdenius (1971; 1972; 1985); Merkelbach and West (1967); Athanassakis (1983); Hamilton (1989; 1990); Solmsen (1990); and Solmsen et al. (1991).

[4] See Garnsey (1988).

[5] On Askra, see the study by Edwards (2004).

[6] See Athanassakis (1992: 171).

[7] See Nelson (1998: 137–8); and Clay (2003).

his brother Perses is described as being over the division of inherited land (*W.D.* 37–9). Perses is said to have bribed the *basileis* and, thus, distorted straight *dikē*. Having lost the case against his brother, Hesiod laments the distorting social role of the greedy and corrupt *basileis*. Zinon Papakonstantinou has, in fact, interpreted the key influence of this 'litigation' in Hesiod's poem as a claim for 'true justice' amidst a conception of 'legal norms' that are contestable – a version of 'justice' that 'has to struggle in order to prevail and get reinstated into the human world' (2008: 37 41–5).[8] This would be the perspective of the owner of an *oikos* of middling size who works on the land himself, together with a few servants, slaves and animals, rather than the more aristocratic viewpoint often evident in the Homeric poems and prevalent in Hesiod's time. Papakonstantinou writes: 'the poetry of Hesiod . . . is somewhat subversive to the aristocratic paradigm of justice, without however completely challenging the ideal of law, order and stability provided by the charismatic leader' (ibid.).[9] For my purposes, leaving Papakonstantinou's translation of 'justice' and 'law' aside, it is notable that the remarkable survival of this account of an archaic inheritance dispute (*W.D.* 30–9, 395–9) is ingeniously utilised by Hesiod, who presents this conflict as a wider platform upon which to promulgate his advice for a fairer divine and mortal order. The *Theogony* – and the same is true of the *Work and Days* – centres on a new cosmic, as well as social, order presided over by Olympian Zeus, within which the *moira* (lot, portion) and the force of the gods, as well as that of the mortals, is depicted as relatively immanent in the world.[10] Ordering in this manner centres on the avoidance of the transgression of boundaries by mortals and gods. In this sense, the *Theogony* is at the same time a *cosmonomy*, wherein a characteristic divine act of Zeus, in the establishment of the Olympian order, is

---

[8] I do not engage in this work with the particular uses of *dikē* in Homer, Hesiod and more generally.

[9] See *Th*. 81–90; see also Papakonstantinou (2012: 23).

[10] See Nelson (1998: 61–3); on Zeus as presiding, see Hes. fr. 174: 'Seeing all things, the eye of Zeus, if he desires to, observes each situation, nor does this type of *dikē* that our polis finds itself in escape his notice' (my translation).

the distribution of powers and *timas* ('honours'), through the division [*diedassato*] of prefectures and prerogatives (*Th.* 885).[11]

In Hesiod, several words of the group *nemō/nomos* are encountered, for instance δυσνομίη (*dusnomiē*), εννομίη (*eunomiē*), νέμω (*nemō*), Νέμεσις (*Nemesis*), νεμεσσάω (*nemessaō*), νόμος (*nómos*) and νομός (*nomós*). Hence, *nemō* is encountered in the sense of 'to dwell' (for example, W.D. 119; 231), 'to dispense' (ἐνέμοντο, *enemonto*) among a group and 'to distribute' or 'apportion' (*W.D.* 224). In particular, in *Works and Days* (224), *nemō* is used in direct relation to *dikē*, being used of 'men who devour bribes and who have not distributed a straight *dikē*'. In a similar sense, we meet the expression ἔργα νέμονται (*erga nemontai*) in *Works and Days* (231), where the sense of its use lies in the dispensing, among those who work the field, of the 'fruits of the fields'. *Nemō* continues to have the sense already noted in Homer regarding a customary or conventional practice, possibly indicating the effect of a 'possession'-usage of a certain kind. In Hesiod, further, one observes the middle voice of *nemesthai* becoming a fixed term for the work in the fields (for example, in *W.D.* 119), as well as in relation to pasture and grazing cattle (Pohlenz [1948] 1965: 138). Max Pohlenz, in fact, writes: 'the noun *Nomos* is already familiar in Hesiod's time as a "special way of life, a regular form of life"' (for example, fr. 221; *Th.* 417; Pohlenz [1948] 1965: 138–9).

If there is, in this context, an 'expansion' in Hesiod in the usage of *nemō/nomos*, it appears to be mostly in the sense of a relatively widened scope, but still within the plateaux of worship 'rites'/'rules' and other fundamental norms in the social life of mortals. In addition, when we encounter in Hesiod the earlier form of *nomós*, a similar use to the Homeric can be observed. Hesiod, for instance, uses the sense of 'range' (*W.D.* 403: ἀχρεῖος δ᾽ ἔσται ἐπέων νομός [*nomós*], 'the field of your words will be useless');[12] as well as the sense of the

---

[11] Compare Hom. *Il.* 15.189.

[12] Perhaps the sense of a 'pasturage' of words is present here; compare Hom. *Il.* 20.246–9 and 249, in particular: ἐπέων δὲ πολὺς νομὸς ἔνθα καὶ ἔνθα; Svenbro (1993: 112–13) disputes the accent and reads *nómos* instead, since there is attestation of it in the manuscripts, to signify a 'flow of words'. The sense of a 'distribution' (of words) is to my mind

'course' of the north wind (*W.D.* 526: οὐδέ οἱ ἠέλιος δείκνυ νομὸν [*nomón*] ὁρμηθῆναι, 'for the sun shows him no pastures to make for'). Thus, the Hesiodic uses with regard to 'a place of pasture', a 'habitat' or 'feeding place' are in proximity to the Homeric uses. Finally, in Hesiod's famous *shield* description (at 461–2), we read: διὰ δὲ μέγα σαρκὸς ἄραξε | δούρατι νωμήσας [*nōmēsas*], ἐπὶ δὲ χθονὶ κάββαλε μέσσῃ (indicating the position of the combatant when the spear thrust had cast him flat upon the ground).

The composite nouns δυσνομίη (*dusnomiē/dusnomia*, for example, *Th.* 230) and εὐνομίη (*eunomiē/eunomia*) can be understood, though perhaps not before their sixth-century BC uses, as meaning 'disorder' and 'order' (in the concrete sense of an arrangement) in a relatively broad sense, and this is possibly further facilitated in Hesiod through their mythographic personification.[13] *Dusnomiē*, which is very rarely used, is the offspring of Strife (Ἔρις, *Eris*), who gives birth, inter alia, to Famine and War (*Th.* 230), while, crucially, *Eunomiē* is the daughter of Zeus and Themis (*Th.* 902). In fact, *Eunomia* along with *Dikē* and *Eirēnē* is said to be one of the *Horai*, the famous daughters of Zeus and Themis, who oversee seasonal work. The personifications prevalent in Hesiod lend a cosmological, as well as an *ethological*, sense to these nouns. While not certain, this arguably adds some potential grounding to the etymological derivation from *eu-* and the root **nem* (meaning, early on, to 'allot', 'apportion'), bringing *eunomia* closer to the apportionment noted earlier in relation to *moira/moirai*. Zeus acts in such a manner when he 'apportions', in an act comparable to later uses of *eunomia*, when, for example, he distributes *timas* – although *nemein* as such is not utilised here (*Th.* 885: ὃ δὲ τοῖσιν ἑὰς διεδάσσατο τιμάς [*diedassato timas*]). *Dusnomia*, in this manner, may be linked to the overstepping of boundaries or marks (and hence could be read as proximate to *hubris*).

---

clear in these passages. If the accent is accepted in *nómos* instead of *nomós*, this may be an early example of the etymological link between *nómos* and 'distribution-sharing'.

[13] Another poet, Tyrtaeos, is said to have composed a work titled *Eunomia* that described the origin and nature of the Lacedaemonian political constitution, of which only ten verses survive; see Arist. *Pol.* 5.6.2.

Perhaps, then, the historical uses of *nemō* as encountered in Hesiod and other fragments of lyric poetry encompass both a further multiplication of the sense(s) of the word and the related milieu and an extension of its usages. In addition, the worship-related uses are maintained centre stage, as manifested in the divisions of *moirai*, the presence of the *horai* and so forth, which in the *Theogony* are characteristic acts of Zeus in particular, who is, for that matter, prefigured as Zeus Νεμέτωρ (*Nemetōr*). While such an etymological hypothesis is not proof of the formation of these two composites,[14] some of the key characteristics of *eunomia* appear to be 'non-arbitrariness', a (fair) 'distribution/sharing' and a 'common' (i.e. a characteristic or manner amidst a group of living beings). Indeed, these characteristics appear to signify *nómos* itself, which in Hesiod seems to entail them even more explicitly than elsewhere. It seems, further, that the act of distribution is not necessarily what exhausts the meaning of *eunomia* (nor perhaps that of *nomos* too); it involves, in a wider sense, a composition, a dwelling or a manner of being. If *eunomia* characterises a certain ordering of living beings in their habitus, the term *anomón* (which we encounter first in Hesiod's *Theogony* in one of its very rare appearances in Greek literature) describes inhuman behaviour, or ways of being. Thus, in the *Theogony*, Hesiod describes Typhaon, a monstrous being that is half-human and half-snake, as *anomón* (at 306–7): τῇ δὲ Τυφάονά φασι μιγήμεναι ἐν φιλότητι | δεινόν θ᾽ ὑβριστήν τ᾽ ἄνομόν [*anomón*] θ᾽ ἑλικώπιδι κούρῃ. The adjective *anomón* has been translated at times as 'normless', in a general sense (while at times also with a more pronounced, though unlikely, 'juridical' sense). Its use tends more towards what is non-human, in the manner of being outside of a certain human normalcy. That said, it remains possible, as Gregory Vlastos has argued, to view *anomón* as the opposite of *eunomia* (rather than *nómos*) but also to imagine a sense of unwritten 'law' (*agraphos nómos*) present within it (1953: 350). Nonetheless, the nouns *anomia* (see the first use of it in Aeschylus, examined in Chapter Nine) and *dusnomia* (in Hesiod and Solon)

---

[14] See Heinimann ([1945] 1965/1972: 64).

seem to have appeared during different periods and hence were most unlikely to be synonymous. The adjective *anomón* in its earliest use in Hesiod appears to be related to violence (*bia*) and *hubris*, as particular characteristics of a non-human creature. It is thus possible that *anomón* refers to the absence of human 'norms' or, better, normalcy.

2. Hesiodic *nómos*

It is worth examining some key passages in Hesiod to explore more closely the uses of the word *nómos*.

(a) In perhaps the most famous passage regarding *nómos* in Hesiod, we read in *Works and Days* (274–85):

ὦ Πέρση, σὺ δὲ ταῦτα μετὰ φρεσὶ βάλλεο σῇσι,
καί νυ δίκης ἐπάκουε, βίης δ᾽ ἐπιλήθεο πάμπαν.
τόνδε γὰρ ἀνθρώποισι νόμον διέταξε Κρονίων,
ἰχθύσι μὲν καὶ θηρσὶ καὶ οἰωνοῖς πετεηνοῖς
ἔσθειν ἀλλήλους, ἐπεὶ οὐ δίκη ἐστὶ μετ᾽ αὐτοῖς·
ἀνθρώποισι δ᾽ ἔδωκε δίκην, ἣ πολλὸν ἀρίστη
γίγνεται· εἰ γάρ τίς κ᾽ ἐθέλῃ τὰ δίκαι᾽ ἀγορεῦσαι
γι[γ]νώσκων, τῷ μέν τ᾽ ὄλβον διδοῖ εὐρύοπα Ζεύς·
ὃς δέ κε μαρτυρίῃσι ἑκὼν ἐπίορκον ὀμόσσας
ψεύσεται, ἐν δὲ δίκην βλάψας νήκεστον ἀάσθη,
τοῦ δέ τ᾽ ἀμαυροτέρη γενεὴ μετόπισθε λέλειπται·
ἀνδρὸς δ᾽ εὐόρκου γενεὴ μετόπισθεν ἀμείνων.

In translation:

> But you, Perses, lay up these things within your heart
> and listen now to [*dikē*], ceasing altogether to think of
>   violence.
> For the son of [*Kronos*] has ordained this [*nómon*] for men,
> that fishes [fish] and beasts and winged fowls [birds]
> should[15] devour one another [each other], for [*dikē*] is not
>   in [among] them;

---

[15] The 'should' is not necessary in this verse: one can, instead, read 'eat one another'.

but to mankind [human beings] he gave [*dikē*] which
   proves [by] far the best.
For whoever knows the [*dikai*; what is *dikē*] and is ready to
   speak it,
far-seeing Zeus gives him prosperity;
but whoever deliberately lies in his witness [swears a
   false oath] and foreswears himself,
and so hurts [harms] [*dikēn*] and sins beyond repair,
that man's generation [family] is left obscure thereafter.
But the generation [family] of the man who swears [the
   oath] truly is better thenceforward.[16]

It seems that one encounters in these verses the first, and at the
same time the widest, early description of a sense of *nómos*.
The famous verse, among these dense lines, is of course the
statement as to how *dikē* is the divine gift to human beings in
opposition to other animals. Mortals are able to and obliged
to avoid violence if they are to respect the *nómos* of Zeus.
Mortals are, however, capable of failing in this and force or
violence thus ensues (i.e. 106–201). In these emblematic verses,
Perses is advised to pay attention to *dikē* and refrain from
violence/force (βίης, *biēs*), for Zeus has appointed (arranged/
disposed) such a *nómos* to mortals, in contrast to fish, birds
and other animals that devour each other and live without
dikē (i.e. *dikē* is not in/with them). Unlike human beings, other
animals do not have the *dunamis* (or the *adunamia*, to recall
Aristotle) to refrain from violence.[17] To mortals, Zeus gave
dikē, which is 'by far the best' because the one who knows *dikē*
can then voice it in the *agora*.[18] *Dikē* is directly opposed to war

[16] Translated by Evelyn-White (1914); my comments in brackets.
[17] Arist. *Pol.* 1253a31–3, 37: ὥσπερ γὰρ καὶ τελεωθεὶς βέλτιστον τῶν ζώων
    ἄνθρωπός ἐστιν, οὕτω καὶ χωρισθεὶς νόμου καὶ δίκης χείριστον πάντων
    . . . ἡ δὲ δικαιοσύνη πολιτικόν (Just as *anthrōpos* is the best of animals
    when perfected, he is the worst of all, when separated from *nómos* and
    dikē . . . *dikaiosunē* is political [i.e. at the heart of the polis]).
[18] A significant aspect of this passage with regard to the role of the oath
    cannot be engaged with here; instead, I focus on verses 274–9. The thing
    to note, however, is the clear boundary which marks *dikē* from perjury
    and which, once crossed, remains an incurable dishonour for the person
    and his family. One's lot or *moira* lies within one's actions, or one's
    dunamis. On the central importance of the oath, see Burkert ([1977] 1985:
    252f) and Agamben (2011).

or violence, and it is for this reason that Zeus' *nómos* is to be followed. So how can this *nómos* against annihilation through war be understood in these verses?

It would, in a sense, be misleading to imagine *nómos* here as a *nómos*-law. A 'law' that is ordained by Zeus, perhaps in the form of a divine 'law' or 'command', could be understood in the archaic milieu as related to the passage to adulthood (and the voicing of *dikē*, its linguistic counterpart) so that mortals can shape their *moira* by following the path of *dikē* through their capacity to act/speak, in so far as they do act/speak. What is characterised as a *nómos*, with, perhaps, indirect allusions to distribution-sharing of pasture and sustenance, is the way of life that is marked by a proper arrangement (of *dunamis*, power) among mortals who abide by *dikē* (the divine order), which thus ensures a peaceful and prosperous common life. The divine dispensation by Zeus here implies that every living being receives a portion, or way of life, and, by extension, that these ways of life are inseparable from one another. If it is a divine ordering, it can be said that it is so because it protects the common ordering (and the demarcation) of different ways and (plural) *dunameis* of living amidst other beings. It would be simplistic, in this account, if such a *nómos* were simply to be read as the 'law-giving command of an omnipotent god', or as anything other than the marking and ordering of, and in this sense the bordering between, human and animal life, as well as (among mortals) between a life that follows *dikē* and the one that does not. While in these verses the divine sanction appears evident, the ordering of life is not by any means the exclusive domain of a divine power. Ostwald is to the point, in this regard, when he suggests that this *nómos* relates to a behaviour, a manner of living, rather than an ordinance or 'law' (1969); though indeed, *nómos*, in Hesiod, is not limited to just this sense.[19] In Hesiod, for instance, *nómos* is also described in relation to the activities of agriculture (*W.D.* 388) and 'sacrifices' (*Th.* 416–17), each time intimately attached to the *dunamis* of mortals (and their ability or power to resort to violence). Thus, the divine *nómos* is not sufficient in itself (in its delimitation of a power or *dunamis*). Rather, it is the taking of

---

[19] See Hirzel (1907: 366–8, n. 2); and Stier (1928: 232).

a sacred oath that is the means through which a binding takes place between mortal power (*dunamis*), and its communicative actualisation (the very experience of linguistic being and living that must name *dikē*) has to assume this 'ritual' bind, this form, if the path to *dikē* is to be abided by and, crucially, be voiced in the *agora*. The oath ensures, perhaps, the binding of one's genealogy to *dikē*, or indeed its utter destruction, if the dispensation of one's power is not fulfilled.

Giorgio Camassa, more recently, read the phrasing of νόμον διέταξε (*nómon dietaxe*, at 276, which Evelyn-White in the translation referred to above rendered as 'ordained') as 'he [Zeus] established a law'. For Camassa, this leaves no doubt that the verb διατάσσω (*diatassō*) signifies the act of 'law-giving or law-disposing', and he thereby believes that it shows Hesiod's awareness of a sense of 'law', or at least a sense of a 'natural' law (2011a: 470–3).[20] In this regard, Camassa appears to go a little over the more conservative interpretation that I propose at this point. The verb *diatassō* does not presuppose or provide a clear or necessary juridical or natural syntagma. Instead, as mentioned earlier, it entails indirect allusions to pasturing, land use and subsistence, or better, in a wider sense, an arrangement of each creature's *dunamis*. This is sanctioned according to a power or capacity to follow (or not) *dikē*. This does not mean, however, that a potential later sense of a particular 'legal' arrangement, or ordering, could not have derived its uses in/from such poetic allusions to *nómos*. Camassa writes:

> It can therefore be argued that νόμος became established and spread like wildfire as a term suitable to define the law (written) from the time the polis tries to give itself a clear appearance, to intervene on their own destiny through a legal system – already more or less elaborate, distributing itself evenly among the persons entitled and by laying down the powers of each, indicating a way out over conflict permanent. The traces of this are already in Hesiod. (2011a: 473)

---

[20] See also Shipp (1978), who argues that this can be understood, instead, as 'law'.

Whether these 'traces' are already evident in Hesiod will necessarily remain open to further debate, but Camassa's hypothesis retains its speculative possibility if one understands that, already prior to 'written law' and the use of *nómos* as 'law', Hesiod shows a clear appreciation of the gift of a *dunamis* to speak, to name and to order life (*dikē*). Michael Gagarin and Paul Woodruff suggest, to an extent in agreement with Camassa, that Hesiod 'is appealing to *nomos* as the gift of a norm (for human beings, justice) that is enforced by a god and ought to be enforced by human judges. In the end, the distinction between such a gift and divine law is a small one' (2007: 21). It could be said, however, that Zeus is dispensing, in the expressed grant or gift to mortals, the demarcation of (different/better) ways or powers of being, rather than the sanction of a 'divine' or 'natural' 'law'. The necessary caution as to the use of the term 'natural' here remains ever worthwhile: if it was 'natural' for human beings to 'have' *dikē* instead of devouring each other, it appears that Hesiod's description would lose its (in my view) formative (and radical) sense: the mortal way or *form* of life has to be made/formed.

Did Zeus, in his act of *nemein*, grant mortals 'justice'? It seems to me that it would be further misleading to translate *dikē* as 'justice'. Instead, one could think of a marking, a limit-setting, perhaps an *indication* of a mark (Benveniste 1968: 107–10), or a 'form' to the *dunamis* of mortal life. It is a marking or limit that could have been long recognised as an 'ordering-arrangement' between animal and human living, or, to arguably anticipate Aristotle, in one sense between *zōē* and *bios*: still, less a juridical ordinance than a demarcation of a way of life for mortals, as well as a distinct one for other animals. It is mortals that need to *abide* by a form of life (*dikē*). The way of being of mortals and other animals is their *nómos* (and in this sense both 'have' an apportioned *nómos*). *Dikē* does not, however, merely indicate a norm or an ordinance, but a concrete way of living through its experience, a normalcy or *ēthos* that is considered 'best' for the singular-as-common life of the polis (*bios*).

As a way of life, it appears to be a description or demarcation of an *ēthos*, rather than a set 'law' (whether in the sense of *Satzung*, a statute set, or a divine/customary/natural law).

175

When Erik Wolf (who was appointed Dean of the Faculty of Law in Freiburg by Martin Heidegger) suggested that this *nómos* has the sense of 'the essence of an individual being' and that *nómos* is meant as 'objectively valid' (in opposition to a 'subjective *Dikē*', as he put it), he seems to stretch the meaning of *nómos* too far, as well as to anachronistically limit the sense of *dikē* to a subjective realm (1950–70: I 151). *Nómos*, as Wolf writes, may be seen as a kind of 'natural order' or, in his Heideggerian expression, a 'being-in-order', but, I would add, only if understood in the sense of an *ēthos*, a way of being, a form of life: the form must accord to the living and vice versa. *Dikē* is not somehow normatively 'integrated' (ibid.) into human coexistence; rather, it demarcates the *ēthos* and, in this sense, the particular existence of mortals who are bound to the experience of a polis, of a political life according to *dikē*. Birds, in this manner, have their own *nómos*, but not *dikē* (that is, arguably, they lack the indication of the particular – vocal – marking within which human coexistence appears to live best).[21]

Interestingly, *dikē* (like *dais* noted in the examination of feasts in Chapter One, but also elsewhere) marks the divide between human beings and other animals (Rundin 1996: 188–9) at the moment of the binding (through an oath) of human potentiality (*dunamis*) to a particular socio-political and vocal form. It is an indication of a mark that suggests, in one view, the presence of a remarkable early 'anthropological' and *glossological* sense in Hesiod. Thus, Hesiod can be said to be marking not just a way of life for mortals (the *anthroponomikon*, as I have called it in the Preface), but also what is best or 'proper' as an established or preferred *ēthos* that (the Hesiodic-anthropomorphic) Zeus dispenses against *anthropophagia* (the refraining from violence among mortals being particularly marked in the prohibition of not 'sacrificing' members of one's community), as well as *aglossia*.[22] *Dikē* may be one of many possible *nómoi* or orderings, arrange-

---

21 The relevant verses are 524–6: ὅτ᾽ ἀνόστεος ὃν πόδα τένδει | ἔν τ᾽ ἀπύρῳ οἴκῳ καὶ ἤθεσι λευγαλέοισιν. | οὐδέ οἱ ἠέλιος δείκνυ νομόν [νομόν] ὁρμηθῆναι. The boneless octopus was thought to be able to eat its own 'foot' given its lack of a *nomós*, in the sense of the availability of 'pasture'.

22 See Heinimann (1945: 62–3, n. 14); and similarly, Hdt. 4.106; Hes. *Th.* 54.

ments, but, for Hesiod, it is the one allotted for mortals. As Aristotle puts it much later: ὁ δὲ μὴ δυνάμενος [*dunamenos*] κοινωνεῖν ἢ μηδὲν δεόμενος δι᾽ αὐτάρκειαν οὐθὲν μέρος πόλεως, ὥστε ἢ θηρίον ἢ θεός ('But he who is unable to live in a community, or needs no part of the polis by reason of self-sufficiency, that one is either a beast or a god'; *Pol.* 1253a27–9).

(b) In *Works and Days* 388–9, we read: οὗτός τοι πεδίων πέλεται νόμος οἵ τε θαλάσσης | ἐγγύθι ναιετάουσ᾽ οἵ τ᾽ ἄγκεα βησσήεντα ('this is the *nómos* of the plain and of those who dwell near the sea and on rich land far from the sea, to plough and sow and reap lightly clad if success in farming is to be achieved'). In these verses, *nómos* is used to refer to a description of a way of doing something, a manner of acting or a related behaviour, in this particular case, the *nómos* of the plains (πεδίων νόμος, *pediōn nómos*). Again, an action of normalcy is described, the way in which something is done: 'the regular order and necessity that the farmer fulfils [in] his seasonal work' (Ostwald 1969: 23). Hesiod is suggesting the way in which a farmer ought to strip the land for ploughing and harvesting, with a sense of what is normal or proper in going about such farming activity. Indeed, as Emmanuel Laroche has noted, in Hesiod we locate *nómos* as an indication of a regular ordering (1949: 13–15). In contrast, George P. Shipp, in his brief but emphatically argued study, has proposed that this regularity can, in fact, be perceived as much more proximate to a 'legal' sense: that is, even as one 'transferred' from the 'legal sphere' (1978: 12). Indeed, one could read here an idea of 'a concrete set of rules' about a particular activity, although I think this is more so in the sense of everyday peasant life 'norms', 'customs' or 'conventions'. As Karl-Joachim Hölkerskamp suggests, this is akin to the 'rules' or 'customs' described in relation to 'sacrificial' uses, or modes of work (2000: 73–6).[23]

(c) In verse 66 of the *Theogony*, we read: [Μοῦσαι] μέλπονται πάντων τε νόμους καὶ ἤθεα κεδνά. In this verse, *nómos* (in the plural *nómous*) is encountered in its first extant plural form,

---

[23] See Hes. fr. 248 and *Th.* 417. For an argument that reads this as referring to 'laws' on the basis that Hesiod is acting as a kind of 'legislator' procuring advice and particular rules throughout his poem, see Shipp (1978).

indicating a multiplicity of arrangements or 'distributions' (ways of being). This use of *nómos* refers to 'the ways of the gods', also alluding to their 'haunts' and 'ranch'-pasture. The proximity here of the *nómoi* and the *ēthea* (ἤθεα) is possibly also semantic (though not an identification). It is worth reading verses 65–75 in full:

ἐν θαλίης: ἐρατὴν δὲ διὰ στόμα ὄσσαν ἱεῖσαι
μέλπονται πάντων τε νόμους καὶ ἤθεα κεδνὰ
ἀθανάτων κλείουσιν, ἐπήρατον ὄσσαν ἱεῖσαι.
αἳ τότ᾿ ἴσαν πρὸς Ὄλυμπον ἀγαλλόμεναι ὀπὶ καλῇ,
ἀμβροσίῃ μολπῇ: περὶ δ᾿ ἴαχε γαῖα μέλαινα
ὑμνεύσαις, ἐρατὸς δὲ ποδῶν ὕπο δοῦπος ὀρώρει
νισσομένων πατέρ᾿ εἰς ὅν: ὃ δ᾿ οὐρανῷ ἐμβασιλεύει,
αὐτὸς ἔχων βροντὴν ἠδ᾿ αἰθαλόεντα κεραυνόν,
κάρτει νικήσας πατέρα Κρόνον: εὖ δὲ ἕκαστα
ἀθανάτοις διέταξεν ὁμῶς καὶ ἐπέφραδε τιμάς.

In translation:

And they, uttering through their lips a lovely voice,
sing the [*nómous*] of all and the goodly ways
of the immortals, uttering their lovely voice.
Then went they to Olympus, delighting in their sweet
    voice,
with heavenly song, and the dark earth resounded about
    them
as they chanted and a lovely sound rose up beneath their
    feet
as they went to their father. And he was reigning in
    heaven,
himself holding the lightning and glowing thunderbolt,
when he had overcome by might his father [Kronos];
and he [distributed/ordered] fairly to the immortals
their portions and declared their [*timas*].[24]

For my purposes, the key verse is 74, where another use of the verb διέταξεν (*dietaxen*) is met, in the sense of an apportion-

---

[24] Translated by Evelyn-White (1914).

ment or arrangement among the community, in this instance that of the gods.[25] It is perhaps implied in this passage that the ways of the gods and the ways of the mortals are not that remote.[26] Eric A. Havelock noted the proximity between *ēthea* and *nómos* in Hesiod, which arguably survives all the way to Plato's *Laws* (1963: 62). Havelock writes:

> *Nomos* and *ethos* signify in their original usage not prin-
> ciples or beliefs but localised human activities, that of
> distributing or managing land in the case of *nomos*, and
> that of living in a place or a haunt in the case of *ethos*. Their
> inspiration is behaviouristic, not philosophic, legal, or
> moralist. (1963: 63, n. 10)

Not yet *mores naturam* (Propertius), then, but not too distant from such either. In Hesiod, the *ēthos* is still very much a place, a local abode, a way or dwelling, that signifies a dispo-sition as a habitus. This appears to be so in at least two further verses: in τοῖς δὲ δίχ' ἀνθρώπων βίοτον καὶ ἤθε' ὀπάσσας (*W.D.* 167), 'by giving them food and shelter separate from mortals'; and in Hesiod's iconic description of Pandora as having received, as a gift from Hermes, an (ἐπίκλοπον) ἦθος (*ēthos*) (*W.D.* 67, 78).[27] This 'local' sense could be said to have been gradually forgotten, however, and perhaps already so in Hesiod's time, and to be transitioning towards a broader meaning, though still suggesting something inherent in a way of being or acting.

(d) In a similar sense to verse 66, in verses 416–17 of the *Theogony*, one encounters the formulaic phrase κατά νόμον (*kata nómon*):

καὶ γὰρ νῦν, ὅτε πού τις ἐπιχθονίων ἀνθρώπων
ἔρδων ἱερὰ καλὰ κατὰ νόμον ἱλάσκηται,
κικλήσκει Ἑκάτην.

In translation:

---

[25] See Heinimann (1945: 63, n. 15).
[26] See Havelock (1963: 62).
[27] See Hirzel (1907: ch. 4.2).

Whenever any one of mortal men
offers fair sacrifice and begs favour according to [*nómon*]
he calls upon Hecate.[28]

Some have read the use of *nómos* [*nómon*] at this point in a
fairly clear sense of 'law'.[29] The offering to the gods *kata nómon*
– that is, according to the *nómos* – can be instead understood
as 'according to a custom, rule or a certain ordering' that is
common to the polis (akin to the sense of *nómos*, in fact, in fr.
20, which I discuss below). It is important to appreciate that
for the early Greeks a *nómos* is a kind of 'rule', whether in the
sense of a customary practice, or a social-worship convention in a manner that cannot be determined as 'legal' in any
formal or direct sense. In the prepositional expression *kata
nómon*, which Hölkerskamp notes and which appears in the
extant literary evidence for the first time in Hesiod, what is
indicated above all is a particular way or ordering, in a wider
(2000: 78) and yet still practical sense, but one that remains
within the range of a way of acting or living.[30]

(e) Finally, Hesiod's fr. 20 is generally accepted as genuine
in the form in which it was preserved by Porphyrius (*De
abstin.* ii.18): ὥς κε πόλις ῥέζῃσι, νόμος [*nómos*] δ' ἀρχαῖος
ἄριστος ('howsoever the city does ['sacrifice'], the ancient
nómos is best'). *Nómos* here appears, in perhaps its clearest
form, as *nómos* in the sense of the ancient manner, or way,
with particular regard to the distributive practice of 'sacrifice'. It can be read as paying tribute and conforming to the
ancient way or usage, a custom or convention that has stood
well through time and which is considered to be the most
'proper' (though not necessarily because of its longevity). I
showed earlier in Chapter One, with regard to the Homeric
poems, that 'sacrificial' practices are central to the social-
worship plateau that forms one (if not *the*) nucleus of life in
this period (and beyond). The reference to 'sacrifice' can thus
be understood not just as a random milieu among others
(although, as has already been shown, *nómos* is used in relation to varied practices), but as one of the most (or even *the*

---

[28] Translated by Evelyn-White (1914).
[29] See the discussion in Ostwald (1969).
[30] See also Heinimann (1945: 63).

most) revered practice of distribution/arrangement/ordering. This sacrificial practice is also at the heart, to the extent that one can speculate about such a matter, of the early notion of *nómos*, long before *nómos*-law becomes commonplace, as it does in the classical period. *Nómos*, then, once more, does not appear to have a direct formalised sense of 'law', but more of a manner of usage or practice, which, in Hesiod in particular, acquires a more pronounced notion of 'propriety and validity': a 'proper' usage or practice according to convention or the 'rules' of a particular milieu of normalcy.

3. Alcman, Alcaeus, Archilochus and Theognis

It is useful to turn, briefly, to some of the surviving instances of the further uses of *nomos* in post-Homeric and post-Hesiodic poetry in order to observe whether and how the uses of the word and its relations are expressed.[31] Here, I can only offer some indications through an eclectic range. It appears that post-Homeric poetry is generally proximate to the uses of the *nemein* family of words, though, as has already been seen, *nómos* is only directly evident in use after Homer. It has been argued by scholars that one finds, in, for instance, the poets Archilochus, Alcaeus and Theognis in particular, an oscillating meaning of *nómos* between worship rites and other conventions or customs, with some potential proximate signification of *nómos*-'law'.

In one characteristic use of *nómos* in poetry (as mentioned above), *nómos* can denote a way of being or a 'proper' manner. Alcman, an exceptional poet of 'the language of the birds' (*mousikē*) of the late seventh century BC, is often considered to be Lacedaemonian[32] (or, according to others, Lydian, though

---

[31] On Greek elegy and iambos, see generally Edmonds ([1922–7] 1945; 1931); Campbell (1967); West (1974; 1989); Bowie (1993: 90–101); and Gerber (1999). On lyric poetry, see Campbell ([1967] 1990); Jakobson (1979); Burnett (1983); Hutchinson (2001); and Budelmann (2009).

[32] Alcman provides a radically different account of the isolated and austere Spartan society as conventionally presented. In addition, it is worth noting that the discovery and publication of the second century AD *P. Oxy.* 24 (in 1957), n. 2390, frag. 2 = fr. 5 (Page 1962a) has revealed, through the scholiast's allegorical summary, who describes the poet as a φυσικός (*phusikos*; fr. 2 col. ii 25–6), a ritual cosmogonic poem attributed to

in any case quite certainly active in Sparta) and is believed to be the earliest of the so-called nine lyric poets. He writes in fr. 40: ϝοῖδα δ' ὀρνίχων νόμως [*nómōs*] | παντῶν.[33] In this ornithological expression, common to Alcman and other poets, *nómos* appears to be used in the sense of the ways of birds, or more likely in the musical sense of *nómos* (the musical modality of the birds' singing [κακκαβίδων, *kakkabidōn*], which I examine in more detail in Chapter Ten).[34]

As a young boy, we are told by testimonies, another famous poet of the seventh century BC named Archilochus received his calling from the Muses while his father had sent him to tend animals (as was the case for Hesiod).[35] In Archilochus, considered the first or one of the earliest lyric poets (as well as the inventor of the *Iambos*) and a near contemporary of Hesiod, we encounter various uses of *nomos*. In fr. 74.7 we find a metaphorical use of the oxytone *nomós*, as follows: μηδ'

Alcman. In this poem, undifferentiated matter (ἄπορον and ἀτέκμαρτον, *aporon* and *atekmarton*) is described as subject to the genetic, creative power (*genesis panton*; though not *ex nihilo*) of Thetis (τίθημι, *tithēmi*) that found its narrow way (πόρος, *poros*) and the *tekmōr* (τέκμωρ), the limit (τέλος, *telos*) or limit-setting of its 'generative way' (compare Hes. *Th.* 116). It could even be said that *poros* is here the *archē* of the creative *dunamis*, while *tekmōr* is the limit of this power (its binding to its limit). *Thetis* is not an anachronistic demiurge, but a shape-shifting sea power, a distributor of 'generative order' that creates in a manner akin to a moulding technician/artisan (τεχνίτης, *technitēs* 19) who gives shape to bronze (see Vernant 1970: 219–33; and Most 1987: 1–19). If it is true that Alcman wrote such a poem (or that the allegorical summary depicts it faithfully) then, astonishingly, it may precede the cosmogonic verses of the Miletian 'pre-Socratic philosophers' (Thales, Anaximander and Anaximenes). Most likely, it seems to me, Alcman did not write what the scholiast describes (later sources do not mention him in this regard), but a poem akin to the inspired commentary could very well have been composed by him, though what it contained exactly remains unknown.
[33] See Kousoulini (2013: 429).
[34] See Vlastos (1953: 349–50, n. 41); and, generally, Calame (1983); Budelmann (2009). It can be noted that the *Moirai* and the *Muses*, in lyric poetry and beyond, can be said to be proximate as the ones that 'bring or dispense' *eunomia*; see Chapter Ten.
[35] According to the inscription at Archilochus' shrine in Paros, the so-called *Archilocheion*. See Treu (1955: 40–54); and Kontoleon (1956: 29; 1964). On Archilochus, see Treu (1959); Pouilloux et al. (1963); West (1985; 1989); Burnett (1983); Bossi (1990; 1976); Berranger (1992); Aloni (2007: 205–37); and Ornaghi (2009).

ὅταν δελφῖσι θῆρες ἀνταμείψωνται νομὸν [*nomón*]; whereby dolphins are said 'to be roaming the mountains or plains'. In fr. 12, we read the phrase νομίμου ταφῆς, (*nomimou taphēs*), probably referring to ways or rules as to a burial custom; similarly so in fr. 230 [Bude], where one finds reference to, most probably, 'customs' rather than 'laws'. It is also worth turning at this point to an enigmatic short fragment that has given rise to differing interpretations as to the use of the term *nómos*. In fr. 133 [Bergk] (= 232 West) we read: Νόμος δὲ Κρητικὸς διδάσκεται; or Νόμους δὲ Κρητικοὺς διδάσκεται.[36] This fragment can be translated as 'one is taught of the Cretan *nómos* or *nómoi*'. Camassa has, in fact, questioned the way in which one is to understand this fragment:

> Since Crete is celebrated for its legislative wisdom which is traced back a long way (. . . given also the substantial remains of inscriptions legal provisions dating back to the Archaic period), it is tempting to understand *nomos* or *nomoi* to which word the poet of Paros surely refers as 'law' or 'laws', though possibly in a mocking manner. But are we entitled to attribute this meaning for the age of Archilochus? (2011a: 471)

I will engage a bit further with the 'laws' of Crete in Chapter Ten, but for now, it can be noted that Cretan *nómoi* appear to be the earliest such reference we have (note *Il.* 2.648). Camassa rightly disputes the 'evolutionary' perspective whereby customs 'evolved' into laws (as in Gagarin 2008: 33–4) and suggests that if one accepts that *nómos* means (also) 'law' during the seventh century BC, then it is possible that Archilochus is also referring to Cretan 'law or laws' in this fragment, rather than custom or customs. Camassa argues that the recent evidence as to the contact between the islands of Crete and Paros may suggest, by implication, that Archilochus would have become aware of the famous Cretan 'laws', thus warranting such a reference in his poetry (2011a: 473). The interpretation of *nómos* (or the plural *nómous*) in this fragment as 'laws', or at least as customary 'rules/laws',

---

[36] See Camassa (2011b: 97, n. 258).

remains possible, and it may be so contra Ostwald (1969), who reads 'practice' for *nómos* in this fragment, thus rendering it the first extant indication of the use of *nómos* as some form of 'law'; in this case, reflecting a contentious change in social conventions or institutions.[37] Even so, the sense of 'law' at this point should not be confused with the direct sense of *nómos*-law of the classical period. After all, in Archilochus, similarly to in Hesiod, the *nómos* is marked by Zeus' observation of *hubris* and *dikē* (ὕβρις τε καὶ δίκη μέλει; fr. 177 West),[38] which echoes the *eunomia* which the gods observe in Homer (i.e. *Od.* 17.487: ἀνθρώπων ὕβριν τε καὶ εὐνομίην [*eunomiēn*] ἐφορῶντες) and which does not seem to refer to 'law'.[39]

In the surviving fragments of another important poet, Alcaeus of Mytilene (c. 620 BC), we meet a number of different uses of *nómos* and *nemō*.[40] In fr. 6 (Campbell [1982] 1993: 238), we read τόδ' αὖτε κῦμα τῶ προτέρω νέμω [*nemō*]. This can be translated as 'this wave in turn comes (like?) [the previous one]', signifying 'movement' (though νέμω [*nemō*] or νόμω [*nómō*] are here uncertain). In fr. 35 (= *P. Oxy.* 1233 fr. 14 = G.1.25 [Lobel-Page]) we find the negative expression κὰν νόμον (*kan nómon*), possibly meaning 'without custom' or perhaps 'without law-norm' of a certain kind. Similarly, we encounter the same expression in its negative form in fr. 129, at 25 (Voigt 1971 = *P. Oxy.* 2165 fr.1): οὐ κὰν νόμον (*ou kan nómon*), which David A. Campbell translates as 'unlawfully' in relation to the act of 'sacking or devouring' a city ([1967] 1990: 299). It remains uncertain to what extent Alcaeus is referring to a *nómos*-law in these fragments, whereas the sense of *nómos*-'custom/norm' is more clearly evidenced in other fragments and via proximate words. Thus, the proposed translation would be 'not according to custom'. In fr. 71.2 (= *P. Oxy.* 1234 fr. 2) we read: οὕτω τοῦτο νομίσδεται [*nomisdetai*]. In translation, this can be rendered as 'such is the

[37] Vlastos, however, argues with good reason that it is hard to see why the Greeks would have come to need a new everyday term for 'custom' as such when they already had *ēthos* (1953), though perhaps the subtlety of different uses allowed for such variation.
[38] See the discussion in Gagarin (1974: 186–97).
[39] The oxytone *nomós* is also found in fr. 122 West: μηδ' ἐὰν δελφῖσι θῆρες ἀνταμείψωνται νομὸν [*nomón*].
[40] On Alcaeus, see Page (1955); and Burnett (1983).

custom', in the milieu of feasts and with possible regard to a contrast with excessive drinking. It is worth noting that the development of the word into νομίζω (*nomizō*), which is not met with in Homer and Hesiod, appears to be an expression that indicates the sense of 'such is the way'. In two further fragments, where the context is missing, we can observe two other interesting instances. In fr. 72.6 (= *P. Oxy.* 1234 fr.2 = 45.5) we read: ἔνθα νόμος [*nómos*] θάμ' ἐν . . . ('where the custom is to . . .'); and in fr. 181 (= *P. Oxy.* 2295 fr. 41) we find ενος νόμω [*nómō*], which Campbell translates as 'custom' ([1982] 1993, 317). Finally, in fr. 382, as quoted in Hesychius (E 5076), we meet the expression νόμισμ' [*nomism'*] ἐπινέοισα (or ἐπ' οἱ πνέοισα), referring possibly to a custom or tradition (in the milieu of some kind of 'discipline').

I turn, lastly, to the poet Theognis (c. 552–41 BC),[41] who follows in the steps of Hesiod and whose era was marked by significant social instability.[42] Theognis, a rich aristocrat from Megara adjacent to the Isthmus of Corinth, often describes himself as in exile from his homeland after he has lost his influence and property, possibly residing in Thebes (as well as elsewhere, including Sparta, Euboea and Sicily). Theognis was a particularly famous poet in his time and beyond for his ethical elegies and, some would say, even his 'legislative' advice, to the extent that Xenophon would describe his poetry as a 'treatise on people' (σύγγραμμα περὶ ἀνθρώπων, *suggramma peri anthrōpōn*), 'just as if a horseman were to write about horsemanship' (Stob. 4.29.53). Friedrich Nietzsche in 1864, at the age of twenty, devoted his early thesis (*Valediktionsarbeit*) to Theognis and located, among other ideas, an early inspiration for his 'genealogy of morals' in Theognis' 'revaluation of values'.[43] A central thread in Theognis' poetry is his criticism of the social 'base'

---

[41] Perhaps closer to 600 BC; in any case, Theognis probably composed in the late archaic period, while it is also important to note that his poetry was widely re-edited during the classical period.

[42] On Theognis, see Harrison (1902); Allen (1905: 386–95); Carrière (1948); Figueira and Nagy (1985); Nagy (1985: 22–81); Gerber (1991: 186–214); Selle (2008); on Theognis and 'law', see Papakonstantinou (2004: 5–17; 2008: 108–12).

[43] See Nietzsche (1867; 1869); Negri (1985); Colli and Montinari (2006: 420–62).

(κακοί, δειλοί; *kakoi, deiloi*), which took power in the polis and which, as the poet states (at 54), οὔτε δίκας [*dikas*] ᾔδεσαν οὔτε νόμους [*nómous*], 'knew [in the past] neither *dikas* nor *nómous*'.[44] Meanwhile in the verses immediately following (55–6) he describes that they 'wore out goat skins clothing their sides; They dwelt there like deer beyond this city.' It is worth noting, in passing, the related use of *enemonto* in verse 56: ἔξω δ᾽ ὥστ᾽ ἔλαφοι τῆσδ᾽ ἐνεμοντο πόλεος. Furthermore, the base, for Theognis, acted in 'a vain/hopeless way' (ἄνθρωποι δὲ μάταια νομίζομεν [*nomizomen*], εἰδοτες οὐδέν; at 141). In this case, the sense of *nómous* (at 54) appears to refer to the ordered normalcy that is disrupted, as well as the 'norms' of the polis.

While some may be tempted to translate, in these verses, *nómous* or *nómos* as 'law' or 'laws', the social/political nature of the passage and the analysis of Hans Erich Stier (despite it being a predominantly moral reading) appear to lend weight to an understanding akin to that of 'customs or social conventions/norms' (1928: 236; but it is once more important to note that these are categorisations that are not easily translatable or separable, if at all). A comparison with the *Iliad*'s (9.214) ἄνδρα [. . .] ἄγριον οὔτε δίκας εὖ εἰδοτα οὔτε θέμιστας could be juxtaposed, whereby Theognis (at 54, as we saw earlier) could be said to 'replace' the Homeric *themistas* with *nómous*. Yet the 'replacement', if it is one, does not necessarily seem to alter the sense of *nómous* as 'sacred' social-political conventions and norms. Such *nómoi* appear to have had a character of (objective) validity, yet they are not to be understood as (written) 'laws', or equally to be confused with 'morals' either, since in the poems there is a frequent opposition between *nómoi* and *ēthē*. We observe perhaps a proximate terminological development to a notion of 'law-norm', but not quite as yet. More so, in Theognis, *nómos* emerges, at least by implication, as a collection of social or political 'norms': that is, as 'ideals' that can include certain elements of practical rules or conventions.

Finally, we read in verses 279–80 of how Theognis characterises the 'base's' view of *dikē*: εἰκός τοι κακὸν ἄνδρα κακῶς

---

[44] For an introduction to Theognis in relation to his political views, see Papakonstantinou (2008: 105–26).

τὰ δίκαια νομίζειν [nomizein], | μηδεμίαν κατόπισθ᾽ ἀζόμενον νέμεσιν [nemesin]. This could be rendered as: 'It is usual for a bad man to enact the bad as *dikaia*, and have no fear of *nemesis* thereafter.' It can be noted that the sense of *nomizein* appears to signify a certain paradigmatic shift to a way of thinking, a certain 'attitude' or 'view'. A little further on, in verses 289–90, we read: νῦν δὲ τὰ τῶν ἀγαθῶν κακὰ γίνεται ἐσθλὰ κακοῖσιν | ἀνδράσιν· ἡγέονται δ᾽ ἐκτραπέλοισι νόμοις [nómois]. Here, the lower social classes and their leaders are opposed to the old noble ways by rejoicing in perverted *nómois* (meaning perverted ways, customs or norms). The older norms or normal order of things (*nómoi* and *dikē*; whereby *nómoi* most likely refer, again, to ways or social norms) are said to have been perverted by the prevalence of insolence and 'out of bounds behavior'.[45] Such a reversal of social order is rather vividly described in verses 677–8: χρήματα δ᾽ ἁρπάζουσι βίη, κόσμος δ᾽ ἀπόλωλεν, | δασμὸς δ᾽ οὐκέτ᾽ ἴσος γίνεται ἐς τὸ μέσον; here, the base and its leaders are depicted as seizing possessions (*chrēmata*) by force (*biē*), so that order (*kosmos*) has been reversed or destroyed. There is no longer respect for the supposedly equitable or fair division (of such 'possessions'), nor regard for the common interest. We read, for instance, in this sense, of a divine *eunomia* in verse 1142: οὐκέτι γινώσκουσ᾽ οὐδὲ μὲν εὐνομίας (*eunomias*).[46] Divine *nemesis* is supposedly no longer to be greatly feared (οὐ νέμεσις πρὸς θεῶν γίνεται οὐδεμία, at 1182), and the 'weak', we could hear Theognis bemoan, have overtaken the world.

---

[45] See also Laroche (1949: 173).
[46] See the potentially similar use of (divine) *eunomia* in Tyrtaeus, Arist. fr. 4 West; Strab. 8.362 and 8.4.10, who also places him as holding an important position in the Spartan army.

Seven

The Nomos of Heraclitus

ἔστι που νέων ξύνεσις καὶ γερόντων ἀξυνεσίη.
χρόνος γὰρ οὐ διδάσκει φρονεῖν,
ἀλλ᾽ὡραίη τροφὴ καὶ φύσις.
Her. fr. 183[1]

ἀθάνατοι θνητοί, θνητοὶ ἀθάνατοι,
ζῶντες τὸν ἐκείνων θάνατον,
τὸν δὲ ἐκείνων βίον τεθνεῶτες.
Her. fr. 62[2]

οὐκ ἐμοῦ, ἀλλὰ τοῦ λόγου ἀκούσαντας
ὁμολογεῖν σοφόν ἐστιν ἓν πάντα εἶναί.
Her. fr. 50[3]

1. Kosmology

At the threshold of the sixth and fifth centuries BC, there lived a philosopher named Heraclitus in the area of Ephesus on the coast of Asia Minor, north of Miletus.[4] We do not know much

---

[1] 'There is, I suppose, an intelligence of the young and an unintelligence of the aged. For it is not time that teaches wisdom, but early nourishment and *phusis*.'

[2] 'Mortals are immortals and immortals are mortals, the one living the other's death and dying the other's life.'

[3] 'Listening not to me but to the *logos* it is wise to agree that all things are one.'

[4] On Heraclitus' fragments and thought, see: Diels (1901); Lassalle ([1858] 1920); Gigon (1935); Brecht (1936); Wolf (1950–70); Burckhardt (1952); Cornford ([1912] 1957); Axelos (1962); Guthrie (1962: I); Wheelright (1964); C. H. Kahn (1964; 1979); Brun (1965); Mourelatos (1965); Snell (1965); Heidegger and Fink (1970/1979); Veikos (1988; [1979] 1985); Ramnoux

about him, but he was possibly of aristocratic descent, or sympathetic to the aristocracy. It is also said that he refused to take part in the legislature of Ephesus, or engage in politics (unlike, for example, Solon[5]), instead at times preferring to play with children.[6] Later sources record that Heraclitus was, in fact, the author of a book or treatise titled Περὶ Φύσεως (*Peri Phuseōs*), though this remains uncertain.[7] For my purposes, Heraclitus is of particular interest not only owing to his surviving fragments about *nómos*, but also because one can observe in his thought uses of the term *nómos* that can be interpreted in an almost 'philosophical' manner. In this sense, Werner Jaeger perhaps exaggerated when he wrote that Heraclitus 'is actually the first man to approach the problem of philosophical thought with an eye to its social function', and that in him it is for the 'first time that the idea of "law" has appeared in philosophic thought' (1947: 115). *Nómos*, in Heraclitus, is of course neither an ideal nor an abstract concept, if these are what we are accustomed to designate as the ingredients of 'philosophy'. Jaeger, further, maintained that not only is this 'the first time that the idea of "law" has appeared in philosophic thought', but 'what is more, it is now regarded as the object of the highest and most universal knowledge; the term is not used in the simple political sense but has been extended to cover the very nature of reality itself' (ibid. 115).

It is worthwhile noting that for Heraclitus there is not yet a division between *phusis* and reality, nor a distinction between 'facticity' and 'normativity'. There is *kosmos-logos* and, if his thought is to be characterised, it could be named as a *kosmology*. Thus, when Jaeger states that Heraclitus' 'divine law' (*theios nómos*) is 'something genuinely normative' (in

---

(1968); Stokes (1971); Barnes (1979); Colli (1980); Kirk et al. ([1957] 1983); Jeannière (1985); Wright (1985); Robinson (1987); Dumont (1988); Boudouris (1989); Dilcher (1995); Bremer (1996); Bollack and Wissmann ([1972] 2001); Geldard (2001); Diels and Kranz ([1903] 1952/2004); and Mouraviev (1999–2008, 2006: vol. III.3.B/i).

[5] Parmenides, another pre-Socratic philosopher, was also said to be a giver of laws; see Diog. Laert. 9.23; and Strabo 6.1.1.

[6] See fr. 52: αἰὼν παῖς ἐστι παίζων, πεττεύων· παιδὸς ἡ βασιληίη ('time is a child playing draughts, the kingly power is a child's').

[7] See Diog. Laert. *Vit.* 9.5; and Arist. *Rhet.* 1407b11.

arguable contrast to a so-called 'law of nature' or law of *phusis*), or that 'It is the highest norm of the cosmic process, and the thing which gives that process its significance and worth' (1947: 116), he could be misread in part as interpreting the Heraclitean sense(s) of *nómos* as if akin to a 'transcendental' imperative realm that is not of course proximate to Heraclitus' time. In contrast, it is the Stoics who would establish a proximate sense of *nómos* in a manner akin to the one Jaeger describes. Charles H. Kahn (1979) will, hence, urge caution as to the identification of *nómos*, in some juridical manner, with *theios* (the 'divine').

There is a relation between the divine (or the divine *nómos*) and the mortal *nómoi* of the polis, but how this is to be interpreted in Heraclitus' surviving fragments remains a complex question. Michael Gagarin, for example, has suggested that already, from the end of the seventh century BC, the 'emphasis on procedure' in Greek law may have had a significant influence on so-called pre-Socratic thought (2002: 23).[8] Roman Dilcher, instead, saw the polis and its *nómos* as an amalgamated total of 'rules, customs and forms of behaviour that are valid and followed in one city' (1995: 49). The matter of the so-called 'divine law' will prove to be even more of a difficult notion to decipher. This was evidently the subject of ancient questioning, as indicated in a fragment ascribed to Pythagoras which states:

> *Themis* in the realm of Zeus, *Dikē* in the world below, hold the same place and rank as *Nómos* in the cities of men; so that one who does not justly perform his appointed duty, may appear as a violator of the whole order of the universe. (Cornford [1912] 1957: 54)

Thus, I will revisit in more detail the key uses of *nómos* in Heraclitus and, crucially, the particular reference to the divine (*nómos*).

---

[8] On the pre-Socratics, see indicatively: Burnet (1945); Nietzsche (1962); Kirk et al. ([1957] 1983); Barnes (1983); Mourelatos (1994); Hussey (1995); and Diels and Kranz ([1903] 1952/2004).

2. *Nemō*

In Heraclitus' fr. 11, we encounter the verb νέμω (*nemō*) in the form of νέμεται (*nemetai*): πᾶν γὰρ ἑρπετὸν πληγῇ νέμεται (*plegē nemetai*).[9] It is worth referring first to the apparently unique source of the fragment that is considered to be a pseudo-Aristotelian cosmological treatise titled *De Mundo* (Περὶ Κόσμου), usually translated into English as *On the Universe*, and that should not be mistaken for Aristotle's *De Caelo* (Περὶ οὐρανοῦ; *On the Heavens*).[10] The authenticity of the treatise, in fact, was not questioned until the fifth century AD, and doubt intensified much later when it was considered that, in *De Mundo*, the god Aristotle allegedly presents in this text is significantly different from the non-creator and non-providential god of Aristotle's other work.[11] Yet in *De Mundo*, god is arguably not portrayed as a creator at all, but only as the source of all power (and phenomena), that is, of all vital force. In *De Mundo* at 400b31–401a11, the Heraclitean fragment in question is cited at the closing of a passage, which is rendered as follows:

Ἡγουμένου δὲ ἀκινήτως αὐτοῦ (*scil,* τοῦ θεοῦ) καὶ ἐμμελῶς ὁ σύμπας οἰκονομεῖται διάκοσμος [*ho sumpas oikonomeitai diakosmos*] οὐρανοῦ καὶ γῆς, μεμερισμένος κατὰ τὰς φύσεις πάσας διὰ τῶν οἰκείων σπερμάτων εἴς τε φυτὰ καὶ ζῷα κατὰ γένη τε καὶ εἴδη · καὶ γάρ ... τῶν τε ζώων τά τε ἄγρια καὶ ἥμερα, τά τε ἐν ἀέρι καὶ ἐπὶ γῆς καὶ ἐν ὕδατι βοσκόμενα, γίνεται καὶ ἀκμάζει καὶ φθείρεται τοῖς τοῦ θεοῦ πειθόμενα θεσμοῖς· πᾶν γὰρ ἑρπετὸν [τὴν γῆν] πληγῇ νέμεται, ὡς φησιν Ἡράκλειτος.[12]

Under the motionless and harmonious god the whole ordering [*diakosmos*] of heaven and earth is administered [*oikonomeitai*], apportioned according to [*phusis*] through

---

[9] All references to the fragments are from Diels and Kranz ([1903] 1952/2004).

[10] See Lallot (1972: 109–15).

[11] See Kraye (1990: 342).

[12] Bekkeri ([1831] 1987: 156) renders the crucial fragment as τὴν γῆν νέμεται (*tēn gēn nemetai*).

the seeds [*spermata*, of life] in plants and animals, between 'genera' and 'species' . . . and animals, both wild and tame, feeding in the air or on the earth or in the water, are all born and come to their prime and decay in obedience to the *thesmoi* of god for, in the words of Heraclitus, 'every creeping thing is driven to pasture [with a blow]'.[13]

In the treatise, the 'world' is the ordering or arrangement (*kosmos*) of all things (and their vital force or power) preserved by and through god (at 391b11–12). As will be seen later, this is not remote from Heraclitus' expressed thought on the One, god and *kosmos*. While I must here leave aside the differences between the Heraclitean and the pseudo-Aristotelian cosmological accounts, suffice it to note that the milieu within which the fragment of Heraclitus is referred to does appear proximate enough to the *theios nómos* (divine *nómos*) that I discuss below, as well as the central principle of the Heraclitean unity (and not identity) of differences among all existent beings and things.

The closing part of the fragment in question can be rendered in English as: 'every creeping thing is driven to pasture with a blow'. The use of *nemetai* in a pastoral sense is a use which is already familiar in the epics. It straightforwardly refers to all creeping things grazing, which embraces all animals that can creep, including human animals. Similarly, in Empedocles, the pre-Socratic philosopher who lived in the fifth century BC in southern Sicily, we encounter the description of shellfish as 'ocean-dwellers', which 'range the bottom of the sea', with the remarkable use of *nomōn*: τοῦτο μὲν ἐν κόγχαισι θαλασσονόμων [θαλασσονόμοις, *thalassonomois*] βαρυνώτοις (fr. B75).[14] It is true that at least another recording of the Heraclitean fragment renders it, instead, as νέμεται τήν γῆν (*nemetai tēn gēn*),[15] as indicated in brackets in the *De*

---

[13] For the Greek text, see Lorimer (1924–5; 1933); for an alternative translation, though proximate, see Thom (2014).

[14] On Empedocles, see Bollack (1965–9; 2003); O'Brien (1969; 1981; 1995); Gallavotti (1975); van der Ben (1975); Wright (1981); Inwood ([1992] 2001); Rossetti and Santaniello (2004); Trépanier (2004); and Casertano (2007).

[15] Kapp (1792: 309) renders τὴν γῆν (*tēn gēn*).

Mundo extract quoted, although this is not accepted by most later commentators, who accept, instead, the rendering of πληγῇ νέμεται (*plēgē nemetai*; i.e. Stobaeus; Apuleius; Diels, 80.1.8).[16] William L. Lorimer (1933: 98), to whom we owe the most detailed study and translation of this important treatise, accepts Diels' rendering.[17] Returning to this matter more recently, the French Hellenist and specialist in ancient Greek grammar Jean Lallot (1972) studied the extant manuscripts of *De Mundo* and reported that all the Greek manuscripts transmit the sentence in question in an identical form (with *plēgē*), and notes in particular the evidence in the Armenian, Syrian and Latin translations. Yet he also observed that there is another tradition that has *tēn gēn* instead of *plēgē*. As to the former, *plēgē* appears to be the rendering of Stob. 1.1.36, as well as of two sources outside of the pseudo-Aristotelian: Pl. *Critias*, at 109c, and in the late fourth to early third century BC the *Hymn to Zeus* by Cleanthes, a stoic philosopher who succeeded Zeno (at 5–12).[18] The sense attested here is that all beings are 'persuaded' by Zeus, the holder of the lightning. These late renderings have indeed convinced most interpreters, including the seminal editor and translator of the Heraclitean fragments Geoffrey Kirk ([1954] 1975: 258), who considered the two possible renderings of the fragment and reluctantly accepted *plēgē*.

If πληγῇ (*plēgē*) is accepted, then the fragment refers to a blow, which would most likely be a reference to the commonplace kick that one might give to a cow or donkey in a pastoral milieu (Kirk [1954] 1975: 260). If, instead, we were to read the fragment as merely referring to 'grazing the land', then the 'coherence' of the extract from the treatise would

---

[16] Tricot's French translation of *De Mundo* (1990: 202) renders it as '*car toute bête est poussée au pâturage par des coups, comme le dit Héraclite*'; the same is the case in Loffredo's Italian translation (1974: 184–5); and in the German translation by Strohm (1970, 258). The exceptional study of the treatise by Thom (2014: 54–5) accepts *plege nemetai* as well and translates the fragment as: 'For every animal is driven to pasture by a blow, as Heraclitus says.'

[17] Heidegger and Fink at the *Heraclitus Seminar* (1966/1967) appear to have read the standard rendering of the fragment as πληγῇ νέμεται (1979/1970: 31–2).

[18] See Lallot (1972: 110–11), with further references.

perhaps be distorted. Just before Heraclitus is quoted, the treatise describes the grazing of animals on land and in air and water that reach their prime and then decay according to the *thesmoi* (the 'sacred ordinances') of 'god'. Further, the presence of the word πειθόμενα (*peithomena*) is relevant – a word that we also meet in the epics and that entails a sense of being 'induced', 'led' or 'persuaded'.[19] Thus, perhaps it makes good sense to the author of the treatise to read in Heraclitus the term *plēgē*, at least in a parallel regard to 'being driven to pasture'.

Lallot critically notes the particular uses of this commonplace phrase, as for example in the *Critias*, where Plato differentiates mortals from animals on the basis that the stick is to cattle what (divine) persuasion is to mortals (1972: 112). He adds, however, that nothing in the *De Mundo* passage refers to a 'divine violence', so as to justify the *plēgē* (ibid.).[20] The alternative rendering of τήν γήν (*tēn gēn*), Lallot proposes, better relates to the context of the fragment. Heraclitus distinguishes the walking animal (*herpeton*; i.e. with its trunk parallel to the earth) from other animals by a single plateau or 'environment' – the surface of the earth – and by a particular affinity with the 'element of the earth' (ibid. 112–13). Lallot argues that *plēgē*, as recorded in Stobaeus and indirectly attested in the extant Armenian manuscript, could be explained as a late copying error 'itself facilitated by the existence of the quasi-proverbial expression πληγή νεμόμενα [*plēgē nemomena*]' (ibid. 112, n. 21).

Furthermore, for Lallot, Heraclitus' use of *herpeton*, in a broad sense, excludes the possibility of *nemetai* as meaning 'to graze' or 'feed'. Instead, he argues (in agreement with Laroche and Benveniste) that the 'primary value' of the root **nem-* (as 'regulated distribution'; note also the use of *memerismos* in the *De Mundo* passage), from which the pastoral senses later developed, is the early sense that Heraclitus

---

[19] In this regard, we can note the use of πείθεσθαι in fr. 33: νόμος καὶ βουλῆ πείθεσθαι ἑνός, 'there is also *nomos* in obeying the will of one' (Jaeger 1947: 127); or 'and it is *nomos*, too, to obey the counsel of one'.

[20] Lallot (1972: 113, n. 26) traces further the expression of *tēn gēn nemetai* in the neo-Platonic philosopher Aeneas of Gaza (c. 518 BC; Boissonade 1836: 10).

employs in the fragment: 'every being which, to move, finds
support on the earth, is, by right, sharing the land' (ibid. 113).
This interpretation matches, Lallot argues, the sense that the
author of *De Mundo* also employs, evidently, in the expression ὁ σύμπας οἰκονομεῖται διάκοσμος [*ho sumpas oikonomeitai diakosmos*]. For Lallot, it is 'by legal attribution (of the god)
that the *herpeta* occupy the earth. The land is their *nomós*
(*canton*) under a *nómos* (law)' (ibid. 113, n. 26). The manner
of the attribution as 'legal' in Lallot's use should be perhaps
understood in the general regulatory-distributory/sharing
sense of *nemein* we have repeatedly encountered, though to
what extent such a juridical (or other) sense of 'ordering the
universe' can be attributed to Heraclitus remains a question.

In the alternative rendering (with *plēgē*), human animals
(or their 'foolish majority') could, according to some commentators, be imagined as being driven (i.e. as being in need
of 'convincing') towards understanding of the heraclitean
logos.[21] While the author of the treatise may have had a
stronger sense in mind, it would not, perhaps, be Heraclitean
to consider such a 'being driven' in an absolute manner,
though this would not be due to the endorsing of a beating.
It would not be entirely un-Heraclitean (though, perhaps,
more so Orphic),[22] given that Heraclitus does bemoan the
deviation of human beings from the *logos* and of the *nómoi*
from the divine *nómos*, respectively (Kirk [1954] 1975: 262).
It is possible then, that the 'kick' as a 'kick of god' is not
Heraclitean, since one does not find support for this in any
of the other fragments, but rather an expression that fitted
the intention of the author of *De Mundo* (ibid. 261). That said,
an early sense of the relativity and non-absolutely obliging
sense of the human *nómoi* is quite evident in the fragment. In
any case, and for our purposes, it is probably best to separate
the fragment from the treatise and read it on its own. The
Heraclitean fragment uses *nemetai*, it seems to me, both in the
commonplace sense of 'grazing', with a possible extended
sense of 'being driven', and in the sense of 'an attribution'
and a 'distribution/sharing', though not necessarily in the

---

[21] See Kirk ([1954] 1975: 262).
[22] On the Orphic influence see, for example, the discussion in Heinimann
([1945] 1965/1972: 67–9).

strong sense of Lallot's interpretation (i.e. a *legal* attribution/ distribution), and we do know that the two senses merge later on to convey a notion of 'being steered' in the 'political'-rhetorical milieu of Heraclitus.[23]

More significantly, in Heraclitus, as well as in other so-called pre-Socratic philosophers, being 'driven' has the sense of being stirred up by the variously named 'rule or regularity' of the phenomena (*nómos*, *dikē*, *logos*, etc.). Crucially, as we shall see, this stirring up is immanent in the world, though dynamically so: that is, in constant (be)coming. It rests by changing. Thus, Lallot (1972) proposes an alternative, and still plausible, extension of interpretation. In Heraclitus' fr. 11, Lallot notes, the use of the article (*tēn*) before *gēn*: *tēn gēn*, if accepted, refers emphatically to earth as a cosmological 'state', rather than as a 'physical element' (like water, fire and air). That is, it is used in the sense of a state in the *palintropy* of becoming (similarly so in fr. 66; ibid. 114–15). The *tēn gēn* (the earth) in the fragment, then, refers to the earth as the pole of the *kosmos* that acts as a force on beings (opposed, Lallot states, to the 'ascensional force of the Fire') enabling them to inhabit the earth and share it (*nemesthai*; ibid.). Individuation in the common plateau of the earth happens only because of the counter-ascensional force that the Earth (*tēn gēn*) enables in the becoming of beings.

3. *Nomizein*

It is worth noting in passing, that in the Heraclitean fragments we also meet the verb νομίζειν (*nomizein*) in fr. 14 (τὰ γὰρ νομιζόμενα κατ' ἀνθρώπους μυστήρια ἀνιερωστὶ μυεῦνται), which was preserved by Clement of Alexandria (*Protr.* 22). The context of Clement's reference to Heraclitus is the patristic polemic against mystery cults and pagan divinatory practices.[24] In English, it can be rendered as 'the mysteries [possibly, of initiation] among men are recognised/

---

[23] For instance, the sense of steering (ἐκυβέρνησε, *hekubernēse*) in fr. B41, which is the only instance of this word in Heraclitus; or in Anaximander, fr. A15; and Parmenides, fr. B12.3.

[24] On the context, see Valentin (1958). On the cults, see, for instance, Burkert (1987).

practised in an impious (non-*hiera*) manner',[25] which may be read as an indication of the critical stance that Heraclitus appears to have held regarding, for instance, bloody 'sacrifices' (e.g. fr. 5) and other cult practices.[26] Incidentally, the interest of Heraclitus in cult practices is evident in five other fragments that directly refer to them: frs 5, 15, 68, 69 and 92.[27] In Clement's passage, which includes fr. 14, we read:

τίσι δὴ μαντεύεται Ἡράκλειτος ὁ Ἐφέσιος; νυκτιπόλοις, μάγοις, βάκχοις, λήναις, μύσταις· τούτοις ἀπειλεῖ τὰ μετὰ θάνατον, τούτοις μαντεύεται τὸ πῦρ· τὰ γὰρ νομιζόμενα κατ' ἀνθρώπους μυστήρια ἀνιερωστὶ μυοῦνται.

To whom does Heraclitus of Ephesus prophesy? To night-wanderers: Magi, Bacchants, Maenads, initiates in the mysteries. To these he threatens what comes after death, to these he prophesies the fire. For they are initiated impiously into the mysteries recognized/practiced among men.[28]

It is particularly difficult to determine which parts of this passage can be attributed to Clement and which to Heraclitus (other than perhaps most of the last sentence), although there are good indications that some elements of the preceding sentences are also Heraclitean given, for example, the reference to πῦρ (*pur*, fire).[29] For our purposes, the νομιζόμενα (*nomizomena*), in this fragment, probably refer to what is 'current' in the practices in question, or what is 'recognised' as such,

---

[25] For a detailed analysis of translation issues, see Babut (1975: 36).

[26] See fr. 5; on differing views on Heraclitus' 'critique' of such practices, see, for instance, Marcovich (1967); C. H. Kahn (1979: 263–6); and Conche (1986: 173).

[27] On Heraclitus and his stance on 'religion' as an early attempt at a 'philosophy of religion', see Adomènas (1999: 88–113).

[28] Modifying Most's translation (2013: 8).

[29] See Most (2013: 8–9). The famous fragment of Heraclitus as to fire (πῦρ) is fr. 30: κόσμον (τόνδε), τὸν αὐτὸν ἁπάντων, οὔτε τις θεῶν, οὔτε ἀνθρώπων ἐποίησεν, ἀλλ' ἦν ἀεὶ καὶ ἔστιν καὶ ἔσται πῦρ ἀείζωον [*pur aeizôon*], ἁπτόμενον μέτρα καὶ ἀποσβεννύμενον μέτρα. 'The ordering [*kosmos*], the same for all, neither god nor man has made, but it ever was, is and will be. Ever-living fire, kindled in measures and in measures extinguished.'

with a direct sense of customary conventions or norms among the *anthrōpoi* (mortals). In fact, in the extant fragments of another pre-Socratic philosopher, Empedocles, we find three relevant instances of such use in *nómos/nomimon*. In fr. 135, the *nomimon* appears to refer to a wide-ranging or universal *nómos* against, possibly, bloody 'sacrifice':

ἀλλὰ τὸ μὲν πάντων νόμιμο(ν) διά τ' εὐρυμέδοντος
αἰθέρος ἠνεκέως τέταται διά τ' ἀπλέτου αὐγῆς.

But the wide *nomimo*[n] of all extends throughout
Broad-ruling ether and the vast white sky.

Similarly, though in a more vivid distinction with *themis* (what is prescribed as 'sacred right'), in fr. 9 (at 5) we read: ἣ θέμις [οὐ] καλέουσι, νόμωι [*nómōi*] δ' ἐπίφημι καὶ αὐτός. Here, Empedocles says that while it is not *themis* to speak of dissolution as a dreadful fate, he will instead follow the *nómos*, namely what is customary common usage (*nomize-tai*), and do so. Finally, in fr. 17 (at 22) we read: ἥτις καὶ θνητοῖσι νομίζεται [*nomizetai*] ἔμφυτος ἄρθροις (she [Love] is acknowledged even by mortals to be inborn in their limbs).[30]

4. Fr. 114

We can now turn our attention to the most significant fragment, fr. 114, which is preserved in Stobaeus as follows:

ξὺν νόῳ λέγοντας ἰσχυρίζεσθαι χρὴ τῷ ξυνῷ πάντων,
ὅκωσπερ νόμῳ πόλις καὶ πολὺ ἰσχυροτέρως· τρέφονται
γὰρ πάντες οἱ ἀνθρώπειοι νόμοι ὑπὸ ἑνὸς τοῦ θείου·
κρατεῖ γὰρ τοσοῦτον ὁκόσον ἐθέλει καὶ ἐξαρκεῖ πᾶσι καὶ
περιγίνεται.[31]

Kirk translated the fragment in the early 1950s in the following way:

---

[30] Inwood ([1992] 2001: 59–60).

[31] On this fragment, see Gigon (1935: 13–14); Mourelatos (1965: 258–66); and Marcovich (1999: 95).

Those who speak with sense must rely on what is common to all, as a city must rely on its law, and with much greater reliance: for all the laws of men are nourished by one law, the divine law; for it has as much power as it wishes and is sufficient for all and is still left over. ([1954] 1975: 48)

It is necessary to consider some of the fragment's key terms in some detail, while noting with caution that it is probably impossible to determine whether this fragment is to be read as a unit or, instead, as a part of a composition of numerous other fragments.[32] The importance of the fragment is obvious and, for Jaeger, as noted earlier, this is the point where for 'the first time' the idea of 'law' (νόμῳ, *nómō*) has appeared in philosophical thought as the 'the object of the highest and most universal knowledge', and, yet, he adds, this is not a political *nómos*. Instead, this shift in meaning, Jaeger writes, 'has already been foreshadowed by the designation of the world as an ordering-together or *kosmos*' (1947: 115–16). In this sense, for Jaeger, the *theios nómos* or 'divine law' is to be understood normatively as a kind of 'law of all laws' (ibid. 116). For Felix Heinimann, too, human *nómos* is an objective order 'above the individual and even over the community and it governs their lives' ([1945] 1965/1972: 66). Such human *nómos* is 'nourished by the divine law' but is not, however, identical with the superior divine *nómos*. *Theios nómos* lies high above all human *nómoi* and it stands as the one, *xunos*, the common, *logos* that Heraclitus invites citizens to understand in order to enhance their intelligence (ibid. 67).

Let us begin our reading anew in order to consider first how the term *nómos* is utilised in the fragment. For Kirk, agreeing with Heinimann, the term *nómos* functions in the fragment as a simile. Thus, Heraclitus' key point is that those with intelligence will do well to order their thought according to what is *xunon* ('common'; and for Kirk, this is no other than the *logos*) and to do so in a manner akin to the way in which a city orders or structures itself according to its *nómoi*.[33] Kirk's emphasis rests on the manner or intensity of this similitude: citizens should order their thought even more

---

[32] See Schofield (2015: 48, n. 1).
[33] See also Mourelatos (1965: 251).

199

so (than the city orders itself by *nómos*), since human laws are inferior to the absolute 'law' of the One, god ([1954] 1975: 51–5). For Kirk, the laws (*nómoi*) of the city are common to the citizens of a particular city-state, while what is common to all (beyond the particular city-state) is the *logos* (as expressed in, for instance, fr. 1). This means that *logos* is 'operative' in all things, and as such it ensures the unity of all different things (ibid. 55). While Kirk and Heinimann understood *nómos/nómoi* as 'law/laws', Karl Reinhardt argued that the *nómoi* of the city refer, instead, to the precepts or habits of human beings in general ([1916] 2012: 215–16); and Olof Gigon understood as *nómoi* a plural form of the *xunon*, and thus 'the whole genus of common truths and realities' (1935: 14). In any event, the Heraclitean plea is that 'men should follow the *xunon*' (Mourelatos 1965: 258).

Alexander Mourelatos writes: 'What is novel in the fragment is the conception of the relation of human intelligence to the [*xunon pantōn*]' (1965: 259). Given that there is no explicit reference to the 'divine law' in the fragment, it is possible to understand it as referring to the *xunon* or *logos*[34] that need not be identified with a/the 'divine law'. As Mourelatos points out, it remains possible to read the designation τοῦ θείου [*tou theiou*] in a manner similar to that of fr. 32: ἓν τὸ σοφὸν μοῦνον λέγεσθαι οὐκ ἐθέλει καὶ ἐθέλει Ζηνὸς ὄνομα

---

[34] *Logos*, from the verbal noun *legō*, early on meaning 'to recount, gather or collect' (in Homer and Hesiod) and in the derived sense of 'to speak' (for example, *Od.* 1.56 and *Il.* 15.393). In Heraclitus *logos* is not a *nómos*-law (an idea, instead, which is probably neo-Platonic) or reason. Crucially, too, the Heraclitean *logos* indicates an action, expressed in poetic-experiential terms, with possible Pythagorean influence. The action in question is most likely the action of the living *kosmos*, in the breath of everything living wherein change is inherent in the unifying ordering of the juncture between all things. In this sense, if it is proximate to a *nómos* then it is to the *nómos* understood as usage, norms of experience. It would be a mistake, in my view, to read Heraclitus as the thinker of change; if he was interested so vividly in the musical rhythm of strife and differentiation, it was because he was in search of regularity and *harmonia* (*harmoniē*): or rather, the fact that identity and difference are inseparable, to use Heidegger's phrase, since it is the 'world that worlds', 'without why' (1991: 112–13). On *logos* in Heraclitus, see Minar (1939); Verdenius (1966; 1967); Heidegger and Fink (1970/1979); Veikos ([1979] 1985); Darcus (1979a; 1979b); Bartling (1985); Heidsieck (1986); and Bollack (1990).

('wisdom is one only; it is willing and unwilling to be called by the name of Zeus'). The divine, in other words, is the One (ἓν, hen; to which I turn below), the *xunon pantōn*, the One-All, the *logos*.[35] The *logos* is not a juridical 'law', but in the use of the simile in this fragment it could be said that the law's relation to the *xunon* serves as a convenient analogy for the *logos* of the *kosmos*: the cosmological source of All, including the *nómoi*.[36] The *xunon* can be understood as a 'law', in the sense of a cosmological *nómos*, which is the One and the most common among different things/beings at the same time (a *kosmonomos*).[37] Human *nómoi* are particulars, while the divine One or *Nómos*, the One-All (*Hen-Pan*), is, in a sense, 'universal'. On this basis, some have argued for the 'variability' or 'relativity' of human *nómoi*, which differ from community to community, and, as the only genuine commonality of sense, the *theios* (the 'divine').[38] A reference to intelligence, or the *noos*, is made here in one interpretation, through the etymologising Heraclitean word-play between ξυνῶι (*xunōi*, 'common') and ξὺννόωι (*xunnoōi*, 'with sense'). What is held as the most common, the 'divine', is in this manner inherent in all beings (Kirk [1954] 1975: 52–4).

It is then to the understanding of the *theios* (divine *nómos*) that we need to turn, if we are to advance our understanding further. Yet the fragment is not very clear on this. Kahn writes in this regard:

> We can see why the *nomos*, the public law and moral tradition of a city like Ephesus, should be chosen as an illustration of what produces sound thinking, but why it is only an illustration. It is common, but not common enough: common to all Ephesians but not common to all men and all things. As a result, in the search for soundness of mind one must hold on to something stronger, the source not

[35] See Minar (1939).
[36] See ibid. 259.
[37] See Heinimann ([1945] 1965/1972: 65–6), Jaeger (1947: 115) and Kirk ([1954] 1975: 48–56), who reach the same conclusion, though in differing ways, as to the *xunon* being the one and common *nómos* in the fragment.
[38] See Kirk ([1954] 1975: 52 and 54); and Bollack and Wismann ([1972] 2001: 317–18).

only of this but of 'all human laws' . . . Heraclitus hints at, but does not express the notion of a 'divine law' *theios nomos*. Instead he leaves us with a characterization of the common as 'the divine one'. (C. H. Kahn 1979: 118)

What does the *theios* refer to? Not a higher 'law'. Gigon (1935) went so far as to compare the *theios* (*nómos*) to the *agraphos nómos* (unwritten 'law'). It is not, however, entirely clear whether one could understand Heraclitus to mean by the term 'divine' a 'divine law' (surmised by the arguable distinction in the fragment between it and human *nómoi*), or the higher or 'divine' dimension of existence/reality (which the last line of the fragment, characterising the *theios* as impervious, may suggest). Irrespective of which is more fitting, Malcolm Schofield maintains that what is key to the fragment is the relation between the two, the human *nómoi* and the *theios* (*nómos*), and that, in fact, the 'divine' marks and maintains the human 'law' (2015: 52). Kirk writes:

Men who want to behave intelligently must base their behaviour on the formula or rule which operates in (and can be detected in) all things. So, in the narrower social sphere, citizens base their behaviour on that which is accepted to be of universal application in all local matters, namely the law of their city. But the reason for following the rule underlying all things is even stronger than for obeying city laws: city laws are not shared in common by and applicable to all men absolutely, but only to the citizens of a particular city-state, while 'what is common to all' (that is, the *logos* of fr. B1) has no such restrictions, but is analogous to the single divine law of which particular codes of law are merely offshoots. Being such, it is even more to be relied on in determining behaviour in its sphere than are city laws in their sphere. ([1954] 1975: 51)

The human *nómoi*, to be effective, Schofield proposes, need to coincide with the one 'law' which 'controls not merely a particular society of men but the whole complex of existing things, animate and inanimate' (2015: 54). But, as he writes, 'the relationship was not simply one of imitation on the part of human laws: divine law played its part in a concrete

manner, as is implied by the term τρέφονται [*trephontai*]'
(ibid.).

It is to the latter characterisation of the relation between
human *nómoi* and the divine that I turn next. For a moment,
suffice it to note that in all such interpretations the supremacy
of the *theios* (*nómos*) is not placed in doubt. Schofield puts
it somewhat anachronistically: 'In the final sentence of the
fragment the relationship implied here is elucidated by the
characteristics of complete power and sufficiency which are
those of a *theos*' (2015, 53); perhaps, as Theophilos Veikos had
written earlier, the '*Theios nomos, logos, xunon, panta*, etc., are
names for the impersonal absolute' ([1979] 1985: 411).

For Mourelatos, further, this comes close to signifying a
relation of 'subjects' to a 'sovereign' power. In the last sentence of the fragment – which he translates as 'For it rules
as far as it wills and succeeds in defending all (laws) and
prevails over (them)' – Mourelatos finds the manner of a
sovereign power with unlimited jurisdiction: 'it protects, but
also controls. It both guarantees all human laws, but can also
overrule them on appeal' (1965: 262).[39] The terms he uses
are, it seems to me, quite misleading, while it is in any case
uncertain, to say the least, whether Heraclitus would utilise
such an analogy of a near 'juridical sovereignty' in the first
place. For Heraclitus, the divine (*nómos*) is not a pattern or an
objective order to be imitated or adapted in mortal reality.[40]
The boundary, if there ever was one, between the divine and
the mortals, or, equally, *phusis* and the mortal *nómoi*, is not a
'juridical' problem that needs to be 'constitutionally' solved:
the *nómos* and the *nómoi*, *phusis* and 'culture' are con-figured
or com-posed.

It is worth examining the peculiar term τρέφονται (*trefon-*
tai) at this point to seek further clues for the interpretation

---

[39] Mourelatos's warning is worth noting: 'it is important to note that when
the [pre-Socratic] Pluralists speak of a δύναμις [*dunamis*] or "power"
present in a fundamental constituent they must be taken to imply a
power that is continuously, even eternally manifest; nothing like the
Aristotelian scheme of potencies that are triggered into actualities can
be presupposed . . .' (1986: 135). In this regard, it is perhaps pertinent to
suggest that Mourelatos's own conception of a 'sovereign' power betrays
his warning of separating the divine from mortal powers.

[40] Contrast the reading by, for instance, McKirahan (1994: 148).

of the fragment. Many scholars have translated this term as meaning 'nourished' or 'fed' – for example, among others, Kirk ([1954]/1962: 48–50); Guthrie (1962); Burnet (1945); and Kahn (1973: 43). In contrast, Mourelatos reads the Homeric roots of the use of the word in Heraclitus and prefers the supposedly earlier understanding: neither 'nurtured', nor 'brought up', nor 'feeding'. Instead, he favours 'protected' or 'guarded' (1965: 262–3): 'the core idea of τρέφω [*trephō*] is "to shelter, to protect, to keep safe, to preserve intact"'; in some contrast to what Benveniste (1966: 93) thought when he translated it as 'to promote natural growth'.[41] The earlier pastoral context was intact in Homeric usage: the sense is akin to that of the herdsman in relation to his cattle. Thus, Mourelatos concludes: 'Human laws are immature, tender and weak and they are "under the wardship" of divine law' (1965: 264). The divine *nómos* is 'the τροφός [*trophós*] of human institutions: it guards their integrity; preserves them inviolate' (ibid. 264). Mourelatos translates the fragment as follows:

> Those who gauge things with intelligence must rely on what to all is common, as the city relies on law, and even more firmly: for all human laws are under wardship to one, the divine (law); for it rules as far as it wills and protects all (laws) and prevails over (them). (1965: 265)[42]

Shirley Darcus (Sullivan), in turn, adds, along similar lines:

> Men must speak with *noos* and base their strength on what is common to all just as does a city in its law and much more firmly. For all the human laws are nurtured under the one divine law; for it rules as far as it wishes and suffices for all and prevails. (1974: 402)[43]

This fragment indicates that the human and the divine were held by Heraclitus as distinct, while intimately related. The

[41] For a discussion of the significance of τρέφονται [*trephontai*], see Kirk ([1954] 1975: 53–5); Mourelatos (1965: 262–4); and Marcovich (1999: 95).

[42] See Kahn (1973: 43).

[43] On *noos/noein*, see von Fritz (1945/1946); Kirk ([1954] 1975: 48–56); and Marcovich (1999: 91).

theios nómos stands apart from the *anthrōpeioi nómoi*, but it is their 'source and guardian'.[44] For Darcus, this means that, as she put it: 'It is in its *nómoi* that a city comes into contact with the source of its laws, the one Divine *Nómos*. The city by its laws shares in the nature of Divine in its aspect as *Nómos*' (1974: 404). This relation is not one of sustenance or 'juridico-political sovereignty', however, but of cosmological exis-tential power (as the terms κρατεῖ [*kratei*] and περιγίνεται [*periginetai*] imply).[45]

For a better understanding of the fragment we need to inquire further into the Heraclitean One (*hen*). To begin with, it is important to note that the notion of the One in Heraclitus is central to his thought with regard to a par-ticular kind of dynamic unity, as is illustrated by numer-ous fragments, such as 2, 10, 32, 88, 89, 106 and 114.[46] The divine (*nómos*) is singular and not directly comprehensible by mortals (e.g. fr. 86), given that it is not determined by human knowledge (e.g. fr. 50), though inherent in it. The *theion* or 'god' in Heraclitus is not anthropomorphic and is not a principle, other than the dynamic unity (*xunon*) and marking of all opposites (most expressly present in the indifferent *polemos*), for which Heraclitean thought is well-known (e.g. fr. 67: ὁ θεὸς ἡμέρη εὐφρόνη, χειμὼν θέρος, πόλεμος εἰρήνη.). It may or may not be called 'Zeus', as it is called in the Homeric epics, but in Heraclitus it surpasses the human naming of the One. The world, as fr. 84 states, μεταβάλλον ἀναπαύεται καὶ κάματός ἐστι τοῖς αὐτοῖς μοχθεῖν καὶ ἄρχεσθαι. The *hen* rests (*anapauetai*), we read here, as it becomes or turns (*metaballon*). The divine *nómos*, in this sense, can be said to be unable to rest without opposi-tion and the opposites (or relative singularities) cannot be so without the dynamic harmony that unites them (without, nonetheless, reducing them into an identity). Fragment 124

---

[44] In fr. 78 Heraclitus distinguishes, arguably similarly, between the *theion ēthos* (divine *ēthos*) and *anthrōpeion ēthos* (human *ēthos*).

[45] Compare the interpretations by Mouraviev (1999–2008, 2006: vol. III.3.B/i, 291); Graham (2010: I 175); Mansfeld and Primavesi (2011: 285); and Schofield (2015: 52–5).

[46] Indirect reference to the *Hen* or One is made in frs 1, 8, 10, 51, 90, 91, 102 and 103.

states: 'The fairest order [*kosmos*] in the world is a heap of random sweepings.'[47] But it is an ordering.

This is the heart, if there is such a thing, of Heraclitean thought, in fact, the *Hen-Pan* (One-All), the *kosmos*, the *theios nómos* are different names of the Same. It is τὸ πᾶν διαιρετὸν ἀδιαίρετον, γενητὸν ἀγένητον, θνητὸν ἀθάνατον . . . (fr. 50).[48] From all is one and from the one are all: '. . . καὶ ἐκ πάντων ἐν καὶ ἐξ ἑνός πάντα' (fr. 10).[49] I propose, thus, that fr. 33, 'νόμος καὶ βουλῇ πείθεσθαι ἑνός', be understood in this manner: 'and it is *nómos* to follow the counsel of the One'.[50] While in Homer there are 'political' connotations to the metaphoric use of the *nemein* family of words (Mourelatos 1965: 258–66),[51] and while some such use is maintained in Heraclitus, the primary sense in which his thought is to be understood is cosmological or *cosmonomical*. Kahn observes: 'the most familiar of all the overtones of the phrase "the *boulē* of one" is "the plan of Zeus" (*Dios boulē*) announced in the proem to the *Iliad*, the plan and power of the supreme deity' (C. H. Kahn 1979: 181).[52] But the *theion* is not an absolute or a plan in Heraclitus, but the dynamic *Hen-Pan*, the One-All that is the *xunon* ('which wants to be called Zeus as much as not so'). In this particular sense, fr. 33 does indeed 'echo the thought' of fr. 114 (C. H. Kahn 1979: 179).

While the reference to the human *nómoi* in fr. 114 may be a simile, it is not just a simile. We learn from fr. 114 that the human *nómoi* find their source in and are guarded by the one divine *nómos*, the One-All, bringing the 'juridico-political' and the cosmic into unity (rather than mere opposi-

---

47 '. . . ὥσπερ σάρμα εἰκῇ κεχυμένον ὁ κάλλιστος, φησὶν Ἡράκλειτος, [ὁ] κόσμος.' The translation is C. H. Kahn's (1979).

48 In full the fragment reads: Ἡ. μὲν οὖν ἔνφησιν εἶναι τὸ πᾶν διαιρετὸν ἀδιαίρετον, γενητὸν ἀγένητον, θνητὸν ἀθάνατον, λόγον αἰῶνα, πατέρα υἱόν, θεὸν δίκαιον· οὐκ ἐμοῦ, ἀλλὰ τοῦ λόγου ἀκούσαντας ὁμολογεῖν σοφόν ἐστιν ἐν πάντα εἶναί.

49 On Heraclitus' One, see also Papamichael-Paspalides (2005: 41–54); and Axelos (1962).

50 Jaeger, for instance, translates it as 'there is also *nomos* in obeying the will of one' (1947: 127). While a 'juridico-political' interpretation remains possible, of course, the sense proposed here is cosmological.

51 See also Dilcher (1995: 50–1); and the discussion in Schofield (2015).

52 See also Marcovich (1967: 537).

tion). Schofield insists that it is crucial not to misunderstand Heraclitus as if he were a 'simple fatalist' (2015: 56), since he holds 'that the people must do all they can to ensure that the rule of law is upheld' (ibid.).[53] Indeed, 'the paradoxical message' that Heraclitus conveys 'is quite the opposite of that, subverting expectation as we know him to do. Human law is not merely human. It is maintained by divine power, which accomplishes whatever is the divine will' (ibid.). The human *nómoi* are limited, in comparison to the divine, and they deviate from the cosmic *nómos*, yet in this context they are not separated or merely differentiated from the cosmic *nómos*, but instead remain a part of it – a part of what is most powerfully common (*xunon*).

5. *Palinomia*

Martin Heidegger, with reference to fr. 114, writes in *An Introduction to Metaphysics*:

> *Eon*, being [*das Seiend*], is according to its nature *xunon*, assembled presencing [*gesammeltes Anwesen*]; *xunon* does not mean the 'universal', but that which in itself gathers and holds it together. Such a *xunon* is, for example, according to Fragment 114, the *nomos* of the polis, the statute (institution as con-vention), the inner structure of the polis, not a universal, not something that hovers over all and touches none, but 'the original unifying unity of what tends apart' [*die ursprünglich einigende Einheit des Auseinanderstrebenden*]. ([1953] 1959: 100)

In Heidegger's sense, the *nómoi* (or laws) of the polis are not 'common' in the manner of an equivocal distribution, but as what gathers or assembles (*legein*) all differences into the common that the polis itself is: a *nómos*, however, that is mythologically crafted as the *agrapha nomima*. The *nómos* (which Heidegger problematically translates also as 'statute' [*Satzung*]) does not pre-exist the polis, it is cosmologically composed with it; the *nómos* is, in other words, 'a convention

---

[53] See fr. 44.

... which arises through the convening of human beings' (Schufreider 1981: 34). The *nómos* does not pre-exist the *kosmos* of human beings (a 'convening' that *is*, for Heidegger, *polemos*-strife). Such convening, which is, crucially, understood as other than an indifferent unity or a universal, is the *xunon*, which is, in turn, no other than the *theios* (*nómos*) or 'god'. The *theios nómos* finds its dynamic place and source in the *kosmos* (a *kosmos* that is 'neither mortal nor god-created'). Similarly, strife (*polemos*) is not 'political' or 'social', but a cosmological power, a *dunamis*. If there is *harmonia* in the world it is the same as the harmony of the universe (*sum-pan*): namely, a dynamic unity of differences and discordances.

The high importance of *nómos*, for Heraclitus, becomes ever clearer in fr. 44: μάχεσθαι χρή τὸν δῆμον ὑπὲρ τοῦ νόμου ὄκωσπερ τείχεος. The fragment is also rendered by Diogenes Laertius as: μάχεσθαι χρὴ τὸν δῆμον ὑπὲρ τοῦ νόμου ὑπὲρ τοῦ γινομένου ὅκως ὑπὲρ τείχεος.[54] We can translate the fragment, without much significant variation between the two renderings, as follows: 'the *dēmos* must fight for the *nómos* as they would for the walls (the fortifications) of the polis'. Here, we cannot miss the importance of the *nómos*; the supposed action (and role) of the mortals in defending it; and the necessity of such action or strife. Schofield locates, at this point, a sense in which the *nómos* gives the city strength, while its people (the *dēmos*) must fight vigorously for its defence (2015: 58). As he puts it, this implies that 'for Heraclitus one way in which the divine will maintaining a city's law will prevail is through human attempts to live in accordance with law and to do what they can to ensure that their political communities are law-governed' (ibid.). But which 'law'?

The sense of *nómos* in the fragment is open to multiple interpretations. It could refer to the 'law' of the polis, but equally to the customs, norms or conventions of usage and living. Lastly, it could be understood as referring to the *nómos* of the cosmic ordering. For Erik Wolf, it would be wrong to understand such a cosmic order as a kind of 'world law' (1950–70: 269, n. 3). The *nómos*, he writes, is 'an original bond to the *Logos* ... [and] *Nomos* also has the sense of historical-

---

[54] See Marcovich (1999: xii–xiv).

political existence, self-realization, what enables the polis to be in order' (ibid. 271). Heinimann understands *nómos* in this fragment as referring to 'the customs and universally recognized standards of thought' ([1945] 1965/1972: 68), which are at the same time the binding ordinances of the *theios nómos*. Further, he reads a possible Orphic influence in the high regard for the *nómos* and suggests that Heraclitus points to the insight 'that the actual human *nómoi* are not absolutely obliging' and hence must be defended (ibid.). Meanwhile, the intensity with which the need to defend the *nómos* is expressed in the fragment may suggest that what is at stake is not, merely, the human *nómoi* of the polis (or their relativity), but their original common grounding and vital force, the *theios nómos*, of which and in which mortals are.

The sense of *nómos* in Heraclitus, Eric Voegelin has proposed, attests to a number of uses:

(1) *Nomos* as the transcendent divine order; (2) We are like the constitutional and legal order of a polis in conformity with the transcendent order – the *nomos* by which the people should fight as if it were their wall (B 44); (3) *Nomoi* in the plural, meaning the multiplicity of orders of the historically existing poleis; (4) We are like the historical order of the polis, independent of its conformity with the divine *nomos*; (5) We are as the order that can live in a man, a *nomos emphysicos* – as it may appear in a *nomothetēs*, or the platonic king-philosopher . . . [B33]; and (6) *Nomoi* in the plural, which quite possibly takes the association of *nomoi* in the sense of statutes, as has become usual from the reform of Cleisthenes, replacing the ancient *thesmoi*. (1956: 306)

Voegelin's schematic list is not, however, to be understood as a categorisation of unrelated notions of *nómos*. While the difference between human *nómoi* and the divine *nómos* is present in Heraclitean thought, in one sense, it is so in order to indicate something other than a constitutional differentiation or hierarchy. In contrast to the ancient doxographic accounts of Heraclitus' thought, as well as its late modern compartmentalisation by philologists and philosophers, Heraclitus was neither a philosopher of *phusis* nor a philosopher of the polis:

neither a theologian nor a legal philosopher. This is so since in his thought the polis and *phusis* are not separable, and thus we cannot understand his thought if we think of it as, say, an early episode of the *nómos–phusis* debate of the fifth century BC, or equally as the separation of a transcendent and an immanent *nómos*.

Kostas Axelos is the philosopher who observed the non-compartmentalisation of Heraclitus' thought most attentively, in his *Héraclite et la Philosophie* (1962). Nowhere does Heraclitus speak of what ought to be, of an absolute normativity. What is must be as it is (or becomes), since it is as such that it forms a part of the *sum-pan* (σύμπαν [*sum-pan*], the co-versing of the uni-verse). When Heraclitus says that the people must defend or protect the *nómos* as if it were their polis or the walls of the polis, he is not, I would maintain, referring to the *nómoi* of the polis, the statutes or rules that his fellow citizens had made or the ones that they unconvincingly asked him to devise. It is not these *nómoi* that need to be defended, since such *nómoi* can easily be corrupted or misapplied. There is, at the same time, no Archimedean point in Heraclitus' thought that would need to be 'defended' either. There is primarily *polemos*: his most fundamental thought. Such 'strife' shows not the royal road to 'justice' or to the coherence of the *nómos* of the universe with the *nómos* of the polis and vice versa. Rather, 'strife' itself is the juncture where these roads meet, each time; and it is the harmony of 'strife' that needs to be heard, rather than a dystopic or utopian resolution of it in the disparity of differences.

Instead of some kind of fatalistic or revolutionary ideal of 'freedom' or 'justice', Heraclitus observes what binds and unbinds the mortals to the polis and what binds the polis to the divine or co-versing *nómos*. At this binding juncture and disjuncture, the human *nómos* pursues indefinitely the divine (*nómos*), through strife or discord, that is, life and death.[55] Which is to say that the nature of *polemos*, which *is* the polis, the *nómos* and *dikē* (the essence of *nómos*), is irreparably imperfect. As fr. 45 states: ψυχῆ πείρατα ἰὼν οὐκ ἂν ἐξεύροιο, πᾶσαν ἐπιπορευόμενος ὁδόν· οὕτω βαθὺν λόγον ἔχει ('you

---

[55] See Axelos (1962: especially ch. 2).

cannot find the ends of the *psuchē*, whichever direction you travel towards'). The *theios nómos* is dynamically immanent (it is, after all, strife as such), and that is also what unites the inherently discordant juncture of the polis. Kahn writes then that, for Heraclitus, 'there is no split in principle between *nómos* and nature. As an institution, law is neither man-made nor conventional: it is the expression in social terms of the cosmic order' (C. H. Kahn 1979: 15). If this is so, it is in the sense that Heraclitus' *nómos* is dynamically *palintropos*,[56] a *palinomia*, a dynamic rhythm which must be heard in his uses of *nómos*.[57]

---

[56] *Palintropos* (παλίντροπος) is primarily 'back-turning', in the sense of moving to a contrary or opposite direction, signifying change and by extension possibly reversal. In Heraclitus, the central phrasing is *palintropos harmoniē*, and here as ever *harmoniē* means primarily fittingness, adaptation or adjustment with and through change. Physical, but also crucially cosmological (strife), in the sense in which I read Heraclitus more generally here. On *palintropos*, see also frs 94 and 120, Parm. B6, 9 and C. H. Kahn (1979: 199), as well as the Theophrastian synonym *enantiotropēs* (Diog. Laert. 9.7).

[57] I thank Giovanni Panno for our discussion of this chapter. My initial inspiration for a reading of Heraclitus I owe to Kostas Axelos.

Eight
Nomos Basileus

Πλάτων καὶ Πίνδαρος πολλαχῆι μὲν καὶ ἄλληι σοφοί
Ael. Arist. *Or.* 34. 5[1]

Μαντεύεο, Μοῖσα, προφατεύσω δ'ἐγώ
Pind. fr. 150 [Snell-Maehler][2]

εἶα τειχίζωμεν ἤδη ποικίλον
κόσμον αὐδάεντα λόγων
Pind. fr. 194 [Schröder] 1–3[3]

1. Pindar's *nemein*

Pindar, one of the greatest poets of the ancient world, was born of a noble family between c. 522 and 518 BC at Cynoscephalae, near Thebes, the capital of Boeotia in central Greece. He never, so far as we know, describes himself as a poet. Instead, he does, on occasion, call himself a prophet (προφάτας, *prophatas*; *Pae.* 6.6; fr. 150). This may approximate, to an extent, the manner of a poet, in that the poetic and the prophetic were closely identified in the fifth century BC.[4] He was trained in music in Athens (in the flute and the lyre) and he later became a professional composer of lyrics (hymns, *partheneia*,

---

[1] 'Plato and Pindar in various different respects are *sophoi*.'
[2] 'Conduct the divination, Oh Muse, I, as prophet.'
[3] 'Come then: let us now build a variegated, sounding ornament [*kosmon*] of words.'
[4] See Duchemin (1955); Theunissen, in his seminal study *Pindar: Menschenlos und Wende der Zeit*, calls Pindar a 'poet-thinker' (*dichterdenker*) (2000: 7). On the prophetic and the poetic, see, for instance, Nagy (1990); and Détienne (1996).

dithyrambs, paeans, *hyporchēmata, encomia,* dirges and odes).[5] His work, comprising at least seventeen books, once collected at the great library at Alexandria, is largely lost to us. Only four of these books survive today, along with various fragments preserved by scholiasts and later authors' quotations, and through the work of archaeologists at the excavations near Oxyrhynchus (modern El-Bahnasa) in Egypt, who discovered papyri containing remnants of Pindar's work at an ancient rubbish dump.

I begin by examining the key instances of the *nemein/nemō* family of words and the related, which are of particular interest in the Boeotian poet.[6] The use of the verb *nemō,* in the sense of 'watching over' or 'keeping', is, for example, met with in *O.* 2.12, ὦ Κρόνιε παῖ Ῥέας, ἕδος Ὀλύμπου νέμων [*nemōn*] (and also in *O.* 3.36; 10.13; 13.27; *Isthm.* 1.67; *P.* 3.70). In the sense of 'to cultivate' and possibly 'to inhabit fields of land', we find the verb used in *P.* 4.150: ἀγρούς τε πάντας, τοὺς ἀπούρας ἀμετέρων τοκέων νέμεαι [*nemeai*] (also in *O.* 9.27); and in *P.* 11.55, where dwelling peacefully [*nemomenos*] in the marshes is said to avoid *hubris:* τίς ἄκρον ἑλὼν ἡσυχᾷ τε νεμόμενος [*nemomenos*] αἰνὰν ὕβριν ἀπέφυγεν. In the further sense of 'directing or placing' parts of the body, in particular the feet, we read in *N.* 6.15: ἴχνεσιν ἐν Πραξιδάμαντος ἑὸν πόδα νέμων [*nemōn*] (also met with in *Isthm.* 2.22).[7]

We also meet the use of νωμάω (*nōmaō*), meaning 'to ply, wield, or yield' (Slater 1969) within a range of acts, such as chariot-driving in reference to animals: ἀνία τ᾽ ἀντ ἐρετμῶν δίφρους τε νωμάσοισιν [*nōmasoisin*] (*P.* 4.18).[8] Metaphorically

---

[5] On these biographical details, see Norwood (1945: 1–43). On Pindar's poetry more generally, see Gundert (1935); Perotta (1935); Burton (1962); Bowra (1964); Farnell (1965); Crotty (1982); Croiset (1985); Bundy (1986); Burnett (2005); Currie (2005).

[6] For Pindar's text, I follow Snell and Maehler ([Pindar] 1997) and for the fragments, Maehler (1975; 2001), unless otherwise indicated. I also consulted, in particular, Bowra (1964); Bundy (1986) and Race (1997). All translations are by Svarlien (1991), unless otherwise indicated. Note that I omit from consideration the uses of *nómos* in the sense of a 'tune' or 'melody'; on these, see Chapter Ten.

[7] Slater (1969). We also find the use of the verb in a variety of fragments, such as in fr. 215b9 (νέομαι, *neomai;* νέμομαι, *nemomai*), though not certain; and similarly, in fr. 333d (ἀρετάν τε νέμεις; *aretan te nemeis*).

[8] See also I. 2.22: νεῖμ᾽ [*neim'*] ἀπάσαις ἀνίαις.

the same act is expressed in ἀνία τ᾽ ἀλλοτρίαις οὐ χερσὶ νωμάσαντ [*nomasant'*] ἐθέλω - ἐναρμόξαι μιν ὕμνῳ (*Isthm.* 1.15) to signify managing 'the reins' with one's own hands as opposed to another's. Similarly, the 'wielding' of weapons, in this case a shield, is expressed in θαέομαι σαφὲς δράκοντα ποικίλον αἰθᾶς Ἀλκμᾶν᾽ ἐπ ἀσπίδος νωμῶντα [*nōmōnta*] (*P.* 8.47); as well as (with possible reference to Heracles' famous club) in πολλὰ δ᾽ ἕλκε ἔμβαλλε νωμῶν [*nōmōn*] τραχὺ ῥόπαλον (fr. 111, 2). In a wider frame, we find the same sense in terms of 'steering' an army in: νώμα [*nōma*] δικαίῳ πηδαλίῳ στρατόν ('steer your men with the helm of *dikē*'; *P.* 1.86) and in the sense of 'dispensing': ἀργυρέαισι δὲ νωμάτω [*nōmatō*] φιάλαισι βιατὰν ἀμπέλου παῖδ (*N.* 9.51). We also meet the use of νέμονται (*nemontai*) in *N.* 3.82 (κραγέται δὲ κολοιοὶ ταπεινὰ νέμονται), in the sense of how 'chattering daws stay closer to the ground'.

Νόμος (*nómos*), in more than one sense perhaps approximating to 'law' in the sense of 'custom, norm or tradition', is met with a number of times in Pindar: for instance, with reference to funeral rites that are performed according to a *nómos* and in which 'even the dead have a share' (i.e. in the sense of custom/tradition) in ἔστι δὲ καί τι θανόντεσσιν μέρος κὰν νόμον [*nómon*] ἐρδόμενον (*O.* 8.78).[9] In the sense of a 'tradition or customary' practice, we also find the use of νομίζων (*nomizōn*), for instance, in ἱπποτροφίας τε νομίζων ἐν Πανελλάνων νόμῳ [*nómō*] (*Isthm.* 2.38); here, the upholding of a particular Pan-Hellenic custom or practice is mentioned in relation to the rearing of horses. Equally, it is found in relation to 'worship/consider/honour' in: Θεία, σέο ἕκατι καὶ μεγασθενῆ νόμισαν [*nomisan*] χρυσὸν ἄνθρωποι περιώσιον ἄλλων ('Theia of many names, for your sake men honour gold as more powerful than anything else'; *Isthm.* 5.2).

With reference to 'sacred laws', in particular, we meet the plural νόμοις (*nómois*) in οὔτ᾽ ἐν ἀνδράσι γερασφόρον οὔτ ἐν θεῶν νόμοις ('honoured neither by men nor by the *nómoi* of the gods'; *P.* 2.43). Here, the birth of Kentauros, from the union of Ixion with a cloud, is described as not being *en theōn nómois*, that is, as not being divinely sanctioned. Likewise,

---

[9] See also fr. 215.2, ἄλλα δ᾽ ἄλλοισιν νόμιμα [*nomima*], σφετέραν δ αἰνεῖ δίκαν ἀνδρῶν ἕκαστος.

in the singular, we meet *nómos* in: γάμον δαίσαντα πὰρ Δὶ Κρονίδα σεμνὸν αἰνήσειν νόμον [*nómon*][10] (N. 1.72); 'the celebration of a wedding-feast, in the presence of Zeus, the son of Kronos, honours the sacred *nómon*'. In a worship milieu, a personified *Nemesis* is also encountered in Pindar in two instances with the sense of 'apportionment', or as 'the one who apportions' (O. 8.86 and P. 10.44).[11]

In a possibly more direct sense of ordinances-'laws', two particular uses are encountered. First, in P. 1.62: πόλιν Ὑλλίδος στάθμας Ἱέρων ἐν νόμοις [*nómois*] ἔκτισσε; where *Hierōn* is said to have founded the city with 'god-built freedom, in accordance with the *nómoi* of the rule of Hyllus'. However, most probably the sense of *nómos* here is geographical rather than 'juridical or political'. More certain is its use in the second instance, τρὶς μὲν ἐν πόντοιο πύλαισι λαχών, τρὶς δὲ καὶ σεμνοῖς δαπέδοις Ἀδραστείῳ νόμῳ [*nómō*] (N. 10.28), where it is said that Theaeus of Argos won in wrestling, 'at the gates of the sea, and three times on the sacred ground', according to the ordinance (*nómō*) of Adrastus. In addition, we find *nómon*, in the sense of the 'rules/traditional practices' of medicinal remedies, in the remarkable reference to Cheiron teaching Asclepius 'the gentle-handed *nómoi* of remedies': Ἀσκλαπιόν: τὸν φαρμάκων δίδαξε μαλακόχειρα νόμον [*nómon*] (N. 3.55). In an explicit 'political' sense, we encounter the use of *nómon* in reference to a (political) 'regime/tradition', a form of 'governance', with particular regard to 'good order' (akin, perhaps, to a later sense of *eunomia*), in: ἐν πάντα δὲ νόμον [*nómon*] εὐθύγλωσσος ἀνὴρ προφέρει, παρὰ τυραννίδι, χὠπόταν ὁ λάβρος στρατός, χὤταν πόλιν οἱ σοφοὶ τηρέωντι ('under every type of *nómon* the man who speaks straightforwardly prospers: [both] in a tyranny, and where the raucous masses oversee the state, and where men of skill do'; P. 2.86). Similarly, we read: ἀδελφεοῖσί τ᾽ ἐπαινήσομεν ἐσλοῖς, ὅτι ὑψοῦ φέροντι νόμον [*nómon*] Θεσσαλῶν αὔξοντες ('we shall further praise his noble brothers, because they exalt and strengthen the traditional *nómon* of the Thessalians'; P. 10.70).

---

[10] Following Snell and Maehler ([Pindar] 1997) in reading νόμον [*nómon*] for δόμον [*dómon*].

[11] Slater (1969); Slater locates also the use of νεμεσάω (*nemesaō*) in Pind. *Isthm.* 1.3 with the sense of 'to reproach'.

The oxytonic νομός (*nomós*) is encountered in Pindar, too – for instance in *O*. 7.33, εἶπε Λερναίας ἀπ᾽ ἀκτᾶς εὐθὺν ἐς ἀμφιθάλασσον νομόν [*nomón*], where a ship is described as voyaging from 'the shore of Lerna straight to the pasture land that is surrounded by sea'.[12] Similarly, a herbage is indicated in fr. 153, preserved by Plutarch, that reads δενδρέων δὲ νομὸν [*nomón*] Διώνυσος πολυγαθὴς αὐξάνοι, ἁγνὸν φέγγος ὀπώρας, wherein Dionysus is described as 'the power [*nomón*] in the tree'[13] when he is praised as follows: 'may gladsome Dionysus swell the fruit upon the trees, the hallowed splendour of harvest time'.[14] In a pastoral milieu, we meet also the use of νομεύω (*nomeuō*) to express the act of 'putting to graze': νόμευε δ (in fr. 15 [Schröder]). Finally, we encounter the use of the word νομάδες (*nomades*, 'nomads') in two instances; a use, it should be noted, which we did not meet in Homer. First, in the sense of nomadic being, we meet the word in νομάδεσσι [*nomadessi*] γὰρ ἐν Σκύθαις ἀλᾶται στρατῶν (fr. 105b, 1); and, second, we meet it in the direct reference to a Libyan nomad tribe of horsemen in: παρθένον κεδνὰν χερὶ χειρὸς ἑλὼν ἆγεν ἱππευτᾶν Νομάδων [*Nomadōn*] δι᾽ ὅμιλον ('took the noble girl's hand in his hand and led her through the crowd of Nomad horsemen'; *P*. 9.123).[15]

2. *Nomos basileus*

The most famously controversial reference to *nómos* in Pindar is located in fr. 169a. Early on, the fragment was constructed from a composite of a Platonic quotation (*Gorgias* 484b) and a description by Aelius Aristides (*Or*. 45.52; 2.68–9 [Dindorf]). Yet since the 1960s, the interest in the fragment has been replenished upon the discovery of a significant first or second

---

[12] See also Pind. *Pae*. 4.51: ἔα δὲ νομὸν [*nomón*] Περιδάιον.

[13] See also Pind., fr. 140 [Bowra].

[14] In Plu. *Mor*. 365a = *Isis and Osiris* 35; see also Plu. *Mor*., 675f. Plutarch preserves another fragment of Pindar's which states: ἐαν δὲ νομὸν [*nomón*] Κρήτας περιδαῖον; fr.23 [Böckh], II, 631.

[15] In Pindar, we also meet Νόμιος (*Nomios*), with reference to Zeus as the guard of flocks, in *P*. 9.650; ἐπίνομος (*epinomos*), meaning neighbouring, in *P*. 11.7; ἔννομος (*ennomos*), probably in the sense of 'duly ordered', in *P*. 9.57; as well as the composite ἀστυνόμος (*astunomos*), in the sense of a city dweller, in *N*. 9.31.

century AD papyrus (*P. Oxy.* 2450), which adds over twenty-four verses to the original seven or eight.[16] I will thus explore the famous fragment incrementally. First, I examine the most famous lines with regard to *nómos*, in order to question how the term *nómos* could be understood. Then, I turn to the fuller recomposed extract within its heroic milieu in order to investigate some of the further complications of interpretation that arise, in particular, with regard to the relation between *nómos*, *bia* and the *dikaion* (commonly translated, though not unproblematically, as 'law/sovereign power', 'force/violence' and 'justice/right'). The famous 'opening' verses are rendered [Bergk] as follows:

> Νόμος ὁ πάντων βασιλεὺς
> θνατῶν τε καὶ ἀθανάτων
> ἄγει . . .

These verses can be translated as:

> *Nómos* the king of all
> both mortals and immortals
> steers . . .

The primary question is: what is meant by *nómos* in this fragment's introductory gnome? Could it be a sense of 'law' or 'custom' or 'a belief . . . an intellectual attitude' (Ostwald 1969: 109–38)? This question has been one of the most intensely debated among philologists and theorists. In fact, during the last hundred years, most interpreters have sided with either of two core viewpoints. On the one hand stand those that attribute to *nómos* the sense of an 'abstract universal principle'; on the other, those that consider *nómos* to refer to 'custom or tradition'.

The sense of *nómos* as an 'abstract principle' (for some, of a 'universal' modality) is, in one way or another, advanced by the majority of interpreters, though on differing grounds. A wide variety of such 'abstract' *nómoi* are seen as plausible by

---

[16] The *Oxyrhynchus Papyri* (*P. Oxy.*) 2450 (Lobel 1961: 141, Plate XV, A and B); with significant restorations in Page (1962a: 49–51). Other editions of the fragment can be found, among else, in Bowra (1947); and Snell (1955).

many: for instance, 'natural law', 'divine law', 'fate' and so forth. In Plato's *Gorgias* (as will be seen in more detail below), the Pindaric *nómos* is arguably equated with a certain conception of 'natural law', in order to assert that, essentially, 'might is right' (*nómos* here replacing the earlier more commonplace sense of *phusis*; 482e–4c); however, it should be noted from the outset that this is not the sense that Pindar has available to him.[17] In any case, in this manner of interpretation, as D. L. Pike notes, *nómos* is perceived as an 'objective' phenomenon, that is, as 'the normal and inevitable way in which any given class of creatures naturally behaves' (1984: 20). For Pike, the Pindaric *nómos* is singular and king of all (1984: 20–2). For Hans Erich Stier, among others, such a *nómos* is an 'order' that is inviolable and central to the belief and will of god(s), as well as mortals (1928: 227, 238).[18] Hugh Lloyd-Jones famously espouses this camp by supporting the view that *nómos* refers to an 'inviolable principle' and, more specifically, that *nómos* means 'law', that is, *nómos* is 'the law of the universe, and particularly the law of Zeus' (1972: 56). *Nómos* is, in one sense, here identified with the 'will' (or *nómos*) of Zeus.

Further, Marcelo Gigante also interpreted *nómos* as the 'law of Zeus': an 'absolute *nómos*' that governs the world ('*Nomos è il principio assoluto della divinità*'; 1956: 111), linking Pindar's *nómos* to Heraclitus' *nómos* in fr. 114,[19] while also suspecting Orphic or Pythagorean influence in Pindar's use (ibid. 75). Earlier, scholars such as Wilhelm Nestle (1911: 251), Otto Schröder (1917: 202), Victor Ehrenberg (1921: 120) and Felix Heinimann ([1945] 1965/1972: 68–70) concurred that such influence, whether Orphic or Pythagorean, was indeed likely to one degree or another. Eric R. Dodds, however, suggested that the alleged evidence for such influence is 'too late to be trustworthy' (1959: 270).[20] Proximate, while differentiated, views were advanced by August Böckh ([1811–19, 1821]

---

[17] See the discussion in Pavese (1968: 52–4); see, further, Lesky (1949: 588f); for the possible Orphic influence, see Guthrie ([1952] 1993: 236f).

[18] For views that agree with Stier, see Untersteiner (1954: 297, n. 30); Fränkel ([1951] 1962: 545–6); and Treu (1963: 212).

[19] Though, as has been seen earlier in this work, the Heraclitus fragment does not refer to 'divine laws' as such.

[20] Gigante (1956) compiles the various interpretations up to the mid-1950s.

2013: 642), Wilhelm Nestle ([1942] 1975: 160) and Emmanuel Laroche (1949: 174–5), considering the understanding of *nómos* as a 'law of Fate' in the sense of *Moira* or Ἀνάγκη (*Anangkē*). Everyone, god and mortal, must remain within the *nómos* of the region or the apportionment within which one is. However, Carlo Pavese, considering the wider point of view, held that there seems to be meagre support in the earlier usage of the word *nómos* for such a universal 'abstract' conception of it (1968: 48). In addition, Poulheria Kyriakou, in her recent contribution, considered that *nómos* 'as divine justice or universal order is not convincing' (2002: 196–7).

In contrast, other interpretations have posited the view that *nómos* refers to custom, tradition or convention. At times, Herodotus understood *nómos* in this manner (for example, at 3.38.4). In Hesiod (as noted in Chapter Six) *nómos* can refer to a 'custom' based on tradition, whether in terms of a worship rite or another type of 'rule'. Ehrenberg, with special emphasis on the use of *nómos* in relation to worship rites, and akin to Laroche's view (1949), inferred the early application of *nómos* with regard to 'custom or tradition' (1960: 98). For Ulrich von Wilamowitz-Moellendorff (with whom Wilhelm Theiler (1965) and Cecil M. Bowra (1964) concurred), *nómos* 'is that which is accepted as right in the opinion and general belief of people' (1920: 96). Furthermore, Max Pohlenz, at the end of the Second World War, argued that the oxytonic νομός (*nomós*) with its central meaning being 'the allotted part of land', as we met it in Homer, was the 'earlier' word in the family of words that I examine in this work, and it was on this basis that the sense of a 'regionally delimited way of life of the inhabitants' (1948: 142) was later added to it, which then took a distinct baritone form. In this regard, the earlier form of *nómos* is said to be localised and customary.

We do find, in Pindar, as was noted earlier, the manner of a 'convention' (with regard to funeral rites in particular) or customs and tradition, as well as possibly, in one way at least, the sense of some kind of 'law' or 'ordinance-norm', and so it remains possible that the usage of *nómos* here conforms to the commonplace range of Pindar's time. Pavese proposed an adjustment to this strand of interpretation by suggesting that 'the usage of Pindar conforms to the same range of meanings' (1968: 54; with particular reference to fr. 215), while drawing attention to the fact that such use 'emphasizes the binding character of the received custom in a given circle' (ibid. 55). Thus, in Pindar: 'The notion inherent in the word has an obligatory force to start with. *Nómos* is not simply "custom", but the custom accepted by the community and determining individual behaviour' (ibid.).

Meanwhile *nómos*, in this line of interpretation, has been described as, to one extent or another, a 'subjective' phenomenon (Pike 1984: 20). That is, it is considered as an attitude of 'convention' that can take the form of a 'norm' suited to a particular set of people or a community. Pike claims that, for this camp of thought, such a *nómos* is the 'subjective attitude' and not the 'norm' itself (ibid.). Probably, as I have suggested, the line between a 'mere' local custom and one that is recognised more widely is a thin, if at all decipherable, one. Yet no matter to what degree, the understanding of *nómos* as a matter of 'custom or convention' has had a number of adherents. In differing ways, the earlier scholars, Gennaro Perotta (1935: 109), Kurt Latte (1946: 73) and Alfred Croiset (1985: 233), among others, arrived at a similar view. Of the more recent interpretations, along similar lines but with a distinct path of argumentation centring on 'tradition and customary' application (or 'social' recognition), particularly prominent is that of Martin Ostwald (1965: 124–31).[21] As Ostwald put it, *nómos* refers here to 'the attitude traditionally or conventionally taken to a norm' (ibid. 134). To this view I return at the end of this chapter.

This way of interpretation is not without its own limits. For Pavese, for instance, the emphasis on 'custom' appears to be irrelevant in the particular milieu of the fragment (1968: 48). Dodds arrived at a similar conclusion when he claimed that Heracles' actions, to which the fragment refers, 'can scarcely be adduced as an apt paradigm of the customary' (1959: 270). Nor, as Kyriakou suggests with good reason, can Pindar 'be identified with Callicles in the *Gorgias* (484b), since the latter speaks within the sense of the sophistic antithesis between νόμος and φύσις' (2002: 198, n. 5).[22] She crucially adds: 'At any

---

[21] See Stefou (2015: 1–11) for a more recent summary of the differing views, as well as his own well-reasoned analysis.

[22] See, further, for Kyriakou's critical commentary and related references concerning more recent adherents (though few) to this view.

rate, for the Greeks, the "existing state of affairs" is usually determined by the gods or fate, or both in cooperation' (ibid. 196, n. 3). The crucial question then remains: how could one disentangle the intersections between 'custom', *nómos* and those particular views of *nómos* as a 'universal principle'? One perhaps does not have to. While customs, for instance, as Kyriakou notes, may at times not have anything to do with the gods, it could be said that the extent to which 'tradition' and 'worship' are barely separable during the archaic period (and beyond) may suggest that some coexistent plausibility could be afforded, at least to a degree, as to both points of view: not perhaps in the manner of 'synthesis', but of inter-relation. That said, this should not be stretched to the point of over-accommodating the many differing views on Pindar's *nómos*, whether on the level of their core line or, indeed, in terms of their differing aspects on the detail.

Given the level of nuance in each account – with which I have, however, only engaged in a brief schematic sense – this is most probably a debate that will persist; though one may wonder with what further distinct possibility of any substantial revelation, given all that has already been attempted. I do not think that there is a case for a discernible third interpretation; instead, there are some views which propose the inhabitation of ambiguity. Marian Demos, in her analysis following Kevin Crotty, claims that such ambiguity is present in Pindar's use of *nómos* in this particular fragment, to the extent that it refers to both a notion of *nómos* (akin to that of a divine *nómos*) and to social custom or usage, and she makes reference to the etymological link of *nómos/nemein* with an 'allotment or apportionment' (1991: 63–5). Crotty had earlier attempted to find a middle point of reconciliation between the two core interpretations ('universal principle' and 'custom'), suggesting that in Pindar's era these two senses coexisted (1982: 106). After all, as Lloyd-Jones has stressed, 'human law was only an extension of the divine law' (1972: 56).

We can perhaps gain a reasonably modest perspective by examining what Pindar actually provides in the fragment in question. For Lloyd-Jones, the opening lines poetically purport to 'dignify some particular abstraction by confer-ring on it Zeus' title of "ruler of gods and men"' (1972: 48). Indeed, *nómos* was not only semantically polyvalent, but also a commonplace word in Pindar's time. Zeus as the king of gods, too, was equally unexceptional and in the Pindaric poems this is especially so (for example, in *O*. 7.34 and *N*. 5.35). Pavese brings the two together when he writes '*Nomos* is personified as a king', though noting that '[n]ormally the deity that represents the law of King Zeus is his spouse Themis, the Olympian goddess appointed to watch over the execution of his decrees [θέμιστες, *themistes*] in heaven and on earth' (1968: 55).[23] During Pindar's age, it is possible that *nómos* was already beginning to replace *themis* and *dikē* with reference to what is 'right' or the 'norm', but this is difficult to establish. More importantly, it is *nómos* that is called 'a king' here, and in this context the question has been inevitably raised as to whether we should infer a direct personification of *Nómos*. As Pavese notes, there is no clear precedent regarding this, 'unless one resorts to late Orphic sources' (1968: 55). In any case, the more crucial matter remains that gods, as much as mortals, are said to 'abide' by the *nómos basileus*.

What can be learned from the designation of *nómos* as *basileus* (king)? The earlier Hesiodic formula for Zeus is commonly θεῶν βασιλῆα (-ῆι) καὶ ἀνδρῶν, that is, 'king of gods and mortals' (*Th*. 827; 923). Pavese notes that this appears to be isometric to the even earlier Homeric form of Δία Κρονίωνα ἄνακτα (*Dia Kroniōna anakta*; ἄναξ, *anax*, *Od*. 9.145; 1993: 145) and, he continues, '*Nomos* is an abstract idea personified, or rather deified, on the model of an epic formula for Zeus' while '[t]he title βασιλεύς is usually given to the god in power in the so-called succession myth' (ibid.). It is also noticeable that the word ἄγει (*agei*), which is used to describe *Nómos* as 'steering', is a term that is frequently used in Pindar for 'leading' by a divine agency (for example, in *P*. 5.76). In the Orphics, as far as we know, there is reference to *Nómos* becoming a *paredros* of Zeus (ibid. 145–6), though this appears to be late. It is, however, conceivable that *Nómos* as king would resonate with Pindar's audience. Pavese even goes so far as to suggest that here, perhaps, *Nómos* refers to a particular decree of Zeus (1968: 56), if not his general

---

[23] Pindar testifies to this in *I*. 8.31; *O*. 3.8; and fr. 30.1; see the discussion in Pavese (1968).

authority.[24] Yet as Kyriakou cautiously writes: 'The only certain thing about νόμος is what Pindar himself says about it, namely that it is an all-pervasive power governing with extreme violence the affairs of both gods and men' (2002: 198, n. 5). I turn next to the matter of the 'violent hand', but for now it can be noted that such a *nómos* reigns above all: that is, it governs mortal and immortal matters and is most powerful, perhaps even in the sense of being inescapable (ibid. 199).

3. Heracles

It is now time to examine the extended version of the text that was recomposed in the 1960s upon the discovery of the papyrus fragments, whereby Pindar recounts the brutal deeds of the demigod Heracles against Geryon and Diomedes. The discovery of the *Oxyrhynchus Papyri* enabled the so-called 'new version' of the fragment to include substantial additional portions of Pindar's poem. The papyrus in question was published, extensively analysed and commented on by Edgar Lobel (1961) (Part 2450 of the *P. Oxy.*, n. 2, pl. XV, A and B). The first lines of the papyrus coincide with the famous lines of fr. 169a. That Heracles is designated as violent is not in doubt, but the debate rests on how and why his 'vicious' acts are, for some, 'justified', or 'enabled' by Zeus, or by convention (*nómos*). For some interpreters, the question is a genuine Pindaric one, since the poet himself appears to interrogate these deeds, at least to an extent. The answer to this question is not, in any case, straightforward given the ambiguity evident in the fragment between the violation of the *nómos* by Heracles and the protection or 'toleration' afforded, arguably, by the *nómos*.

The ambiguity is registered, early on, in the later reference that Herodotus makes to the famous phrase '*Nómos* is king of all' (at 3.38), with regard to the violent deeds of the Persian King Cambyses. The last two lines refer to Pindar directly: οὕτω μέν νυν ταῦτα νενόμισται [*nenomistai*], καὶ ὀρθῶς μοι δοκέει Πίνδαρος ποιῆσαι νόμον [*nómon*] πάντων βασιλέα

---

[24] Pavese agreed with the earlier interpretations by Kerényi (1955) and Lesky (1949).

φήσας εἶναι ('and it is, I think, rightly said in Pindar's poem that [*nómos*] custom is lord of all').[25] Not without controversy, the Herodotean reference has been read as a misunderstanding of the Pindaric poem (for example, by Gigante 1956; and Bloomer 1993), or, in contrast, as a sophisticated reference (for instance, by Ostwald 1965). Irrespectively, the sense of *nómos* as 'localised custom' remains quite distinctly Herodotean. No matter which side one takes, the question remains: what is the relation between *nómos*, *bia* and *dikē*? It is with this in mind that I propose to return once more to the subject of the nature of *nómos* in Pindar.

The transcript is reproduced below, with Pavese's rendering of the lection signs (1968: 48–50):

Νόμος ὁ πάντων βασιλεύς
Θνατῶν τε καὶ ἀθανάτων
ἄγει δικαιῶν τὸ βιαιότατον
ὑπερτάτα χειρί. Τεκμαίρομαι
ἔργοισιν Ἡρακ | λέος
ἐπεὶ Γαρυόνα ⌋ βόας
Κυκ | λωπεί ⌋ ων ἐπὶ π | ροθύρων Εὐρυσθέος
ἀναίρει τε κ ⌋ αἱ ἀπ | ριάτας ἔλασεν.
........] Διομήδεος ἵππους
......μ]όναρχον Κικόνων
παρὰ] Βιστο ⌋ νίδι λίμνα
χαλκοθώρ]ᾱκος Ἐνναλίου
..............] ἔκπαγ | λον υἱόν,
................]. ραντα μέγαν,
οὐ σὺν κό]ρῳ ἀλλ᾽ἀρετᾷ.
........γ]ὰρ ἁρπαζομένων τεθνάμεν
........]μάτων ἢ κακόν ἔμμεναι.
........] ἐσελθών μέγα
......ν]υκτὶ βίας ὁδόν
..........]ρεν, λαβὼν δ᾽ ἐν[α] φ[ῶτ]α πεδάρσι[ον
φά[τ | ναις] ἐν λιθίναις βάλ[ε − ◡ ◡ −
ἱππ. [.....]έναν φρέ[ν ◡ −
καὶ ν[ιν.....].ζον. ταχέως
δ᾽ἀράβη[σε] διὰ [λ]ευκῶν

----

[25] Translated by Godley (1920).

ὀστέ[ων] δοῦπος ἐ[ρ]<ε>ικομένων.
ὁ δ᾽ἀφ[αρ π]λεκτόν τε χαλκόν
ὑπερη [..].ε τραπεζᾶν
προβά⌐τω⌐ν ἀλυσιωτόν
δι᾽ἐρκ[ἐ]ων, τεῖρε δὲ στελεῶ
ἄλλαν [μ]ὲν σκέλος, ἄλλαν δὲ πᾱ[χυν,
τὰν δὲ πρυμνὸν κεφαλᾶς
ὀδ[ὰ]ξ α[ὐ]χένα φέροισαν.
.ρ.μι[.]. ὅμως ἐ[οῖ]σ᾽ ὑπα.[.].θυ.[
πικρο[τά]ταν κλάγεν ἀγγε[λία]η
ζαμενε[. . .] τυρανν[.....]
...]κί..[..ἐ]κ λεχέω[ν ἀπέ]δ{ε}ιλ[
..........]ν καθε.[....]ς ῥα.[
..........].ιον κακ[.....]
........].ον ἐ[
...
.νατ[ ]ν.[

ἔμολε [κ]αὶ παῖδα[ ]
Ἡρακ | λ[έ]ος εξαρ.θ.[.].[ ]
τεταγ | μένον τοῦτ᾽ἀρ[α δωδ]έκατο[ν
Ἥρας ἐφετ | μαῖς Σθενέλοιό μιν
υἱὸς κέ[λ]ευσε<ν> μόνον
ἄνευ συ[μμ]αχίας ἴμεν.
καὶ Ἰόλαο[ς ἐ]ν ἑπταπύλοισι μένω[ν τε
Θήβαις Ἀ]μ⌐ φιτρύωνί τε σᾶμα χέω[ν
..........]μιᾷ δ᾽ἐπὶ θήκᾳ
..........]ν καλλικέρας
..........]άδις οὒς <τ>οι
..........]ου στρατὸς οὐκ ἀέκ[ων
...].αθ[.......]ον[..]κ[..].ᾷ ²⁶

Pavese's translation (1968: 85) of the extended fragment, with
minor modifications indicated in brackets, is as follows:

Law, king of all, mortals and immortals, leads, bringing violence to justice,²⁷ with highest hand. I judge from

---

²⁶ See also the rendering and commentary by Ostwald (2009: 96–104), who
follows the restorations proposed by Page (1962a), with some divergence.
²⁷ Ostwald translates instead: '[Nomos] brings on with sovereign hand what
is most violent and makes it just' (2009: 104; see further, ibid. 104–5).

Heracles' deeds. For Geryon's cattle he seized and drove to the Cyclopean doorway of Eurystheus without price paid, and Diomedes' (fierce) mares (he subdued, after he had slain) near the Bistonian marsh the chief of the Cicones, the terrible [formidable (*ekpaglos*)] son of (bronze)-armed Enyalius, (rousing) his great (anger), not with battle lust [*koros*], but with valor [*aretē*]. For (he preferred) to be dead, (his) goods being seized away, rather than to be a coward [*kakos*].

Having entered the large (mansion, the hero quickly) at night found a way of force [*bia*]; he took a man aloft and threw him into the stone cribs, (to divert the fierce) mares' (alert) senses, and they (devoured) him. Forthwith a noise cracked through the shattered white bones. He there-upon tore off, from underneath the animals' tables, the entwined bronze, fastened to links along the stable, and stung them with his club, while one was carrying off a leg, one a forearm, another in her teeth the head, by the root of the neck.

. . .

she screamed the bitterest news, (and aroused) the mighty lord from his various-colored couch, unshod . . . he slew (?) . . .

. . .

came also the son . . . ranked as a supernumerary (?) of Heracles. This as a twelfth, at Hera's behests, Sthenelos' son bade him, to go alone without help. And Iolaus remaining in seven-gated Thebes and heaping a mound for Amphitryon . . . in one tomb . . . the beautiful-horned . . . the folk not unwilling...

. . .

It is helpful to examine, first, the three characters mentioned in the fragment in some more detail. First of all, the figure of Heracles, who is central to Pindar's narration in the praising of his deeds and rewards against numerous animal and hybrid powers (usually understood as *hubristai*, i.e. as acting or being in *hubris*), is prominent.[28] One perhaps characteris-

---

[28] See Nieto Hernandez (1993). The theme of Heracles' deeds and eventual apotheosis traverses Greek literature; see, for instance, Schweitzer (1922);

tic reference to the Heraclean labours is found elsewhere, in Pindar's *N*. I, at 61–72:

γείτονα δ᾽ ἐκκάλεσεν Διὸς ὑψίστου προφάταν ἔξοχον,
ὀρθόμαντιν Τειρεσίαν: ὁ δέ οἱ φράζε καὶ παντὶ στρατῷ,
  ποίαις ὁμιλήσει τύχαις,
ὅσσους μὲν ἐν χέρσῳ κτανών,
ὅσσους δὲ πόντῳ θῆρας ἀϊδροδίκας:
καί τινα σὺν πλαγίῳ
ἀνδρῶν κόρῳ στείχοντα τὸν ἐχθρότατον
φᾶσέ νιν δώσειν μόρῳ.
καὶ γὰρ ὅταν θεοὶ ἐν πεδίῳ Φλέγρας Γιγάντεσσιν μάχαν
ἀντιάζωσιν, βελέων ὑπὸ ῥιπαῖσι κείνου φαιδίμαν γαίᾳ
  πεφύρσεσθαι κόμαν
ἔνεπεν: αὐτὸν μὰν ἐν εἰράνᾳ καμάτων μεγάλων ἐν
  σχερῷ
ἁσυχίαν τὸν ἅπαντα χρόνον ποινὰν λαχόντ᾽ ἐξαίρετον
ὀλβίοις ἐν δώμασι, δεξάμενον θαλερὰν Ἥβαν ἄκοιτιν καὶ
  γάμον
δαίσαντα, πὰρ Δὶ Κρονίδᾳ σεμνὸν αἰνήσειν νόμον.

In translation:

> And he called his neighbour, the outstanding prophet of
>   Zeus the highest,
> the truthful seer Teiresias. And the prophet told him and
>   all the men what fortunes the boy would encounter:
>   how many he would slay on land,
> and how many lawless [ἀϊδροδίκας: ignorant of *dikē*]
>   monsters at sea.
> And he told of a certain one, most hateful, who walked
>   with crooked insolence
> towards men, whom the boy would send to his doom.
> For he said that when the gods meet the giants in battle
>   on the plain of Phlegra,
> the shining hair of the giants will be stained with dirt
>   beneath the rushing arrows of that hero.
> But he himself will have allotted to him in peace, as

Ehrenberg (1946); Galinsky (1972); Carter Philips (1978); Brommer (1986); Uhlenbrock (1986); and Padilla (1998).

an extraordinary reward for his great hardship,
continuous peace for all time among the homes of the
blessed.
He will receive flourishing Hebe as his bride and
celebrate the wedding-feast,
and in the presence of Zeus the son of Cronus he will
praise the sacred *nómon*.[29]

A few lines earlier in the ode, Pindar narrates how Chromios,
Hiero's general, welcomes and praises Heracles.[30] Pindar
refers to Heracles' famous strangling of Hera's snakes and
Ampitryon, it is stated, witnessed the ἐκνόμιον λῆμά τε καὶ
δύναμιν (*eknomion lēma te kai dunamin*) of his son, that is,
his 'unnatural spirit' and power (56–7). The description of
Heracles' power as one that lies outside of the *nómos* (*eknomion*) needs to be kept in mind. The demigod Heracles
is of 'extra-ordinary', 'uncustomary', *ek-nomian* 'nature'. If
his power and 'nature' are such – that is, if the source of his
power and 'nature' lies outside of the *nomos* – how will his
deeds conform to the (mortal) *nómos*? If *nómos* signifies one's
apportionment (or, as some argue, 'fate'), then Heracles'
nómos may be in contrast to that of mortals in that his *nómos*
'permits' excessive violence and power. To act violently is
the norm for him and he will do so, Teiresias states in the
last verse, *while* praising the sacred *nómos* (the divine dispensation of norms/normalcies).[31] Heracles' *nómos* may be a
Pindaric paradigm of the sacred *nómos*.

The Heraclean theme is too extensive in the Greek literature to be summarised, let alone analysed, in any adequate
detail, but some key aspects are worth noting. Heracles is
renowned for being a violent, vengeful figure and Pindar
depicts a number of such acts in his odes. For instance, in *O.*
10.27–44, where Heracles slays the two Moliones (*Molionidai*)
and King Augeas, or in *Isthm.* 4.57, where he battles against
Antaeus, an ogre; as well as in *N.* 4.25–6, where Heracles leads

---

[29] Translated by Svarlien (1990/1991); reading, with Snell, νόμον (*nómon*) for
δόμον (*dómon*).
[30] Chromios is the victor celebrated in the ode against the Carthaginians
and the Etruscans, while Heracles here is, arguably, paralleled with him.
[31] See Ostwald (1965: 29).

a military expedition to Troy. While Pindar does not provide a full account of Heracles' labours, Heracles is described as being of divine origin (Hernandez 1993: 76);[32] his character is said to be of great valour and bravery; and, further, he is said to be the founder of the Olympian festival.[33] The hero is repeatedly praised for his labours. His characterisation as a benefactor of mortals and as a 'civilizing hero' is clear (ibid.). It is in this sense that he plays a characteristic role in the battle of the gods against the giants (N. 7.90), which, as Hernandez notes, by the fifth century BC had become a clichéd reference to the battles of the Greeks against the barbarians (ibid.).[34]

Heracles enjoys extra-ordinary dominion by being the 'master of animals'[35] and 'the lord of waters' (Nieto Hernandez 1993: 88). The latter is most famously depicted in his victory against the Lernian Hydra, an aquatic or swamp monster; not to mention his famous pillars that were placed 'at the outermost of the then known sea', whereby the sea has the sense of a 'creative principle' or force, signifying the 'origin of life' (ibid. 95).[36] At the same time, Pindar appears to avoid mention of other mythical aspects of his character: 'his excessive appetite, his sexual incontinence (comparable only to that of his father Zeus), his quarrels with the gods, and so forth. Pindar, in fact, omits the hero's frightful death and his self-immolation on Mount Oeta' (ibid. 77). Yet it should be borne in mind that some of these characteristics are not met with before the time of Sophocles.[37] That said, it is worth adding, as Pavese notes, that βία (bia) often has a 'positive connotation', and that is always so for Pindar, 'except in P. 8.15'. He then goes on to say: 'He often calls his admired heroes βιαταί: Patroclus at O. 9.75, Jason at P. 4.236, Antilochos at P. 6.28, Achilles at Pae. 6.84' (1968: 72). In contrast, βίαιος (biaios) is a 'deprecatory epithet always designating an hubristic quality' (ibid.).[38]

---

[32] For example, O. 10.44; P. 9.84ff; N. 1.36; 10.12ff; Isthm. 7.5ff.

[33] ibid., for example, O. 1.5–7, 2.2–4, 3.11–35, 4.67–8, 10.24ff; N. 10.32–3, 11.27–8.

[34] See also Vian (1952: 288).

[35] See Burkert (1979: 78).

[36] See O. 3.43–5; N. 3.20–3; Isthm. 4.11–12.

[37] See Shapiro (1983: 7–18).

[38] Though it has to be said that Pavese states this in relation to his particular

In this manner, with Pindar's usually enthusiastic encomium of Heracles in mind, Heracles is depicted 'as an instrument of the will of Zeus and as the benefactor of mankind who
eliminates monstrous opponents' (Kyriakou 2002: 195).[39] Yet
as Kyriakou notes attentively, while some interpreters (for
example, Pavese 1968: 48) appreciate Heracles' violent deeds
as subject to divine favour, the gods, other than Zeus at least,

> did not customarily favour Heracles: Hera, whose bidding
> is mentioned in this fragment too . . . was his archenemy
> and Ares was Diomedes' father; Poseidon was the grand-
> father of Geryon and Heracles fought against him as well
> as Apollo and Hades at Pylos (*O.* 9.29–35). (2002: 196, n. 3)

Kyriakou adds:

> Zeus' goodwill toward Heracles was definitely not cus-
> tomary but a manifestation of paternal affection which
> ensured the hero's survival. Even if the gods can be said
> to have customs, the favour toward Heracles cannot count
> among them and thus cannot exemplify the supposed rule
> of custom over the gods. Those who understand νόμος as
> the fated order of the universe or the law of Zeus suggest
> that violence is ultimately part of the plan of fate or Zeus
> for the just administration of the world. (2002: 196, n. 3)

In this light, it is worth examining the Heraclean deeds mentioned in the particular fragment with regard to the specific
ways in which the victims of Heracles' labours are depicted
in Pindar, but it is worth pointing out, following Pavese in
that regard, that some of his deeds are in honour of the gods,
such as the assembling of the large herd in Cyclopean Tiryns
or Mycenae (in the Eurystheus incident) which, according
to Apollonius 2.5.10, he 'then sacrificed . . . to Hera' (Pavese
1968: 63). In addition, Pavese adds, cattle-raiding, according
to heroic customs, 'is not dishonourable in itself; the Dioscuri

---

interpretation of the way in which Heracles' deeds are described as
violent in the fragment, and in order to dissociate his 'way of force' from
the term 'violence' at the much-debated verse 3, to which I return below.
[39] See Gigante (1956: 56–71).

indulged in it, along with the Alpharetidae, and so did Achilles, when he raided Aeneas on the slopes of Ida' (ibid. 67–8).[40] Above all, while Heracles is not portrayed by Pindar in entirely favourable terms, he remains a highly favoured son of Zeus carrying out the god's will.[41]

4. Diomedes and Geryon

Let us now turn to examine how Heracles' victims are described in Pindar. Much of the debate as to the interpretation of the fragment involves the question as to whether the victims of Heracles' deeds, as described in the fragment, are portrayed as monstrous *hubristai* (and therefore as receiving fated retribution), or as honourable characters faced with unilateral Heraclean aggression. We saw earlier how Teiresias emphasises that Heracles will confront, in his labours, the *hubristai* (those who know no *dikē*) and act with valour, while praising the sacred *nómos* (or Zeus).[42] In the extended fragment as preserved in the papyrus, Heracles drives off the cattle and horses without making payment and kills their owners Diomedes and Geryon.[43]

Diomedes is described as having defended his property and showing *aretē*. Nick Fisher, in fact, notes another fragment (fr. 81[S]) that 'seems to start to praise Geryon, and then to draw back in face of Zeus' favouritism towards Heracles' (1992: 235). Yet of this fragment only a single sentence has survived and it is not advisable to draw a sustainable interpretation on its basis. Diomedes is known in the literature as the king of Thrace, whose man-eating mares, which Heracles

---

[40] See Hom. *Hym. to Herm.*

[41] See Pike (1984: 17–19). The role of Athena is also depicted in *P. Oxy.* 2617, fr. 3, in her conversation with Poseidon, who is told, possibly, to not intervene and save Geryon; see, further, Barrett (2007).

[42] See also the discussion in Fisher (1992: 233).

[43] Plato describes Heracles as 'neither purchasing nor Geryon giving' (οὔτε πριάμενος οὔτε δόντος τοῦ Γηρυόνου; *Gorg.* 484b11); the *scholium* on Aristides' *On Rhetoric* 52 states that Heracles 'neither asked for nor purchased' the cattle (οὔτε αἰτήσας οὔτε πριάμενος; Dindorf, III, 408). It should be noted that in the Pindaric fragment it is not clear from the surviving text whether Heracles kills Diomedes or whether he was devoured by his own monstrous horses.

captured, devoured passing strangers. Diomedes is known to be the son of the god Ares, of renowned warlike spirit. Kyriakou has noted that the scholiast of the papyrus (at 15) could be relied upon as evidence that Diomedes is commended for resisting the theft of his property, and Heracles' act is explicitly said to be an act of 'injustice' (2002: 200): 'for [it is better] to die while [possessions] are being carried off than to be a coward' ([κρέσσον γ]ὰρ ἁρπαζομένων τεθνάμεν | [× χρη]μάτων ἢ κακὸν ἔμμεναι; 16–17).

Fisher notes, in contrast, that Geryon was a monstrous character who 'was related to many other figures of monstrous shape and unpleasant habits, that Heracles, and others like Perseus, dealt with' (1992: 235).[44] Geryon is, indeed, described as a monster (θῆρας ἀϊδροδίκας).[45] We learn from Hesiod (*Th.* 309 and 333), Pavese writes, that Geryon is the grandson of Poseidon and the son of Chrysaor ('who sprang from the blood of Medusa, the daughter of Phorkys and Keto who were children of Pontus and Gea') and the Oceanine Callirrhoe:

> and [he] lives beyond the Ocean streams on the island Erythia, which is where Heracles kills him beside his misty dwellings. His sister is Echidna who had children with Typhon (i.e. Geryon's dog Orthos, Cerberus and the dragon of the Hesperids). (1968: 61 and n. 39)[46]

Thus, for some interpreters, Geryon's *hubris* lies in his being a monster (ibid. 68). It is on this basis that, with Geryon and Diomedes depicted as 'outlaws' and monsters, interpreters (for example, Lloyd-Jones) find that Zeus would 'tolerate' their slaughter by Heracles.[47] But it would, perhaps, be misleading to read here an anachronistic logic of 'justification', since the traditional general attitude of all 'to events that violate their sense of justice' was, it seems, to 'keep a resigned

[44] See Pavese (1968: 61).
[45] See Pind. *I.* 1.13 and Hes. *Th.* 289–94 and 981–3.
[46] Pindar also refers to Geryon in *I.* 1.13. Geryon is described as a most formidable opponent with three bodies and six warlike arms; Stesichorus describes him as having wings, as Pavese observed (1968: 61, n. 42).
[47] See Kyriakou (2002: 201).

and prudent silence in the face of superior powers' (Kyriakou 2002: 202–3). On the other hand, Geryon and Diomedes were not mere mortals, which could reverse this argument.

The perplexity, arguably expressed in Pindar, lies in the fact that Heracles is depicted in these verses as the unprovoked aggressor. By the sixth century BC, Geryon was described in a more sympathetic light, as, for instance, in Stesichorus' *Geryonis* (fr. 15, 13 and 11), while, in turn, Heracles is described in a less encomiastic manner.[48] Stesichorus, the earliest lyric poet, describes Geryon as a legitimate defender of his possessions against a plundering Heracles. However, Heracles still benefits from Zeus' favour, despite his violent and unjust deeds. Pindar, on the other hand, while praising Geryon, does not wish to pass 'judgment' on Zeus' will (σὲδ' ἐγὼ παρά μιν αἰνέω μέν, Γηρυόνα, τὸ δὲ μὴ Δί φίλτερον σιγῶμι πάμπαν·; 'I, on the one hand, praise you, Geryon, in comparison to [Heracles], but I should keep silence entirely about what is not dear to Zeus'; in fr. 70b).[49] If Stesichorus' depiction of Geryon was a precedent that Pindar had in mind when he was composing his poem, then it may be possible to suggest that Pindar confronts the paradox between Heracles' brutality and the sacred *nómos* (of Zeus). In *N.* 1.70–2 Heracles is said to praise that sacred *nómos*: δεξάμενον | Θαλερὰν Ἥβαν ἄκοιτιν καὶ γάμον | δαίσαντα πὰρ Δὶ Κρονίδα, σεμνὸν αἰνήσειν νόμον [*nómon*] ('after welcoming Hebe as his wife and celebrating his marriage beside Zeus, son of Kronos, he [Heracles] will praise his holy *nómos*'). Even if Pindar is not praising Heracles directly, as would be his usual manner, he does appear to specifically praise Zeus' *nómos*. It is also worth noting that generally in the lyrical tradition, Geryon

---

[48] Stesichorus (630–555 BC) was a remarkable lyric poet, born in Metauros in southern Italy. On Stesichorus, see Robertson (1969); Page (1973); Lerza (1978); Walcot (1979: 326–51); Tsitsibakou-Vasalos (1990); Lazzeri (1995: 93–9); Barrett (2007); and Curtis (2011); see also the fragments of Megacleides in Janko (2000: 138–43). Heracles is also described as a violent transgressor in Apollonius; on this, see Levin (1971: 23).

[49] See the discussion by Segal (1985: 190–5). Kyriakou notes that Segal makes an argument regarding Geryon's death being a form of 'divine fate or justice' on the basis that S15 in Stesichorus describes one of the arrows of Heracles piercing Geryon's skull as 'δαίμονος αἴσαι', that is, 'in accordance with divine fate' (2002: 201, n. 13).

and Diomedes are depicted as villains (Pike 1984: 19–20). Kyriakou stresses then that despite the partly complimentary description of Geryon as the legitimate defender of his possessions: 'it is very implausible that Pindar would not be more explicit about such an important factor in the story and would instead choose to suggest the monstrosity of Heracles' opponents by stressing their legitimate rights and even their nobility' (2002: 197).[50]

5. *Bia* and *dikē*

It is time now to turn to the interpretation of the most controversial line in the fragment, which states δικαιῶν τὸ βιαιότατον [*dikaiōn to biaiotaton*], and which Pavese translates, as noted earlier, as 'bringing violence to justice'. Pavese's minority interpretation begins by noting that δικαιῶν τὸ βιαιότατον, as encountered in the fragment, is not identical to the phrasing in Plato's *Gorgias* (484b), which reads βιαίων τὸ δικαιότατον [*biaîōn to dikaiotaton*]. This, Pavese notes, is 'opposed to all other sources, except Libanius, *Ap. Socr.* 87' and he asks: 'is this a misquotation or a playful paraphrasing?'[51] For Pavese, 'the translation of the phrase cannot be along the lines of "justified" or "to claim or demand as a right"' (1968: 58). Pavese asks, in this regard, who is ἄγει(ν) [*agei(n)*]? And he answers: *Nómos* ('the verb governs a noun as an object'; ibid. 58). Δικαιῶν (*dikaiōn*) has a factitive sense and *agei* is transitive, taking the same object as *dikaiōn*.[52] For the poet, he adds, δικαιῶν = το βιαιότατον (ibid. 59). Pavese, then, concludes his 1968 attempt with the following:

> Surely Pindar meant 'Rule, king of all, leads, bringing violence to justice, with highest hand.' ... He imagines *Nomos* sitting on its throne and dispensing its decrees in the attitude of a king, as Rhadamanthys is pictured so doing in Hades. (ibid.)

[50] See also Fisher (1992: 235).
[51] The reference to the Pindaric fragment is frequent: see Plato's *Prot.*, 337d; *Symp.*, 196b and Aristotle's *Rhet.*, 140a22. On the possibility of deliberate misquotation in Plato, see Dodds (1959: 270–2); Pavese (1968: 69–70); Demos (1994: 85–107; and, more generally, 1999); and Grote (1994: 21–31).
[52] On this point, see Wilamowitz-Moellendorff (1920: 96).

Lloyd-Jones, in contrast, rejected Pavese's sense of some type of implied 'punishment' in the sense of 'bringing violence to justice', while Pavese himself, in a later response, admitted that his earlier interpretation of this line was perhaps 'far-fetched' (1993: 143–57). For Lloyd-Jones, the aggressor is clearly Heracles, while Diomedes is acting out of *aretē* (and not *hubris*), which means that the fragment's line can be rendered as 'making just what is most violent' (1972: 45–56). It would, however, be misleading to overemphasise this line of argument and turn it into an early instance of a conflict between 'rights or justices' (i.e. between Heracles and Diomedes and so forth). *Nómos*, for Lloyd-Jones, is an abstract title, rather than a personification conferred on Zeus as he governs gods and mortals. Thus, for Lloyd-Jones the object of *agei* is derived from θνατῶν τε καὶ ἀθανάτων.[53] In his view, as a result, the disputed verses of the fragment should be translated as follows: the superior *nómos* 'guides all mortals and immortals according to its will' (1972). For others, such as Dale Grote, *agei* does not have an object, and as a result he translates the opening lines, leaving the verb untranslated, as: 'the law, which is the king of all, mortals and immortals, ἄγει, justifying violence . . .' (1994: 23).

Pike, noting the ambiguity of δικαιῶν (*dikaiōn*; δικαιόω, *dikaioō*), illustrated that it can be interpreted in the sense of a 'justification' (whereby the *nómos* of Pindar would be rendering a violent act as just – an interpretation that Pike seems to prefer), as well as in the sense of a 'punishment' (i.e. bringing violence before justice, *bia* before *dikē* – whereby Heracles would be said to 'enact' that 'punishment'; 1984: 19).[54] In one way or another, Heracles is depicted in this sense as the one who brings, or 'justifies', justice and order with his violent hand against the *hubristai*, whether out of his own will or as the pursuer of the will of Zeus. Ostwald finds that the object is τὸ βιαιότατον (1965: 117). For him,

> the point of the poem is that, although the theft of Geryon's cattle and of the mares of Diomedes was accomplished by violence, we must not object to it, since they are generally

---

[53] Demos (1994: 94) agrees.
[54] See also Stefou (2015: 9).

held to be glorious labours of Heracles; and what is generally believed to be right has royal, that is legitimate and
not tyrannical, power and this power is recognized by both
gods and men. (1969: 38)

On the other hand, Fisher notes, even if *nómos* is understood
as 'custom or recognised opinion', *nómos* 'may on occasion
conflict with strict justice' (1992: 234). However, the sacred
nómos, as in the final line of *N.* 1, cannot be perceived as a
form of 'partial justice'.[55] Once more, this would risk reading
Pindar in a tragic or otherwise anachronistic modality.

Lastly, for Kyriakou, δικαιῶν (*dikaiōn*), despite its ambiguity, can be understood in the following sense:

Νόμος, the sovereign power, claims extreme violence as
its prerogative, reserves it as its right in order to fulfil its
ends ... Νόμος empowers or perhaps forces Heracles to
act violently, i.e. unjustly. It does not make violence just, it
only makes use of violence. Heracles' injustice is not justified but shown to be the means that a sovereign, amoral
power uses to bring about the implementation of its will.
(2002: 200)

Nómos, in other words, is an 'absolute' power (ibid. 201), in
contrast to Treu, who earlier argued that *nómos* is a 'limited'
power on the basis of a 'tragic reading' of the fragment (1963:
211–14). Thus, it is not a matter of the justification of violent
deeds or of a mere favouritism by Zeus for one of his sons.
Rather, it is an acceptance of the supremacy of the sacred
nómos. 'Justice' (*dikē*) and 'violence' (*bia*) are not opposed in
Nómos-basileus – as they are in Hesiod (see Chapter Six with
reference to *W.D.* 276–80). Kyriakou concludes:

Pindar may have meant to suggest that the most salient
characteristic of the ultimate authority is violence and
not justice. This universal authority, νόμος, is a sovereign
ordinance, a norm that everybody has to obey and a fate
that nobody can escape ... In frag. 169a Pindar suggested

---

[55] See Fisher (1992: 235).

that, on some occasions at least, νόμος reserves the right to enforce the use of extreme violence and to overrule justice. (2002: 206)[56]

It is a worthwhile excursus, thus, at this point to note the manner in which the early Greeks think of *bia*. In her personification as a deity, *Bia* is a winged *daimon* of power and force and she stands beside Zeus' throne as one of the four enforcers of his will (her siblings being *Nikē*, *Kratos* and *Zēlos*; Hes. *Th*. 385). This is perhaps not the earliest use of the word. In Hesiod's *Theogony*, the guardians are wonderful, while for Plato's *Protagoras* they are terrible (at 321d). It is worth noting then that, for instance, βία (βίη; *bia*, *biē*) in Pindar, but also in Homer, is ever associated with 'power', and especially physical strength (for example, in *O*. 1.88; *P*. 4.212; *N*. 11.22), rather than necessarily or exclusively with 'violence'. It is on the basis of the subsequent understanding of an exertion of physical strength (as force) that *bia* will be opposed in Plato's *Phaedrus* to 'acting out of will' (ἑκών, *hekōn*): πρὸς βίαν βουληθῆς μᾶλλον ἢ ἑκὼν λέγειν (236d2–3); while in Aristotle, *bia* will be opposed to *phusis* in *Physics* (at 4.8.215a1). It is of interest, however, in this regard, that the word *bia* etymologically is thought to originate from the proto-Indo-European *$g^w eih_3 w$- ('to live', *$guiuos$*). The etymological link between *bia* and *bios* is itself telling, as it is so in other languages (i.e. *vis* and *vita* in Latin and, as noted above, the Indo-European *$guiuos$* and *$guiie$*). In Greek, one of two words that signify life is βίος (*bios*), which early on means *a way* of living, in the sense of 'surviving'. It is in this guise that it is opposed to the other word for life in Greek, *zōē*, which usually signifies animal life (approximating to the notion of natural or 'biological life' to a degree), and it is in this manner, too, that Aristotle will write in *De Generatione Animalium* that the foetus 'lives the [way of] life of a plant' (ζῆν [*zēn*] τὰ τοιαῦτα φυτοῦ βίον; *GA* 736b13),

---

[56] While it is notable that Kyriakou writes of a 'right' to the use of violence and of an 'overruling' of justice, in a somewhat anachronistic manner, this is to emphasise her point. Kyriakou also notes, with good reason, that Pindar's *nómos* 'can be contrasted with the paradigmatic just kings that avoid violence in Homer, *Od*. 19.109–114; and Hesiod *Th*. 81–92; *W.D*. 225–247' (2002: 205).

utilising both words in order to establish the clarity of his distinction.[57]

Kyriakou, interestingly, is not a long way from at least a component of the interpretation by, for instance, Demos, whereby the apportionment of *nómos* (whether understood as 'fate' or as another universal *nómos*) is inescapable: *nómos* is the 'ultimate' power (Demos 1994: 98). Despite the reprehensibility of Heracles' actions, to mortal eyes at least, *nómos* has the ultimate power to act as a 'king' (*basileus*), whether by 'overruling' such reprehension or by using violent means.[58] To this question I return to anew below, with particular regard to the way in which the philosopher Giorgio Agamben has recently reread the famous fragment. Suffice to say that it should not be forgotten that Heracles is a demigod of the heroic age, an age where his actions, while violent, would not have been considered unusual (i.e. as against *nómos*, custom, whether of Heracles or of the heroes more generally), but rather intrinsic to heroism.[59] Perhaps, after all, the behaviour of a hero in the heroic age should not be assumed uncritically, as if echoed in the time of Pindar, let alone later that of Plato.[60] Pindar's attitude towards Heracles' deeds can to an extent be seen as ambiguous, yet at the same time commonplace: if a demigod, Heracles, is pursuing the will of Zeus in his heroic labours, then, while he may act wrongly, that is, outside of (mortal) custom or convention, he ever remains *ek-nomios* (by his 'nature' or *moira*). Ultimately, Pindar seems to be telling us that he has acted justly according to *Nómos-basileus*.[61] The paradox or ambiguity may at the same time be here read as a matter of fact: Heracles was violent *and* just.

---

[57] Socrates in Plato's *Phaedrus* will, in a comparable sense, describe how the good *logoi* must be composed as a living creature: δεῖν πάντα λόγον ὥσπερ ζῷον [zōon] συνεστάναι σῶμα (at 264c).

[58] See the valuable recent discussion by Stefou (2015: 1–11); compare Pindar's fr. 70b.

[59] See White (2001: 31–7).

[60] It should be noted that in Plato's *Seventh Letter*, at 334c, he advises: μὴ δουλοῦσθαι Σικελίαν ὑπ᾽ ἀνθρώποις δεσπόταις, μηδὲ ἄλλην πόλιν, ὅ γ᾽ ἐμὸς λόγος, ἀλλ᾽ ὑπὸ νόμοις· οὔτε γὰρ τοῖς δουλουμένοις οὔτε τοῖς δουλωθεῖσιν ἄμεινον. That is, that it is preferable to enslave Sicily under *nómois*, rather than under arbitrary human rule.

[61] See Lloyd-Jones (1972: 55–6) and also fr.81.

6. Agamben's *nomos basileus*

Agamben has more recently drawn remarkable philosophical attention anew to the Pindaric fr. 169a, for the purposes of inquiring into 'the most ancient recorded formulation' of the 'principle' and 'paradox of sovereignty' (1998: 30). Relying on the reconstruction by August Böckh,[62] Agamben renders the translation of the opening lines as follows:

> The *nomos* sovereign of all,
> Of mortals and immortals,
> Leads with the strongest hand,
> Justifying the most violent [*giustificando il più violento*].
> I judge this from the works of Heracles.

For Agamben, Pindar 'defines the sovereignty of the *nomos* by means of a justification of violence' (1998: 31). This Agamben considers to be beyond doubt, given the reference to Heracles' deeds.[63] We have already seen that it may not, for Pindar, be a matter of 'justification' as such, let alone of 'sovereignty' per se; his *nómos* could be said to be, according to Hesychius, *kata tēn phusin*, and, as stated earlier, Pindar praises Heracles in emphatic ways (for example, in *N*. 1.33f).[64] Yet the ambiguity in the Pindaric formulation, due mostly to the extant manuscripts and their differences, could be retained. In any case, what is to be considered is the relation between the 'two essentially antithetical principles that the Greeks called *Bia* and *Dikē*, violence and justice' (ibid. 31).

Agamben writes of their 'scandalous unification' in the

---

[62] Agamben omits the full reference to the German classicist August Böckh (1785–1867), who collected, edited and commented upon the works of Pindar; the reference is probably to the commentary in Böckh ([1811–19, 1821] 2013: v.2, 641–3).

[63] The scholiast to Pindar's *N*. 9.35 writes in this regard: ο δὲ ἰσχυρός ἀνὴρ τὸ προυπάρχον δίκαιον καταπαύει (Böckh ([1811–19, 1821] 2013: v. 2, 640; 'the strong man cancels the current or pre-existing *dikaion*'; my translation). Agamben's justification on the basis of Heracles' deeds has been long accepted by classicists, see, for instance, Schröder (1917: 201).

[64] '*Basileus*' refers to the kingdom of *nómos*, a sense that we meet numerous times. For example, consider the reference to Alcidamas in Aristotle's *Rhet.* 1406a23, which states: οἱ τῶν πόλεων βασιλεῖς νόμους.

sense of an 'Aristotelian conjunction of opposites' (ibid.).
Aristotle produced a systematic analysis of opposites in
Chapters 10 and 11 of his *Categories*. Among the four categories of opposites that he delineated, 'contraries' entail
the type of opposition that characterises the disjunction
of violence and *dikē* ('justice', in Agamben's rendering).
Contraries are, for Aristotle, not interdependent, since the
excess of one leads to the annihilation of the other. In this
sense, the excess of violence can be said to lead to the annihilation of *dikē*. A conjunction of opposites would mean that
a complete or near-unification (fusion) of the two would
lead to the scandal in question, whereby *dikē* = violence and
vice versa.[65] In Agamben's analysis of the fragment, it is
nómos that stands for the power which 'with the strongest
hand' achieves the 'paradoxical union of these opposites'
(ibid. 31). Such a *nómos* collapses the earlier Hesiodic differentiation between the *nómos* of beasts and the *nómos* of
mortals and renders violence and *dikē* at a point of 'indistinction', in the name of the kingdom or sovereignty of
nómos (*W.D.* 275–9; Agamben 1998: 32).[66] Agamben explains
then that sovereignty is 'the threshold on which violence
passes over into law and law passes over into violence'
(ibid.). We have seen earlier that *nómos* does not necessarily stand for 'law' in the Pindaric use, though perhaps
it does so, in one sense, when seen as a 'sacred' *nómos*. In
addition, let me add, it is not 'law and violence', in this
regard, that Pindar depicts as in an arguable conjunction,
but *dikē* (which is not exactly 'law' or 'right') and *bia* (which
is not just 'violence'). That said, the interpretative uncer-
tainty with regard to Pindar's use of *nómos* does allow room
for the penetrating theoretical assumptions that Agamben
employs. Agamben, in fact, refers to Solon's expression
κράτει νόμου (*kratei nómou*) whereby, he writes, the specific
'force' of law was identified in the connection of violence
(*bia*) and *dikē* (ταῦτα μὲν κράτει | νόμου βίην τε καὶ δίκην
συναρμόσας | ἔρεξα καὶ διῆλθον ὡς ὑπερχόμην; 'with the

---

[65] In a different sense, we read in Aristotle that the opposites are co-present
(ἐνούσας), *Metaph.* L. 2.1069, 6, 19–24 and *Phys.* 1.4.187, a20–3.

[66] On the antithesis of *bia* and *dikē*, see Hom. *Il.* 16.387–8; and Solon fr. 24.16
[Diehl].

force of the *nómos* I have connected violence [*biēn*] and *dikē'*)
(ibid. 31).[67]

It is at this point in his explication of the fragment that
Agamben refers to the German lyric poet Friedrich Hölderlin
(1770–1843) and his translation of and commentary on the
Pindaric fragment, titled *Das Höchste* (*The Highest*). Famously,
the text of *Das Höchste*, from approximately 1805, begins with
a translation of the Pindaric fragment:

Das Gesez,[68]
Von allen der König, Sterblichen und
Unsterblichen; das führt eben
Darum gewaltig
Das gerechteste Recht mit allerhöchster Hand.[69]

The law,
Sovereign/King of all,
both mortals and Immortals; it is for that reason
that it compellingly/violently guides,
The most just justice/Right with a supreme hand.[70]

Richard Pierre has noted that the source that Hölderlin used
for his translation of the Pindaric fragment 'was a two-volume
text he owned (dated 1560), edited by Henricus Stephanus'
(2016: 30).[71] It is important to note that the Stephanus edition,
as Pierre adds, did not contain the 'longest extant version'
(ibid. 30) and that it juxtaposes the Latin translation whereby,
for example, *ius* and *lex* correspond to *nómos* and *dikē* (ibid.).
Agamben notes, further, that Hölderlin probably had reference to Plato's *Gorgias*, where the phrasing *biaiōn ton dikaiotaton* (doing violence to the most just) is met at 484b1–10. For
Agamben, the Platonic citation in the *Gorgias* 'consciously
alters the Pindaric text' (1998: 33), rendering the fragment as
follows:

---

[67] Solon fr. 24 [Diehl]; Arist. *Resp. Ath.* 5.
[68] '*Gesez*' is an earlier spelling for '*Gesetz*'.
[69] (2004: 229–30).
[70] (2004: 229–30; my translation); Adler (1984: 43) translates the last verse as
'The rightest right with the very right hand'.
[71] See Bartel (2000: 10–12).

The *nomos*,
sovereign of all
mortals and immortals
Leads with the strongest hand
Doing violence to the most just.

Agamben, thus, emphatically comments:

> Only an acute *coniunctivitis professoria* was able to induce phi-
> lologists (in particular, the editor of the now aged Oxonian
> critical edition of Plato) to correct the more authoritative
> manuscripts' phrase, *biaion to dikaiotaton*, in accordance
> with the letter of Pindar's text (*dikaion to biaiotaton*). Ulrich
> von Wilamowitz-Moellendorff has justly observed (1920:
> 95–7), *biaion* is too rare in Greek to be explained by a lapse
> of memory (let alone a *lapsus calami*), and the meaning of the
> Platonic wordplay is perfectly clear: here the 'justification
> of violence' is at the same time a 'doing violence to the most
> just', and the 'sovereignty' of the nomos of which Pindar
> speaks consists in this and nothing else. (1998: 33–4)[72]

It is worth returning to the *Gorgias* to examine this in a bit
more detail. This is what we find in the *Gorgias* at the point
when Callicles refers to Pindar (484b1–c3 [Dodds]):

> δοκεῖ δέ μοι καὶ Πίνδαρος ἅπερ ἐγὼ λέγω ἐνδείκνυσθαι
> ἐν τῷ ᾄσματι ἐν ᾧ λέγει ὅτι –νόμος ὁ πάντων βασιλεὺς
> θνατῶν τε καὶ οὗτος δὲ δή, φησίν, ἀθανάτων ἄγει δικαιῶν
> τὸ βιαιότατον [Bergk; or βιαίων τὸ δικαιότατον?] ὑπερτάτᾳ
> χειρί· τεκμαίρομαι ἔργοισιν Ἡρακλέος, ἐπεὶ – ἀπριάτας
> – λέγει οὕτω πως – τὸ γὰρ ᾄσμα οὐκ ἐπίσταμαι – λέγει
> δ' ὅτι οὔτε πριάμενος οὔτε δόντος τοῦ Γηρυόνου ἠλάσατο
> τὰς βοῦς, ὡς τούτου ὄντος τοῦ δικαίου φύσει, καὶ βοῦς
> καὶ τἆλλα κτήματα εἶναι πάντα τοῦ βελτίονός τε καὶ
> κρείττονος τὰ τῶν χειρόνων τε καὶ ἡττόνων.

---

[72] Though as Agamben stresses, Plato's aim is to undermine this conflation of *bia* and justice. Agamben finds this aim expressed also in Plato's
Protagoras, 337c and in the *Laws*, 690b–c. On the latter, see the analysis
below. As to the rarity of the *biaiōn*, it should be said that it obviously
does not exclude the possibility of its use.

And it seems to me that Pindar adds his evidence to what I say, in the ode where he says – Law [*nómos*] the sovereign of all, Mortals and immortals, which, so he continues, carries all with highest hand, justifying the utmost force: in proof I take the deeds of Heracles, for unpurchased – the words are something like that – I do not know the poem well – but it tells how he drove off the cows as neither a purchase nor a gift from Geryones; taking it as a natural right that cows or any other possessions of the inferior and weaker should all belong to the superior and stronger.

Agamben's interpretation (though not his reading as a whole) rests on the acceptance of βιαίων τὸ δικαιότατον (*biaiōn to dikaiotaton*) in line 3, as opposed to, perhaps, Pindar's rendering. He follows Wilamowitz-Moellendorff, who notes Plato's correction of βιαίων (*biaiōn*) with βιαιῶν (*biaiōn*; 1920: 95–105).[73] The most authoritative manuscripts of the *Gorgias*, as Ostwald has shown, render line 3 as βιαίων τὸ δικαιότατον (*biaiōn to dikaiotaton*; 1965: 32, n. 8) – apart from one, he notes, that of Parisinus, which renders in a marginal note δικαιῶν τὸ βιαιότατον (*dikaiōn to biaiotaton*; ibid.; this is also the case with Pavese's reproduction of the papyrus text which I referred to extensively earlier). Aelius Aristides (117–181 BC) in *To Plato: In Defence of Oratory*, arguing against Callicles, renders it as δικαιῶν τὸ βιαιότατον (*dikaiōn to biaiotaton*; 52.14 Jebb; Ael. Arist. *Or.* 45. 52–3) and refers the *biaiotaton* to Heracles' deeds. If that is the case, as Konstantinos Stefou notes, agreeing with Ostwald (2009: 95, n. 8), then the change in the majority of the manuscripts is a case of 'spoonerism' (2015: 4; a view which, in contrast to Agamben, he agrees with).

It has to be stressed that it is Callicles speaking in the *Gorgias*, and he is referring to the Pindaric fragment in order to bolster his thesis over the 'natural justice' of the 'right' (*dikē*) of the most powerful as against the mortal *nómoi*.[74] Callicles

---

[73] Lloyd-Jones also agrees that Plato writes *biaiōn to dikaiotaton*, but underlines that this was not what Pindar had written (1972: 48). Pike (1984: 19), Demos (1994: 95–106) and Grote (1994: 22) also accept this as deliberate in Plato. See Stefou (2015: 4–5) for a discussion.

[74] See Demos (1994); Grote (1994); for the wider context see Ehrenberg (1921); and Heinimann ([1945] 1965/1972).

defends, in other words, 'might is right' as a matter of *dikaion* ('natural justice') against the posited *nómoi* of the many who, as he says, are ἀσθενεῖς (*astheneis*, weak; 483b5). This sense is, arguably, also encountered in Euripides' *Hecuba* at 798–605:

ἡμεῖς μὲν οὖν δοῦλοί τε κἀσθενεῖς ἴσως:
ἀλλ᾽ οἱ θεοὶ σθένουσι χὠ κείνων κρατῶν
Νόμος: νόμῳ γὰρ τοὺς θεοὺς ἡγούμεθα
καὶ ζῶμεν ἄδικα καὶ δίκαι᾽ ὡρισμένοι:
ὃς ἐς σ᾽ ἀνελθὼν εἰ διαφθαρήσεται,
καὶ μὴ δίκην δώσουσιν οἵτινες ξένους
κτείνουσιν ἢ θεῶν ἱερὰ τολμῶσιν φέρειν,
οὐκ ἔστιν οὐδὲν τῶν ἐν ἀνθρώποις ἴσον.

I may be a slave and weak as well,
but the gods are strong,
and *Nomos* too which prevails over them,
for by *nomos* it is that we believe in them and set up
boundaries of right [*dikai*] and wrong [*adika*] for our lives.
Now if this principle, when referred to you, is to be set at
nothing, and they are to escape [*dikē*] who murder guests
or dare to plunder the temples of gods,
then all fairness in human matters is at an end.[75]

In other words, for Callicles, Pindar's *nómos*, from which he claims to draw support for his thesis, is the *nómos* of *phusis* that grounds the *dikē* of the *bia* of the strong over the weak. In this manner, as Stefou argues, Callicles can in fact be said to be following the edict of the earlier Homeric ethics, which

dictates the behaviour that 'justifies the most violent act' (δικαιῶν τὸ βιαιότατον), because the νόμος that it imposes accepts wrongdoing with the aim of defending what is at the heart of the value system of the Homeric heroes, namely honour (τιμή). Based on the Homeric ethics, it constitutes justice (δίκη) of the Homeric good man (ἀγαθός) to perform unjust deeds with the aim of maintaining his τιμή and avoiding being reproached by others. (2015: 7)

[75] Translated by Coleridge (in Oates and O'Neill (1938: I)), who translates '*nómos*' as 'custom'.

Callicles defends the aristocratic viewpoint, a viewpoint that Pindar was certainly familiar with, if not attached to. But this is not all, since it is not, as seen earlier, unproblematic to merely accept that Pindar voices an aristocratic 'ideology'.

If the majority of the manuscripts of the *Gorgias* are to be followed, then it still needs to be noted that the Pindaric fragment is reread by Agamben with an eye clearly devoted to its Platonic-Calliclean rendering, which, as mentioned above, is distant from the original fragment as well as, crucially, Pindar's post-Homeric context. Yet to what extent the poet reaches a different conclusion to that of Plato may remain a question. While it can be said that the poet's understanding does not leave room for the immediacy of 'justice' that, according to one interpretation, Plato's philosopher-king in the *Republic* would hold, and if Agamben is, further, right (1998: 33) as to Plato aiming to undermine the coincidence of *bia* and *nómos* (which seems to be the case), then some convergence between the poet and the philosopher may be possible. Socrates, it ought to be noted, will successfully refute Callicles' thesis by stating that *nómos* is best and ultimately leads to εὐδαιμονία (*eudaimonia*), not when it is derived from mighty power, but rather when it derives from the soul under the principle of the ἄρχων ἑαυτοῦ (being the *archōn* of one's self).[76] Hence, if it is a 're-arrangement' in Plato, then it is for the purposes of Callicles' thesis not Socrates (Plato's), nor, indeed, Pindar's.

Whichever view as to the differing manuscripts is adopted, the fact remains that Plato's reference to Pindar's *nómos*, whether through 'wordplay' or not, leads to the undermining of the principle or *nómos* that underlies the rendering of *biaiōn to dikaiotaton*. Agamben locates, further, this undermining in Plato's *Laws* at 690b–c, where the Athenian states: κατὰ φύσιν δέ, τὴν τοῦ νόμου ἑκόντων ἀρχὴν ἀλλ᾽ οὐ βίαιον πεφυκυῖαν ('but rather according thereto – the natural rule of law [*nómou*], without force, over willing subjects').[77] This can, further, be supplemented with reference to 714e–15a, which Agamben does not refer to though he is of course aware of

---

[76] See the attentive discussion in Stefou (2015: 9–10).
[77] Translated by Bury (1967–8).

it, where it is stated in 'response' to the matter discussed in 690b as to Pindar's *nómos* that αὐτῶν τοῦτο, καὶ ἔφαμέν που κατὰ φύσιν τὸν Πίνδαρον ἄγειν δικαιοῦντα τὸ βιαιότατον, ὡς φάναι ('to quote Pindar the law marches *kata phusin* when it justifies the right [*dikē*] of might').[78] Indeed, while the sense remains with regard to 'might is right', the phrasing in this passage appears to reveal the conscious 'wordplay' or the 'purposeful paraphrasing' of Plato's rendering of the fragment, since here we read instead δικαιοῦντα τὸ βιαιότατον (*dikaiounta to biaiotaton*).

7. Hölderlin's un-Heraclean *nomos*

It is of further interest, for my purposes, that Plato's ultimate aim at this point in the *Gorgias* is to emphasise the preference for knowledge (σοφία, *sophia*). It is, then, worth following Hölderlin's commentary to his translation of the fragment to see why that may be the case for the German poet also. Hölderlin writes:

> *Das Unmittelbare, streng genommen, ist für die Sterblichen unmöglich, wie für die Unsterblichen; der Gott muß verschiedene Welten unterscheiden, seiner Natur gemäß, weil himmlische Güte, ihret selber wegen, heilig sein muß, unvermischet. Der Mensch, als Erkennendes, muß auch verschiedene Welten unterscheiden, weil Erkenntnis nur durch Entgegensetzung möglich ist. Deswegen ist das Unmittelbare, streng genommen, für die Sterblichen unmöglich, wie für die Unsterblichen.*
> *Die strenge Mittelbarkeit ist aber das Gesetz.*
> *Deswegen aber führt es gewaltig das gerechteste Recht mit allerhöchster Hand.*
> *Die Zucht, sofern sie die Gestalt ist, worin der Mensch sich und der Gott begegnet, der Kirche und des Staats Gesetz und anererbte Satzungen (die Heiligkeit des Gottes, und für den Menschen die Möglichkeit einer Erkenntnis, einer Erklärung), diese führen gewaltig das gerechteste Recht mit allerhöchster Hand, sie halten strenger, als die Kunst, die lebendigen Verhältnisse fest, in denen, mit der Zeit, ein Volk sich begegnet*

---

[78] ibid.

hat und begegnet. »König« bedeutet hier den Superlativ, der nur das Zeichen ist für den höchsten Erkenntnisgrund, nicht für die höchste Macht. (2004: v. 11, 229–30)

The immediate [*Das Unmittelbare*], strictly speaking, is impossible for mortals, as it is for the immortals; a God must distinguish different worlds, according to his nature, since heavenly goodness, because of itself, must be sacred, unmixed. Human beings, as knowing creatures, must also distinguish different worlds, because knowledge is only possible through opposition [*Entgegensezung*]. For this reason, the immediate [*das Unmittelbare*] is, strictly speaking, impossible for mortals and immortals.

However [*aber*], strict mediacy [*die strenge Mittelbarkeit*], is the law [*das Gesetz*]. That is why, compellingly, it guides the justest justice with a sovereign hand.

Discipline, in so far as it is form in which human beings and the gods meet, the law [*Gesetz*] of Church and State and inherited statutes [*Sazungen*] (the god's sanctity, and for human beings the possibility of recognition, an elucidation), these compellingly guide the justest justice with a sobering hand, more strictly [*strenger*] than arts they stabilise those vital matters [*lebendige Verhältnis*] in which, in time, a people has encountered itself and continues to encounter itself. 'King' here means the superlative that is only the sign for the supreme ground for cognition, not for the highest power.[79]

What would the immediate (*das Unmittelbare*) 'be', if it were accessible? Richard Pierre suggests that it would 'eliminate the need for such justification entirely, by directly joining the law of justice (*Recht*) and enacted law (*Gesetz*)' (2016: 23–4). But the poet, having declared that this remains impossible for both mortals and immortals, has no interest in that possibility and, instead, aims to undermine it. Crucially, too, the poet is not referring to matters of 'power' or 'law', but instead rereads the

---

[79] Translated by Hamburger in Hölderlin (1994: 639); with some modifications. For an extensive study of the translation and commentary, see Schestag (1999: 375–411); see also, Killy (1954); Baum (1963/1964); and Franz (1988).

Pindaric fragment as a claim to the 'supreme ground for cognition'. *Das Höchste* grammatically refers to an abstract concept, not a person (ibid. 28). The claim rests with regard to the aporetic ground of knowledge (taking the aporia, in fact, to its full range as to the unmediated as much as to the mediated).

Let us unpack this a little further. For Hölderlin, both gods and mortals must endure opposition or differentiation, albeit for different reasons. Gods must encounter differentiation for by 'nature' they must remain unmixed, while mortals are cognisant only in opposition to all, while remaining ever-mixed. As a result, immediate (direct) knowledge is impossible, for both. Mortal law and immortal Law (*das Gesetz*, but also *Recht*) are always mediated (in this sense: *nómos* as a 'convention', or as Herodotus later has it, 'custom'). Neither the gods nor mortals could ever have 'power' or 'sovereignty' over the immediate *nómos* (in the poet's sense of *Gesetz*, akin, it could be suggested, to Pindar's *nómos-basileus*), which remains ever inaccessible and supreme. Yet for this reason, it joins mortals and immortals at the same time as it disjoins them both from itself – perhaps a 'juncture' along the lines of the poet's other poem, *Brod und Wein* (*Bread and Wine*), which states:

> at noon or just before midnight,
> Whether it's early or late, always a measure [*ein Maß*]
> exists,
> Common to all, though his own to each one is also
> allotted
> Each of us makes for the place, reaches the place that he
> can.[80]

In this sense, *nómos* is the 'highest' condition for both mortals and immortals.

Moreover, as the poet writes in his essay *Über Religion* (*On Religion*, 1796), the 'law(s)' of mortals (whether of the church or posited statutes), mediated as they have to be, can only render a universal claim under the 'structure of necessity' to which all cognition is subject and beyond which it

---

[80] Hölderlin (2004: 9, 137ff); '*Bis in die Mitternacht, immer bestehet ein Maß,* | *Allen gemein, doch jeglichem auch ist eignes beschieden,* | *Dahin gehet und kommt jeder, wohin er es kann*'.

cannot reach (Hölderlin 1943–85: IV, 276). In contrast, while
the importance of posited institutions remains, another type
of laws, spiritual laws, that cannot be cognised ('*nicht blos
gedacht warden*'; ibid.), remains, one could say, 'the highest'
juncture/disjuncture for mortals. Mortal *nómos*, as well as
divine *nómos*, can only be a sign of the supreme ground of
cognition (*Erkentnißgrund*): it marks it by being related to it,
as much as it is, as a result, simultaneously marked by it.

Such a supreme ground is not, however, an ideal *nómos*,
or an overpowering force (*Macht*), but instead the pathway
(reminiscent, perhaps, of Parmenides' *palintropos*) whereby
'absoluteness' (to paraphrase Heraclitus) likes or prefers to
hide: it is *mediation without ends*.[81] Even the *nómos-basileus*
is not the sign of 'the highest', but the sign *für den höchsten
Erkenntnisgrund* ('the highest epistemic ground'). For the
poet, it is only in this manner that the possibility of encoun-
tering oneself arises ever-mediately. The immediate remains
necessary for the encounter, if forever withdrawn from
sight, and even its withdrawal can only be cognised medi-
ately. This is then the poet's, albeit tragic, reading of Pindar
and the φύσις (*phusis*) of the cosmic *nómos*.[82] In this way,
the *nómos-basileus* of Pindar's can be said to live through the
German poet's Apollonian inspiration in the only experience
that maintains itself in the unmixed most meditatively (even
if ever-failingly): *das Höchste der Kunst* ('the Highest in Art').[83]
What characterises, perhaps, the immediate is a structure of
negativity, the highest *nómos of nihilism*.

Martin Heidegger, in his reading of Hölderlin's fragment
in *Elucidations of Hölderlin's Poetry* (delivered in the 1970s but
first published in 1981) and his interpretation of the immediate in the poet's translation, writes: 'The immediate is itself
never something mediate; on the other hand, the immediate,
strictly speaking, is the mediation, that is, the mediatedness

---

[81] See the discussion, along similar lines, by Bartel (2000) and Stergiopoulou
(2014).

[82] See Hölderlin's notes (1988: v. 16); Lacoue-Labarthe 1989; and Agamben's
commentary (1999b: 90–1).

[83] See the discussion in Stergiopoulou (2014: 112–17). The 'highest' in art,
arguably poetry for Agamben though not named in these terms, holds
central importance for a philosophical understanding of the experience
of language and of negativity; see, further, Agamben (1991).

of the mediated, because it renders the mediated possible in its essence' (1981/2000: 84). In Heidegger's reading, it is 'nature' (which Heidegger understands 'deconstructively' as φύσις/*phusis*) that is the 'all-mediating mediatedness': the *nómos* (ibid. 84). In this regard, Heidegger refers to another poem by Hölderlin titled *Wie wenn am Feiertage* (*As when on a Holiday*), which could be said to contain an implied reference to the Pindaric fragment:

> *Jetzt aber tagts! Ich harrt und sah es kommen,*
> *Und was ich sah, das Heilige sei mein Wort.*
> *Denn sie, sie selbst, die älter denn die Zeiten*
> *Und über die Götter des Abends und Orients ist,*
> *Die Natur ist jetzt mit Waffenklang erwacht,*
> *Und hoch vom Aether bis zum Abgrund nieder*
> *Nach festem Gesetze, wie einst, aus heiligem Chaos gezeugt,*
> *Fühlt neu die Begeisterung sich,*
> *Die Allerschaffende, wieder.*

> But now day breaks! I awaited and saw it come,
> And what I saw, may the holy be my word,
> For she, she herself, who is older than the ages
> And above the gods of Occident and Orient,
> Nature is now awakening with the clang of arms,
> And from high Aether down to the abyss,
> According to firm law, as once, begotten out of holy Chaos,
> Inspiration, the all-creative,
> Again feels herself anew.[84]

Heidegger seems to suggest that in the poet's 'nature' (*Natur*), chaos and *nómos* are indistinct. This is not the chaos that mortals appreciate as a form of lawlessness (*anomia*), but instead, as Hölderlin describes it, as 'holy wilderness' (ibid.) It is worth quoting a characteristic part of Heidegger's commentary in full:

> Nevertheless, chaos; signifies first of all the yawning, gaping chasm, the open that first opens itself, wherein

---

[84] Translated by Hoeller in Heidegger (1981/2000: 83).

everything is engulfed. The chasm affords no support for anything distinct and grounded. And therefore, for all experience, which only knows what is mediated, chaos seems to be without differentiation and thus mere confusion. The 'chaotic' in this sense, however, is only the inessential aspect of what 'chaos' means. Thought in terms of nature [φύσις] chaos remains that gaping out of which the open opens itself, so that it may grant its bounded presence to all differentiations. Hölderlin therefore calls 'Chaos' and 'confusion' 'holy'. Chaos is the holy itself. Nothing that is real precedes this opening, but rather always only enters into it. All that appears is already surpassed each time by it. Nature is, 'as once', prior to and above everything. She is the former – and that in a double sense. She is the oldest of every former thing, and always the youngest of subsequent things. By awakening, nature's coming, as what is most futural, comes out of the oldest of what has been, which never ages because it is each time the youngest. (ibid. 84)

Only the poets, for Heidegger, can embrace the light of the 'originary' φύσις (reinterpreting the distinction between the poet's *Natur* and *phusis*), which remains forever unmixed, in the sense that it exists as the Open (*das Offene*), a gap as a 'juncture' (*dikē*), while nonetheless inaccessible (ibid. 85). In this reading, it could be said that it is this *phusis* which, as the *nómos* of the All, leads with the supreme hand or *bia*. For Heidegger's reading, the holy is the unsettling (*Entsetzliche*) itself (1981/2000: 85), the clearing (*die Lichtung*).[85] To this 'originary' unsettlement, the showing of a limit, mortal and immortal laws can only identify a void that must be filled, a need that must be satisfied. The meaningless must be full of meaning. As a result, their ever-failing claim to universality (to 'say' Being or to 'see' the Open) hides behind the structure of mediate necessity.[86] *Phusis* is 'the rising into the

---

[85] For a well-known critique, see de Man (1983: 259). For a recent critical outline of Heidegger's reading and de Man's critique, see Shaw (2015), whom I thank for sharing his work with me.

[86] See Hölderlin (1943–85: IV, 276–8). For a recent reading, see Cooper (2012: 195–211). Cooper presents a critical differentiation of Hölderlin from Agamben's reading, in particular relation to Hölderlin's tragic reading

open: the lighting of that clearing into which anything may enter appearing, present itself in its outline, show itself in its "appearance" (*eidos, idea*) and be present as this or that' (Heidegger 1981/2000: 79). It is in this manner that *phusis* as the clearing of the Opening (*Das Offene*), in Heidegger's interpretation, is the *nómos-basileus* of all.[87]

8. Cosmonomy

Agamben's own reference to Hölderlin can be further elucidated when juxtaposed to the philosopher's critique of Carl Schmitt's reading (and criticism) of Hölderlin's translation of the fragment. Schmitt, in *Der Nomos der Erde* in 1950, critiques the poet for mistranslating *nómos* as *Gesetz*, 'even though he knows that, in the strictest sense, law is rigorous mediation [*das Gesetz die strenge Mittelbarkeit ist*]' (1974: 42).[88] Schmitt wants, in fact, to reread the poet's translation along the lines of his own understanding of *Gesetz*. For Schmitt, *Gesetz* is a derivative convention which is posited (constituted) and which, crucially, is preceded by a 'constitutive historical event' which remains the unmediated original principle (*nómos*) (ibid.). For, Schmitt writes, *nómos*

of Sophocles, as well as with regard to the ultimate law in Hölderlin (love), which is remarkably close to Paul's messianic *plēroma* of the law: 'For Hölderlin the opening of representation – its cut, where it is revealed to itself as ending, as unfolding in messianic time – is an opening into a determinate social reality, an *ethos*. Representation's ending is revealed in the moment poetry adverts to life, and, in that moment, reveals life as both restricted, marked by the wound of separation and the diminishments of need, and as a result of that restriction free from need, part of the "sphere of relation" whose ultimate law – of love – is infinite' (2012: 201). While Cooper is right in noting differences between Hölderlin and Agamben in this respect, one has to note the crucial convergence in Agamben's critique of the onto-theological structure of relation or negativity, and the further scope for their approximation in the conception of 'love'; see Agamben (1995b: 61; 1999a: 114–15).

[87] In this regard, it would be interesting to compare Heidegger's reading with Maurice Blanchot's reflections on the German poet in general and the Pindaric fragment in particular, in, for instance, [1949] 1995: 111–31 and elsewhere.

[88] Modifying the translation as in Agamben (1998).

is precisely the full immediacy [*Unmittelbarkeit*] of juridical power not mediated by laws [*Gesetze*]; it is a constitutive, historical event [*ein konstituierendes geschichtliches Ereignis*], an act of *legitimacy* which alone gives the legality of mere law [*des bloßen Gesetzes*] its meaning. (ibid.)

Agamben proceeds to critique Schmitt's own misinterpretation of the poet as follows:

Here Schmitt completely misinterprets the intention of the poet, which is directed precisely against every immediate principle. In his commentary, Hölderlin defines the *nomos* (which he distinguishes from law) as rigorous mediation (*strenge Mittelbarkeit*): 'The immediate', he writes, 'is, taken in the rigorous sense, impossible for mortals as for immortals; the god must distinguish different worlds, according to his nature, since the heavenly goods must be holy for themselves, unmixed. Insofar as he knows, man too must distinguish different worlds, since knowledge is only possible through opposition' (*Sämtliche Werke*, p. 309). (1998: 32–3)

Schmitt confuses the poet's *Gesetz* with his own object of critique of positivist law, and Heracles' deeds, which he perceives as higher than *Rechtskraft*, with Pindar's *nómos-basileus*. As Katerina Stergiopoulou comments: 'What Schmitt does not want to argue about with Hölderlin is the challenge that Hölderlin's understanding of *Gesetz* and of *Mittelbarkeit* (mediation) might pose to his own reading of *nomos*' (2014: 112). For the German jurist, Heracles, as depicted in the remainder of the Pindaric fragment, is the mythical 'founder of order' [*Ordnungsstifter*], since he 'creates right' (*schafft Recht*) through his *nehmen-nemein*, the naming of the *nómos* (i.e. the apportionment or partition of land that in itself is not enough, but has to be named and claimed; 2003: 342).[89]

For the poet, instead, no Heracles (sovereign) can 'save us',

---

[89] See the discussion by Stergiopoulou (2014: 112–15). For an attentive reading of Hölderlin's *nómos* in relation to the tragic and the *Antigone* in particular, see Panno (2004), whom I thank for sharing and discussing his work with me.

in direct contrast to Schmitt's reconceptualisation of *nómos*. Agamben comments: 'Hölderlin displaces a juridico-political problem into the sphere of the theory of knowledge: What is more original and stronger than law is not (as in Schmitt) the *nómos* as sovereign principle but rather the mediation that grounds knowledge' (1998: 33). For according to the poet, any attempt to let violence and law (*Gesetz*) coincide with the highest ground of knowledge is not only impossible, but ever-undermined when attempted. The poet, it appears, is the (German) jurist's most cunning enemy. Not a *nómos-basileus*, but a *kosmos basileus*, perhaps, or an imagined sense when the two were indistinguishable.

Jean-Luc Nancy, in fact, is the French philosopher who has reflected on the Pindaric fragment in a cosmological, or *cosmonomical* manner (and from whom Agamben borrows for his critique of sovereign power). Nancy's reading approximates, as his title suggests, '*Cosmos Basileus*', the sense of what I call a *cosmonomy*, as the 'ground of knowledge'. For Nancy, the differentiation or partitioning/sharing of the world (which is nothing but its 'diversity of worlds') is the 'law of the world' and it 'does not have a sovereign' (2000: 185). Instead, Nancy writes, '*Cosmos, nomos*' (ibid.). *Nómos*, Nancy adds, is 'the distribution, apportionment, and allocation of its parts' (ibid.). Such distribution/sharing, however, is not absolutely accomplished, or the apportionment out of essences or natures never ends. The world itself is 'the giving (*le don*)' (ibid.). Such a sharing/giving is what a singular existence is itself, too, whereby its own 'giving' is its own 'condition of possibility', as well as 'detachment' (impossibility):

> Each existence [*existant*] appears in more ensembles, masses, tissues, or complexes than one perceives at first, and each one is also infinitely more detached from such, and detached from itself. Each opens onto and closes off more worlds, those within itself just as much as those outside, bringing the outside inside, and the other way around. (ibid. 187)[90]

---

[90] '*Chaque existant appartient à plus d'ensembles, de masses, de tissus ou de complexes qu'on ne l'aperçoit d'abord, et chacun aussi s'en détache plus, et se détache de lui-même, infiniment. Chacun ouvre et ferme sur plus de mondes, en*

9. Neither a *nomodicy*, nor a *nomomachia*

As far as Pindaric *nómos* is concerned, in contrast to Schmitt's, *nómos* is not the immediate act/event, or the (albeit inaccessible) condition that grounds law (or right) in the sense of a sovereign law in the polis, but one can still see why Schmitt read Pindar the way he did. There is, further, nothing explicit in Pindar's fragment that suggests that *nómos* is to be understood as common to a community (mortals and immortals do not appear to form such a community).[91] Meanwhile, Ostwald has insisted that *nómos* in Pindar's fragment does not appear as the 'law of fate' or the 'will of Zeus' (2009: 109–10); but, for the Greeks, it may well have been possible to consider Zeus' will as 'subject' to the 'universal *nómos*', or as its 'voice'.[92] In addition, as seen earlier, *nómos* is not always said to be of divine derivation in Pindar. In some degree of contrast to Agamben too, Pindar's *nómos* is 'the earliest formulation of the paradox of sovereignty' if in the sense of the most vivid early expression of the ambiguity and, crucially, supremacy of the 'holy' *nómos* in relation to both mortals and immortals.[93]

---

lui comme hors de lui, creusant le dehors dedans, et réciproquement' (Nancy 1998: 95).

[91] On the same point, see Ostwald (2009: 109).

[92] I thank Poulheria Kyriakou for very kindly discussing this question, and the fragment more generally, with me.

[93] Compare and contrast the later Stoic Chrysippus, who seems to refer to the Pindaric fragment in his *Nómos*, with a clear metaphysico-political sense in the post-Pindaric dissolution of the pre-Socratic distinction between *phusis* and *nómos*: ὁ νόμος πάντων ἐστὶ βασιλεὺς θείων τε καὶ ἀνθρωπίνων πραγμάτων· δεῖ δὲ αὐτὸν προστάτην τε εἶναι τῶν καλῶν καὶ τῶν αἰσχρῶν, καὶ ἄρχοντα καὶ ἡγεμόνα καὶ κατὰ τοῦτο κανόνα τε εἶναι δικαίων καὶ ἀδίκων καὶ τῶν φύσει πολιτικῶν ζῴων προστακτικὸν μὲν ὧν ποιητέον, ἀπαγορευτικὸν δὲ ὧν οὐ ποιητέον ('*Nómos* is the king of all, both divine and human. It ought to preside over the noble and the base, as chief and hegemon and thus accord what is *dikaion* and *adikon*, prescribing to animals that are by nature political what they should do, and prohibiting them from what they should not do'; Marcian, *Inst. I.* (Momsen, 11, 25)); see also Stob. 2.96.10–12 (SVF 3613), 2.102.4–9 (SVF 3614). Along similar lines, but with an even clearer sense of the supremacy of Zeus and of *nómos* as according to *phusis*, we read in Cleathes' *Hymn to Zeus*: Κύδιστ' ἀθανάτων, πολυώνυμε, παγκρατὲς αἰεί, | Ζεῦ, φύσεως ἀρχηγέ, νόμου μέτα πάντα κυβερνῶν, | χαῖρε· σὲ γὰρ πάντεσσι θέμις θνητοῖσι προσαυδᾶν; SVF I, 537, 1–3 ('Most honoured among the immortals, Possessor of many names,

Yet what is this *nómos*? Can we imagine Pindar, in his age, prescribing that the *nómos* of 'might is right' should be followed universally?[94] Equally, is *nómos* a matter of 'custom'? Both could be maintained, to an extent, if not read anachronistically – that is, as a hint to the range of practices/habits that define particular (or a plurality of) mortal or immortal beings (with regard to a 'convention' of experience). In one sense, the *nómos* in the fragment does appear to emphasise the 'validation' of a 'mere' custom or 'fact of experience'.[95] But it remains possible that Pindar, to an extent idiosyncratically, is expressing and divinising a universal *nómos*, that is, poetically utilising Heracles as a paradigm for it. In a sense, Pindar does not, however, compose a *nomodicy*, and neither does he describe a *nomomachia* (a conflict of *nómoi*). The 'reconciliation' of *bia* and *dikē* takes place under the name of *nómos*, most probably – at least in part – in the sense of the remembrance and acceptance by Pindar's audience of the earlier heroic *ēthos* or *nómos*. *Nómos*, in agreement with Ostwald in this regard, needs to be read in the particular poetic milieu and not be extracted as a self-evident precursor of the classical *nómos–phusis* debate or, indeed, as a 'universal' form of 'law' in the sense of sovereign power/law.[96] Pindar is not Euripides.[97] If *nómos* is to be understood as some kind of a 'universal' *nómos* or 'ordering' that apportions and binds the gods as much as mortals, then it may be the poetic explication of a *nómos* that pre-dates any later opposition to it (whether in the name of *phusis* or otherwise). It is *nómos*, the tradition of a past (or at least passing) age, perhaps to an extent explicitly

Ever Almighty, Zeus, Chief of *phusis*, you govern/steer with Your *nómos* over all things, hail to You. For to address You, it is *themis*, for all mortals' [my translation]); for a commentary and an alternative, though proximate, translation, see Meijer (2007: 209–28). For a general discussion, see the useful analysis by Domaradzki (2012: 125–48).

[94] As Gigante (1956: 91) claims for instance; a view that Ostwald finds objectionable (2009: 112, n. 81).

[95] See the discussion in Ostwald (2009: 114–15).

[96] As it may be implied to some extent in, for instance, Plato's *Protagoras*, where it is said that 'man' is the only animal who believes in the gods because of the συγγένεια [*suggeneia*] (commonality of *genos*) between gods and 'men' (322a3).

[97] See Ostwald (2009: 123); and Euripides' tragedy *Children of Heracles* (*Heraclidae*).

noted already in Pindar as unpleasant, and yet for the poet it is a *nómos* that can still be heard, as well as accepted.

Ἓν ἀνδρῶν, ἓν θεῶν γένος· ἐκ μιᾶς δὲ πνέομεν
ματρὸς ἀμφότεροι· διείργει δὲ πᾶσα κεκριμένα
δύναμις, ὡς τὸ μὲν οὐδέν, ὁ δὲ χάλκεος ἀσφαλὲς αἰὲν
ἕδος
μένει οὐρανός. ἀλλά τι προσφέρομεν ἔμπαν ἢ μέγαν
νόον ἤτοι φύσιν ἀθανάτοις,
καίπερ ἐφαμερίαν οὐκ εἰδότες οὐδὲ μετὰ νύκτας
ἄμμε πότμος
ἄντιν' ἔγραψε δραμεῖν ποτὶ στάθμαν.
Pind. N. 6.1–7[98]

---

[98] 'There is one *genos* among god and men. From the same mother we draw breath. Yet a wholly distinct power [*dunamis*] separates us, for one *genos* is nothing, whereas the bronze sky remains an ever-unshakeable abode. Though we do resemble the immortals in some way, in greatness of *noon*, or in *phusis*, neither by day nor at night do we know what befalls [*potmos*].'

Nine

The Nomos *of the Tragedians*

ὅστις νέμει [*nemei*] κάλλιστα τὴν αὐτοῦ φύσιν,
οὗτος σοφὸς πέφυκε πρὸς τὸ συμφέρον
Eur. *Polyidus* fr. 634[1]

τὸν αὐτὸν ἐκείνῳ λόγον ἡ θνητὴ φύσις
ζητεῖ κατὰ τὸ δυνατὸν ἀεί τε εἶναι καὶ ἀθάνατος.
δύναται δὲ ταύτῃ μόνον, τῇ γενέσει,
ὅτι ἀεὶ καταλείπει ἕτερον νέον ἀντὶ τοῦ παλαιοῦ . . .
Pl. *Sym.* 207d1–3[2]

1. Prologue

Between the sixth and fifth centuries BC, during what is understood to be a transitional period, the polis of Athens was rendered first under the rule of an aristocracy and later under a democracy in which the *dēmos* held a famously decisive role.[3] Meanwhile, the wider use of written 'laws'[4] perhaps challenged the understanding of the transmission and use of traditions, as well as the relation between 'law' (in a wider sense)

---

[1] 'The one who distributes well his own *phusis* is *sophos* ['wise'] to his own benefit.'

[2] 'Mortal *phusis* ever seeks, to the extent possible, to be immortal. Yet it can only be so in one way, that is, by generation [*genesis*], since in this manner it ever leaves behind the new in place of the old.'

[3] See Ostwald (1969); and Humphreys (1988). Athenian democracies were of various types that traverse several periods within the era that cannot, however, be treated here in adequate detail.

[4] See, for instance, Thomas (1992); and Gagarin (2008: 39–66); see also the analysis by Svenbro (1976; [1988] 1993: 123–36) as to *nómos* being a 'law' that was 'read', in the use of, for example, *ananemein* and *aponemein*, or later in Herodotus' *ananemesthai* ('to recite from memory'; 1.173).

and the ancestral 'customs' and worship rites. *Nómos* appears to be used, during the fifth century BC, to describe 'laws' that are inscribed (though not exclusively) and that still receive their authority from the gods, but now also, crucially, through binding conventions and contingent rules.[5] This shift is also inferred from the way in which the term used for '(divinely) established ordinances' or 'laws', *thesmos*, is thought to have been overtaken by *nómos* as the more frequently used term to denote 'legislation' (and its more collective endorsement).[6] Furthermore, within the auspices of this development we can posit the – in many respects crucial – opposition between *phusis* and *nómos* that, perhaps, 'begins' with the pre-Socratic philosophers and reaches its highest point in the Sophists, the Socratics and the Cynics, as well as, arguably, beyond them.[7] Yet *nómos*, as it will be seen, never becomes, exclusively, a designation of 'law', let alone of 'written law', in the tragedians. The persistent multi-layeredness of the word *nómos* (as well as of the eventual 'juridical' senses of the word) will be traced through an examination of its particular uses in the tragedian poets who traverse this period of so-called transition. The tragedians, it ought to be remembered, do not resolve such (falsely conceived as strictly bipolar) debates, but instead strike a questioning tragic attitude, inter alia, towards and within *phusis* and *nómos*.

Tragedies[8] (but also comedies)[9] frequently engage with political and quasi-'legal' situations, and one can also

---

[5] See Hölkeskamp (2000: 73–96).

[6] Ehrenberg (1921: 109); and Ostwald (1969: 12–19); see also Harrison (1955); and MacDowell (1978). How gradual or accurate this 'shift' is remains open to question.

[7] See, for instance, Heinimann (1945); Guthrie (1971); Kerferd (1981); and Rankin (1983). I have excluded any substantive engagement, in this work, with the *phusis–nómos* 'debate'.

[8] The literature on tragic drama is vast. See, for instance, Murray (1913); Lucas (1950); Vickers (1973); Reinhardt (1976); Winnington-Ingram (1980); Segal (1981/1999; 1986); Goldhill (1986); Heath (1987a); Loraux (1987; 2002); Vernant and Vidal-Naquet (1988); Easterling (1997); Hall (1997; 2006); Pelling (1997); Griffin (1998); Seaford (2000); Sommerstein (2002); Kitto (2003); Sourvinou-Inwood (2003); Beer (2004); Gregory (2005); Carter (2007); and Mastronarde (2010). On tragedy and law, see two recent studies by Harris (2004) and Allen (2005).

[9] I examine *nómos* in comedy in a forthcoming work.

observe a broader relation between theatre and 'law'. Sally Humphreys writes: 'the experiences of watching plays and judging court cases were closely connected; dramatists and orators illuminate each other's texts' (1988: 482).[10] Yet this does not mean that the tragedies should be read as predominantly 'political' or 'legal', or that their differences in form and content should be downplayed. Analogously, echoing the ancient relation between poetry and 'religion', there is also a close connection between tragedy and 'religion' (and, indeed, one between *nómos* and worship rites as such), but this does not render the plays 'theological' treatises. Instead, one could maintain an attentive open stance towards the interwovenness of living in the social experience that the tragedies were, within the worship milieu in which they were presented and experienced.[11] My more modest aim here, however, remains the outline study of the instances and the configuration of the uses of *nómos* and its family of words, in order to appreciate their coeval complexity and poetic diversity.[12]

2. *Nemein*

2.1 *Aeschylus*

Aeschylus was probably born around 525 BC in Eleusis, near Athens, and he died in 456 BC. The verb νέμω (*nemō*) is encountered in a number of passages and uses in the works of Aeschylus, who wrote over eighty plays. I will examine his uses of the word *nómos* in some detail, but for now it is worth

[10] See also Allen (2005: 374).

[11] It is also worth noting that there is no engagement with tragedy at a 'philosophical' level among the classical Greek philosophers, other than a poetic one or a critique of 'political', 'moral' and 'religious' views expressed in the plays. A 'philosophy of the tragic' is a modern (predominantly German) understanding, as Peter Szondi has shown, that takes its flight from Aristotelian poetics for entirely different purposes ([1961] 2002). For my purposes, both poetic and philosophical accounts of tragedy remain of implied interest, but they do not form the direct object of this study; see Schmidt (2001); Krell (2005); and Lambropoulos (2006).

[12] On the poetics of tragedy and philosophy, see, for instance, Leonard (2012). It should be noted that I have omitted from consideration in this chapter the musical uses of *nómos* in the tragedians, some of which I refer to in Chapter Ten.

observing that a possible connection in use between the *nemō* verb and *nómos* can already be shown in a key expression in the *Suppliants*,[13] at 670–4, where it is said that Zeus rules by an ancient *nómos*:

τὼς πόλις εὖ νέμοιτο
Ζῆνα μέγαν σεβόντων,
τὸν ξένιον δ᾽ ὑπερτάτως,
ὃς πολιῷ νόμῳ αἶσαν ὀρθοῖ.

This can be translated as:

> may their polis be regulated/ruled [εὖ νέμοιτο, *eu nemoito*] well,
> if they hold in awe mighty Zeus,
> and, above all, Zeus the warden of guests,
> who by πολιῷ νόμῳ [*poliō nómō*] guides *aisa* straight.
> (Smyth 1926)

Herbert W. Smyth translated the expression πολιῷ νόμῳ (*poliō nómō*) as 'venerable enactment' (1926).[14] Martin Ostwald noted that the double reference to *nemō* may imply the etymological connection between *nemō* and *nómos* (1969: 9) in uses that are 'religious' in context (as are, here, the 'origins' of *hikesia*-supplication).[15] The phrase is used when the Danaids bless Argos in the form of a prayer and refer to an ancient ordinance/regulation (of Zeus *Xenios* regarding his direction of *aisa*), which the Argives ought to respect. It is in their prayer that we meet, too, the eunomic reference, at 670, while there is no reference to *nómos* as 'law'. The phrase *poliō nómō* can perhaps be translated as a 'venerable enactment' (Smyth 1926), whereas Ostwald reluctantly translates it as a 'hoary

---

[13] The *Suppliant Women* is based on the foundation myth of Mycenaean Argos in the Pelopponese. The myth involves the fifty daughters of Danaus (the Danaides) who form the chorus of the play and who, in fleeing along with their father in order to escape their forced marriage to the fifty sons of King Aegyptus (Danaus' brother), flee to Argos and appeal to King Pelasgus for protection.

[14] I have slightly modified the translation.

[15] On *hikesia*, see Kopperschmidt (1967); and Naiden (2006). I devote a forthcoming work to the ancient Greek practices of supplication.

ordinance' (1969: 28) that may be implied to stand above
Zeus. Yet Ostwald notes that this is probably not meant to be
so, given that in the play one does not find any order that is
'higher' than the gods, in at least this sense (ibid.). The ordinance, guiding *moira*, is probably meant at this point in the
sense that it is binding among mortals and that, when so, the
polis is well-ordered or -apportioned.

In another passage, at 504–5, the chorus states:

τούτῳ μὲν εἶπας, καὶ τεταγμένος κίοι
ἐγὼ δὲ πῶς δρῶ; ποῦ θράσος νέμεις [nemeis] ἐμοί;

The *basileus* ('king') replies, at 506:

κλάδους μὲν αὐτοῦ λεῖπε, σημεῖον πόνου.

In translation, the chorus states: 'As you told him, let
him go as instructed. Yet how am I to act? Where do you
dispense [νέμεις, *nemeis*] my safety?' To which the king
replies: 'Leave your boughs here, tokens of your distress.'
The verb *nemō* is used here in the commonplace sense of 'to
dispense'. The older sense of *nemō* regarding 'apportioning
shares' is met at 403, when the chorus states: ἀμφοτέροις
ὁμαίμων τάδ' ἐπισκοπεῖ | Ζεὺς ἑτερορρεπής, νέμων
[nemōn] εἰκότως. This can be translated as: 'Kindred to both
in blood Zeus oversees the two sides equally, apportioning
to each.' Similarly, in the *Eumenides*,[16] at 727, the chorus

---

[16] The *Eumenides* concludes the *Oresteia* trilogy. Orestes, still pursued by the
Erinyes for the murder of his mother, receives refuge at the Apollo temple
in Delphi, before he makes his way to Athens. The Erinyes, however, surround him and Orestes seeks Athena's intervention. Athena surmounts
a jury in Athens (at the Areopagus) and she presides over a 'trial', where
eventually the 'jury' is hung, while Athena convinces the Erinyes to
accept her casting of a vote in favour of Orestes. It is worth noting that
four years before the *Eumenides* was produced in 458 BC, the Areopagus
court, which was a historical and predominantly aristocratic court (with
political and juridical powers though limited 'jurisdiction' – on homicide, arson, wounding, etc.), had been affected by extensive reforms that
deprived it of its more extensive powers. On the trial of Orestes and Attic
law, see Sommerstein (2010: 26–7); and Leâo and Rhodes (2010: 47–8).

refers to παλαιὰς διανομὰς [*palaias dianomas*] in the sense of dispensations: σύ τοι παλαιὰς διανομὰς καταφθίσας | οἴνῳ παρηπάτησας ἀρχαίας θεάς, which can be translated as: 'It was you [Apollo] who destroyed the old dispensations when you beguiled the ancient goddesses with wine.' Wine-dispensing is the milieu of one of the oldest uses of the verb, as shown once more in fr. 55.2: κρᾶσιν ἥρωσιν νέμω [*nemō*] ('wine I distribute/allot to the Heroes').

At 716, we also meet the chorus referring to the 'dispensing' of prophecies in this manner: μαντεῖα δ' οὐκέθ' ἁγνὰ μαντεύσῃ νέμων [*nemōn*] ('you will prophesy, dispensing prophecies that are no longer pure').[17] At 401, the sense of 'an assignment of a portion of land' is expressed in: ἔνειμαν [*eneiman*] αὐτόπρεμνον ἐς τὸ πᾶν ἐμοί | ἐξαίρετον δώρημα Θησέως τόκοις· ('they assigned to me [a great portion of their spoils], a gift to Theseus' sons'). In a related, approximate, sense of 'what is due', we read at 624: φράζειν Ὀρέστῃ τῷδε, τὸν πατρὸς φόνον | πράξαντα μητρὸς μηδαμοῦ τιμὰς νέμειν [*nemein*]. Here, the chorus, addressing Apollo, asks whether Orestes is to be told, following Apollo's oracle, to avenge his father's murder and disregard the honour (*timas*) due to his mother. Finally, at 747, the chorus states: ἡμῖν γὰρ ἔρρειν, ἢ πρόσω τιμὰς νέμειν [*nemein*] ('yes, and we will be ruined, or maintain our honours further [in the sense of extending their privileges further]').

In *Prometheus Bound*,[18] in three passages, we find the related sense of 'apportionment' expressed more directly. At 527, the chorus states: μηδάμ' ὁ πάντα νέμων [*nemōn*] | θεῖτ' ἐμᾷ γνώμᾳ κράτος ἀντίπαλον Ζεύς ('may Zeus, who apportions everything, never set his power in conflict with my purpose'). Earlier, at 229–30, Prometheus addresses Zeus: ὅπως τάχιστα τὸν πατρῷον ἐς θρόνον | καθέζετ', εὐθὺς δαίμοσιν νέμει [*nemei*] γέρα | ἄλλοισιν ἄλλα, καὶ διεστοιχίζετο ('As soon as he had seated himself upon his father's throne, he immediately assigned to the deities their several privileges and

---

[17] Translated by Smyth (1926).
[18] In *Prometheus Bound*, Zeus' agents chain Prometheus to a rock as punishment for providing fire to mortals. The Ocean nymphs (the chorus) hear Prometheus narrate the titanomachy and his benefactions against Zeus' will.

apportioned to them their proper powers').[19] At 292, Oceanus arrives to aid Prometheus and he tells him: χωρίς τε γένους οὐκ ἔστιν ὅτῳ | μείζονα μοῖραν νείμαιμ' [*neimaim'*] ἢ σοί. Here, Oceanus, whom Homer once characterised as 'the genesis of all gods' (*Il.* 14.201, 246) and whose compassion, by definition, is key, states: 'Blood ties (*genos*), I think, constrain me; and, apart from blood ties, there is none to whom I should give more due (*moira*; the assignment of a share) than to you.' At 442, one also encounters the use of 'to hold' or 'to occupy': Καυκάσου πέλας νέμονται (*nemontai*; i.e. a citadel near the Caucasus). In this sense, the bee-keepers, associated with Artemis, are named μελλισσονόμοι (*mellissonomoi*), in fr. 87.

In *Agamemnon*,[20] we meet the use of *nemō* in relation to the guidance of the mind. At 802, Aeschylus uses the following commonplace phrasing: οὐδ' εὖ πραπίδων οἴακα νέμων [*nemōn*]. In translation, this can be rendered as 'not rightly guiding the helm (the handle) of your mind'. Similarly, at 685, this phrasing is applied to the guiding or wielding of the tongue: αισι τοῦ πεπρωμένου | γλῶσσαν ἐν τύχᾳ νέμων [*nemōn*]; 'was it some power invisible guiding his tongue aright by forecasting of destiny?'[21] Lastly, we meet the sense of 'holding or supporting', at 75: ἰσόπαιδα νέμοντες [*nemontes*] ἐπὶ σκήπτροις ('supporting on our canes a strength akin to a child's').

Further, it is worth noting that in *Choephoroi*[22] one encounters the wider sense of living a particular life (*bios*), which is close to the sense of *nemō* as in 'dwelling'. An example occurs in the phrasing of Orestes, βίον νομίζων [*bion nomizōn*], at 1003. The clearest example of this sense of 'living or residing' is perhaps found in the *Eumenides*, at 1016: δαίμονές τε καὶ βροτοί, | Παλλάδος πόλιν νέμον- [*nemon-tes*] | τες ('*daimones* and mortals, dwelling/living in Pallas' polis'). In

---

[19] ibid.

[20] *Agamemnon*, the first part of three tragedies that compose the *Oresteia*, narrates the ending of the war in Troy and the return of King Agamemnon to Argos, where his wife Klytemnestra waits to kill him.

[21] Translated by Smyth (1926).

[22] The *Choephoroi* is the second part to the *Oresteia* trilogy, which narrates how Orestes kills his mother; an act that will, as a result, subject him to the curse of the Erinyes, when he flees to Argos.

this way, we also find in Aeschylus the composite ἔννομος (*ennomos*), meaning 'to live', 'to inhabit', as well as in a more technical sense in ἐννόμιος (*ennomios*) in relation to pastures (for example, Aes. *Sup.* 384, 404, 547, 565; *Choe.* 483). Here, the meaning is close to 'duly ordered', whereby, as in Hesiod, the meaning of order is 'the middle' between the disorder of masterlessness and the extreme order of the despot (for example, *Eum.* 529ff). In fr. 198, the Scythians are described as well-ordered in the manner of 'fair pasture lands' (εὔνομοι; *eunomoi*): ἀλλ'ἱππάκης βρωτῆρες εὔνομοι Σκύθαι (Strab. *Geog.* 7, 3.7.301). This eunomic sense, akin to the sense I noted in Pindar (for example, *N.* 9.29), is perhaps also indicated in the expression *horthonomoi* (*Eum.* 964): ὀρθονόμοι. Lastly, it should be emphasised that when Aeschylus describes the 'function' of the gods, implied in relation to the guiding of the Athenian polis, he uses the verb *nemō*, for example in the *Eumenides* at 918–19: τὰν καὶ Ζεὺς ὁ παγκρατὴς Ἄρης τε | φρούριον θεῶν νέμει [*nemei*], | ῥυσίβωμον Ἑλλάνων ἄγαλμα δαιμόνων ('Zeus the omnipotent and Ares, holds as a fortress of the gods, the bright ornament that guards the altars of the gods of Hellas');[23] and in *Seven against Thebes*, one can sense the same indirectly, at 234: διὰ θεῶν πόλιν νεμόμεθ᾽ [*nemometh'*] ἀδάματον ('that our polis is *adamaton* – unconquered – we owe to the gods').

2.2 *Sophocles*

Sophocles was born in 495 BC and probably died in 406. He is said to have been the author of over one hundred plays. In Sophocles, we meet the later sense of *nemō* in the manner of 'I consider, I think, I believe' and so forth. For example, in *Ajax*[24] Agamemnon tells Odysseus, at 1331: φίλον σ᾽ ἐγὼ μέγιστον Ἀργείων νέμω [*nemō*] ('since I consider you my greatest friend among all the Argives').[25] In another example

---

[23] Translated by Smyth (1926).
[24] In *Ajax*, we find Odysseus and Ajax at Troy, when, upon Achilles' death, they compete for his armour; Ajax's loss leads to his attempt to slaughter the Greek leaders. Meanwhile, Athena replaces the leaders with cattle and sheep.
[25] Soph. *Aj.* 265 πότερα δ᾽ ἄν, εἰ νέμοι [*nemoi*] τις αἵρεσιν, λάβοις ('and

of this use, in *Electra*,[26] at 150, we read: Ἰὼ παντλάμων Νιόβα, σὲ δ' ἔγωγε νέμω [*nemō*] θεόν, | ἅτ' ἐν τάφῳ πετραίῳ ('Ah, all-suffering Niobe, I count you [consider, believe you to be] divine, since you weep forever in your rocky tomb').[27] Later, in the same play, we can note the use of 'to believe or think'. At 599, Electra states against her mother: Καί σ' ἔγωγε δεσπότιν | ἢ μητέρ' οὐκ ἔλασσον εἰς ἡμᾶς νέμω [*nemō*], | ἢ ζῶ βίον μοχθηρόν, ἔκ τε σοῦ κακοῖς ('I think [I believe] that you are no less a mistress to me than a mother; so wicked is the life that I live'). Also, in a wider use in *Oedipus Colonus*[28] the chorus states, at 879: Τάνδ' ἄρ' οὐκέτι νεμῶ [*nemō*] πόλιν ('Then I think/consider this city no longer exists'). In the *Trachiniae*, at 483, we also read: εἴ τι τήνδ' ἁμαρτίαν νέμεις [*nemeis*] ('if you regard [consider] this in any way an error'); and at 57: νέμοι [*nemoi*] τιν' ὥραν τοῦ καλῶς πράσσειν δοκεῖν (perhaps in the sense of he 'deemed [believed, thought] to fare well').[29]

The older sense of 'to distribute/share' (and by extention 'to give, to dispense') is met with a number of times in Sophocles. In *Ajax*, at 1351, Odysseus states: Ἀλλ' εὖ λέγουσι τοῖς φίλοις τιμὰς νέμειν [*nemein*] ('But it is easy to grant dispensations [*timas*] to friends when they advise well'). At the beginning of the play one finds the use of 'assigning responsibility/blame' for a deviation, at 28: Τήνδ' οὖν ἐκείνῳ πᾶς τις αἰτίαν νέμει [*nemei*] ('all men assign responsibility to him'). The archetypical act of the distribution of drinking cups is described at 1200: Ἐκεῖνος οὐ στεφάνων οὔτε βαθειᾶν |

---

which, if the choice were given you, would you choose – to distress your friends, and have joy yourself, or to share the grief of friends who grieve?'); translated by Jebb (1893).

26 *Electra* narrates the aftermath of Orestes' father's murder upon the former's return to Mycenae.

27 In this sense, one can also observe the use of *nomizomena*: for example, *El.* 327 and *OC* 1603.

28 *Oedipus at Colonus* revisits Oedipus anew, who is now wandering blind. His fate is to be decided by King Theseus, who grants him sanctuary. The king of Thebes, Kreon, in the meantime, demands that Oedipus return to the city and captures his daughters (Antigone and Ismene).

29 See further examples in *OT* 39; 516; 549; 551; and 610. *Oedipus Tyrannos* has Oedipus, years after he has committed his infamous deeds (killing his father and marrying his mother), solving the riddle of the Sphinx and becoming king of Thebes.

κυλίκων νεῖμεν [*neimen*] ἐμοὶ τέρψιν ὁμιλεῖν | οὔτε γλυκὺν
αὐλῶν ὄτοβον, δύσμορος ('No delight in garlands, or deep
wine-cups did that miserable man give me, no sweet din
of flutes'). Meanwhile in the *Trachiniae*[30] the same sense
is used with regard to 'providing/giving' the truth at 398,
when Delaneira asks: Ἦ καὶ τὸ πιστὸν τῆς ἀληθείας νεμεῖς
[*nemeis*]; ('Will you give me the honest truth?')[31] In *Oedipus
Tyrant* we can note its use regarding the distribution of *Tuchē*,
that should not be dishonoured, at 1080–1: Ἐγὼ δ' ἐμαυτὸν
παῖδα τῆς Τύχης νέμων [*nemōn*] ('I, who hold myself son of
Tuchē [approx. 'fortune']'). A rare sense, possibly metaphorical, of 'to read-distribute' (νέμει, *nemei*) can be read in fr. 144
[Nauck]: νεμεῖς τίς οὐ πάρεστι, τίς ξυνώμοσεν.[32]

The distribution or assignment of one's fortune/destiny
is described as a function of Zeus in the *Trachiniae*, at 1022:
βιότου τοιαῦτα νέμει [*nemei*] Ζεύς ('so strong is the destiny
apportioned by Zeus'). A little later, at 1238, Heracles states:
Ἀνὴρ ὅδ' ὡς ἔοικεν οὐ νεμεῖν [*nemein*] ἐμοὶ | φθίνοντι
μοῖραν ('The man will offer no due respect to my diminish-
ing *moira*'). Similarly, with regard to the granting of honour
(*timē*, *geras*) to Odysseus, we find him state in *Philoctetes*,[33] at
1062: τιμὴν ἐμοὶ νείμειεν [*neimeien*], ἣν σὲ χρῆν ἔχειν ('the
time that ought to have been one's own'). The same sense can
be found in further contexts, such as when we encounter the
expression in 'assigning or allotting' a mother to someone in
fr. 24: Πολυκράτης μητέρα νέμει [*nemei*] ('Polucrates allots
a mother [to you]'); or in *Oedipus Tyrant*, at 240: χέρνιβος
νέμειν·[*nemein*] with reference to allowing or apportioning a

---

[30] In the *Trachinian Women*, the wife of Heracles, Deianeira, was earlier
sought by Nessos, a centaur, whom Heracles would kill. A long time
later, as a result of another of Heracles' violent deeds, she became an exile
along with her children in Trachis (a polis in central Greece).

[31] This may be the sense in *Phil.* 393: ἃ τὸν μέγαν Πακτωλὸν εὔχρυσον
νέμεις ('the great Pactolus distributes/rolls a golden [stream of] sands').

[32] See the discussion in Svenbro ([1988] 1993: 110), who suggests that the
addressing with *nemeis* at the start signifies 'Read!' and may indicate the
passage 'from orality to writing'. See also the analysis by Catenacci (1999:
49–61).

[33] Philoctetes is the invaluable warrior who was sorely missed by the
Greeks during the decade in which they were attacking Troy and whom
they had banished to a remote island (Lemnos).

share (a libation with 'sacred' water) in a purification rite.[34]
Also, in *Ajax*, at 513: ὑπ' ὀρφανιστῶν μὴ φίλων, ὅσον κακὸν
| κείνῳ τε κἀμοὶ τοῦθ', ὅταν θάνῃς, νεμεῖς [*nemeis*], where,
upon the death of the king, his son, now an orphan, would
have bestowed upon him the fate of being tended by guardians who are neither family nor friends.[35]

The sense of 'to wield', in this case fiery lightning, is met
with in *Oedipus Tyrant*, at 201: τόν, ὦ <τᾶν> πυρφόρων |
ἀστραπᾶν κράτη νέμων [*nemōn*], | ὦ Ζεῦ πάτερ, ὑπὸ σῷ
φθίσον κεραυνῷ ('you who wield the powers/forces of fiery
lightning, Zeus our father, slay him beneath your thunderbolt').[36] A few verses later, at 237, we encounter the sense of
'ruling' a land: κράτη τε καὶ θρόνους νέμω [*nemō*]. Similarly,
at 579, Kreon asks: Ἄρχεις δ' ἐκείνῃ ταὐτὰ γῆς ἴσον νέμων
[*nemōn*]; ('Do you rule the land as she [Jocasta] does, with
equal sway?'). Furthermore, in a pastoral sense, the verb is
used for the grazing of cows in, for example, fr. *Ich.* 397:
πολλαὶ βόες νέμουσι [*nemousi*].[37] In addition, in *Oedipus
Tyrant*, at 1118, there is reference by the chorus to πιστὸς ὡς
νομεύς [*nomeus*] ἀνήρ ('as trustworthy a man as any herds-
man/shepherd'); and this use, with reference to a herdsman
roaming freely with his herd, is also seen at 761 in the utilisa-
tion of νομάς (*nomas*): ἀγρούς σφε πέμψαι κἀπὶ ποιμνίων
νομάς. In Sophocles, we can also note a related composite:
the *agronomoi* (upland pastures), at 1102: τῷ γὰρ πλάκες
ἀγρόνομοι πᾶσαι φίλαι· ('dear to him are all the upland pastures'). Lastly, the rarer use of νέμος (*nemos*) is found in the
sense of wooded pastures in *Ajax*, at 413: πόροι ἁλίρροθοι
| πάραλά τ' ἄντρα καὶ νέμος [*nemos*] ἐπάκτιον. Richard
Claverhouse Jebb (1893) translates this verse as follows: 'you
paths of the sounding sea, you tidal waves and wooded pastures by the shore'.[38]

---

[34] Such a rite is described in detail in *OC* 466ff; on pollution and purification, see Parker (1983).

[35] See also, Soph., fr. 144, from the lost *Gathering of the Achaians*: νέμ' εἴ τις
οὐ πάρεστιν ὃς ξυνώμοσεν.

[36] Translated by Jebb (1887).

[37] See the uncertain fr. 959 [Jebb], ἣν ὁ βούκερως Ἴακχος αὐτῷ μαῖαν
ἡδίστην νέμει [*nemei*], where the bucolic sense appears linked to cult
worship; Strab. 687; Jebb (1917 in Pearson (ed.): Vol. 3).

[38] In *OT* 1118, we meet the semantically related use of νομεύς [*nomeus*],

2.3 *Euripides*

Euripides was born in 480 BC and is said to have died in 406, after having written over ninety plays. The senses of 'to distribute/share', 'dispense' and 'to give' or 'grant' are encountered numerous times in his works. In *Iphigeneia in Tauris*,[39] prophesies are described as being distributed, at 1255: μαντείας βροτοῖς θεσφάτων νέμων [*nemōn*] ('distributing prophecies from the gods to mortals').[40] Similarly, in *Orestes*,[41] at 592, prophecies are said to be distributed to mortals by Apollo, who sits at the navel of the earth: ὁρᾷς δ᾽ Ἀπόλλων᾽, ὃς μεσομφάλους ἕδρας | ναίων βροτοῖσι στόμα νέμει [*nemei*] σαφέστατον. In *Electra*,[42] at 1169, the chorus states: νέμει [*nemei*] τοι δίκαν θεός, ὅταν τύχῃ· ('the god distributes justice, whenever it befalls'). In the *Suppliant Women*,[43] at 380, we can see an example of 'distributing or dealing out' where the chorus expresses the dealing out of defeat to *adikia*, with *dikē* revered: σύ τοι σέβεις δίκαν, τὸ δ᾽ ἧσσον ἀδικίᾳ | νέμεις, δυστυχῆ τ᾽ ἀεὶ πάντα ῥύῃ ('I know that you revere *dikē*, and you deal out – *nemeis* – defeat to *adikia*, protecting the afflicted at all times').[44] Finally, in two fragments of Euripides we can note two further uses: from the lost Euripidean play *Antiope*, fr. 184 entails νέμων [*nemōn*] τὸ πλεῖστον ἡμέρας ('distributing, giving, devoting the most part of the day [to something]'); while the lost play *Telephus*, fr. 702 includes νείμωσιν [*neimōsin*] θεοί ('gods distributing/ giving [harsh treatment]').

In a 'political' sense, the granting of the throne by a

---

when the chorus states: πιστὸς ὡς νομεὺς ἀνήρ ('trusty as any shepherd').

[39] Iphigeneia, who did not die in Aulis, is at the temple of Artemis, where she is to sacrifice the Greeks who arrive in Tauris (Crimea).

[40] Translated by Potter (1938).

[41] Orestes and Electra are hoping that their death sentence from the Argives will be halted by Menelaos's intervention.

[42] In *Electra*, Electra and her brother Orestes conspire and kill their mother, Klytemnestra, to avenge the murder of their father, Agamemnon.

[43] In the *Suppliant Women*, the mothers of the dead led by the king of Argos, Adrastos, plead at Eleusis for Theseus to aid them in offering proper burial to their dead.

[44] See also 611, 616, and 241.

deceased father is expressed in *Heracles*,[45] at 463: σοὶ μὲν γὰρ Ἄργος ἔνεμ᾽ [enem'] ὁ κατθανὼν πατήρ, while in *Phoenician Women*[46] the dispensing of army companies and their captains is described at 1093: λόχους ἔνειμεν [eneimen] ἑπτὰ καὶ λοχαγέτας. In the wider sense of 'ruling the polis' we meet the use of the verb in *Rhesus*[47] at 475, where Hector states: πόλιν νεμοίμην [nemoimēn] ὡς τὸ πρίν ποτ᾽ ἀσφαλῇ. Furthermore, with regard to giving or resigning one's share, we find two examples. In *Iphigeneia in Aulis*[48] at 499, one resigns one's share into another's hands: σοὶ νέμω [nemō] τοὐμὸν μέρος. And in the *Phoenician Women*, Jocasta states, in a similar thematic, at 548: σὺ δ᾽ οὐκ ἀνέξῃ δωμάτων ἔχων ἴσον | καὶ τῷδε νεῖμαι [neimai]; κᾷτα ποῦ 'στιν ἡ δίκη; ('will you not be content with your fair share of your heritage and give the same to him?'). Finally, we also see the negation of the sense of 'distribution or allowance', in *Hippolytos*,[49] at 745: ναύταις οὐκέθ᾽ ὁδὸν νέμει [nemei] ('forbids further passage to sailors').

The sense of 'thinking, believing, considering or revering' is encountered in a number of passages. It occurs. for example, in *Helen*,[50] at 917–18: οὔκουν χρή σε συγγόνῳ πλέον

---

[45] In *Heracles*, during Heracles' absence from Thebes, his wife (Megara) and children are about to be killed by a usurper to the throne (Lykos), only to be temporarilly saved by Heracles' return. Hera sends Lyssa ('Madness') to Heracles, who then kills his family.

[46] In *Phoenician Women*, Oedipus and Jocasta are alive in Thebes; Oedipus has cursed his sons that they will share the 'inheritance' between them with the use of violence. One of his sons, Polyneikes, had been ruling, when, the other son, Eteokles, arrives to sack his own homeland with the aid of an Argive army.

[47] Possibly by Euripides, this play is based on Homer's *Il.* 10, or a more archaic version of it (in any case an independent part to the *Iliad* in Euripides' time). Rhesus is the divine king, a Thracian hero, who inspires the warring tribes.

[48] For Agamemnon to receive advantage for his ships on the way to Troy, he must sacrifice his daughter, Iphigeneia, to the goddess Artemis. Klytemnestra seeks Achilles' help to save Iphigeneia, but to no avail. Indeed, Iphigeneia offers herself to be sacrificed.

[49] In *Hippolytos*, the son of Theseus serves Artemis. Aphrodite reacts by leading his stepmother, Phaedra, to fall in love with him against her will. When this is revealed to Hippolytos, Phaedra, in fear of Theseus, kills herself. Theseus curses and banishes his son, who upon exile dies.

[50] In *Helen*, Helen is in Egypt. Menelaos, shipwrecked on the Egyptian

| νέμειν [nemein] ματαίῳ μᾶλλον ἢ χρηστῷ πατρί ('thus you should not esteem a thoughtless brother more than a good father').[51] In a similar manner, and in the sense of revering the mob (ὄχλος, *ochlos*) owing to fear, we note the verb's use in *Hecuba*,[52] at 868: ἐπεὶ δὲ ταρβεῖς τῷ τ' ὄχλῳ πλέον νέμεις [nemeis]. From the lost play titled *Chrysippus*, fr. 839 includes the phrasing: μήτηρ πάντων νενόμισται [nenomistai] ('considered to be the mother of all'). Within this semantic sphere, we can also note, in Euripides, the use of *nomizein* (νομίζειν)/*nomimon*: for instance, in the *Bacchae*[53] at 7, τὰ νομισθέντα [nomisthenta] γὰρ ἀεί; and at 895, τό τ' ἐν χρόνῳ μακρῷ νόμιμον [nomimon]. Characteristic uses are also found in *Iphigeneia in Aulis*, at 33: τὰ θεῶν οὕτω νενόμισται [neno-mistai]; and in *Electra*, at 234, with direct reference to *nómos*: νομίζων νόμον πόλεως [nomizōn nómon poleōs]. In these uses, what is shown is what is conventionally accepted as a *nómō* (νόμῳ). This has an extended social or political sense that becomes most apparent in the expression found in the *Bacchae*, at 430–1: τὸ πλῆθος ὅ τι | τὸ φαυλότερον ἐνόμισε [enomise] χρῆ- | ταί τε, τόδ' ἂν δεχοίμαν (where it is stated that 'it is wise to accept those things that have been conventionally practised by the multitude [*plēthos*]').

Finally, in the pastoral sense of 'herding, or feeding', we observe the early uses of the verb enduring in Euripides. In the *Cyclops*,[54] at 28, it is stated νέμουσι [nemousi] μῆλα

---

coast, brings with him a woman who to him is Helen. He then meets the real Helen and together they seek the assistance of the sister of the king of Egypt (Threnoe) in order to flee.

51 Slightly modifying the translation by Coleridge (1938).

52 In *Hecuba*, Troy has fallen and Hecuba, along with the rest of the captured women, begins the journey to Greece. At Thrace, Hecuba finds out that her son (Polydoros) has been killed by the king of Thrace, Polymestor, and that her daughter, Polyxena, was sacrificed as an offering to the dead Achilles. Hecuba wishes to give her daughter a proper burial. Agamemnon decides the matter and finds for Hecuba.

53 The *Bacchae* is a late play of Euripides, produced posthumously, and considered to be his most vigorous achievement. In the play, a young Dionysus arrives at the palace of Thebes to take revenge on the house of Cadmus. Having gathered a cult of female worshippers (the Bacchae), he leads the Theban women to ecstatic frenzy and the young King Pentheus declares a ban on his worship.

54 In *Cyclops*, the only surviving satyr play, Euripides parodies Homer's *Od.*

νέα νέοι πεφυκότες ('we now herd the flocks'), while in the *Bacchae*, at 735, we read: αἰ δὲ νεμομέναις [*nemomenais*] χλόην ([the heifers][55] browsing the grass).[56] In *Electra*, we find the sense of 'roaming or ranging through the woods' at 1163: δρύοχα νεμομένα [*nemomena*]. We also see the related sense of 'to dwell' or 'to inhabit', whether directly or metaphorically, in a number of passages. Some key examples are found in the *Bacchae*, at 404–5: ἵν᾽ οἱ θελξίφρονες νέμον- [*nemon-*] | ται θνατοῖσιν Ἔρωτες, with reference to Cyprus, the island of Aphrodite 'where the Erotes, who soothe mortals' hearts, dwell';[57] and in *Rhesus*, at 700, where a dweller is described in a seacoast town of Locris as *nemomenos*: παραλίαν Λοκρῶν νεμόμενος πόλιν [*nemomenos polin*]. In a metaphoric use in *Trojan Women*[58] at 1088, the positioning/standing of the Cyclopian walls of stone that reach up to heaven is expressed as follows: λάινα Κυκλώπι᾽ οὐράνια νέμονται [*nemontai*]. Once more, the sense of 'dwelling' is evident in the lost play *Polyidus*, fr. 636.7: νομὸν βίου [*nomón biou*] ('haunts, dwellings').

3. *Nōmaō/Nōmōn*

The form of νωμάω (*nōmaō*; also: νώμα, *nōma*, -άτω, -atō; νωμῶν, *nōmōn*, -ῶντα, -ōnta) can be also traced in the tragedians in its earlier commonplace senses, along with a now-established use of 'to guide', or 'to govern'. Thus, in the sense

9 and centres the play on the encounter of Odysseus with the Cyclops. In a key scene Polyphemos refuses to offer hospitality to Odysseus and his sailors, eats two of the sailors and claims that he has no fear of the gods.

55 Young cows.

56 See also *Cycl.* 49; 50: δρύοχα νεμομένα [*nemomena*], τάδε κατήνυσεν; *Rhet.* 551–2: ἤδη δὲ νέμουσι [*nemousi*] κατ᾽ Ἴδαν | ποίμνια; and *El.* 1164: δρύοχα νεμομένα [*nemomena*], τάδε κατήνυσεν.

57 The relation of *erōs* to *nómos* is widespread in antiquity and its characteristic engagement is to be found in Plato's *Symposion*, as well as in Aristophanes' comedies (for example, in *Birds* 34–41, 324; 411 and 755–6). The stifling *nómos* is often dynamically compared to the natural 'dwelling' of *erōs*. In the *Symposion*, *erōs* is to lead one to one's own (*oikeion*; 193d2), while in *Phaedrus erōs* can become hybristic (i.e. in 237d3–8.4).

58 In *Trojan Women*, upon the fall of Troy, Poseidon and Athena seek to take revenge on the returning Greeks to Athens. Hecuba and the chorus of Trojan women are captured by the Greeks.

of 'to observe' or 'note', we find νωμῶ [*nōmō*] in Euripides' *Phoenician Women*, at 1255: μάντεις δὲ μῆλ᾽ ἔσφαζον, ἐμπύρους τ᾽ ἀκμὰς | ῥήξεις τ᾽ ἐνώμων [*enōmōn*] ὑγρότητ᾽ ἐναντίαν ('the seers/prophets were sacrificing sheep while observing the tongues and forks of fire, the damp reek [which is a bad sign]'). In Sophocles' *Oedipus Tyrant*, at 300–1, we find a wider sense with regard to Teiresias' omniscience: ὦ πάντα νωμῶν [*nōmōn*] Τειρεσία, διδακτά τε | ἄρρητά τ᾽ οὐράνιά τε καὶ χθονοστιβῆ ('Teiresias, you who dispose/observe/grasp all things, those that can be explained and those unspeakable, things in heaven and things that move on earth'). Perhaps the sense here comes close to a sense of 'judging' or 'dividing' ('discerning'). Not far from this semantically, we meet the verb in the manner of 'to guide', or, perhaps, 'to lead'. In Aeschylus' *Seven against Thebes*, at 24–6, we read:

νῦν δ᾽ ὡς ὁ μάντις φησίν, οἰωνῶν βοτήρ,
ἐν ὠσὶ νωμῶν [*nōmōn*] καὶ φρεσίν, πυρὸς δίχα,
χρηστηρίους ὄρνιθας ἀψευδεῖ τέχνῃ·

In translation:

Yet now, as the seer, the herdsman of birds, informs us,
guided by his ears and his mind to understand with
    unerring skill
the prophetic birds unaided by ['sacrificial'] fire.

Comparably, within a wider sphere, *Dikē* is said to guide all things to their highest end or limit in Aeschylus' *Agamemnon*, at 781: πᾶν δ᾽ ἐπὶ τέρμα νωμᾷ [*nōma*]. This sense of 'observation' becomes assimilated to the sense of 'governance', whereby perhaps to some extent 'omniscience' points to a certain sense of 'omnipotence'. In an unattributed fragment Zeus is said 'to govern or to direct' life and death: Ζεὺς ὁ καὶ ζωῆς καὶ θανάτου πείρατα νωμῶν [*nōmōn*].[59] But one meets this sense already in Aeschylus' *Seven against Thebes*, at 2–4: ὅστις φυλάσσει πρᾶγος ἐν πρύμνῃ πόλεως | οἴακα νωμῶν [*nōmōn*], βλέφαρα μὴ κοιμῶν ὕπνῳ ('he who guards from

---

[59] Stob. *Ecl.* 1.1.9; but note that this may not be a 'tragic' fragment.

the stern the concerns of the polis and guides its helm with sleepless eyes').[60]

In composite form in *Prometheus Bound*, Aeschylus uses (or possibly invents) the composite οἰακονόμοι (*oiakonomoi*; οἰκονόμος, *oikonomos*), at 148, to signify a helmsman in metaphoric usage for the one who 'governs or pilots'. This use can be juxtaposed with the synonymous οἰακοστρόφος (*oiakostrophos*) expressed by the chorus in the same play, at 515, to indirectly signify the action of a pilot.[61] In the earlier and common use of the verb with the sense of 'to wield', we encounter its use in Aeschylus' *Persae*, at 321: Ἄμιστρις Ἀμφιστρεύς τε πολύπονον δόρυ | νωμῶν [*nōmōn*] ('Amistris, and Amphistreus, wielder of a painful spear'); and in *Choephoroe* at 163: νωμῶν [*nōmōn*] ξίφη ('wielding a sword'). Finally, we also meet the early use of the verb to signify the plying of the feet in Sophocles' *Oedipus Tyrranus*, at 468: πόδα νωμᾶν φυγᾷ πόδα νωμᾶν [*nōman*]; as well as in Aeschylus' *Choephoroe*, at 288: ὁρῶντα λαμπρόν, ἐν σκότῳ νωμῶντ' [*nōmōnt'*] ὀφρύν ('he sees lucidly, even though he moves his eyebrows in the dark [unable to sleep]').

4. *Nómos*

In the tragedians, we meet the word *nómos* in the singular and the plural in a variety of uses, indicating the persistence of the multiplicity of the word's semantics, as well as some furthering of the earlier uses in question. Hence, I examine below the surviving plays of the three tragedians in turn in order to consider the variety and the form of these uses.

4.1 *Aeschylus*

In Aeschylus' *Choephoroe*, at 93, we meet *nómos* in the sense of 'custom' or 'common use': ἢ τοῦτο φάσκω τοὖπος, ὡς νόμος βροτοῖς ('I utter the words that men are accustomed to use'). In a worship context, here the *nómos* of a prayer (an offering at the tomb of a dead father) is claimed to accord with the manner or *nómos* of mortals, that is, their proper

---

[60] On the use of οἶακος [*oiakos*], see Aes. *Sup.* 717; and *Ag.* 663.
[61] See also Aes. *Sept.* 62; the composite is also met in Eur. *Med.* 523.

way. This proper way is in the manner of 'reciprocity' as a 'custom' among mortals, to the extent that one may appreciate here a claim that *nómos* equals 'reciprocity'. Likewise, at 150, it is stated that it is a *nómos* to accompany the paean to the deceased with wailings. It is *nómos*, a proper, due 'custom', to lament: ὑμᾶς δὲ κωκυτοῖς ἐπανθίζειν νόμος. At 400, the chorus, refers to *nómos*, in the plural, with reference to ancestral *nómoi*, according to which blood spilled on the ground demands blood (vengeance): ἀλλὰ νόμος [*nómos*] μὲν φονίας σταγόνας | χυμένας ἐς πέδον ἄλλο προσαιτεῖν. Further, a few verses later, at 424, a particular *nómos* (in a close musical sense) is referred to with regard to Kissian female mourners who beat their breasts and sing an Arian dirge: ἔκοψα κομμὸν Ἄριον ἔν τε Κισσίας | νόμοις [*nómois*] ἰηλεμιστρίας. The sense of burial 'customs' among mortals who dwell together is referred to, at 483, by Orestes: οὕτω γὰρ ἄν σοι δαῖτες ἔννομοι [*ennomoi*] βροτῶν.[62] The chorus uses the interesting expression συννόμους [*sunnomous*] βροτῶν, at 598, perhaps in the sense of shared woes (*atai*) in respect of the ways, or by implication the destiny, of mortals (in this case, the 'passions of women as leading mortals to ruin'). We are, perhaps, a little closer to a sense of a 'rule' in *nómos* at 989–90, with regard to Aegisthus' death, which Orestes declares to have been according to *nómos*: ἔχει γὰρ αἰσχυντῆρος, ὡς νόμος, δίκην. | ἥτις δ' ἐπ' ἀνδρὶ τοῦτ' ἐμήσατο στύγος ('he [Aegisthus] has suffered the [*dikē*] held as *nómos* for adulterers'). The killing of an adulterer is said to be devoid of retribution: a *nómos*, perhaps, in this case, still within the wide range of a social 'custom' or commonly-held convention.

In the *Agamemnon*, we meet three characteristic examples

---

[62] Similarly, at *Sup.* 405, we read: ἄδικα μὲν κακοῖς, ὅσια δ' ἐννόμοις ('the *adika* to the wicked and the honourable to the ἐννόμοις'; i.e. those that share in the *nómos*). The sense of the composite is wide and it can involve those that share in the polis or the *oikos*, as in *Sup.* 547 and 565, in the sense of those who inhabit or dwell together. In the sense of a customary rite, we meet the use of *nomimōn* (νομίμων) by the chorus at *Sept.* 333–5: κλαυτὸν δ' ἀρτιτρόποις ὠμοδρόποις | νομίμων προπάροιθεν διαμεῖψαι | δωμάτων στυγερὰν ὁδόν (Smyth translates: 'it is a lamentable thing that modest girls should be plucked unripe, before the customary rites, and should make a loathsome journey from their homes'; 1926).

of *nómos* as a 'custom', or as an extended 'custom' in the sense of what the norm is in a particular situation. At 1207, the chorus questions Cassandra, ἤ καὶ τέκνων εἰς ἔργον ἤλθετον νόμῳ [*nómô*], asking whether her union with Apollo resulted in children. Ostwald notes that the use of νόμῳ [*nómô*] at this point refers to a normalcy (that the union between two sexes results in children; 1969: 22). At 312, Klytemnestra refers to λαμπαδηφόρων νόμοι, that is, the *nómoi*, the usual ways or methods, of torch-bearers. The sense of being unsuited, in this case, for a proper 'sacrifice'/feast is found in a line of the chorus, at 151: σπευδομένα θυσίαν ἑτέραν ἄνομόν τιν' (urging another sacrifice, one that knows no *nómos*; *anomon*). Finally, at 594, Klytemnestra refers to the offering and then the 'sacrificial' cry (ὀλολυγμὸν, *ololugmon*) that she addressed to the gods (over the fall of Troy) as a female *nómō*: ὅμως δ' ἔθυον, καὶ γυναικείῳ νόμῳ [*nómō*]. In this instance, one can perceive a sense of *nómos* as a 'usual way', a 'customary role' or a 'norm' that applies to women in particular, in their very being as women (understood in a strong sense, though one that can include rebellious overstepping). It is worth noting too that, in the play, Klytemnestra is regularly depicted as a 'deceiving woman'. In *Oedipus Tyrranus*, we find a notion of *nómos* with regard to 'speaking properly with regard to the truth' at 322, where Oedipus tells Teiresias: οὔτ' ἔννομ' [*ennom'*] εἶπας οὔτε προσφιλῆ πόλει ('you did not speak properly, or with love for the polis').

In the *Eumenides*, the contravention of the religious *nómos* of the gods is expressed, at 169–72, as follows:

ἐφεστίῳ δὲ μάντις ὢν μιάσματι
μυχὸν ἐχράνατ' αὐτόσσυτος, αὐτόκλητος,
παρὰ νόμον [*para nómon*] θεῶν βρότεα μὲν τίων,
παλαιγενεῖς δὲ μοίρας φθίσας.

In translation:

Although he is a prophet, he has stained his sanctuary
with pollution at its hearth, at his own urging, at his own
   bidding;
against the *nómos* of the gods, he has honoured mortal
   things

and caused the ancient allotments [*moiras*] to
  decay.[63]

The violation of the *nómos* of the gods consists in the honouring, here, of what is in the 'mortal domain'. Apollo has
honoured Orestes, a mortal, at Delphi, contravening the
limits, the portions, of the *moira* of the gods. This is a case
of pollution, since Orestes is polluted following the matricide. The ancient *nómos* in question is the *nómos* of *Moira*,
which allotted to immortals (and to mortals) particular
limits or portions that are not to be exceeded.[64] The Erinyes
claim that Apollo violates the *nómos* of the ancient gods by
receiving the polluted matricide Orestes at Delphi (171–2).
More specifically, it violates *Moira*'s 'laws' and their own.
The Erinyes specify that they are the ancient and divine
embodiment of *Dikē*, the representatives of the age-old 'law'
dispensed by *Moira*; they even perceive Apollo's (and later
also Athena's) action as a dishonouring of their personal
'rights'.[65] At 448–9, the ancient *nómos* is mentioned, in a
religious context, according to which one is not permitted
to utter words before being properly cleansed: ἄφθογγον
εἶναι τὸν παλαμναῖον νόμος [*nómos*], | ἔστ' ἂν πρὸς ἀνδρὸς
αἵματος καθαρσίου ('the one who is defiled by the shed-
ding of blood is barred from speaking until sprinkled with
ritually cleansing blood'). The 'custom' of supplication is,
further, invoked by Apollo to refer to Orestes as a suppliant by *nómos* after confirming that Orestes was purified
according to what is proper, at 576: ἔστι γὰρ νόμῳ [*nómō*] |
ἱκέτης. Finally, at 778, we read: ἰὼ θεοὶ νεώτεροι, παλαιοὺς
νόμους [*nómous*] | καθιππάσασθε κἀκ χερῶν εἵλεσθέ μου
('younger gods, you have ridden down the ancient 'laws'
[regarding vengeance following a homicide] and have taken
them from [the] hands [of the Erinyes]!')[66] Here, the chorus
(Erinyes), lamenting their defeat in the newly-found court,
attended by mortals and by immortals, state that the ancient
nómoi have been dishonoured by the younger gods, which

---

[63] Translated by Smyth (1926).
[64] See also Laroche (1949: 190–1).
[65] For example, 778–9 = 808–9; 780 = 810; 792 = 822; 839 = 872; 845–6 = 879–80.
[66] Translated by Smyth (1926); this phrase is repeated at 808.

threatens the *nómos* of the universe itself as much as that of the polis.[67] A similar critique of the younger gods and the new *nómoi* of Zeus is notable in *Prometheus Bound*, at 148–51: νέοι γὰρ οἰα- | κονόμοι [*oiakonomoi*] κρατοῦσ' Ὀλύμπου· | νεοχμοῖς δὲ δὴ νόμοις [*nómois*] Ζεὺς | ἀθέτως κρατύνει, | τὰ πρὶν δὲ πελώρια νῦν ἀιστοῖ ('For there are new rulers in Olympus, and Zeus holds sway with despotic 'customs'; that which was mighty before he now reduces to nothing'). The *nómoi* of Zeus are, in fact, characterised as 'despotic or self-appointed', at 404: ἰδίοις νόμοις [*idiois nómois*].

Some of the most interesting uses of *nómos*, and arguably the earliest 'political use' (Ostwald 1969: 44f) of the word, are to be found in the *Suppliants*. At 220, the customary-'religious' *nómoi* of the Greeks are identified by Danaus in relation to the worship of Hermes: Ἑρμῆς ὅδ' ἄλλος τοῖσιν Ἑλλήνων νόμοις [*nómois*] ('here is Hermes, according to Hellenic "customs"'). The religious or ritual sense of *nómos* is prevalent in 240–2, with regard to the supplication rite: κλάδοι γε μὲν δὴ κατὰ νόμους [*nómous*] ἀφικτόρων | κεῖνται παρ' ὑμῖν πρὸς θεοῖς ἀγωνίοις: here, the king addresses the chorus and refers to (probably olive) branches which are said to be *kata nómon* (i.e. usually carried by the suppliants) by their side before the assembly of the gods.[68]

The instance that Ostwald (1969) considers to be the earliest (464–3 BC) use of *nómos* in a directly 'political or juridical' sense is encountered at 387–91, where Pelasgus states:

εἴ τοι κρατοῦσι παῖδες Αἰγύπτου σέθεν
νόμῳ πόλεως [*nómō poleōs*], φάσκοντες ἐγγύτατα γένους
εἶναι, τίς ἂν τοῖσδ' ἀντιωθῆναι θέλοι;

---

[67] It is of interest that the Erinyes appear, to some extent, to conflate the use of *thesmos* (divine ordinances) with *nómos* at this point; though a full conflation would presuppose a scission between *kosmos* and *nómos*, which has yet to take place, if it ever fully did so.

[68] Supplication was well established as a customary practice before the fifth century BC; it involved the observance of a sacred *nómos* (see, for instance, Hdt. 5.71; Thuc. 1.134) under the protection of Zeus *hikesios*, whereby the suppliant by remaining within the precinct of a temenos would become *hieros*; it is worth noting that Antigone invokes the principle but is never portrayed as a suppliant (1663); see Schlesinger (1933); Kopperschmidt (1967); and Naiden (2006).

δεῖ τοί σε φεύγειν κατὰ νόμους [*kata nómous*] τοὺς
οἴκοθεν,
ὡς οὐκ ἔχουσιν κῦρος οὐδὲν ἀμφὶ σοῦ.

In translation:

If the sons of Aegyptus exert their authority
according to the *nómos* of your polis, who would contest
   your relatives
claiming as they are the next of kin [*genos*]?
You surely must invoke according to the *nómoi* of the land
you have fled, that they have no sway over you.

Ostwald considers that *nómos* at this time may or may not
refer to 'written law',[69] but this remains, in one sense, beside
the point for my purposes. In any case, while a poetic imitation of a technical reference to a *nómos* appears possible at this
time, the milieu remains customary (and Aeschylus, it should
be noted, never directly refers to 'written law'). However,
what scholars agree on is that it is increasingly evident in this
period (end of the sixth or beginning of the fifth century BC)
that *nómos* as a kind of 'law' (whether written or not) replaces
the earlier use of *thesmos* ('ordinance') to refer to certain types
of 'laws'.[70] Finally, the predominantly worship-related uses
of *nómos* in relation to the divine power of Zeus, as seen in
Prometheus Bound, are poignantly described in the *Suppliants*,
at 670–3, in ways that are reminiscent of Hesiod, and possibly
Pindar:

τῶς πόλις εὖ νέμοιτο [*eu nemoito*]
Ζῆνα μέγαν σεβόντων,
τὸν ξένιον δ' ὑπερτάτως,
ὃς πολιῷ νόμῳ [*poliō nómō*] αἶσαν ὀρθοῖ.

This can be translated as:

---

[69] Ostwald (1969: 44ff). Ostwald discusses three (legal) inscriptions from
near Athens that were most likely contemporary with the play.
[70] See Ostwald (1969: 12–19); for the 'shift', see Arist. *Ath. Pol.* 4.3; 3.4; 4.1;
7.1; and Hdt. 1.59.6.

Thus may their polis be governed well [*eu nemoito*],
if they are in awe of the mighty Zeus,
who, above of all, is the warden of the *xenos*,
and where by old *nómō* he guides destiny [*aisa*] straight.

Before I turn to Sophocles and his particular uses of *nómos*, it
is worth noting that in Aeschylus one can observe the widest
variety of composite words utilising *nómos*. For instance, a
'pastoral' sense is preserved in composites such as: 'dwelling in the plain', expressed in πεδιονόμος (*pedionomos; Sept.*
272); the αγρονόμος (*agronomos*), 'dwelling in fields' (*Ag.* 142);
the ανθονόμος (*anthonomos*), 'feeding on flowers' (*Sup.* 43,
539); the ποιονόμος (*poionomos*) and the πρόνομος (*pronomos*)
who are 'grazing' (*Ag.* 1169; in the plural at *Sup.* 50); the
γαιονόμος (*gainomos*) 'dwelling the earth' (in the plural at
Sup. 54); and the βούνομος (*bounomos*) of oxen grazing (fr.
249). The flock is expressed as νόμευμα (*nomeuma*) (*Ag.* 1416);
and the 'land army' is called πεζονόμος (*pezonomos*) (*Per.* 70).
The sense of 'dwelling or guarding' is expressed in composites like αστυνόμος (*astunomos*), a 'dweller guarding' (*Ag.* 88).
A 'companion' is called ξύννομος (*xunnomos*) (*Sept.* 354). The
'wielder of a weapon' is described as σιδηρονόμος (*siderono-
mos*) (*Sep.* 788), while the act of 'arranging' is expressed in
πεσσονομέω (*pessonomeō*) (*Sup.* 12). The frequent sense of a
particular 'custom or a way of life' is expressed, for instance,
in περσονομέω (*personomeō*), 'to live as Persians do' (*Per.* 585,
919),[71] and πολισσονόμος (*polissonomos*) (*Per.* 852). Finally,
being an outcast from the polis and its customary way of life
is emphatically signified in ἐκνομος (*eknomos*) (*Eum.* 92). This
complex of composites enhances further the coexistence of a
wide variety of uses and functions of the word and its family
in ways that are not strictly distinguished.

4.2 *Sophocles*

In Sophocles' *Oedipus Tyrant*, at 865–6, we encounter the
distinct expression νόμοι ὑψίποδες (*nómoi hupsipodes*). The

---

[71] The *Persians*, possibly the earliest surviving tragedy, is based on the historical events of the Greco-Persian wars and in particular the defeat of the
Persians, led by Xerxes, at the Battle of Salamis in 480 BC.

passage where the chorus praises such *nómoi* (involving, for instance, 'respect for the gods and parents') is at 863–71:

εἴ μοι ξυνείη φέροντι
μοῖρα τὰν εὔσεπτον ἁγνείαν λόγων
ἔργων τε πάντων, ὧν νόμοι [*nómoi*] πρόκεινται
ὑψίποδες, οὐρανίαν
δι᾽ αἰθέρα τεκνωθέντες, ὧν Ὄλυμπος
πατὴρ μόνος, οὐδέ νιν
θνατὰ φύσις ἀνέρων
ἔτικτεν οὐδὲ μή ποτε λάθα κατακοιμάσῃ·
μέγας ἐν τούτοις θεὸς οὐδὲ γηράσκει.

In translation:

May, as it is my *moira*,
my words and my deeds be praised of their purity
– for those are sanctioned
by the highest [*hupsipodes*] *nómoi*,
born in the aether, their father Olympus alone.
Their father was not a mortal,
nor would oblivion [*lēthē*] ever lay them to sleep:
a mighty god [*megas*] lies within them and never grows old.

The milieu appears to be the transgression committed and the plague that has as a result affected the polis. Here, the chorus refers to *nómoi* which are of divine origin, that is, divine *nómoi*, by which the chorus, praising them, wish to abide. The *nómoi*, the chorus states, are not born on earth or created by mortals, but instead in the aether, the separate sphere of the eternal and the divine.[72] Such ancestral *nómoi* sanction a purity that the chorus refers to, and they are the same unwritten *nómoi* that Antigone will abide by, as will be seen later.

---

[72] In Euripides' lost play *Melanippe Wise*, fr. 487, the sacred aether is described as Zeus' dwelling (ἱερὸν αἰθέρ᾽, οἴκισιν Διός). In fr. 919 (= Auge F265a), from an unidentified play of Euripides, the aether is described as the gods' summit that surrounds the earth (κορυγὴ δὲ θεῶν ὁ περὶ χθόν᾽ ἔχων φαεννὸς αἰθήρ). On the separation of different types of 'laws', see Harris (2010: 124).

The world is ordered by these 'laws', eternal, universal and unwritten as they reside in the *phusis* of things, in the sense of a cosmic, divine *nómos*.[73] Reverence for these 'laws', the chorus holds, is necessary if one is to avoid destruction. In *Oedipus Colonus*, at 1381–2, *Dikē* is named as *sunthronos* on the ground of ancient, 'primordial' *nómoi* in an analogous sense: εἴπερ ἐστὶν ἡ παλαίφατος | Δίκη ξύνεδρος Ζηνὸς ἀρχαίοις νόμοις [*archaiois nómois*] ('if in fact ancient *Dikē* sits beside Zeus, sharing the throne as is said by ancient *nómoi*').

Such *nómoi* are distinct, in one sense, from the local 'customs' that are, for instance, expressed in fr. 937 (Jebb): νόμοις [*nómois*] ἔπεσθαι τοῖσιν ἐγχώροις καλόν. For instance, in *Oedipus Colonus*, which is largely concerned with the matter of supplication,[74] it is a mortal sacred *nómos* that Oedipus is told by the chorus to abide by, namely adhering to the 'custom' of speaking from a particular place and not from upon the 'sacred' (*abatōn*) ground; at 168 the chorus states: . . . ἀβάτων [*abatōn*] ἀποβάς, | ἵνα πᾶσι νόμος [*nómos*] | φώνει· (leave the forbidden ground, and speak from where it is *nómos* to do so). Speech is intimately linked, for Charles Segal, with a proper realm (1999: 373), perhaps of *nómos* as such, though the *abatōn* is not necessarily anomic. In the *Trachiniae*, at 1177–8, Heracles cautions Hyllus towards being obedient to one's father, since this is the best *nómos*: νόμον [*nómon*] | κάλλιστον ἐξευρόντα, πειθαρχεῖν πατρί.[75] In a similar manner, Delaneira asks Lichas to abide by the proper *nómos* of a messenger, in the sense of a traditional norm or 'custom' of behaviour.[76] In the *Ichneutae*, a satyr play which reworks the Homeric *Hymn to Hermes*, a hunt that proceeds in a 'proper' way is referred to as being κατὰ νόμον [*kata nómon*] (at 195).

---

[73] Ryzman reads at this point a fusion of *phusis* and *nómos* (1992: 99).

[74] On supplication, as intimately linked to human and religious *nómoi*-customs, see Harris (2012: 295–9); and, see generally, Naiden (2006).

[75] See also 1224, and 1229. Such obedience can be contrasted with the *anomia* of the Centaur: ὑβριστὴν ἄνομον (*hubristēn anomon*; at 1096). In the *Trachiniae* it is of interest to compare the depiction of Heracles to earlier depictions of the hero, such as in Pindar. On Heracles in Sophocles, see Calame (1998).

[76] At 616–17: Ἀλλ' ἕρπε καὶ φύλασσε πρῶτα μὲν νόμον, | τὸ μὴ 'πιθυμεῖν πομπὸς ὢν περισσὰ δρᾶν· ('but go; and adhere, first, to the rule that messengers should be unwilling to act excessively').

These 'customs', in a wider sense, can also refer to the ways of a whole country. In the uncertain fr. 937 (Jebb) we read: νόμοις [*nómois*] ἐπεσθαι τοῖσιν ἐγχώροις καλόν. Here the meaning appears proverbial in the sense of 'one follows the local "customs"'.[77] In *Oedipus at Colonus*, at 337, Oedipus refers to the *nómoi* of the Egyptians (as well as to the composite σύννομοι, *sunnomoi*, at 340):

> ὦ πάντ᾽ ἐκείνω τοῖς ἐν Αἰγύπτω νόμοις [*nómois*]
> φύσιν κατεικασθέντε καὶ βίου τροφάς:
> ἐκεῖ γὰρ οἱ μὲν ἄρσενες κατὰ στέγας
> θακοῦσιν ἱστουργοῦντες, αἱ δὲ σύννομοι [*sunnomoi*]
> τἄξω βίου τροφεῖα πορσύνουσ᾽ ἀεί.

In translation:

> . . . the 'customs' [ways] of Egypt
> that are such in *phusin* and *bios*.
> There the men sit weaving inside the house,
> while their wives [*sunnomoi*]
> go outside to procure the daily life's means.

It is not certain, perhaps, whether these refer to 'laws', 'customs', or conventions, in the Egyptian context. Yet the milieu appears to be one of tradition or 'custom', a way of life centred on the particular gender roles that were prevalent in Egypt. It should be noted that the sense of *sunnomoi* is, specifically, of a husband and wife in an intimate relationship, though it can express a bond more generally; that is, one that is largely based on the earlier, or even perhaps earliest, uses of *nómos* with regard to 'eating and feeding' (as, for example, in *Philoctetes*, at 1436: ὡς λέοντε συννόμω [*sunnómō*]).

At first sight, at 548, the reference to *nómos* presents some difficulty of interpretation, with regard to whether its sense is 'juridical or religious', but this, as suggested earlier, may be a false dichotomy. Oedipus pleads, with regard to the killing of his father Laius in ignorance, as follows: νόμω [*nómō*] δὲ καθαρός, ἄϊδρις εἰς τόδ᾽ ἦλθον ('pure before the *nómos*,

---

[77] Stob. *Flor.* 43.25 [4.7, 9 Hense]; Jebb (in Pearson (ed.) 1917: I, 104).

ignorant in the act, I have come to this'). The act of self-defence
follows Laius' attempt to murder Oedipus, to which the latter
reacted with fatal consequences.[78] Here, the καθαρός (*katharos*)
may refer to 'innocence' more generally, but perhaps, more so,
to the ritual purity of being free from pollution. Oedipus, in
any case, claims that he is innocent because he did not know
that he was killing his father (and this was an established principle, too, according to Athenian law) – a claim, in fact, that
the chorus eventually accepted.[79] In the context of this play the
reference to *nómos* is most likely 'religious' rather than 'juridical' (though the intimate relation between the two remains
more important than marking their delimitation).

In a possible 'political or juridical' sense, Theseus states
at 907–8: νῦν δ᾽ οὔσπερ αὐτὸς τοὺς νόμους [*nómous*] εἰσῆλθ᾽
ἔχων, | τούτοισι κοὐκ ἄλλοισιν ἁρμοσθήσεται ('now, by just
such *nómoi* as he [Kreon] himself has brought, will he be
ruled'). At this point, the sense of *nómos* appears to refer
to Kreon's duplicitous acts (i.e. his violent attempt to seize
Oedipus), his ways with his *nómoi*. This use of *nómos* is supported a few verses later, at 913–18, when Theseus adds:

ὅστις δίκαι᾽ ἀσκοῦσαν εἰσελθὼν πόλιν
κἄνευ νόμου [*nómou*] κραίνουσαν οὐδέν, εἶτ᾽ ἀφεὶς
τὰ τῆσδε τῆς γῆς κύρι᾽, ὧδ᾽ ἐπεισπεσὼν
ἄγεις θ᾽ ἃ χρῄζεις καὶ παρίστασαι βίᾳ [*bia*],
καί μοι πόλιν κένανδρον ἢ δούλην τινὰ
ἔδοξας εἶναι κἄμ᾽ ἴσον τῷ μηδενί.

In translation:

You came to a city that exercises *dikai*
and does nothing without *nómos*,

[78] For an analysis of this in relation to *OT* and Athenian homicide law, see
Harris (2010: 131–40).
[79] See Harris (2010: 137–8 and 144, n. 51, in particular). Compare *OT* on the
question of whether the killing of Laius was justified. For Vernant and
Vidal-Naquet, on the basis of a distinction he draws between two different *nómoi/dikai*, one can be 'innocent and pure from the human point of
view', but 'guilty and polluted from the religious point of view' (1972:
110–11), and vice versa; consider, also, to an extent whether and how
such a distinction could apply to Antigone.

but you have spurned these [*nómoi*]
and you have taken what you need with force/violence
    [*bia*],
taking captives and enslaving them,
as if this polis was devoid of men, or manned by slaves,
and as if I was equal to naught.

The use of *nómos* with regard to 'what is proper' in the sense of 'the way of doing something or being' is, in fact, prevalent in *Ajax*. At 350, Aias addresses the chorus:

ἰώ
φίλοι ναυβάται, μόνοι ἐμῶν φίλων,
μόνοι ἔτ᾽ ἐμμένοντες ὀρθῷ νόμῳ [*orthō nómō*],
ἴδεσθέ μ᾽ οἷον ἄρτι κῦμα φοινίας ὑπὸ ζάλης
ἀμφίδρομον κυκλεῖται.

In translation:

Ah,
sailor friends, only you among my friends,
still singularly abide by the straight [proper] *nómos*,
look now at the wave that is breaking and
receding around me, in the murderous storm.

The characterisation of *nómos* as *horthos*, in the classical period, appears to have attained a further aspect, from its earlier 'uprightness' to a direct sense of 'correctness or rightness'.[80] The *nómos* in question is perhaps the conventional principle that one expects companions or friends to properly uphold (possibly in the manner of 'loyalty'). At 548, Ajax remarks regarding his son: ἀλλ᾽ αὐτίκ᾽ ὠμοῖς αὐτὸν ἐν νόμοις [*nómois*] πατρός (he must be forthwith steeped in the rough *nómoi* of his father). The sense of *nómos* here is that of a proper way of behaviour or being. Similarly, this notion of what is a proper way or manner is encountered at 1130, with regard to the divine or daimonic *nómoi* over the proper burial of the dead (δαιμόνων νόμους, *daimonōn nómous*). This is also

---

[80] For a semantic analysis of *horthō*, ranging from 'upright' to 'justice', see Coin-Longeray (2013).

seen at 1344, when Odysseus refers to τοὺς θεῶν νόμους, 'the *nómoi* of the gods' that would be destroyed if, under a decree of non-burial, the dead were not buried (in this case the burial of Ajax), which is defended by Agamemnon. With some similarity to *Antigone*, as will be seen later, the decree is, as a result, considered impious.

At 1246–9, the sense of what is proper is utilised by Agamemnon, but this time with direct reference to accepting the 'adjudications' on what is due:

ἐκ τῶνδε μέντοι τῶν τρόπων οὐκ ἄν ποτε
κατάστασις γένοιτ᾽ ἂν οὐδενὸς νόμου [*nómou*],
εἰ τοὺς δίκῃ νικῶντας ἐξωθήσομεν
καὶ τοὺς ὄπισθεν εἰς τὸ πρόσθεν ἄξομεν.

In translation:

At a place where these ways prevail,
there could be no settlement of any *nómos*,
if we were to thrust those who prevail in *dikē* aside
and bring forth those in the rear.

Such a decision, one that settles which is the winning side in a dispute, needs to find acceptance if *nómos* is to prevail among a community. A similar strong defence of *nómos*, though in a different context, is found in *Electra* at 1506, when Orestes remarks to Aegisthus that to avoid wrongdoing one must be punished (by death) when in breach of the *nómos*: ὅστις πέρα πράσσειν τι τῶν νόμων [*nómōn*] θέλει, | κτείνειν: τὸ γὰρ πανοῦργον οὐκ ἂν ἦν πολύ. Earlier, at 1043, Electra tells Chrysothemis that she does not wish to live in a place where certain (dishonourable) *nómoi* abide (τούτοις ἐγὼ ζῆν τοῖς νόμοις [*nómois*] οὐ βούλομαι). Here the sense could be that of 'custom' or 'way'. Finally, we encounter a clearer sense of the latter at 576–81, when Klytemnestra is warned that the murder of Agamemnon (in revenge for Iphigeneia's death) may set a *nómos*/'custom' (of, most likely, 'retaliation') that could turn against her:

εἰ δ᾽ οὖν, ἐρῶ γὰρ καὶ τὸ σόν, κεῖνον θέλων
ἐπωφελῆσαι ταῦτ᾽ ἔδρα, τούτου θανεῖν

χρῆν αὐτὸν οὕνεκ᾿ ἐκ σέθεν; ποίῳ νόμῳ [*nómō*];
ὅρα τιθεῖσα τόνδε τὸν νόμον [*nómon*] βροτοῖς
μὴ πῆμα σαυτῇ καὶ μετάγνοιαν τιθῆς.

In translation:

> But, as you see, if his motive was this [to help his brother]
> should you have killed [Agamemnon]?
> According to what *nómos*?
> Beware that by laying down such a *nómos* for mortals
> [retaliation?],
> you do not in fact lay down trouble and remorse for
> yourself.

Antigone's *nómos*

Burial

It is pertinent now to turn to one of the most intriguing and celebrated plays, *Antigone* (c. 443 BC).[81] It is worth outlining the core elements of the play at this point before I turn to examine the uses of *nómos* within it.[82] Thebes has been defeated by the Argive army and Oedipus' sons (Eteocles and Polyneices) killed each other while fighting on opposing sides. King Kreon (their uncle, the brother of Jocasta, Oedipus' wife) declares that Eteocles should be buried properly, since he fought to defend the kingdom, while Polyneices fought for the enemy and should be left unburied, exposed to the dogs and birds of prey. Antigone, the sister of the two fallen brothers (and Kreon's niece), after failing to convince her sister, Ismene, to support her in defying the king's decree, takes it upon herself to try to bury her brother's body. As she is attempting to perform the required funeral rite she is, however, caught and sentenced to being walled up in a cave.

---

[81] The literature on the *Antigone* is vast. Some of the more recent readings are: Bowra (1944); Else (1976); Steiner (1984); Ostwald (1986: 148–61); Bushnell (1988); Sourvinou-Inwood (1989: 134–48); Foley (1996); Griffith ([1999] 2003); Holt (1999); Benardete (1999); Butler (2000); and Lloyd-Jones ([1994] 2002).

[82] The background to this play is reimagined in Eur. *Phoen.*, as well as in Aes. *Sept.*, which I referred to earlier.

Towards the end of the play, the prophet Teiresias warns Kreon that he has defied the world of the dead, as much as that of the living, by not observing proper burial practices and as a result the city is polluted. In the end, Kreon proceeds to bury the body of Polyneices and attempts to release Antigone, only to discover that she has taken her own life. His son attacks him (but does not kill him) and then kills himself. Upon hearing the devastating news, Kreon's wife (Eurydike) also takes her own life. The gods, who did not intervene to save Antigone, thus impose this severe punishment upon Kreon, completing the twists that make up one of the most vivid tragic complexes.

There are several noteworthy elements to the play, but one of the most important is the 'custom' or *nómoi* of burial.[83] The matter of burial and the honouring (or dishonouring) of the dead arises a number of times in Sophocles (for example, in *Ajax*, 1336–65). In *Antigone*, the daughter of Oedipus defends her purpose as regards burying her brother, even though she does not actually bury him properly (while, however, fulfilling, contrary to ritual 'custom', the main part of the burial).[84] Earlier (predominantly aristocratic) family 'customs' regarding burial are increasingly affected by democratic legislation during the classical period, enabling interpreters to read this as a battle between kinship and the so-called state, between the family[85] and the 'law', the aristocratic *oikos* and the demo-

---

[83] Indicatively, see Ostwald (1986: 150, 156–7 and 160).

[84] Antigone is initially observed covering the body with dust, which was a token act of burial, an 'honouring' when proper burial could not be performed. In a later play (*OC*) Sophocles describes how Antigone promised her brother that she would bury him if he were to die as was fated (1399–1413). In *Antigone*, Antigone does not actually perform the burial 'proper', i.e. to completion; see especially 54–60 and 421–31. On the role of women in preparatory funeral rites, in particular, see Kurtz and Boardman (1971: 143–4); Loraux (1998); and Alexiou (2002: 14–23). It should be emphasised that, on the basis of the extant evidence, the central role in the performance of funeral rites was in the classical period preserved for men. On this and a comparative analysis of the examples of Klytaimestra, Medea and Antigone, see Hame (2008). By implication, what Antigone actually did in relation to the burial seems to be assumed as sufficient as far as the play is concerned; see, for example, 245–7, 395–6 and 404–5. This should not, however, be taken as evidence of actual practice; see Sourvinou-Inwood (1995).

[85] On the family and the *oikos* in classical Greece, see Lacey (1968).

cratic polis, the ancient 'customs'/*thesmoi*/*nómoi* and the new *nómoi*, and so forth.[86] As Katerina Zacharia writes, this was 'to interfere in the most intimate area of all: the family. In Greek terms, what we are dealing with is the gradual encroachment of the polis (city-state) on the *oikos* (family or household)' (2009: 56). Christiane Sourvinou-Inwood (1995) identified a shift in the way in which burials (and death more generally) are already perceived during the seventh century BC, leading to the impetus for funerary *nómoi* in the polis.[87] In this connection, Bonnie Honig (2009) has suggested that Antigone is the late claimant of the Homeric and 'aristocratic worldview' at a time of 'post-Homeric' democratic Athens.[88] Hence, Kreon has been read as a representative of democratic politics, though to an extent misleadingly so given that in the play he is later exposed as a tyrant. However, he is the ruler (the victorious general) who assumes power in the aftermath of a painful civil war, and the chorus describe him, at 155, as an ἄρχων νεοχμός (*archōn neochmos*, a ruler of 'a new kind').[89]

The burial of the dead was crucial in this later period, but its roots are perhaps already to be seen in Homer, since unritualised death was one of the key threatening events of pollution and, in the classical period, it becomes a task undertaken by the polis to provide for and observe the funerary norms (the *patrios nómos*, as Thucydides refers to it, at 2.34.1).[90] It has been suggested that to deny burial altogether

---

[86] This is not to disregard the various polarities that can be read valuably in the play for the varied purposes of interpretation, but to focus on what the play actually expresses. Nor, for that matter, should certain conflicts, such as the particular gendered roles that are explicitly or implicitly assigned in the play, be downplayed. For classic readings that in one way or another identify Kreon quite strongly with the 'state', see Hirzel (1900: 65ff); Schmid (1903); Meyer-Benfey (1920: 31ff); and Wilamowitz-Moellendorff (1921: 517). For critical readings of this position, see Bowra (1944); Whitman (1951); Lesky (1952); Jens (1952); Weinstock (1955); Ehrenberg (1956); Mette (1956); and Ostwald (1986).

[87] See also Parker (1996: 50).

[88] On the ethical transformations at this time and the role of Sophocles, see Blundell 1989.

[89] See Pritchett (1985: 246–9); and Podlecki (1986).

[90] On *patrios nómos* and state burial, see Jacoby (1944) and Clairmont (1983); on death in general, see Garland (1985).

was in a certain sense 'religiously' and socially unthinkable,[91] though in *Antigone* it remained a possibility with regard to traitors, among, perhaps, other enemies of the city and its *eunomia*. Wicked traitors (at 518) of the Athenian polis were not allowed burial, as can be surmised by peripheral evidence and what was considered accepted military practice, but this, perhaps, did not necessarily forbid burial outside of the walls of the polis.[92] There is no definitive literary evidence as to this, though what there is may be sufficient.[93] To be precise, Kreon himself does not refer to any specific *nómoi* of the polis as a precedent for his decree against the burial of Antigone's brother, other than his own authority on the matter and more generally;[94] nor does he defend it extensively throughout the

[91] As Zacharia points out, to be reduced to a state of powerlessness was the most severe experience that any Greek could suffer, and especially so when dead (2009: 58); but this does not mean that the practice of non-burial was not widespread.

[92] On the pan-Hellenic custom of burying the dead, see Kurtz and Boardman (1971: 143, 360); Rosivach (1983); and Rehm (1994: 181, n. 9). The early studies on non-burial are by Vischer (1865: 44–52) and Hester (1971: 19–21 and 55). More recent studies include Foley (1995: 134); Lindenlauf (2001); Patterson (2006); and Hame (2008). Among the ancient sources, see Xen. *HG*: 1.7.22; Thuc. 1.138.6; Plut. *Phoc.* 33.3; Din. 1.77. Rosivach notes that beyond Attica there are references in Phrynichus, Plutarch and Diodorus Siculus of an absolute refusal of burial to, for example, temple robbers (1983: 194); while in terms of the war-dead, he notes, *anairesis* allowed the losing side to bury its dead (see, for instance, Thuc. 5.74.2); yet earlier, as in the *Iliad*, the mistreatment of corpses is frequent (for example, 22.395ff; 24.14ff); note some later instances as well (for example, Eur. *El.* 855–98). We will encounter later on the justification of burial in Euripides' *Suppliants*. When Rosivach turns to the situation in the *Antigone*, he notes that Kreon is not obliged on the basis of *anairesis* to bury Polyneices, but only to allow the retrieval of his body (1983: 207), which is not, however, an issue raised in the play. He has no obligation, as a ruler, to bury him in Athens as he was a traitor, while as a member of Polyneices' family he has an obligation that he is not, however, necessarily due to perform himself (yet notably, he is the only surviving male member of the *oikos*).

[93] To an extent there is sufficient evidence as to the custom of non-burial with regard to not extending to burial outside of the homeland, as far as Attica is concerned in, for instance, Xen. *Hell.* 1.7.22; Plut. *Phoc.* 37.3–5; Lyc. *Leoc.* 113–14; and Thuc. 1.138.6.

[94] It is worth noting that there was no formal distinction between a decree and a *nómos*, at least before the reforms of 402/403 in Athens; see Quass (1971: 1–20) and the discussion in Fletcher (2012: 228). One must be careful to distinguish between a decree issued unilaterally with regard to

play (other than by referring to his word, at 657). However, this is not to say that it was not a reasonable, honourable and expected ban as regards someone who was an enemy as well as a traitor (even though also kin).[95] In this respect, to tackle this issue as (or through) an elaborate, even exclusive, 'legal' argumentation remains quite misleading. Meanwhile, Vincent Rosivach contends that Kreon's manner of executing this ban, in particular through the exposure of the corpse to birds and dogs of prey, would not be acceptable to the Athenians, since it was a form of impiety (1983: 210).[96] The burial or non-burial context is, then, the milieu in which Sophocles' poetic genius will reveal that neither of the two main tragic characters, Kreon and Antigone, are simple moral (or, indeed, nomological) agents.[97]

Hupsipolis
The uses of *nómos* in the *Antigone* merit appreciation both for their centrality and for their complexity (if not aporia).[98] In offering this, however, it is not particularly helpful to read the play, and the uses of *nómos* in particular, as a matter of an overtly structural conflict or contrast between, for instance, one kind of *nómos* and another (or any other duality for that matter, such as, most famously, that found in Hegel's dialectical reading of the opposition between the *oikos* and the polis, an opposition which, however, leads him to support the now classic juridicalisation of Antigone and Kreon's conflict as a conflict between two right(s) positions: a juridical

a particular contingency, as seems to be the case here, and one that was voted as such by the assembly. Fletcher notes that a *psēphisma* (a voted decree) is referred to as a *nómos* in Euripides (for example, *Ion* 1250–6); 2012: 231, n. 24).
[95] On the burial and reburial of Antigone's brother, see Whitehorne (1983: 129–42).
[96] See Teiresias' accusation at 1015ff.
[97] See the analysis of this complexity in Hester (1971); for a more recent contribution to this, see Harris (2004); for the later uses of the *Antigone* during the classical period and in particular in Demosthenes' oration, see Ferrario (2006).
[98] For readings with a particular emphasis on Antigone's *nómos* see, for instance, Hamilton (1991: 86–98); Douzinas and Warrington (1994); Harris (2003: 19–56); Ost (2004: 153–203); Nonet (2006); Fletcher (2008); Etxabe (2009; 2013).

scission between the self and the polis).[99] Nor shall I read the uses of *nómos* as an opposition between different *nómoi*, or an implied struggle between the political centre of the polis and its marginal other (or its outside).[100] Such readings, while engaging in other respects, tend to reduce the uses and the meanings of *nómos* to a structural dualism, whether dialectical or not, which often presupposes or leads to anachronistically polarised understandings of the uses of *nómos*, beyond what is actually found in the tragic texts. The more modest aim in my approach is, so far as is possible, not to go beyond the textual evidence and to observe the coexistent multiplicity of the uses of *nómos* and its family of words.

Antigone, in her initial address to and dialogue with her sister Ismene, refers to Kreon's decree against the burial of her traitor brother as a κήρυγμα (*kērugma*; a decree, to which I return below) and states (23–30):

Ἐτεοκλέα μέν, ὡς λέγουσι, σὺν δίκης [*dikēs*]
χρήσει [*chrēsei*] δικαίᾳ [*dikaia*] καὶ νόμου [*nómou*] κατὰ
    χθονὸς
ἔκρυψε τοῖς ἔνερθεν ἔντιμον νεκροῖς·
τὸν δ᾽ ἀθλίως θανόντα Πολυνείκους νέκυν
ἀστοῖσί φασιν ἐκκεκηρῦχθαι τὸ μὴ
τάφῳ καλύψαι μηδὲ κωκῦσαί τινα,
ἐᾶν δ᾽ ἄκλαυτον, ἄταφον, οἰωνοῖς γλυκὺν
θησαυρὸν εἰσορῶσι πρὸς χάριν βορᾶς.

---

[99] Hegel translated *Antigone* at the age of sixteen and her presence traverses his work. For instance, Antigone appears at crucial moments in the *Phenomenology of Spirit* (paras 429–76) and in *The Philosophy of Right* (para. 166); see Hegel (1962; 1997; 1991). In the Hegelian system 'bipolarity' is a necessary framework for the dialectic, yet what is dialectically maintained for Hegelian purposes has also been misunderstood in readings that anachronistically impose, instead, a rather rigid opposition or contradiction between a divine *nómos* and a mortal *nómos*, or, as they claim, 'family' and the 'state'.

[100] Such a dualism, among others, informs, to a significant extent, a seminal reading within the field of legal theory by Douzinas and Warrington (1994a: 187–226), along with its further elaboration in (1994b: 25–92). Their reading is, in large part, influenced by Hegel and Heidegger, as well as Lacan, and it purports to show that the philosophy and ethics of law are bound to the tragic. I owe thanks to both authors for inspiring my early engagement with the play during my legal studies.

Jebb (1891) translates:

Eteocles, they say, with due observance
of right and 'custom', he has laid in the earth
for his honour among the dead below;
as for the poor corpse of Polyneices, however,
they say that an edict has been published to the
    townsmen
that no one shall bury him or mourn him,
but instead leave him unwept, unentombed,
for the birds a pleasing store as they look to satisfy their
    hunger.

The very first use of *nómos* in the play, at 24, relates to Eteocles'
burial, which is said to be according to *nómos* and *dikē (dikaia)*.
Nómos here refers to the valid observance of a 'custom' of a
burial rite. Equally, Antigone will claim later, the burial of
Polyneices is also a matter of honour and *nómos*. Yet before I
turn to Antigone's statements, it is worth revisiting Ismene's
and Kreon's initial reactions.

At 59, Ismene warns Antigone of the fate in store for those
who disobey the decree of non-burial (death):

νῦν δ᾽ αὖ μόνα δὴ νὼ λελειμμένα σκόπει
ὅσῳ κάκιστ᾽ ὀλούμεθ᾽, εἰ νόμου βίᾳ [*nómou bia*]
ψῆφον τυράννων [*psēphon turannōn*] ἢ κράτη [*kratē*]
παρέξιμεν.

In translation:

Now, we two who are all alone, consider
how much worse we shall be destroyed, if in defiance of
    the *nómos*
we overstep a tyrant's decree or his powers.

Ismene states the 'ground' upon which she refuses to assist
her sister's defiance and act against (*bia*) the *nómos* of a tyrant.
(By attempting to bury her brother, Antigone has arguably
also acted against the gendered authority that required the
male kin to be responsible for the burial.) Already, at 74–7,
Antigone states that her act in defiance of the *nómos* was

according to the honour of the gods (at 77: τὰ τῶν θεῶν ἔντιμ'), setting the stage for the conflict that revolves throughout the play. Ismene is at this point conventionally portrayed as considering *nómos* and authority/ruling to be identifiable (the *psêphos, kêrugma* of Kreon's = *nómos*), while also expressing the will of the polis (79).[101]

Kreon's first statement in the play is introduced at 175–7:

ἀμήχανον δὲ παντὸς ἀνδρὸς ἐκμαθεῖν
ψυχήν τε καὶ φρόνημα καὶ γνώμην, πρὶν ἂν
ἀρχαῖς [*archais*] τε καὶ νόμοισιν [*nomoisin*] ἐντριβὴς φανῇ.

Kreon speaks of the fact that one is unable to ascertain one's own capabilities (his *psuchên*, his *phronêma* and his *gnômên*) before one has been steeped in the *archai* and the *nómois*, thus putting to the test one's legislative and ruling capacities. Presumably, Kreon is referring to the capabilities of a democratic citizen subject to the legislation and rule of the polis, while it could be said that he impliedly refers also to his own position as the ruler of the polis. For my purposes, the noun of interest that Kreon uses is νόμοισιν (*nomoisin*), a noun which, so far as I know, is only used twice in Sophocles (and three times in Euripides). The second use of *nomoisin* is met a few verses later when Kreon states: τοιοῖσδ᾽ ἐγὼ νόμοισι τήνδ᾽ αὔξω πόλιν ('by such *nómoi* I benefit the polis'). Such *nómoi* possibly refer to the *nómoi* of the polis. While Antigone (and not only Antigone) calls Kreon's decree as to the non-burial of traitors a *kêrugma*, the decree echoes, perhaps, relevant *nómoi* of the Athenian polis of this period, and it can be noted that the *kêrugma* is said, at 7, to have been declared πανδήμῳ πόλει (*pandêmô polei*). On the basis of this identification, some scholars, such as Sourvinou-Inwood, have read Kreon as representing the polis (1989: 135–7), the 'state'. In such a reading, with good reason, Kreon, as the rightful (albeit peculiar) successor to the throne and head

---

[101] See Democritus 68 B47 D–K; compare with Menelaus in *Aj.* 1073ff. On the identification of the citizens with the polis see, for instance, Thuc. 7.77.7. Later in the play, Ismene will 'shift' towards the *philia* of her sister (538–9).

of the household, represents the 'civic order'.[102] Kreon identifies himself (and his own decrees) with the *nómoi* of the
polis (175–91) and the honouring of the πάτρας (*patras*; 182),
while the *nómos* regarding non-burial is described as a *nómos*
by Ismene (59).

Comparably, at 211–14, the chorus refers to a ruler's *nómoi*
by telling Kreon:

σοὶ ταῦτ᾽ ἀρέσκει, παῖ Μενοικέως Κρέον,
τὸν τῇδε δύσνουν κἀς τὸν εὐμενῆ πόλει:
νόμῳ δὲ χρῆσθαι [*nómō de chrēsthai*] παντί που πάρεστί
   σοι
καὶ τῶν θανόντων χὠπόσοι ζῶμεν πέρι.

In translation:

That is what you wish, Kreon,
as to the polis' enemy and its friend
you may use any *nómos* you will
as to the dead and those of us that live.

The chorus states that Kreon, as a ruler, is able to utilise
any *nómos* he wishes over the living and the dead. Yet it
seems to me it would be misleading to suggest that the
chorus expresses here a strong position as to whether Kreon's
nómos (or decree) receives its authority (or legitimacy) from
the polis. It is equally possible to suggest that the chorus
impliedly at this point refers to Kreon's *nómoi* as the *nómoi* of
a man who is in power, an autocrat who legislates with whatever decrees he so wishes.[103] Or perhaps this remains open
for the audience. But, in any case, the chorus will characterise
whoever breached the *nómos* of non-burial (for they are not
yet aware of Antigone's act) as an ἄπολις (*a-polis*), that is, as
someone who is outside the polis (at 370).

The 'religious' undertone of the *nómoi* as to burial that are
mentioned in Sophocles are perhaps most closely depicted in
relation to the gods at 284–7, where Kreon responds angrily,
and to an extent provocatively, just after the chorus speaks of

---

[102] See Sourvinou-Inwood (1989); and Whitehorne (1983: 137).
[103] See Thuc. 3.37.3.

the possibility of the burial of Polyneices being the result of a divine intervention by asking:

πότερον ὑπερτιμῶντες ὡς εὐεργέτην
ἔκρυπτον αὐτόν, ὅστις ἀμφικίονας
ναοὺς πυρώσων ἦλθε κἀναθήματα
καὶ γῆν ἐκείνων καὶ νόμους [*nómous*] διασκεδῶν;

In translation:

Was it in high esteem for his benefactions
that they [the gods] sought to hide [bury] him,
when he had come to burn their columned temples,
their dedications and their land, and disperse its *nómoi*?

Kreon is self-characterised at this point as the protector of the *nómoi* of the polis against anyone who threatens to dissolve them (διασκεδῶν, *diaskedōn*; at 287).[104] Mortals are characterised by the ability to do good and evil (at 366) as part of their most δεινόν (*deinon*) character (at 332–3).[105] Within the characterisation of the fractured nature or power of mortals as positioned somewhere between the admirable and the terrible lies the ordering of the polis by *nómoi*. At 355–60, it is stated:

καὶ φθέγμα καὶ ἀνεμόεν φρόνημα καὶ ἀστυνόμους
[*astunomous*]
ὀργὰς ἐδιδάξατο καὶ δυσαύλων
πάγων ὑπαίθρεια καὶ δύσομβρα φεύγειν βέλη
παντοπόρος· ἄπορος ἐπ᾽ οὐδὲν ἔρχεται
τὸ μέλλον·

In translation:

---

[104] See Knox (1964: 102).
[105] The most significant philosophical reading of the *deinon*, in the *Antigone*, remains that of Heidegger ([1953] 1959: 149–63): 'The strangest (man) is what it is because, fundamentally, it cultivates and guards the familiar, only in order to break out of it and to let what overpowers it break in' (ibid. 163). Note that, in this work, Heidegger does not engage with Antigone's *nómos* as such; for a critique of Heidegger's translation, see Sauge (2014).

Speech, and thought like the wind, and the tempers that
    order the polis,
these he has taught himself,
and how to avoid the arrows of harsh frosts and those of
    rain storms.
He is ever resourceful. Whatever the future brings, he
    strides resourcefully.

At 368, Sophocles describes someone who is an *υψίπολις*
(*hupsipolis*) as one who abides by the *nómoi* of the polis and
the oath-bound *dikē* of the gods (νόμους [*nómous*] παρείρων
χθόνος | θεῶν τ' ἔνορκον δίκαν [*henorkon dikan*]). It is worth
reading the relevant verses that surround this designation at
365–75, where the chorus states:

σοφόν τι τὸ μηχανόεν τέχνας ὑπὲρ ἐλπίδ᾽ ἔχων
τοτὲ μὲν κακόν, ἄλλοτ᾽ ἐπ᾽ ἐσθλὸν ἔρπει,
νόμους [*nómous*] γεραίρων [*gerairōn*] χθονὸς θεῶν τ᾽
    ἔνορκον δίκαν,
ὑψίπολις [*hupsipolis*]: ἄπολις [*apolis*] ὅτῳ τὸ μὴ καλὸν
ξύνεστι τόλμας χάριν. μήτ᾽ ἐμοὶ παρέστιος
γένοιτο μήτ᾽ ἴσον φρονῶν ὃς τάδ᾽ ἔρδει.

Jebb (1891) translates:

Possessing resourceful *technas*, a subtlety beyond
    expectation
he moves now to evil, now to good.
When he honours the *nómoi* of the land and the *dikē* of the
    gods to which he is bound by oath [*horkon*],
his city prospers. But banned from his city is he who,
    thanks to his rashness,
couples with disgrace. Never may he share my home,
never think my thoughts, who does these things.

It should be noted that Jebb renders γεραίρων (*gerairōn*) in place
of παρείρων (*pareirōn*; to render complex). It is also of interest
to note the contrasting of *hupsipolis* with *apolis*. *Hupsipolis* is
only met once in the poet, and means the one who 'holds the
polis high', that is the one who honours the polis. This is in
comparison to the *apolis* that commonly denotes the one who is

a-polis, that is without a polis, or who, by implication, breaches the *nómoi* of the polis.[106] That one can be either *hupsipolis* or *apolis* can be read in parallel with the power to do good or evil, and in this context it is crucial to realise that the *technai* are the effects of mortal powers, the *deinon* character (that renders one equally *pantoporos* and *aporos*). The power of mortals is characterised by a scission, for good and evil, and as such is subject to overstepping and change (in this manner, mortal power is comparable to the non-static and non-absolute power of the gods). Finally, the statement of the *nómoi* in conjunction with the oath to the gods (in their totality) suggests that the chorus does not separate the mortal from the immortal *nómoi* at this point, or at least implies their intimate relation.[107] In fact, the chorus speaks of the *nómoi* of the land – νόμους χθονός (χθών, *chthōn*; chthonian). It is for these ancestral ties, on the basis of which the polis thrives, that the chorus sings. The citizen, in other words, is not conceivable without a share in the land (*chthōn*), and, perhaps as a result, the *nómoi* of the polis and the ancestral *nómoi* cannot be separated: the *nómoi* are, after all, earth-born. Indeed, at the conclusion of the play, Antigone calls herself a shareholder when she describes herself as a metic during her *katabasis*, at 868 (ἐγὼ μέτοικος ἔρχομαι).[108]

At 382, Antigone is characterised by the chorus as being disobedient and as acting in contravention of the royal *nómoi*:

οὐ δή που σέ γ᾿ ἀπιστοῦσαν
τοῖς βασιλείοισιν ἄγουσι νόμοις [*nómois*]
καὶ ἐν ἀφροσύνῃ καθελόντες;

This can be translated as follows: 'are they not bringing you captive for defying the king's *nómoi* and being caught acting in folly?' The characterisation of the *nómoi* appears to be political: they are the *nómoi* of the king. This can be coupled with Kreon's statement, at 449, when he asks Antigone: καὶ

---

[106] See Else (1976: 46).

[107] In arguable contrast, Kreon can be said to be pointing to a distinction between the Olympian and the cthonian gods, for instance in his oath at 758; see also 736, where the polis is not differentiated from the χθών (*chthōn*).

[108] On the metic, see Whitehead (1977); and Mueller (2011: 421–2).

δῆτ᾽ ἐτόλμας τούσδ᾽ ὑπερβαίνειν νόμους [*nómous*]; ('and so you dared to transgress the *nómoi*?'). This accusation of transgressing the *nómoi* of the polis (in Kreon's statement) leads to his characterisation of Antigone's act as *hubris*, at 480–1: αὕτη δ᾽ ὑβρίζειν μὲν τότ᾽ ἐξηπίστατο, | νόμους [*nómous*] ὑπερβαίνουσα τοὺς προκειμένους. It is also of interest for my purposes that Kreon here names the *nómoi* that Antigone 'transgresses' as προκειμένους (*prokeimenous*), which can be understood as the 'laid out *nómoi*', the *nómoi* at hand in the sense of 'the set or prescribed' *nómoi* (here, the implication of written or published *nómoi* remains uncertain). I return to this below, but first it is important to turn to Antigone's uses of *nómos*.

Antigonomia
Antigone claims to be following the honour (or will) of the gods (77) and later to be acting in accordance with another *nómos* that is superior to the *nómoi* of the polis, or at least, to Kreon's decree, which she contravenes. Consider the famous verses 450–5, where Antigone states:

Οὐ γάρ τί μοι Ζεὺς ἦν ὁ κηρύξας [*kēruxas*] τάδε,
οὐδ᾽ ἡ ξύνοικος τῶν κάτω θεῶν Δίκη·
οὐ τούσδ᾽ ἐν ἀνθρώποισιν ὥρισαν νόμους [*nómous*]·
οὐδὲ σθένειν τοσοῦτον ᾠόμην τὰ σὰ
κηρύγμαθ᾽ ὥστ᾽ ἄγραπτα [*agrapta*] κἀσφαλῆ θεῶν
νόμιμα [*nomima*] δύνασθαι θνητὸν ὄνθ᾽ ὑπερδραμεῖν.

In translation:

It was not Zeus that declared [*kēruxas*] this decree,
nor did chthonian *Dikē*
define such *nómoi* among mortals;
nor did I consider that your decrees [*kērugmath'*] could be
of such force so to override the unwritten [*agrapta*] and
firm [*kasphalē*] nomima of the gods.

Antigone continues to characterise these *nomima*, at 456–62:

οὐ γάρ τι νῦν γε κἀχθές, ἀλλ᾽ ἀεί ποτε
ζῇ ταῦτα, κοὐδεὶς οἶδεν ἐξ ὅτου 'φάνη.

τούτων ἐγὼ οὐκ ἔμελλον, ἀνδρὸς οὐδενὸς
φρόνημα δείσασ᾽, ἐν θεοῖσι τὴν δίκην
δώσειν· θανουμένη γὰρ ἐξῄδη, τί δ᾽ οὔ;
κεἰ μὴ σὺ προὐκήρυξας. εἰ δὲ τοῦ χρόνου
πρόσθεν θανοῦμαι, κέρδος αὔτ᾽ ἐγὼ λέγω.

In translation:

> [these *nomima*] have a life that is not of now or of
>   yesterday, but of all time,
> and no one knows when they first appeared.
> Given this, I did not wish to suffer any
> divine *dikē* by fearing the mind of a mortal.
> Die I must, I knew that.
> If I were to die prematurely, even without regard to your
>   decree.
> But if I do die then I consider this to be a gain.

The *nomima* are described as having a life, in that it is possible they are principles ordering human life, at least in some
contrast to the 'commands' or decrees of a king. They are
eternal and unwritten. Antigone seems to describe them as
one of the highest *nomima* (which are 'high' because they are
'earth-bound', as in her claim to chthonian *dikē*; at 451). Such
nomima are repeatedly contrasted with Kreon's ephemeral
decrees, and Antigone states that she would rather breach
the mortal decree than contravene the *nomima* of the gods.
Perhaps the distinction can be said to be also between breach-
able *nómoi* and unbreachable *nomima*. The *nomima* prescribe a
way of life that is according to a cosmic order, in one sense.
Irrespective of circumstances, such *nomima* must be adhered
to and be honoured.[109] The implication of the chthonian
(lower) *nomima* being 'higher' than the mortal decrees (or
perhaps *nómoi*), and hence as transcending them, has been
interpreted as another 'moral viewpoint', or as a 'natural law'
in a more or less strong sense.[110] This is one interpretation

---

[109] For Harris, the unwritten laws were not separate from the *nómoi* of the
city, but rather their 'foundation' (2006: 54–6); for the seminal treatment,
see Hirzel (1900).

[110] See Aristotle's reading of *Antigone* in *Rhetoric,* as asserting a 'right' by

that has been quite commonplace in readings of the play, especially those that read Antigone, rather anachronistically, as a heroic dissident torn between different 'worldviews' or moral 'rights'. Yet it seems to me that the manner here is cosmological, rather than predominantly 'political or moral': it is the chthonian cosmology of the *nómoi* that Antigone claims to abide by (and they are not a form of 'natural law': the *nomima* are of the gods). In this manner, Antigone is not 'partly right and partly wrong', but abides by *nómoi* that are, in a way, superior on the surface of the earth. Furthermore, complicating any attempt at a mere opposition of different orders or 'rights', the *nomima* for Sophocles and his time are not higher (as in separate) than the *nómoi* of the polis, but their foundation (Bowra 1947: 1001). Hence, the opposition of a 'partial right and a partial wrong' (regarding Kreon as much as Antigone) that the Hegelian-inspired readings, among others, advance, or opposition between 'one right versus another right', is not adequate if Sophocles' (and Antigone's) 'religious' sensibility is appreciated cosmologically. While, at first, Sophocles poetically portrays the two 'rights' or *nómoi* in opposition to each other for the purposes of the play's tragic conflict, the position that Antigone upholds is, it seems

nature and in accordance with 'natural law' (1373b1–13 and 1375a31–75b2); though note that Aristotle does not refer to a 'natural law', but to the 'common law' (*koinos nómos*) that is *kata phusin* (at 1375a32). That said, the possibility of a parallel between Aristotle's interpretation of the *nómos agraphos* which Antigone abides by and his *koinos nómos* remains plausible, though not in the anachronistic sense of 'natural law'. It has already been indicated that Antigone's 'defence' is at this point cthonic, earth-bound and in this sense, it is also *kata phusin* (and as such non-arbitrary, whether in terms of her will or that of the gods); see Guthrie (1971: 117–31). On 'natural law' and the *Antigone*, see Burns (2002). Nonet, in a philosophical reading of the play, relies on Aristotle's reading of the *Antigone* in order to understand the *nomimon* that she abides by as a *nómos* that 'sways over the gods themselves' (2006: 320), since no one knows of their 'origin'. I cannot align this understanding in my reading, since such supposed indeterminacy can and does refer to the divine power (and primarily that of Zeus); though in Nonet it has to be read in conjunction with what he suggests is to be understood as *kata phusin*, in his rereading of Aristotle's *koinos nómos*. For Nonet, Antigone's 'law' is *phusis, to eon, kosmos* (ibid. 323) and yet not in the sense of a *lex naturalis*, or an 'essential nature', or 'law of nature' in the sense of a causal rule (ibid.). I return to Nonet's reading below.

to me, the only one available to a Greek of Sophocles' time. Antigone's courage is derived from the heart of the absolute *nomima* of the gods, and this may also be the ground upon which, by the end of the play, Antigone will 'reconcile' her 'duty' with her 'love'.[111]

The uses of *nomima* and *nómos* are open to different interpretations. Firstly, it is crucial to turn our attention to the characterisation of the *nomima* as *agrapta* (unwritten). Without entering the debate as to the birth and form(s) of written law in ancient Greece, it is worth emphasising that an understanding of the unwritten character of the *nomima*, as in some direct or indirect opposition to a strong ('legitimatory') sense of written law, would be misleading.[112] Even in the complex period of Athenian democracy, the forms and uses of written laws continued to be ambivalent and the relationship of tradition to unwritten law remains unclear (especially given the lack of evidence).[113] It is relatively well-established that the term 'unwritten law' (ἄγραφος νόμος, *agraphos nómos*) appears in the mid to late fifth century BC.[114] Ostwald, *contra* Rudolf Hirzel's early and still relevant study (1900), has shown that at that time the references to unwritten *nómos* do not cohere into a 'concept'.[115] I suggested above that tentative

---

[111] For a reading that is, to an extent, close to this interpretation, even if in large part a christological reading, see Weil (1957: 18–23). In this sense Antigone, also, is neither female nor male (as subject to an opposition), but rather, in one sense at least, androgynous.

[112] On the important question of the 'birth' of written law in Ancient Greece, see, indicatively, Gagarin (1986); Camassa (1988: 130–55); Humphreys (1988: 645–93); and Hölkeskamp (1992b: 87–117). On anachronistic readings of *Antigone* regarding the opposition between *nómos* and tyranny, natural law and positive law and so forth, see Stolfi (2014).

[113] While it is known that in 403 BC the use of unwritten laws was subject to a certain form of ban, so far as their use by magistrates was concerned (Andoc. I 85 and 87), Aristotle will still refer to unwritten customary laws as higher than written *nómoi* in *Pol.* 1287b. For a helpful discussion on orality and the *mnēmones*, see Thomas (1989); see also Cerri (1979); and Bakker (1997).

[114] See Gagarin (1986: 25 and n. 21). On *agraphos nómos* see Hirzel (1900); Bowra (1944: 169ff); Ehrenberg (1956: ch. 2, app. A); Knox (1965: 95–8); Guthrie (1971: 117–30); Lloyd-Jones (1971: 109ff); Ostwald (1973: 70–104); Gigante ([1956] 1993: 202–9). See also the particularly illuminating study by Cerri (1979: especially chs 2 and 4).

[115] Hirzel (1900); see also Ostwald (1973: 70–104).

references to written *nómos*-'law' can be found in Aeschylus, though I noted that they are not absolutely certain. Moreover, as Rosalind Thomas has shown in her lucid work, it is possible that the so-called late reference to an *agraphos nómos* may be a 'reaction' to the emergence of written law (1995b: 64–6). In other words, it may be that the long-held use and validity of customary *nómos* (enduring in the fifth century BC) eventually encounter the need to reflect on its relation to written *nómoi*: 'You do not distinguish unwritten laws from written until you are beginning to see written law as a definite category' (Thomas 1995b: 64). Yet here, there is, in fact, no clear indication in the use of the word *nómos* to refer to 'written law'.[116]

In any case, for Sophocles, the unwritten *nomima* are not portrayed as anything other than ancestral and superior, and yet as widely knowable. They are not anarchic, as Kreon suggests of Antigone's transgression (672), but in contrast for Sophocles the *archē* of all *nómoi*. Rather than being weak, dark and unknowable, as Hegel would have it (1997: 286–7), the *nomima* are, for the poet, the ancestral 'customs', the *archē* and the basis upon which *nómoi* are cognised (and then differentiated). These *nómoi* are the divine order of the cosmos, Victor Ehrenberg writes, and are the core motivation of Antigone, rather than kinship, which, instead, is overshadowed (1954: 33–4). Ehrenberg noted that these are the same as the *nómoi* in *Electra* at 1093f, in *Oedipus Colonus* at 1381f, and in *Oedipus Tyrant* at 865, which I examined earlier (ibid. 36). They are also the same, in this sense, as the one *nómos* in Heraclitus.[117]

Philippe Nonet, linking Antigone's *nómos* with that of Heraclitus, centres his attention on the character of *agraphos* and proposes to read it not as a reference to a mere contingency (of its being unwritten), but rather to its incapacity for being

---

[116] See Ostwald (1969: 44). The earliest certain reference to written *nómos* is the late inscription of 418/7, *IG* I^3 84. See Humphreys (1988) and the discussion by Thomas (1995b: 65). The unwritten character of the *nomima*, however, does not necessitate a reading that locates here the 'unconscious' of *nómos*; for an (in part) critical reading, see Butler (2000).

[117] Though Ehrenberg distinguishes between divine and human *nómoi* quite sharply (1954).

written, its 'unsayability' (2006: 324). Yet such an incapacity only matters to the emergent powers of writing (and written 'laws'). To the inevitable metaphysics of writing (including the metaphysics of Western conceptions of 'natural law' in this regard), Nonet contrasts the 'unsayability' of the *nomima*. It can be accepted that, to some extent, Antigone's *nómos* is abiding by a cosmological rather than a distinctly 'political or juridical' order, yet it remains the case that, in itself, Nonet's reading, with its emphasis on the unsayability of Antigone's *nómos*, remains entangled with a metaphysical negativity of *phusis* that is not Sophoclean, but rather the critical premise of a Heideggerian Aristotelianism. For Nonet, the *phusis* in question is the *phusis* of 'being in its totality (*das Seiende im Ganzen*)' (2006: 328). Hence, Nonet writes:

> *Das Ereignis*, as the law, is then nothing other than the joining of the unity of belonging together of φύσις, which grants beings (*das Seiende*) to rise out of darkness into light, and ἀλήθεια, namely unconcealment as the clearing in which man stands as guardian of the radiance of being (*das Sein*). (2006: 334)

However, Antigone's *nomima* are the observances of the transmission of tradition, the ancestral sacred 'customs' that acknowledge the distance between the divine and the mortal, not a 'higher moral law or a natural law' (or an unsayable 'Law of law'). They are neither necessarily unsayable nor merely contingently unwritten.

Is Antigone's claim a 'legal claim', as Edward Harris (2012), among others, suggests? Julen Etxabe, for instance, has argued that 'Antigone's *nómos* addresses the specific issue of her disobedience (and not the absolute right of burial)' and that her disobedience, against Kreon as much as the polis, is not to be explained on the grounds of necessity, equity or heroism (2009: 63).[118] For Etxabe, with good reason, Antigone does not rely on the divine *nomima* in order to adduce extra 'legitimacy' to her action, for she is aware that she lacks such legitimacy (and, in fact, accepts Kreon's 'sovereign power';

---

[118] See also the more extensive treatment in Etxabe (2013).

2009: 65). It seems to me, however, that, to an extent, Etxabe succumbs to the appeal of a juridical dualism as if between opposed *nómoi*, which leads his reading anew to the categorisation of Antigone's 'case' as a 'hard case', that is, as one torn between two different *nómoi* that cannot be simply contrasted or conciliated, and, while these are speculative observations, any interpretation of Antigone's situation as a legal 'battle' misses the primarily non-juridical sense in which Sophocles' Antigone speaks. Rather than a juridical antinomy, one encounters, perhaps, Antigone's nomotropism for the needs of the play's central (initial) conflict between the mortal decree and the customary/'religious' *nomimon*. If Antigone is not claiming 'legitimacy', it is because the order of the cosmos is not in her control and Kreon, as is evident to her (and the audience), has overreached his civic authority. Her prudence is not a 'jurisprudence' of 'jurisdiction', but an act of reverence to the gods as much as to the polis's ancestral 'customs'. And it is noteworthy, equally, that throughout the play she never rejects the polis.

Autonomos
At 605–14, the chorus addresses Zeus as follows:

τεάν, Ζεῦ, δύνασιν τίς ἀνδρῶν ὑπερβασία κατάσχοι;
τὰν οὔθ᾽ ὕπνος αἱρεῖ ποθ᾽ ὁ πάντ᾽ ἀγρεύων,
οὔτε θεῶν ἄκματοι μῆνες, ἀγήρῳ δὲ χρόνῳ
δυνάστας κατέχεις Ὀλύμπου μαρμαρόεσσαν αἴγλαν.
τό τ᾽ ἔπειτα καὶ τὸ μέλλον
καὶ τὸ πρὶν ἐπαρκέσει
νόμος [*nómos*] ὅδ᾽, οὐδὲν ἔρπει
θνατῶν βιότῳ πάμπολύ γ᾽ ἐκτὸς ἄτας.

Jebb (1891) translates:

Your power, great Zeus – what human overstepping can
    check it?
Yours is power that neither Sleep, the all-ensnaring,
nor the untiring months of the gods can defeat.
Unaged through time, you rule by your power and
dwell thereby in the brilliant splendor of Olympus.
And through the future, both near and distant,

as through the past,
shall this law [*nómos*] prevail: nothing that is vast
comes to the life of mortals without ruin [*atas*].

The *nómos* that the chorus refers to is the ancestral divine *nómos*, the *archē* of life (and death) that orders or governs life throughout time and without exhaustion,[119] and which determines that mortal life cannot avoid *atē*[120] (as, for example, inflicted in and by Antigone's family). Transgressing the cosmic order, overstepping the *moira*, the limit of one's portion, leads to ruin, but is that avoidable? Antigone's *atē*, from the start, is indicated as that of her family following from Oedipus' self-inflictions and blinding, the suicide of Jocasta and the deadly battle between her two brothers. Antigone's *atē*, as inherited (at 856) as self-afflicted while engaged by an Erinys (idiocy and madness), is implicitly declared as such by Kreon, too, earlier at 485: εἰ ταῦτ' ἀνατεὶ τῇδε κείσεται κράτη. *Atē* is not an exceptional event, but one that characterises mortal life in contradistinction to divine power (as the chorus seems to suggest at 613–14).[121] Mortal life is ephemeral, finite and fragmented, and this is exposed in particular when mortals transgress the divine *nómos* of cosmic order. Mortal life cannot absolutely escape the transgressive act. It is of interest that this *nómos* which the chorus refers to appears indistinguishable from the *nomima* that Antigone claims she abides by. And it is further noticeable that it is the same *atē* according to the same *nómos* that will ruin Kreon in the end.

The chorus, quite disapprovingly, following her encomium, describes Antigone's act, at 821–2:

ἀλλ' αὐτόνομος [*autonomos*] ζῶσα μόνη δὴ
θνητῶν Ἅιδην καταβήσει.

In translation:

Guided by your own *nómos*, living-dead
you will descend to Hades.

---

[119] See also *OT* 863–71.
[120] See Doyle (1984).
[121] On divine power, see also *Ant.* 604 and 624.

Antigone's act is described by the chorus as an *autonomos* one in which, apparently, no other force played a part but her own.[122] This is the earliest and, so far, unique use of the word αὐτόνομος (*autonomos*) with regard to individual action in the extant Greek texts. It is first important to note that it is not Antigone who describes herself in this manner, but the chorus. The chorus appears to intend to describe Antigone's act as a 'personal' quality, signifying an 'unconstrained' action, but it is, furthermore, a reference to her passion in particular and her living-dead status,[123] rather than a reference to her as a 'political entity'. The chorus, utilising the word *autonomos* in this passage,[124] does not seem to have understood Antigone's act, yet it does imply that her act (as *autonomos*) remains an arguably honourable deed of defiance. Perhaps, Sophocles entertains the sense of her act as being one of unconstrained defiance of a superior order or *nómos*; while the word *autonomos* also indicates her giving a *nómos* to herself, living according to her own *nómos* (which, as the chorus stated in the first stasimon, is, by implication, different from or opposed to the *nómos* that is identified with the polis).[125] In the eyes of the chorus, Antigone, by acting the way she did, both acknowledges and defies the *nómos* of the polis (or of Kreon), and the chorus, as a result, both acknowledges and criticises her for this.

It is also worth noting that the uses of *autos-* in this play[126] tend to refer to the fate of Antigone's family: the *autos-* perhaps also indicates the same/the sameness, that is, the shared heredity of the family's tragic fate. The *autos-* is inevitably open to speculation at this point, but it is probably a key tropism that indicates the poetic complexity of the tragedy of Antigone's ways (as well as by implication Kreon's), rather than the mere sense of a unilateral act (given, in fact, that Antigone herself is never concerned with her own 'will' in the play), especially since it is implied she is 'fated' to act in

---

[122] On the use of the *autos-*, see also 875: *autognōtos* ('self-made' [decision]); and the treatment of this, as well as an analysis of its further uses, in Loraux (1986).

[123] See, also 857–71.

[124] For a discussion, see Ostwald (1982: 10–12).

[125] On 'autonomy' in Sophocles and more generally, see Ostwald (1982); from a philosophical perspective, see Castoriadis (2001; 2004).

[126] See 51; 52; 56; 172; 864.

the way she does. It is particularly significant that Antigone is marked in this way, with her threshold existence character-ised as 'living-dead'. In that threshold of being, in between life and death, her 'will' is earlier described by the chorus as an *erōs* (220) for the καλόν (*kalon*; 73–4), the highest honouring of 'the good' (913). Ultimately, Antigone, like her father, can neither be wholly 'autonomous' (in the sense of 'self-caused') nor be able to heroically overcome her *moira* and fulfil an end that stands beyond her finite existence.

In one sense, Antigone could be read as being described as someone who gives a 'law' to herself, or as claiming some 'proto-natural right'. Nonet translates the *autonomos* as 'as yourself-a-law-to-yourself' (2006: 324) and writes: 'Antigone's living law is Antigone. If that law is the law of φύσις, then Antigone is a *Gestalt* of φύσις as law' (ibid.). Indeed, Antigone is a child, παῖς (*pais*), a young girl. Her knowing of this 'law' does not emerge from any prior expe-rience in 'worldly matters' (ibid.). She also does not delib-erate or question herself. She is not, however, acting on the ground of some 'principle' or 'right'. Nonet here notes a self-known ὀργή (*orgē*; meaning, in its Doric form, what 'rises from earth'), and ὀργάς (*orgas*), a plot of 'fertile land' (ibid. 325). The verb ὀργάν (*organ*) signifies, Nonet adds, '"to grow fertile, to ripen, to swell", and for man, "to swell with desire"' (ibid.). Antigone's knowing rises 'out of the earth that brings it forth'. *Contra* Hegel, and all readings that centre on a duality structure between two orders in conflict, Nonet maintains, in a primarily Heideggerian reading, that Antigone's *nómos* does not grow out of the necessity of her defending herself against the civic order, but out of the earth (ibid. 327). Antigone's *nómos*, in this reading, is not posited, but it appears and orders, that is, it holds sway over mortals and immortals. Her *nómos*, like she herself, is, for Martin Heidegger's reading, 'authentically uncanny' (*eigentlich unhe-imlich*; 1984; 1996).[127] Still, it is worth remembering that this

---

[127] Heidegger's interpretation of Antigone's *nómos* is that her *nómos* is the polis, wherein entities manifest, or appear, themselves and where they are joined in a finite swirl (*Wirbel*) in the *unheimisch* (unhomely) (1984: 81 and 61); Heidegger's reading is indebted to Hölderlin's translation (1988); on Hölderlin's reading and translation, see Schrader (1933).

interpretation extends quite far from the sense in which the word is used by the chorus in this passage.

In my reading, the one thing that mortals and immortals cannot override is their *moira*, that is, their life – to each what is due as their 'own' life. A good life, a life of pleasure, the *kalon*, is measured ultimately by the wondering errancy which is immanent in one's acts. But this is shown to be an open question that can only remain ever open, beyond 'judgment' and 'right'. Antigone is led to the realisation of her fate through her 'own' act. At 847, Antigone asks (suggesting, among other things, that the chorus has not understood her act and motivation) οἵα φίλων ἄκλαυτος, οἵοις νόμοις ('unwept by loved ones, by what *nómoi* . . .?'). Antigone asks the chorus according to what *nómoi* she suffers her lonely exile and her untimely death. As Antigone lives in exile, at the threshold, between the mortals and the immortals, Kreon's *nómoi* (Antigone names them as such this time, echoing the phrase of the chorus about her acting 'autonomously') have interrupted not only her brother's proper burial, but also her own death.[128] Meanwhile, she admits that she hears disapproval from the citizens and that she has acted against the *nómos* of Kreon (and, perhaps only in that sense, the *nómos* of the polis).[129]

In a similar self-address, though directly this time, Antigone asks, at 908: τίνος νόμου δὴ ταῦτα πρὸς χάριν λέγω; (according to what *nómos* do I say this?). It is worth reading the relevant passage in full (905–15):

οὐ γάρ ποτ᾽ οὔτ᾽ ἄν, εἰ τέκνων μήτηρ ἔφυν,
οὔτ᾽ εἰ πόσις μοι κατθανὼν ἐτήκετο,
βίᾳ [*bia*] πολιτῶν τόνδ᾽ ἂν ἠρόμην πόνον.
τίνος νόμου [*nómou*] δὴ ταῦτα πρὸς χάριν λέγω;
πόσις μὲν ἄν μοι κατθανόντος ἄλλος ἦν,
καὶ παῖς ἀπ᾽ ἄλλου φωτός, εἰ τοῦδ᾽ ἤμπλακον,
μητρὸς δ᾽ ἐν Ἅιδου καὶ πατρὸς κεκευθότοιν
οὐκ ἔστ᾽ ἀδελφὸς ὅστις ἂν βλάστοι ποτέ.
τοιῷδε μέντοι σ᾽ ἐκπροτιμήσασ᾽ ἐγὼ
νόμῳ [*nómō*] Κρέοντι ταῦτ᾽ ἔδοξ᾽ ἁμαρτάνειν
καὶ δεινὰ τολμᾶν, ὦ κασίγνητον κάρα.

[128] See Goheen (1951: 89).
[129] See the analysis by McDevitt (1982).

Jebb (1891) translates:

> Never, if I had been a mother of children,
> or if a husband had been rotting after death,
> would I have taken that burden upon myself in violation
> of the citizens' will.
> For the sake of what law [*nómou*], you ask, do I say that?
> A husband lost, another might have been found,
> and if bereft of a child, there could be a second from some
> other man.
> But when father and mother are hidden in Hades,
> no brother could ever bloom for me again.
> Such was the law whereby I held you first in honour,
> but for that Kreon judged me guilty of wrongdoing
> and of dreadful outrage, dear brother!

Antigone responds to the chorus by implying that her act was, in fact, truly pious, because honouring her brother more than any other relative (child or husband) is in fact a *nómos* that exceeds self-interest (as well as that of the political *nómoi*). Her defiance would not have been exercised against the polis and its citizens, if it were not for the fact that her brother could never be replaced (unlike a child or a husband). That is the *nómō* (νόμῳ) of her action, for which, in contrast, Kreon's decree declared her guilt.

For Etxabe, in his at times nomological reading, these verses show that Antigone's act of defiance is declared 'legitimate' (rather than 'necessary, heroic or equitable') with regard to transgressing a particular decree or *nómos* (of Kreon's) for the sake of her brother, rather than anyone else. It is an act, Etxabe argues, that does not aim at a total conflict with the polis's *nómos*, but towards the preservation of the honour of her lineage (*oikos*):[130]

> This claim is not a particular exemption (necessity) or rectification (equity) of the law, whereby the definition of the law stands as before. Nor is it a heroic call to disregard ordinary norms and constraints. Rather, the claim for legitimacy is an

---

[130] On the latter, see MacDowell (1989).

attempt to redefine the normative realm by bringing to the public eye what a given society fails to recognize as the law (but nonetheless ought to). This is, in my view, the implicit claim Antigone makes in branding her argument a *nomos* and submitting it to the scrutiny of the 'wise citizens' [904]. Antigone wants the citizens to know that her disobedience is also defensible from their perspective. (2009: 66)

But Etxabe's analysis ventures a bit too far if it supposes that Antigone is arguing 'as if' in court, necessitating the con-struction of a 'legal argument', let alone of a self-willed *nómos* that will legitimate and validate her act with the force of a considerable counter-law. Antigone's *nómos* is not her 'own' *nómos* (nor is she aiming to merely honour her lineage or *oikos* out of self-interest), contrary to what the chorus claimed earlier. She is abiding by the *nómos agraphos*, the ancestral *nómos* of the gods that, as seen earlier, mortals did not con-struct. She does so with, in fact, some disregard for her *oikos*. While Etxabe notes that Antigone's actions do not contradict her reverence for the unwritten *nómoi*, but instead enunciate the 'true complexity' of her act, he still seems to suppose that Antigone needs to justify herself 'juridically'.

Antigone, it seems to me, acknowledges that there are other 'perspectives' to her act, but she maintains that the deed was genuinely pious according to a *nómos* that can neither be breached nor adjudicated ('her' *nómos* admits no abstrac-tion or jurisprudential elaboration and recategorisation). The *nómos* she abides by does not require 'legitimisation'. It is worth remembering, at this point, that Kreon will be ruined on the basis of his own transgression of the same *nómos* that Antigone claims to be abiding by and for which there is and there cannot be, in principle, deliberation or jurisprudential conflict. Whether or not this *nómos* of Antigone represents the aristocratic defence of blood lineage, the fact remains that 'her' *nómos* is not 'political or juridical' (nor, for that matter, is it a 'scandal').[131] Antigone remains aware of her

---

[131] The French psychoanalyst Jacques Lacan, reflecting on Goethe's perplex-ity over such a 'scandalous' line, read these verses as pointing not to a scandal, but to the singularity of 'bare' existence; yet this limit-existence (Lacan's 'signifying void') remains too uncertain for a reading of these

act's irreparable consequences from the start. The endpoint of the play is not *dikē* (in a 'juridical or political' sense), I would suggest, but cosmic order (the sacred ground upon which the polis and the *nómos* dwell). In Athens, everything began with a prayer or a 'sacrifice' and it is this proverbial tone that signifies the milieu within which the play unfolds.

At 1113–14, Kreon acknowledges that the divine *nómos* that Antigone abided by is part of the 'laws' (*nómoi*) that are the established order of things: δέδοικα γὰρ μὴ τοὺς καθεστῶτας νόμους [*nómous*] | ἄριστον ᾖ σῴζοντα τὸν βίον [*bion*] τελεῖν. Jebb (1891) translates as follows: 'I am held by the fear that it is best to keep the established laws to life's very end.' The conflict between divine *nómos* and the *nómos* of the polis is not a conflict as such for Antigone, but an essential relation to a distance that separates and enjoins the earth and the sky. Kreon becomes aware of the cosmic order that he has violated and of its equally irreparable consequences for Antigone.[132] The chorus's final turn in this regard is clear too, instructing him to bury Polyneices and to free Antigone. The foremost 'law' (which, I believe, is not the Athenian 'rule of law', as Harris suggests; 2012: 290), for all times, is that mortal power cannot escape its *moira*; the sacred apportionment of *nómos* remains an enduring *archē*. Overstepping a limit produces Antigone's act and Kreon's decree and leads them both into the abyss of the living-dead (at 1288), namely, a life without pleasure. Yet the limits that the two characters overstep are qualitatively different.

Ultimately, for Sophocles, it should not be forgotten that it is Kreon who is to be exposed and torn apart. Earlier, Kreon

verses, at least for my purposes; see Lacan (1992: 243–90). Equally, on the other hand, a search for certainty, for a relatively clear-cut explanation as to why Antigone says she would do this for her brother, but not for a dead husband or child, is not that helpful either; see Nussbaum (1986). What remains for my consideration is what Antigone actually says. In my view, she is making neither a certain nor an uncertain *general* statement of 'principle' that would, for instance, apply to all brothers or all siblings and close relations. For an illuminating reading of this contingency, see Mader (2005). It remains possible, of course, to reread Lacan in this light, whereby his contingency and singularity would be enjoined in analytic schematism.

[132] On 'order' in *Antigone*, see Kirkwood (1991); on the gods' destructive power, see Padel (1995).

had characterised the civic *nómoi* that he was protecting as προκειμένους (*prokeimenous*), even though his authority is eventually shown to be probably self-asserted. In *Oedipus Tyrant*, it is of interest to note that the *nómoi* that are described, instead, as *prokeimenoi* are the unwritten *nómoi* (865), the *hupsipodes nómoi*. It would thus perhaps be reasonably cautious to hold that, in any case, the line that separated the two types of *nómoi* implied at this point and earlier on in the play was an uncertain one (and perhaps this was Sophocles' key dramatic matter). Kreon will, now, accept that the *nómoi* that Antigone abided by (the unwritten *nómoi*) are in fact καθεστῶτας (*kathestōtas*) and hence superior.[133] Yet it is crucial to note that the ending of the play entails not a resolution, as in a juridical conflict, nor the *mimēsis* of the scales of justice, but, rather, the learning – established in life, usage,[134] and erring – which is not other than the *poiēsis* of life as an ever-generative *ēthos* before the gods. Contrary to an overtly nomic recomposition, what we are left with is a question, which, just as the tragic play ends, remains open.

4.3 *Euripides*

I turn, finally, to Euripides (484–407 BC) to examine his uses of *nómos* in his extant tragedies (produced between 438 and 408 BC), as well as in some of the surviving fragments from his myriad lost plays. It is fair to note that the majority of the uses of *nómos* in Euripides refer to customary practices, 'laws' or conventions, traditional 'morality', but also to a universal *nómos* (as in *Hecuba*). Euripides 'speaks' to his social milieu without, however, pointing to anything teleological, other than a plurivocity of forces and practices. In *Alcestis*,[135] at 56–7, in the dialogue between Apollo and Death, Death refers to *nómos* in the following manner:

---

[133] See Honig (2009: 9–10).

[134] Heidegger translates *nómos* in Antigone (449–57) as '*der weisende Brauch*' ([1953] 1959: 219); for a discussion of this translation, see Nonet (1995: 994).

[135] In *Alcestis*, Admetos, with the aid of Apollo, would have his wife, Alcestis, die in his place, which Alcestis accepts on the condition that her husband would not remarry.

Ap. κἂν γραῦς ὄληται, πλουσίως ταφήσεται.
De. πρὸς τῶν ἐχόντων, Φοῖβε, τὸν νόμον [*nómon*] τίθης.

In translation:

Ap. And yet if she dies old, she will receive a rich burial.
De. The *nómos* you are positing, Phoebus, is to the
advantage of the rich.

Here, Death accuses Apollo of establishing a *nómos* according to which older people would receive richer funerals than the young. The use of *nómos*, at this point, is in the sense of a norm. In a relatively similar manner and with a clearer sense of a customary norm, Pheres states that he does not accept it as an ancestral *nómos* (whether *patrōon* or Hellenic) that fathers should die for their children. At 683, we read: οὐ γὰρ πατρῷον τόνδ' ἐδεξάμην νόμον [*nómon*], | παίδων προθνῄσκειν πατέρας, οὐδ' Ἑλληνικόν ('I did not receive this as a family *nómos*, fathers dying for their children, nor as a Hellenic one either').

In *Medea*,[136] at 238, Medea speaks of the hard *moira* that one receives when one comes before new *ēthē* ('ways') and *nómoi*: ἐς καινὰ δ' ἤθη καὶ νόμους ἀφιγμένην. The reference here is to a woman who marries and has to adopt new ways of life ('customs') in the sense of norms of conduct.[137] At 537–9, Jason speaks of the blessings that he has brought to Medea, within which lie her awareness of how to live an eunomic life by using and respecting the *nómoi* (νόμοις χρῆσθαι, *nomois chrēsthai*) that do not permit the use of brute force: γαῖαν

---

[136] The plot centres on Medea's revenge due to Jason's marriage to King Kreon's daughter. She receives sanctuary from the king of Athens (Aigeus), while she plots and then executes her revenge by killing Jason's bride, her children and Kreon.

[137] In relation to marriage, one can observe further a couple of relevant uses of *nómos* in *Iphigeneia in Aulis*. The custom (*nómos*) of a proper marriage, where the mother gives her child away, is mentioned at 734, when Klytemnestra tells Agamemnon: οὐχ ὁ νόμος οὗτος οὐδὲ φαῦλ' ἡγητέα ('this is not the custom [*nómos* as to the arrangement of marriage] but you think lightly of such things'). At 694, she tells him that his grief due to Iphigeneia's impending marriage will be alleviated by 'custom' (*nómos*) and *chronos* ('time'): ἀλλ' ὁ νόμος αὐτὰ τῷ χρόνῳ συνισχανεῖ.

κατοικεῖς καὶ δίκην ἐπίστασαι | νόμοις [nómois] τε χρῆσθαι
μὴ πρὸς ἰσχύος χάριν· | πάντες δέ σ' ἤσθοντ' οὖσαν Ἕλληνες
σοφήν. Finally, at 812, the chorus appeals to the mortal *nómoi*
in order to dissuade Medea from murdering her children:
νόμοις [nómois] βροτῶν ξυλλαμβάνουσα.

In the *Heraclidae*,[138] at 141–2, the *nómoi* according to which
the polis condemns the Argives (who become fugitives)
to death are mentioned as follows: νόμοισι [nomoisi] τοῖς
ἐκεῖθεν ἐψηφισμένους | θανεῖν· ('sentenced by the *nómoi* of
that polis to die'). The central question in the play concerns
the due treatment of suppliants who claim asylum at the altar
of the gods (*temenos*), in line with the Hellenic higher *nómos*
('custom') and the polis. Here, the herald claims that the suppliants must be extradited on the grounds of the local *nómoi*
(in the sense of decreed laws) of the polis of Argos, which
condemn fugitives to death, and, thus, he uses excess force
in an attempt to remove them from the altar. The reference
to ἐψηφισμένους (*epsēphismenous*; voted, sentenced) does not
appear to refer to a democratic process, given that I surmise
in the context of the play that this is the edict of a self-serving
tyrant's decree (1003; 186) against the children of Heracles,
who are, we are told, innocent. At 292, the chorus, in response
to the herald, refers to *nómos* in the following way: πᾶσι
γὰρ οὖτος κήρυξι νόμος [nómos], | δὶς τόσα πυργοῦν τῶν
γιγνομένων ('for this is the manner of heralds, to proclaim a
nómos, twice as large as the truth'). The sense of *nómos* in this
passage could reside both in the idea of the *nómos* on which
the herald grounds his claim as to extradition and in the
playful notion of telling/decreeing a tale that is exaggerated.

Lesser forms of *nómos*, whether by decree or by a herald's 'custom' or 'way', are open to variation and excess,
whereas the 'higher law' of divine *nómos* takes priority and
remains absolute. At 963, Alcmene asks the servant: εἴργει
δὲ δὴ τίς τόνδε μὴ θνήσκειν νόμος [nómos]; ('what *nómos* is it
that prevents his being killed?'). The *nómos* referred to here,
the servant explains, is the *nómos* against killing an enemy

---

[138] In the *Heraclidae*, the king of Mycenae, Eurystheus, pursues the children
of Heracles who have taken refuge at the altar of Zeus at Marathon. A
battle ensues and Eurystheus is captured. Heracles' mother, Alkmene,
demands and receives his execution.

captured alive in battle (966), since this is the *nómos* of the
land. Thus, Eyrustheus, who was pursuing the fugitives and
aimed at enforcing his *nómos* even outside of his 'jurisdiction', as well as against the 'higher' (for the Athenians) *nómos*
of sanctuary, will, when captured, also claim protection
under the Hellenic *nómoi*. Thus, at 1009–11: νῦν οὖν ἐπειδή μ'
οὐ διώλεσαν τότε | πρόθυμον ὄντα, τοῖσιν Ἑλλήνων νόμοις
[*nómois*] | οὐχ ἁγνός εἰμι τῷ κτανόντι κατθανών· ('now, since
they did not kill me on the battlefield, when I was willing to
die, by the *nómoi* of the Greeks, my death, for the man who
kills me, is impure'). This *nómos* is a sacred *nómos* of the gods
that the polis upholds.[139] This forms, in a sense, yet another
example of the intimate relation of divine *nómos* with the
nómoi of the polis.

In *Hippolytos*, the young self-righteous bastard son of
Theseus, Hippolytos, is held to be in breach of the *nómos*
regarding his oath to speak the truth and his disrespect for
family and the polis. At 91, the servant addressing Hippolytos
concerning his exclusive devotion to one goddess refers to a
nómos that is observed by all mortals: οἶσθ' οὖν βροτοῖσιν ὃς
καθέστηκεν νόμος [*nómos*]. The *nómos* in question is described
by the servant as relating to εὐπροσηγόροισίν (95): that is, the
nómos concerning 'affability', being courteous towards the
gods, which is established among mortals in accordance with
divine *nomos*, and which Hippolytos doubts, unless humans
are to follow heavenly *nómos* (in 'usage'), at 98: εἴπερ γε θνητοὶ
θεῶν νόμοισι [*nomoisi*] χρώμεθα [*chrōmetha*]. Hence, the question involves whether one should be affable even towards
someone to whom one has no inclination (in Hippolytos' case,
Aphrodite). Hippolytos' stance is informed by the view that
one cannot worship Artemis (who will eventually reveal his
innocence) and Aphrodite (who had made Hippolytus fall in
love with Phaedra, Theseus' wife) at the same time (102–4).
Between 'passion' and 'reason' (*sophrosunē*), Hippolytos lives
on the threshold of mortal tragedy.[140]

Contrary to such revered *nómoi*, perhaps as a result of
another *nómos* (convention/'custom') we read at 459–61
regarding Phaedra's stance towards the yielding to sup-

---

[139] For further analysis, see Burnett (1976).
[140] See the discussion in Lattimore (1962) and Berns (1973).

pliants: χρῆν σ᾽ ἐπὶ ῥητοῖς ἄρα | πατέρα φυτεύειν, ἢ ᾽πὶ δεσπόταις θεοῖς | ἄλλοισιν, εἰ μὴ τούσδε γε στέρξεις νόμους [*nómous*] ('your father, then, should have begotten you on fixed terms or with a different set of gods in heaven if you are going to refuse abiding by these *nómoi*'). Here, the sacred *nómos* concerning supplication is assumed to be reasoned on the hypothetical basis of an upbringing that abided by different 'norms' (*nómoi*) and gods. The emphasis on this is due to the fact that Phaedra's stance towards Aphrodite, as well as that of Hippolytos, would mean that one would be rejecting both the *oikos* and the polis (as they are interdependent). The next reference to *nómos* is found at 1046, where Theseus tells Hippolytos that his dishonouring of his father and of his oath to the gods has been on the basis of a self-proclaimed *nómos* against his own self: ὥσπερ σὺ σαυτῷ τόνδε προύθηκας νόμον [*nómon*]. Finally, at 1328–9, Artemis will state that she cannot interfere with Aphrodite's wishes, since: θεοῖσι δ᾽ ὧδ᾽ ἔχει νόμος· [*nómos*] | οὐδεὶς ἀπαντᾶν βούλεται προθυμίᾳ ('amidst the gods the *nómos* ['custom'] is as such: no god attempts to cross the will of another').

In the *Suppliants*, the central theme is the proper treatment of the war-dead.[141] At 311–13 Aethra states: νόμιμά [*nomima*] τε πάσης συγχέοντας Ἑλλάδος | παῦσαι: τὸ γάρ τοι συνέχον ἀνθρώπων πόλεις | τοῦτ᾽ ἔσθ᾽, ὅταν τις τοὺς νόμους [*nómous*] σώζῃ καλῶς ('the confounding of the Hellenic *nomima* must be stopped, since this is what holds the mortal *poleis* together, when the *nómoi* are adhered to by all'). The *nómoi* in question are the sacred Pan-Hellenic 'customs/ rites' of proper burial. In a similar manner, and with regard to the divine sanction of such *nómoi*, the chorus states at 378: νόμους [*nómous*] βροτῶν μὴ μιαίνειν ('so not to desecrate the *nómoi* of mortals'). Another use of *nómos* of particular interest is made at 430–4, when Theseus, addressing the Theban herald, states:

ὅπου τὸ μὲν πρώτιστον οὐκ εἰσὶν νόμοι [*nómoi*]
κοινοί, κρατεῖ δ᾽ εἷς τὸν νόμον [*nómon*] κεκτημένος
[*kektēmenos*]

---

[141] On the treatment of burial in stages at Athens, see Garland (1985: 14ff).

αὐτὸς παρ' αὑτῷ· καὶ τόδ' οὐκέτ' ἔστ' ἴσον.
γεγραμμένων [*gegrammenōn*] δὲ τῶν νόμων [*nómōn*] ὅ τ'
ἀσθενὴς
ὁ πλούσιός τε τὴν δίκην ἴσην [*dikēn isēn*] ἔχει[,]

In translation:

[in Thebes] there are, to start with, no *nómoi* common to
all,
but one man is tyrant, in whose keeping and in his alone
the *nómos* resides,
and in that case there is no equality.
But when the *nómoi* are written down,
both the weak and the rich enjoy equal *dike*[,]

In these verses, Euripides appears as the earliest poet to refer
to written *nómoi* ('laws'), while praising them as a defence
against tyranny. In a polis that observes (a relative) equality, written laws are a shared possession and defence against
self-serving exploitation and rule. At 524–7, the claim is made
that conserving the *nómoi* of all Hellas[142] requires that the
dead be buried properly:

νεκροὺς δὲ τοὺς θανόντας, οὐ βλάπτων πόλιν
οὐδ' ἀνδροκμῆτας προσφέρων ἀγωνίας,
θάψαι δικαιῶ, τὸν Πανελλήνων νόμον [*nómon*]
σῴζων.

Edward P. Coleridge (1938) translates:

but still I think it right to bury the fallen dead, not
injuring any polis
nor yet introducing murderous strife [*agōnias*],
but preserving the *nómon* of all Hellas.

Similarly, at 670–2: ἡμεῖς ἥκομεν νεκροὺς μέτα, | θάψαι
θέλοντες, τὸν Πανελλήνων νόμον [*nómon*] | σῴζοντες,
οὐδὲν δεόμενοι τεῖναι φόνον. If such a *nómos* were introduced

---

[142] On Panhellenic *nómoi*, see Thuc. 3.56.2; 3.59; 3.67; 4.97.8; 4.98.2; 4.98.8;
and Loraux (1998).

it would allow cowardice to prevail, as stated at 541–2 by Theseus: τοῖς ἀλκίμοισιν οὗτος ἦν τεθῆ νόμος [*nómos*]. | κἀμοὶ μὲν ἦλθες δεῖν' ἀπειλήσων ἔπη, ('if such a *nómos* is posited, it will turn to cowards, the stoutest'), while at 562–3 it is stated that ὡς εἰς ἔμ' ἐλθὼν καὶ πόλιν Πανδίονος | νόμος παλαιός [*nómos palaios*] δαιμόνων διεφθάρη ('[For never shall it be proclaimed] that the ancient *nómos* of the gods [regarding burial of the dead] was set at nothing, when it devolved on me and the city of Pandion'). Theseus, who is the least orthodox character in the play, does not refer to the divine at any other point except this passage (and the implication at 195ff), but his is clearly a reference to the well-established convention that sees in the gods the origin of human *nómoi* ('customs').[143]

It is time now to turn to what for my purposes is one of the most interesting plays. In *Hecuba*, the form and justification of *nómos*, in its various political and 'moral' divine forms, is at the heart of the play – similarly, in fact, to *Antigone*.[144] The Trojan Hecuba attempts to persuade the 'sovereign' ruler (Odysseus) to save the life of her daughter (Polyxena). The tragic circumstances involve the Greek army forming an anachronistic democratic assembly at Thrace and voting to sacrifice an innocent Trojan girl, Hecuba's daughter (107–9). Further, of significance is the later discovery of a corpse, that of her son Polydorus, who had been murdered by another king, Polymestor. This leads to Hecuba's attempt to persuade Agamemnon to support her in taking revenge against Polymestor. The play culminates in quasi-'juridical' fashion with a trial before Agamemnon as a rather partial judge deliberating over Hecuba's revenge against an ally of the Greeks.[145]

---

[143] See Conacher (1956).

[144] Fletcher notes: 'In *Antigone*, the edict of Kreon is a unilateral decision that bypasses any democratic process. In *Hecuba*, the decree is created in a democratic forum that resembles the Athenian assembly. A most significant difference is that Hecuba, who seems to share Antigone's understanding of *nomos*, enacts brutal retaliation with the blinding of Polymestor and the murder of his children' (2012: 232). In this regard, it could be suggested that Hecuba's references to *nómos* are even more interesting than those of Antigone.

[145] It is crucial to note that in this play, most vividly, three worlds meet: the

We first meet, once more, a reference to *nómos* with regard to the shedding of blood in the act of homicide at 291–2, where Hecuba states: νόμος [*nómos*] δ' ἐν ὑμῖν τοῖς τ' ἐλευθέροις ἴσος | καὶ τοῖσι δούλοις αἵματος κεῖται πέρι ('the same *nómos* holds among you, equally for free and slave, as to the shedding of blood'). Perhaps, Hecuba is making an implied reference to Athenian homicide laws, given that she seems to infer that her daughter's 'sacrifice' is, in fact, murder, in conflict with the assembly's decree. But, indeed, her reference to a *nómos* that is, crucially, *isos* ('equal' to both free and slave) makes it quite clear that her *nómos* here is a 'religious' reference to a universal *nómos* (rather than the *nómoi* of the polis), expressing the fact that human 'sacrifice' goes against a universal way of being, of conduct, as does the forceful extraction of a suppliant from the altar (288–90). Odysseus rejects her plea, rendering, in his eyes at least, the voted decree of the assembly (as to the 'sacrifice' of Polyxena) superior to the alleged universal *nómos* that Hecuba appeals to (303–1).

With regard to her son, Polydoros, Hecuba appeals to Agamemnon at 799–801:

ἀλλ' οἱ θεοὶ σθένουσι χὡ κείνων κρατῶν
νόμος [*nómos*]· νόμῳ [*nómō*] γὰρ τοὺς θεοὺς ἡγούμεθα
καὶ ζῶμεν ἄδικα καὶ δίκαι' ὡρισμένοι·

In translation:

> but the gods are strong, and *nómos* ['custom'] prevails
>   over them;
> for by *nómos* ['custom'] we believe in them
> and set up boundaries of 'right' [*dikaia*] and 'wrong'
>   [*adika*] in our lives.

As seen earlier, Hecuba, the one-time queen of Troy and now a slave, earlier invoked a universal *nómos*, a religious 'custom' or convention that would apply equally to slaves and the

Greeks, the Trojans and the Thracians, who – in the order named – depict the distinction of 'civilised' to less 'civilised' or 'barbarian' peoples. This distinction is ingeniously questioned by Euripides.

free. In this latter passage, in her appeal to Agamemnon (as part of a long supplication rite)[146] with regard to his intervention for the avenging of her murdered son, she claims that this universal *nómos* is of equivalent 'validity' (especially in respect of the impious murder of guests and the destruction of altars; at 803–5). In addition, this *nómos* is, arguably, described as one that rules over the gods themselves, and in addition, it is, at the same time, by this *nómos* that mortals believe in the gods and distinguish the *dikaion* and the *adikon*. The interpretation of *nómos* in this passage is more complex than it may at first seem. *Nómoi* regarding homicide were the subject of Attic homicide law, and it is in theory possible to interpret this later use of *nómos* (as a 'custom' or sacred *nómos*) in a direct or implied relation to Attic law (after all, laws most often placed their grounding in the gods).[147] Yet it is probably unlikely that Hecuba would appeal to Attic law, being a Trojan avenger.

The sense of *nómos* in this passage remains, it seems to me, predominantly 'religious', while still open to some question with reference to the 'grounding' of the 'belief' in the gods. Felix von Heinimann (1945: 121–2), with good reason, reads this use of *nómos* in a 'religious' sense, while adding that Hecuba 'undercuts' it by claiming that the grounding of the belief in the gods is on the basis of a 'custom' or popular practice (i.e. a convention).[148] Ulrich von Wilamowitz-Moellendorf, in turn, draws an indirect relation to Pindar's fr. 169a, though the differences between the two are perhaps more important than he assumed ([1895] 1959: 97). In some proximity, Marcelo Gigante interprets *nómos* as a universal *nómos*/'law' that overpowers the gods (1956: 220–1). Whether Euripides aims at expressing such an overpowering character, though, remains in doubt. It is perhaps possible to suggest that the 'laws' of the gods are more likely meant here, rather than a 'law' above their power, or that what is anterior to them could be implied to be an impersonal cosmic 'law' (i.e.

---

[146] On the ritual, see Pedrick (1982); and Freyburger (1988).

[147] For a discussion, see Mossman (1995); for an earlier reflection, see Kirkwood (1947).

[148] Read in this manner, also, though with differing approaches, by Nussbaum (1986: 400) and Segal (1989a: 71).

Hecuba's universal *nómos*). Furthermore, νόμῳ (*nómō*) could be a reference to a sacred *nómos* or convention following such an anterior cosmic 'law' (Nestle 1940/2: 499). Ehrenberg interprets *nómos*, in this regard, as a norm which in effect renders the gods moral and credible and which can then be the basis of the measure of a proper vow (1923: 140–1).[149] In any case, the 'impersonal' and 'personal', so far as the gods were concerned, and as Segal has argued, are divided by a thin line when it comes to their depiction in Euripides (1989a: 11–12).

The universal *nómos* that Hecuba pronounces in this passage (at 799–801, and also at 802–5) is fundamentally, it seems, derived from a divine, cosmic order, which forms the ground of mortal 'customs' and *nómoi* (including the divine *nómoi*). That said, ultimately the cosmic and the divine were indistinguishable, since the higher universal *nómos*, in effect, evidences, for Hecuba, the belief in the gods and the mortals' distinction between the *dikaion* and *adikon*. Meanwhile, one must bear in mind that Agamemnon, to whom the plea of a powerless slave is addressed, is described as someone who can destroy *nómos* (in the 'civic' sense), hence Hecuba's need to appeal to him in the name of a divine, superior (certainly over his power), universal *nómos*. Most likely, Hecuba's appeal to the universal *nómos* is akin to the *nómos agraphos* that Antigone appealed to: that is, the unwritten, universal *nómos* regarding supplication, hospitality, burial and so forth, which received divine sanction.[150]

But how is one to understand Hecuba's supposed twist in her reference to *nómos* when she states that it is by *nómos* that mortals believe in gods and define what is *dikē* and what is not? It could be suggested that Hecuba at this point is a sophist who disputes the existence of the gods, suggesting that 'religion' is a matter of 'custom' or convention. But while she expresses a form of scepticism, Hecuba's dramatic vision is not, overall, relativistic, since at no point does she dispute the superior value of the universal *nómos* to which she appeals (even if in her acts she then betrays it). Segal notes that Hecuba

---

[149] See, further, Lanza 1963, 416–39.
[150] See Segal (1989a: 70).

skips over the problem of multiple, relative *nomoi* among the different societies and races of mankind and turns to a single unifying *nomos* as a stable moral principle, without which 'nothing is safe' (805). But she exploits a certain ambiguity in the notion of *nomos* (universal law, relativistic custom-law). This hint of ambiguity prepares us for her betrayal of the very principle that she here affirms so nobly. (1989b: 71)

Her claim, and the play more generally, rests on the conflict of traditional assumptions of *nómos* being turned, in Hecuba's words, into a more developed universal *nómos*. Meanwhile the gods, as much as the mortals, can appear subject to perhaps potential conflict with mortal decisions, as well as with the universal *nómos*. And all this in an ambiguous fashion that was, most likely, intentionally achieved through Euripides' tragic genius.[151] When the chorus adds its voice to this conundrum, it states, at 846–9:

δεινόν [*deinon*] γε, θνητοῖς ὡς ἅπαντα συμπίτνει,
καὶ τὰς ἀνάγκας οἱ νόμοι [*nómois*] διώρισαν,
φίλους τιθέντες τούς γε πολεμιωτάτους
ἐχθρούς τε τοὺς πρὶν εὐμενεῖς ποιούμενοι.

It is strange (*deinon*, terrible) how each extreme is met with in human life. *Nómoi* (in the sense of mortal, civic, 'customs' or conventions of the *poleis*) determine even our natural (*philia*) ties, rendering the most bitter foes friends, and regarding as foes those who formerly were friends. Here, the chorus appears to complain about the *nómoi* that require one to view an enemy as a friend and vice versa, and this as a matter of necessity (*anangkē*). In other words, 'civic' *nómoi* (crucially in the plural) form contingencies that become necessity (i.e. Hecuba's appeal to someone who is her enemy – Agamemnon). Perhaps there is here a clearer indication of the conflict between tradition and the new ways of the mortal *nómoi*, indicating, as Judith Fletcher suggests, the gradual separation of divine and mortal *nómoi* at the time (2012), or,

---

[151] See Heinimann (1945: 121–2); and Heath (1987b: 67–8).

rather, let me add, a new form of relation between them. In any case, Euripides does not explicitly suggest this. Instead, he shows us a plurivocal world that does not yet seem able to accomodate the coexistence of a universal *nómos* and a seemingly distinguished mortal contingency.

It is of further interest, in this regard, that a few verses later, at 865–7, Hecuba's lamentation includes the following reference to *nómos*:

ἢ χρημάτων γὰρ δοῦλός ἐστιν ἢ τύχης,
ἢ πλῆθος αὐτὸν πόλεος ἢ νόμων γραφαὶ [*nómōn graphai*]
εἴργουσι χρῆσθαι μὴ κατὰ γνώμην τρόποις.

This can be translated as:

for he is a slave either to money or to fortune [*tuchē*],
or else the people [*plēthos*], or the fear of 'public
  prosecution'
prevents him from following the dictates of his way
  (*gnōmē*).[152]

In this passage, in evidently gnomic mode, Hecuba's 'anti-democratic' (for some interpreters)[153] lament for mortal servility (and in particular Agamemnon's) declares that no one is free. Clearly, Hecuba criticises the 'laws' in favour of an unwritten traditional universal *nómos*. And the reference to *nómoi* here, instead, is relative to the *graphai*, namely, the written 'laws'.

How much, then, can we make of this reference to written *nómoi* in Euripides? Euripides does not seem to show explicit or strong interest – nor perhaps should one expect him to – in the *nómos–phusis* debate that marked the classical period. What, instead, seems to attract his attention is the appeal of a harmony between *phusis* and the *kosmos*, hence the interest in and the ambiguous references to a universal *nómos* in contradistinction to the *nómoi* of the polis.[154] Mortal beings, as Segal notes, are still trapped in their contingency, their *nómoi*

---

[152] Translated by Coleridge (1938), slightly modified.
[153] On this, see Morwood (2014).
[154] See Lanza (1963: 416–39).

(be they slaves or free, rich or poor). Meanwhile, Hecuba's appeal to a universal *nómos* (perhaps one that the world in question was not yet ready for) proves less persuasive in the end (Segal 1989b: 75, 82). The *nómoi* can turn into savagery and the savages can appeal to the *nómoi* (or the universal *nómos*). For Euripides, *contra* Nietzsche, the appeal to a superior *nómos* in the encounter of mortal contingency appears pertinent against social disintegration.[155]

The final reference to *nómos* in the play is quite straightforward. At 973–5, Hecuba states: ἀλλ᾽ αὐτὸ μὴ δύσνοιαν ἡγήσῃ σέθεν, | Πολυμῆστορ ἄλλως δ᾽ αἴτιόν τι καὶ νόμος [*nómos*], | γυναῖκας ἀνδρῶν μὴ βλέπειν ἐναντίον. This can be translated as: 'do not think it ill will towards you, Polymestor; there is another cause as well, the *nómos* ['custom'] which does not allow women to meet men's gaze'. *Nómos* here refers to a 'custom' regarding an impropriety of conduct. In *Heracles*, at 778–80, the chorus states: νόμον [*nómon*] παρέμενος, ἀνομίᾳ χάριν διδοὺς | ἔθραυσεν ὄλ- | βου κελαινὸν ἅρμα ('disregarding *nómos* for the sake of *anomia*, he destroys the black chariot of prosperity').[156] The disregard for *nómos*, says the chorus in its condemnation, leads to the shattering of prosperity. The reference to prosperity is, here, a powerful decrying, since prosperity was considered one of the key competitive excellences of the so-called highest Greek values. The reference to *nómos* appears to be in the sense of 'custom' or convention. At 1316–17, in the final part of the play, Theseus, Heracles' friend, addressing the hero turned suppliant, speaks of the gods and asks: οὐ λέκτρ᾽ ἐν ἀλλήλοισιν, ὧν οὐδεὶς νόμος [*nómos*], | συνῆψαν; ('have they [the gods] not intermarried in ways that *nómos* forbids?'). Here the gods, like mortals, are said to be subject to misfortune and, like mortals, this is due to their deeds (in this case, incestuous unions against the norm). This is, further, said in Theseus' attempt to support Heracles' own tragic misfortune, though Heracles will not accept what is said regarding the gods' anomic deeds (1341–6). Finally, at 1360–1, Heracles states: δὸς τούσδε τύμβῳ καὶ περίστειλον νεκροὺς | δακρύοισι τιμῶν - ἐμὲ γὰρ οὐκ ἐᾷ νόμος [*nómos*]

---

[155] For a discussion along these lines, see Segal (1989a: 72–82).
[156] The chorus refers to *anomia* once more, at 757: τίς ὁ θεοὺς ἀνομίαι χραίνων, θνατὸς ὤν.

('give them burial, and lay the dead with the honour of a tear, for my doing so is forbidden by *nómos*'). Here, Heracles is unable to bury his own children, being their murderer, as this would be impious and against 'custom' (*nómos*).[157]

In *Trojan Women* at 266–7, Hecuba states: ἀτὰρ τίς ὅδ᾽ ἦ νόμος [*nómos*] ἢ τί | θέσμιον, ὦ φίλος, Ἑλλάνων; ('what "custom", or what ordinance is this among Hellenes, friend?'). The use of the disjunctive in this instance is double, and it can indicate a close relation (for some, an identification), or a further specification in the second instance. The earlier differentiation, so far as one can tell, between *nómos* as a fact of tradition that institutes a 'natural' order and *thesmos* as an enactment or imposition that is 'arbitrary' (an ordinance or, later, a posited legislation) shifts during the fifth century BC (with preference given to *nómos* over *thesmos*' earlier significations, especially since *nómos*, in the Sophists, was counterposed to *phusis*). The terms are eventually used interchangeably (Hölkeskamp 2002: 123–6), while during the fifth century BC the word *nómos* is also used in close relation to *psēphisma* (decree) to refer to a vote at the assembly and, in particular, to its content. In these verses, however, Hecuba is not drawing a relation (or distinction) between *nómos* and *thesmos*, as the reference to a Pan-Hellenic *nómos* or *thesmion* (*thesmos*) indicates that the sense is probably that of a 'custom' or convention; reversing, here crucially, the usual distinction between the Hellenes and the barbarians, which Hecuba uses to suggest her horror regarding her daughter's monstrous fate as a prize for a hero (Achilles, who is, in fact, dead). The clear sense of 'custom' is found in other passages, such as: 323–4, where Cassandra, the delirious prophetess, states: παρθένων ἐπὶ λέκτροις | ἇι νόμος [*nómos*] ἔχει – referring to a 'custom' or rite at the maiden's wedding, as it is 'custom' (*nómos*); or at 1031–2, where Menelaus is advised by Hecuba to establish a *nómos*

---

[157] In *El.* 234, Orestes states: οὐχ ἕνα νομίζων φθείρεται πόλεως νόμον ('he languishes about, not adhering to the customs of any polis'). For the sake of completion, it is worth noting another reference to *nómos*, at 1268–9, where the Dioskouroi state a juridical or quasi-juridical *nómos*: καὶ τοῖσι λοιποῖς ὅδε νόμος τεθήσεται, | νικᾶν ἴσαις ψήφοισι τὸν φεύγοντ᾽ ἀεί ('and this *nómos* will be established for posterity, that the accused will always win if he has equal votes').

that all unfaithful wives are to be killed: νόμον [*nómon*] δὲ τόνδε ταῖς ἄλλαισι θές | γυναιξί, θνήσκειν ἥτις ἂν προδῷ πόσιν. Finally, at 1210, Hecuba describes horsemanship and archery as *nómoi* honoured by the Phrygians (Φρύγες νόμους; *Phruges nómous*).

In *Iphigeneia in Tauris*, we encounter a series of 'religious' uses of *nómos*. For instance, at 34–5, one can observe the incidence of *nomoisi* in terms of rites: ναοῖσι δ' ἐν τοῖσδ' ἱερέαν τίθησί με·| ὅθεν νόμοισι [*nomoisi*] τοῖσιν ἥδεται θεὰ ('[Artemis] has made me the priestess in this temple. Here I begin the rites, which the goddess delights in'). Further, Iphigeneia states, at 38: θύω γὰρ ὄντος τοῦ νόμου [*nómou*] καὶ πρὶν πόλει ('I sacrifice according to earlier *nómos* of the polis', namely, the manner/'custom' of 'sacrifice'). At 464–6, the leader of the chorus addresses Artemis and states: πόλις ἥδε τελεῖ, δέξαι θυσίας, | ἃς ὁ παρ' ἡμῖν νόμος [*nómos*] οὐχ ὁσίας | ἀναφαίνει ('if this polis carries out the rites [*thusias*], accept the victims, which "custom" [*nómos*] holds to be impious'). This is probably in relation to a general 'custom' (*nómos*) with regard to purification rites and 'sacrifices' of arriving strangers to Artemis. At 959, the 'religious' practice, initiated by Orestes, is described as a *nómos*: τελετὴν γενέσθαι, κἆτι τὸν νόμον [*nómon*] μένειν; while at 1189, Iphigeneia states: τὸν νόμον [*nómon*] ἀνάγκη τὸν προκείμενον σέβειν ('it is necessary to show reverence to the standing [*prokeimenos*] *nómos*'). Finally, at 1458–9: νόμον [*nómon*] τε θὲς τόνδ'·ὅταν ἑορτάζῃ λεώς, | τῆς σῆς σφαγῆς ἄποιν' ἐπισχέτω ξίφος ('posit this *nómos*: whenever the people keep the festival, let a sword be held').

In *Cyclops*, at 229–30, Odysseus calls it a *nómos* for mortals to receive the shipwrecked suppliants: νόμος [*nómos*] δὲ θνητοῖς, εἰ λόγους ἀποστρέφῃ, | ἱκέτας δέχεσθαι ποντίους ἐφθαρμένους ('there is a *nómos* among mortals, if you are deaf to these considerations, that one must receive shipwrecked suppliants'). Odysseus refers here to the well-established ancestral (divine) *nómos* of the duty of hospitality, the *nómoi* of ξενία (*xenia*).[158] In contrast, in a simulation of a commonplace antithesis between *nómos* and *bia* or *anomia*, the Cyclops Polyphemos states, at 338–41:

---

[158] See, further, 316–46.

οἳ δὲ τοὺς νόμους [*nómous*]
ἔθεντο ποικίλλοντες ἀνθρώπων βίον [*bion*],
κλαίειν ἄνωγα: τὴν <δ᾽> ἐμὴν ψυχὴν ἐγὼ
οὐ παύσομαι δρῶν εὖ, κατεσθίων γε σέ.

This can be roughly translated as: 'As to those who have posited *nómoi* and rendered complex the lives of mortals, they can go weep. I will not stop giving pleasure to my heart, by eating you.' Here, Polyphemos, read by some as echoing a sophistic discourse, and by others as a self-serving tyrant,[159] declares that he denounces all those who devise *nómoi* over the living. Instead, unrestrained by *nómoi* and 'civilisation', Polyphemos opts to satisfy his impulsive anomic desire. The use of *nómoi*, at this point, may be that of 'laws', though more likely in the wider sense of social conventions or norms – not necessarily sophistic or tyrannical perhaps, then, but in fact, an old Homeric antithesis. In a similar sense, though in a rather different context, the chorus, in *Iphigeneia in Aulis*, laments that anomic conduct could become stronger than the *nómoi*, at 1095–6: Ἀνομία δὲ νόμων κρατεῖ [*Anomia de nómōn kratei*].

In *Helen*,[160] at 800, we meet the reference to νόμοισι βαρβάροις [*nomoisi barbarois*] by Menelaos, referring to the 'customs' or ways of the barbarians. At 871, Theone speaks of offering her *nómos* ('rites') to the gods: νόμον [*nómon*] δὲ τὸν ἐμὸν θεοῖσιν ἀποδοῦσαι πάλιν. At 1240–1, Theoklymenos asks: τί δ'; ἔστ' ἀπόντων τύμβος; ἢ θάψεις σκιάν; ('What? Is there a tomb for the absent or will you bury a shadow?'); to which Helen replies: 'it is customary among the Hellenes, whenever someone dies at sea': Ἕλλησίν ἐστι νόμος [*nómos*], ὃς ἂν πόντῳ θάνῃ. Closely linked to this, at 1277, Menelaos tells Theoklymenos that it is dictated (customarily) *nomima* that the dead shall not be tricked of their due (ἐν εὐσεβεῖ γοῦν νόμιμα [*nomima*] μὴ κλέπτειν νεκρῶν).[161]

---

[159] For a discussion of both the 'sophistic' readings and an analysis of Polyphemos as a tyrant, see O'Sullivan (2005).
[160] See note 50 above.
[161] Burial rites are richly described in this play. In fact, a unique, description of a symbolic burial rite is offered (on land, 1059–60; as well as another at sea, 1063–4). The cenotaph (κενός τάφος, *kenos taphos*) is mentioned at

At 1246, the practice of burying the shipwrecked is referred to as a 'custom' (*nómos*) of the Hellenes (ἐν Ἕλλησιν νόμων [*nómōn*]). Theoklymenos, at 1258, refers to the barbarian 'custom' (*nómos*) with regard to 'sacrificing' a horse or a bull: ἐν βαρβάροις μὲν ἵππον ἢ ταῦρον νόμος [*nómos*]. At 1270, the Hellenic 'custom' is called a *nomimon* (Ἑλλὰς νόμιμον) with regard to burial as far away from the coast as possible so that pollution is not washed back ashore.[162] This is justified, further, at 1277, on the ground of respecting what is due (*nomima*) to the dead: ἐν εὐσεβεῖ γοῦν νόμιμα [*nomima*] μὴ κλέπτειν νεκρῶν. At 1429, Theoklymenos states that he has no time for the 'customs' (*nómoi*) of the Pelops: ἀλλ᾽ εἴα: τοὺς μὲν Πελοπιδῶν ἐῶ νόμους [*nómous*]. Finally, at 1561, we note the description of a bull that refused to be brought aboard the ship, as a result of which the herald and the other men present are urged to carry it on their shoulders according to Ἑλλήνων νόμῳ (Hellenic *nómō*, 'custom').

In the prologue to *Ion*,[163] Hermes describes Apollo's plan following his rape of Kreousa, the Queen of Athens, and her secret (from her husband, Xouthos) pregnancy, whereby he instructed Hermes to bring the infant to Delphi so that he can be raised as a temple servant, only to return the son to Xouthos as 'his child'. Ignorant of this and the child's identity, Kreousa attempts to kill him. At 19–21, Hermes

1057–8. This is a practice that stretches back to Homeric times (see, for example, *Od.* 4.584; 9.64–66; 11.75–6) and we have encountered it also in the *Antigone*, at 245–56; see also Plut. *Mor.* 870e–f). For an analysis, see Vermeule (1979: 187); and on burial, in particular, see the classic study by Kurtz and Boardman (1971: 71–108).

[162] It should be noted that I have omitted here a detailed examination of the numerous uses of *nomizein* and *nomimos* in Euripides. For *nomizein*, see, for instance, *Hec.* 326; *Med.* 493; *Alc.* 644; *Rh.* 868; *Her.* 313; *I.T.* 471; and *He.* 307; while for *nomimos*, see: *Phoen.* 822 and 347 and 541; *Ba.* 894; 1008; *He.* 1286 and 1293; *Sup.* 19 and 311. I have also omitted the examination of the instances of the use of *nemēsis* and *nomas*. As to instances of *nemēsis*, see the singular use in Aes. *Sept.* 235 that occurs in proximity to νεμόμεθα [*nemometha*]; Soph. *Or.* 1362; *El.* 1467; *Phil.* 602; *OC* 1753; and Eur. *Phoen.* 183–4. On *nomas*, see, for instance Eur. fr. 636; and Hom. *Il.* 1–3: τὸν ἀκταῖς νομάδα [*nomada*].

[163] Kreousa plots to kill Ion, not knowing that he is her son. The plot fails and Ion makes his way to take revenge against Kreousa, while Kreousa finds refuge at the altar of Apollo.

states: κοίλης ἐν ἀντίπηγος εὐτρόχῳ κύκλῳ, Ι προγόνων νόμον [nómon] σῴζουσα τοῦ τε γηγενοῦς Ι Ἐριχθονίου. κείνῳ γὰρ ἡ Διὸς κόρη ('there [Kreousa] exposed him [the infant] to die in the round circle of a hollow cradle, adhering to the "custom" [nómos] of her ancestors, and of Erichthonius, the earth-born'). The nómos, 'custom', here appears to refer to the myth of Erichthonius (mentioned in Homer at *Il.* 2.547–8). The mythical King Erichthonius of Athens (possibly earlier a serpentine deity) was said to be the progeny of Athena's seed (while escaping Hephaestus, the goddess's seed fell on the earth). Erichthonious, Athena's child, grew out of the earth (just like a plant). As such, the mythologeme becomes the myth of the autochthony of the polis of Athens, establishing citizenship on the ground of the Attic earth.[164] In *Ion*, the Athenians are described as such (i.e. as the people of the earth), at 29–30: λαὸν εἰς αὐτόχθονα [autochthona] Ι κλεινῶν Ἀθηνῶν. A few verses later the nómos is explained clearly, at 24–6: ὅθεν Ἐρεχθείδαις ἐκεῖ Ι νόμος [nómos] τις Ι ἔστιν ὄφεσιν ἐν χρυσηλάτοις Ι τρέφειν τέκνα ('from which the Erechthidae [the sons of Erechtheus] have a "custom" [nómos] to rear their children in gold serpents'). The 'custom', in other words, entails giving children golden serpents as charms (associated perhaps with the ornaments used for burial, pointing to the despair of Kreousa, who does not expect the infant to survive), a nómos of the ancestors regarding the earth-born, the *autochthonous*.[165]

At 230–1, the chorus refers to a nómos as follows: ἔχω μαθοῦσα· θεοῦ δὲ νόμον [nómon] Ι οὐ παραβαίνομεν ('I know; I do not wish to transgress the nómos of the god'). This nómos refers to the 'custom' that one should not approach the altar at the temple before a sacrifice (in this case of sheep) is properly offered. With reference to the gods being the authors of the mortal nómoi (and the fact that their transgression incurs an *anomia*), we meet, at 443–4, Ion contemplating his address to Apollo and stating in a remarkable semi-'juridical' manner: πῶς οὖν δίκαιον τοὺς νόμους [nómous] ὑμᾶς βροτοῖς Ι γράψαντας, αὐτοὺς ἀνομίαν [anomian] ὀφλισκάνειν; ('how is it *dikaion* for you to write the nómoi of mortals, while you incur

---

[164] See Loraux (1981: 37ff); Montanari (1981); and Rosivach (1987).
[165] See also Soph. *Aj.* 202; and Hdt. 1.171–2, 4.197.2.

an *anomia*?'). Here, Ion implies that, since mortals are always
punished for wicked acts that transgress the (divine) *nómoi*,
Apollo should seek virtue, even though he has the power to
do otherwise (440) because, perhaps, the poetic implication
is that the gods would have to compensate the mortals. We
meet this complaint once more at 1312–13: δεινόν γε, θνητοῖς
τοὺς νόμους [*nómous*] ὡς οὐ καλῶς | ἔθηκεν ὁ θεὸς οὐδ᾽ ἀπὸ
γνώμης σοφῆς ('It is strange [*deinon*] that the god has given to
men these *nómoi*, which are bad or without wisdom'). It is of
interest, then, that at 642–4 we find an explicit reference to the
relation between *phusis* and *nómos* before the gods:

ὃ δ᾽ εὐκτὸν ἀνθρώποισι, κἂν ἄκουσιν ᾖ,
δίκαιον εἶναί μ᾽ ὁ νόμος [*nómos*] ἡ φύσις [*phusis*] θ᾽ ἅμα
παρεῖχε τῷ θεῷ. ταῦτα συννοούμενος

This can be translated as: 'What men ought to wish for, even
if they are unwilling – "custom" [*nómos*] and my nature
[*phusis*] made [it] *dikaion* before the god.' *Nómos* and *phusis*
are juxtaposed here, but not in an antithesis. Instead, they
are posed in a relation that points to a common ground
between them, a cosmic order wherein the mortal *nómoi* are
conjoined. At 1258, Kreousa states: τῷ νόμῳ [*nómō*] δέ γ᾽
ὄλλυμαι ('though by the *nómos* I am destroyed'). Kreousa
initially responds with some hesitation to the advice of the
chorus that she escape to the altar of the temple and become
a suppliant, since it is not *themis* ('right') to kill a suppliant
– advice that Kreousa will follow. It is possible to read at
this point a distinction, between the ordinance (*themis*) and
the social 'custom' (*nómos*). Furthermore, at 1047, there is
an adverbial reference to how a social *nómos* ('custom',
perhaps) cannot stop one from mistreating an enemy.[166]
Thus, the old tutor will tell Kreousa: ὅταν δὲ πολεμίους
δρᾶσαι κακῶς | θέλῃ τις, οὐδεὶς ἐμποδὼν κεῖται νόμος
[*nómos*]. While a direct reference to a 'religious' *nómos* is
made, at 1322, the Pythian priestess of Apollo at the Delphic
shrine is described as guarding the ancient *nómos* of the

---

[166] See also, from an unidentified Euripidean play, in fr. 1091: νόμος τὸν
ἐχθρὸν δρᾶν, ὅπου λάβῃς, κακῶς ('it is *nómos*-custom to harm one's
enemy, wherever you catch him'); Collard and Cropp (2008: 611).

tripod. The 'religious' *nómos* referred to here appears to be the high authority regarding the dispensing of oracles: Φοίβου προφῆτις, τρίποδος ἀρχαῖον νόμον [*archaion nómon*] | σώζουσα.

In the *Bacchae*, central to which is Dionysus, *nómos* is used especially in the choral odes and in relation to Pentheus, who is branded *anomos*, even though he considers himself to be a pious ruler of Thebes. Early on, at 331, Cadmus states οἴκει μεθ' ἡμῶν, μὴ θύραζε τῶν νόμων [*nómōn*] ('dwell with us, not outside the *nómoi*') in the sense of 'customs'. Dwelling and the customary *nómoi*, as a way of life, are directly juxtaposed here, where the reference to the *nómoi* is to the long-standing tradition of the ancestors (which Teiresias describes, at 201, as *patrious paradochas*). At 386, the chorus refers to Pentheus' insolence and his ignorance of the universal *nómoi* (i.e. universal Dionysian *phusis*) as an anomic conduct: ἀνόμου [*anomou*] τ' ἀφροσύνας. Here *anomia* is equated with dysnomic *aphrosunē*, senselessness (the opposite of Dionysian *sophrosunē* and *eunomia*, in the sense, for the chorus, of customary knowledge that it is necessary to learn if suffering is to be avoided). Dionysian knowledge or learning does not extend here beyond the earthly knowledge of mortals.

When, at 484, *nómos* is referred to as οἱ νόμοι [*nómoi*] δὲ διάφοροι, Dionysus differentiates the 'customs' of barbarians (regarding his worship) from those of the Hellenes (doing so against Pentheus, who proposed that the barbarians are worse than the Hellenes) by stating that *nómoi*, in the plural, indicate a community or collective which merely follows different *nómoi* that, however, are not less worthy. At 890–2, the chorus states: οὐ | γὰρ κρεῖσσόν ποτε τῶν νόμων [*nómōn*] | γιγνώσκειν χρὴ καὶ μελετᾶν ('it is better not to propose or plan anything that exceeds the *nómoi*'). Which *nómoi*? The chorus answers this question in an iconic statement in the next few verses, at 896–7: τό τ' ἐν χρόνῳ μακρῷ νόμιμον [*nomimon*] | ἀεὶ φύσει τε πεφυκός ('that which has been *nómos* for a long time is grounded in *phusis*'). These are the same *nómoi* of the *patrious paradochas* that Teiresias referred to earlier – the ancestral tradition – which in the Dionysian manner do not contradict the *nómoi* of the polis or *phusis*, but instead point to the unity of *phusis* and *nómos* in (Dionysian)

harmony.[167] The *nómos* that Pentheus ignores is the higher
nómos that receives its ancestral grounding from *phusis*
(*phusis* = *Themis*; 416), implying that the polis's *nómoi* have
to yield to the higher *nómos*. Thus, at 991–6 (= 1011–16) the
chorus states: ἴτω δίκα φανερός, ἴτω ξιφηφόρος | φονεύουσα
λαιμῶν διαμπάξ | τὸν ἄθεον ἄνομον ἄδικον [anomon adikon]
Ἐχίονος | γόνον γηγενῆ ('let manifest [phaneros] dikē come
forth, let it slay through, with sword in hand, the throat, this
impious [atheon], outside the *nómos* [anomon], unjust [adikon],
earth-born offspring of Echion'). In addition, at 997, such an
anomos (Pentheus) is also described as παρανόμῳ [para-nómō];
while the higher *nómos* is described, at 1009–10, as *dikē*: τὰ δ᾽
ἔξω νόμιμα [nomima] | δίκας [dikas] ἐκβαλόντα τιμᾶν θεούς
('the "customs" that are outside *dikē* are banished for the
honour of the gods').

In *Orestes*, at 429, we meet a reference to a 'religious' *nómos*
regarding purification, and in particular the cleansing of
the hands of blood, when Menelaos asks: οὐδ᾽ ἥγνισαι σὸν
αἷμα κατὰ νόμον [kata nómon] χεροῖν; ('have your hands not
been cleaned of blood, according to *nómos*?'). The customary
nómos is referred to, at 495, as the common, universal *nómos*
of the Hellenes: τὸν κοινὸν Ἑλλήνων νόμον. An ancestral
nómos is, perhaps, mentioned by implication, also, at 502–3,
when Tyndareus tells Menelaus that if, instead of killing her,
Orestes had banished his mother from his *oikos*, he would
have conformed to the standards of proper conduct (*nómos*):
τὸ σῶφρόν τ᾽ ἔλαβεν ἀντὶ συμφορᾶς | καὶ τοῦ νόμου [nómou]
τ᾽ ἂν εἴχετ᾽ εὐσεβής τ᾽ ἂν ἦν ('he would have gained wisdom
instead of trouble, by adhering to the *nómos* [i.e. probably in
the sense of ancestral 'custom' concerning the relations of
children with their parents] and showing piety').

The wider use of *nómos* regarding a people's customary
ways of living and conducting itself is evident when the *nómoi*
of the Phrygian people are mentioned, at 1426: Φρυγίοισι
νόμοις [nómois]; similarly, describing the barbarian way as
βαρβάροις νόμοισιν (barbarois nomoisin; at 1430); and again,
at 1507, with reference to the ways of supplication of barbarians: νόμοισι βαρβάροισι. In *Phoenician Women*, we encounter

---

[167] See Heinimann (1945: 166ff).

a proximate reference by the chorus to the Phoenician way (*nómos*) of bowing down before royalty: γονυπετεῖς ἕδρας προσπίτνω σ', ἄναξ, | τὸν οἴκοθεν νόμον [*nómon*] σέβουσ' (at 294). In juxtaposition to the Hellenic ways, we can note similar uses in *Andromache*. For example, with reference to the barbarian lack of a *nómos* against incest and the murdering of family members, we read, at 175–6: κόρη τ' ἀδελφῷ, διὰ φόνου δ' οἱ φίλτατοι | χωροῦσι, καὶ τῶνδ' οὐδὲν ἐξείργει νόμος [*nómos*] ('brother with sister, nearest kin murder each other, and there is no *nómos* to stop any of this'). The barbarian way of life ('custom'/convention) is also referred to by Hermione, in contradistinction, at 243: οὐ βαρβάρων νόμοισιν [*nomoisin*] οἰκοῦμεν πόλιν ('we do not dwell here with barbarian "customs"').

In *Orestes*, the sense of *nómos* as, arguably, 'custom-law' is implied at 487 when Tyndareus responds to Menelaos' view that family must come first with καὶ τῶν νόμων [*nómōn*] γε μὴ πρότερον εἶναι θέλειν ('and another "custom" is to willingly yield to the *nómoi*'), that is, not to behave as if above the *nómos*. More direct references are attested in a range of other instances. Yet the sense of *nómos* as 'custom-law' may not be 'juridical'. For instance, at 571, Orestes states τόνδ' ἔπαυσα τὸν νόμον [*nómon*] ('to put an end to the *nómos*'), that is, to the *nómos* of women murdering their husbands, which he claims to have stopped by his own act of murdering Klytemnestra. Meanwhile, at 892–3, the messenger states ὅτι καθισταίη νόμους [*nómous*] | ἐς τοὺς τεκόντας οὐ καλούς, whereby if Orestes were to kill his mother, it would be an act 'that would threaten to establish *nómoi* that would not be good regarding the relation between sons and parents'. At 941, it is implied that the murder of one's parent, if not punished, would lead to the relaxation of the 'law' (ὁ νόμος ἀνεῖται; *ho nómos aneitai*) against it, with perhaps a clear reference to homicide *nómos* at this point (similar to, for instance, *Hec.* 291).

Finally, it is worth observing some of the general uses of *nómos* in the surviving fragments of Euripides, before I also turn to briefly examine the more political or 'juridical' uses. It is worth starting with an example of the etymological relation between *nómos* and the verb *némein*, which is evidenced in fr. 1064.1–2 from an unidentified play of Euripides. Here, we read that to hold a mother dear is *nómos*, and in the next line one can note the use of *nemein* (προσφιλῆ νέμειν ἀεί) in the sense of 'to return' (Colland and Cropp 2008: 601), or possibly with the meaning of 'to (re)distribute' (i.e. the honour for being born). Uses of *nómos* in the sense of 'custom' or convention can be seen in a number of other fragments. For instance, in fr. 141 illegitimate children are said to not be inferior to legitimate children, but are considered unequal by νόμῳ νοσοῦσιν [*nómō nosousin*], that is, by convention.[168] A fragment from the lost play *Archelaus*, fr. 228.8, includes the following verse: Δαναοὺς καλεῖσθαι νόμον [*nómon*] ('the *nómos* ['rule', 'custom'] to call [the Pelasgians] "Danaans"'). In another lost play, *Augē*, we find, fr. 265a (= 920N), ἡ φύσις ἐβούλεθ', ἣ νόμων [*nómōn*] οὐδὲν μέλει ('*phusis* willed it, which cares not for convention/"custom"'); the convention refers here to the sexual submission of women, which is said to be so 'by *phusis*'). From *Theseus*, fr. 388.3 contains a wish that τόνδ' εἶναι νόμον [*nómon*], τῶν εὐσεβούντων οἵτινές τε σώφρονες ('this as a rule, to love those who are pious and temperate').[169] We can also include, in this regard, two further examples. The first is from the lost play *Ino* where, in fr. 402.1, we read: νόμοι [*nómoi*] γυναικῶν (which probably refers to *nómoi* made regarding wives, i.e. the ability to have many wives). The second is from the lost play *Cretan Women*, contained in fr. 469: ... νόμος [*nómos*] δὲ λείψαν' ἐκβάλλειν κυσίν ('the habit/"custom" of throwing the remains of a meal to the dogs'). 'Customs' can extend to particular ways of conduct, as seen earlier, and to particular practices. Thus, from the lost play *Bellerophon*, fr. 286b.5 (= 292N) includes the following line: τῷ νόμῳ [*nómō*] ἰώμεθ' αὐτάς ('we treat [illnesses] according to the rule of practice or convention' [i.e. not by giving random remedies]).

Of the wider uses of *nómos* to refer to the 'customs' or ways of a people, we have examples such as the one from the lost play *Autolycus*, at fr. 282.13: τὸν Ἑλλήνων νόμον [*nómon*] ('the *nómos* of the Greeks [to honour athletes]'); or in the lost play *Meleager*, fr. 530.9: Αἰτωλοῖς νόμος [*nómos*] ('the *nómos* ['custom'] for all Aitolians [to keep, in warring,

---

168 See Stob. 4.24.45.
169 See Stob. 1.9.4b.

their right foot bare]').[170] In a fragment of the play *Dictys*, fr. 337, there is a reference to the ancestral *nómos* that we have encountered before: σέβειν δὲ τοὺς κρατοῦντας ἀρχαῖος νόμος [*archaios nómos*] ('the ancient *nómos* is to honour those in power [kings]'). Ancestral and universal is also the *nómos* that we find in another fragment of the same play, fr. 346: ἔστι κοινὸς ἀνθρώποις νόμος [*koinos anthrōpois nómos*] ('one single *nómos* common to all mortals', i.e. the love which all living creatures have for their offspring); and the fragment, notably, ends with: τὰ δ' ἄλλα χωρὶς χρώμεθ' ἀλλήλων νόμοις ('for all else, different mortals have different *nómoi* from one another').

If we turn to the more political or 'juridical' occurrences of *nómos* in the extant fragments there are some additional interesting uses to note. With regard to anomic situations, in fr. 172 we read: οὔτ' εἰκὸς ἄρχειν οὔτ' ἐχρῆν ἄνευ νόμων [*nómōn*] τύραννον εἶναι. That is, 'it is neither reasonable to rule, nor ought there to be a king, without laws'.[171] We also meet some references to situations of 'exception', where the non-observance of *nómos* is warranted: for example, in the lost play *Oedipus*, fr. 597: τὸν νόμον [*nómon*] χαίρειν ἐῶν ('to leave the *nómos* ['law'] aside [in order to effect summary justice]'). Meanwhile, from an arguably semi-'juridical' perspective, we can observe a reference to 'necessity' in the lost play *Hippolytus Veiled*, fr. 433: ἐγωγέ φημι καὶ νόμον γε μὴ σέβειν | ἐν τοῖσι δεινοῖς τῶν ἀναγκαίων πλέον ('I say, do not even honour *nómos* ['law'] under circumstances of necessity [i.e. honour necessity instead]').[172]

The relation between anomy and *nómos* is well observed in fr. 597[N], attributed to Euripides as a verse from a play titled *Pirithous*, though it remains uncertain (it may possibly be by his contemporary Critias). Here, good character is described as safer than a *nómos* (τρόπος δὲ χρηστὸς ἀσφαλέστερος νόμου [*nómou*]). In *Sisyphus*, also possibly attributed to

---

[170] Similarly, from the lost Euripidean play *Telephus*, perhaps, we read in fr. 727b: νόμ[ο]ις Ἑλληνικοῖς (Hellenic *nómoi*, [customs]); and from another unidentified play of Euripides, fr. 853 includes: νόμους τε κοινοὺς Ἑλλάδος ('common *nómoi* of Hellas').

[171] Translated by Collard and Cropp (2008: 167); similarly, in *Sup.* 429–32.

[172] See Stob. 3.12.10.

Critias, though still uncertain, we read at 19.9–10 (= Critias fr. 1N) ἔπειτ' ἐπειδὴ τἀμφανῆ μὲν οἱ νόμοι [*nómoi*] | ἀπεῖργον αὐτοὺς ἔργα μὴ πράσσειν βίᾳ [*bia*] ('Then, when the laws were preventing men from doing violence openly, but they did it in secret' (Collard and Cropp 2008: 673); *nómos* can here be seen as a reference to a 'convention'). A few verses below, at 19.40, we also read: τὴν ἀνομίαν τε τοῖς νόμοις κατέσβεσεν ('*anomia* was quenched with the *nómoi*').[173] The praise of *nómoi* is paradigmatic in a fragment from the lost play *Archelaus*, fr. 252, where we read of the attribution to *nómoi* of the power to foster great improvements for mortals: ἐκ τῶν δικαίων γὰρ νόμοι [*nómoi*] ταὐξήματα | μεγάλα φέρουσι, πάντα δ' ἀνθρώποις <καλά> | τάδ' ἐστὶ χρήματ', ἢν τις εὐσεβῇ θεόν ('Laws bring about great increase as a result of "just" actions, and thus make everything [good?] for mortals. This is genuine wealth: respect for god [divine power]').[174]

During the fifth century BC *nómos* becomes associated with contingent, posited 'juridical' *nómoi*, as well as, crucially, with a universal *nómos* that is at least speculated as being applicable to 'all' Greeks (and even allegedly to barbarians), for instance in relation to matricide, supplication and burial. However, it cannot be concluded that the word *nómos* (and its family) had semantic uses restricted to 'juridical or political' senses; uses which, indeed, the word acquires more concretely during this period. Thus, as has been shown, *nómos* continues to refer to social 'customs', moral principles and worship rites, among other things. Meanwhile, in the tragedians, the relativity and contingency of the *nómoi* of mortals in the polis is portrayed not as a sign of a monocular 'progress', but rather as a prime site of tragic conflict. *Nómos*, in the tragedians, becomes ever more particular, while at the same time it becomes ever more 'universal', 'living' or 'worldly'. The *muthos* of tragedy is, in this sense, the *muthos* of *nómos*: *Eudaimonia–Eunomia*.

If there are higher laws that determine the more infinite nexus of life [*jenen unendlichern Zusammenhang des*

---

[173] Translated by Collard and Cropp (2008: 677); translation slightly modified.

[174] Translated by Collard and Cropp (2008: 251).

Lebens], if there are unwritten divine laws, the ones of which Antigone speaks when in spite of the strict public prohibition she buries her brother – and there must be such laws if that higher nexus is not a mere phantasm – I say, if there are such laws, then they are in any case insufficient [*unzulänglich*], insofar as they are represented as being *merely* for themselves and not as caught up in life [*im Leben begriffen*] . . . Thus, even if it were a universal law for all civilised peoples, the law could never be thought at all in abstraction from a particular case. It could never be thought if one were unwilling to take into account its very own peculiarity [*Eigentümlichkeit*], namely its intimate imbrication [*innige Verbundenheit*] with the sphere in which it is exercised. (Hölderlin 1992: v. 2, 54–5)

Ten

Nomos Mousikos

ποιεῖν κατὰ φύσιν ἐπαΐοντας
Her. fr. 112 [DK][1]

ὁ Μοισαγέτας με καλεῖ χορεῦσαι
Pind. fr. 94c[2]

ὕμνον ἀείδουσιν, . . . πάντων δ' ἀνθρώπων φωνὰς
καὶ κρεμβαλιαστὺν μιμεῖσθ' ἴσασιν
Hom. *Hym. to Apollo*, 162–3[3]

γραμμάτων τε συνθέσεις, | μνήμην ἁπάντων,
μουσομήτορ᾽ ἐργάνην.
Aes. *PB* 460–1[4]

1. *Bios mousikos*

Mousikē is of the same *genos* as human *phusis*, says Aristotle.[5] In Plato's *Philebus*, at 62c, Socrates asks Protarchos whether *mousikē* is necessary for the adequate mixture essential to a desirable life; to which he replies that he certainly considers *mousikē* to be necessary, 'if our life [*bios*] is really to be a life of some [proper] kind' (ἀναγκαῖον φαίνεται ἔμοιγε, εἴπερ

---

[1] 'To do according to *phusin*, listening.'

[2] '[Pindar is Apollo, invoked as] the guide of the Muses, inviting [the poet] to dance.' The Muses here are, most likely, a female chorus.

[3] '[The maidens] in song can imitate the voices of all mortals and their clattering sounds.'

[4] '[T]he syntheses of letters (into written words) is the instrument of the memory of all things, and the mother of the Muse(s).'

[5] *Pol.* 1340b: καί τις ἔοικε συγγένεια ταῖς ἁρμονίαις καὶ τοῖς ῥυθμοῖς εἶναι.

γε ἡμῶν ὁ βίος ἔσται καὶ ὁπωσοῦν ποτε βίος). Furthermore, in the *Phaedo*, at 61a, Socrates while in prison will be told in a recurring dream that *ὡς φιλοσοφίας μὲν οὔσης μεγίστης μουσικῆς* ('philosophy is the highest *mousikē*'). In what sense is this meant, he wonders? Is it in the sense, perhaps, of shaping a way of life, an *ēthos*, as a continuous becoming of a philosophical search/initiation (*muēsis = mousikē*)? Socrates disputes this initial understanding and suggests to himself that what he was, in fact, told to do is to practise *mousikē* in the ordinary sense. But, of course, the answer to the question cannot be understood as if it were a contemporary dilemma, or as falling into the late supposedly neat modern scission between abstract philosophy and ordinariness. Socrates is well aware that the practice of *mousikē* and philosophical understanding are united before the experience of the happening of sound and 'language'. These two events are so intimately linked that philosophy must undertake to study them and protect them from erosion. The two coeval *anthropogenic* events of the occurrence of the *phōnē* (or 'voice, sound') and of the 'word' (*logos*), at a time when these are not yet separated, are the inspiration and measure of the 'highest philosophy' (= *mousikē*).

Rather than consider Socrates to be in conversation with his 'bad conscience', as Friedrich Nietzsche would perhaps have it, it is of interest to imagine the way in which *mousikē* was experienced; that is, the experience that actually enables such a Socratic expression in the first place. While doing so it is worth keeping in mind what Plato understood as the *astheneia* of philosophy, its 'privation' (not in the sense of a mere weakness, but rather as a searching reflection, a receptivity and a re-articulation: *διάρθρωσις, diarthrōsis*)[6] – a searching-turn to its original inspiration, which is no other than *mousikē*. Socrates is told, while questioning his own reflection, that he should practise *mousikē*, and the impression remains that so

---

[6] It is of interest that Aristotle defines the *phōnē* of certain animals that have *glōtta* and lungs as *ἀσθενῆ φωνήν* (*asthenē phōnēn*; weak voice); *Anim.* 4.9.536a. At 4.9.535a–b, Aristotle, famously, defines *dialektos* ('language') as: *ἡ τῆς φωνῆς ἐστι τῇ γλώττῃ διάρθρωσις* ('the glottis's articulation of the voice'). Animals that have no voice or language can still produce sound, hence 'voice and sound are two different things, while language is a third' (*Φωνὴ καὶ ψόφος ἕτερόν ἐστι, καὶ τρίτον διάλεκτος*).

he would. Irrespective of which interpretation of his questioning dream one prefers, it remains the case that a relation or analogy between philosophy and *mousikē* continued to influence philosophical, as much as 'musical', thought. For instance, Aristides Quintilianus, during the third century BC. in his treatise *Peri mousikēs* (Περί Μουσικῆς) at III, 27.133–20, describes *mousikē* as providing the foundation of all learning (all *paideia*, including *philosophia*). But the relation of *mousikē* and the *logos* was much more than a mere analogy. As will be seen, for the Greeks, *mousikē* had a much wider experiential significance as a *technē* ('art'), in that it set the conditions for the 'highest learning' and *ēthos*.

It is, then, worth outlining the importance of *mousikē* for the Greeks prior to the time of Plato and Aristotle.[7] The starting point has to be a clarification as to the word itself: *mousikē*. *Mousikē* is not reducible to what is commonly understood as music.[8] Nor is *mousikē* reducible to a *technē* (at least not before the fourth century BC) – if perceived in its formal technical aspects – or to an object (of music). We are, further, accustomed to think of *mousikē* under the poetic image of the (nine) Muses famously depicted in Hesiod, yet *mousikē* was a wider dynamic plateau of experience. Penelope Murray and Peter Wilson write:

---

[7] The literature on different aspects of *mousikē* is extensive. On ancient Greek music, see indicatively and generally Gevaert (1875–81); Weil and Reinach 1900; Grieser (1937); Wegner (1949); Düring (1956); Koller (1963); Lippman (1975); Michaelides (1978); Chailley (1979); Comotti ([1979] 1991; 1989); West (1992); Neubecker (1994); Gentili and Pretagostini (1998); Landels (1999); Mathiesen (1999); Meriani (2003). See, further, Pöhlmann and West (2001); Pöhlmann (1970), on the extant melodies and fragments; Murray and Wilson (2004), on the culture of *mousikē* in classical Athens; Rocconi (2003) on the formation of the technical terminology; West (1981), on Homer and song in relation to early Greek music; Georgiades (1949; 1958), on *mousikē* and rhythm, and (1982) on *mousikē* and language; Barker (1984), on the musicians; Barker (1989) on harmonic and acoustic theory; Griffin (2009) and Hagel (2009), on the technical history; Papadopoulou (2004a), on instruments in cult and (2004b) on the more general history; Kowalzig (2007), on performance; Pearson (1990), on Aristoxenus; Anderson (1994), Bélis (1999) and Gibson (2005), on the musicians; and Anderson (1966), on *ēthos* and education.

[8] For an essential account of the concept of *mousikē*, see Koller (1963: 5–16); also, Kaden (2004: 67–9); and Murray and Wilson (2004: 1–5).

In its commonest form, *mousikē* represented for the Greeks a seamless complex of instrumental music, poetic word, and coordinated physical movement. As such it encompassed a vast array of performances, from small-scale entertainment in the private home to elaborate festivals in which an entire polis was involved. *Mousikē* was an endlessly variegated, rich set of cultural practices, with strongly marked regional traditions that made them a valuable item of local self-definition as well as a means for exchange and interaction. (2004: 1)

It is worth emphasising the mixture of dance, song and word, while observing that such a mixture amounted also to an ordering of a 'proper' life more generally; that is, the domain of the foremost social education in *ēthos* and pleasure.[9] One of the most vivid traditions of this experience was celebrated in one of the most remarkable (though often idealised) regions of ancient Greece, Arkadia. Polybius, relying probably on Aristoxenus, famously describes the Arkadian *politeia* as one where *mousikē* provided the ideal ordering and education (4 at 20.7: εἰς τὴν ὅλην πολιτείαν τὴν μουσικὴν παραλαβεῖν).[10] So important was *mousikē* for the life of the Greek polis that its absence was marked as exceptional or abnormal.

Before *mousikē* was perhaps perceived as a technical *technē* (from, possibly, the fourth century BC), it was a key component of 'ritual' practice and social ordering, inseparable from the transmission of a way of life (*ēthos*). It is possible to presume that *mousikē* was significant long before the archaic period, given

---

[9] Fitton (1973: 259) writes: 'The protoplasm of Greek lyric poetry was a song-and-dance. The integrated nature of the performance is reflected in the word μολπή [*molpē*].' The word, from the verb μέλπω [*melpō*], is already attested in Homer (e.g. *Il.* 18.572 and *Od.* 6.101).

[10] See Murray and Wilson (2004: 2), who indicate: 'Their state-funded programme of socialization on a grand scale included musical training for males until the age of thirty, demanding instruction and demonstration in instrumental performance and dance as well as vocal expertise.' On the centrality of *mousikē* in education, see, for the classical tradition, Pl. *Prot.* 326ab; *Tim.* 80b; and *L.* 654a–d, 672e and 666d. For the special case of the *polis* of Sparta, see Calame (1977). More generally, see Marrou (1965); and Anderson (1966).

that archaeological research has established that all the key instruments had been in existence since the early bronze age (Younger 1998). This may indicate a strong continuity between the earlier periods, as well as the later transformations in the archaic, classical and Hellenistic periods, along with extensive interactions with eastern civilisations in the Mediterranean.[11] The most important stringed instruments were the tortoise-shell *chelys*, the round *phorminx*, the square *kithara*, the standard lyre known as the *lyra* and, finally, its large variation, the *barbitos*. Stringed instruments, lyre-singing (*kitharōidia*), as well as instrumental performance (*kitharistikē*), were central to the experience of *mousikē*.[12] The other key instruments were the pipes (*auloi*), which facilitated a long tradition of pipe music, as a counterpart to kithara music (*auloidikē* with song and the instrumental *aulētikē*) that was particularly associated with the notion of order (and, for that matter, with the elegy).[13]

It would be anachronistic to perceive the wide practices of *mousikē* as 'artistic', since *mousikē* forms (orders) activities and events as varied as a civic celebratory *ēthos* or military formations in war (Huchzermeyer 1931: 48). Indeed, *mousikē* included the exclusively male domain of singing the epics (an idiosyncratic practice that for some, perhaps, Homer performed himself, though this remains speculative), the carrying out of rituals (which were the most significant motors of group-sanctioned norms), victory celebrations (which included odes, the *epinikia*), the practice of *symposia*, different kinds of processions[14] and, essentially for the

---

[11] See Franklin (2016).

[12] The lyre is vividly portrayed in Homer's *Il.* 1.600–5 and in Pind. *P.* 1.1–12 as 'golden and divine'. See also Hom. *Hym. to Apollo* 130–2, as well as Apol. Rhod. *Argo.* 1.496–504, for a key description of the Orpheus myth. On the instruments in ancient Greece, see, for instance, Huchzermeyer (1931); Haldane (1966); Maas and Snyder (1989); Sarti (1992); Frontisi-Ducroux (1994); Wilson (1999); and Papadopoulou and Pirenne Delforge (2001),

[13] For a classic view on this see Arist. *Prob.* 10.9.28.

[14] Another key formative development during this period is the widespread establishment of public contests, including specifically musical contests (for instance, in Delphi and Argos) that eventually acquire a Panhellenic form (the Pythian games being among the most famous, before the Athenian *Panathinaia*). On musical contests and the *Panathinaia*, in particular, see Kotsidu (1991); and Shapiro (1992).

purposes of this work, poetry.[15] A central worship-experience itself, *mousikē* was at the same time, already in Homer and Hesiod, a dynamically *cosmopoietic* sphere of knowledge, while during the sixth century BC (though possibly earlier too) *mousikē* is commonly thought of in ever more elaborate ways as to its *cosmopoietic* power (most famously under the Pythagorean doctrine of *harmonia*).[16] Music, poetry and dance were inseparable from the life of the polis, which was itself indissociable from worship and cult, as well as from the *nomothetic* tradition of myth.[17] It is here worth noting that 'dance' was also considered as primarily musically significant sound performance (Lonsdale 1993; Kowalzig 2007; Barker 2010). Lastly, the significance of the uses of *mousikē* in a period that is predominantly oral, and thus essentially acoustic, should not be underestimated,[18] while the use of writing would be a key means for its later theoretical study.[19]

From early on, *mousikē* is a widespread activity and the plateau of social knowledge and 'order'. *Mousikē's* essential link to language and to poetry was audible to the archaic ear. It is of paramount importance to appreciate that poetry originates within the experience of *mousikē*.[20] Greek poetry

---

[15] For an introduction, see West (1992: 4–8); and Landels (1999). For the evidence, see Barker (1984; 1989).

[16] See Plato's awareness of this in, for instance, *Ion* 531c; and *Tht.* 173e.

[17] It is important to note that in the early archaic period there is no term for 'poet' other than the tuneful singer (ἀοιδός, *aoidos*), in the sense of performance, rather than composition; see Gentili (1988) and Maslov (2009); in this work, I use imprecisely the terms 'poet' and 'poetry' for the convenience of a general understanding. On dance, see Lawler (1964); Prudhommeau (1965); Dale (1969); Fitton (1973); Delavaud-Roux (1991); Lonsdale (1993); Henrichs (1994–5); Kowalzig (2004); Zafiri (2007). An ancient source that vividly links *mousikē* with movement of the face and the feet is Ath. I.21f; I.22c. On poetic performance, see Edmunds and Wallace (1997).

[18] See Havelock (1963; 1982) and the revision of his earlier theses (1986).

[19] On writing, the invention of prose and orality, see generally Havelock (1982; 1986); Thomas (1992); and Goldhill (2002).

[20] On poetry and its craft, as well as its relation to *mousikē*, see generally Del Grande (1932); Fowler (1954); Koller (1956); Snell (1961); Page (1962b); Murray (1981); Campbell ([1982] 1993); Calame (1983; 1986; 1995); Gostoli (1986); Bartol (1992a; 1992b); West (1993); Segal (1994a); Gentili and Perusino (1995); Thomas (1995a); Miller (1996); Nagy (1996; 2002); Edmunds and Wallace (1997); Bolonyai (1998); Pinault (2001); Garcia (2002); Clay (2004); Bowie (2009); Brillante (2009); and Ornaghi (2009).

was divided into a wide variety of forms, for instance, dithyrambs, *prosodia, partheneia, thrēnoi,* paeans and so forth (Furley and Bremer 2001: 10–13). Lyrical, or elegiac poetry, is perhaps linked to the aedic, the rhapsodic and to the famous choral performances of Attic drama. As Claude Calame (1997: 9) has exceptionally shown, poetry is not a mere accompaniment to the key events of a political community but formed by, as much as forming, a social act. Greek poetry from the Mycenaean to the classical period was predominantly sung, though the epic and the melic were probably distinguished in their customary traditions.[21] Formulaic diction was, thus, necessary, if the singer (*aoidos*) was to be enabled to perform well (in Homer we encounter two famous performances by a θεῖος ἀοιδός (*theios aoidos*), such as Demodocus, Phemius and Thamyris).[22] The practice of memorising poetry for the purposes of performance was perhaps one of the reasons, too, as to why the Muses were associated with the transmission of social memory (*mnēmosunē*), as well as why poet-singers enjoyed an exceptional status.[23] Ultimately, *mousikē* in the poetic experience forms one of the most exceptional, yet commonplace, experiences of 'music': 'the complete combination of poetry, melody, and dance . . . was the ideal type of music as well as the predominant type . . . wordless music was regarded as inferior' (Lippman 1964: 52–4).[24]

2. A note on 'ritual' *mousikē*

Mousikē was neither a mere accompaniment to processes and events nor a mere amusing supplement to entertainment. It could be said that no social process/event, no expression of authority and normalcy, could be voiced without

---

[21] See Lang (1969); Durante (1976); West (1988: 156–9); and Mathiesen (1999: 24), who remains uncertain.
[22] See Franklin (2003); Wilson (2010: 209); and also, for a useful discussion in relation to law, Mittica (2015).
[23] See Hom. *Il.*1.1; *Od.*1.1; Hes. *Th.* 1–115; see, further, Ziegler (2007).
[24] This created music with a 'single rhythmic expression' and a 'remarkably definite physical nature' (ibid. 54). Similarly, a τέλειον μέλος (*teleion melos*) comprised melody, poetic text and dance, while μέλος (*melos*) indicated an instrumental piece or a song; Mathiesen (1999: 25).

mousikē.[25] In the polis, in joyous events (i.e. marriages, *symposia*, harvests), as much as in funerals and wars, there is an immersion in *mousikē* and the vector of a series of traditions that reach and surpass the classical period. It is instructive, in this regard, that the intersection between *mousikē* and ritual is just as complex and extensive. Ritual practices connected to song are evident in the epic: for instance, in Homer, the noteworthy scene of the Linos-song (*Il.* 18.561–72), or the singing of the paean (*Il.* 1.472–4).[26] It is famously reported by Aristotle that tragedy originated in the performance of those who led the dithyramb (dedicated to Dionysus; *Poet.* 1449a10–1; though this remains in dispute). The word 'tragedy' itself (τραγωδία, *tragōdia*: *tragos* = 'he-goat', *hōdē* = 'song') may indicate the link to (Dionysian) worship (Latacz 1993–2003: 53–65). In tragedy, the primary agents were the choral singers (who had to compete with other choruses) and even later, in the fourth century BC, Plato refers to the tragic poets as 'singers' (*L.* 7. 817b7–8).[27]

It is, then, of crucial importance to observe the integration of poetry, dance, music and worship practices in a ritual milieu (within which concern as to the 'effects' of *mousikē* becomes understandable and wherein, perhaps, lies the reason why Plato will be ready to censor some of its forms in his *Laws*). Thus, within its ancient roots, the dithyramb is not just a choral song expressed with instrumental music and dancing, but also, in one sense, a (Dionysian) ritual. In fact, what happens to the dithyramb by the time of the sixth century is also instructive as regards the understanding of *mousikē* itself. It is worth noting that by the sixth century BC, as Martin L. West has shown, the dithyramb becomes fully

---

[25] Koller (1965: 277–85) has argued that an early poet-singer, but also a later one, would specifically be *thespis aoidos*, singer of the sacred word.

[26] See Nagy (1974); and Calame (1977). The uses of song in relation to military events, and feasts (e.g. *Od.* 17.271), is also met with in epic; see Mathiesen (1999: 23–4).

[27] On ancient Greek 'song culture' and its connection with the Athenian audience's experience of tragedy, see Herington (1985: 3–5); Bacon (1994); and Revermann and Wilson (2008). The 'goat' element is disputed, but not the 'religious' milieu of tragedy; see Pickard-Cambridge ([1927] 1962); and Vernant and Vidal-Naquet (1988).

institutionalised and reorganised within the system of the annual festivals (1992: 16–18). Once the festivals and contests were restructured, it is believed that musical performances became gradually semi-detached from the ritual context in which they were born (Barker 1990: 50–1). Yet from early on, all poetry in rituals had a worship/'ceremonial' character or relation, be it, for instance, the *prosodia*, hymns or paeans, where the intersection of poetic word, song and worship is most evident (West 1992: 15).[28] Hymns, too, would preface melic poetry and form the central kernel of the poetic experience, indissociably from the experience of worship (Nagy 1990b: 360).[29]

Jana Kubatzki (2016), in her insightful recent contribution to the study of the function of music in ancient Greek cults, has shown that music played a key and substantial role in multiple ways, while, in her earlier work, she analytically examined fifty texts from between the eighth and the fourth centuries BC with reference to cult practices involving music (2015).[30] As she writes: 'Hymns must be regarded as the predominant song type in cult performance, since they were sung in all parts of the cult ritual: during the procession, before the sacrifice and during the feast and the contest' (2016: 1). Similarly, the processional songs *prosodia* (προσόδοις, *prosodois*) honouring the gods were self-evidently ritual enactments. Indeed, Kubatzki writes that the 'most important musical act in cults was singing' (ibid. 4). Music intersects with rituals in a variety of life practices, which suggests the close relation (perhaps indissociably so) between *mousikē*, ritual, language, ordering and magic. Hence, magical music 'ritual' elements were practised in medicinal acts, as in relation to Odysseus' wound (*Od.* 19.457), while 'purgatory effects' were induced by music in cult practices (Lippman 1964). *Mousikē*, inseparable from worship song-dances (ἄσματα ὑπορχήματα; *asmata hyporchēmata*) and ritual processes was prominent in all mystery rites (Strab. 10.3.9–16), while ritual sacrifices

[28] See also Symonds (1873: 292).
[29] On hymns, in this regard, see, for instance, Keyssner (1932); West (1965); Furley (1993); Furley and Bremer (2001); and Vamvouri Ruffy (2004).
[30] On *mousikē*, musicians, musical instruments and cult worship, see also Nordquist (1994); Brand (2000); and Papadopoulou (2004a).

involved music as an essential part of the preparatory and executory stages (West 1992: 15; Hdt. 1.132.1).[31]

Kubatzki (2016) sheds further light on the importance of the use of music in sacrificial rituals with regard to the particular function of music as a means for the mimetic interaction and communication with the divine, a function served by the acts of poet-singers as much as by the mimetic experience of the worshipping audience (Furley and Bremer 2001: 59). The power of music to induce, for example, *mania* (an altered state of consciousness), or to lead, more commonly, to imitation of the divine, was common knowledge (Arist. *Pol.* 1342a–b); as was, also, the power of music to institute that common knowledge (*homoiōsis*) or community through *mimēsis*.[32] In fact, the importance of imitation, as a way of transformation, was a primary device for the experience of the divine within one's self (ἔνθεος; *entheos*).[33] Kubatzki refers to a characteristic passage of the *Bacchae* (2016: 152–66):

Ὦ ἴτε βάκχαι,
ὦ ἴτε βάκχαι,
Τμώλου χρυσορόου χλιδᾷ
μέλπετε τὸν Διόνυσον
βαρυβρόμων ὑπὸ τυμπάνων,
εὔια τὸν εὔιον ἀγαλλόμεναι θεὸν
ἐν Φρυγίαισι βοαῖς ἐνοπαῖσί τε,
λωτὸς ὅταν εὐκέλαδος
ἱερὸς ἱερὰ παίγματα βρέμῃ, σύνοχα
φοιτάσιν εἰς ὄρος εἰς ὄρος: ἡδομέ-
να δ'ἄρα, πῶλος ὅπως ἅμα ματέρι
φορβάδι, κῶλον ἄγει ταχύπουν σκιρτήμασι βάκχα.

This can be rendered in English, following Kovacs' translation (2002) along with Kubatzki's attentive corrections (2016: 12), as follows:

---

[31] Pl. *Rep.* 395a–e; Hdt. 1.132.4; see also Quasten (1930: 6–9, 42ff.).
[32] Aristotle follows Plato in this; Plato mentions *mimēsis* at *Rep.* 3.392c11–4b1 and in *L.* 2.655d5–6; 7.798d8–9. On the social significance, see Brand (2000: 118); and Goulaki-Voutira (2004: 372).
[33] See Koller (1954); Halliwell (2002); Rocconi (2014); and Kubatzki (2016: 9); the famous view on *mimēsis* is Aristotle's, in his *Poet.* 1447a13–16.

Oh bacchants,
oh bacchants,
pride of the River *Tmōlos* that runs with gold:
sing Dionysus' praises
to the deed-roaring frame drums [ὑπὸ τυμπάνων],
making ecstatic cries to the god of ecstasy
with Phrygian shouts and exclamations,
when the lovely *aulos* shrills,
all holy, its holiness sings in concert
with those who go to the mountain, to the mountain!
Hence in joy, like a colt with its grazing mother,
the bacchant leaps and gambols on nimble legs.[34]

Imitation, an altered state of consciousness, and divine *mimēsis* are combined through the magical medium of *mousikē* (song–dance–word–rite), when in appropriate rhythm and intonation (Kaden 2004: 74–7).[35] For Kubatzki, then, *mousikē*, from the eighth century BC and onwards, is not a mere supplement to ritual practice, but in fact a direct expression, and, I would add, 'formation', of the divine nature of creativity as such.

3. Διὰ μούσας[36]

If all instruments had their origin in the gods, so all poem-songs had their origin in the divine Muses, who, it could be said, were *mousikē* (Kubatzki 2012: 28). Kubatzki refers to the famous statement by Strabon, following Hermann Koller (1963: 158), who describes this relation as follows:

The muse directs the sense of the human labor, but the true sense directs it to the divine. The enthusiasm seems to be a divine enthusiasm . . . and to approach the visionary. The veil of the mystical cult, however, makes the divine more

---

[34] Compare the earlier iconic passages describing the dance and song of the Muses in Hesiod's extended hymn at the start of the *Theogony* at 2.7–14, 39–43 and 68–70.

[35] See Koller (1963: 153), who explains that the body is understood as the instrument of the soul and music is the mimetic (acoustic) expression of the soul. This is comparable to a large variety of cultural practices; see Mauss (2007: 67ff.).

[36] [*Dia mousas*]; Eur. *Alc.* 962, 'through the Muse[s] [or the poem-song]'.

sublime, expressing its essence, which escapes our perception, in play. The music, however, which includes dance, rhythm, and melody, connects us to the divine through pleasure and artistic perfection for the same reason. (Strab. X 3, 9; ibid.)

It is not possible to appreciate the interwoven experience of *mousikē* for the Greeks without an inquiry into the Muses.[37] As with most Greek traditions, the depiction of the Muses is extensively varied. This is, in fact, in some contrast to the Hesiodic representation of the dominant image of the nine Muses, the daughters of Zeus and *Mnēmosunē* (with Apollo named as their leader in song, though this was probably after he had taken over the Delphic shrine).[38] Crucially, in the proximate Homeric tradition, *Mnēmosunē* is not mentioned once and the Muses are enumerated as nine (*Od.* 24.60). At least to an extent, the ancient (as well as scholarly) tendency has been to reduce variation by concentrating on the common elements of an evidently polymorphic tradition.[39] Thus, the parentage of the Muses by Zeus and *Mnēmosunē* 'is a construct, a derivative of the gradual and heterogeneous process of eliminating the rare and untypical elements in favour of the common and similar ones' (Mojsik 2011: 11).[40] However, we do know of the older Muses that were said to be born out

---

[37] The literature on the Muses is vast, see, indicatively, Mayer (1933); Boyancé (1937; 1972); Notopoulos (1938); Otto ([1955] 1961); Accame (1963a; 1963b); Barmeyer (1968); Stroh (1976); Neitzel (1980); Barchiesi (1991); Nagy (1992; 1996); Brillante (1994); Pretagostini (1995); Rudhart (1996); Camilloni (1998); Détienne (1999); Hardie (2004; 2006; 2009); Murray and Wilson (2004); Murray (2005); Assaël (2006); Heiden (2007); Pucci (2007); and Pucci (2013).

[38] The nine Muses were said to be: *Kalliopē* ('the beautifully [sweet] voiced/ faced', related to speech, epic and poetry), *Kleiō* (related to history), *Eratō* (related to love or erotic poetry), *Euterpē* (related to music and lyric poetry), *Melpomenē* (related to tragedy), *Poluhumnia* (related to sacred song, lyric and rhetoric), *Terpsichorē* (related to choral song and dance), *Thalia* (related to comedy and bucolic poetry) and *Ourania* (related to the sky and astronomy; see Pl. *Phdr.* 259d). For an analysis of Apollo and *mousikē*, especially in the Hellenistic period, see Bing (1988: 124–31).

[39] See Murray and Wilson (2004); Murray (2005; 2014); Hardie (2000; 2006; 2009); and the extensive recent treatment in Mojsik (2011).

[40] See, further, the recent re-examination by Maslov (2016).

of *Ouranos* and *Gē*, long before their existence was entrenched within the Olympian kingdom after the dominance of the pan-Hellenic Olympian worship (Otto [1955] 1961: 26; Diod. Sic. 4.7.1; Pind. *N.* 3.1–12), which may also suggest even earlier chthonic mythical origins.[41]

Tomasz Mojsik has recently examined the key genealogies of the Muses, and it is worth outlining some of his findings. The first extant mention of the Muses' genealogy is found in epic poetry with Homer and Hesiod, though in significantly differing ways. In the *Iliad*, in book two (at 491–2 and 598) the Muses are depicted as Olympian, of an indefinite number, their father being Zeus (while, at the same time, a singular unnamed Muse is described as the daughter of Zeus in the *Odyssey* at 8.488 and, as singular, once more, in *Il.* 2.761, the other instance being *Od.* 1.1).[42] Homer never mentions their mother. For Mojsik, the Homeric depiction may suggest an earlier genealogy of the Muses, but it is hard to ascertain that reliably (2011: 15, 21–2). In contrast, Hesiod depicts the Muses as Heliconian goddesses (*Th.* 1), as Olympian (*Th.* 25), and as daughters of Zeus, born of *Mnēmosunē*, whose mother was *Ge* (*Th.* 52–62, 75–9; notably here, the location shifts from Olympus to Pieria).[43] Furthermore, consider the genealogy which derives the Muses from Apollo and has Apollo named as *Mousagetēs*.[44] Another version of the genealogy can be traced in Euripides, who describes the Muses as originating from Pieria and as brought to life by *Harmonia* above the ether of Attica (*Med.* 824–32). The latter may be a later legend, but it is of particular interest as one of the clearest indications of the equation of the Muses with *mousikē* (and *harmonia*),

---

[41] On the divine presence of the Muses, see Barmeyer (1968: 55–68).

[42] On Zeus, see Stehle (1997: 205).

[43] See Mojsik (2011: 22–5). Pieria and *Olympos* are two key geographical locations for the Muses' genealogy, but there are others (Helikon, the river Amnisos in Crete and so forth); see Calame (1997: 31).

[44] This name with reference to Apollo is found in Pl. *L.* 654a, 665a. In the Orphic *Hymn to Apollo* [Kern] it is rendered as Μουσαγέτα [*Mousageta*] at 6. In the Orphic *Hymn to Nómos* [Kern], *Nómos* is personified and described as the one who ensures the stability of *phusis* with *nómois*, at 3, as well as an ἀστροθέτην [*astrothetēn*], at 2, 'the one who sets the stars'. The link to *cosmopoiesis* appears common between *nómos*-song and *nómos*-'law' (of *phusis* or the gods).

with significant – and thus persistent through time – political (and musical) consequences.[45] Already, the genealogies are too many to bypass the variations. However, what appears most probable is that from the start the Muses are a collective, a chorus (Murray 2014: 15), as in the *Iliad* (1.604), where they perform on *Olympos* as a chorus (*khoros*).

Mojsik has also examined the names given to the Muses across archaic and classical poetry. Notably, the Muses are frequently described as *korai, parthenoi* (girls, virgins; 2011: 56), while, as seen earlier, the first ever mention of named Muses is found in Hesiod (Th. 77–9).[46] West has indicated, in detail, that the remarkable Hesiodic names stem from preceding verses that connect particular attributes to the Muses (1966: 18off).[47] Indeed, Mojsik has shown that the invocation of the unnamed Muses (whether in the singular or plural) remained, in fact, the norm (2011: 56). Hence, while in the Hesiodic tradition one derives the most eloquent depiction of the connection between the Muses and the process of creativity in *mousikē*, song or poetry (which are, as stated earlier, not strictly distinguishable), their names and number vary throughout even the late classical tradition, suggesting that their genealogies and naming remained fluid.[48] Thus, what was common to the Muses was not, in fact, their names, number or particular attributes.

There are several mythological divinities that relate, in one way or another (mostly in the sense of being singers/dancers), to *mousikē*; from the Nereids to the Charites, the Nymphs, the Erinyes and the Sirens, although the most crucial figures, in this

---

[45] See, further, Mojsik (2011: 46); also, Hardie (2004); and Wilson (2004).

[46] See Roscher (1904) and Slater (1969).

[47] See also Murray (2005: 152). On the relation of the Muses to the Nymphs, see Camilloni (1998: 25–7). Hesiod names, in the *Theogony*, one of the Muses as *Ourania*, whom he also lists as a nymph, possibly indicating a much earlier tradition; see, further, West (1966: 181).

[48] See Mojsik (2011: especially chs 3 and 4). Usener compared what for him is the common movement from unity to multiplicity between the Muses, the *Moirai*, the Nymphs and so forth (1903: 357–8). For Plutarch, the Muses were also called *Mneiai* ('Memories'), Plut. *Mor.* 743d, notably linked to 'persuasion'; while for Pausanias there were three and their names were: *Meletē* ('study, practice'), *Mnēmē* ('memory') and *Aoidē* ('song'), Paus. 9.29.2–3.

regard, remain the Muses (Barker 2010).[49] The divine nature of the Muses is particularly poignant from Hesiod onwards, but their divinity can be variously speculated as being pre-Olympian, natural-elemental, chthonic and mythical. Barker noted the particular tradition that has the Pierian Muses not as deities but as the young daughters of a man called Pieros (Pausanias 9.29.1–5; Barker 2010: 2). The young chorus may be the source of the iconic depiction in the *Theogony* whereby the Muses are seen dancing in the vicinity of the streams of Mount Helicon and then performing their choral song on the highest peak. Andrew Barker has identified that what the different traditions have in common is that the Muses are, at most times, a company of singers-dancers who are

> always placed outside the civilised world, in the wild places on mountains, among the rocky peaks and streams and forests [. . .] they sometimes sing in the palace of the gods on Olympus, and in the human world their sanctuaries were often close to cities or even inside them; but their imagined lives are not centred on the cities like those of the Olympians and some minor divinities, nor on the cultivated farmlands; and their homes are not in temples or houses or, indeed, palaces. This is a feature they share with all other groups of beautiful, immortal young women, Charites, Oreads, Oceanides, Nereids, and so on, and with any number of nymphs of the hills and woodlands. In origin, all these beings are spirits of the untamed world of nature, and the Muses in particular are creatures of the mountain-tops and springs. (2010: 2–3)[50]

It is also worth pointing out that what the Muses actually do is perform the dance–song and their action is, each time,

[49] On the comparable Nymphs, see the recent study by Larson (2001) and the earlier seminal work by Otto ([1955] 1961: 9–20; 29–35); the earliest association was provided by Farnell ([1896] 1909: 5, 435).

[50] Barker (2010: 9–10) refers to the long tradition of animals that sing, which, for instance, in the case of the cicadas, are described as the Muses' prophets, as in Pl. *Ph.* 259b–d; while the association of *mousikē* with natural elements (mountains, springs, rocks and so forth) is often noted; see Hardie (2006: 53–7) with special reference to 'territory formation'; and Lonsdale (1993: 262–8).

mousikē. That is, speculatively, the initiation necessary for human beings to become human, where *mousikē* may be one of the earliest initiations, led by choruses of young women, not of a mysterious and concealed content in the 'untamed nature', but the (divine) *phusis* of living (and of 'enunciating' or, more generally, 'sounding' the divine).

For the Muses, *mousikē* is their plateau. Yet *mousikē* is not a detachable domain of activity in the life of the Greeks. It is intimate with the ordering of the cosmos, the polis and the *ēthos* (Halliwell 2012: 23). The gods are themselves depicted as being in need of *mousikē*. For instance, in Pindar's fr. 31 [SM], the Muses are brought into being to satisfy a divine request to 'adorn' (κατακοσμεῖν) Zeus' world order in song and *mousikē* [51] – an order that the Muses are classically depicted as celebrating with their divine voice (*Th.* 43–4: θεῶν γένος αἰδοῖον πρῶτον κλείουσιν ἀοιδῇ).[52] Furthermore, the absence of *mousikē*, as has already been noted, is of an utmost negative character. *Amousia*, in fact, is formed in direct relation to the term 'Muse'. Stephen Halliwell has analysed the encounter of the adjectives *amousos* or *apomousos*, as in, for instance, Empedocles at 81B74 [DK], who describes a fish as ἄμουσον [*amouson*], possibly in the sense of lacking the capacity of speech and *mousikē* more generally.[53] In Euripides, too, *mousikē* is contrasted with the neglect (ὧν μουσῶν ἀμελεῖ) of the Muses that leads to perishing (Eur. fr. 1028). Halliwell writes: '*Amousia* can be thought of, in that sense, as the condition of a life and its values as a whole' (2012: 21).

The manifestation of the song of *logos* is tantamount to existence, to a proper *bios*. *Bios* is a *mousopoieia*, as Sophocles will depict the musician Thamyras carry out in his musico-*poiesis* (fr. 245.5).[54] The association of the Muses with learning perhaps begins here, especially for the classical period in particular, when the term 'Muse' is etymologised from μυέω (*mueō*, 'initiate in the mysteries', which perhaps included

---

[51] See Ael. Ari. *Orat.* 2. 470; for a discussion, see Snell (1976: 82–94); and Hardie (2000: 33).

[52] See Kritzias (1980).

[53] See Assaël (2006: 256, n. 12).

[54] For other examples, see Hardie (2002: 193; 2009: 48–51; 2012); and, generally, Brillante (1991; 2013/2014).

both silence [the closed mouth] and *mousikē*), that signifies a key part of *paideia*, which itself extends from the mysteries to philosophy and mathematics that are themselves, in this sense, inseparable (Hardie 2004). *Mousikē* is an initiatory act in living, a force of regeneration and inspiration, as is most evident, perhaps, in tragedy, where the song of the chorus reminds the tragic cosmos of its regenerative domain in *mousikē*, as well as of the scission between *phōnē* and word. Not having a voice, this is the tragedy of a human being who speaks. Tragedy must arouse the emotions so as to arouse the soul to 'remember' its original existence and inspiration in *mousikē* – the 'original' event of the linguistic experience of the non-linguistic.

It could be philosophically said that what is handed down to the polis and its members each time is not 'memory' in general, but (the 'tragedy' of mortal) voice;[55] the existence of the heroes in a *bios mousikos*, whereby between silence and *mousikē* (or *phōnē*) the self is lost-and-found and vice versa.[56] In tragedy, then, and in philosophy *mousikē* is not the 'other' of *logos*, but the 'open' (that I call the *chaosmos*) within which the *logos* finds (and loses) its own-most domain. As Giorgio Agamben has written, 'the primary opening of man in the world is not logical but musical' (2016a: 138, my translation). If the original event of the word, for a human being, is musical (hence the place of the Muse's inspiration), his or her experience of language is inherently poietic, as opposed to that of other animals, which have only song. If the poet, and every human being, feels the need to sing, it is, the philosopher writes, in order to remember that she/he lives 'in language without being able to hear [or have] his voice' (ibid. 137). The Muse is, then, the name for the event of attempting to remember the advent of the word, its musical *cosmopoiesis*, as I have called it. But all there is now is the word-song, or the nine modes of the Muses.

It is worthwhile, in this sense, to refer to the varied etymologies of the term *Mousa* (the term is also encountered in

---

[55] For the essay that inspired, in more than one way, my genealogy, see Agamben (1995a: 79–80). I would like to thank Giorgio Agamben for the discussions on *mousikē* and *nomos* more generally.

[56] See, Agamben and Ferrando (2014).

dialect variants such as the Aeolian *Moisa* or the Doric *Mōsa*). In her excellent analysis, Jacqueline Assaël (2000) has shown the variety and complexity of the most prevalent etymological derivations.[57] Assaël locates the two main derivations as being from the root *μοντ- (*Mont*), evident in the Latin word *mons* (mountain) and from the Indo-European root *my/men/mn*, which indicates the notion of an 'intellectual activity' (Assaël 2000: 12–16), and this seems to be the dominant scholarly view.[58] Yet Assaël, for good reason, finds this schematism, between a mountain deity and a deity of intellectual-poetic activity, rather simplistic. As regards the latter derivation, the only ancient etymological attempt can be found later in Plato's *Cratylus*, where Socrates states that the word 'Muse' is related to the desire towards creativity, which, since the epic poets, was related to the charm of *erōs*: τὰς δὲ 'Μούσας' τε καὶ ὅλως τὴν μουσικὴν ἀπὸ τοῦ μῶσθαι, ὡς ἔοικεν, καὶ τῆς ζητήσεώς τε καὶ φιλοσοφίας τὸ ὄνομα τοῦτο ἐπωνόμασεν ('As for the "Muses" and *mousikē* in general, out of their desired [*mōsthai*], it seems, search and love of *sophia*, this name was given to them'; at 406a). Assaël explains that 'to establish this etymology, the philosopher refers to a Dorian verb form, μῶσθαι (*mōsthaï*). In this dialect, the Muse is called Μῶσα (*Mōsa*), facilitating rapprochement with the infinitive in question' (2000: 17), the fundamental meaning of this root being *mōsthai*, that is, 'to investigate', 'to meditate', or 'to aspire to' (2000: 27).[59] For Assaël, despite the lateness of the sources:

> The etymology of the *Cratylus* reflects conceptions shared by authors of archaic and classical epochs that are illustrated in genres as different as cosmogonic poetry, lyricism

---

[57] My translation.
[58] Referring to the etymological studies of Boisacq (1923) and Snell (1993). The original etymological analysis is by Brugmann (1894: 255); but see also Camilloni (1998: 7). In agreement with Brugmann are also Wilamowitz-Moellendorff (1956–9: 1, 246); Otto ([1955] 1961: 26–7); and Nagy (1974: 249); see also the discussion in Hardie (2009). On mountains, the muses and the gods more generally, see Burn (1949); Brown (1961); Bintliff (1996); Hurst and Schachter (1996); Calame (1996); and Clarke (1997). On the philosophers and the Muses, see Boyancé (1937).
[59] See also Thgn. 769–72.

or philosophy. It thus touches on an essential feature of the Muse, and psychoanalysts still defend the idea that inspiration feeds on a form of desire. (2000: 27)

On the other hand, different linguistic presuppositions suggest that the mountains, in particular, remain crucial to the understanding of the origin of the term 'Muse'.[60] Along these lines there is the derivation from the root *$\mu o \nu \tau$- (* *mont*-), present in the Latin *mons-montis*,[61] but Assaël notes that no other Greek word appears to be derived from this alleged origin (2000: 28). However, Muses are frequently described as 'of the mountains' ($\dot{o} \rho \varepsilon \iota \dot{\alpha} \delta \varepsilon \varsigma$), linking them directly to the mountain nymphs (Koller 1963: 17–48). Mythological references to the elemental natural realm and being of the Muses (and related lesser deities) are evident, while designations of their domain as Helicon in Boeotia (Hesiod), or, alternatively, in the north of Pieria (Pausanias), may signal worship traditions in competition with each other, possibly related to the historical establishment of a cult in a particular region. Notably, archaeological research has not confirmed either geographical derivation thus far. It may be that, as Assaël suggests, the cult of the Muses prior to the literary period remained 'esoteric in which case it would be understandable that nothing had been disclosed about the modalities of religious rites connected with the search for inspiration' (2000: 33). Yet it is probably upon such older traditions (similar or related to the other female singing/dancing deities) that the epic poets would draw, even if they were to represent them in differing ways. It may be the case, at the same time, that their essential elemental significance would be the initiating ordering power of the wor(l)d-song, the poietic origin in the voice of the *kosmos*, rather than from the later senses of 'inspiration', or the desire for 'investigative intellectual activity'.

According to Assaël, the most prevalent etymological derivation is the one that links the word *mousa* to the root *$\mu o \nu / \mu \varepsilon \nu / \mu \nu$ (**mon/men/mn*), which can in turn be associated

---

[60] This connection is discussed in detail in Wilamowitz-Moellendorff (1925: 103–18).

[61] See Dodds (1951: 99); Duchemin (1955: 26 and 290); Wackernagel (1955: 1207); and Koller (1963: 38).

with meditative reflection or memory, as can be seen in relation to the verb (*mimnēskō*), indicating 'to bring to mind/
memory': 'since this term is constructed on the zero degree
of the same root' (2000: 41).[62] The names of the Hesiodic nine
Muses, in this manner, may be lexicographic signatures of
the poet's re-imagining of tradition(s), indicating the early
appreciation of the divine nature of poetic creativity (though
this is more evident in relation to lyric poetry than in earlier
forms). For example, the regenerative power of the prophetic
(revelatory in the sense of annunciatory/enunciatory) vision
of *Mnēmosunē* (memory) is a Homeric tradition, but most
probably it contains traces of a much earlier divine function.
This is seminally expressed by Jean-Pierre Vernant in the following way:

> What then is the function of memory? . . . By bringing
> down the barrier that separates the present from the past,
> it bridges the gap between the world of the living and that
> beyond . . . The privilege that *Mnemosune* confers . . . is that
> of a contact with the other world, the possibility of enter-
> ing and returning freely. The past appears as a dimension
> of the hereafter. Memory and its divinities have a magical
> virtue which makes them the dispenser of immortality.
> (1983: 71)[63]

---

[62] *Mnēmē*, in the classical period, a synonym of *Mnēmosunē* (and in some
sources the mother of the Muses; the father being Zeus; see Hes. *Th.* 53–4,
54–65 and 915–16), becomes a *technē* of memorisation during the fifth
century BC. It later becomes a device of rhetoric; see Hardie (2006: 45, n.
31, 46). On the central 'religious' importance of memory, see Effenterre
(1973: 39); and Thomas (1996: 22). On its relation to *dikē*, see Sol. 1.1–17;
and in relation to political-juridical decision-making, the *mnamon*
and the *mnēmones* in Crete, see Thomas (1992: 69ff; 1995b: 66ff); and
Papakonstantinou (2008: 78, n. 23). For the earlier sense of the Muse as a
'reminder' (from *mon-t-yai*), see Détienne (1996: 39–52); and Nagy (1974:
249). One ancient source can be seen in Pausanias 9.29.2, where *Mnēmē* is
named as one of three Muses.

[63] Compare to the transmission by a seer; see Dodds (1951: 81); Flower
(2008: 22); Fontenrose (1978); Nagy (1990a). See, also, Hes. *Th.* 27–8,
30–65; Pindar brings the two together in fr. 150 S: μαντέυεο, Μοῖσα,
προφατέυσω δ'ἐγώ. See, further, Brillante (2013/2014). On prophecy and
poetry, as well as the relation of poets to initiation rites, see Fascher
(1927); Chadwick (1942); and Dickie (1998). Note also that in Muse cults,

Thus, the derivation from the root *μον/μεν/μν (*mon/men/
mn) is supported by both 'mythical genealogies and the
forms of archaic thought' (Assaël 2000: 51–2). Mousikē (=
the Muse) influences, or composes, the human poietic mind
between vision and voice (the two most significant means
of the Greek 'reflective' experience).[64] This is the experience
of the sweet fruit of the poet's mind (Pindar O. 5.8: γλυκὺν
καρπὸν φρενός), his/her dunamis that attempts to make musically possible the linguistically impossible – that sound and
word, phōnē and logos may once again coincide.[65]

The open mouth relates dynamically to the closed mouth.
Memory is the experience of regeneration. Neither merely
passive nor merely active (autochthonous), the 'mind' (or at
least its particular dunamis, the φρήν [phrēn]) is receptive of
the chasm of the kosmos (Snell 1978: 54). The Muses are the
divine gift of a dunamis ('power'), one which is not, early
on, exclusively 'human', but which is the power to transmit
logos in vision–voice–song–dance. It is a logopoietic dunamis
that in the poet, however, will find its characteristic minister-
messenger (the ἄγγελος, aggelos), a sacred transmission-
dunamis that can rarely be withdrawn.[66] It is a power, in one
sense, which initially the poets share with the gods (Pind. fr.
31).[67] It is divine and mortal life experiences in poetic glory –
it is cosmopoietic aural existence, as such.

That said, the link to poetic enunciation and the initiation
of remembrance is a construction of the poets, and, while
the etymological inquiry remains unclear, the possible
earlier divine function of the choral deities (be they Muses,

the oracular manner was associated with the sacred site of their worship;
see Hardie (2004: 57); and, for an ancient source, see Plut. De Pyth. 17,
402c–d.

[64] It cannot be measured with accuracy, but the differentiation between the
'human' and the 'divine' in, for instance, Homeric times was not rigid,
but dynamic.

[65] Φρένες [Phrenes] in archaic poetry often signifies the means of action
(frequently associated with speech); see Biraud (1984: 1.27–49); and, generally, Ireland and Steel (1975).

[66] See Koller (1963: 39–48); Devereux (1987); and Meriani (2006); the exception, in the literary period, is Thamyris, who is punished by the Muses so
that he forgets his ability (dunamis) to play the kithara in Il. 2.599ff.

[67] See, generally, Hardie (2000).

Nymphs or others) suggests a pre-poetic plateau for what later became the annunciatory act of the song of the Muses. That the inspiration–initiation of the Muses takes place at a young age (whether of the collective of the singers, or of the singer-poet) is, in this sense, significant: if there is something that the human *phōnē* lacks, and which requires a divine gift (the *archē*, in other words, may be essentially *acoustically* received; while *Archē*, it is worth noting, is later the name of one of the Ciceronian Muses),[68] then that is *mousikē* – the attempt to compose the unity of word with song-speech set to the regenerative divine rhythm of living. However, this is a supposed unity that, according to this later tradition, does not originally belong to it. Now, it must be 'received' so that the singer can attain perfection and become a θεῖος ἀοιδός [*theios aoidos*], a divine poet (Brillante 2013/2014: 48). This is only made possible if the poem-song can perform its mimetic spellbinding power between word and sound (the base stratum of truth-making; Détienne 1999). The primary power of the Muses is perhaps, then, at least from the archaic period onwards, not memory but truth-binding, or, better, memory as the enunciatory act of truth-binding. It is the poietic order of things, which early on remembers its song, yet has no masters, as Hesiod sang.[69] Before the *kosmos* was the subject of prose (i.e. philosophy, rhetoric and so forth), poetry encountered its original inspiration in the yawning gap of the *chaosmos*, the one that mythology retold in the *titanomachia* and that the earlier female natural deities sang of. The original divine domain of *chaos* was acoustic (neither silent, nor void), as indicated by Titan Typhoeus' 'multiplicity of sounds and voices' (Weber 2014: 76, referring to Goslin 2010).[70] Indeed, Owen Goslin has argued that the *titanomachia* was (also) a battle over ordering sound, through which Zeus' defeat of Typhoeus (and his reduction to *aphōnia*, 'voiceless-

---

[68] Cic. *N.D.* 3.21.

[69] See Vernant (2006: especially ch. 17); for the relation to the power of kings as poet-kings and *thaumatourgoi* in the delivery of *dikē*, see the discussion by Mittica (2015: 34–7), with further references; and Clay (1988: 327, n. 20).

[70] The only immortal, in Homer and Hesiod, to be described as having a tongue and *phōnē*; see, further, Goslin (2010).

ness') imposes sonic order and establishes the Muses so as to mediate between the (clear) voice of the immortals and the voice of mortals and thus turn mortal voice into the aspiring inspiration of song (2010: 359–69). Tellingly, in the pre-poetic world, *Mnēmosunē*, for Friedrich Hölderlin, was a Titan, the daughter of *Ouranos* and *Gē*.[71]

Alcman famously compares the 'clear voice' of the Muses to that of the Sirens (fr. 30 = Calame 86): ἁ Μῶσα κέκλαγ᾽, ἁ λίγηα Σηρήν, though the Sirens are rather different from the Muses and are not singers as such.[72] As Brillante has noted, the verb κλάζω [*klazō*], used here to describe the voice of the Muses, is at first sight peculiar, since it was, among other things, associated with the cry of animals. In Alcman, it seems to indicate the strangeness of the voice of the Muses in its extraordinary splendour (Brillante 2013/2014: 43): a strangeness that perhaps echoed still the earlier natural deities' singing, before the poetic spell emerged. As a result, the poets were highly trained *phoneticians* (Starobinski 1971), for their poetry was composed of not one, but two 'languages' or voices. One was the everyday speech and the other was the *mousikē*, and it was only the latter that had *alethophoric dunamis*: the power to (transmit) reveal what is real (Bennett 2016: 3). In the *mesocosm*, which was the human world for the Greeks, the trained poet-singer could hear the acoustic signature of the *cosmopoietic* choral agencies (earlier uranian, natural and chthonian) of *mousikē*. Fionn Bennett, in fact, with reference to Plato's *Laws* (653d–4b), emphasises that in the archaic period (but perhaps also beyond it) the only reliable means to hear and express that *cosmopoietic* signature was *mousikē* (2016: 6). As he puts it: 'words had to mean what their expressive powers were incapable of expressing' (ibid. 9). A word was not a word, if it did not signify the 'reality' of the thing of which it spoke, and only *mousikē* could convey that for mortals. For an essentially oral culture, it can be appreciated, further, why the poet in the archaic period would need to invoke the clear voice of the Muse(s) so as to ritually and mimetically bridge the yawning gap between *phōnē* (sound)

---

[71] (1969: 198–9); see Plutarch, who associates the Muses with cosmic regions; Plut. *Quaes. Conv.* 9, 4.3.745a–c.

[72] See Calame (1983: 467f).

and word. This could also, perhaps, explain why in the literary period the spellbinding means of poetic-song transmission of *alētheia* would become open to challenge (as in Plato) for constructing its own *kosmos* as a *muthos*.[73]

Finally, the particular context for this 'proto-institution' of poetic-song transmission, which is another form of the transmission of *aletheic* tradition in more general terms, remains to be clarified.[74] When we meet the Muses in the mid to late archaic and classical periods, it ought to be kept in mind that the earlier tradition(s) has been challenged and reshaped. Calame (1977), in a remarkable study of the institution of the chorus, has shown that the social role of the lyric chorus is clearly comparable to an initiation ritual. We could speculate that the Muses are the ritual and worship practice of such an initiation into the acoustic image of the *kosmos* imitated in the voice, an image which, in the classical period, undergoes further transition during the emergence of prose. The wide variety of female mythical groups, such as the Nymphs, the Nereids, the Emathides, the Charites, the Amazonides and so forth, has already been noted. It is worth emphasising once more, though, that they were choral collectives (Calame 1977: 30), suggesting that the Muses must have borrowed from these earlier traditions and could have been collectives themselves. Accordingly, in Pindar's Fifth *Nemean*, Apollo conducts the singing of the Muses, who form a chorus (ἄειδ' ὁ χορός)[75] and sing παντοίων νόμων (various 'songs' – *nómōn*; to which I turn in more detail below; ibid. 50).[76]

These predominantly female choruses are, at times, depicted as being in musical competition with each other

---

[73] See Baxter (1992).
[74] It is worth noting the obvious fact that the transmission of tradition was by its nature conservative and, therefore, its protection by the divine Muses became, perhaps, a necessary personification following the logic of earlier personifications in cult worship.
[75] See also the description in Hes. *Th.* 7f: χορούς ἐνεποιήσαντο καλούς.
[76] If the *choros* (chorus) of the tragic plays was – well through the classical period – the central kernel of a tragedy's structure and performance, it is in this sense also the literary period's highest *mousikē paideia* (though, notably, performed by an all-male group of actor-singers). On the chorus, see Webster (1970); Calame (1977); Mullen (1982); Bacon (1994); Wilson (2000); Athanassaki and Bowie (2011); and Peponi (2013).

(Calame 1977: 50).[77] It was noted earlier that the Muses were often called daughters (θύγατρες, *thugatres*), young girls (κόραί, *korai*), virgins (παρθένοι, *parthenoi*), indicating their choral community as one of adolescent girls performing an initiation rite, possibly imitating earlier female collective deities, such as the Nymphs.[78] The role of the Muses as a chorus of singers could be understood as the ritual of a divine chorus that initiates the dance–song (Calame 1997: 52).[79] The poet, later on, could be said to act as an instructor, led himself/herself by the invocation of the Muse(s), acting as the initiator (conductor) giving the tonal direction to the song of the chorus.[80] If, as Calame has shown, the ritual activity of adolescent girls in the lyric chorus is entirely comparable to the institution of the earlier rituals of tribal initiation (1997: 262), then it is possible to suggest that the choral Muses are a mythical/religious image of the ritual of social initiation or instruction.[81] In this light, the close relation of the Muses with cult practices further exemplifies the relation between ritual, *mousikē* and social ordering (as well as the experience of creativity and expression more widely). *Mousikē* was the primary means for the ritual transmission (and later 'education') of social norms, mythological and religious authority or

[77] See Eur. *I.A.* 1054ff; Pind. *P.* 9.112f.
[78] See Pind. *Pae.* 7b.15–17, who describes *Mnēmosunē* as such; see, further, Jeanmaire (1939); Eliade (1958); Cohen (1964); Brelich (1969); Popp (1969); Calame (1977); Chirassi-Colombo (1979); Foley (1981); Loraux (1981); Sourvinou-Inwood (1988); Dowden (1989); Lonsdale (1993); Zweig (1999); Ingalls (2000); and Dillon (2002).
[79] Calame cites Stesichorus, who describes the Muse as ἀρχεσίμολπος (*archesimolpos*; μόλπη, *molpē*), 'initiator of the song and the dance' in Stes. fr. 250P, cited by Ath. 5.180e. On the relation between choral performance, competition and ritual rites (initiation), see Calame (1997: 89–206); and the earlier study by Lonsdale (1993: 169–205). The origins of such choral performance may be Cretan, see Hom. *Il.* 18.590ff.
[80] See Calame (1997: 230), citing Alcm. fr. 26P[= 90C]; fr. 14(a)P[= 4C] and fr. 27P[= 84C].
[81] In this regard, there may have been a possible early relation between songs composed for female choruses, which eventually became known as the *Partheneia* (performed in 'coming of age' ceremonies), and which barely survive in the fragments of Alcman and Pindar (Ps. Plut. *Mus.* 17, 1136f); Calame (1977) suggests, inter alia, that the term *Partheneion* is of late coinage. Virgin songs are mentioned in Hom. *Il.* 16.180–3; and *Od.* 6.102–8, 154–7.

patrimony, and in turn, for adolescent girls in particular, the sacred transition from adolescence to maturity (ibid. 261–2). The relationship between the Muses, *mousikē* and ritual initiation should not, then, be perceived as 'intellectual', 'symbolic' or 'metaphoric' (a relationship that perhaps reached its peak, with Orphic influence, during the fifth century BC; Hardie 2004: 13–14), but as dynamically immanent in the musical experience of the divine cosmic sound in the transmission, and *astheneia*, of the mortal voice.[82]

4. *Harmonia*

The role of the divine musical instruments should not be underestimated. In the Homeric *Hymn to Hermes*, for example, the lyre is clearly attested as such, indicating an archaic, but also possibly a pre-archaic, tradition of pre-poetic cult practices. This may also be one of the key stratums upon which mythology places Orpheus of Thrace in the early heroic age, as the celebrated singer (only appearing in literary evidence in the sixth century BC) who utilised his magical lyre to charm animals, vegetables and rivers (Kern 1922).[83] The articulation of sound was, in this sense, the mimetic – relational – articulation of the divine domain and sacred life. This may be the ground upon which, later, the quintessential Greek notion of *harmonia* over all aspects of living found its roots. The word *harmonia*, John C. Franklin has shown, may have an Indo-European background (2002), but, in any case, it is not attested in the sense of tuning or scale before the sixth century.[84] Franklin notes the early archaic links between the lyre, the bow and *mousikē* in epic (e.g. *Od.*

---

[82] Athenian philosophy schools would conduct their learning under the cult of the divine Muses; see Hardie (2004: 15). *Sophia* was associated with the Muses at least since Pindar (ibid. 24); while, crucially, melic and elegiac poets referred to poetry by the term *sophia*. On the Orphic influence, see Graf (1974).

[83] On Orpheus, see the seminal studies by Graf (1974; 1995); see also, Linforth (1941); Guthrie ([1952] 1991); West (1983); Segal (1989b); Henry (1992); and Parker (1995: 483–510). As to the chronology and the myth of Orpheus, see Warden (1982).

[84] Unless the implied reference in Sappho is considered to be such; fr. 70.9–11 [Voigt], from the seventh century BC; see, also, Franklin (2003: 302, n. 11).

21.406–11), as well as in Heraclitus (22B51 [DK]; Franklin 2002: 17–18). The link between the instrument and the ordering of life is, thus, prevalent in a range of practices, from (musical) purification to initiatory and communal formation and regeneration.

A musical instrument is an instrument for mimetically conducting the *kosmos*. If there is 'mystery' to the song, it is only in the ritual of the song's mimetic performance of ordering and restoration.[85] This may be the early basis for Aristotle's invocation of the notion of *harmonia* in a political-ethical ideal form (*Eth. Nic.* 1131a–4b);[86] Plato, too, bases upon it his utopian polis, whereby *harmonia* is a limit as much as a foundation of unity and order. Earlier, though, *harmonia* is an infinite (circular) consonance, an articulation of cosmic sound, the 'hidden' attunement that can still be heard in Heraclitus.[87] It is this *harmonia*, a circular tensional system of ordering the *kosmos*, that will later be broken down to intervals in succession by Pythagoras and Aristotle (with traces of this already, perhaps, in the pre-Socratics), in order to reorganise the way in which the *archē* of music and cosmic order were to be thought of. In other words, earlier, *harmonia* may be the composite result of the transmission of sound in its mimetic juxtaposition with the *kosmos*.[88] Harmony was not a matter of giving shape to *chaos*, in the sense of its quantifiable (geometric or dynamic) measurement and limitation, but of hearing the *chaosmos* and annunciating it in the first place. Thus, it could be better understood why *mousikē* eventually became the great political and *ēthos*-forming educator, as well as a technical episteme uniting mathematics and philosophy, among other things. Walter F. Otto writes:

[85] Plut. *Agis* 799f; Ps. Plut. *Mus.* 1134b, 1146bc; see further, Franklin (2002), with further references; the earlier, Burkert ([1984] 1992: 42 and 16), as well as Gostoli (1988). On the 'mystery' of the lyre, see *Anth. Pal.* 2.111–16.

[86] On *mousikē* and *paideia*, see Arist. *Pol.* 8, 5.1340a18–40, where *mousikē* tends to *ēthos* and the soul.

[87] See Milani (2007); Mittica (2015: 30) refers to Milani and discusses *harmonia*. See the essential study by Wersinger (2008); also, Franklin (2002); and Barker (1978a; 1978b; 2007). In the *Tim.* 35b–6b, Plato gave music universal philosophical significance as the articulation of the World-Soul, in direct relation to mathematics and musical scales.

[88] On the influential Pythagorean development of *harmonia* beyond the Greeks, see the wonderful study by Heller-Roazen (2011).

music is thus the great educator, the source and symbol of all order in the world and in the life of mankind. Apollo the musician is identical with the founder of the ordinances, identical with him who knows what is right, what is necessary, what is to be. In this accuracy of the god's aim Hölderlin could still recognize the archer . . . (1954: 77)

Eventually, the centrality of *mousikē* and the instruments acquired an even wider political and philosophical significance (Franklin 2006). Lukas Richter has suggested that this later understanding of *harmonia* could be rooted in the *cosmopoietic* microcosm of a living *harmonia*, within which the human body and soul are, first, consonant songs (1999: 289–306). It is in this sense that one can hear anew Nietzsche's musings when, in *The Birth of Tragedy*, he writes that in (Dionysian) music's inmost kernel we hear 'the roaring desire for existence pouring from [the heart chamber of the world will] into all the veins of the world, as a thundering current, or as the gentlest brook, dissolving into mist' (1967: 21). *Mousikē* is the continuous *genesis* (to paraphrase Aristotle) of the *kosmos* and the mimetic practice of *mousikē*, as a result, can only be a continuous activity of regeneration.

Such *cosmopoiesis* needs to be understood in the particular human relation to *mousikē*, that is language as such. Levin's reflections on the nature of *mousikē* (2009) are attentive to the significance of the Greek understanding of the experience of *phōnē*/sound in this sense (the continuous movement of the aether to the ear).[89] In the classical period one can hear, perhaps, now with another ear, Aristotle's statement that

ἡ δὲ φωνὴ ψόφος τίς ἐστιν ἐμψύχου· τῶν γὰρ ἀψύχων οὐθὲν φωνεῖ, ἀλλὰ καθ' ὁμοιότητα λέγεται φωνεῖν, οἷον αὐλὸς καὶ λύρα καὶ ὅσα ἄλλα τῶν ἀψύχων ἀπότασιν ἔχει καὶ μέλος καὶ διάλεκτον. ἔοικε γάρ, ὅτι καὶ ἡ φωνὴ ταῦτ' ἔχει. (*De anima* 420b5–6)

In translation:

---

[89] For Aristoxenus, the primary matter that harmonics study is the movement (*kinesis*) of the voice into pitch; see Barker (1989: 119–84), with reference to Book 1.

phōnē is a living sound that is met in living beings, and that all inanimate objects, such as the *aulos* and the *lura* [instruments], can only [are built to] have *phōnē* by imitation; and all those inanimate things that are said to have *melos* and *ekphrasis* [*melos* and expression/enunciation] can be said to have a *phōnē*, [only] because *phōnē* has those capacities [elements].

Indeed, as Flora R. Levin writes, 'That this was so is because the ancient Greek language was itself a form of melodious expression' (2009: xiii). Similarly, Aristoxenus of Taras (Tarentum, southern Italy), the most famous musical theorist of the classical period and beyond, described everyday speech as akin to, though not identical with, a *melos* (a song/melody; ibid. xiv, n. 1).

We have already seen how the relation between variable accent (which itself was musical, prosodiac – προσᾴδεται, *prosadetai*) and semantic meaning was commonplace and crucial to the Greek experience (i.e. *nómos* and *nomós*).[90] If the Greeks developed, with Pythagoras and Aristoxenus, an acoustical *theory* of *mousikē*, this was not due to a lack of an essentially acoustic (musical) experience of life and language, but in order to reshape its principles and paideutic ordering. In a remarkable study conducted during the late 1950s, the lucid Greek musicologist, historian of the Greek language, pianist and engineer Thrasybulos Georgiades was able to show that the essence of every (poetic) act was broadly musical for the Greeks, not in the sense of a work, or an object of work, but as a cosmic activity at play, where no distinction is made between 'language' and *mousikē* (1982: 134). What was determined phonetically in the 'Greek language' early on was identifiable as a determined sound, which was in itself systematised towards the *mimēsis* of the ordering forces of the *kosmos*. As Johannes Lohmann has shown, for instance, the *stoicheion*, that is, a letter matched to a measure of sound, does not just signify an alphabetic sound determination but, primarily, the shadows cast by the solar *gnomon* at different hours (1970: 4–5).[91]

---

[90] Stanford (1967) has illustrated thousands of such variations in Greek.

[91] See also Koller (1955); on Anaximander as the first creator of a *gnomon*, see Diog. Laert. 2.1.7.

Mousikē (in the non-onomastic sound) coexisted with the onomastic word (and the two co-inhabit the verse). Thus, *mousikē*, because of its *cosmopoietic* manner, could not be altered by independent musical-rhythmic setting: 'The rhythmic principle of antiquity is based not on the distinction between the organisation of time (the measure, system of accents) and its filling in (with various note values) but rather on intrinsically filled-in time' (Georgiades 1982: 4–5). Unlike modern Western languages, which can set a verse to music in a number of different ways, Georgiades explains, 'the Greek word's syllables could neither be extended or abbreviated, but were perceived as inflexible elements' (ibid. 4) – they were either long or short. Which is to say that their rhythm did not conform to a pre-existing pattern in a predetermined system of time (i.e. measurement of time), but simply to the quantity of duration. This quantitative rhythm was determined 'by the language; it was a characteristic of the Greek language [up until the fourth century BC]' (ibid. 5). The Greek word *phōnē* indicates in itself both the voice and the acoustic phenomenon, to the point that the phenomenon is in fact a *phonemenon*, a rhythmic movement (*kinēsis*) of the *phōnē*.[92] Such a movement is mimetic, not in the sense of representing something, but in the sense of making something appear in its (poietic) existence (Koller 1954). Everything lies in the imitation, in one regard, in voicing, and so one finds *phōnē* in the sound of the world (Pl. *Phileb.* 17b). The orbit–song–dance of one's soul and body, like the orbit of the stars, the song of the rivers and so forth, is *phonological*. The philosophers will, for instance, think of the voice (*phōnē*) in its physical sense as breath (*pneuma*), impelled from the mind through the mouth, and, physiologically, as a shock propagated by the aether through the ears and brain and blood to the soul.[93] It is worth noting that the Muse called *Mnēmosunē* is described as a breath (ἄνασσαν, *anassan*) in the Orphic *Hymn to Mnēmosunē* [Kern] at 1. To be concordant with the world is the acoustic experience of adhering to the cosmic *harmonia* (Pl. *Tim.* 47b–e);

[92] See Giordano (1999); and Gera (2003).
[93] The intricate link, often implied, between the soul (psyche) and learning, as much as that between rhetoric, philosophy and poetry, is frequent in Greek thought (from Plato and Aristotle to Hellenistic poetics).

thus, in order to show the cosmic significance of anything, it was best to do so in *mousikē* (Pl. *Rep.* 530d–1d). *Harmonia* is generative-mimetic, closer to a cosmic dance than to a system of signification. It may be that, early on, (melic) *logos* and *mousikē* are indistinguishable (and, still, in Plato never strictly separable).[94] Therefore, as Koller (1963) has shown, though drawing particularly on later classical to second century BC sources, the ordinary everyday language of the early Greeks remained understood as based on rhythmic and tonal forms that were matched to the melodic compositions.[95] 'Being', one could say, for the early Greeks, is not only 'said in many ways', but is *rhythmopoietic*. The *kosmos*, in this sense, has an acoustic-melic signature which was heard in everyday speech, or *mousikē*.[96]

The threshold of indistinction between language, poetry, song, dance and *alētheia* can be observed vividly in both ordinary speech and in *mousikē*, to the extent that *mimēsis* is, in fact, an indication of the experience of language as much as of the experience of living (including, later, the root perhaps for that Greek modality of the living-song that is the tragedy, which Aristotle famously defined as a *mimēsis praxeōs*; *Poet.* 6.1449b24), namely, as essentially visual and acoustic (until, perhaps, the time of Euripides).[97] Language as an experience, is, in this manner, inseparable from the *nomós* (arrangement and song) of ritual action. If ordinary everyday speech was

---

[94] See Nef (1919); and Georgiadis (1949).
[95] *Phōnē* is understood as instrumental or vocal. For Koller, if ordinary language (*eggramatos phōnē*) was produced through *rhēma, onoma, sullabai* and *grammata*, melodic arrangement (tonal *phōnē, emmelēs phōnē*) was correspondingly produced through the combination of *sustēmata, diastēmata* (interval flows) and *phthoghoi* (audible sounds); Koller (1955). For Koller, the two are related and he adds a third stratum, which is the metric poetic (*poiēma*) composition that is produced by the combination of *rhuthmos, sullabai* and the *dunameis* of the *stoicheia*; Koller (1955); see Bennett (2016), for a discussion. On the relation between prosody and linguistic expression, see Devine and Stephens (1994).
[96] On the complex relationship between the divine gift of speech and the epic, see Johnstone (2009). On the divine voice and its relation to the voice of mortals, see Lazzeroni (1957); and Détienne and Hamonic (1995).
[97] See also his view on melodies as the imitations of *ēthos*-dispositions, *Pol.* 1340a18–40. That such imitations entailed, early on, a certain magical character is repeated in Pl. *L.* 659e.

itself doxastic, song and hymn-prefaced poetry, in turn, had a hieratic function as *alētheia*-bearing (Georgiades 1958: 41f). This may be the primary sense of the widespread use in antiquity of the verb *deiknumi* (*deixis*: to show, to indicate, to reveal): to bring forth song, hymn or *melos*. Such an act of indication could be directly related to the Muses, as, perhaps, in Alcman 59b3 [Davies = 149 Calame]: ἔδειξε Μωσᾶν δῶρον ('indicate [*edeixe*] this gift of the Muses').[98] Perhaps, then, my own speculation is also meaningful amidst the numerous hints that, for the Greeks, the arrangement of *mousikē* had *cosmopoietic* power. The indication of the phenomenon was the *phonemenon* of the *kosmos*: its *alētheia* in/is song.

5. *Mousikos nómos*

At some uncertain point during the archaic period, novel musical intonation conventions developed,[99] perhaps linked to the evolution of the musical *melos* (μέλος) along with the development of the performance of epic poetry (though the latter was not, properly, sung).[100] One of the most famous musicians of the seventh century BC, Terpandros (Terpander),[101] is described as having sung the Homeric epic with the aid of new *citharodic nómoi*, which he named as such, whereby, according to a certain new lyric *nómos* (*kata nómon*), he would wrap melodies around the verses.[102] What was the importance of this *nómos*-song as it acquired a new technical

---

[98] See also Ael. Arist. *Or.* 3. 620 [Lenz-Behr]: μουσικὰν ὀρθὰν ἐπιδεικνυμένου [*mousikan orthan epideiknumenou*].

[99] See West (1992: 214–17 and 327–85).

[100] How epic poetry was sung by the *rhapsōdoi* is discussed in detail by Nagy (2002).

[101] Terpandros (Τέρπανδρος, Terpander; c.712–c.645 BC) is said to have been born in ancient Antissa on the Greek island of Lesbos and to have been active in Sparta, Lydia and Delphi. His fame extends further throughout the classical period as he is favourably mentioned by, for instance, Plutarch and Pindar; see, Pind. *Eulogies*, 125–6; Gostoli (1990); also, Heraclides of Pontus of the fourth century BC, in fr. 157 [Wehrli 1969]; Ath. 14.635e; on Heraclides, see Grieser (1937: 46); van Groningen (1955); Barker (1984: 211, n. 42); and Ercoles (2014).

[102] Heraclid. Pont. fr. 157 [= Ps. Plut. *Mus.* 1132c]. The parts of the citharodic *nómos* as defined by Terpander are: ἀρχά ('beginning'), μεταρχά ('after-beginning'), κατατροπά ('down-turn'), μετακατατροπά ('after-

significance? It is worth looking into the 'musical' uses of *nómos* in order to appreciate its particular sense and potential relations with the examined uses and the wider family of words that I have been investigating throughout this book (including the question of whether this *nómos* can be linked to the sense of *nómos*-'law', or 'rule'). It is possible, even if in a speculative manner, that the close pattern between speech and song or melody, referred to earlier, may have been the elemental fertile ground upon which the specific musical *nómos* was experienced.

It is useful to try to gather as many preliminary definitional elements to the *nómos* as possible.[103] Thomas J. Mathiesen calls *nómos* 'the most intriguing' of all the *musicopoietic* forms of ancient Greek music (1999: 58),[104] and he adds that the *nómos* had 'great complexity' and was associated in particular with 'virtuoso performers' (ibid.). For the purposes of attempting to understand the musical *nómos* in a schematic way, he also identifies four types (following the four classes of competition in religious festivals): two accompanied by a *kithara* or an *aulos* and another two that were solo performances (ibid. 59): on the one hand νόμοι κιθαρῳδικοί [*nómoi kitharōdikoi*] and αὐλῳδικοί [*nómoi aulōdikoi*], and on the other νόμοι κιθαριστικοί [*nómoi kitharistikoi*] and αὐλητικοί [*nómoi aulētikoi*].[105] The difficulty remains, however, that as regards the archaic period, during which significant innovation is said to have taken place, the evidence is limited, while what we can learn from the classical period (which often refers back to the archaic past of *mousikē*) we encounter more often than not in fragmented or distorted accounts. We do know, nonetheless, that the archaic musical traditions, at least in part, did survive during the classical epoch and so,

---

down-turn'), ὀμφαλός ('centre or navel'), σφραγίς ('seal'), ἐπιλογός ('conclusion'); Poll. *Onom.* 4.66 = Terp. *test.* 39 [Gostoli 1990].

[103] For an extensive description, see Barker (1984; especially App. A).

[104] For a discussion and evidence about the *nómos*, see Crusius (1888); Wilamowitz-Moellendorff (1903: 83–105); Del Grande (1932); Grieser (1937); Fleming 1977; Barker (1984: 249–55); Nagy (1990b); and Hordern (2002: 15–32). For a recent detailed engagement with the ancient Greek modes and scales, see West (1992: 160–89); on the linguistic and etymological analysis, see Laroche (1949: 166–71).

[105] See Laroche (1949: 167), who refers to the *Schol.* to Aristoph. *Eq.* 9.

from Plato to Aristoxenus, we can still hear the *mousikē* of the past, as could they. Irrespective of this, it would be mistaken to expect a neat schema of the archaic *nómos*, or to imagine an over-systematised way of understanding the conception and practising of the musical *nómoi* (Barker 1984: 249–55). *Nómos* as a musical tune that can be conventionally formed, while open to local variation, may approximate to the oral customary variation among, for example, partly isolated geographical regions and *poleis*, in the 'experience of language' as such.[106]

For Max Pohlenz, since 'time immemorial' the word *nomós* was the name of a basic musical form to which a composer and performer had to conform ([1948] 1965: 334).[107] Gagarin notes that the word *nomós* entailed a 'special musical use . . . for a "tune" as the "customary intonation of certain words"' evidenced as early as in the *Homeric Hymn to Apollo* (at 20: νομός [. . .] ᾠδῆς, *nomós ōdēs*; Her. I.24; 2008: 34).[108] Here, the sense of *nomós* is that of hymn-song, conventionally estab-

---

[106] See West (1992: 215–17); and, earlier, Grieser (1937).
[107] On the *nómoi*, see Monroe (1894); Grieser (1937); Chailley (1956); Bartol (1998); Almazova (2001; 2014a; 2014b); Firinu (2009); and Pöhlmann (2010–11).
[108] The accent on *nomos* is disputed, while earlier scholars have rendered the term in the plural (*nómoi*). Many scholars suggest that the *nómos* is a 'literary development of a cultic "hymn"'; Fleming (1977: 223, n. 4), with further references. A possible root may be the Homeric Hymn, or an earlier form. Rocconi has noted the interchangeable use of *nómos* and *humnos* to mean '*harmonia*', that is, 'attunement, musical scale' (2016: 75); she also refers to the dithyrambographer Telestes of Selinus (fifth–fourth century BC), fr. 810[*PMG*]: πρῶτοι παρὰ κρατῆρας Ἑ ἄνων ἐν αὐλοῖς | συνοπαδοὶ Πέλοπος Ματρὸς ὀρείας | Φρύγιον ἄεισαν νόμον· | τοὶ δ' ὀξυφώνοις πηκτίδων ψαλμοῖς κρέκον | Λύδιον ὕμνον ('First of all, Greeks, the comrades brave of Pelops, | Sang o'er their wine, in Phrygian melody [*nómon*] | The praises of the mighty Mountain Mother; | But others, striking the shrill strings of the lyre, | Gave forth a Lydian hymn'; [Bohn]; see Rocconi (2016: 74). See, further, Laroche (1949: 167, n. 24). Lastly, it is worth noting that Apollo is occasionally named with the epithet *Nomios* [Νόμιος], god of order, as well as *mousikē*; see Farnell ([1896] 1909: 4.123) and Dowden (2007: 50); this has, in fact, led some scholars to suggest that the root may be pastoral, with some reason; see Duchemin (1960: 87–126); for a critique, see Laroche (1949: 167–71). The personification *Nomios* is used as to other gods as well, for example, with reference to Pan in the Orphic *Hymn to Pan*, 1, with a clear pastoral sense.

lished as part of ritual worship-singing in praise of Apollo. Gagarin, in this regard, discerns that musical *nómoi* referred to either 'melodies' (*nómoi*) or general 'rules', particularly relevant to musical education (ibid. 35). Here, then, the early ritual context of the birth of *nómos* in the musical uses appears possible and, in fact, occurs in choral performances accompanied by the *aulos* or the *kithara* (Procl. 32q–33, prior to the reforms of Chrysothemis). One of the great classicists of modern times, Martin L. West, proposed that the word probably involved two main uses. On the one hand there was a technical use that 'must have implied a particular rhythm or sequence of rhythms' (1992: 242). Its scope of application was narrow: 'It referred to a specific, nameable melody, or a composition in its melodic aspect, sung or played in a formal setting in which it was conventionally appropriate: a sacrifice, a funeral, a festival competition, or a professional display.' West adds: 'It was not, initially, genre-specific: the word could be applied to melodies accompanying hexameter poetry, elegy, iambic verse, lyric narrative, epinicians, dithyrambs' (1992: 216).[109] On the other hand, we have a non-technical use, favourable to the poets with regard to 'any melody with a definite identity or character: the songs of different birds, a mourner's song, the various songs in a particular musician's repertory, and so forth' (ibid.).[110] Both uses are of interest, if only for the reason that it is most likely that they could not have developed without regard to each other, even if they each adopt different roles at different periods.

It should be noted that there is hardly any substantial evidence of the word *nómos* in its musical sense(s) before the fifth century BC (Barker 1984, I: 254). Whether this evidence can be considered substantial depends on whether one expects a systematised technical use or not. As will be seen, there were music-related uses of *nomos* in the archaic period, even if their exact use may remain obscure, yet this hardly amounts to 'no evidence' whatsoever. We do not know how the archaic *nómoi* were composed or organised, yet eventually

---

[109] On the dithyrambs, see Pickard-Cambridge ([1927] 1962: 112–24).

[110] For instance, West (1992: 215–16) refers to: Pind. *N.* 5. 35; fr. 35c; Aesch. *Supp.* 69; *Ag.* 1142, 1153; *Choe.* 424, 822; Ps. Aesch. *P.V.* 575; Soph. fr. 245; 463; 861; Eur. *Hec.* 685 and *Hel.* 188.

nómoi (music 'modes/rules') became extended compositions, organised in several sections. In the time of the *mousikoi*, their complexity and virtuosity became renowned.[111] John Landels (1999: 5) writes: 'The compositions they wrote and performed were called "kithara-singers' *nomoi*"; this was the genre in which the most famous innovators made their mark, and to excel in [them] was their ultimate ambition.' He adds: 'The woodwind players were not left out either; they performed solos which were known as "Aulis-players' *nómoi*" – extended instrumental pieces with a number of "movements", some of which seem to have been in the nature of programmatic music.'[112] One famous example (the *Puthikos nómos*) told, in five sections, 'the story of the victory of Apollo over the mythical monster called the Python at Delphi' (1999: 5).[113]

Perhaps we will never know the exact development of the (collective) experience of poem-singing and of *mousikē* more generally, but what can be appreciated is that performance was recreative/regenerative (Nagy 1996).[114] As we shall see, the variation of the *nómoi* appears to have been subject to regional (melodic) traditions, while recognition of a conventional form coexisted with such differentiation. In this sense, *nomos*, if the etymological link to 'allotment/distribution-sharing' is correct, could also refer to the conventional form of a melodic practice (i.e. its melodic distribution), while at the same time being susceptible to regional conventions of interpretation (similar, in fact, to non-musical *nómoi*).[115] The regional variation is notable with regard also to the way in

---

[111] See Lippman (1975: 78–86); Strab. 9.13.10.

[112] See Mathiesen, who writes that '*Nomoi* for solo instruments were a later development, undoubtedly reflecting the rising prominence of a professional class of artists. The Puthic [*Puthikos*] Nomos . . . is an example of the third type, the auletic *nomos*, an extended composition for solo *aulos* in which the music itself is highly descriptive or evocative. Auletic *nomoi* and a fourth type, the kitharistic *nomos*, were introduced at the Pythian Games in 586 and 558 BCE' (1999: 59). On the *Puthikos*, see Kolk (1963: 41–7); West (1992: 212–14); D'Angour (1997: 338); and Mathiesen (1999: 64 and 178).

[113] To the various types of *nómoi* I turn below.

[114] On the recreative *dunamis* of *mimēsis*, see Koller (1954).

[115] See Mathiesen (1999: 59ff.).

which *mousikē* was said to affect the *ēthos* in a particular polis, both in the sense of education and also, widely, in the sense of influencing the audience's way of being (Gostoli 1988: 231–7).

It is often said that the *nómoi* were 'conservative in their tradition' (Fleming 1977: 223). Yet we do not know enough to be able to ascertain whether the earlier (archaic) *nómoi* were considered to be strict forms. 'Strictness' in modality, given their regional and functional variation, could not mean lack of adaptability and innovation (for instance, shifting *harmoniai* within a *nómos*).[116] Nor did the *nómos* encompass the ways of *mousikē* as a whole, whether formalised or otherwise.[117] The term *nómos* was probably used to refer to an extensive range of musical performances, which were not necessarily as strict early on as they later became. To get a sense of this, it is worthwhile to turn to the infamous late-antiquity (most probably neo-Platonic) definition of *nómos* at the start of the sixth chapter (1133 B) of the Ps. Plutarchean treatise *On Music*.[118] The key passage is as follows:

Τὸ δ' ὅλον ἡ μὲν κατὰ Τέρπανδρον κιθαρῳδία καὶ μέχρι τῆς Φρύνιδος ἡλικίας παντελῶς ἁπλῆ τις οὖσα διετέλει· οὐ γὰρ ἐξῆν τὸ παλαιὸν οὕτω ποιεῖσθαι τὰς κιθαρῳδίας ὡς νῦν, οὐδὲ μεταφέρειν τὰς ἁρμονίας καὶ τοὺς ῥυθμούς· ἐν γὰρ τοῖς νόμοις ἑκάστῳ διετήρουν τὴν οἰκείαν τάσιν. διὸ καὶ ταύτην <τὴν> ἐπωνυμίαν εἶχον· νόμοι γὰρ προσηγορεύθησαν, ἐπειδὴ οὐκ ἐξῆν παραβῆναι <τὸ> καθ' ἕκαστον νενομισμένον εἶδος τῆς τάσεως.[119]

---

[116] See Ps. Plut. *Mus.* 1134c; Procl. *Chre. Ap.* in Phot. *Bibl.* 320b12–18. In Proclus, we also meet reference to the possible Cretan origin of the musical *nómos*, in *ap.* Phot. *Bibl.* 320 [Bekker]; see also Swindler (1913: 57) and Rutherford (1995). Incidentally, ancient Greek harmonics develop into a 'science' of the arrangement of notes in scales and with regard to their relationships; on this, see West (1992: 5).

[117] This is still attested in the classical period, in, for instance, Pl. *L.* 700a–b, where the *nómoi* are described as 'another' type of song, among others; while Plato refers to how the form or rule of the *nómos* was eventually fixed and was to be followed strictly.

[118] See, further, Weil and Reinach (1900); Winnington-Ingram (1936); Lassèrre (1954); Gamberini (1979); Gostoli (1982); Comotti (1994); and Pöhlmann (2011).

[119] Bartol's translation is as follows: 'Some compositions belonging to citharodic poetry have been called *nomoi*, since the τάσις, which was

375

In this passage, with particular reference to Terpander's older (archaic) *kitharōdia* (citharody) and its differentiation from the new *kitharōdia*, within which lies a particular type of *kitharōdia*, that of *nómos*, *nómos* is described as a form that was 'seeking to preserve traditional, melodious as well as rhythmical, patterns' (Bartol 1998: 302). As Thomas J. Fleming notes, *nómos* 'in some senses . . . is not much different from *harmonia* or *melos*' (1977: 222). Yet as Krystyna Bartol explains,

> it would appear that the tendency to maintain modes and rhythms that were established for each *nomos* was nothing else than compliance with the appropriate (οἰκεία) τάσις of a *nomos*. This τάσις, as can be assumed from the text, consists of ἀρμονία and ῥυθμός. It concerns therefore not the subject-matter but the form of a *nomos*. It seems that in this definition of *nomos* the adjective οἰκεία, qualifying the noun τάσις, is of crucial importance. Its use with reference to the melodic structure of the *nomos* allows us to assume that this structure might have been strictly subordinated to the *nomos*' function, since the word οἰκεῖος in literary criticism, from Plato onwards, denotes first of all the appropriateness of the form of an artistic work for the function, which this work intends to perform towards its addressees. (1998: 305)

It was the manner, linked in one sense to the *ēthos*, that was adequate in terms of its designated function or occasion which was to be 'performed' in a particular way.[120] In her conclusion, Bartol writes:

> the point of Ps.-Plutarch's definition of *nomos* is expressed by the . . . οἰκείαν τάσιν, which emphasises that the essence of this *citharodic* genre [*nomos*] was its exceptional immu-

observed throughout these compositions, was appropriate for their functions. This observance, respecting form as well as functions, caused *nomoi* to become conservative in respect to the form. And this became the main principle, the law (νόμος) according to which *nomoi* were composed and delivered' (1998: 306).

[120] See Ps. Plut. *Mus.* 33, 1143B; and the discussion in Bartol (1998: 305), with further references; on *ēthos* and *mousikē*, see Anderson (1966).

tability of the traditional emotional content of particular *nomoi*. This was retained by using certain formal devices concerning the rules of their composition. (1998: 306)

The 'strictness', then, or the conformity to the form or rule of a *nómos*, entailed the observance of a particular compositional function, which, each time, was due to a determined τάσις (*tasis*). Meanwhile, the early *nómoi* appear to have been semi-structured modal compositions (Grieser 1937). Nonetheless, apart from the fact that the *nómos* eventually acquired particular forms, Plutarch's definition does not provide a direct explanation as to how it came to be called *nómos* in the first place.[121] Could it be because it was obvious to his audience that *nómos* was a *nómos mousikos*, a 'way of song'?

Before I continue this exploration of the sense in which *nómos* was used in relation to this particular musical mode, it is worth noting the wide variety of *nómoi* that have been attested. There were many different modalities of *nómoi* (songs and instrumental – mimetic – compositions in a particular 'tune' or 'melody')[122] which were practised between the archaic and the classical period and beyond, which, however, are not easy to classify into neat categories. As seen earlier, an instrumental classification, for example, establishes 'the citharodic, citharistic, aulodic, and auletic *nomoi*' (West 1992: 216).[123] The earliest *nómos*, so far as we can tell, is the kitharodic (for example, Terpander), with the auletic *nómoi* following on

---

[121] For *nómos* as a set-piece, see Ps. Plut. *Mus.* 1133b.

[122] See Pindar, παντοίων νόμων ('songs of all kinds') N. 5.25; and νόμων ἀκούοντες θεόδματον κέλαδον, in fr. 35c. Incidentally, Ps. Aristotle states that because of their mimetic manner, these *nómoi* were astrophic, *Prob.* 19.15 (at 918b13). On Aristotle's views on *mousikē*, with which I cannot engage in this work, see, for example, Depew (1991); and Jones (2012).

[123] See West (1992), for the detailed sources; also, Mathiesen (1999: 58–71). For example, the *citharodic* is attested, here and elsewhere, in Hdt. 1.24.5; Clonas is said to have composed *aulodic nómoi* in Heraclid. Pont. fr. 157 [Wehrli 1969 = Ps. Plut. *Mus.* 3, 1132C], among which note two particular *nómoi* named *Apothetos* (secret) and *Schoinion* (rope-like). It is possible that the elegy may have been originally composed as an aulodic *nómos* (Ἔλεγοι, *Elegoi*); see Ps. Plut. *Mus.* 8; and *Mor.* 1134A. On the classification of the *nómoi*, see Rutherford (1995); and on the early Greek elegy, see Bowie (1986).

later (e.g. Clonas and Ardalus of Troezen).[124] Most, if not all, of these were probably associated with a particular god (e.g. Apollo or Pan),[125] while others are determined by geographic location (e.g. Aeolian or Phrygian).[126] In addition, *nómoi* are identifiable by the composer (νομοποιός, *nomopoios*) who supposedly created them (hence, Terpandrean, Olympian and so forth). Another way of classification is by their function, or the occasion on which they were performed. West notes, for example: '*Kradias* [fig-branch flagellation of scapegoat figure], *Epitymbidios* [funeral], *Elegoi, Iamboi, Kuklios* [dithyrambic], *Komarchios* [starting the revel], *Exodios* [exit of a chorus]' (1992: 216). Still other *nómoi* were named according to their particular rhythm (e.g. *Puthikos*, or *Trochaikos*), or by some other musical feature (e.g. '*Oxys* [high-pitched], *Orthios* [steep], *Kolobos* [truncated], *Polukephalos* [many-headed], *Schoinion* [drawn out like a rope], *Trimelēs* [three-mode], *Tetraoidios* [four-note]' and so forth; ibid.).[127] With such variation in type, instrument and function (along with different ethical effects), as well as customary localised characteristics, it is possible, for West, to emphasise that, while some formal precision is identifiable, variation was 'possibly available' (1992: 217) and in different ways (i.e. rhythmic, modal, lyric, etc.), and especially so when the *nómoi* apparently started to semi-detach from the central worship or ritual functions for which they were originally created.[128]

---

[124] See Del Grande (1923).

[125] West (1992: 216) notes that the *nómos* of Athena was standard during the *Panathinaia*; see also Barker (1990: 50–1); Kotsidu (1991); and Kowalzig (2004).

[126] See Ps. Plut. *Mus.* 1132d; and Ath. 14.625c–6a. For example, the Phrygian mode (*nómos*) was 'appropriate to a range of moods, from cheerful bonhomie or piety to wild excitement or religious frenzy'; West (1992: 180). The Boeotian *nómos* is met with in Soph. fr. 966: Βοιώτιον νόμον (tune, *Boiōtion nómon*; possibly auletic), which had apparently proverbial use to suggest also 'things which are mild at the outset, but become severe or vehement as they go on' [Jebb, III, 124].

[127] For instance, on the *trimelēs* (tri-modal), see Ps. Plut. *Mus.* 1134ab. The *polukephalos nómos* was attributed to Athena, Olympus or Krates; see Mathiesen (1999: 64 and 178); see, further, Schlesinger ([1939] 1970); Barker (1984: 57–8); Clay (1992); Frontisi-Ducroux (1994); and Papadopoulou and Pirenne Delforge (2001).

[128] West (1992: 217) refers to the example of Timotheus' *Persae*, the only, so

For the non-technical uses of the musical *nómos*, I turn once more to the poets and the tragedians.[129] The earliest instance of the word in a supposed musical (probably non-technical)[130] sense is generally accepted to be the phrasing of Alcman's ϝοῖδα δ᾽ ὀρνίχων νόμως | παντῶν ('I know the *nómoi* [*nómōs*] of all kinds of birds'; *PMGF* fr. 40).[131] Alcman appears to relate bird song to human song (alternatively: their 'ways'), implying that each bird has its own *nómos* [way] of singing.[132] Eleonora Rocconi has observed that the musical sense in this fragment 'can only be assumed'. Yet as she adds, another fragment (*PMFG* fr. 39) offers some support, since the poet 'names himself as the "discoverer" of words and melody that put into human language the voices of partridges': ϝέπη τάδε καὶ μέλος Ἀλκμὰν | εὗρε γεγλωσσαμέναν | κακκαβίδων ὄπα συνθέμενος. This may suggest, in a general sense, 'the musical nuance of the term *nomos* also in fr. 40.7' (2016: 73–4). Hence, while the context remains unknown, a musical sense

far, extensive *nómos* fragment that seems to contain substantial metrical variation. On Timotheus' *Persae*, see Ebeling (1925); Longman (1954); Korzeniewski (1974); Cricca (1984; 1985); Janssen (1984); and Hordern (1999; 2002). This may have been the case, also, with the earlier archaic *nómoi*. Pindar's *polukephalos nómos* (κεφαλᾶν πολλᾶν νόμον; *P.* 12.23) may signify melodic variation, as well as its theme: the many-headed serpent (see, also, πάμφωνον μέλος [*pamphōnon melos*] in *P.* 12.19). This may also be, as Rocconi (2016: 75) states, the only technical use in Pindar.

[129] The distinction between technical and non-technical uses remains uncertain, especially in the archaic period. More so, as noted earlier, the distinction between, for example, 'religious' and so-called secular poems is very hard to establish, if at all possible. For instance, a hymn (essentially in praise of the gods in choral performance) is not characterised by any particular metre, or compositional technique to distinguish it from other poetry; see Furley and Bremer (2001).

[130] See Barker (1984: 250).

[131] Alcman was active in Sparta, in the late seventh century BC. References to birds are very common in Alcman and in other poets; for example, Pratinas characterises a bird as ἀδύφωνον (*aduphōnon*, 711 *PMG*); while Pind. *O.* 2.86–8 refers to: παγγλωσσίᾳ κόρακες; for a discussion of these and Alcman more generally, see Calame (1983); Ferrari (2008); and Kousoulini (2013: 429). In Euripides, swans are noted as musical, as, for example, in Eur. *El.* 150ff; and as related to the Muses in *I.T.* 1104ff.

[132] Rocconi (2016) notes the longevity of this particular 'relation', present in Homer (*Od.* 21.406–11) and the Mycenaean period; see Anderson (1994: 4–7); compare Aristoph. *Av.* 1342.

is generally accepted (Heinimann [1945] 1965/1972: 65).[133]
While some, on the basis of the literary evidence, insist that
there is no proof of the (technical) musical sense of *nómos*
before the classical period, the general musical sense of the
poets is entirely possible.

In fact, John Chadwick has not only accepted the 'clear'
musical sense in the Alcman fragment, but also challenged
the conventionally accepted etymological analysis of the
word *nomos* more generally, to ask whether it is not possible to find the musical *nómos* prior to the so-called legal
nómos (in the sense of 'rule' or 'law'; 1996: 206ff), which, at
some level, may be plausible. Chadwick maintained that the
same is true of the *Homeric Hymn to Apollo* (at 20): πάντη γάρ
τοι, Φοῖβε, νόμος βεβλήατ᾽ἀοιδῆς ('for everywhere upon you,
Phoebe, all range of song [*nómos*] has been cast'). The poet's
song 'travels' and so needs to cater for the range of songs
appropriate to all places.[134] The context of singing a hymn
to praise a god aids this reading, though it is worth noting
briefly that in this passage whether the word *nómos* is to be
rendered in the singular or the plural, and more crucially
whether it refers to places of pasturage, or a type of melody,
remains open to question. We have encountered, already,
Hesiod's reference to *nómos* in the *Theogony* at 60: μέλπονται
πάντων τε νόμους καὶ ἤθεα κεδνὰ. We have seen that, for
some, this is the earliest 'legal' sense of *nómos* (= 'laws'), and
yet the only certain thing is that these *nómoi* (most likely not
'laws' in the strict sense, but 'domains' or 'spheres of action')
are sung by the Muses.[135] While I agree with Rocconi (2016)
that the evidence regarding the archaic period is limited and
unclear, and hence may only indicate the more general experience of melody, the use of the word *nómos* in the vicinity of such an experience (Hesiod), or in its very expression
(Alcman), could suggest that the *mousikē* of the early Greeks

---

[133] Heinimann ([1945] 1965/1972: 64ff) argues for the fixity and regularity of
such a *nómos*.
[134] On the wandering poets, see Bowie (2009: 105–36); and Prauscello (2009:
168–94).
[135] For Chadwick, a musical sense of *nómos* preceding that of 'law' remains
possible here (1996: 206ff); in any case, it is probably safer to presume
that the sense of *nómoi* here is not that of 'laws' (perhaps instead approximating to 'customs, ways, conventions').

may have reflected a fundamental genetic relation between the (poetic) word and rhythmic sound. Later, this may be present in Pindar's verse where Muses sing the παντοίων νόμων (*pantoiōn nómōn*, 'all kinds of song'; *N.* 5.21), albeit in a (most probably) non-technical sense.[136]

In addition, the references to *nómos* in a musical sense in the dramatists are worth noting. Suffice it to mention some characteristic instances.[137] In Euripides' *Helen*, at 185–90, we meet the νόμον γοερόν [*nómon goeron*] ('loud woe *nómon*'; expressed here by a Nymph), as well as Hecuba's desperate musical νόμον βακχεῖον, *nómon bakcheion* in *Hec.* 684–7. We have already seen how in Aeschylus' *Agamemnon*, at 150–1, the chorus describes the sacrifice of Iphigenia as a θυσίαν ἑτέραν ἄνομόν τιν', ἄδαιτον ('a sacrifice without song [*anomon*] and feast').[138] In the same play, 'a *nómos* of women' is described at 594 as γυναικείω νόμω (*gunaikeiō nómō*), in relation to a ritual 'female cry' (*lugmos*).[139] Finally, in Sophocles' fr. 861 [Jebb = 407 Dindorf] one reads: Σειρῆνας εἰσαφ<ικόμην> | Φόρκου κόρας, θροοῦντε τούς Ἀιδου νόμους. The Sirens are presented as singing fatal tunes (*nómoi*). While in some cases the dramatists relate the use of *nómos* to the more direct political sense, their common use remains that of a 'localized melodic idiom' (Rocconi 2016: 73 and 75).

For Emmanuel Laroche, the uses of musical *nómos* are

---

[136] See the engaging discussion in Rocconi (2016: 73–4), who refers, also, to the 'uncertain' use in Pindar's *O.* 1, ἱππίω νόμω (*ippiō nómō*), though it ought to be remembered that Pindar was a *mousikos*.

[137] See, for example, Pickard-Cambridge ([1927] 1962); Gould and Lewis (1968); Fleming (1977); Pintacuda (1978); Richter (1983); Herington (1985); Wiles (1990); Prins (1991); West (1999); and Wilson (1999).

[138] See Fleming (1977: 223), who suggests that the reference at this point is possibly to a paean; on which, see Fairbanks (1900); Käppel (1992); also, Lloyd-Jones' primary reading of the musical sense (1953: 46). On 'sacrifice' and the origin of poetry, see Svenbro (1984). See also the possibly musical use in *Ag.* 1142, as to Cassandra's *nómos anomos* (comparable to *eknomos* in *Ag.* 1472–4). In addition, see as to the *thrēnoi*, Aes. *Choe.* (423–4): νόμοις ἰηλεμιστρίας [*nómois hiēlemistrias*]; and, earlier, *Od.* 22.347. Lamentations are chanted, earlier, at *Choe.* 150. In fact, in *Choe.* the Chorus states, at 823, νόμον θήσομεν [*nómon thēsomen*], which has, perhaps, a musical sense, too. On Aeschylus and *mousikē*, see Moutsopoulos (1959a); Haldane (1965); and Prins (1991).

[139] See Segal (1994b).

dual, and in fact he separates two distinct meanings. One use is technical and prevalent in prose, the *nómos*, while the other is 'general and quite vague', used in poetry to signify 'tune sung' (*air chanté*; 1949: 166). According to the evidence of the poets (and later on the philosophers), on which Laroche relies for the most part, it would appear that the rather abstract use (or more specifically the general reference to song) is more ancient. While some would urge caution given the poetic nature of the sources, at the same time, if the *nómos* was originally a hymn and its roots lie there, the poetic sources are not only the most reliable, but also essential. The development of a more fixed technical use of the *nómos* makes sense, too, from within this domain of ritual musical composition and poetic performance.[140] Laroche notes that the *nómos* is, after all, a song (ἄεισμα, *aeisma*; ᾠδή, *ōdē*) characterised by its essential elements: 'the harmony (σύστημα, *sustēma*; ἁρμονία, *harmonia*), the pace or extent (ῥυθμός, *rhuthmos*; μέτρον, *metron*), and finally by the height tone (τάσις, *tasis*; ἀνάτασις, *anatasis*). We know further that the *nómos* was a variety of μέλος [*mēlos*] word, with which *nomos* trades often' (ibid. 169). The variation, then, that marks the definition of *nómos* is that of 'the intervals of the notes', the *melody* (ibid.).[141] The *nómos* is, in this wider sense, musical.

The etymology of the musical use remains rather unclear and, given the limited evidence, will most likely continue to be so. Laroche's meticulous study accepts neither the sup-

---

[140] On early hymns and the emergence of choral song, see Richardson (2011). In hymns, the tradition of myth, divine praise, related practices and ritual meet in a way that is exemplary of their inseparability in a social dynamic context. See, also, the pioneering work of Calame (1977), who emphasises the political role of choral performances; as well as the recent study by Kowalzig (2007), on which I rely here.

[141] The source for this is Pl. *Mus.* 1133c6: Τὸ δ᾽ ὅλον ἡ μὲν κατὰ Τέρπανδρον κιθαρῳδία καὶ μέχρι τῆς Φρύνιδος ἡλικίας παντελῶς ἁπλῆ τις οὖσα διετέλει· οὐ γὰρ ἐξῆν τὸ παλαιὸν οὕτως ποιεῖσθαι τὰς κιθαρῳδίας ὡς νῦν οὐδὲ μεταφέρειν τὰς ἁρμονίας καὶ τοὺς ῥυθμούς· ἐν γὰρ τοῖς νόμοις ἑκάστῳ διετήρουν τὴν οἰκείαν τάσιν. Διὸ καὶ ταύτην [τὴν] ἐπωνυμίαν εἶχον· νόμοι γὰρ προσηγορεύθησαν, ἐπειδὴ οὐκ ἐξῆν παραβῆναι [τὸ] καθ᾽ ἕκαστον νενομισμένον εἶδος τῆς τάσεως. Τὰ γὰρ πρὸς τοὺς θεοὺς ὡς βούλονται ἀφοσιωσάμενοι, ἐξέβαινον εὐθὺς ἐπί τε τὴν Ὁμήρου καὶ τῶν ἄλλων ποίησιν. Δῆλον δὲ τοῦτ᾽ ἐστὶ διὰ τῶν Τερπάνδρου προοιμίων.

posed (by some) pastoral origins (i.e. *Nomios*; though there seems to be some relation) nor the attempts that associate *nómos*, all too readily, with fixity or obligation (*nómos*-law) (1949: 170). In addition, the root that points to a sense of 'distribution' (that, in fact, the ancients themselves attempted to trace, for example, Archytas) is, for Laroche, quite particular to the designated action (i.e. with regard to an effect on the soul; ibid.). Thus, it seems that the original, to an extent technical, use of the *nómos* as a melody (in the same group of early Greek words such as *metron*, *melos* and so forth) signifies a particular 'form' sung, initially probably with the lyre, a 'form' which entails 'the order, the place and the succession of notes' (ibid.). This can suggest that, etymologically, *nómos* relates to the act of 'disposing', 'ordering', or the 'ruling' of something (sung) at least, at first in a non-highly specified manner. The earlier, and possibly primary, semi-technical use then designates a tune sung in a melodic manner, which remained, at the same time, quite abstract; while later it was combined into a more technically determined use which appears to have acquired a certain rigidity (and even to have replaced *melos*), which may itself be related, to some extent, to the gradual use of *nómos* as a 'rule' and eventually 'law'. While Laroche's analysis may, at times, be blurred, its overall reasoning remains fairly consistent at a linguistic analytical level. Thus, with good reason, Laroche insists that 'it [the use of *nómos* as a 'rule' or 'law'] cannot be explained by it [its musical sense and uses]' (ibid. 171), not, at least, with certainty.

If the etymological analysis of *nemein* that relies on 'distribution/sharing' is correct, it may be possible, in one approach, to interpret the musical use of *nómos* rather widely, with regard to the distribution/diffusion of sound and voice, though this remains, in part, merely speculative. In any case, a less delimited approach is probably better. Given the prevalence of *mousikē* in early and later Greek societies, it is possible to speculate that the word was used in a musical sense in a manner comparable to the wide uses I have already examined: that is, with regard to an idiom, a way of being or acting (including singing and dancing), a custom or convention and in some cases a more specified (over time) 'rule/manner' that is proper and that is to be followed. It is thus potent to suggest, if my hypothesis in this work is correct, that these (wide but concrete) uses precede (historically and etymologically) those of *nómos*-'law' encountered in the sixth and fifth centuries BC. While it is not possible to ascertain with absolute certainty whether the stricter ordered-regulatory or the wider (though not 'abstract') customary/idiomatic uses historically came first, or indeed how exactly they relate to each other, the multi-threaded inquiry I have followed allows for an understanding whereby the idiomatic uses were the multi-versal plateau in which the later, more visibly 'juridico-political' (at least to a modern eye) uses were enveloped, or at least parallelised, rather than 'progressively' collapsed.

That in the classical period some (most notably Plato) would, in part polemically, relate the musical use to a 'juridico-political' *nómos* and, indeed, highly effectively (and poetically) so remains testimony to the multi-threaded uses of *nómos and nomós* (indicating the existence of more than a singular 'word'). Hence, this complexity and coexistence of uses, which persists in the later periods, is yet another indicator of the integral multi-threadedness in the expression of Greek ways of living and creating more generally. Like the nightingale (ἀηδόνα, *aēdona*),[142] in Hesiod's *Works and Days*, at 203, the *bios* was *mousikos*. It was sung in many ways, to paraphrase Aristotle, and had a ποικιλόδειρον (*poikilodeiron*, varied) sound. However, in the insistence of the jurists for the origin of *nómos*-'law', the danger is, as ever, to mistake a complex situation for a more familiar one.

6. The early law-givers' song

In Ps. Aristotle's *Problemata* at 919b38–920a2, we read:

Διὰ τί νόμοι καλοῦνται οὓς ᾄδουσιν; ἢ ὅτι πρὶν ἐπίστασθαι γράμματα, ᾖδον τοὺς νόμους, ὅπως μὴ ἐπιλάθωνται, ὥσπερ ἐν Ἀγαθύρσοις ἔτι εἰώθασιν; καὶ τῶν ὑστέρων οὖν ᾠδῶν τὰς πρώτας τὸ αὐτὸ ἐκάλεσαν ὅπερ τὰς πρώτας.

---

[142] It was not uncommon for poets and singers to be called a nightingale; the two words are very close (*aoidos* 'singer' and *aēdon* 'nightingale'); see Nagy (1996: especially ch. 3).

Why are the *nómoi* which are sung so called? Is it because before they could write, they sang their *nómoi* so not to forget them, as they do among the Agathursoi? So they gave the same name to the most important of their later songs that they gave to their first songs.

The passage is unclear. The peripatetic author refers to the *Agathursoi* (a tribe in what is now known as Romania), who apparently sang their *nómoi*. The author does not directly explain why these people sang their *nómoi* and how this related to the Greek experience, though perhaps it is suffi-ciently implied that this is a practice of concern to the Greeks given the open question that initiates the passage, as well as that the explanation somehow lies in the experience of 'law-making' (before writing was introduced) and the song's mnemonic benefit. Now, amidst the mythopoetic remarks and stories with regard to the early Greek 'law-givers', as they are often called, as well as their close relation to poetry (e.g. Solon, Charondas) there are explicit or implicit refer-ences to the role and effect of *mousikē*.[143] This should not come as a surprise when poetry, dance and song (*mousikē*) were so closely intertwined, as were 'law', 'magic' and worship practices (Govaert 1964). What all of them have in common, it seems, is, in one sense, *mousikē* and more generally the social character of their function. Calame has shown that archaic poetry had an inherently social function, in contrast to the contemporary understanding of poetry (1997: 9), and I have maintained the same as to *mousikē*. Indeed, there appears to

---

[143] According to Aristotle, the first 'law-giver' was Onomacritus, a poet (*Pol.* 1274a26). For the unreliability of the biographical sources as to the early 'law-givers', see Szegedy-Maszak (1978: 210ff.). For the purposes of a schematic orientation, despite the absence of precise chronological figures, note that 650 BC is the approximate time of the inscription of Dreros and it is within this time that Lycurgus, law-giver of Sparta (though uncertain) and Zaleucus, law-giver of Locri Epizephyrii, are active. By 621 BC, possibly, Dracon composes his famous laws in Athens, while around the same time Charondas acts as the law-giver of Catana. Solon is active in 594 BC in Athens. The so-called 'code' of Gortyn is placed in 450 BC (though uncertain); and Plato writes the *Laws* in 340 BC; see, Lewis (2007). The 'judicial' officials were, notably, later often called *mnēmones* ('rememberers') or *hieromnēmones* ('sacred rememberers'); see Arist. *Pol.* 1321b, 34–40; and Plut. *Mor* 297e–f.

have been a 'Poet-King', or 'law-giver instructed by poet' model, and the link to poetry (most notably in Solon) coheres with the link to *mousikē*. After all, Crete was famous for its *mousikoi*, who apparently taught the art of 'law-giving' that was linked to the legend of King Minos (Mittica 2015: 37–8).[144]

Some of the important, but not so well-known, early 'law-givers' who were active in the seventh or sixth centuries BC were Charondas of Catana and Zaleukos of Locris, along with the better-known (though probably mythical) Lycurgus of Sparta and Solon of Athens.[145] Biographical information regarding all the early law-givers is unreliable, yet it is widely reported that they all travelled extensively within the range of the Greek *poleis* and beyond, and they are said to have been to Crete (which, as already noted, was considered at the time to be the 'cradle' of 'law-making'; Strab. 10.4.19; Hölkeskamp 1992a: 52).[146] It is important to note that these early law-givers do not call their 'laws' *nómoi*, as they emerge within the 'religious' context of the *themistes* and, thus, early on, we only find the term *thesmoi* instead. George Pelham Shipp (1978: 17) argues that, nonetheless, the laws of Zaleucus and Charondas 'are indeed called *nomoi*', but he does so with reliance on a late source, Aristotle's *Politics* 1319a. More peculiarly, Shipp seems to translate all law-related (in one sense or another) Greek terms with the word *nómos* throughout his study,

---

[144] In the Ps. Pl. *Minos*, 318d, the Cretans are described as having the oldest *nómoi* of the Hellenes. In the *Laws*, King Minos is named as the son of Zeus and Europa and as Zeus' legislator, at 624b (= Paus. 3.2.4). On Minos, see Aris. *Pol.* II. 10.1271.30; Diod. Sic. I.94.23; and Strab. 14. 2.38.762c, who describes Minos as the oldest 'legislator' of the mortals.

[145] For an extensive bibliography and exegesis, see Camassa (1987: 613–56). In this work, I do not engage with the early or later law-givers in any substantial detail; a separate work will examine some of their uses of the term *nómos*, in more detail, including a consideration of Solon's poetry; see Dunbabin (1948: 68–75); Gagarin (1986/1989: ch.3; 2008, ch. 3); Irwin (2005); and Blok and Lardinois (2006).

[146] See Hdt. 1.65.4; Plut. *Lyc.* 4.1; Solon, 2.1; Ps. Pl. *Minos*, 318c–d; Arist. *Pol.* B 1269– 70a and 1274; for a discussion, see Adcock (1927: 95–109) and Camassa (1988: 150ff). Camassa considers the link with rhythmic sonorous speech as clearly evident in its link with law-making (1996: 561–76); see, further, the discussion in Mittica (2015: 40). Gagarin (2008) remains sceptical, even though the evidence appears quite sufficient for a reasonable speculation.

which is entirely misleading.[147] Indeed, we know that Solon, for instance, refers to his 'laws' as *thesmoi* (fr. 36.18; Plu. *Sol.* 3.5) and Dracon, another famous law-giver, described his homicide 'law' as a *thesmos* too (*IG* I3 104.20 = *Nomima* I.02 = *IGT* 11). As has been seen earlier, it is most likely that *nómos* begins to be used in some sense of 'law' around the mid-fifth century BC, and probably, in the particular sense of 'written law', in the post-403 constitution era (Andoc. I. 85, 87).

In their travels, as legend has it the 'law-givers' also met with philosophers – most famously, Lycurgus met Thaletas, as did Zaleucus (who is said later to have taught Charondas; Hölkeskamp 1992a: 52).[148] Another legend has Charondas and Zaleucus as pupils of Pythagoras, who was regarded as a 'law-giver' himself (ibid.).[149] Andrew Szegedy-Maszak has shown, further, that 'the Greeks had a well-known tendency to ascribe the creation of their various institutions to a single person', while emphasising that the creation of *nómos*

---

[147] It is worth noting, also, that, for Shipp, these two law-givers use *nómos* in the sense of 'legal distribution' for the first time in its *legal* sense (1978: 15) and with particular emphasis on the colonial explanation of the emergence of written laws: 'In these new organized settlements, with new lands and under new conditions of life, sometimes founded by the combined enterprise of more than one home state, there would be the most obvious need for conscious and systematic lawgiving, and a new conception of law would develop, producing an institution which could no longer be denoted satisfactorily by the old terms, *themis*, *thesmos* or whatever they might be' (ibid.). While the link to the new colonies' experience and needs is plausible in part, Shipp's understanding limits the semantic field of *nómos* to that of, generally, 'distribution', while it has been shown already that the uses of *nómos* were polyvalent and coexistent, beside and beyond the sense of the distribution-sharing of land.

[148] Disputed already in antiquity, most notably by Aristotle in *Pol.* 1274a 28–31. On Zaleucus, see van Compernolle (1976: 329–400; and 1981: 759–69), as well as von Fritz (1983); and Adcock (1927: 100–1).

[149] For Pythagoras as a 'lawgiver', see Iambl. *Vit. Pyth.* 25; Porph. *Vit. Pyth.* 17; Diog. Laert. 8.3; see also Burkert (1972); and Szegedy-Maszak (1978: 202–6). Aristoxenos of Taras (fourth century BC) considered Charondas and Zaleucos to be Pythagoreans (fr. 43 [Wehrli]). Damon of Athens, a contemporary of Socrates, was considered a Pythagorean and, among other things, was revered for his systematic consideration of *harmonia* and *ēthos*, possibly in some relation to the 'order' of the polis; see Pl. *Rep.* 400a, and the discussion in Mathiesen (1984). On *harmonia* in Plato, see the excellent analysis by Tsimbidaros (2011).

remained a human act, even if divinely inspired or protected (1978: 208).[150] As to their key purpose, 'lawgivers are often presented as arbitrators in an attempt to reconcile conflicting class interests that threaten the social stability of their communities. The most notable example of an appointment of a lawgiver as a result of social strife is Solon' (Papakonstantinou 2008: 64).[151] Zinon Papakonstantinou adds that Solon 'In fr. 37 . . . asserts that he "stood in no-man's-land between them (i.e. the rich and the poor) like a boundary marker"', while

> in principle, there was nothing unusual when in a number of archaic communities, the *dēmos* and the aristocracy agreed to endow a widely acceptable individual with extraordinary political and legislative powers. What was unusual in the case of the lawgivers was the circumvention of the normal law-making procedures already in place in a particular polis with the appointment of an individual with restricted tenure and exceptional powers to promulgate law. (2012: 67)

Tradition has it that Zaleucus was possibly a Locrian, the first 'law-giver', devising (and writing) 'laws', later adopted elsewhere, for the colony Locri Epizephyrioi in southern Italy.[152] Given our earlier discussion of the pastoral uses of *nomos*, it is worth mentioning that Zaleucus is described as a shepherd by a scholiast of Pindar, most likely as a way of indicating his middle-class status.[153] It is also said, by Hermippos of Smyrna, that Zaleucus' laws (called *nómoi*

---

[150] In the legends, there is often mention of a relation with Apollo, or with the Oracle in Delphi, though this must have been after Apollo took over the shrine; see Koller (1963: 71–2). On the wider traditions of divine inspiration, see Plut. *Num.* 4.7; and the discussion in Liou-Gille (2000: 174–7).

[151] On Solon, see Linforth (1919); Ruschenbusch (1966); Hölkeskamp (2005); and, for a legal historical approach, see Blok and Lardinois 2006; Brisson and Pradeau (2007); and Mittica (2015: 48–52); on Solon as a singer, see Anhalt (1993).

[152] See Ephorus *FGrHist.* 70F 139 (= Strab. 6.1.8); see also, for example, Ael. *V.H.* 13, 24; Dem. 24. 139–41.

[153] See Schol. *ad* Pind. *O.* 10.17; Aris. *Pol.* 6.4.2, 1296a; for a discussion, see Camassa (1988: 135–6).

only in the later source) were sung in Athens at sympotic events, which, if true, indicates their poetic-musical form and function.[154]

We also learn, from the late work of Strabo, that when the people of Mazaka (Cappadocia) employed Charonda's *nómoi* (Χαρώνδα νόμοις, *Charōnda nómois*), they had a νομῳδός (*nomōdos*) sing them (12.2.9): νομῳδόν [*nomōdon*], ὅς ἐστιν αὐτοῖς ἐξηγητὴς τῶν νόμων [*exēgētēs tōn nómōn*].[155] In the word *nomōdos*, in which *nómos* is obviously related to the verb ᾄδω (*adō*; 'to sing', 'to praise'), we find the best linguistic evidence of the link between *nómos* and *mousikē*, or singing in particular (Camassa 2014), as well as a link to the possibly primary sense of *adō* as resounding/singing with a human voice (also noted in Mittica 2015).[156] In this vein, we also have two further reports of laws being rendered into poetry or song. Plutarch, quite reliably, writes that Solon versified his laws (which he refers to as *nómois*) into ἔπος (*epos*) before he published them (Sol. 3.5). Michael Gagarin (1986/1989: 54, n. 10) has disputed this, largely on the basis of the lateness of the sources. Similarly, and perhaps even more famously, Terpander, in the seventh century BC, is reported by Clement of Alexandria to have versified the laws of Sparta (for which as a practice there is reliable evidence; Gagarin 1986/1989: 54, n. 10).[157] In some contrast to Gagarin's overall sceptical view, Giorgio Camassa finds such practice unsurprising, given that in the archaic period 'law' was predominantly administered orally. Camassa refers to the Cretan tradition (with regard also to Ephoros in the fourth century BC), according to which children would learn the laws μετά τινος μελῳδίας [*meta*

---

154 *FGrHist.* 1026 F 5, Ath. 6.19b: ἤδοντο δὲ Ἀθήνησι καὶ οἱ Χαρώνδου νόμοι παρ' οἶνον, ὡς Ἕρμιππός φησιν ἐν ἕκτῳ περὶ Νομοθετῶν [*Nomothetōn*].

155 For a discussion of these sources, among other things, see Arnaoutoglou (2004).

156 See, further, Piccirilli (1981); though doubted by Gagarin (1986/1989: 54), who does not accept that 'laws' were or could have been 'the subject of song'; see further, Weiss (1923: I, 113–17); Mühl (1929: 105–24, 432–46); Triantaphyllopoulos (1983: 27–34); Camassa (1988: 140ff); Thomas (1995b: 62–4; 1996, 14–19); Ruzé (2001); Arnaoutoglou (2004: 2–4); and Ellinger (2005).

157 Clem. Alex. *Strom.* 1.16.78; see, further, Gostoli (1990); and Mittica (2015: 44–6).

tinos melōdias], for *mousikē* had, at least, *psychagogic* and *mnemonic* effects (1988: 145).[158]

Perhaps the relationship between *nómos* and *mousikē* did itself undergo a transition during the period of the appearance of written 'ordinances/legislation' (responding to particular problems);[159] nevertheless, customary practices of poetic (re)production, whether for the purposes of poetic creation, praise of the gods, learning or, indeed, 'law-giving' (all of which could not be easily distinguished) did not and could not vanish. Written legal norms, which, however, early on were not called *nómoi*, emerge around the middle of the seventh century BC, happily coexisting with oral 'laws'. Papakonstantinou's approach explains this not as a developmental, progressive schema, but as a break with some of the traditional practices (2008: 48–9):

> More specifically, the evidence for seventh century Greece (including written statutes and late traditions regarding the legal reforms of various lawgivers) suggests a widespread transition from a set of orally transmitted norms, whose validity was accepted by the majority of social actors and which were enforced usually by the decisions of the aristocratic courts and social pressure, to a set of written prescriptions that, as far as we know, were enacted through a deliberative process that at times involved a number of social groups. Deeply embedded custom is, in other words, now articulated as written statutory law.

The extent to which custom is articulated as 'written law' is unclear. Still, it is possible that, before they were systematised

---

[158] The source is Ael. *V.H.* 2.39: Κρῆτες δὲ τοὺς παῖδας τοὺς ἐλευθέρους μανθάνειν ἐκέλευον τοὺς νόμους μετά τινος μελῳδίας, ἵνα ἐκ τῆς μουσικῆς ψυχαγωγῶνται καὶ εὐκολώτερον αὐτοὺς τῇ μνήμῃ παραλαμβάνωσι καὶ ἵνα μή τι τῶν κεκωλυμένων πράξαντες ἀγνοίᾳ πεποιηκέναι ἀπολογίαν ἔχωσι ('The Cretans had the young children of the free citizens to learn the *nomoi* according to a musical melody, for they would receive *psuchagogia* from the music and would better register them in their *mnēmē*, and so that if they committed a forbidden act they would not be able to plead "ignorance" [ἀγνοία; agnoia]').

[159] See Whitley (1997: 655); and, generally, for a critique see Papakonstantinou (2002).

in writing, at least in part, or with regard to specific issues, 'laws' may have been sung in order to be disseminated, learnt and preserved (Thomas 1995b: 63). Rosalind Thomas further speculates that it was perhaps these sung oral laws that were later written down, though there is not enough evidence to suggest that such a practice, as reported in late sources, precluded or excluded the existence of already-written laws.[160]

Paola Mittica, in her recent contribution, follows the esoteric philological advice of not proposing that legal *nómoi* simplistically derive from musical *nómoi*, or, equally, that musical *nómoi* derive from legal ones. She suggests instead that the relation between the two is to be understood analogically, whereby 'the paths' through which the two types of *nómoi* developed are kept independent of each other (2015). For Mittica, the only thing that can explain this relation is 'the complex semantics of the root of these *nomoi*' (2015: 31; though in my view these semantics can only be understood in the coeval uses in which we find them). That is, it can be held that there is a certain degree of 'appropriateness', of an abiding by a certain apportionment, a 'rule' (Chantraine) whereby it is, in one sense, the musical *nómos* that 'borrows' from the 'legal specification' (ibid. 32). It is noteworthy, however, as Mittica points out, that for Chantraine (1968–2009) the musical sense of *nómos* is found at least as early as in the seventh century BC, and thus pre-dates the 'legal' sense of *nómos* (fifth century BC) (2015: 32). Mittica asks: did the notion of a 'rule' develop in relation to music before that of 'law'?

It has already been seen that customary practices, a way of behaving and a certain sense of ordering or appropriateness pre-exist the 'legal' sense of 'rule-making' in oral, polyvalent and not over-systematised milieux during the archaic period.

---

[160] The earliest inscribed text with legal content is the decree from Dreros in Crete (mid to late seventh century BC; *BCH* 61 (1937), 334 = *Nomima* I.81); see Papakonstantinou (2008: 50), who notes other early evidence, including the famous Gortyn stone blocks (IC IV 72), possibly of the late sixth century BC (though perhaps later); see also the most recent extensive treatment in Gagarin and Perlman (2016: 57 and 197–221). It remains possible that inscriptions on other material, such as wood, were used in other areas, including Athens. On written law, see, for example, Camassa (1988: 130–55); Hölkeskamp (1992b: 87–117); and the earlier Stroud (1979), with particular reference to Solon and Dracon.

It may also be the case that what Mittica (2016) refers to is an analogous duality that was not necessarily perceived as such by the Greeks. In this sense, the notion of a customary or conventional practical 'rule', or better, 'way', does seem to pre-exist (or at least coexist with) 'law'. Yet such taxonomic genealogy is responding to a characteristically modern anxiety, with regard to so-called 'primitive communities' in particular, and, more generally, the categorisation of whatever pre-dates 'law' ('pre-law', 'proto-law' and so forth) that tends to overwrite its own concerns regarding the evidence (or lack of evidence) it interprets.[161] This, to an extent, remains inevitable. Gagarin, for example, who has strongly argued for an early appearance of *nómos* = law, does so by dividing the time in question into three 'eras', such as a 'pre-law', a 'proto-law' and a 'law' period, and does so, among other reasons, because he presupposes a trans-historical Hartian schematism (1986/1989; 2008). More particularly, he believes that, when it comes to *nómoi*-laws in the musical sense (as in the late second century BC – αδόμενοι νόμοι, *adomenoi nómoi*, in Ath. 619b), these were perhaps only rendered into musical form for didactic (2008: 52) and, perhaps, mnemonic reasons.

In some contrast, Thomas has argued for 'law' as musically sung (1995a, b), whereby the practice of singing rendered these (customary) 'laws' into distinctive rules in a polis. The socio-'religious' importance of *mousikē* for the Greeks, as seen earlier, warrants the speculation that the intersection of social ordering, ritual practices, poetry-singing and instrumental experience would be the conventional milieux for the early appearance of a variety of means and forms of 'ordinances'. It is not necessarily the case that singing a 'law' (norm, tradition, etc.) rendered it into a 'law' as such (as some kind of exclusive means to an

---

[161] On 'pre-law', see the seminal Gernet ([1948–9] 1951: 3); Burchfiel (1993); Cantarella (1987); and Détienne (1969: 203–4). The epistemological mistake is to suggest that what precedes, for instance, archaic or classical 'law' is a more primitive form of 'law', using the terms that later draw a nascent legal definition to describe what precedes its creation. Even to the extent that Gernet uses the term 'pre-law' to represent a period in which what later became distinguishable as 'law' and 'religion' were still indistinguishable, the term remains a modern, and in that regard to some extent a misleading, cartography.

end). That a 'law' was sung in order to be rendered 'real', understood, communicated, protected and praised in a *bios* that was *mousikos* in more ways than one is a ripe ground for speculation. At the same time, I would maintain that there is a polyvalence of uses for the word *nómos*, whereby νόμος ᾠδῆς (*nómos hōdēs*)[162] referred to a rule of song, to use a shorthand, and sung *nómoi*. If the tradition is to be accepted, at least in a vague general sense, this was a practice that simultaneously satisfied creative, communicative, mnemonic and social-ordering purposes. The evidence does suggest some eventual analogy to the technical sense of *nómos*, or to *nómos*-rule or convention, a way of acting. Yet the earlier relation between ordering, *nómos* and *mousikē* cannot be known in any reliable sense, nor, at the same time, can it be subsumed under the later modes of understanding *mousikē* and *nomōdia*, let alone the 'strict' sense of 'juridical systematisation'.

It is thus quite appropriate to bring this preliminary discussion to a close with reference to Plato. Plato expresses his (in part) conservative attitude towards the so-called 'new music' (innovating instruments, rhythms and melodies)[163] during the latter part of the fifth century BC and, in particular, in his dialogue *Nómoi* (*Laws*).[164] Plato had already emphasised, in the *Republic* (at 4.424c), what was common knowledge – that music is the most important means of social 'ordering' (*harmonia*) – by paying particular attention to the educational musical norms/modes which he held preferable (for example, the Dorian over the Lydian scales/*harmoniai*; 398d–9c; also in the *L.* 799a–811e). In the *Laws*, Plato refers, with approval, to

162 See Laroche (1949: 171).
163 This was not an ancient term, see D'Angour (2006). For the ancients, particular concern arose specifically with the rise of dithyrambic and theatre music. On the so-called 'new music', see Pickard-Cambridge ([1927] 1962)); Del Grande (1946); Richter (1968a; 1968b; 1983); Fleming (1977); West (1992: 349–50, 365–6); Zimmermann (1992); D'Angour (1997; 2011); Csapo (1999–2000; 2004); Wilson (2003; 2004); Barker (2004); and Battezzato (2005).
164 The intersection of *mousikē* and *nómos* in Plato's *Laws* is much richer than I can explore in this work; see, further, Moutsopoulos (1959b); Bertrand (1999); Mathiesen (1999: 60–1); Brann (2004); Rocconi (2012); Peponi (2013); and Murray and Wilson (2004).

Egyptian *nómoi* over music, limiting their potential reform (at 657a–c), though there does not appear to be reliable evidence as to comparable legislative attempts in the Greek *poleis*. It is obviously significant that Plato devotes a large part of his *Laws*, a fundamentally political work, to the importance of *mousikē*, indicating how its older sense of proper (and divine sanctioned) order had remained significant in the classical period (at 700–1c). However, clearly, Plato's (as well as Aristotle's) stance remains representative of a late fifth century milieu (West 1992: 369ff).[165] Furthermore, Plato's famous analogies between *nómos* and *mousikē*, as Rocconi has shown in her analysis, are quite unusual, if not unprecedented (2016: 72). In particular, Plato equates following the 'rules' appropriately (*orthotēs*) of the musical *nómoi* with the ordering (*nómon* and *taxin*) of the polis (*L.* 657b).[166] But I wonder whether we are missing the point if we insist on literary precedent and miss the tradition that Plato and Aristotle, for that matter, transmit to their time and ours: music was at the heart of the original experience of political *poiēsis*.

That his use of technical musical terms (and the *nómoi*) is pre-emptively set to suit his own critical purposes is shown best, as Rocconi has illustrated, in Book 7 of the *Laws*:

> [Here] Plato lists some specific laws – calling them also models (*tupoi*) and moulds (*ekmageia*) – related to music (τῶν περὶ μοῦσαν νόμων καὶ τύπων), most of which have to do more with the religious and civic purposes of music performances than with specific technical aspects inherent in them. (2016: 79; Pl. *L.* 801c–d)

Plato ties appropriate musical performances to the religious calendar, and states

> the norm according to which 'the poet shall compose nothing beyond what is deemed lawful (νόμιμα; *nomima*) and right (δίκαια; *dikaia*) and fine (καλά; *kala*) and good (ἀγαθά; *agatha*) by the city', and that such compositions

[165] See, further, Lippman (1975); and Butti di Lima (2012).
[166] See the discussion in Rocconi (2016: 77–8); and Plato's *Rep.* 425a, on the relation between *mousikē* and *eunomia*.

must be approved by 'those who are appointed as judges in these matters . . .' (Rocconi 2016: 79; at 801c–d)

Plato, then, wishes to legislate (νομοθετεῖν, *nomothetein*) the appropriate *harmoniai*, rhythms and purpose of songs (at 802d–e).[167] Even if Plato is expressing particular political views on *mousikē* (and for that matter *nómos*), it is clear that he does so not in order to disregard or reduce the social function of *mousikē* as such, but to elevate the pursuit of the good away from the tragedians and the poets and place it at the heart of the divine gift of *phronēsis* which, as he implies, is musically conditioned.[168]

This, then, not only signifies the continuing role of *mousikē* (and of *nómos mousikos*) for the archaic and classical Greeks, but also serves as a corrective to the mistaken impression that one can understand what role *mousikē* entailed for the Greeks by resort, merely, to the classical context, let alone the technical one. Equally, for my purposes, the way in which Plato plays with the polyvalence and openness of the word *nómos* confirms that the coexistence of multiple uses of *nómos* was not a mere archaic 'developmental' stage that ultimately leads us to the simplistic equation *nómos* = law (especially so, when *nómos* as 'law' remains still a relatively open question for Plato and for those who followed him). Before Plato's *Laws*, possibly indicating the ancient tradition(s) through poetic licence, Pindar in his *First Hymn* (of which only a few lines survive) portrayed *mousikē* in, perhaps, cosmogonic terms whereby Zeus and Apollo bestow *mousikē* upon mortals and immortals (in the context of the sacred marriage of Cadmus and Harmonia), in order for the *kosmos* to be properly ordered and completed (frs. 29–35c [M]).[169] Zeus is said to produce his god-built noise, the *nómoi* (fr. 35c [M]: νόμων ἀκούοντες θεόδματον κέλαδον, *nómōn akouontes theodmaton keladon*). Implicitly, at least, the *kosmic nómos* or ordering has

---

[167] Plato, apparently, refused to be a *nomothetēs* for Cyrene and Megalopolis, Plut. *Adv. Col.* 32; D.L. 5.4; Ael. *V.H.* 12.54.

[168] See Rocconi (2016: 82–3). I thank Eleonora Rocconi for her generous advice on an earlier draft of this chapter. On Plato and the poets, see the collected essays in Destrée and Herrmann (2011).

[169] See the seminal study of the fragments by Snell ([1946] 1953: 71–89).

an essentially aural life: the god bestows, precisely, sound of *nómoi*. This was not just the poetic-musical ordering of a *kosmos-mousikos*, but also the means within which the peculiarity of the mortal (and immortal) *phōnē* could render itself effectively into the artifice of the word; and, for the philosophers, into the acoustic thought that Heraclitus still heard. It is a sound (*nómos*) that 'loves to hide', for this is its peculiar *dunamis*. *Nomos* was, after all, to be sung and heard.

Νόμους τὰς ᾠδὰς ἡμῖν γεγονέναι
Pl. *L*. 799e[170]

δικαίῳ τῷ στόματι ᾄδειν
Plut. *De Super.* 116b1[171]

---

[170] 'Our songs are our *nómoi*.'
[171] 'Sing with a fair/just mouth'; *dikaiō* here could be read as the 'fair indicative mouth'.

Bibliography

Accame, S. (1963a) 'L'invocazione alla Musa e la verità in Omero e in Esiodo (Prima Parte)', *Rivista di Filologia e di Istruzione Classica*, 41: 257–81.

Accame, S. (1963b) 'L'invocazione alla Musa e la verità in Omero e in Esiodo (Seconda Parte)', *Rivista di Filologia e di Istruzione Classica*, 41: 385–415.

Adcock, F. E. (1927), 'Literary tradition and early Greek code-makers', *Cambridge Historical Journal*, 2: 95–109.

Adkins, A. W. H. (1960), *Merit and Responsibility: A Study in Greek Values*, Oxford/London: Clarendon Press.

Adkins, A. W. H. (1968), 'Moira', *Classical Review*, 18(2): 194–7.

Adler, J. (1984), 'Philosophical Archaeology: Hölderlin's "Pindar Fragments"', *Comparative Criticism* 6: 23–40.

Adomènas, M. (1999), 'Heraclitus on religion', *Phronesis*, 44(2): 88–113.

[Aeschylus] (1926), *Aeschylus*, H. W. Smyth (trans.), 2 vols, Cambridge, MA: Harvard University Press.

Agamben, G. (1991), *Language and Death: The Place of Negativity*, K. E. Pinkus and M. Hardt (trans.), Minneapolis, MN: University of Minnesota Press.

Agamben, G. (1995a), *Homo sacer – il potere sovrano e la nuda vita*, Torino: Einaudi.

Agamben, G. (1995b), *Idea of Prose*, M. Sullivan and S. Whitsitt (trans.), Albany, NY: State University of New York Press.

Agamben, G. (1998), *Homo sacer: Sovereign Power and Bare Life*, D. Heller-Roazen (trans.), Stanford, CA: Stanford University Press.

Agamben, G. (1999a), *Potentialities: Collected Essays in Philosophy*, D. Heller-Roazen (trans.), Stanford, CA: Stanford University Press.

Agamben, G. (1999b) *The End of the Poem: Studies in Poetics*,

D. Heller-Roazen (trans.), Stanford, CA: Stanford University Press.

Agamben, G. (2008), *Signatura rerum – Sul metodo*, Torino: Einaudi.

Agamben, G. (2009), *The Signature of All Things: On Method*, Luca D'Isanto with Kevin Atell (trans.), New York: Zone Books.

Agamben, G. (2011), *The Sacrament of Language: An Archaeology of the Oath*, A. Kotsko (trans.), Stanford, CA: Stanford University Press.

Agamben, G. (2016a), *The Use of Bodies*, A. Kotsko (trans.), Stanford, CA: Stanford University Press.

Agamben, G. (2016b), *Che cos'è la filosofia?*, Macerata: Quodlibet.

Agamben, G. and M. Ferrando (2014) *The Unspeakable Girl: The Myth and Mystery of Kore*, L. De La Durantaye and A. J. Wyman (trans.), London: Seagull Books.

Alexiou, M. (2002), *The Ritual Lament in Greek Tradition*, Lanham, MD/Oxford: Rowman & Littlefield.

Allen, D. (2005), 'Greek tragedy and law', in M. Gagarin and D. Cohen (eds), *The Cambridge Companion to Ancient Greek Law*, Cambridge: Cambridge University Press, 374–93.

Allen, T. W. (1905), 'Theognis', *Classical Review*, 19(8): 386–95.

Almazova, N. (2001), 'Instrumental "nomos": some considerations', *Hyperboreus* 7: 80–90.

Almazova, N. (2014a), *Ancient Greek Writers on their Musical Past: Studies in Greek Musical Historiography*, Pisa/Roma: Fabrizio Serra Editore.

Almazova, N. (2014b), 'Harmateios nomos', *Music and Arts in Action*, 66: 518–38.

Aloni, A. (2007), 'Appendice: storie di telefo a paro. la "nuova" elegia di Archiloco (P. Oxy 69, 4708)', in A. Aloni and A. Iannucci (eds), *L'Elegia Greca e l'Epigramma dalle Origini al V Secolo*, Florence: Le Monnier Università, 205–37.

Anderson, W. D. (1966), *Ethos and Education in Greek Music: The Evidence of Poetry and Philosophy*, Cambridge, MA: Harvard University Press.

Anderson, W. D. (1984), *Greek Musical Writings: I. The Musician and his Art*, Cambridge: Cambridge University Press.

Anderson, W. D. (1994), *Music and Musicians in Ancient Greece*, Ithaca, NY: Cornell University Press.

Ando, V. (2004), 'Vino e sistema di valori nei poemi Omerici', *Thalassa* 1: 87–99.

Andrewes, A. (1938), 'Eunomia', *Classical Quarterly*, 32: 89–102.

Anhalt, E. K. (1993), *Solon the Singer, Politics and Poetics*, Lanham, MD: Rowman & Littlefield.

Anwander, A. (1949–50), 'Schicksal-Wörter in Antike und Christentum', *Zeitschrift für Religions- und Geistesgeschichte*, 2: 48–54, 128–35.

Applebaum, H. A. (1992), *The Concept of Work: Ancient, Medieval, and Modern*, Albany, NY: State University of New York Press.

[Apollonius Rhodius] (1990), *Apollonius Rhodius: Argonautica*, R. C Seaton (trans.), repr. edn, Cambridge, MA: Harvard University Press (Loeb).

[Apollonius Rhodius] Hunter, R. L. (1993), *The Argonautica of Apollonius: Literary Studies*, New York: Cambridge University Press.

Arend, W. (1933), *Die typischen Scenen bei Homer* (Problemata, 7), Berlin: Weidmann.

Aristides Quintilianus (1983), *On Music*, T. J. Mathiesen (trans. and ed.), New Haven, CT: Yale University Press.

Aristophanes (1979), *Aristophanes*, 3 vols, Cambridge, MA: Harvard University Press (Loeb).

Aristotle (1926), *Nicomachean Ethics*, H. Rackham (trans.), Cambridge, MA: Harvard University Press (Loeb).

[Ps.] Aristotle (1936), *Problems*, W. S. Hitt (trans.), 2 vols, Cambridge, MA: Harvard University Press (Loeb).

Aristotle (1938), *The Athenian Constitution*, H. Rackham (trans), Cambridge, MA: Harvard University Press (Loeb).

Aristotle (1967), *Politics*, H. Rackham (trans.), Cambridge, MA: Harvard University Press (Loeb).

Aristotle (1975), *The Art of Rhetoric*, J. H. Freese (trans.), Cambridge, MA: Harvard University Press (Loeb).

Aristoxenus (1902), *The Harmonics of Aristoxenus*, H. S. Macran (ed. and trans.), Oxford: Clarendon Press.

Aristoxenus (1997), *Elementa Rhythmica*, L. Pearson (trans.), Oxford: Clarendon Press.

Arnaoutoglou, I. (2004), 'Aspects of oral law in archaic Greece', in D. L. Cairns and R. A. Knox (eds), *Law, Rhetoric, and Comedy in Classical Athens. Essays in Honour of Douglas M.*

Bibliography

MacDowell, Swansea: Classical Press of Wales, 1–13 = id. in (1995), '*Bulletin of the Institute of Classical Studies*, 40: 59–74.

Arnheim, M. T. W. (1977), *Aristocracy in Greek Society*, London: Thames & Hudson.

Asheri, D. (1966), *Distribuzioni di terre nelle antica Grecia.* Torino: Memorie dell'Accademia delle Scienze *di Torino*.

Assaël, J. (2000), 'Poétique des etymologies de μοῦσα (mousa), la muse', *Noesis*, 4: 11–53.

Assaël, J. (2006), *Pour une poétique de l'inspiration, d'Homère à Euripide*, Coll. d'Études Classiques 21, Louvain: Peeters.

Athanassaki, L. and E. Bowie (eds) (2011), *Archaic and Classical Choral Song: Performance, Politics and Dissemination – Trends in Classics*, Supp. v. 10, Berlin: De Gruyter.

Athanassakis, A. N. (trans.) (1983) *Hesiod: Theogony, Works and Days, Shield*, Baltimore, MD: Johns Hopkins University Press.

Athanassakis, A. N. (1992) 'Cattle and honour in Homer and Hesiod', *Ramus* 21: 156–86.

Athanassakis, A. N. (2004), *The Homeric Hymns*, Baltimore, MD: Johns Hopkins University Press.

Athanassakis, A. N. and B. N. Wolkow (eds and trans) (2013), *The Orphic Hymns*, Baltimore, MD: Johns Hopkins University Press.

Athenaeus (1854), *The Deipnosophists. Or Banquet of the Learned of Athenaeus*, Henry G. Bohn (trans.), 3 vols, York Street, Covent Garden.

Athenaeus (1950), *The Deipnosophists*, C. B. Gulick (trans.), 7 vols, Cambridge, MA: Harvard University Press (Loeb).

Autenrieth, G. ([1877] 1960), *An Homeric Dictionary*. London: Macmillan.

Avagianou, A. A. (ed.) (2002), *Λατρείες στην 'Περιφέρεια' του Αρχαίου Ελληνικού Κόσμου*, Athens: National Institute of Research (EIM).

Avilés, D. (2010) *Altgriechische Gesetze, Natur und Entwicklung eines Rechtsinstituts*, Dissertation zur Erlangung der Doktorwürde an der Philosophischen Fakultät der Universität Freiburg, Schweiz.

Axelos, K. (1962), *Héraclite et la philosophie*, Paris: Les Éditions de Minuit.

Axelos, K. (1969), *Le jeu du monde*, Paris: Les Éditions de Minuit.

Babut, A. D. (1975), 'Héraclite et la religion populaire, Fragments 14, 69, 68, 15 et 5 Diels-Kranz', *Revue des Études Anciennes*, 77: 27–62.

Bacon, H. (1994), 'The chorus in Greek life and drama', *Arion* 3, 1: 6–24.

Bakker, E. J. (1997), *Poetry and Speech: Orality and Homeric Discourse*, Ithaca, NY: Cornell University Press.

Bakker, E. J. (2013), *The Meaning of Meat and the Structure of the Odyssey*, Cambridge: Cambridge University Press.

Barchiesi, A. (1991), 'Discordant muses', *Proceedings of the Cambridge Philological Society*, 37: 1–21.

Barker, A. (1978a), 'Music and perception: a study in Aristoxenus', *Journal of Hellenic Studies*, 98: 9–16.

Barker, A. (1978b), 'Hoi kaloumenoi harmonikoi: the predecessors of Aristoxenus', *Proceedings of the Cambridge Philological Society*, 24: 1–21.

Barker, A. (1984), *Greek Musical Writings, 1: The Musician and his Art*, Cambridge: Cambridge University Press.

Barker, A. (1989), *Greek Musical Writings, 2: Harmonic and Acoustic Theory*, Cambridge: Cambridge University Press.

Barker, A. (1990), 'Public music as "fine art" in archaic Greece', in J. W. McKinnon (ed.), *Antiquity and the Middle Ages: From Ancient Greece to the 15th Century*, Basingstoke: Palgrave Macmillan, 45–67.

Barker, A. (2004), 'Transforming the nightingale: aspects of Athenian musical discourse in the late fifth century', in P. Murray and P. Wilson (eds), *Music and the Muses: The Culture of 'Mousike' in the Classical Athenian City*, Oxford: Oxford University Press, 185–204.

Barker, A. (2007), *The Science of Harmonics in Classical Greece*, Cambridge: Cambridge University Press.

Barker, A. (2010), 'The music of the Muses', *VIS: Rivista do Programma de Pós-Graduação em Arte da Universidade de Brasilia*, 9(2): 11–19.

Barmeyer, E. (1968), *Die Musen: Ein Beitrag zur Inspirationstheorie*, München: Fink.

Barnes, J. (1979), *The Presocratic Philosophers*, I. *From Thales to Zeno*, London/New York: Routledge.

Barnes, J. (1983) *The Presocratic Philosophers*. London/New York: Routledge.

Barrett, W. S. (2007), 'Stesichorus, Geryoneis, SLG 11', in

W. S. Barrett and M. L. West (eds) (2007) *Greek Lyric, Tragedy, and Textual Criticism: Collected Papers*, Oxford: Oxford University Press.

Bartel, H. (2000), *Centaurengesänge: Friedrich Hölderlins Pindarfragmente*, Würzburg: Königshausen und Neumann.

Bartling, H.-M. (1985), *Der Logosbegriff bei Heraklit und seine Beziehung zur Kosmologie*, Göppingen: Kümmerle.

Bartol K. (1992a), 'How was iambic poetry performed? A question of Ps.-Plutarch's reliability: (De mus. 1141 A)', *Euphrosyne* 20: 269–76.

Bartol, K. (1992b), 'Where was iambic poetry performed? Some evidence from the fourth century BC', *Classical Quarterly*, 42: 65–71.

Bartol, K. (1998) 'The importance of appropriateness. Rethinking the definition of nomos', *Philologus*, 142: 300–7.

Battezzato, L. (2005), 'Lyric', in J. Gregory (ed.), *A Companion to Greek Tragedy*, Oxford: Wiley Blackwell, 149–66.

Baudy, G. (1983), 'Hierarchie oder: Die Verteilung des Fleisches', in B. Gladigow and H. G. Kippenburg (eds), *Neue Ansätze in der Religionswissenschaft*, München: Kosel, 131–74.

Baum, M. (1963/1964), 'Hölderlins Pindar-Fragment "Das Höchste"' *Hölderlin-Jahrbuch* 65–76.

Baxter, T. (1992), *The Cratylus: Plato's Critique of Naming*, Leiden: Brill.

Beekes, R. (1885), *Etymological Dictionary of Greek.; Lexicon Homericum*, 2 vols, H. Ebeling (ed.), vol. 1, London.

Beekes R. and L. van Beek (2010), *Etymological Dictionary of Greek*, 2 vols, Leiden/Boston, MA: Brill.

Beer, J. (2004), *Sophocles and the Tragedy of Athenian Democracy*, Westport, CT: Praeger.

Bekkeri, I. ([1831] 1987), *Aristotelis Opera*, III, Berlin/New York: De Gruyter.

Bélis, A. (1999), *Les musiciens dans l'antiquité*, Paris: Hachette.

Bendall, L. M. (2001), 'The economics of Potnia in the Linear B documents: palatial support for a Mycenaean deity' in R. Laffineur and R. Hägg (eds), *Potnia: Deities and Religion in the Aegean Bronze Age* (Aegaeum 22) Liège/Austin, TX: 445–52.

Bendall, L. M. (2007), *Economics of Religion in the Mycenaean World: Resources Dedicated to Religion in the Mycenaean Palace*

Economy, Monograph No 67, Oxford: Oxford University School of Archaeology.

Bendall, L. M. (2013) 'Wanax', *The Encyclopedia of Ancient History*, London: John Wiley, 7.044–5.

Bennet, J. (1992), 'Collectors or owners? An examination of their possible functions within the palatial economy of LM III Crete', in J.-P. Olivier (ed.), *Mykenaïka* [Actes du IXe Colloque international sur les textes mycéniens et égéens = *Bulletin de Correspondance Hellénique*, Suppl. 25], 65–101.

Bennett, E. L. (1956), 'The landholders of Pylos', *American Journal of Archaeology*, 60: 103–33.

Bennett, F. (2016), 'Music and language in ancient verse: the dynamics of an antagonistic Concord', *Humanities*, 5, 1: 1–13.

Benveniste, É. ([1948/1975] 1993), *Noms d'agent et noms d'action en indo-européen*, Paris: Adrien Maisonneuve.

Benveniste, É. (1966) *Problèmes de Linguistique générale*, I, Paris: Gallimard.

Benveniste, É. (1968) *Le vocabulaire des institutions indo-europeennes, vol. 2: Pouvoir, droit, religion*, Paris: Éditions de Minuit.

Benveniste, É. (and J. Lallot) (1973), *Indo-European Language and Society*, Coral Gables, FL: University of Miami Press.

Bergk, T. (1866), *Poetae Lyrici Graeci*, Vol. 1, Lipsiae: Teubner.

Bergk, T. (1882), *Poetae Lyrici Graeci*, Vol. 3, Lipsiae: Teubner.

Bergquist, B. (1967), *The Archaic Greek Temenos: A Study of Structure and Function*, Lund: Gleerup.

Bergren, A. (2008), 'Language and the female in early Greek thought', in A. Bergren (ed.), *Weaving Truth: Essays on Language and the Female in Greek Thought (Hellenic Studies 19)*, Washington, DC: Center for Hellenic Studies, 13–40.

Bernardete, S. (1999), *Sacred Transgressions: A Reading of Sophocles' Antigone*, South Bend, IN: St Augustine's Press.

Berns, G. (1973), 'Nomos and physis (an interpretation of Euripides' Hippolytos)', *Hermes*, 101(2): 165–87.

Berranger, D. (1992), *Recherches sur l'histoire et la prosopographie de Paros à l'époque archaïque*, Clermont-Ferrand: Presses Universitaires Blaise Pascal.

Berry, E. G. (1940), *The History and Development of the Concept of ΘΕΙΑ ΜΟΙΡΑ and ΘΕΙΑ ΤΥΧΗ down to and including Plato*, dissertation, Chicago.

Bibliography

Berthiaume, G. (1982), *Les rôles du mágeiros. Étude sur la boucherie, la cuisine et le sacrifice dans la Grèce ancienne*, Leiden: Brill.

Bertrand, J.-P. (1999), *De l'écriture à l'oralité – lectures des Lois de Platon*, Paris: Publications de la Sorbonne.

Bianchi, U. (1953), Διὸς αἶσα – *Destino, uomini e divinità nell'epos, nelle teogonie e nel culto dei Greci*, Studi Pubblicati dall'Istituto Italiano per la Storia Antica 11, Rome.

Bing, P. (1988), *The Well-Read Muse: Present and Past in Callimachus and the Hellenistic Poets*, Göttingen: Vandenhoeck & Ruprecht.

Bintliff, J. L. (1982), 'Settlement patterns, land tenure and social structure: a diachronic model', in C. Renfrew and S. Shennan (eds), *Ranking, Resource and Exchange: Aspects of the Archaeology of Early European Society*, Cambridge: Cambridge University Press.

Bintliff, J. L. (1996), 'The archeological survey of the Valley of the Muses and its significance for Boeotian history', in A. Hurst and A. Schachter (eds), *La montagne des Muses*. (Recherches et Rencontres, 7.) Geneva: Librairie Droz, 193–224.

Biraud, M. (1984), 'La conception psycholagique A l'époque d'Homère: les organes mentaux', *Cratyle* 1: 27–49.

Biscardi, A. (1982), *Diritto greco antico*, Firenze–Milano.

Biscardi, A. (1999), *Scritti di diritto greco*, E. Cantarella and A. Maffi (eds), Università degli Studi di Milano, Facoltà di Giurisprudenza, Pubblicazioni dell'Istituto di Diritto Romano, 34, Milano: Giuffrè.

Blanchot, M. 'The "sacred speech" of Hölderlin' in M. Blanchot ([1949] 1995), *The Work of Fire*, Stanford, CA: Stanford University Press.

Blok, J. H. and A. Lardinois (eds) (2006), *Solon of Athens, New Historical and Philological Approaches*, Leiden/Boston, MA: Brill.

Bloomer, W. M. (1993) 'The superlative *Nomoi* of Herodotus's *Histories*', *Classical Antiquity*. 12: 30–50.

Blundell, M. W. (1989), *Helping Friends and Harming Enemies. A Study in Sophocles and Greek Ethics*, Cambridge: Cambridge University Press.

Blusch, J. (1970), *Formen und Inhalt von Hesiods individuellem Denken* (Abh. z. Kunst-, Musik- u. Literaturwiss., 98), Bonn: H. Bouvier.

Boardman, J. (1999), *The Greeks Overseas*, 4th edn, London: Thames & Hudson.

Böckh, A. ([1811–19, 1821] 2013) *Pindari opera quae supersunt*, 2 vols, Leipzig, with I. A. Gottlob Weigel, Cambridge: Cambridge University Press.

Boisacq, E. (1923), *Dictionnaire étymologique de la langue grecque, étudiée dans ses rapports avec les autres langues indo-européennes*, Heidelberg: Cari Winter's Universitatsbuchhandlung/ Paris: Klincksieck.

Boissonade, J.-F. (ed.) (1836), *Aeneas Gazaeus et Zacharias Mitylenaeus de immortalitate animae et mundi consummatione*, Paris: Mercklein.

Bollack J. (1965–9), *Empédocle*, I–III, Paris: Éditions de Minuit.

Bollack J. (2003), *Empédocle. Les Purifications*, Paris: Seuil.

Bollack, J. (1990) 'Réflexions sur les interprétations du logos héraclitéen', in J. F. Mattéi (ed.), *La Naissance de la raison en Grèce*, Paris: PUF, 165–85.

Bollack, J. and H. Wissmann ([1972] 2001) *Héraclite, ou, La separation*. Paris: Éditions de Minuit.

Bolonyai, G. (1998), 'Lyric genres in Aristotle's Poetics', *Acta Antiqua Academiae Scientiarum Hungaricae*, 38: 27–39.

Borecký, B. (1963), 'The primitive origin of the Greek Conception of equality', in L. Varcl and R. F. Willets (eds), *Geras: Studies Presented to George Thomson on the Occasion of his 60th Birthday*, Acta Universitatis Carolinae, Philosophica et Historica I, Graecolatina Pragensia II, Prague: Universita Karlova, 41–52.

Borecký, B. (1965), *Survivals of Some Tribal Ideas in Classical Greek*, Acta Universitatis Carolinae, Philosophica et Historica Monographia X, Prague: Universita Karlova.

Borecký, B. (1971), '*Die politische Isonomie*', *Eirene* 9: 5–24.

Bossi, F. (1976), 'Alcune recenti edizioni di Archiloco (1968–1972)', *Atene e Roma*, 21: 1–18.

Bossi, F. (1990), *Studi su Archiloco*, Bari: Adriatica Editrice.

Boudouris, K. J. (ed.) (1989), *Ionian Philosophy*, Athens: Kardamitsa Institute.

Bowie, E. (1986), 'Early Greek elegy, symposium and public festival', *Journal of Hellenic Studies*, 106: 13–35.

Bowie, E. (1993), 'Lyric and elegiac poetry', in J. Boardman, J. Griffin and O. Murray (eds), *The Oxford History of the Classical World*, Oxford: Oxford University Press, 90–101.

Bowie, E. (2009), 'Wandering poets, archaic style', in R. Hunter and I. Rutherford (eds), *Wandering Poets in Ancient Greek Culture*, Cambridge: Cambridge University Press, 105–36.

Bowie, E. (2011), 'Alcman's First Partheneion and the song the sirens sang', in E. Bowie and L. Athanassaki (eds), *Archaic and Classical Choral Song: Performance, Politics and Dissemination*, Berlin: De Gruyter, 33–66.

Bowra, C. M. (1944), *Sophoclean Tragedy*, Oxford: Oxford University Press.

Bowra, C. M. (1947), *Pindari carmina cum fragmentis*, Scriptorum Classicorum Bibliotheca Oxoniensis, Oxford: Clarendon Press.

Bowra, C. M. (1964), *Pindar*, Oxford: Oxford University Press.

Boyancé, P. (1937), *Le Culte des Muses chez les philosophes grecs, Études d'histoire et de psychologie religieuses*, Paris: De Boccard.

Boyancé, P. (1972), *Le culte des Muses chez les philosophes grecs*, Paris: De Boccard.

Brand, H. (2000), *Griechische Musikanten im Kult*, Dettelbach: Verlag J. H. Röll.

Brann, E. (2004), *The Music of the Republic: Essays on Socrates' Conversations and Plato's Writings*, Philadelphia, PA: Paul Dry Books.

Brecht, F. (1936), *Heraklit – Ein Versuch über den Ursprung der Philosophie*, Berlin.

Brelich, A. (1969), *Paides e Parthenoi*, Roma.

Bremer, D. (1996), 'Heraklit', in F. Ricken (ed.), *Philosophen der Antike*, Stuttgart/Berlin/Köln, I, 73–93.

Bremmer, J. N. (1994), *Greek Religion*, Cambridge: Cambridge University Press.

Bremmer, J. N. (1998), '"Religion", "ritual", and the opposition "sacred vs. profane"', in F. Graf (ed.), Ansichten griechischer Rituale: Geburtstags-Symposium für Walter Burkert, Castelen bei Basel, 15 bis, 18 March 1996, Stuttgart, 9–32.

Bremmer, J. N. (2007), 'Greek normative animal sacrifice', in D. Ogden (ed.), *A Companion to Greek Religion*, Boston, MA/Oxford: Blackwell, 132–44.

Breniquet, C. and C. Michel (eds) (2014), *Wool Economy in*

the Ancient Near East and the Aegean: From the Beginnings of Sheep Husbandry to Institutional Textile Industry, Ancient Textiles Series 17, Oxford/Philadelphia, PA: Oxbow Books.

Brillante, C. (1991) 'Le muse di Thamyris', *Studi classici e orientali*, 41: 429–53.

Brillante, C. (1994), 'Poeti e re nel proemio della Teogonia esiodea', *Prometheus* 20: 14–26.

Brillante, C. (2009), *Il cantore e la Musa. Poesia e modelli culturali nella Grecia arcaica*, Pisa: Edizioni ETS.

Brillante, C. (2013/2014), 'La voce delle muse nella poesia greca arcaica', *I Quaderni del Ramo d'oro*, 6: 34–51.

Brisson, L. and J.-Fr. Pradeau (2007), *Les Lois de Platon*, Paris: Presses Universitaires de France.

Brock, R. (2013), *Greek Political Imagery from Homer to Aristotle*, London: Bloomsbury.

Brommer, F. (1986), *Heracles: The Twelve Labors of the Hero in Ancient Art and Literature*, New Rochelle, NY: A. D. Caratzas.

Brown, A. D. (1961), 'Muses on Pindos', *Greece and Rome*, 8: 22–6.

Brown, N. O. (1947), *Hermes the Thief – The Evolution of a Myth*, Milwaukee, WI: University of Wisconsin Press.

Brown, W. E. (1956), 'Land-tenure in Mycenaean *Pylos*', *Historia*, 5: 384–400.

Brugmann, K. (1894), 'Μοῦσα, τρίαινα, θρῖναξ, θρῖνακίη, ἤνεικα', *Indogermanische Forschungen*, 3: 253–64.

Brun, J. (1965), *Héraclite ou le philosophe de l'éternel retour*, Paris: Seghers.

Bruns, G. (1970), *Küchwesen und Mahlzeiten – Archaeologia Homerica: Die Denkmäler und das frühgriechishe Epos*, vol. 2, Q, Göttingen: Vandenhoeck & Ruprecht.

Budelmann, F. (ed.) (2009), *The Cambridge Companion to Greek Lyric*, Cambridge: Cambridge University Press.

Bundy, E. L. (1986), *Studia Pindarica*, Berkeley, CA: University of California Press.

Burchfiel, K. J. (1993), 'The myth of pre-law in early Greece', in G. Thür (ed.) *Symposion, Vorträge zur griechischen und hellenistischen Rechtsgeschichte* (Graz-Andritz, 12–16 September 1993), Köln/Weimar/Wien, 79–104.

Burckhardt, G. (1952), *Heraklit – Urworte der Philosophie, griechisch und deutsch*, Wiesbaden.

Burford, A. (1993), *Land and Labor in the Greek World*. Baltimore, MD/London: Johns Hopkins. University Press.

Burford, A. (1977), 'The family farm in Greece', *Classical Journal*, 73: 162–75.

Buriks, A. A. (1948), *ΠΕΡΙ ΤΥΧΗΣ – De ontwikkeling van het begrip Tyche tot aan de Romeinse tijd hoofdzakelijk in de philosophie*, Dissertation, Leiden.

Burke, B. (1999), 'Purple and Aegean textile trade in the early second millennium B.C.', in P. P. Betancourt, V. Karageorghis, R. Laffineur and W.-D. Niemeier (eds), *Meletemata: Studies in Aegean Archaeology Presented to Malcolm H. Wiener as He Enters his 65th year*, Liège/Austin, TX: Université de Liège/University of Texas, 75–82.

Burkert, W. (1972), *Lore and Science in Ancient Pythagoreanism*, Cambridge, MA: Harvard University Press.

Burkert, W. ([1972] 1983), *Homo Necans – The Anthropology of Ancient Greek Sacrificial Ritual and Myth*, P. Bing (trans.), Los Angeles, CA/London: University of California Press.

Burkert, W. ([1977] 1985), *Greek Religion – Archaic and Classical*, J. Raffan (trans.), Maiden, MA/Oxford: Blackwell/Harvard University Press.

Burkert, W. (1979), *Structure and History in Greek Mythology and Ritual*, Sather Classical Lectures, 47, Berkeley, CA: University of California Press.

Burkert, W. ([1984] 1992), *The Orientalizing Revolution: Near Eastern Influence on Greek Culture in the Early Archaic Age*, Cambridge, MA: Harvard University Press.

Burkert, W. (1987), *Ancient Mystery Cults*, Cambridge, MA: Harvard University Press.

Burn, A. R. (1949), 'Helicon in history: a study in Greek mountain topography', *Annual of the British School at Athens*, 44: 313–23.

Burnet, J. (1945), *Early Greek Philosophy*, with corr. by W. L. Lorimer, London: Macmillan.

Burnett, A. P. (1976), 'Tribe and city, custom and decree in children of Heracles', *Classical Philology*, 71(1): 4–26.

Burnett, A. P. (1983), *Three Archaic Poets: Archilochus, Alcaeus, Sappho*, Cambridge, MA: Harvard University Press.

Burnett, A. P. (2005), *Pindar's Songs for Young Athletes of Aigina*, Oxford: Oxford University Press.

Burns, T. (2002), 'Sophocles' Antigone and the history of the concept of natural law', *Political Studies*, 50: 545–57.

Burton, R. W. B. (1962), *Pindar's Pythian Odes: Essays in Interpretation*, Oxford: Oxford University Press.

Bury, R. G. (ed. and trans.) (1967–8), *Plato* [Plato in Twelve Volumes], vols 10 and 11 Cambridge, MA/London: Harvard University Press/William Heinemann.

Bushnell, R. W. (1988), 'Speech and authority: "Antigone"', in R. W. Bushnell (ed.), *Prophesying Tragedy: Sign and Voice in Sophocles' Theban Plays*, Ithaca, NY/London: Cornell University Press, 43–66.

Butler, J. (2000), *Antigone's Claim: Kinship between Life and Death*, New York: Columbia University Press.

Butti di Lima, P. (2012), 'Tra legislatore e poeta: un dialogo all'interno delle Leggi di Platone', in R. Cavalluzzi, P. Guaragnella and R. Ruggiero (eds), *Il diritto e il rovescio*, Pensa, 33–50.

Cairns, D. L. (1993), *Aidōs: The Psychology and Ethics of Honour and Shame in Ancient Greek Literature*, Oxford: Oxford University Press.

Cairns, D. L. (1996), 'Hybris, dishonour, and thinking big', *Journal of Hellenic Studies*, 116: 1–32.

Calame, C. (1977), *Les Choeurs de jeune filles en Grèce archaïque. I: morphologie, fonction religieuse et sociale*, Rome: Edizioni dell'Ateneo.

Calame, C. (ed.) (1983), *Alcman*, Roma: Edizioni dell'Ateneo.

Calame, C. (1986), *Le récit en Grèce ancienne*, Paris: Meridians Klincksieck.

Calame, C. (1995), *The Craft of Poetic Speech in Ancient Greece*, 2nd edn, Ithaca, NY/London: Cornell University Press.

Calame, C. (1996), 'Montagne des Muses et Mouséia: la consécration des travaux et l'héroïsation d'Hésiode', in A. Hurst and A. Schachter (eds), *La montagne des Muses*, Genève: Librairie Droz, 43–56.

Calame, C. (1997), *Choruses of Young Women in Ancient Greece: Their Morphology, Religious Role, and Social Function*, Lanham, MD: Rowman & Littlefield.

Calame, C. (1998), 'La Poésie lyrique grecque, un genre inexistant?', *Littérature* 111: 87–110.

Caldwell, R. (1989), *The Origin of the Gods – A Psychoanalytic*

Study of Greek Theogonic Myth, Oxford: Oxford University Press.

Camassa, G. (1987), 'La codificazione delle leggi e le istituzioni politiche delle città greche della Calabria in età arcaica e classica', in S. Settis (ed.), *Storia della Calabria. La Calabria Antica*, I, Roma: Reggio Calabria, 613–56.

Camassa, G. (1988), 'Aux origines de la codification écrite des lois en Grece', in M. Détienne (ed.), *Les savoirs de l'écriture en Grèce ancienne*, Lille: Presses Universitaires.

Camassa, G. (1996), 'Leggi orali e leggi scritte. I legislatori', in S. Setis (ed.), *I Greci. Storia-Cultura-Arte-Società*, 2.i, Torino, 561–76.

Camassa, G. (2011a), 'Μίνως πρακτικός τε ἅμα καὶ νομοθέτης σπουδαῖος. Le leggi cretesi attraverso la lente di Archiloco e le prime fasi della storia di nomos', in F. Carinci, N. Cucuzza, P. Militello and O. Palio (eds), *Κρήτης Μινωιδός: Tradizione e identità minoica tra produzione artigianale, pratiche cerimoniali e memoria del passato, Studi offerti a Vincenzo La Rosa per il Suo 70° compleanno*, Studi di Archeologia Cretese 10, Padova: Bottega d'Erasmo, 469–76.

Camassa, G. (2011b), *Scrittura e mutamento delle leggi nel mondo antico*, Roma: L'Erma di Bretschneider.

Camassa, G. (2014), 'Eforo e l'invenzione della legge', *Quaderni di storia*, 40, 80: 71–94.

Camilloni, M. T. (1998), *Le Muse*, Rome: Editori Riuniti.

Campbell, D. A. ([1982] 1993), *Greek Lyric – The New School of Poetry and Anonymous Songs and Hymns*, vols I–V, Cambridge, MA: Harvard University Press (Loeb).

Campbell, D. A. (1967), *Greek Lyric Poetry – A Selection*, Cambridge, MA/London: Harvard University Press.

Campbell, D. A. (ed.) ([1967] 1990), *Greek Lyric Poetry*, 5 vols, London/Bristol: Bristol Classical Press/Macmillan.

Cantarella, E. (1979), *Norma e sanzione in Omero – Contributo alla protostoria del diritto greco*, Milano: Istituto di Diritto Romano Milano.

Cantarella, E. (1984), 'A proposito di diritto e prediritto', *Studi Storici*, 1: 75–82.

Cantarella, E. (1987), 'Tra diritto e prediritto: un problema aperto', *Dialogues d'histoire ancienne*, 13: 149–60.

Cantarella, E. (1994) *Diritto greco*, Milano: Libreria CUEM.

Cantarella, E. (2001), 'Modelli giurisdizionali omerici: il

giudice unico, la giustizia dei vecchi', *Symposion* 1997, Köln, 3–19.

Cantarella, E. (2002a), 'Dispute settlement in Homer – once again on the Shield of Achilles', in G. Vlachos and Dimakis, P. D. (eds), *Mélanges en l'honneur Panayotis D. Dimakis: Droits Antiques et Société*, Athens, 2002, 147–65.

Cantarella, E. (2002b), *Itaca – Eroi, donne, potere tra vendetta e diritto*, Milano: Feltrinelli.

Carlier, P. (1984), *La royauté en Grèce avant Alexandre*, Strasbourg: Etudes et Travaux Association pour l'Étude de la Civilisation Romane.

Carlier, P. (1987), 'À propos des te-re-ta', in P. Ilievski and L. Crepajac (eds), *Tractata Mycenaea*, Proceedings of the Eighth International Colloquium on Mycenaean Studies, Ohrid (15–20 September 1985), Skopje: Macedonian Academy of Sciences and Arts, 65–73.

Carlier, P. (1992), 'Les collecteurs sont-ils fermiers?', in J.-P. Olivier (ed.), *Mykenaïka*, Actes du IXe Colloque international sur les textes mycéniens et égéens (= *Bulletin de Correspondance Hellénique*, Suppl. 25), 159–66.

Carpenter, M. (1983), 'KI-TI-ME-NA and KE-KE-ME-NA at Pylos', *Minos*, 18: 81–8.

Carrière, J. (1948), *Théognis de Mégare: Etude sur le recueil élégiaque attribué à ce poète*. Paris: Bordas.

Carter, D. M. (2007), *The Politics of Greek Tragedy*, Phoenix: Bristol Phoenix Press.

Carter Philips, F. (1978) 'Heracles', *Classical World*, 71: 431–40.

Cartledge, P. (1998b), 'Writing the history of archaic Greek political thought', in N. Fisher and H. van Wees (eds), *Archaic Greece: New Approaches and New Evidence*, London: Classical Press of Wales/Duckworth, 379–99.

Cartledge, P. (2002), *The Greeks – A Portrait of Self and Others*, 2nd edn, Oxford: Oxford University Press.

Casabona, J. (1966), *Sacrifices: Recherches sur la vocabulaire des sacrifices en grec des origins á la fin de l'époche classique*, Aix-en-Provence: Publications des Annales de la Faculté des Lettres.

Casertano, G. (ed.) (2007), *Empedocle tra poesia, medicina, filosofia e politica*, Proceedings of the International Conference, Napoli.

Casevitz, M. (1985) *Le vocabulaire de la colonisation en grec ancien: étude lexicologique: les familles de ktizo et de oikeo-oikizo*, Paris: Klincksieck.

Cassola, F. (1964), 'Solone, la Terra e gli Ectemori', *La Parola del Passato*, 19: 26–68.

Castoriadis, C. (2001), 'Αισχύλεια Ανθρωπογονία και σοφόκλεια αυτοδημιουργία του ανθρώπου', [Aeschylean Anthropology and Sophoclean Self-Creation of Anthropos], in id. Ανθρωπολογία, πολιτική, φιλοσοφία. Πέντε. διαλέξεις στην Βόρειο Ελλάδα, Athens: Ypsilon, 11–36.

Castoriadis, C. (2004), *Ce qui fait la Grèce*, vol. 1, Paris: Seuil.

Cavalli, M. V. (2008–9), 'The Homeric aristocratic Oikos: a model of socio-economical aggregation', *Gaia*, 12: 69–76.

Cerri, G. (1979), *Legislazione orale e tragedia greca. Studi sull'Antigone di Sofocle e sulle Supplici di Euripide*, Napoli: Liguori.

Chadwick, J. (1958), *The Decipherment of Linear B*, Cambridge: Cambridge University Press.

Chadwick, J. (1979), 'Land-holding at Pylos', *Bulletin of the Institute of Classical Studies*, 26: 130–2.

Chadwick, J. (1996), *Lexicographica Greca: Contributions to the Lexicography of Ancient Greek*, Oxford: Oxford University Press.

Chadwick, N. K. (1942), *Poetry and Prophecy*, Cambridge: Cambridge University Press.

Chailley, J. (1956), 'Le mythe des modes grecs', *Acta Musicologica*, 28: 137–63.

Chailley, J. (1979), *La Musique grecque antique*, Paris: Les Belles Lettres.

Chang, C. and H. A. Koster (1986), 'Beyond bones: toward an archaeology of pastoralism', in M. B. Schiffer (ed.) (1986), *Advances in Archaeological Method and Theory*, vol. 9, New York: Academic Press, 97–148.

Chaniotis, A. (1988), 'Habgierige Götter, habgierige Städte. Heiligtumsbesitz und Gebietsanspruch in den kretischen Staatsverträgen', *Ktema* 13: 21–39.

Chaniotis, A. (1995), 'Problems of "pastoralism" and "transhumance" in classical and Hellenistic Crete', *Orbis Terrarum*, 1: 39–89.

Chantraine, P. (1936), 'Homérique Μερόπων ἀνθρώπων' in F. Cumont (ed.), *Mélanges (Annuaire de l'Institut de philologie et d'histoire orientales et slaves*), vol. I, *Bruxelles*: Université Libre de Bruxelles, 121–8.

Chantraine, P. (1968–2009), *Dictionnaire étymologique de la langue grecque – Histoire des mots*, Paris: Librairie Kliencksieck.

Cherry, J. (1988), 'Pastoralism and the role of animals in the pre- and protohistoric economies of the Aegean', in C. R. Whittaker (ed.), *Pastoral Economies in Classical Antiquity*, Cambridge Philological Society Supplementary 14, Cambridge: Philological Society, 6–34.

Chirassi-Colombo, I. (1979), '*Paides* e *Gynaikes*: note per una tassonomia del comportamento rituale nella cultura attica', *QUCC* 30: 25–58.

Chroust, A.-H. (1947), 'Anonymous treatise on law: the pseudo-Platonic dialogue Minos', *Notre Dame Law Review*, 23(1): 47–53.

Clairmont, C. W. (1983), *Patrios Nomos: Public Burial in Athens during the Fifth and Fourth Centuries B.C.*, 2 vols, Oxford: Oxford University Press.

Clarke, M. (1997), 'Gods and mountains in Greek myth and poetry', in A. B. Lloyd (ed.), *What Is a God: Studies in the Nature of Greek Divinity*, London: Duckworth, 65–80.

Clay, D. (2004), *Archilochos Heros – The Cult of Poets in the Greek Polis*, Washington, DC/Cambridge, MA: Harvard University Press.

Clay, J. S. (1988), 'What the muses sang: Theogony 1–115', *Greek Roman and Byzantine Studies*, 29: 323–33.

Clay, J. S. (1992), 'The World of Hesiod', *Ramus*, 21: 131–55.

Clay, J. S. (1994), 'The dais of death', *Transactions of the American Philological Association*, 124: 35–40.

Clay, J. S. (2003), *Hesiod's Cosmos*, Cambridge: Cambridge University Press.

Cobb, W. S. (1998), 'Plato's Minos', *Ancient Philosophy*, 8: 187–207.

Cohen, D. (1989), 'Greek law: problems and methods', *Zeitschrift der Savigny-Stiftung für Rechtsgeschichte*, 106: 81–105.

Cohen, D. (1995), *Law, Violence and Community in Classical Athens*, Cambridge: Cambridge University Press.

Cohen, Y. A. (1964), *The Transition from Childhood to Adolescence: Cross-cultural Study of Initiation Ceremonies, Legal Systems, and Incest Taboos*, Chicago, IL: Aldine.

Coin-Longeray, S. (2013), 'Ὀρθός chez Eschyle: dressé, exact, juste', *Syntaktika*, 44: 1–15.

Collard, C. and M. Cropp (eds and trans) (2008) *Euripides, Fragments*, vols 7 and 8, Cambridge, MA: Harvard University Press (Loeb).

Colli, G. (1980), *La sapienza greca, III. Eraclito*, D. Del Corno (ed.), Milano: Adelphi Edizioni.

Colli, G. and M. Montinari (eds) (2006), 'Friedrich Nietzsche: De Theognide Megarensi', *Kritische Gesamtausgabe* (KGW) Berlin: De Gruyter, 3: 420–62.

Comotti, G. ([1979] 1991), *La musica nella cultura greca e romana*, Turin: EDT.

Comotti, G. (1989), *Music in Greek and Roman Culture*, R. V. Munson (trans.), Baltimore, MD: Johns Hopkins University Press.

Comotti, G. (1994), 'Note a Ps.-Plutarch De Musica', *Museum Criticum*, 29: 259–61.

Conacher, D. J. (1956), 'Religious and ethical attitudes in Euripides' suppliants', *Transactions and Proceedings of the American Philological Association*, 87: 8–26.

Conche, M. (1986), *Heraclite – Fragments*, Paris: Presses Universitaires de France.

Cooper, I. (2012), 'Law, tragedy, spirit: Hölderlin contra Agamben', *Journal of Literary Theory*, 6, 1: 195–211.

Cornford, F. M. ([1912] 1957), *From Religion to Philosophy*, New York: Harper.

Cornford, F. M. (1952), *Principium Sapientiae. The Origins of Greek Philosophical Thought*, Cambridge/New York: Cambridge University Press.

Cricca, E. (1984), 'Note ai Persiani di Timoteo (fr. 15 P.) I', *Giornale Filologico Ferranese* 7: 105–9.

Cricca, E. (1985), 'Note ai Persiani di Timoteo (fr. 15 P.) II', *Giornale Filologico Ferranese* 8: 9–14.

Crielaard, J. P. (1995), 'Homer, history and archaeology. some remarks on the date of the Homeric world', in J. P. Crielaard (ed.), *Homeric Questions*, Amsterdam: JC Gieben, 201–88.

Croiset, A. (1985), *La poésie de Pindare et les lois du lyrisme grec*, Paris: Librairie Hachette.

Crotty, K. (1982), *Song and Action: The Victory Odes of Pindar*, Baltimore, MD/London: Johns Hopkins University Press.

Crusius, O. (1888), 'Über die Nomosfrage', Verhandlungen

der 39, Versammlung der deutschen Philologen und Schulmänner in Zürich, 28 September, Leipzig, 258–75.

Csapo, E. (2004), 'The politics of the new music', in P. Murray and P. Wilson (eds), *op. cit.*, 207–48.

Csapo, E. (1999–2000), 'Later Euripidean music', in M. Cropp, K. Lee and D. Sansone (eds), *Euripides and Tragic Theatre in the Late Fifth Century*, Illinois Classical Studies, 24–5: 399–426.

Cunliffe, R. J. ([1924] 2012), *A Lexicon of the Homeric Dialect*, expanded edn, Norman, OK: University of Oklahoma Press.

Cunliffe, R. J. (1963), *A Lexicon of the Homeric Dialect*, Norman, OK: University of Oklahoma Press.

Currie, B. (2005), *Pindar and the Cult of Heroes*, Oxford: Oxford University Press.

Curtis, P. (2011), *Stesichoros's Geryoneis*, Mnemosyne Supplements, 333, Leiden/Boston: Brill.

Curtius, L. (1903), *Die antike Herme*, Leipzig.

Dale, A. M. (1969), 'Words, music and dance', in A. M. Dale, *Collected Papers*, Cambridge: Cambridge University Press, 156–69.

D'Angour, A. (1997), 'How the dithyramb got its shape', *Classical Quarterly*, 47: 331–51.

D'Angour, A. (2006), 'The new music – so what's new?', in S. Goldhill and R. Osborne (eds), *Rethinking Revolutions through Ancient Greece*, Cambridge: Cambridge University Press, 264–83.

D'Angour, A. (2011), *The Greeks and the New. Novelty in Ancient Greek Imagination and Experience*, Cambridge: Cambridge University Press.

Darcus (Sullivan), S. (1974), '"Daimon" as a force shaping "ethos" in Heraclitus', *Phoenix*, 28, 4: 390–407.

Darcus (Sullivan), S. (1979a), 'A person's relation to ψυχή in Homer, Hesiod, and the Greek lyric poets', *Glotta*, 57: 30–9, 159–73.

Darcus (Sullivan), S. (1979b), 'Logos of psyche in Heraclitus', *Rivista Storica dell'antichita*, 9: 89–93.

de Coulanges, F. (1903), *La Cité Antique. Étude sur le culte, le droit, les institutions de la Grèce et de Rome*. 18th edn, Paris: Librairie Hachette et Cie.

de Fidio, P. (1977), *I Dosmoi Pilii a Poseidon: una terra sacra di età micenea*, Rome: Edizioni dell'Ateneo and Bizzarri.

de Fidio, P. (1987), 'Palais et communautés de village dans le royaume mycènien de Pylos', P. H. Ilievski and L. Crepajac (eds), *Tractata Mycenaea* – Proceedings of the Eighth International Colloquium on Mycenaean Studies, Ohrid, 15–20 September 1985, Skopje: Macedonian Academy of Sciences and Arts, 129–49.

de Man, P. (1983), 'Heidegger's exegesis of Hölderlin', W. Godzich (trans.), in P. de Man, *Blindness and Insight: Essays in the Rhetoric of Contemporary Criticism*, 2nd edn, Minneapolis, MN: University of Minnesota Press.

de Romilly, J. (1971), *La loi dans la pensée grecque des origines à Aristote*. Paris: Les Belles Lettres.

Deger-Jalkotzy, S. (1983), 'Zum Charakter und zur Herausbildung der mykenischen Sozialstruktur', in *Res Mycenaeae: Akten des VII. Internationalen Mykenologischen Colloquiums in Nürnberg, 6–10 April 1981*, A. Heubeck and G. Neumann (eds), 89–111, Göttingen: Vandenhoeck & Ruprecht.

Del Grande, C. (1923), 'Nomos citarodico', *Rivista Indo-Greco-Italica* 7: 1–17.

Del Grande, C. (1932), *Espressione musicale dei poeti greci*, Napoli: Ricciardi.

Del Grande, C. (1946), *Ditirambografi – Testimonianze e frammenti*, Napoli: Loffredo Editore.

Delavaud-Roux, M.-H. (1991), *Recherches sur la danse dans l'Antiquité grecque*, Dissertation, 3 vols, Université d'Aix-Marseille.

Deleuze, G. ([1968] 1994), *Différence et répétition*, Paris: Presses Universitaires de France.

Deleuze, G. and F. Guattari (1981), *Mille plateaux*, Paris: Éditions de Minuit.

Della Volpe, A. (1994), 'Τέμενος: an Etymological Study', *Twenty-first LACUS Forum* 21: 626–34.

Della Volpe, A. (2004), 'A vestige of land tenure in Homer', *General Linguistics*, 41: 113–33.

Demand, N. H. (1990), *Urban Relocation in Archaic and Classical Greece: Flight and Consolidation*, Norman, OK: University of Oklahoma Press.

Demos, M. (1991), *Lyric Quotation in Plato*, dissertation, Harvard University.

Demos, M. (1994), 'Callicles' quotation of Pindar in the Gorgias', *Harvard Studies in Classical Philology*, 96: 85–107.

Demos, M. (1999) *Lyric Quotation in Plato*, Lanham, MD: Rowman & Littlefield.

Demosthenes (1949), *Orations*, N. W. De Witt (trans.), 7 vols, Cambridge, MA: Harvard University Press (Loeb).

Depew, D. (1991), 'Politics, music and contemplation in Aristotle's ideal state', in D. Keyt and F. D. Miller jr (eds), *A Companion to Aristotle's Politics*, Oxford: Oxford University Press, 346–80.

Destrée, P. and F.-G. Herrmann (eds) (2011), *Plato and the Poets, Mnemosyne Supplements*: Monographs on Greek and Latin Language and Literature, 328, Leiden/Boston, MA: Brill.

Détienne, M. (1969) 'Gernet (Louis), Anthropologie de la Grèce antique', *Archives des sciences sociales des religions* 28: 203–4.

Détienne, M. (1977), *The Garden of Adonis: Spices in Greek Mythology*, J. Lloyd (trans.), 'Introduction' by J. P. Vernant, Sussex: Harvester Press.

Détienne, M. (1996/1999), *The Masters of Truth in Archaic Greece*, J. Lloyd (trans.), New York: Zone Books.

Détienne, M. and Hamonic, G. (eds) (1995), *La déesse parole – Quatre figures de la langue des dieux*, Paris: Flammarion.

Détienne, M. and J.-P. Vernant (eds) (1989). *The Cuisine of Sacrifice among the Greeks*, P. Wissing (trans.) Chicago, IL: Chicago University Press.

Devereux, G. (1987), 'Thamyris and the muses (an unrecognized Oedipal myth)', *American Journal of Philology*, 108: 199–201.

Devine, A. M. and L. D. Stephens (1994), *The Prosody of Greek Speech*, New York/Oxford: Oxford University Press.

Dickie, M. (1998), 'Poets as initiates in the mysteries: Euphorion, Philicus and Posidippus' *Antike und Ahendland*, 45: 49–77.

Diels, H. (1901), *Herakleitos von Ephesos*, Berlin: Weidmann.

Diels, H. and Kranz, W. (eds) ([1903] 1952/2004), *Die Fragmente der Vorsokratiker*, 6th edn, Berlin/Zurich: Weidmann.

Dietler, M. and B. Brian Hayden (eds) (2001), *Feasts:*

Archaeological and Ethnographic Perspectives on Food, Politics, and Power, Washington, DC: Smithsonian Books.

Dietrich B. C. (1962), 'The spinning of fate in Homer', *Phoenix*, 16, 2: 86–101.

Dietrich, B. C. (1964), 'The judgement of Zeus', *Rheinisches Museum für Philologie*, NF 107: 97–125.

Dietrich, B. C. (1965), *Death, Fate and the Gods: The Development of a Religious Idea in Greek Popular Belief and in Homer*, London: Athlone Press.

Dietrich, B. C. (1974), *The Origins of Greek Religion*, Berlin/New York: De Gruyter.

Dietrich, B. C. (1988) 'The instrument of sacrifice', in R. Hägg, N. Marinatos and G. Nordquist (eds), *Early Greek Cult Practice*, Proceedings of the Fifth International Symposium of the Swedish Institute at Athens, SkrAth 4, 38, Stockholm. 35–50.

Dilcher, R. (1995), *Studies in Heraclitus*, Hildesheim/Zürich/New York: Georg Olms Verlag.

Dillon, M. (2002), *Girls and Women in Classical Greek Religion*, London: Routledge.

Dilts, M. R. (1971), *Heraclidis Lembi Excerpta Politiarum*, Durham, NC: Duke University Press, no. 20.

Dindorf, W. (1855), *Scholia graeca in Homeri Odysseam ex codicibus aucta et emendata*, 1, Oxford.

Dittrich, O. (1926), *Geschichte der Ethik*, Leipzig: F. Meiner.

Dodds, E. R. (1951), *The Greeks and the Irrational*, Berkeley/Los Angeles, CA: University of California Press.

Dodds, E. R. (1959), *Plato: Gorgias*, Oxford: Clarendon Press.

Domaradzki, M. (2012), 'Theological etymologizing in the early Stoa', *Kernos*, 25: 125–48.

Domínguez, A. (2011) 'The origin of Greek colonization and the Greek *polis*: some observations', *Ancient West and East* 10: 195–207.

Donlan, W. (1970), 'Changes and shifts in the meaning of demos in the literature of the archaic period', *La Parola del Passato*, 135: 381–95.

Donlan, W. (1982a), 'Reciprocities in Homer', *Classical World*, 75(3): 137–75.

Donlan, W. (1982b), 'The Politics of Generosity in Homer', *Helios*, n.s. 9: 1–15.

Donlan, W. (1985), 'The social groups of dark age Greece', *Classical Philology* 80(4): 293–308.

Donlan, W. (1989a), 'Homeric temenos and land tenure in dark age Greece', *Museum Helveticum*, 46(3): 129–45.

Donlan, W. (1989b), 'The pre-state community in Greece', *Symbolae Osloenses: Norwegian Journal of Greek and Latin Studies*, 64(1): 5–29.

Donlan, W. (1993), 'Duelling with gifts in the Iliad: as the audience saw it', *Colby Quarterly*, 29(3): 155–72.

Donlan, W. (1997), 'The Homeric economy', in I. Morris and D. Powell (eds), *A New Companion to Homer*, Leiden/New York/Cologne: Brill, 649–67.

Donlan, W. (1998), 'Dark age Greece: Odysseus and his hetairoi', in C. Gill, N. Postlethwaite and R. Seaford, *Reciprocity in Ancient Greece*, Oxford: Oxford University Press, 51–71.

Dougherty, C. (2001), *The Raft of Odysseus: The Ethnographic Imagination of Homer's Odyssey*, Oxford: Oxford University Press.

Douglas, G. E. (ed. and trans.) (1999), *Greek Elegiac Poetry: From the Seventh to the Fifth Centuries BC*, Cambridge, MA: Harvard University Press (Loeb).

Douzinas, C. and R. Warrington (1994a), 'Antigone's law: a genealogy of jurisprudence', in C. Douzinas, P. Goodrich and Y. Hachamovitch (eds), *Politics, Postmodernity and Critical Legal Studies*, London: Routledge.

Douzinas, C. and R. Warrington (1994b), *Justice Miscarried: Ethics, Aesthetics and the Law*, Hemel Hempstead: Harvester Wheatsheaf.

Dowden, K. (1989), *Death and the Maiden: Girls' Initiation Rites in Greek Mythology*, London: Routledge.

Dowden, K. (2007), 'Olympian Gods, Olympian Pantheon', in D. Ogden (ed.), *A Companion to Greek Religion*, Oxford: Blackwell, 41–55.

Doyle, R. E. (1984), *Ate: Its Use and Meaning*, New York: Fordham University Press.

Driessen, J. (1992), '"Collector's items": observations sur l'élite mycénienne de Cnossos', in J.-P. Olivier (ed.), *Mykenaïka, Bulletin de Correspondance Hellénique*, Supplement 25: 197–214.

Duchemin, J. (1955), *Pindare: Poète et prophète*, Paris: Les Belles Lettres.

Bibliography

Duchemin, J. (1960), *La Houlette et la lyre: Recherche sur les origins pastorales de la poésie, I: Hermés et Apollon*, Paris: Les Belles Lettres.

Duchemin, J. (1980), 'Personnifications d'abstractions et d'éléments naturels: Hésiode et l'Orient', in J. Duchemin (ed.), *Mythe et Personnification: travaux et mémoires*, Actes du colloque du Grand Palais, Paris, 7–8 May 1977, Paris: Les Belles Lettres.

Duffy, J. (1947), 'Homer's conception of fate', *Classical Journal*, 42(8): 477–85.

Duhoux, Y. (1976), *Aspects du vocabulaire économique mycénien (cadastre – artisanat – fiscalité)*, Amsterdam: Hakkert.

Dumont, J.-P. (1988), 'Héraclite', in J.-P. Dumont, *Les Présocratiques*, Paris: Bibliothèque de la Pléiade/Gallimard.

Dunbabin, T. J. (1948), *The Western Greeks*, Oxford: Oxford University Press.

Duplouy, A. (2006) *Le Prestige des Élites: Recherches sur les modes de reconnaissance sociale en Grèce entre les Xe et Ve siècles avant J.-C.*, Paris: Les Belles Lettres.

Durante, M. (1976), *Sulla preistoria della tradizione poetica greca. Parte seconda: risultazione della comparazione indoeuropea*, Roma: Edizioni Dell'Ateneo.

Düring, I. (1956), 'Greek music: its fundamental features and its significance', *Journal of World History*, 3: 302–29.

Earle, T. (2011) 'Redistribution in Aegean palatial societies. Redistribution and the political economy: the evolution of an idea', *American Journal of Archaeology*, 115(2): 237–44.

Easterling, P. E. (1997), *The Cambridge Companion to Greek Tragedy*, Cambridge: Cambridge University Press.

Ebeling, H. ([1880–5] 1963), *Lexicon Homericum*, Leipzig: Teubner.

Ebeling, H. L. (1925), 'The Persians of Timotheus', *American Journal of Philology*, 46: 317–31.

Eckels, R. P. (1937). *Greek Wolf-Lore*, dissertation, University of Pennsylvania.

Edmonds, J. M. (ed. and trans.) ([1922–7] 1945), *Lyra Graeca*, 3 vols, New York: G. P. Putnam's Sons (Loeb).

Edmonds, J. M. (ed. and trans.) (1931), *Elegy and Iambus*, New York: G. P. Putnam's Sons (Loeb).

Edmunds, L. and R. Wallace (eds) (1997), *Poet, Public, and*

Performance in Ancient Greece, Baltimore, MD: Johns Hopkins University Press.

Edwards, A. T. (2004), *Hesiod's Ascra*, Berkeley, CA: University of California Press.

Effenterre, H. v. (1973) 'Le contract de travail du scribe Spensithios', *Bulletin de correspondance hellénique*, 97: 31–46.

Ehnmark, E. (1935) *The Idea of God in Homer*, dissertation, Uppsala.

Ehrenberg, V. (1921), *Die Rechtsidee im frühen Griechentum: Untersuchungen zur Geschichte der werdenden Polis*, Leipzig: S. Hirzel.

Ehrenberg, V. (1923), 'Anfange des griechischen Naturrechts', *Archiv für Geschichte der Philosophie*, 35, Neue Folge, 28(1): 12–143.

Ehrenberg, V. (1940), 'S.v. isonomia', *Pauly's Real-Encyclopaedie der classischen Altertumswissenschaft*, Suppl. 7, 293–301.

Ehrenberg, V. (1946), 'Tragic Heracles', in *Aspects of the Ancient World*, New York/Oxford: W. Salloch/Basil Blackwell, 144–66.

Ehrenberg, V. ([1946] 1965), 'Eunomia' in K. F. Stroheker and A. J. Graham (eds) (1965), *Polis und Imperium*, Zurich: Artemis, 139–58.

Ehrenberg, V. (1954), *Sophocles and Pericles*, Oxford: Basil Blackwell.

Ehrenberg, V. (1956), *Sophokles und Perikles*, München: C. H. Beck.

Ehrenberg, V. (1960) *The Greek State*, Oxford: Clarendon Press.

Eidinow, E. (2011), *Fate Luck and Fortune: Antiquity and its Legacy*, London/New York: I. B. Tauris.

Eitrem, S. (1909), *Hermes und Die Toten*, Christiania Videnskabs-Selskabs Forhandlinger, 5.

Ekroth, G. (2007), 'The importance of sacrifice: new approaches to old methods', *Kernos* 20: 287–469.

Ekroth, G. (2008), 'Meat in ancient Greece: sacrificial, sacred or secular?', in W. Van Andringa (ed.), *Sacrifices, marché de la viande et pratiques alimentaires dans les cites du monde romain* [= *Food & History* 5], Turnhout, Brepols, 249–72.

Ekroth, G. (2011), 'Meat for the gods', in V. Pirenne-Delforge and F. Prescendi (eds) '«Nourrir les dieux?» Sacri ce et represen-tation du divin' (*Kernos*, suppl. 26), Liège, Centre International d'Étude de la Religion Grecque Antique, 15–41.

Eliade, M. (1949), *Traité d'histoire des religions*, Paris: Payot.

Eliade, M. (1958), *Birth and Rebirth*, New York: Harper & Row.

Ellinger, P. (2005), 'En marge des lois chantées: la peste et le trouble', in P. Sineux (ed.), *Le législateur et la loi dans l'Antiquité: Hommage à Françoise Ruzé*, Caen: Presses Universitaires de Caen, 49–62.

Else, G. F. (1976), *The Madness of Antigone*, Heidelberg: Carl Winter Universitätsverlag.

Enegren, H. L. (2004), 'Animals and men at Knossos: the Linear B evidence', in *Pecus. Man and Animal in Antiquity: Proceedings of the Conference at the Swedish Institute in Rome, 9–12 September 2002.*

Enegren, H. L. (2008), *The People of Knossos: Prosopographical Studies in the Knossos Linear B Archives*, Uppsala: Acta Universitatis Upsaliensis.

Ercoles, M. (2014), 'Notes on the aulodic nomoi apothetos and schoinion', *Greek and Roman Musical Studies*, 2: 177–83.

Etxabe, J. (2009) 'Antigone's Nomos', *Animus*. 13: 60–73.

Etxabe, J. (2013), *The Experience of Tragic Judgment*, Abingdon: Routledge.

Euripides (1938), *The Complete Greek Drama*, W. J. Oates and E. O'Neill Jr (eds), 2 vols, E. P. Coleridge (trans.), New York: Random House.

Euripides (2002), *Helen, Phoenician Women and Orestes*, D. Kovacs (trans.), Cambridge, MA: Harvard University Press (Loeb).

Evelyn-White, H. G. (1914), *The Homeric Hymns and Homerica*, Cambridge, MA/London: Harvard University Press/ William Heinemann.

Fairbanks, A. (1900), *A Study of the Greek Paean*, Ithaca, NY: Macmillan.

Faraguna, M. (2007), 'Tra oralità e scrittura: diritto e forme della comunicazione dai poemi omerici a Teofrasto', *Etica e Politica*, 9(1): 75–111.

Farnell, L. R. ([1896] 1909), *The Cults of the Greek States*, 5 vols, Oxford: Clarendon Press.

Farnell, L. R. (1965), *Pindar: A Commentary*, Amsterdam: Adolf M. Hakkert.

Fascher, E. (1927), *ΠΡΟΦΗΤΗΣ – Eine Sprach -und religionsge-schichtliche Untersuchung*, Giessen: Töpelmann.

Ferguson, J. (1958), *Moral Values in the Ancient Word*, London: Methuen.

Ferrari, G. (2008), *Alcman and the Cosmos of Sparta*, Chicago, IL: University of Chicago Press.

Ferrario, S. B. (2006), 'Replaying Antigone: changing patterns of public and private commemoration at Athens c. 440–350', in C. B. Patterson (ed.), *Antigone's Answer: Essays on Death and Burial, Family and State in Classical Athens, Helios*, Special Issue, 33: 79–117.

Fiddes, N. (1991), *Meat: A Natural Symbol*, New York: Routledge.

Figueira, T. and G. Nagy (eds) (1985), *Theognis of Megara*, Baltimore, MD/London: Johns Hopkins University Press.

Fine, J. V. A. (1951), *Horoi: Studies in Mortgage, Real Security and Land Tenure in Ancient Athens* 9, Baltimore (Hesperia suppl.).

Finkelberg, A. (1998a), 'On the history of the Greek κοσμος', *Harvard Studies in Classical Philology*, 98: 103–36.

Finkelberg, M. (1998b), 'Timē and Aretē in Homer', *Classical Quarterly*, 48(1): 14–28.

Finley, M. I. (1952), *Studies in Land and Credit in Ancient Athens 500–200 B.C. The Horoi Inscriptions*, New Brunswick, NJ: Rutgers University Press.

Finley, M. I. ([1954] 1977/1988), *The World of Odysseus*, London: Penguin.

Finley, M. I. (1957), 'Homer and Mycenae: property and tenure', *Historia*, 6: 133–59.

Finley, M. I. (1968), 'The alienability of land in ancient Greece', *Eirene* 7: 25–32.

Finley, M. I. (1973), *Problèmes de la Terre en Grèce ancienne*, Paris and The Hague.

Finley, M. I. (1975), *The Use and Abuse of History*, London: Chatto & Windus.

Finley, M. I. (1976), 'Colonies – an attempt at a typology', *Transactions of the Royal Historical Society*, 5th series, 26: 167–88.

Finley, M. I. (1977), *The World of Odysseus*, revised 2nd edn, New York: Viking.

Firinu, E. (2009), 'Il primo stasimo dell'Ifigenia Taurica euripidea e i Persiani di Timoteo di Mileto: un terminus post quem per il nomos?', *Eikasmós*, 20: 109–31.

Fisher, N. R. E. (1979), 'Hybris and dishonour: II', *Greece and Rome*, 26: 32–47.

Fisher, N. R. E. (1992), *Hybris: A Study in the Values of Honour and Shame in Ancient Greece*, Warminster: Aris & Phillips.

Fitton, J. W. (1973), 'Greek dance', *Classical Quarterly*, 23(2): 254–74.

Fleming, T. J. (1977), 'The musical nomos in Aeschylus' Oresteia', *Classical Journal*, 72(3): 222–33.

Fletcher, J. (2008), 'Citing the law in Sophocles' Antigone', *Mosaic: A Journal for the Interdisciplinary Study of Literature*, 41: 66–87.

Fletcher, J. (2012), 'Law and spectacle in Euripides' Hecuba' in D. Rosenbloom and J. Davidson (eds), *Greek Drama IV: Texts, Contexts*, Oxford: Aris & Phillips.

Flower, M. A. (2008), *The Seer in Ancient Greece*, Berkeley/Los Angeles, CA/London: University of California Press.

Foley, H. (1995), 'Tragedy and democratic ideology: the case of Sophocles' Antigone', in B. Goff (ed.), *History, Tragedy, Theory: Dialogues on Athenian Drama*, Austin, TX: University of Texas Press, 131–450.

Foley, H. (1996), 'Antigone as a moral agent', in M. Silk (ed.), *Tragedy and the Tragic: Greek Theatre and Beyond*, New York/Oxford: Clarendon Press/Oxford University Press, 49–73.

Foley, H. P. (ed.) (1981), *Reflections of Women in Antiquity*, New York: Gordon & Breach.

Fontenrose, J. (1978), *The Delphic Oracle*, Berkeley, CA: University of California Press.

Forbes, H. (1995), 'The identification of pastoralist sites within the context of estate-based agriculture in ancient Greece: beyond the "transhumance versus agro-pastoralism" debate', *Annual of the British School at Athens*, 90: 325–38.

Ford, A. (1981), *A Study of Early Greek Terms for Poetry: Aoide, Epos and Poiesis*, dissertation, Yale University.

Foucault, M. ([1970–1] 2011), *Leçons sur la volonté de savoir, Cours au Collège de France 1970–71*, D. Defert (ed.), Paris: Gallimard/Seuil.

Foucault, M. (2007), *Security, Territory, Population: Lectures at the Collège de France 1977–1978*, Michel Senellart (ed.), London: Palgrave Macmillan.

Foucault, M. (2014), *Lectures on the Will to Know: Lectures at the Collège de France*, New York: Palgrave Macmillan.

Fowler, R. L. (1954), *The Nature of Early Greek Lyric – Three Preliminary Studies*, Toronto/London: University of Toronto Press.

Fox, R. S. (2012), *Feasting Practices and Changes in Greek Society from the Late Bronze Age to Early Iron Age*, Oxford: Archaeopress.

Foxhall, L. and A. D. E. Lewis (eds) (1996), *Greek Law in its Political Setting: Justifications not Justice*, Oxford: Clarendon Press.

Fränkel, H. F. ([1951] 1962), *Dichtung und Philosophie des frühen Griechentums: Eine Geschichte der griechischen Epik, Lyrik und Prosa bis zur Mitte des fünften Jahrhunderts*, München: C. H. Beck.

Franklin, J. C. (2002), 'Harmony in Greek and Indo-Iranian cosmology', *Journal of Indo-European Studies*, 30(1–2): 1–25.

Franklin, J. C. (2003), 'The language of musical technique in Greek epic diction', *Gaia – Revue interdisciplinaire sur la Grèce archaïque*, 7: 295–307.

Franklin, J. C. (2006), 'The wisdom of the lyre: soundings in Ancient Greece, Cyprus and the Near East', in E. Hickmann and R. Eichmann (eds), *Musikarchäologie im Kontext: Archäologische Befunde, historische Zusammenhänge, soziokulturelle Beziehungen. Serie Studien zur Musikarchäologie 5*, Rahden: Leidorf, 379–98.

Franklin, J. C. (2016), *Kinyras: The Divine Lyre*, Hellenic Studies Series 70, Washington, DC: Center for Hellenic Studies.

Franz, M. (1988), 'Die Schule und Die Welt: Studien zu Hölderlins Pindar-fragment «Untreue der Weisheit»', in *Jenseits der Idealismus: Hölderlins letzte Homburger Jahre (1804–6)*, C. Jamme and O. Pöggeler (ed.), 139–56 [= *Neuzeit und Gegenwart* 5] Bonn: Bouvier.

Freyburger G. (1988), 'Supplication grecque et supplication romaine', *Latomus*, 47: 501–25.

Frisk H. ([1954] 1960; 1972), *Griechisches etymologisches Wörterbuch*, 3 vols, Heidelberg: Carl Winter, Universitatsverlag.

Frontisi-Ducroux, F. (1994), 'Athéna et l'invention de la flûte', *Musica e Storia*, 2: 239–67.

Furley, W. (1993), 'Types of Greek hymns', *Eos*, 81: 21–41.

Furley, W. and J. M. Bremer (2001), *Greek Hymns: Selected*

Cult Songs from the Archaic to the Hellenistic Period, 2 vols, Tübingen: Mohr Siebeck.

Gagarin, M. (1974), 'Dikē in Archaic Greek thought', *Classical Philology*, 69: 186–97.

Gagarin, M. (1986/1989), *Early Greek Law*, Berkeley, CA: University of California Press.

Gagarin, M. (2002), 'Greek law and the Presocratics', in V. Caston and D. W. Graham (eds), *Presocratic Philosophy: Essays in Honour of Alexander Mourelatos*, Aldershot: Ashgate, 19–24.

Gagarin, M. (2005), 'Early Greek law', in M. Gagarin and D. Cohen (eds), *The Cambridge Companion to Ancient Greek Law*, Cambridge: Cambridge University Press, 82–94.

Gagarin, M. (2008), *Writing Greek Law*, Cambridge: Cambridge University Press.

Gagarin, M. and D. Cohen (eds) (2005), *The Cambridge Companion to Ancient Greek Law*, Cambridge: Cambridge University Press.

Gagarin, M. and P. Perlman (2016), *The Laws of Ancient Crete, c. 650–400 BCE*, Oxford: Oxford University Press.

Gagarin, M. and P. Woodruff (2007), 'Early Greek legal thought', in E. Pattaro, F. D. Miller and C.-A. Biondi (eds), *A Treatise of Legal Philosophy and General Jurisprudence: A History of the Philosophy of Law From the Ancient Greeks to the Scholastics*, vol. 6, Dodrecht: Springer.

Galinsky, G. K. (1972), *The Herakles Theme: The Adaptations of the Hero in Literature from Homer to the Twentieth Century*, Oxford: Basil Blackwell.

Gallavotti, C. (ed.) (1975), *Empedocle – Poema fisico e lustrale*, Milano: Mondadori.

Gamberini, L. (1979), *Plutarco, della musica*, Florence: L. S. Olschki.

Garcia, J. F. (2002), 'Ritual speech in early Greek song', in I. Worthington and J. Miles Foley (eds), *Epea and Grammata: Oral and Written Communication in Ancient Greece*, Leiden: Brill, 29–53.

Garland R. (1985), *The Greek Way of Death*, London: Duckworth/ Cornell University Press.

Garner, R. (1987), *Law and Society in Classical Athens*, London/ Sydney: Croom Helm.

Garnsey, P. (1988), *Famine and Food Supply in the Graeco-Roman*

World: Responses to Risk and Crisis, New York: Cambridge University Press.

Gebauer, J. (2002), *Pompe and Thysia, Attische Tieropferdarstellungen auf Schwarz -und rotfigurigen Vasen*, Münster: Ugarit-Verlag.

Gehrke, H. J. (2000), 'Verschriftung und Verschriftlichung sozialer Normen im archaischen und Klassischen Griechenland', in E. Lévy (ed.), *La codification des lois dans l'antiquité, Actes du Colloque de Strasbourg*, 27–9 November 1997, Paris, 141–59.

Geldard, R. (2001), *Remembering Heraclitus*, Great Barrington, MA: Lindisfarne Books.

Gentili, B. (1988), *Poetry and its Public in Ancient Greece: From Homer to the Fifth Century*, Baltimore, MD: Johns Hopkins University Press.

Gentili, B. and F. Perusino (eds) (1995), *Mousikē: metrica ritmica e musica greca: in memoria di Giovanni Comotti*, Pisa/Roma: Istituti Editoriali e Poligrafici Internazionali.

Gentili, B. and R. Pretagostini (eds) (1988), *La musica in Grecia*, Bari: Laterza.

Georgiades, T. (1949), *Der griechische Rhythmus: Musik, Reigen, Vers und Sprache*, Hamburg: Marion von Schröder.

Georgiades, T. (1958), *Musik und Rhythmus bei den Griechen*, Hamburg: Rowohlt.

Georgiades, T. (1982), *Music and Language*, Cambridge: Cambridge University Press.

Georgoudi, S. (2010), 'Sacrificing to the gods: ancient evidence and modern interpretations', in J. N. Bremmer and A. Erskine (eds), *The Gods of Ancient Greece – Identities and Transformations*, Edinburgh: Edinburgh University Press, 92–105.

Georgoudi, S., R. Koch Piettre and F. Schmidt (eds) (2005), *La cuisine et l'autel: Les sacri ces en questions dans les sociétés de la Méditerranée ancienne*, Turnhout: Brépols.

Gera, D. L. (2003), *Ancient Greek Ideas on Speech, Language and Civilization*, Oxford: Oxford University Press.

Gerber, D. (1991), 'Theognis', *Lustrum*, 33: 186–214 = in id. (ed.) (1997), *A Companion to the Greek Lyric Poets*, Leiden: Brill, 117–28.

Gernet, L. (1917), *Recherches sur le développement de la pensée juridique et morale en Grèce*, Paris: Ernest Leroux.

Gernet, L. (1938), 'Introduction à l'étude du droit grec ancien', *Archives d'histoire du droit oriental*, 2: 261–92.

Gernet, L. ([1948–9] 1951), 'Droit et Prédroit en Grèce ancienne', *L'Année sociologique*, 3rd series, Paris, 21–119.

Gernet, L. ([1955] 1979), *Droit et société dans la Grèce ancienne*, Paris: Sirey/Arno Press.

Gernet, L. ([1968] 1982), *Droit et institutions en Grèce antique*, Paris: F. Maspero/Flammarion.

Gernet, L. (1981), *The Anthropology of Ancient Greece*, S. J. Hamilton and B. Nagy (trans.), Baltimore, MD: Johns Hopkins University Press.

Gernet, L. and A. Boulanger (1932), *Le génie grec dans la religion*, Paris: Renaissance du Livre.

Gershenson, D. (1991), *Apollo the Wolf-God*, Virginia Journal of Indo-European Studies Monograph, 8, McLean, VA: Institute for the Study of Man.

Gevaert, F. A. (1875–81), *Histoire et théorie de la musique de l'antiquité*, Ghent: C. Annoot-Braeckman.

Giannakis, G. (1998), 'The "fate-as-spinner" motif: a study on the poetic and metaphorical language of Ancient Greek and Indo-European I', *Indogermanische Forschungen*, I, 103: 1–27.

Giannakis G. (1999), 'The "Fate-as-Spinner" motif: a study on the poetic and metaphorical language of Ancient Greek and Indo-European II', *Indogermanische Forschungen*, 104: 95–109.

Gibson, S. (2005), *Aristoxenus of Tarentum and the Birth of Musicology*, Oxford: Oxford University Press.

Gigante, M. ([1956] 1993), *Nomos Basileus*, Ricerche filologiche, 1, Napoli: Edizioni Glaux; (1993), 2nd edn, Napoli: Bibliopolis.

Gigon, O. (1935), *Untersuchungen Zu Heraklit*, dissertation, Basel.

Giordano, M. (1999), *La parola efficace – Maledizioni, giuramenti e benedizioni nella Grecia arcaica*, Pisa–Roma.

Giraudeau, M. (1984), *Les notions juridiques et sociales chez Hérodote: études sur le vocabulaire*, Paris: De Boccard.

Glotz, G. ([1926] 1965), *Ancient Greece at Work – An Economic History of Greece: From the Homeric Period to the Roman Conquest*, New York: Barnes & Noble.

Godart, L. (1977), 'Les ressources des palais mycéniens de Cnossos et Pylos', *Les Études Classiques*, 45: 31–42.

Godart, L. (1992), 'Les collecteurs dans le monde égéen', in J.-P. Olivier (ed.), *Mykenaïka*, Actes du IXe Colloque international sur les textes mycéniens et égéens = *Bulletin de Correspondance Hellénique*, Supplement, 25, 254–83.

Goheen, R. F. (1951), *The Imagery of Sophocles' Antigone: A Study of Poetic Language and Structure*, Princeton, NJ: Princeton University Press.

Goldhill, S. (1986), *Reading Greek Tragedy*, Cambridge: Cambridge University Press.

Goldhill S. (2002), *The Invention of Prose*, Oxford: Oxford University Press.

Goslin, O. (2010), 'Hesiod's Typhonomachy and the ordering of sound', *Transactions of the American Philiological Association*, 140: 351–73.

Gostoli, A. (1982), 'Le "invenzioni" di Archiloco nella testimonianza del de musica dello Ps. Plutarco; asinarteti ed epodi', *AION* (Annali), 4–5: 25–36.

Gostoli, A. (1986), 'La figura dell'aedo preomerico nella filologia peripatetica ed ellenistica', in G. Cerri (ed.) (1986), *Scrivere e recitare – Modelli di trasmissione del testo poetico nell'antichità e nel medioevo*, Roma: Edizioni dell'Ateneo, 103–26.

Gostoli, A. (1988), 'Terpandro e la funzione etico-politica della musica', in B. Gentili and R. Prestagostini (eds), *La Musica in Grecia*, Roma/Bari: Laterza, 232–7.

Gostoli, A. (1990), *Terpandro – Introduzione, testo critico, testimonianze e commento*, Roma: Edizioni dell'Ateneo.

Goulaki-Voutira, A. (2004), 'Musik bei öffentlichen und privaten Opfern: Prozession, Opferhandlung, Symposium nach dem Opfer (in Heiligtümern)', in *Thesaurus Cultus et Rituum Antiquorum*. vol. II, Los Angeles, CA: Getty Publications, 371–5.

Gould, J. (2001), *Myth, Ritual, Memory, and Exchange: Essays in Greek Literature and Culture*. Oxford: Oxford University Press.

Gould, J. and D. M. Lewis (1968), *The Dramatic Festivals of Athens*, 2nd edn, London/Oxford: Clarendon Press.

Govaert, C. J. and J. van den Bergh (1964), *Themis En De Muzen – De Functie Van De Gebonden Vormen In Het Recht*, Haarlem: H. D. Tjeenk Willink.

Graf, F. (1974), *Eleusis und die orphische Dichtung Athens in vorhellenistischer Zeit* (RGVV 33), Berlin/New York: De Gruyter.

Graf, F. (1995), 'Orfeo: un poeta tra gli uomini', in D. Restani (ed.) (1988), *Musica e mito nella Grecia antica*, Bologna: Il Mulino, 303–20.

Graf, F. (2002), 'What is new about Greek sacrifice', in H. F. J. Horstmanshoff, H. W. Singor, F. van Straten and J. H. M. Strubbe (eds), *Kykeon: Studies in Honour of H. S. Versnel*, Leiden: Brill, 113–25.

Graf, F. (2008), *Apollo*, London: Routledge.

Graham, A. J. (1964), *Colony and Mother City in Ancient Greece*, Manchester: Manchester University Press.

Graham, A. J. (1982), 'The colonial expansion of Greece: the western Greeks', in J. Boardman and N. G. L. Hammond (eds), *The Cambridge Ancient History: The Expansion of the Greek World, Eighth to Sixth Centuries B.C.*, 3(3): 83–195.

Graham, D. (2010), *The Texts of Early Greek Philosophy*, Cambridge: Cambridge University Press.

Gray, D. H. F. (1955), 'Houses in the *Odyssey*', *Classical Quarterly*, New Series 5(1/2): 1–12.

Greene, W. C. ([1944] 1948), *Moira. Fate, God, and Evil in Greek Thought*, Cambridge, MA: Harvard University Press.

Gregory, J. (ed.) (2005), *A Companion to Greek Tragedy*, Malden, MA: Blackwell.

Grieser, H. (1937), *Nomos – Ein Beitrag zur griechischen Musikgeschichte*, Heidelberg: F. Bilabel.

Griffin, A. (2009), *Ancient Greek Music: A New Technical History*, Cambridge: Cambridge University Press.

Griffin, J. (1980), *Homer on Life and Death*, Oxford: Clarendon Press

Griffin, J. (1998), 'The social function of Attic tragedy', *Classical Quarterly*, 48, 39–61.

Griffith, M. (ed.) ([1999] 2003), *Sophocles: Antigone*, Cambridge: Cambridge University Press.

Grote, D. (1994), 'Callicles' use of Pindar's ΝΟΜΟΣ ΒΑΣΙΛΕΥΣ: Gorgias 484b', *Classical Journal*, 90, 1: 21–31.

Grottanelli, C. (1988) 'Uccidere, donare, mangiare', in C. Grottanelli and N. F. Parise (ed.), *Sacrificio nel società nel mondo antico*, Roma/Bari: Laterza, 1988, 8–16.

Grottanelli, C. and N. F. Parese (eds) (1988), *Sacrificio nel società nel mondo antico*, Roma/Bari: Laterza.

Guiraud, P. (1893), *La Propriètè fonciére en Grèce jusqu'à la Conquête romaine*, Paris: Imprimerie Nationale Librairie Hachette et Cie.

Guizzi, F. (2010), 'Ho visto un re . . . La regalità nello Scudo di Achille', in M. D'Acunto and R. Palmisciano (eds), *Lo Scudo di Achille nell'Iliade – Esperienze ermeneutiche a confronto*, Atti della giornata di studi Napoli, 12 May 2008, Pisa/Roma: Fabrizio Serra, 86–91.

Gundert, H. (1935), *Pindar und sein Dichterberuf*, Frankfurter Studien zur Religion und Kultur der Antike, 10, Frankfurt am Main: Vittorio Klostermann.

Guthrie, W. K. C. ([1952] 1993), *Orpheus and Greek Religion*, Princeton, NJ: Princeton University Press.

Guthrie, W. K. C. (1962), *A History of Greek Philosophy I: The Presocratic Tradition from Parmenides to Democritus*, Cambridge: Cambridge University Press.

Guthrie, W. K. C. (1969), *A History of Greek Philosophy III: The Fifth-Century Enlightenment*, Cambridge: Cambridge University Press.

Guthrie, W. K. C. (1971), *The Sophists*, Cambridge: Cambridge University Press.

Gützwiller, K. (1991), *Theocritus' Pastoral Analogies: The Formation of a Genre*, Madison, WI: University of Wisconsin Press.

Gützwiller, K. (2006a), 'The herdsman in Greek Thought', in M. Fantuzzi and T. D. Papanghelis (eds) (2006), *Brill's Companion to Greek and Latin Pastoral*, Leiden/Boston, MA: Brill, 1–23.

Gützwiller, K. (2006b), 'The bucolic problem', *Classical Philology*, 101(4): 380–404.

Hagel, S. (2009), *Ancient Greek Music – A New Technical History*, Cambridge: Cambridge University Press.

Hägg, R. and B. Alroth (eds) (2005), *Greek Sacrificial Ritual, Olympian and Chthonian: Proceedings of the Sixth International Seminar on Ancient Greek Cult*, Göteborg University, 25–7 April 1997: Sävedalen.

Hahn, I. (1977), 'Temenos and service land in the Homeric epics', *Acta Antiqua Academiae Scientiarum Hungaricae*, 25: 299–316.

Haldane, J. A. (1965), 'Musical themes and imagery in Aeschylus', *Journal of Hellenic Studies*, 85: 33–41.

Haldane, J. A. (1966), 'Musical instruments in Greek worship', *Greece and Rome*, 2nd Series, 13(1): 98–107.

Hall, E. (1997), 'The sociology of Athenian tragedy', in P. E. Easterling (ed.), *The Cambridge Companion to Greek Tragedy*, Cambridge: Cambridge University Press, 93–126.

Hall, E. (2006), *The Theatrical Cast of Athens: Interactions between Ancient Greek Drama and Society*, Oxford: Oxford University Press.

Halliwell, S. (2002), *The Aesthetics of Mimesis: The Ancient Texts and Modern Problems*, Princeton, NJ/Oxford: Princeton University Press.

Halliwell, S. (2012), '*Amousia*: living without the Muses', in I. Sluiter and R. Rosen (eds), *Aesthetic Value in Classical Antiquity*, *Mnemosyne Supplements*, vol. 350, Leiden: Brill, 15–45.

Halstead, P. (1981), 'Counting sheep in neolithic and bronze age Greece', in I. Hodder, G. Isaac and N. Hammond (eds), *Pattern of the Past. Studies in Honour of David Clarke*, Cambridge: Cambridge University Press, 307–39.

Halstead, P. (1987), 'Traditional and ancient rural economy in Mediterranean Europe: plus ça change?', *Journal of Hellenic Studies*, 107: 77–87.

Halstead, P. (1990–1), 'Lost sheep? On the Linear B evidence for breeding flocks at Knossos and Pylos', *Minos* 25–6: 343–65.

Halstead, P. (1992b), 'The Mycenaean palatial economy: making the most of the gaps in the evidence', *Proceedings of the Cambridge Philological Society*, 38: 57–86.

Halstead, P. (1995), 'Plough and power: the economic and social significance of cultivation with the ox-drawn ard in the Mediterranean', *Bulletin on Sumerian Agriculture*, 8: 11–22.

Halstead, P. (1996), 'Pastoralism or household herding? Problems of scale and specialization in early Greek animal husbandry', *World Archaeology*, 28: 20–42.

Halstead, P. (2001), 'Mycenaean wheat, flax and sheep: palatial intervention in farming and its implications for rural society', in S. Voutsaki and J. T. Killen (eds), *Economy and Politics in the Mycenaean Palace States*, Proceedings of Cambridge Philological Society, suppl., vol. 27: 38–50.

Halstead, P. (2012), 'Feast, food and fodder in neolithic–bronze age Greece. Commensality and the construction of value', *eTopoi – Journal for Ancient Studies*, 2: 21–51.

Halstead, P. and V. Isaakidou (2011), 'Revolutionary secondary products: the development and significance of milking, animal-traction and wool-gathering in later prehistoric Europe and the Near East', in T. Wilkinson, S. Sherratt and J. Bennet (eds), *Interweaving Worlds: Systemic Interactions in Eurasia, 7th to 1st Millennia BC*, Oxford: Oxbow Books, 61–76.

Halstead, P. and J. C. Barrett (eds) (2004), *Food, Cuisine and Society in Prehistoric Greece*, Sheffield Studies in Aegean Archaeology 5, Oxford: Oxbow Books.

Hame, K. J. (2008), 'Female control of funeral rites in Greek tragedy: Klytaimestra, Medea, and Antigone', *Classical Philology*, 103: 1–15.

Hamilakis, Y. and E. Konsolaki (2004), 'Pigs for the gods: burnt animal sacrifices as embodied rituals at a Mycenaean sanctuary', *Oxford Journal of Archaeology* 23(2): 135–51.

Hamilton, J. (1991), 'Antigone: kinship, justice, and the polis', in D. C. Pozzi and J. M. Wickersham (eds) (1991), *Myth and the Polis*, Ithaca, NY: Cornell University Press, 86–98.

Hamilton, R. (1989), *The Architecture of Hesiodic Poetry*, Baltimore, MD: Johns Hopkins University Press.

Hardie, A. (2000), 'Pindar's "Theban" cosmogony (the First Hymn)', *Bulletin of the Institute of Classical Studies*, 44: 19–40.

Hardie, A. (2002), 'The Georgics, the mysteries and the Muses at Rome', *Proceedings of the Cambridge Philological Society*, 48: 175–208.

Hardie, A. (2004), 'Muses and Mysteries', in P. Murray and P. Wilson (eds), *Music and the Muses: The Culture of Mousikē in the Classical Athenian City*, Oxford: Oxford University Press, 11–37.

Hardie, A. (2006), 'The Aloades on Helicon: music, territory and cosmic order', *Antike und Ahendland*, 52: 42–71.

Hardie, A. (2009), 'Etymologising the muse', *Materiali e discussioni per l'analisi dei testi classici*, 62: 9–57.

Hardie, A. (2012), '*Hypsipyle*, Dionysus Melpomenos and the

Muse in Tragedy', *Papers of the Langford Latin Seminar*, 15: 143–89.

Harris, E. M. (2003), 'Antigone the lawgiver, or the ambiguities of nomos', in Harris and Rubinstein (eds), *The Law and the Courts in Ancient Greece*, London: Duckworth, 19–56.

Harris, E. M. (2012), 'Homer, Hesiod, and the "origins" of Greek slavery', *Revue des études anciennes*, 114: 345–66.

Harris, E. M. (2004), 'Antigone the lawyer or the ambiguities of nomos', in Harris and Rubenstein (eds), 19–56 [= Harris, E. M. (2006), 41–80].

Harris, E. M. (2006), *Democracy and the Rule of Law in Classical Athens. Essays on Law, Society, and Politics*, Cambridge: Cambridge University Press.

Harris, E. M. (2010), 'What are the laws of Athens about? Substance and procedure in Athenian statutes', *Dike*, 12–13: 5–68.

Harris, E. M. (2012), 'Sophocles and Athenian Law', in K. Ormand (ed.), *The Blackwell Companion to Sophocles*, Oxford: Blackwell, 287–300.

Harris, E. M. and L. Rubinstein (eds) (2004), *The Law and the Courts in Ancient Greece*, London: Duckworth.

Harris, J. (1929), 'The origin of the cult of Hermes', *Bulletin of the John Rylands Library*, 13, 1: 107–22.

Harris, S. (2012), 'From the parochial to the universal: comparing cloth cultures in the bronze age', *European Journal of Archaeology*, 15: 61–97.

Harris, W. V. (1989), *Ancient Literacy*, Cambridge, MA: Harvard University Press.

Harrison, A. R. W. (1955), 'Law making at Athens at the end of the fifth century BC', *Journal of Hellenic Studies*, 75: 26–35.

Harrison, E. (1902), *Studies in Theognis*, Cambridge: Cambridge University Press.

Harrison, J. E. (1912), *Themis: A Study of the Social Origins of Greek Religion*, Cambridge: Cambridge University Press.

Haubold, J. (2000), *Homer's People. Epic Poetry and Social Formation*, Cambridge: Cambridge University Press.

Havelock, E. A. (1963), *Preface to Plato*, Cambridge, MA: Harvard University Press.

Havelock, E. A. (1978), *The Greek Concept of Justice: From its Shadow in Homer to its Substance in Plato*, Cambridge, MA: Harvard University Press.

Havelock, E. A. (1982), *The Literate Revolution in Greece and its Cultural Consequences*, Princeton, NJ: Princeton University Press.

Havelock, E. A. (1986), *The Muse Learns to Write: Reflections on Orality and Literacy from Antiquity to the Present*, New Haven, CT: Yale University Press.

Hawke, J. (2011), *Writing Authority: Elite Competition and Written Law in Early Greece*, DeKalb, IL: Northern Illinois University Press.

Heath, M. (1987a), *The Poetics of Greek Tragedy*, Stanford, CA: Stanford University Press.

Heath, M. (1987b), 'Jure principem locum tenet: Euripides' Hecuba', *Bulletin of the Institute of Classical Studies*, 34: 40–68.

Hedén, E. (1912), *Homerische Götterstudien*, Uppsala.

Hegel, G. W. F. (1962), *Hegel on Tragedy*, A. Paolucci and H. Paolucci (eds), Westport, CT: Greenwood Press.

Hegel, G. W. F. (1991), *Elements of the Philosophy of Right*, A. W. Wood (ed.), Cambridge: Cambridge University Press.

Hegel, G. W. F. (1997), *Phenomenology of Spirit*, T. M. Knox (trans.) Oxford: Oxford Univerity Press.

Heidegger, M. ([1953] 1959), *An Introduction to Metaphysics*, R. Manheim (trans.), New Haven, CT: Yale University Press.

Heidegger, M. (1981/2000), *Elucidations of Hölderlin's Poetry*, Keith Hoeller (trans. and intro.), Amherst, NY: Humanity Books.

Heidegger, M. (1984), *Hölderlins Hymne 'Der Ister'*, Frankfurt am Main: Vittorio Klostermann.

Heidegger, M. (1991), *The Principle of Reason*, Reginald Lilly (trans.), Indianapolis, IN: Indiana University Press.

Heidegger, M. (1996), *Hölderlin's Hymn 'The Ister'*, W. McNeill and J. Davis (trans.), Indianapolis, IN: Indiana University Press.

Heidegger, M. and E. M. Fink (1970/1979), *Heraclitus Seminar 1966/67*, C. H. Seibert (trans.), Tuscaloosa, AL: University of Alabama Press.

Heiden, B. A. (2007), 'The Muses' uncanny lies: Hesiod, Theogony 27 and its translators', *American Journal of Philology*, 128: 153–75.

Heidsieck, F. H. (1986), 'Observations concernant legein et logos chez Héraclite', *Philosophie du langage et grammaire dans l'Antiquité*, Grénoble, 47–56.

Heinimann, F. von ([1945] 1965/1972), *Nomos und Physis: Herkunft und Bedeutung einer Antithese im griechischen Denken des 5, Jahrhunderts, Schweizerische Beiträge zur Altertumswissenschaft*, Heft, 1, Basel: Friedrich Reinhardt.

Heinrichs, A. (2003), 'Writing religion: inscribed texts, ritual authority, and the religious discourse of the polis', in H. Yunis (ed.), *Written Texts and the Rise of Literate Culture in Ancient Greece*, Cambridge: Cambridge University Press 38–50.

Heitsch, E. (1966), *Hesiod*, Darmstadt: Wissenschaftliche Buchgesellschaft (Wege der Forschung 44).

Heller-Roazen, D. (2011), *The Fifth Hammer – Pythagoras and the Disharmony of the World*, New York: Zone Books.

Henrichs, A. (1994–5), '"Why should I dance?": Choral self-referentiality in Greek tragedy', *Arion*, 3rd series, The Chorus in Greek Tragedy and Culture, 3(1) (Fall/Winter): 56–111.

Henrichs, A. (2000), 'Drama and dromena: bloodshed, violence, and sacrificial metaphor in Euripides', *Harvard Studies in Classical Philology*, 100: 173–88.

Henry, E. (1992), *Orpheus with his Lute: Poetry and the Renewal of Life*, London: Bristol Classical Press.

Herington, J. (1985), *Poetry into Drama: Early Tragedy and the Greek Poetic Tradition*, Berkeley/Los Angeles, CA/London: University of California Press.

Hermary, A. et al. (2004) 'Les sacrifices dans le monde grec', *Thesaurus cultus et rituum antiquorum* I: 60–132.

Herodotus (1920), *Histories*, A. D. Godley (trans.), 4 vols, London: William Heinemann.

Herter, H. (1976), 'Hermes: Ursprung und Wesen eines griechischen Gottes', *Rheinisches Museum*, 119: 193–241.

Hesiod (1977), *The Homeric Hymns and Homerica*, H. G. Evelyn-White (trans.), Cambridge, MA: Harvard University Press (Loeb).

[Hesiod] Hamilton, R. (1990), *Hesiod's Theogony*, Bryn Mawr, PA: Bryn Mawr Commentaries.

[Hesiod] Hamilton, R., E. G. Rainis and R. L. Ruttenberg (eds) (1988), *Hesiod's Works and Days*, Bryn Mawr, PA: Bryn Mawr Commentaries.

Hester, D. A. (1971), 'Sophocles the unphilosophical: a study in the Antigone', *Mnemosyne*, 24: 11–59.

Hirzel, R. (1900), 'ΑΓΡΑΦΟΣ ΝΟΜΟΣ', *Abhandlungen der philologisch-historischen Classe der Königlich Sächsischen Gesellschaft der Wissenschaften*, 20(1).

Hirzel, R. (1907), *Themis, Dike und Verwandtes*, Leipzig: S. Hirzel.

Hitch, S. (2009), *King of Sacrifice: Ritual and Royal Authority in the Iliad*, Hellenic Studies 25, Washington, DC: Center for Hellenic Studies, Trustees for Harvard University Press.

Hodkinson, S. (1986), 'Land tenure and inheritance in Classical Sparta', *Classical Quarterly*, 36: 378–406.

Hoffmann, K. F. (1997), *Das Recht im Denken der Sophistik*, Beiträge zur Altertumskunde 104, Stuttgart/Leipzig: Teubner.

Hölderlin, F. (1943–85), *Sämtliche Werke*, Grosse Stuttgarter Ausgabe, F. Beissner and A. Beck (eds), 8 vols, Stuttgart: Kohlhammer Verlag und J. G. Cottasche Buchhandlung Nachfolger.

Hölderlin, F. (1969), *Werke, Briefe, Dokumente*, München: Winkler.

Hölderlin, F. (1988), *Sämtliche Werke*, D. E. Sattler et al. (eds), vol. 16, Frankfurt am Main: Stroemfeld/Roter Stern.

Hölderlin, F. (1992), *Sämtliche Werke und Briefe*, M. Knaupp (ed.), 3 vols, München: Carl Hanser.

Hölderlin, F. (1994), *Poems and Fragments*, M. Hamburger (trans.), London: Anvil.

Hölderlin, F. (2004), *Sämtliche Werke*, D. E. Sattler (eds), 12 vols, Darmstadt: WBG.

Hölkeskamp, K.-J. (1992a), 'Arbitrators, lawgivers and the "codification of law" in Archaic Greece [problems and perspectives]', *Mètis – Anthropologie des mondes grecs anciens*, 7, 1–2: 49–81.

Hölkeskamp, K.-J. (1992b), 'Written law in Archaic Greece', *Proceedings of the Cambridge Philological Society*, 38: 87–117.

Hölkeskamp, K.-J. (1999), *Schiedsrichter, Gesetzgeber und Gesetzgebung im archaischen Griechenland*, Historia-Einzelschrift, 131, Stuttgart: Steiner.

Hölkeskamp, K.-J. (2000), '(In-)Schrift und Monument. Zum Begriff des Gesetzes im archaischen und klassischen Griechenland', *Zeitschrift für Papyrologie und Epigraphik*, 132: 73–96.

Hölkeskamp, K.-J. (2002), 'Nomos, thesmos, und Verwandtes – Vergleichende Überlegungen zur Konzeptionalisierung geschriebenen Rechts im klassischen Griechenland', in D. Cohen (ed.) (2002), *Demokratie und Soziale Kontrollen im Klassischen Athen*, München, 115–46.

Hölkeskamp, K.-J. (2005), 'What's in a code? Solon's Laws between complexity, compilation and contingency', *Hermes*, 133, 3: 280–93.

Holt, P. (1999), 'Polis and tragedy in the Antigone', *Mnemosyne* 52: 658–90.

[Homer] (1942), *The Iliad of Homer*, S. Butler (trans.), New York: W. J. Black, Perseus Digital Library.

[Homer] (1944), *The Odyssey of Homer*, S. Butler (trans.), New York: W. J. Black, Perseus Digital Library.

[Homer] Hammond, M. (2000), *Homer, The Odyssey*, with intro. by J. Griffin, London: Duckworth.

[Homer] Munro, D. B. and T. W. Allen (eds) (1920), *Homeri Opera*, 2 vols: *Iliad*, Oxford: Oxford University Press.

[Homer Scholia] Erbse, H. (1969–88), *Scholia graeca in Homeri Iliadem*, Berlin: De Gruyter.

[Homeric Hymns] (1963), T. W. Allen, W. R. Halliday and E. E. Sikes (eds), *The Homeric Hymns*, Amsterdam.

Honig, B. (2009), 'Antigone's laments, Creon's grief: mourning, membership and the politics of exception', *Political Theory*, 37, 1: 5–43.

Hooker, J. T. (1987), 'Homeric society. A shame-culture?', *Greece and Rome*, 34: 121–5.

Hordern, J. (1999), 'Some observations on the Persae of Timotheus', *Classical Quarterly*, 49: 433–8.

Hordern, J. (ed.) (2002), *The Fragments of Timotheus of Miletus*, Oxford/New York: Oxford University Press.

Hornum, M. B. (1993), *Nemesis, the Roman State, and the Games*, Leiden: Brill.

Horster, M. (2010), 'Religious landscape and sacred ground: relationships between space and cult in the Greek world', *Revue de l'histoire des religions* 4: 435–58.

Huchzermeyer, H. (1931), *Aulos und Kithara in der griechischen Musik bis zum Ausgang der klassischen Zeit*, Emsdetten: Lechte.

Humphreys, S. C. (1971), 'The work of Louis Gernet', *History and Theory*, 10(2): 172–96.

Humphreys, S. (1988), 'The discourse of law in archaic and classical Greece', *Law and History Review*, 7(2): 465–93.

Hunter, V. and J. Edmondson (eds) (2001), *Law and Social Status in Classical Athens*, Oxford: Oxford University Press.

Hurst, A. and A. Schachter (eds) (1996), *La montagne des Muses*, Geneva: Droz.

Hussey, E. (1995), *The Presocratics*, Indianapolis, IN: Hackett.

Hutchinson, G. O. (2001), *Greek Lyric Poetry: A Commentary on Selected Larger Pieces*, Oxford: Oxford University Press.

Hüttl, W. (1929), *Verfassungsgeschichte von Syrakus*, Prague.

Huxley, G. (2000), 'Laistrygonian pasturage: In memory of Gerard Watson', *Hermathena*, 168: 5–9.

Ingalls, W. B. (2000), 'Ritual performance as training for daughters in Archaic Greece', *Phoenix*, 54(1/2): 1–20.

Inwood, B. (1992), *The Poem of Empedocles – A Text and Translation with an Introduction*, rev. edn (2001), Toronto/Buffalo/London: Toronto University Press.

Ireland, S. and F. L. Steel (1975), 'Phrenes as an anatomical organ in the worlds of Homer', *Glotta*, 53: 183–95.

Irwin, E. (2005), *Solon and Early Greek Poetry: The Politics of Exhortation*, Cambridge/New York: Cambridge University Press.

Isaakidou, V. (2006), 'Ploughing with cows: Knossos and the "Secondary Products Revolution"', in D. Serjeantson and D. Field (eds), *Animals in the Neolithic*, Oxford: Oxbow Books, 95–112.

Isocrates (1945), *Isocrates*, vol. III, L. R. Van Hook (trans.), Cambridge, MA: Harvard University Press (Loeb).

Jacoby, F. (1944), 'Patrios nomos: state burial in Athens and the public cemetery in the Kerameikos', *Journal of Hellenic Studies*, 64: 37–66.

Jaeger, W. (1947), *The Theology of the Early Greek Philosophers*, Oxford: Clarendon Press/Oxford University Press.

Jaeger, W. ([1947] 1960), 'Praise of law: the origin of legal philosophy and the Greeks', in P. Sayre (ed.), *Interpretations of Modern Legal Philosophies*, New York: Oxford University Press, 352–75 (= Jaeger, W. (1960) *Scripta Minora*, II, Rome, 319–51).

Jakobson, R. (1979), *The Sound Shape of Lyric*, Bloomington, IN: Indiana University Press.

Janko, R. (1982), *Homer, Hesiod and the Hymns*, Cambridge: Cambridge University Press.

Janko, R. (2000), *Philodemus: On Poems, Book 1*, New York: Oxford University Press.

Janssen, T. H. (1984), *Timotheus 'Persae': A Commentary*, Amsterdam: A. M. Hakkert.

Jeanmaire, H. (1939), *Couroi et Courètes – Essai sur l'éducation spartiate et sur les rites d'adolescence dans l'antiquité hellénique*, Lille: University of Lille.

Jeannière, A. J. (1985), *Héraclite*, Paris: Aubier.

Jebb, R. C. (ed. and trans.) (1887), *Sophocles. The Oedipus Tyrannus of Sophocles*, Cambridge: Cambridge University Press.

Jebb, R. C. (ed. and trans.) (1891), *Sophocles: The Plays and Fragments, III: The Antigone*, Cambridge: Cambridge University Press.

Jebb, R. C. (ed. and trans.) (1893), *Sophocles: The Ajax of Sophocles*, Cambridge: Cambridge University Press.

Jens, W. (1952), *Antigone-Interpretationen*, Baden-Baden: Festschr. O. Weinreich.

Johnson, F. P. (1941), 'Odysseus' livestock', *Classical Philology*, 36: 273–4.

Johnstone, C. L. (2009), *Listening to the Logos – Speech and the Coming of Wisdom in Ancient Greece*, Columbia, SC: University of South Carolina Press.

Jones, E. (2012), 'Allocating musical pleasure: performance, pleasure, and value in Aristotle's *Politics*', in I. Sluiter and R. Rosen (eds), *Aesthetic Value in Classical Antiquity*, Leiden: Brill, 159–82.

Jones, W. (1956), *The Law and Legal Theory of the Greeks: An Introduction*, Oxford: Clarendon Press.

Jones, W. H. S., E. T. Withington and P. Potter (trans.) (1923–2012), *Hippocrates* [Works], 12 vols, Cambridge, MA: Harvard University Press.

Jost, M. (2007), 'The religious system in Arcadia', in D. Ogden (ed.), *A Companion To Greek Religion*, Malden, MA/Oxford/Carlton, Australia: Blackwell, 264–79.

Jouanna, J. (2012), *Greek Medicine from Hippocrates to Galen, Selected Papers*, Neil Allies (trans. and ed.), with preface by P. van der Eijk, Leiden/Boston: Brill.

Kaden, C. (2004), *Das Unerhörte und das Unhörbare – Was*

Musik ist, was Musik sein kann, Kassel: Bärenreiter/ Metzler.

Kadletz, E. (1984), 'The Sacrifice of Eumaios the Pig Herder', *Greek, Roman, and Byzantine Studies* 25: 99–105.

Kahn, C. H. (1964), 'A New Look at Heraclitus', *American Philosophical Quarterly*, 1: 189–203.

Kahn, C. H. (1973), *The Verb 'Be' in Ancient Greek*, Dordrecht: Reidel.

Kahn, C. H. (1979), *The Art and Thought of Heraclitus*, Cambridge: Cambridge University Press.

Kahn, L. (1979), 'Hermès, la frontière et l'identité ambiguë', *Ktema* 4: 201–11.

Kapp, J. C. (1792), *Aristotelis de mundo liber*, Altenburg: Richter.

Käppel, L. (1992), *Paian, Studien zur Geschichte Einer Gattung*, Berlin/New York: De Gruyter.

Kazanskiene, V. P. (1995), 'Land tenure and social position in Mycenaean Greece', in R. Laffineur and W.-D. Niemeier (eds), *Politeia: Society and State in the Aegean Bronze Age* [Aegaeum 12] (Liège) II: 603–11.

Kerényi, K. (1944), 'Hermes der Seelenführer', *Albae Vigiliae*, Neue Folge 1: 105–6.

Kerényi, K. (1955), *La religione antica nelle sue line fondamentali*, D. Cantimori (trans.), Bologna: N. Zanichelli.

Kerényi, K. (1983), *Apollo: The Wind, the Spirit, and the God: Four Studies*, Dunquin Series, Dallas, TX: Spring.

Kerferd, G. B. (1981), *The Sophistic Movement*, Cambridge/ New York: Cambridge University Press.

Kern, O. (1922), *Orphicorum Fragmenta*, Berlin: Berolini Apud Weidmannos.

Kerschensteiner, J. (1962), *Kosmos – Quellenkritische Untersuchungen zu den Vorsokratikern*, München: Beck.

Keuls, E. C. (1985), *The Reign of the Phallus: Sexual Politics in Ancient Athens*, New York: Harper.

Keyssner, K. (1932), *Gottesvorstellung und Lebensauffassung im Griechischen Hymnus*. Stuttgart: Kohlhammer.

Killen, J. T. (1964), 'The wool industry of Crete in the Late Bronze Age', *Annual of the British School at Athens*, 59: 1–15.

Killen, J. T. (1976), *'a-ko-ra-ja/a-ko-ra-jo'*, in A. Morpurgo Davies and W. Meid (eds), *Studies in Greek and Indo-European Linguistics Offered to Leonard R. Palmer on the*

Occasion of his Seventieth Birthday, 5 June 1976, Beiträge zur Sprachwissenschaft 16: 117–25.

Killen, J. T. (1985), 'The Linear B tablets and the Mycenae: an economy', in A. Morpurgo Davies and Y. Duhoux (eds), *Linear B: A 1984 Survey*, Bibliothèque des Cahiers de l'Institut de linguistique de Louvain, 26: 241–305.

Killen, J. T. (1992), 'Observations on the Thebes sealings', in J.-P. Olivier (ed.), *Mykenaïka*, Actes du IXe Colloque international sur les textes mycéniens et égéens, 2–6 October 1990, *Bulletin de Correspondance Hellénique*, Supplement 25, Paris: Diffusion de Boccard, 365–80.

Killen, J. T. (1993), 'Records of sheep and goats at Mycenaean Knossos and Pylos', *Bulletin on Sumerian Agriculture*, 7: 209–18.

Killen, J. T. (1994), 'Thebes sealings, Knossos tablets, and Mycenaean state banquets', *Bulletin of the Institute of Classical Studies*, 39: 67–84.

Killen, J. T. (1995), 'Some further thoughts on "collectors"', in R. Laffineur and W.-D. Niemeier (eds), *Politeia. Society and State in the Aegean Bronze Age*, Aegaeum 12, Liège/ Austin, TX: Université de Liège/University of Texas/PASP, 213–26.

Killen, J. T. (1998), 'The role of the state in wheat and olive production in Mycenaean Crete', *Aevum*, 72: 19–23.

Killen, J. T. (2008), 'Mycenaean economy', in Y. Duhoux and A. Morpurgo Davies (eds) (2008), *A Companion to Linear B: Mycenaean Greek Texts and their World*, Bibliothèque des Cahiers de l'Institut de Linguistique de Louvain 120, Leuven and Dudley, MA: Peeters, 157–200.

Killen, J. T. (2015), *Economy and Administration in Mycenaean Greece, Collected Papers on Linear B* (1962–2012), 3 vols, Maurizio Del Freo (ed.), Rome: CNR – Insituto di Studi Sul Mediterraneo Antico.

Killy, W. (1954), 'Hölderlins Interpretation des Pindarfragments 166 (Schr.)', *Antike und Abendland* 4: 216–33.

Kirk, G. S. (1954/1975), *Heraclitus. The Cosmic Fragments*, Cambridge: Cambridge University Press.

Kirk, G. S., J. E. Raven and M. Schofield ([1957] 1983), *The Presocratic Philosophers*, Cambridge: Cambridge University Press.

Kirkwood, G. M. (1947), 'Hecuba and nomos', *Transactions of the American Philological Association*, 78: 61–8.

Kirkwood, G. M. (1991), 'Order and disorder in Sophocles' Antigone', *Illinois Classical Studies*, 16(1/2): 101–9.

Kitto, H. D. F. (2003), *Greek Tragedy: A Literary Study*, 3rd edn, London: Routledge.

Kitts, M. (2002), 'Sacrificial violence in the Iliad', *Journal of Ritual Studies* 16: 19–39.

Kitts, M. (2005), *Sanctified Violence in Homeric Society – Oath-Making Rituals and Narratives in the Iliad*, Cambridge: Cambridge University Press.

Kitts, M. (2011), 'Ritual scenes in the Iliad: rote, Hallowed, or encrypted as ancient art?', *Oral Traditions* 26(1): 221–46.

Knox, B. M. W. (1964), *The Heroic Temper*, Berkeley/Los Angeles, CA: University of California Press.

Knox, B. M. W. (1965), *The Heroic Temper: Studies in Sophoclean Tragedy*, Berkeley, CA: University of California Press.

Kolk, D. (1963), *Der pythische Apollonhymnus als aitiologische Dichtung*, Meisenheim am Glan: Anton Hain.

Koller, H. (1954), *Die Mimesis in der Antike. Nachahmung, Darstellung, Ausdruck*, Berne: Francke.

Koller, H. (1955), 'Stoicheion', *Glotta*, 34: 161–74.

Koller, H. (1956), 'Das kitharodische Prooimion: Eine formgeschichtliche Untersuchung', *Philologus*, 100: 159–206.

Koller, H. (1963), *Musik und Dichtung im Alten Griechenland*, Bern–München: Francke.

Koller, H. (1965), 'ΘΕΣΠΙΣ ΑΟΙΔΟΣ', *Glotta*, 43: 277–85.

Koller, H. (1968), 'Πόλις Μερόπων Ἀνθρώπων', *Glotta*, 46(1/2): 18–26.

Kontoleon, N. M. (1956), 'Zu den neuen Archilochosinschriften', *Philologus*, 100: 29–39.

Kontoleon, N. M. (1964) 'Archilochos und Paros', in *Archiloque*, Entretiens sur l'antiquité Classique, Geneva: Fondation Hardt, 10: 37–86.

Kopperschmidt, J. (1967), *Die Hikesie als dramatische Form*, Dissertation, University of Tübingen.

Korzeniewski, D. (1974), 'Die Binnenresponsion in den Persern des Timotheos', *Philologus* 118: 22–39.

Kotsidu, H. (1991), *Die musischen Agone der Panathenäen in archaischer und klassischer Zeit: Eine historisch-archäologische*

Untersuchung, Dissertation, München: tuduv-Verlags-Gesellschaft.

Kousoulini, V. (2013), 'Alcmanic hexameters and early hexametric poetry: Alcman's poetry in its oral context', *Greek, Roman and Byzantine Studies*, 53: 420–40.

Kowalzig, B. (2004), 'Changing choral worlds: song-dance and society in Athens and Beyond', in P. Murray and P. Wilson (eds), *Music and the Muses: The Culture of 'Mousike' in the Classical Athenian City*, Oxford: Oxford University Press, 39–65.

Kowalzig, B. (2007), *Singing for the Gods – Performances of Myth and Ritual in Archaic and Classical Greece*, Oxford: Oxford University Press.

Kränzlein, A. (1963), 'Eigentum und Besitz im griechischen Recht des fünften und vierten Jahrhunderts v. Chr.', *Berliner Juristische Abhandlungen* 8: 91–3.

Krause, W. (1936), 'Die Ausdrücke für das Schicksal in Homer', *Glotta*, 25: 143–52.

Kraye, J. (1990), 'Aristotle's god and the authenticity of De Mundo: an early modern controversy', *Journal of the History of Philosophy*, 28(3): 339–58.

Krell, D. F. (2005), *The Tragic Absolute: German Idealism and the Languishing of God*, Bloomington, IN: Indiana University Press.

Kretschmer, P. and E. Locker (1944), *Rückläufiges Wörterbuch der griechischen Sprache*, Göttingen: Vandenhoeck & Ruprecht.

Kritzias, C. (1980), 'Muses Delphiques à Argos', *Bulletin de Correspondance Hellénique*, suppl. 6: 195–209.

Kubatzki, J. (2015), *Die Rolle der Musik in antiken griechischen Prozessionen. Ikonografische Untersuchung griechischer Gefäße mit dem Schwerpunkt im 6. und 5. Jh. v. Chr.*, Dissertation, Philosophischen Fakultät III der Humboldt-Universität zu Berlin.

Kubatzki, J. (2016), 'Music in rites. Some thoughts about the function of music in Ancient Greek cults', *Journal of Ancient Studies*, 5: 1–17.

Kurtz, D. C. and J. Boardman (1971), *Greek Burial Customs*, London/New York: Routledge.

Kyriakidis, E. (2008), 'Who's who: the shepherds in the Cn series at Pylos', *Pasiphae: Rivista di filologia e antichità egee*, 2(1): 449–59.

Kyriakidis, E. (2010), '"Collectors" as stakeholders in Mycenaean governance: property and the relations between the ruling class and the state', *Cambridge Classics Journal*, 56(1): 140–77.

Kyriakou, P. (2002), 'The violence of Nomos in Pindar fr. 169a', *Materiali e discussioni per l'analisi dei testi classici*, 48: 195–206.

Lacan J. (1992), 'The essence of tragedy: a commentary on Sophocles' Antigone', in J.-A. Miller (ed.), *The Ethics of Psychoanalysis, The Seminar of Jacques Lacan, Book VII*, D. Porter (trans.), New York/London: Norton.

Lacey, W. K. (1968), *The Family in Classical Greece*, London/Ithaca, NY: Thames & Hudson/Cornell University Press.

Lacoue-Labarthe, P. (1989), 'The caesura of the speculative', in C. Fynsk (ed.), *Typography: Mimesis, Philosophy, Politics*, Cambridge, MA: Harvard University Press, 208–35.

Lallot, J. (1972), 'La Terre en partage (Héraclite, fr. 11 D.-K.)', *Archiv für Geschichte der Philosophie*, 54: 109–15.

Lambropoulos, V. (2006), *The Tragic Idea*, London: Duckworth.

Lampros, S. P. (1873), *De conditorum coloniarum graecorum indole praemiisque et honoribus*, Dissertation, Leipzig University.

Landels, J. G. (1999), *Music in Ancient Greece and Rome*, London: Routledge.

Lang, M. L. (1969), 'Homer and oral technique', *Hesperia* 38: 159–68.

Lanni, A. (2006), *Law and Justice in the Courts of Classical Athens*, Cambridge: Cambridge University Press.

Lanza, D. (1963), 'Nomos e Ison in Euripide', *Rivista di Filologia e di Istruzione Classica*, 91: 416–39.

Laroche, E. (1949), *Histoire de la racine νεμ- en grec ancien (νέμω, νέμεσις, νόμος, νομίζω). Études et commentaries*, vol. 6, Paris: Librairie C. Klincksieck.

Larson, J. (2001), *Greek Nymphs – Myth, Cult, Lore*, New York: Oxford University Press.

Lassalle, F. ([1858] 1920), *Die Philosophie Herakleitos Des Dunklen von Ephesos*. Leipzig: E. Schirmer.

Lassèrre, F. (1954), *Plutarque, de la musique*, Lausanne: Urs Graf-Verlag.

Latacz, J. (1993–2003), *Einführung in die griechische Tragödie*. Göttingen: Vandenhoeck & Ruprecht.

Latte, K. (1934), 'Τέμενος', *Paulys Realencyclopädie der classischen Altertumswissenschaft*, 2, Reihe, 10, Stuttgart: Halbband, 435–7.

Latte, K. (1946), 'Der Rechtsgedanke im archaischen Griechentum', *Antike und Ahendland*, 2: 63–76.

Lattimore, R. (1962), 'Phaedra and Hippolytus', *Arion*, 1(3): 5–18.

Lattimore, R. (trans.) (1967), *The Iliad of Homer*, Chicago, IL: University of Chicago Press.

Lattimore, R. (trans.) (1991), *The Works and Days, Theogony, The Shield of Herakles*, Ann Arbor, MI: University of Michigan Press.

Lawler, L. B. (1964), *The Dance in Ancient Greece*, Middletown, CT: Wesleyan University Press.

Lazenby, J. F. (1995), 'The archaia moira: a suggestion', *Classical Quarterly*, 45: 87–91.

Lazzeri, M. (1995), 'Osservazioni su alcuni frammenti della Gerioneide di Stesicoro', *Bollettino dei classici*, 3, 16: 93–9.

Lazzeroni, R. (1957), 'Lingua degli dei e lingua degli uomini', *Annali della Scuola Normale di Pisa*, 26: 1–25 (= Bolelli, T. and Sani, S. (eds) (1997), *Scritti scelti di Romano Lazzeroni*, Pisa, 209–35).

Leâo D. F. and P. J. Rhodes (2010) *Law and Drama in Ancient Greece*, London: Bloomsbury.

Lebedev, A. (1994), 'Homo Loquens: K etimologii grech. ΑΝΘΡΩΠΟΣ, ΜΕΡΟΠΕΣ i slav. ČELOVĚKЪ', Balkanskie chteniia 3 – Lingo etnokul'turnaia istoriia Balkan i Vostochnoi Evropy, Tezisy i materialy simpoziuma, Moskva.

Lee, D. J. N. (1960/1961), 'Homeric κήρ and others', *Glotta*, 39(3/4): 191–207.

Leemans, R. A. (1948), 'Rhythme en ϱυθμός', *L'Antiquité Classique*, XVII: 403–12.

Leitzke, E. (1930), *Moira und Gottheit im alten grichischen Epos*, Dissertation, Goettingen.

Lejeune, M. (1972), 'Le damos dans la société mycénienne', *Mémoires de philologie mycénienne*, Rome: Edizioni dell'Ateneo, 3: 137–54.

Leonard, M. (2012), 'Tragedy and the seductions of philosophy', *Cambridge Classical Journal* 58: 147–54.

Lerza, P. (1978), 'Su un frammento della Gerioneide di Stesicoro', *Atene e Roma* 23: 83–7.

Lesky, A. (1949), 'Zum Gesetzesbegriff der Stoa', *Oesterreichische Zeitschrift für öffentliches Recht*, 2: 587–99.

Lesky, A. (1952), 'Zwei Sophoklesinterpretationen', *Hermes*, 80: 91–105.

Levin, D. N. (1971), 'Apollonius' Heracles', *Classical Journal*, 67(1): 22–8.

Levin, F. R. (2009), *Greek Reflections on the Nature of Music*, New York/Cambridge: Cambridge University Press.

Lévy-Bruhl, H. ([1910] 1960), *Recherches sur les actions de la loi*, Paris: Recueil Sirey.

Lewis, J. D. (2007), *Early Greek Lawgivers*, London: Bristol Classical Press.

Lewis, V. B. (2006), 'Plato's Minos: the political and philosophical context of the problem of natural right', *Review Metaphysics*, 60: 17–53.

Lindberg, T. (2007), 'The oldest law: rediscovering the Minos', *Telos*, 138: 43–68.

Lindenlauf, A. (2001), 'Thrown away like rubbish – disposal of the dead in ancient Greece', *Papers from the Institute of Archaeology*, 12: 86–99.

Lindgren, M. (1973), *The People of Pylos: Prosopographical and Methodological Studies in the Pylos Archives*, Uppsala: Uppsala University.

Linforth, I. M. (1919), *Solon the Athenian*, Berkeley, CA: University of California Press.

Linforth, I. M. (1941), *The Arts of Orpheus*, Berkeley, CA: University of California Press.

Link, S. (1991), *Landverteilung und sozialer Frieden im archaischen Griechenland*, Historia, Einzelschriften 69, Stuttgart: F. Steiner.

Liou-Gille, B. (2000), 'La gure du Législateur dans le monde antique', *Revue belge de philologie et d'histoire*, 78(1): 171–90.

Lippman, E. A. (1964) *Musical Thought in Ancient Greece*, New York: Columbia University Press.

Lippman, E. A. (1975), *Musical Thought in Ancient Greece*, New York: Da Capo Press.

Lissarrague, F. (1995), 'Un rituel du vin: la libation', in O. Murray and M. Tecusan (eds), *In Vino Veritas*, London: British School at Rome, 126–44.

Lloyd-Jones, H. (1953), 'Aeschylus Agamemnon 416ff', *Classical Quarterly*, 3(1–2): 96.

Lloyd-Jones, H. (1971), *The Justice of Zeus*, Berkeley/Los Angeles, CA: University of California Press.

Lloyd-Jones, H. (1972), 'Pindar Fr. 169', *Harvard Studies in Classical Philology*, 76: 45–56.

Lloyd-Jones, H. (ed. and trans.) ([1994] 2002), *Antigone – Sophocles*, repr., Cambridge, MA/London: Harvard University Press (Loeb).

Lobel, E. (1961), *The Oxyrhynchus Papyri*, 24, London: Egypt Exploration Society.

Loffredo, L. (ed. and trans.) (1974), *Aristotele, Trattato sul cosmo per Alessandro*, Napoli: Luigi Loffredo.

Lohmann, J. (1970), *Musiké und Logos: Aufsätze zur griechischen Philosophie und Musiktheorie*, Stuttgart: Musikwissenschaftliche Verlags-Gessellschaft.

Longeray C. (1999), 'Ἀπονέμειν/Leggere (Pind. Isthm. 2, 47; Soph. fr. 144 Radt; Aristoph. Av. 1289)', *Quaderni Urbinati di Cultura Classica*, 62(2): 49–61.

Longman, G. A. (1954), 'Timotheus, Persae 162', *Classical Review*, 4: 208–9.

Lonsdale, S. H. (1993), *Dance and Ritual Play in Greek Religion*, Baltimore, MD/London: Johns Hopkins University Press.

Loraux, N. (1981), *Les Enfants d'Athéna. Idées athéniennes sur la citoyenneté et la division des sexes*, Paris: Maspero.

Loraux, N. (1986), 'La main d'Antigone', *Mètis – Anthropologie des mondes grecs anciens*, 1(2): 165–96.

Loraux, N. (1987), *Tragic Ways of Killing a Woman*, A. Forster (trans.) Cambridge, MA: Harvard University Press.

Loraux, N. (1998), *Mothers in Mourning: Moral and Legal Issues (Myth and Poetics)*, Ithaca, NY: Cornell University Press.

Loraux, N. (2002), *The Mourning Voice: An Essay on Greek Tragedy*, Ithaca, NY: Cornell University Press.

Lorimer, W. L. (1924–5), *The Text Tradition of Pseudo-Aristotle 'De Mundo' – Some Notes on the Text of Pseudo-Aristotle 'De Mundo'*, London: Humphrey Milford/St Andrews University Publications/Oxford University Press.

Lorimer, W. L. (ed.) (1933), *Aristotelis qui fertur libellus de mundo*, Paris: Les Belles Lettres.

Lucas, D. W. (1950), *The Greek Tragic Poets*, London: Cohen & West.

Luhmann, N. (1986), 'The autopoiesis of social systems', in F. Geyer and J. Van d. Zeuwen (eds), *Sociocybernetic Paradoxes: Observation, Control and Evolution of Self-Steering Systems*, London: Sage, 172–92.

Luhmann, N. (1995), *Social Systems*, Stanford, CA: Stanford University Press.

Lupack, S. (1999), 'Palaces, sanctuaries and workshops: the role of the religious sector in Mycenaean economics', in M. L. Galaty and W. A. Parkinson (eds), *Rethinking Mycenaean Palaces: New Interpretations of an Old Idea*, Los Angeles, CA: Cotsen Institute of Archaeology, 25–34.

Lupack, S. (2008), *The Role of the Religious Sector in the Economy of Late Bronze Age Mycenaean Greece*, BAR-International Series 1858, Oxford: Archaeopress.

Lupack, S. (2011), 'A view from outside the palace: the sanctuary and the Damos in Mycenaean economy and society', *American Journal of Archaeology*, 115: 207–17.

Lupi, M. (2003), 'L'archaia moira. Osservazioni sul regime fondiario spartano a partire da un libro recente', *Incidenza dell' antico*, 1: 151–72.

Lupu, E. (2005), *Greek Sacred Law. A Collection of New Documents (NGSL)*, Leiden/Boston: Brill.

Lurker, M. (1984), *The Routledge Dictionary of Gods, Goddesses, Devils and Demons*, London: Routledge.

Maas, M. and M. Snyder (eds) (1989), *Stringed Instruments of Ancient Greece*, New Haven, CT: Yale University Press.

MacDowell, D. M. (1978), *The Law in Classical Athens*, London: Thames & Hudson.

MacDowell, D. M. (1989), 'The oikos in Athenian law', *Classical Quarterly*, 39(1): 10–21.

Macé, A. (2014), 'Deux formes du commun en Grèce ancienne', *Annales. Histoire, Sciences Sociales*, 3: 659–88.

Mackowiak, K. (2010), 'De moira aux Moirai, de l'épopée à la généalogie: approche historique et poétique de l'autorité de Zeus, maître du destin (Iliade, Odyssée, Théogonie)', *Dialogues d'histoire ancienne*, 36(1): 9–49.

Mader, M. B. (2005), 'Antigone's line', *Bulletin de la société Américaine de philosophie de langue Française*, 14(2): 18–40.

Maehler, H. (1975), *Pindari carmina cum fragmentis, 2: Fragmenta*, Bibliotheca Scriptorum Graecorum et Romanorum Teubneriana, Leipzig: Teubner.

Maehler, H. (ed.) (2001), *Pindarus II: Fragmenta*, München and Leipzig: Indices.

Mainoldi, C. (1984), *L'image du loup et du chien dans la Gréce ancienne d'Homère à Platon*, Paris: Éditions Ophry.

Malinowski, B. (1926). *Crime and Custom in Savage Society*, London: Routledge & Kegan Paul.

Malkin, I. (1987), *Religion and Colonization in Ancient Greece*, Leiden: Brill.

Malkin, I. (1998), *The Returns of Odysseus: Colonization and Ethnicity*, Los Angeles: University of California Press.

Malkin, I. (1994), 'Inside and outside: colonisation and the formation of the mother city', *Annali di archeologia e storia antica*, 1: 1–9.

Malkin, I. (2009), 'Foundations', in K. A. Raaflaub and H. van Wees (eds), *A Companion to Archaic Greece*, Oxford: Wiley Blackwell.

Manessy-Guitton, J. (1966), 'Temenos', *Indogermanische Forschungen*, 71: 14–38.

Mansfeld, J. and Primavesi, O. (2011), *Die Vorsokratiker: Griechisch/Deutsch*, Stuttgart: Reclam.

Marcovich, M. (1967), *Heraclitus: Greek Text*, Mérida, Venezuela: Los Andes University Press.

Marcovich, M. (1999), *Diogenes Laertius – Vitae philosophorum, I. Libri I–X*, Stuttgart/Leipzig: Teubner.

Marrou, H. I. (1965), *Histoire de l'éducation dans l'Antiquité*, Paris: Seuil.

Martini, R. (2005), *Diritti greci*, Bologna: Zanichelli.

Maslov, B. (2009), 'The semantics of ἀοιδός and related compounds: towards a historical poetics of solo performance in archaic Greece', *Classical Antiquity*, 28: 1–38.

Maslov, B. (2016), 'The genealogy of the muses: an internal reconstruction of archaic Greek metapoetics', *American Journal of Philology*, 137(3): 411–46.

Mastronarde, D. (2010), *The Art of Euripides*, Cambridge: Cambridge University Press.

Mathiesen, T. J. (1984), 'Harmonia and ethos in ancient Greek music', *Journal of Musicology*, 3(3): 264–79.

Mathiesen, T. J. (1988), *Ancient Greek Music Theory*, München: G. H. Verlag.

Mathiesen, T. J. (1999), *Apollo's Lyre – Greek Music and Music*

Theory in Antiquity and the Middle Ages, Lincoln, NE/ London: University of Nebraska Press.

Mauss, M. (2007), *Manual of Ethnography*, D. Lussier (trans.), intro. by N. J. Allen (ed.), New York/Oxford: Durkheim Press/Berghahn.

Mayer, M. (1933), 'Musen (w:)', in G. Wissowa et al. (eds), *Paulys Realencyclopädie*, vol. 16.1, Stuttgart: Metzler, cols 680–757.

Mazarakis-Ainian, A. (1997), *From Rulers' Dwellings to Temples: Architecture, Religion and Society in Early Iron Age Greece (1100–700 BC)*, Jonsered: P. Åströms förlag.

McCorriston, J. (1997), 'The fiber revolution: textile extensification, alienation', *Current Anthropology*, 38: 517–49.

McCullagh, P. F. (1939), *The Meaning of Nomos in Greek Literature and Thought from Homer to Aristotle*, Dissertation, University of Chicago.

McDevitt, A. S. (1982), 'The First Kommos of Sophocles' *Antigone' Ramus* 11: 134–44.

McDonald, W. A., W. D. E. Coulson and J. Rosser (eds) (1983), *Excavations at Nichoria in Southwest Greece, vol. 3: Dark Age and Byzantine Occupation*, Minneapolis, MN: University of Minnesota Press.

McInerney, J. (2010), *The Cattle of the Sun: Cows and Culture in the World of the Ancient Greeks*, Princeton, NJ/Oxford: Princeton University Press.

McKirahan Jr, R. D. (1994), *Philosophy before Socrates: An Introduction with Texts and Commentary*, Indianapolis, IN/ Cambridge: Hackett.

Mehl, V. and P. Brulé (eds) (2008), *Le sacri ce antique: Vestiges, procédures et stratégies*, Rennes: Presses Universitaires de Rennes.

Meier, C. (1988), 'Zu *Carl Schmitts Begriffsbildung* – Das Politische und der Nomos', in H. Quaritsch (ed.), *Complexio Oppositorum – Über Carl Schmitt*, Vorträge und Diskussionsbeiträge des 28, Sonderseminars 1986 der Hochschule für Verwaltungswissenschaften Speyer, Berlin.

Meijer, P. A. (2007), *Stoic Theology. Proofs for the Existence of the Cosmic God and of the Traditional Gods – Including a Commentary of Cleanthes' Hymn on Zeus*, Delft: Uitgeverij Eburon.

Mele, A. (1968), *Società e lavoro nei poemi omerici*, Napoli: Università degli Studi di Napoli.

Mele, A. [and T. Papillon] (2007), 'How archaic Greek colonization developed and what forms it took', *Electronic Antiquity: Communicating the Classics*, 11(1): 1–12.

Meriani, A. (2003), *Sulla musica greca antica: Studi e ricerche*, Napoli: Guida.

Merkelbach, R. and M. L. West (1967), *Fragmenta Hesiodea*, Oxford: Oxford University Press.

Mette, H. J. (1956), 'Die Antigone des Sophokles', *Hermes*, 84: 129–34.

Meuss, H. (1889), 'Vorstellungen von Gottheit und Schicksal bei den attischen Rednern', *Jahrbücher für Classische Philologie* 25: 468–75.

Meyer-Benfey, H. (1920), *Sophokles' Antigone*, Halle: Niemeyer.

Michaelides, S. (1978), *The Music of Ancient Greece: An Encyclopaedia*, London: Faber & Faber.

Mikalson, J. D. (2016), *New Aspects of Religion in Ancient Athens: Honors, Authorities, Esthetics and Society*, Leiden/Boston: Brill.

Milani, R. (2007), 'Storia filosofica del concetto di armonia', in G. Borio and C. Gentili (eds), *Storia dei concetti musicali*, Roma: Carocci, 31–44.

Militello, P. (2007), 'Textile industry and Minoan palaces', in C. Gillis and M.-L. B. Nosch, *Ancient Textiles – Production, Craft and Society*, Ancient Textiles Series 1, Oxford: Oxbow Books, 35–43.

Miller, A. M. (ed.) (1996), *Greek Lyric*, Indianapolis, IN: Hackett.

Minar, E. L. (1939), 'The logos of Heraclitus', *Classical Philology*, 34(4): 323–41.

Mittica, M. P. (2015), 'When the world was mousiké: on the origins of the relationship between law and music', *Law and Humanities*, 9(1): 29–54.

Mojsik, T. (2011), *Between Tradition and Innovation: Genealogy, Names and the Number of the Muses*, M. Fijak (trans.), Akme, Studia historica, Warszawa: Instytut Historyczny, Uniwersytet Warszawski.

Monro, D. B. and T. W. Allen (1920), *Homeri Opera*, vols 1–2, Oxford: Clarendon Press.

Monroe, D. B. (1894), *The Modes of Ancient Greek Music*, Oxford: Clarendon Press.

Montanari, E. (1981), *Il mito dell'autoctonia: linee di una dinamica mitico-politica ateniese*, Roma: Bulzoni.

Montanari, F., S. Matthaios and A. Rengakos (eds) (2009), *Brill's Companion to Hesiod*, 2 vols, Leiden: Brill.

Morris, H. J. (1986), *An Economic Model of the Late Mycenaean Kingdom of Pylos*, Dissertation, University of Minnesota.

Morris, I. (1996), 'The strong principle of equality and the archaic origins of Greek democracy', in J. Ober and C. Hedrick (eds), *Demokratia*, Princeton, NJ: Princeton University Press, 19–48.

Morris, S. P. (1989), 'A tale of two cities: the miniature frescoes from Thera and the origins of Greek Poetry', *American Journal of Archaeology*, 9: 511–35.

Morwood, J. (2014), 'Hecuba and the Democrats: political polarities in Euripides' play', *Greece and Rome*, 61(2): 194–203.

Mossman, J. (1995), *Wild Justice: A Study of Euripides' Hecuba*, Oxford: Oxford University Press.

Most, G. (1987), 'Alcman's "cosmogonic" fragment (fr. 5 Page, 81 Calame)', *Classical Quarterly*, 37(1): 1–19.

Most, G. (2013), 'Heraclitus on religion', *Rhizomata*, 1(2): 153–67.

Mouraviev, S. (2006), *Heraclitea, III.3.B/1: Les vestiges, 3. Les fragments du livre d'Héraclite, B. Les textes pertinents = Recensio, 3. Fragmenta heraclitea, B. Libri reliquiae superstites/ Héraclite d'Éphèse; extraits des sources (II.A et II.B)*, établis, traduits et annotés, Sankt Augustin: Academia Verlag.

Mouraviev, S. (1999–2008), *Heraclitea*, 10 vols, Sankt Augustin: A. Verlag.

Mourelatos, A. P. D. (1965), 'Heraclitus, fr. 114', *American Journal of Philology*, 86(3): 258–66.

Mourelatos, A. P. D. (1986), 'Quality, structure and emergence in later pre-Socratic philosophy', *Proceedings of the Boston Area Colloquium in Ancient Philosophy* 2: 127–94.

Mourelatos, A. P. D. (ed.) (1994), *The Presocratics: A Collection of Critical Essays*, rev. edn, Princeton, NJ: Princeton University Press.

Moutsopoulos, E. (1959a), 'Une philosophie de la musique chez Eschyle', *Revues des Études Grecques*, 72: 18–56.

Moutsopoulos, E. (1959b), *La Musique dans l'oeuvre de Platon*, Paris.

Mueller, M. (2011), 'The politics of gesture in Sophocles' Antigone', *Classical Quarterly*, 61(2): 412–25.

Mühl, M. (1929), 'Die Gesetze des Zaleukos und Charondas', *Klio*, 22: 105–24, 433–63.

Mullen, W. (1982), *Choreia: Pindar and Dance*, Princeton, NJ: Princeton University Press.

Murray, A. T. (1924), *Homer – The Iliad*, 2 vols, Cambridge, MA: Harvard University Press; London: William Heinemann.

Murray, G. (1913), *Euripides and his Age*, London: Williams & Norgate.

Murray, G. (1934), *The Rise of the Greek Epic*, 4th edn, Oxford: Oxford University Press.

Murray, O. (1983), 'The Greek symposion in history', in E. Gabba (ed.), *Tria Corda: Scritti in onore di Arnaldo Momigliano*, Como: Edizioni New Press, 257–72.

Murray, O. (1993), *Early Greece*, 2nd edn, London/Cambridge, MA: Harvard University Press (1st edn 1978).

Murray, O. (2009), 'The culture of the symposion', in K. A. Raaflaub, and H. Van Wees (eds), *A Companion to Archaic Greece*, Chichester: Blackwell.

Murray, P. (1981), 'Poetic inspiration in early Greece', *Journal of Hellenic Studies*, 101: 87–100.

Murray, P. (2005), 'The muses: creativity personified?', in E. Stafford and J. Herrin (eds), *Personification in the Greek World: From Antiquity to Byzantium*, Aldershot: Ashgate, 147–59.

Murray, P. (2014), 'The muses in antiquity', in K. W. Christian, C. E. L. Guest and C. Wedepohl (eds), *The Muses and their Afterlife in Post-Classical Europe*, London: Warburg Institute, 13–32.

Murray, P. and P. Wilson (eds) (2004), *Music and the Muses: The Culture of 'Mousike' in the Classical Athenian city*, Oxford: Oxford University Press; incl. P. Murray, 'The muses and their arts', 365–89.

Musti, D. (2000), 'Musica greca tra aristocrazia e democrazia', in A. C. Cassio, D. Musti and L. E. Rossi (eds), *Sunaulia: Cultura musicale in Grecia e contanti mediterranei*, Napoli: Istituto Universitario Orientale, 7–55.

Myres, J. L. (1927), *The Political Ideas of the Greeks*,

London: Edward Arnold, repub. 1969, Bath: Cedric Chivers.

Naddaf, G. (2006), *The Greek Concept of Nature*, New York: SUNY Press.

Nagler, M. N. (1990), 'Odysseus: the proem and the problem', *Classical Antiquity*, 9(2): 335–56.

Nagy, G. (1974), *Comparative Studies in Greek and Indic Meter*, Cambridge, MA: Harvard University Press.

Nagy, G. (1979), *The Best of the Achaeans*, Baltimore, MD: Johns Hopkins University Press.

Nagy, G. (1985), 'On the symbolism of apportioning meat in archaic Greek elegiac poetry', *L'Uomo*, 9: 45–52.

Nagy, G. (1990a), 'Ancient Greek poetry, prophecy, and concepts of theory', in J. L. Kugel (ed.), *Poetry and Prophecy – The Beginnings of a Literary Tradition*, London/Ithaca, NY: Cornell University Press, 56–64.

Nagy, G. (1990b), *Pindar's Homer: The Lyric Possession of an Epic Past*, Baltimore, MD/London: Johns Hopkins University Press.

Nagy, G. (1992) 'Authorisation and authorship in the Hesiodic theogony', *Ramus*, 21: 119–30.

Nagy, G. (1996), *Poetry as Performance: Homer and Beyond*, Cambridge/New York: Cambridge University Press.

Nagy, G. (2002), *Plato's Rhapsody and Homer's Music: The Poetics of the Panathenaic Festival in Classical Athens*, Washington, DC: Center for Hellenic Studies and Foundation of the Hellenic World/Harvard University Press.

Naiden, F. S. (2006), *Ancient Supplication*, Oxford: Oxford University Press.

Nakassis, D. (2013), 'Individuals and society in Mycenaean Pylos', *Mnemosyne Supplements: History and Archaeology of Classical Antiquity* 358, Leiden/Boston: Brill.

Nakassis, D., M. Galaty and W. Parkinson (eds) (2011), 'Forum: redistribution in Aegean palatial societies', *American Journal of Archaeology* 115(2): 175–244.

Nakassis, D., J. Gulizio and S. A. James (eds) (2014), *KERAMEJA: Studies Presented to Cynthia Shelmerdine*, Philadelphia, PA: INSTAP Academic Press.

Nancy, J.-L. (1998), 'Cosmos basileus', *Lignes* 3, 35: 94–9.

Nancy, J.-L. (2000), *Being, Singular, Plural*, R. D. Richardson and A. O'Byrne (trans) Stanford, CA: Stanford University Press.

Nauck, A. (1889), *Tragicorum Graecorum Fragmenta*, Lipsiae: Teubner.

Nef, K. (1919), *Einführung in die Musik geschichte*, Zürich.

Negri, A. (1985), *Friedrich Nietzsche – Teognide di Megara*, Rome: Laterza.

Negri, A. (2003), *Time for Revolution*, New York/London: Continuum.

Neitzel, H. (1980), 'Hesiod Und Die Lügenden Musen. Zur Interpretation Von Theogonie 27f', *Hermes*, 108: 387–401.

Nelson, S. A. (1998), *God and the Land – The Metaphysics of Farming in Hesiod and Vergil*, New York/Oxford: Oxford University Press.

Nestle, W. (1911), 'Gab es eine jonische Sophistik?', *Philologus* 70: 242–66.

Nestle, W. ([1940/2] 1975), *Vom Mythos zum Logos: Die Selbstentfaltung des griechischen Denkens von Homer bis auf die Sophistik und Sokrates*, Stuttgart: A. Kroner.

Neubecker, J. A. (1994), *Altgriechische Musik – Eine Einführung*, Darmstadt: Wissenschaftliche Buchgesellscha.

Nieddu, G. (1982), 'Alfabetismo e diffusione sociale della scrittura nella Grecia arcaica e classica: pregiudizi recenti e realtà documentaria', *Scrittura e civiltà*, 6: 233–61.

Nieto Hernandez, M. P. (1993), 'Heracles and Pindar', *Mètis* 8(1): 75–102.

Nietzsche, F. (1867), 'Zur Geschichte der Teognideischen Spruchsammlung', *Rheinisches Museum für Philologie*, 22: 161–200.

Nietzsche, F. (1869), 'Teognidis Elegiæ. E codicibus Mutinensi, Veneto 522 Vaticano 915', Ziegler, C. (ed.), Tübingen: Laupp 1868', *Literarisches Centralbla für Deutschland*, 6: 144.

Nietzsche, F. (1962), *Philosophy in the Tragic Age of the Greeks*, M. Cowan (trans.), Washington, DC: Regnery.

Nietzsche, F. (1967), *Basic Writings of Nietzsche*, Walter Kaufmann (ed. and trans.), New York: Modern Library.

Nikoloudis, S. (2006), *The ra-wa-ke-ta: Ministerial Authority and Mycenaean Cultural Identity*, dissertation, University of Texas at Austin.

Nilsson, M. P. (1949), *A History of Greek Religion*, F. J. Fielden (trans.), Oxford: Clarendon Press.

Nilsson, M. P. (1955), *Geschichte der griechischen Religion*, 2 vols, Munich: Beck.

Nonet, P. (1995), 'Judgment', *Vanderbilt Law Review*, 48: 987–1007.

Nonet, P. (2006), 'Antigone's law', *Law, Culture and the Humanities*, 2: 314–35.

Nordquist, G. C. (1994), 'Some notes on musicians in Greek cult', in R. Hägg (ed.), *Ancient Greek Cult Practice from the Epigraphical Evidence*, Proceedings of the Second International Seminar on Ancient Greek Cult, the Swedish Institute at Athens, 22–4 November 1991, 81–93.

Northrup, M. D. (1976), *The Use of Personnification in Hesiod and the Pre-Socratics*, Ann Arbor, MI: University of Michigan Press.

Norwood, G. (1945), *Pindar*, Sather Classical Lectures 19, Berkeley/Los Angeles, CA: University of California Press.

Nosch, M.-L. (2003), 'The women at work in the Linear B tablets', in A. Strömberg and L. Larsson Lovén (eds), *Gender, Cult, and Culture in the Ancient World from Mycenae to Byzantium*, Proceedings of the Second Nordic Symposium on Gender and Women's History in Antiquity, Helsinki, 20–2 October 2000 (SIMA-PB 166), Sävedalen, 12–26.

Nosch, M.-L. (2008), 'Administrative practices in Mycenaean palace administration and economy', *Pasiphae*, 2: 595–604.

Nosch, M.-L (2014a), 'Voicing the loom: women, weaving, and plotting', in D. Nakassis et al. (eds), op. cit., 91–101.

Nosch, M.-L. (2014b), 'The Aegean wool economies of the bronze age', *Textile Society of America Symposium Proceedings*, 900, Lincoln, NE: University of Nebraska.

Nosch, M.-L. (2014c), 'The wool economy in Greece in the end of the II millennium BCE', in C. Michel and C. Breniquet (eds), *Wool Economy in the Ancient Near East and the Aegean: From the Beginnings of Sheep Husbandry to Institutional Textile Industry*, Ancient Textiles Series 17, Oxford: Oxbow Books.

Notopoulos, J. A. (1938), 'Mnemosyne in oral literature', *Transactions of the American Philological Association* 69: 465–93.

Nussbaum, M. (1986), *The Fragility of Goodness – Luck and Ethics in Greek Tragedy and Philosophy*, Cambridge: Cambridge University Press.

O'Brien, D. (1969), *Empedocles' Cosmic Cycle – A Reconstruction from the Fragments and Secondary Sources*, Cambridge: Cambridge University Press.

O'Brien, D. (1981), *Pour interpréter Empédocle*, Paris/Leiden: Les Belles Lettres.

O'Brien, D. (1995), 'Empedocles revisited', *Ancient Philosophy*, 15: 403–70.

O'Sullivan, P. (2005), 'Of Sophists, tyrants, and Polyphemus: the nature of the beast in Euripides' Cyclops', in G. W. M. Harrison (ed.), *Satyr Drama: Tragedy at Play*, Swansea: Classical Press of Wales, 119–59.

Oates, W. J. and E. O'Neill Jr (eds) (1938), *Euripides – The Complete Greek Drama*, 2 vols, London: Random House.

Olivier, J.-P. (1967), 'La série Dn de Cnossos', *Studi Mediterranei ed Egeo-Anatolici*, 2: 71–93.

Onians, R. B. (1954), *The Origins of European Thought*, Cambridge: Cambridge University Press.

Ornaghi, M. (2009), *La lira, la vacca e le donne insolent – Contesti di ricezione e promozione della figura e della poesia di Archiloco dall'arcaismo all'ellenismo*, Alessandria: Edizioni dell'Orso.

Orrù, M. (1985), 'Anomie and social theory in ancient Greece', *European Journal of Sociology*, 26: 3–28.

Osborne, R. (1997), 'Early Greek colonization? The nature of Greek settlement in the West', in N. Fisher and H. van Wees (eds), *Archaic Greece: New Approaches and New Evidence*, London: Duckworth, 251–69.

Osborne, R. (1996/2009), *Greece in the Making, 1200–479 BC*, London/New York: Routledge.

Osborne, R. (2004a), 'Homer's Society', in R. Fowler (ed.), *The Cambridge Companion to Homer*, Cambridge: Cambridge University Press, 206–19.

Osborne, R. (2004b), *Greek History*, London/New York: Routledge

Osborne, R. (2016), 'Sacrificial theologies', in E. Eidinow, J. Kindt and R. Osborne (eds), *Theologies of Ancient Greek Religion*, Cambridge: Cambridge University Press, 233–48.

Ost, F. (2004), 'Au commencement était ma conscience. L'Antigone de Sophocle: Résistance, apories juridiques et paradoxes Politiques', in F. Ost, *Raconter la loi: Aux sources de l'imaginaire juridique*, Paris: Odile Jacob, 153–203.

Oštir, K. (1929), 'Vorgriech μῶλυ', *Donum Natalicium Schrijnen*, Nijmegen–Utrecht, 286–94.

Ostwald, M. (1965), 'Pindar, nomos, and Heracles: (Pindar, Frg. 169 [Snell2]+POxy. No. 2450, Frg. I): dedicated to Harry Caplan', *Harvard Studies in Classical Philology*, 69: 109–38.

Ostwald, M. (1969), *Nomos and the Beginnings of the Athenian Democracy*, Oxford: Oxford University Press.

Ostwald, M. (1973), 'Was there a concept of agraphos nomos in classical Greece?', in E. N. Lee and A. P. D. Mourelatos (eds), *Exegesis and Argument: Studies in Greek Philosophy Presented to Gregory Vlastos*, Assen: Van Gorcum, 70–104.

Ostwald, M. (1982), *Autonomia its Genesis and Early History*. New York: Scholars Press.

Ostwald, M. (1986), *From Popular Sovereignty to the Sovereignty of the Law*, Berkeley, CA/London: University of California Press.

Ostwald, M. (1996), 'Shares and rights: "citizenship" Greek style and American style', in J. Ober and C. Hedrick (eds), *Dēmokratia: A Conversation on Democracies, Ancient and Modern*, Princeton, NJ: Princeton University Press, 49–62.

Ostwald, M. (2009), *Language and History in Ancient Greek Culture, Philadelphia*, PA: University of Pennsylvania Press.

Otto, W. F. ([1955] 1961), *Die Musen und der göttliche Ursprung des Singens und Sagens*, Darmstadt: Wissenschaftliche Buchgesellschaft.

Otto, W. F. (1954), *The Homeric Gods: The Spiritual Significance of Greek Religion*, M. Hadas (trans.), New York: Pantheon.

Padel, R. (1995), *Whom Gods Destroy*, Princeton, NJ: Princeton University Press.

Padilla, M. W. (1998), *The Myths of Herakles in Ancient Greece: Survey and Profile*, Lanham, MD/Oxford: University Press of America.

Page, D. L. (1962a), 'Pindar: P. Oxy. 2450, fr. 1 ', *Proceedings of the Cambridge Philological Society*, 8: 49–51.

Page, D. L. (1955), *Sappho and Alcaeus*, Oxford: Clarendon Press.

Page, D. L. (ed.) (1962b), *Poetae Melici Graeci*, Oxford: Clarendon Press.

Page, D. L. (1973), 'Stesichorus: the Geryoneïs', *Journal of Hellenic Studies*, 93: 138–54.

Palaima, T. G. (1995), 'The nature of the Mycenaean wanax: non-Indo-European origins and priestly functions', in P. Rehak (ed.), *The Role of the Ruler in the Prehistoric Aegean*,

AEGAEUM 11, Liège, Belgium: Université de Liège, 119–42.

Palaima, T. G. (2004), 'Sacrificial feasting in the Linear B documents', in J. C. Wright (ed.), *The Mycenaean Feast*, Hesperia 73, 2, Princeton, NJ: American School of Classical Studies at Athens, 217–46.

Palaima, T. G. (2006), 'Wanaks and related power terms in Mycenaean and later Greek', in S. Deger-Jalkotzy and I. S. Lemos (eds), *Ancient Greece: From the Mycenaean Palaces to the Age of Homer*, Edinburgh Leventis Studies 3, Edinburgh: Edinburgh University Press, 53–71.

Palmer, L. R. (1963), *The Interpretation of Mycenaean Greek Texts*, Oxford: Clarendon Press.

Palmer, R. (1992), 'Wheat and barley in Mycenaean society', *Mykenaika, 9th International Colloquium on Mycenaean and Aegean Texts, Athens, Greece, Oct. 2–6 1990*, J.-P. Olivier (ed.), *Bulletin de Correspondance Hellénique*, supplement, 25: 473–95.

Palmer, R. (1994), *Wine in the Mycenaean Palace Economy*, Aegaeum, 10, Liège/Austin, TX: University of Liège and Austin.

Palmer, R. (1998–9), 'Models in Linear B landholding: an analysis of methodology', in J. Bennet and J. Driessen (eds), *A-NA-QO-TA Studies presented to J. T. Killen, Minos* 33–4, Salamanca 2002, 223–50.

Palmer, R. (2002), 'Models in Linear B landholding: an analysis of methodology', in *A-NA-QO-TA: Studies Presented to J. T. Killen*, J. Bennet and J. Driessen (eds), Salamanca: Ediciones Universidad de Salamanca, 223–50.

Panno, G. (2004), 'Mediazione della parola nel pensiero di Hölderlin: tragico e legge', *Estetica*, 1: 42–57.

Papadopoulou, Z. (2004a), 'I. Musical Instruments in Cult; II. Musicians in Cult; V. B. Music in Processions and Pannychides in 4.c. Music, Greek Music', in: V. Lambrinoudakis and J. C. Balty (eds), *Thesaurus Cultus et Rituum Antiquorum II*, Los Angeles, CA: J. P. Getty Museum, S. 347–64; 375–8.

Papadopoulou, Z. (2004b), 'Hymning the gods, music in the public life of ancient Greeks', in *Gifts of the Muses – Echoes of Music and Dance from Ancient Greece*, Ausstellungskatalog, Athens: Hellenic Ministry of Culture, 46–57.

Papadopoulou, Z. and V. Pirenne Delforge (2001), 'Inventer et réinventer l'aulos: autour de la XIIe Pythique de Pindare', in P. Brulé and C. Vendries (eds), *Chanter les dieux – Musique et religion dans l'antiquité grecque et romaine*, Rennes: Presses Universitaires de Rennes, 37–58.

Papakonstantinou, Z. (2002), 'Written law, literacy and social conflict in archaic and classical Crete', *Ancient History Bulletin* 16(3/4): 135–50.

Papakonstantinou, Z. (2004), 'Justice of the kakoi: law and social crisis in Theognis', *Dike*, 7: 5–17.

Papakonstantinou, Z. (2008), *Lawmaking and Adjudication in Archaic Greece*, London: Duckworth.

Papakonstantinou, Z. (2009), 'Wine and wine drinking in the Homeric world', *L'Antiquité Classique*, 78: 1–24.

Papakonstantinou, Z. (2012), *Lawmaking and Adjudication in Archaic Greece*, London: Bristol Classical Press/Bloomsbury.

Papamichael-Paspalides, E. (2005), 'The concept of the one in Heraclitus', *Revue de Philosophie Ancienne*, 23(1): 41–54.

Pappas, A. (2008), 'Remember to cry wolf: visual and verbal declarations of LYKOS KALOS', in E. A. Mackay (ed.), *Orality, Literacy, Memory in the Ancient Greek and Roman World* (Orality and Literacy in Ancient Greece, vol. 7), Leiden/Boston: Brill, 97–114.

Parker, R. C. T. (1983), *Miasma: Pollution and Purification in Early Greek Religion*, Oxford, Oxford University Press.

Parker, R. C. T. (1995), 'Early Orphism', in A. Powell (ed.), *The Greek World*, London: Routledge, 483–510.

Parker, R. C. T. (1996), *Athenian Religion: A History*, Oxford: Oxford University Press.

Parker, R. C. T. (2004), 'What are Greek sacred laws?', in E. M. Harris and L. Rubinstein (eds), *The Law and the Courts in Ancient Greece*, London: Duckworth, 57–70.

Patterson, C. B. (2006), 'The place and practice of burial in Sophocles' Athens', in C. B. Patterson (ed.) (2006), *Antigone's Answer: Essays on Death and Burial, Family and State in Classical Athens: Helios*, 33: 9–48.

Patton, K. (2009), *Religion of the Gods*, Oxford: Oxford University Press.

Patzer, H. (1952), 'Ῥαψῳδός', *Hermes*, 80: 314–25.

Pavese, C. (1968), 'The new Heracles poem of Pindar', *Harvard Studies in Classical Philology*, 72: 47–88.

Pavese, C. (1993), 'On Pindar, fr. 169', *Harvard Studies in Classical Philology*, 95: 43–157.

Pearson, L. (1990), *Aristoxenus – Elementa Rhythmica*, Oxford: Oxford University Press.

Pedrick J. (1982), 'Supplication in the Iliad and the Odyssey', *Transactions of the American Philological Association*, 112: 125–40.

Pelling, C. (ed.) (1997), *Greek Tragedy and the Historian*, Oxford: Oxford University Press.

Pelloso, C. (2012a), 'Ius, νόμος, ma'at – Inattualitá e alteritá delle esperienze guiridiche antiche, *Lexis – Poetica, retorica e comunicazione nella tradizione classica*, 30: 217–86.

Pelloso, C. (2012b), *Themis e dike in Omero – Ai primordi del diritto dei Greci*, Milano: Alessandria.

Peponi, A.-E. (ed.) (2013), *Performance and Culture in Plato's Laws*, Cambridge: Cambridge University Press.

Perotta, G. (1935), *Saffo e Pindaro: Due saggi critici*, Bari: G. Laterza & Figli.

Piccirilli, L. (1981), 'Nomoi cantati e nomoi scritti', *Civiltà classica e cristiana*, 2: 7–14.

Pickard-Cambridge, A. W. ([1927] 1962), *Dithyramb: Tragedy and Comedy*, 2nd edn, Oxford: Clarendon Press.

Pierre, R. (2016), 'The sovereign translation: mediation and Hölderlin's "Das Höchste"', *Seminar*, 52(1): 22–38.

Pike, D. L. (1984), 'Pindar's treatment of the Heracles myths', *Acta Classica*, 207(184): 15–22.

Pinault, G.-J. (ed.) (2001), *Musique et poésie dans l'antiquité: Actes Du Colloque De Clermont-Ferrand*, Université Blaise Pascal, 23 May 1997, Clermont-Ferrand.

Pindar (1560), *Olympia, Pythia, Nemea, Isthmia. Caeterorum Octo Lyricorm Carmina, Alcaei, Anacreontis, Sapphys, Bacchylidis, Stesichori, Simonidis, Ibyci, Alcmanis, Nonnulla etiam aliorum*, Omnia Graecè et Latinè, H. Stephanus (ed.), vol. 2. Geneva.

Pindar (1915), *The Odes of Pindar*, Sir J. Sandys (trans.), London: William Heinemann.

[Pindar] (1923), A. Puech (trans.), *Pindare*, 4 vols, Collections des Universités de France, Paris: Les Belles Lettres.

[Pindar] A. Turyn (ed.) (1952), *Pindari carmina cum fragmentis*, Oxford: Basil Blackwell.

Pindar (1975, 1989, rev. repr. of Snell's edition of 1964),

B. Snell and H. Maehler (eds), *Pindari carmina cum fragmentis. II. Fragmenta*, Leipzig: Teubner.

Pindar (1997), B. Snell and H. Maehler (eds), *Pindarus, I: Epinicia*, 8th edn, Stuttgart and Leipzig: Teubner.

Pindar (1997a), *Nemean Odes, Isthmian Odes, Fragments*, W. H. Race (ed. and trans.), Cambridge, MA: Harvard University Press (Loeb).

Pindar (1997b), *Olympian Odes, Pythian Odes*, W. H. Race (ed. and trans.), Cambridge, MA: Harvard University Press (Loeb).

Pintacuda, M. (1978), *La musica nella tragedia greca*, Cefalù: Lorenzo Misuraca.

Plato (1946), *Gorgias*, W. R. M. Lamb (trans.), Cambridge, MA: Harvard University Press (Loeb).

Plato (1952), *Laws*, 2 vols, Cambridge, MA: Harvard University Press (Loeb).

[Plato] (1961), W. R. M. Lamb (ed.), *Plato, vol. 5: Lysis, Symposium, Gorgias*, Cambridge, MA: Classical Library, Harvard University Press/Heinemann (Loeb).

Plato (1963), *Republic*, P. Shorey (trans.), 2 vols, Cambridge, MA: Harvard University Press (Loeb).

Plato (1967–8), *Plato in Twelve Volumes*, Cambridge, MA: Harvard University Press; London, William Heinemann.

[Plato] (1997), J. M. Cooper (ed.), *The Dialogues of Plato*, Indianapolis, IN: Hackett.

Plüss, T. (1920), 'Die Deutund des Wortes Phythmus nach griechischer Wortbildung', *Wochenschriff f. Kl. Philol.* 37: 18–23.

Plutarch (1966), *Plutarch's Lives*, B. Perrin (trans.), 10 vols, London: William Heinemann.

[Ps.] Plutarch (1967), *Plutarch's Moralia*, B. Einarson and P. H. De Lacy (trans.), Cambridge, MA: Harvard University Press (Loeb).

Podlecki, A. J. (1986), 'Polis and monarch in early Attic tragedy', in J. P. Euben (ed.), *Greek Tragedy and Political Theory*, Berkeley, CA: University of California Press, 76–100.

Pohlenz, M. ([1948]), 'Nomos', *Philologus* 97: 135–42 [= Pohlenz, M. (1965), 'Nomos', in M. Pohlenz, *Kleine Schriften*, vol. 2, Hildesheim: Olms].

Pöhlmann, E. (1970), *Denkmäler Altgriechischer Musik*, Nuremburg: Verlag Hans Karl.

Pöhlmann, E. (2010–11), 'Pythikos and Polykephalos nomos. compulsory and optional exercise in the Pythian contest', in D. Castaldo, F. G. Giannachi and A. Manieri (eds), *Poesia, musica e agoni nella Grecia antica*, Rudiae 22–3, 271–83.

Pöhlmann, E. (2011), 'A history of oral tradition of ancient Greek music', *Quaderni Urbinati di Cultura Classica*, 99: 11–30.

Pöhlmann, E. and M. L. West (2001), *Documents of Ancient Greek Music: The Extant Melodies and Fragments*, Oxford: Clarendon Press.

Poliziano, A. ([1482] 2004), *Silvae*, Charles Fantazzi (ed. and trans.), I Tatti Renaissance Library, vol. 14, Cambridge, MA: Harvard University Press.

Popp, V. (ed.) (1969), *Initiation – Zeremonien der Statusänderung und des Rollen-wechsels*, Frankfurt am Main: Suhrkamp.

Pötscher, W. (1960), 'Moira, Themis und τιμή im homerischen Denken', *Wiener Studien*, 73: 5–39.

Potter, R. (trans.) (1938), *Euripides. The Complete Greek Drama: vol. 1, Iphigenia in Tauris*, Whitney J. Oates and Eugene O'Neill Jr (eds), New York: Random House.

Pouilloux, J., N. M. Kontoleon, A. Scherer, K. J. Dover, D. Page, W. Bühler, E. Wistrand, B. Snell, O. Reverdin, and M. Treu (eds) (1963), *Archiloque: sept exposés et discussions*, Entretiens sur l'Antiquité Classique, 10, Vandoeuvres–Genève: Fondation Hardt.

Powell, B. (1989), 'Why was the Greek alphabet invented? The epigraphical evidence', *Classical Antiquity*, 8: 321–30.

Prauscello, L. (2009), 'Wandering poetry: travelling music', in R. Hunter and I. Rutherford (eds), *Wandering Poets in Ancient Greek Culture*, Cambridge: Cambridge University Press, 168–94.

Pretagostini, R. (1995), 'L'incontro con le Muse sull'Elicona in Esiodo e in Callimaco: modificazioni di un modello', *Lexis*, 13: 157–72 [= id. (2007), *Ricerche sulla poesia alessandrina, II. Forme allusive e contenuti nuovi*, Roma, 13–25].

Prins, Y. (1991), 'The power of the speech act: Aeschylus' Furies and their binding song', *Arethusa*, 24(2): 177–95.

Pritchett, W. K. (1985), *The Greek State at War: Part IV*, Berkeley/Los Angeles, CA: University of California Press.

Prodi, P. (1992), *Il sacramento del potere: Il giuramento politico nella storia costiuizionale dell'Occidente*, Bologna: il Mulino.

Prudhommeau, G. (1965), *La danse grecque antique*, Paris: Éditions du Centre national de la recherche scientifique.

Pucci, G. (2013), 'C'erano una volta le Muse', in P. D'Angelo, E. Franzini, G. Lombardo and S. Tedesco (eds), *Costellazioni estetiche. Dalla storia alla neoestetica. Studi in onore di Luigi Russo*, Milano: Guerini & Associati, 326–35.

Pucci, P. (2007), *Inno alle Muse (Esiodo, Teogonia, 1–115)*, Pisa/Roma: Fabrizio Serra Editore.

Pullen, D. J. (2011), 'Redistribution in Aegean palatial societies – before the palaces: redistribution and chiefdoms in mainland Greece', *American Journal of Archaeology* 115: 185–95.

Quale, G. R. (1988), *A History of Marriage Systems*, New York: Greenwood.

Quass, F. (1971), *Nomos und Psephisma: Untersuchung zum griechischen Staatsrecht*, München: Verlag Beck.

Quasten, J. (1930), *Musik und Gesang in den Kulten der heidnischen Antike und christlicher Fruhzeit*, Münster: Liturgiegeschichtl. Quellen und Forschungen 25.

Raaflaub, K. A. (1997), 'Homeric Society', in I. Morris and B. Powell (eds), *A New Companion to Homer*, Leiden/New York: Brill, 624–48.

Raaflaub, K. A. and H. van Wees (2009), *A Companion to Archaic Greece*, London: Blackwell.

Race, W. (ed.) (1997), *Pindar*, 2 vols, Cambridge, MA: Harvard University Press.

Ramat, P. (1960), 'La figura di Moira in Omero alla luce dell'analisi linguistica', *Studi italiani di filologia classica*, 32: 215–48.

Ramnoux C. (1968), *Heraclite ou l'homme entre les choses e les mots*, Paris: Les Belles Lettres.

Rankin, H. D. (1983), *Sophists, Socratics and Cynics*, Totowa, NJ: Barnes & Noble.

Ready, J. (2007), 'Toil and trouble: the acquisition of spoils in the "Iliad"', *Transactions of the American Philological Association (1974–)*, 137(1): 3–43.

Redfield, J. (1975), *Nature and Culture in the Iliad*, Chicago, IL: University of Chicago Press.

Rehm, R. (1994), *Marriage to Death: The Conflation of Wedding and Funeral Rituals in Greek Tragedy*, Princeton, NJ: Princeton University Press.

Reinhardt, K. ([1916] 2012), *Parmenides und die Geschichte der griechischen Philosophie*, 5, Auflage VI, 268, Frankfurt am Main: Vittorio Klostermann.

Reinhardt, K. (1976), *Sophokles*, Frankfurt am Main: Vittorio Klostermann.

Renehman, R. (1963), 'The Derivation of ουθμός', *Classical Philology*, 58: 36–8.

Revermann, M. and P. Wilson (ed.) (2008), *Performance, Iconography, Reception: Studies in Honour of Oliver Taplin*, Oxford/New York: Oxford University Press.

Richardson, N. (2011), 'Reflections on choral song in early hexameter poetry', in L. Athanassaki and E. Bowie, *Archaic and Classical Choral Song: Performance, Politics and Dissemination*, Berlin: De Gruyter, 15–32.

Richter, L. (1968a), 'Die Neue Musik der griechischen Antike. Teil II: Die Tondenkmäler', *Archiv für Musikwissenschaft*, 25(2): 134–47.

Richter, L. (1968b), 'Die Neue Musik der griechischen Antike. Teil i: Die Literarische Überlieferung', *Archiv für Musikwissenschaft*, 1–18.

Richter, L. (1983), 'Die Musik der griechischen Tragödie und ihre Wandlungen unter veränderten historischen Bedingungen', in H. Kuch (ed.), *Die Griechische Tragödie in ihrer Gesellschaftliche Funktion*, Berlin: Akademie Verlag, 115–39.

Richter, L. (1999), 'Struktur und Rezeption antiker Planetenskalen', *Die Musikforschung*, 52: 289–306.

Ridgeway, W. (1885), *The Homeric Land System*, Oxford: Oxford University Press.

Riedinger, J. C. (1976), 'Remarques sur la τιμή chez Homère', *Revue des Études Grecques*, 89: 244–64.

Riedinger, J. C. (1980), 'Les deux aidos chez Homere', *Revue de Philologie*, 54: 69–74.

Rihll, T. E. (1996), 'The origin and establishment of ancient Greek slavery', in M. L. Bush (ed.), *Serfdom and Slavery. Studies in Legal Bondage*, London/New York: Longman, 89–111.

Robertson, M. (1969), 'Geryoneis: Stesichorus and the vase-painters', *Classical Quarterly*, 19(2): 217–21.

Robinson, T. M. (1987), *Heraclitus: Fragments*, Toronto: University of Toronto Press.

Rocchi, G. D. (2007), 'Quindici anni di studi sulle frontiere della Grecia antica: alcune prospettive della ricerca', in Ulrich Fellmeth et al. (ed.), *Historische Geographie der Alten Welt: Grundlagen, Erträge, Perspektiven. Festgabe für Eckart Olshausen aus Anlass seiner Emeritierung*, Zurich: Hildesheim, 87–105.

Rocconi, E. (2003), *Le parole delle muse – La formazione del lessico tecnico musicale nella Grecia antica*, Rome: Quasar.

Rocconi, E. (2012), 'The aesthetic value of music in Platonic thought', in I. Sluiter and R. M. Rosen (eds), *Aesthetic Value in Classical Antiquity*, Leiden/Boston: Koninklijke Brill NV.

Rocconi, E. (2014), 'Effetti speciali sonori e mimetismo musicale nelle fonti greche', *Annali della Scuola Normale Superiore di Pisa*, Classe di Lettere e Filosofia, series 5, 6(2): 703–19.

Rocconi, E. (2016), 'The music of the laws and the laws of music: nomoi in music and legislation', *Greek and Roman Musical Studies*, 4: 71–89.

Roscher, W. H. (1904), *Die Sieben und Neunzahl im Kultus und Mythus der Griechen*, Leipzig.

Rose, P. W. (1992), *Sons of the Gods, Children of the Earth: Ideology and Literary Form in Ancient Greece*, Ithaca, NY: Cornell University Press.

Rose, V. (1886), *Aristotelis qui ferebantur librorum fragmenta*, Lipsiae: Teubner.

Rosivach, V. J. (1983), 'On Creon, "Antigone" and not burying the dead', *Rheinisches Museum für Philologie*, Neue Folge, 126(3/4): 193–211.

Rosivach, V. J. (1987), 'Autochthony and the Athenians', *Classical Quarterly*, 37(2): 294–306.

Rosivach, V. J. (1994), *The System of Public Sacrifice in Fourth-Century Athens*, Atlanta, GA: Scholars Press.

Rossetti, L. and C. Santaniello (eds) (2004), *Studi sul pensiero e sulla lingua di Empedocle*, Bari: Levante.

Rougemont, F. (2001), 'Some thoughts on the identification of the "collectors" in the Linear B Tablets', in S. Voutsaki and J. Killen (eds), *Economy and Politics in the Mycenaean Palace States*, Cambridge: Cambridge University Press, 129–38.

Rougemont, F. (2004), 'The administration of Mycenaean sheep rearing (clocks, shepherds, "collectors")', *PECUS, Man and Animal in Antiquity*, in B. S. Frizell (ed.), Proceedings of the Conference at the Swedish Institute in

Rome, 9–12 September 2002, Swedish Institute in Rome: Projects and Seminars, 1, Rome.

Rougemont, F. (2009), *Contrôle économique et administration à l'époque des palais mycéniens (fin du IIe millénaire av. J.-C.)*, Athens: BEFAR 332.

Rousset, D. (2002), *Le territoire de Delphes et la terre d'Apollon*, Paris: De Boccard.

Rowe, C. (2000), 'Cleitophon and Minos', in C. Rowe and M. Schofield (eds), *Cambridge History of Greek and Roman Political Thought*, Cambridge: Cambridge University Press, 303–9.

Roy, J. (1999), 'The Economies of Arkadia', in T. H. Nielsen and J. Roy (eds), *Defining Ancient Arkadia*, Acts of the Copenhagen Polis Centre, 6.

Rückert, B. (1998), *Die Herme im öffentlichen und privaten Leben der Griechen*, Regensburg: Roderer.

Rudhardt, J. (1958), *Notions fondamentales de la pensée religieuse et actes constitutifs du culte dans la Grèce classique; étude préliminaire pour aider à la comprehension de la piété athénienne au IVme siècle*, Genève: Librairie Droz.

Rudhardt, J. (1996), 'Le préambule de la Théogonie. La vocation du poète. Le langage des Muses', in F. Blaise, P. Judet de La Combe and P. Rousseau (eds), *Le Métier du mythe. Lectures d'Hésiode*, Villeneuve d'Ascq: PUS.

Rudhardt, J. and O. Reverdin (eds) (1981), *Le sacrifice dans l'Antiquité: huit exposés suivis de discussions*, 25–30 August, 27, Genève: Entretiens Fondation Hardt.

Ruipérez, M. S. (1957), 'Notes on Mycenaean land division and livestock-grazing', *Minos* 5: 174–206.

Rundin, J. (1996), 'A Politics of eating: feasting in early Greek society', *American Journal Philology*, 117(2): 179–215.

Ruschenbusch, E. (1966), *ΣΟΛΩΝΟΣ ΝΟΜΟΙ – Die Fragmente des solonischen Gesetzwerkes miteiner Text und Überlieferungsgeschichte*, Wiesbaden: Franz Steiner Verlag.

Rutherford, I. (1995), 'Apollo's other genre. Proclus on nomos and his source', *Classical Philology*, 90: 354–61.

Ruzé, F. (2001), 'La loi et le chant', in J.-P. Brun and P. Jockey (eds), *Τέχναι: Techniques et sociétés en Méditerranée, Hommage à Marie-Claire Amouretti*, Paris: MMSH/Maisonneuve et Larose, 709–17.

Ryzman M. (1992), 'Oedipus, nosos and physis in

Sophocles' Oedipus Tyrannus', *L'antiquité classique*, 61: 98–110.

Säflund, G. (1980), 'Sacrificial banquets in the "Palace of Nestor"', *Opuscula Atheniensia*, 13: 237–46.

Saïd, S. (1979), 'Les crimes des prétendants, la maison d'Ulysse et les festins de l'Odyssée', *Etudes de littérature ancienne*, 1: 9–49.

Sarkady, J. (1981), 'Landownership relations in Pylos', *Acta Orientalia Academiae Scientiarum Hungaricae*, 35(2/3): 291–313.

Sarti, S. (1992), 'Gli strumenti di Apollo', *Annali dell'Istituto Universitario Orientale di Napoli* (archeol.), 14: 96–103.

Sauge, A. (2014), 'Le poète contre le philosophe: primauté de la vie sur l'être. Sophocle: Antigone, Choeur, 332 suivants; Heidegger: Einführung in die Metaphysik . . .', *Syntaktika*, 47: 1–32.

Schaefer, H. (1960), '*Eigenart* und Wesenszüge der griechischen Kolonisation', *Heidelberger Jahrbücher*, 4: 77–93.

Scheer, E. (1908), *Lycophronis Alexandra*, vol. 2, Scholia Continens, Berlin: Weidmann.

Scheid-Tissinier, E. (1994), *Les usages du don chez Homère – Vocabulaire et pratiques*, Nancy: Presses Universitaires de Nancy.

Schelling, F. W. J. (1857), 'Philosophie der Mythologie', in K. F. A. von Schelling (ed.), *Sämmtliche Werke*, vol. 2.2, Stuttgart: Cotta.

Schestag, T. (1999), 'The highest', G. Albert (trans.), in A. Fioretos (ed.), *The Solid Letter: Readings of Friedrich Hölderlin*, Stanford, CA: Stanford University Press, 375–411.

Schlesinger, E. (1933), *Die griechische Asylie*, dissertation, Giessen: Töpelmann.

Schlesinger, K. ([1939] 1970), *The Greek Aulos*, London: Methuen.

Schmid, W. (1903), 'Probleme aus der sophokleischen Antigone', *Philologus*, 62: 1–34.

Schmidt, D. J. (2001), *On Germans and Other Greeks: Tragedy and Ethical Life*, Bloomington, IN: Indiana University Press.

Schmitt, C. (1974), *Der Nomos der Erde im Volkerrecht des Jus Publicum Europaeum*, 2nd edn, Berlin: Duncker & Humblot.

Schmitt, C. (1993), 'Appropriation/distribution/production: toward a proper formulation of basic questions of any social and economic order', G. Ulmen (trans.), *Telos*, 95: 52–64.

Schmitt, C. (2003), *The Nomos of the Earth: In the International Law of the Jus Publicum Europaeum*, New York: Telos.

Schmitt, C. (2006), *The Nomos* of the *Earth in the International Law of the Jus Publicum Europaeum*, G. L. Ulmen (trans.), New York: *Telos*.

Schmitt-Pantel, P. (1990), 'Sacrificial meal and symposion: two models of civic institutions in the archaic city?', in O. Murray (ed.), *Sympotica: A Symposium on the Symposium*, Oxford: Clarendon Press, 14–33.

Schmitt-Pantel, P. (1992), *La cité au banquet: histoire des repas publics dans les cités grecques*, Collection de l'École Française de Rome 157, Rome: École Française de Rome.

Schofield, M. (2015), 'Heraclitus on law (fr. 114 DK)', *Rhizomata*, 3(1): 47–61.

Schrader, H. (1933), *Hölderlins Deutung des Oidipus und der Antigone Die anmerkungen im rahmen der klassischen und romantischen deutungen des antik-tragischen*, Mnemosyne, Arbeiten zur Erforschung von Sprache und Dichtung 10, Bonn.

Schröder, O. (1917), 'ΝΟΜΟΣ Ο ΠΑΝΤΩΝ ΒΑΣΙΛΕΥΣ', *Philologus*, 74: 195–204.

Schröder, O. (1918), 'Ρυθμός', *Hermes*, 53: 324–9.

Schufreider, G. (1981), 'Heidegger on community', *Continental Philosophy Review*, 14: 25–54.

Schultz, R. (1910), *Aidos*, Rostock.

Schwartz, E. (1951), *Ethik der Griechen*, Stuttgart.

Schwartz, J. (1960), *Pseudo-Hesiodeia*, Leiden: Brill.

Schweitzer, B. (1922), *Herakles, Aufsätze zur griechischen Religions- und Sagengeschichte*, Tübingen: Mohr.

Scott, M. (1980), 'Αἰδώς and Nemesis in the works of Homer, and their relevance to social or co-operative values', *Acta Classica*, 23: 13–35.

Seaford, R. (1994), *Reciprocity and Ritual: Homer and Tragedy in the Developing City-State*, Oxford: Clarendon Press.

Seaford, R. (2000), 'The social function of tragedy: a response to Jasper Griffin', *Classical Quarterly*, 50(1): 30–44.

Seaford, R. (2004), *Money and the Early Greek Mind: Homer, Philosophy, Tragedy*, Cambridge: Cambridge University Press.

Seebohm, H. E. (1895), *On the Structure of Greek Tribal Society: An Essay*, London/New York: Macmillan.

Segal, C. (1981/1999), *Tragedy and Civilization: An Interpretation of Sophocles*, Norman, OK/Cambridge, MA: University of Oklahoma Press/Harvard University Press.

Segal, C. (1985), 'The Bacchae as metatragedy', in P. Burian (ed.), *Directions in Euripidean Criticism – A Collection of Essays*, Durham, NC: Duke University Press, 156–76.

Segal, C. (1986), *Interpreting Greek Tragedy*, Ithaca, NY: Cornell University Press.

Segal, C. (1989a), 'Law and universals in Euripides' Hecuba', *Sprachaspekte als. Experiment, Annales Universitatis Turkuensis*, Seriers B. 187, Turku, 63–82.

Segal, C. (1989b), *Orpheus: The Myth of the Poet*, Baltimore, MD: Johns Hopkins University Press.

Segal, C. (1994a), *Singers, Heroes and Gods in the Odyssey*, Ithaca, NY: Cornell University Press.

Segal, C. (1994b), 'The gorgon and the nightingale: the voice of female lament and Pindar's twelfth Pythian ode', in L. Dunn, and N. Jones (eds), *Embodied Voices: Representing Female Vocality in Western Culture*, Cambridge/New York: Cambridge University Press, 17–34.

Segal, C. (1999), *Tragedy and Civilization: An Interpretation of Sophocles*, Norman, OK: University of Oklahoma Press.

Selle, H. (2008), *Teognis und die eognidea*, Berlin: De Gruyter.

Shapiro, A. (1992), 'Mousikoi agones: music and poetry at the Panathenaia', in J. Neils (ed.), *Goddess and Polis: The Panathenaic Festival in Ancient Athens*, Princeton, NJ: Princeton University Press, 53–76.

Shapiro, H. A. (1983), 'Héros theos. The death and apotheosis of Héraclès', *Classical World*, 77: 7–18.

Shaw, B. (2015), 'Semele's Ashes: Heidegger's Interpretation of Hölderlin's "As When on a Holiday ...."', *Epoché: A Journal for the History of Philosophy*, 20(1): 169–93.

Shelmerdine, C. W. (1999), 'Administration in the Mycenaean palaces: where's the chief?', in M. L. Galaty and W. A. Parkinson (eds), *Rethinking Mycenaean Palaces: New Interpretations of an Old Idea*, Los Angeles, CA: Cotsen Institute of Archaeology, 19–24.

Shelmerdine, C. W. (2006), 'Mycenaean palatial administration', in S. Deger-Jalkotzy and I. S. Lemos (eds), *Ancient*

Greece: From the Mycenaean Palaces to the Age of Homer, Edinburgh: Edinburgh University Press, 73–86.

Shelmerdine, C. W. (2008), 'Mycenaean society', in Y. Duhoux and A. Morpurgo Davies (eds), *A Companion to Linear B: Mycenaean Greek Texts and Their World*, Bibliothèque des Cahiers de l'Institut de Linguistique de Louvain 120, Leuven/Dudley, MA: Peeters, 115–58.

Sherratt, A. (1981), 'Plough and pastoralism: aspects of the secondary products revolution', in I. Hodder, G. Isaac and N. Hammond (eds), *Pattern of the Past: Studies in Honor of David Clarke*, Cambridge, MA: Cambridge University Press, 261–305.

Sherratt, A. (1983), 'The secondary exploitation of animals in the Old World', *World Archaeology*, 15: 90–104.

Sherratt, S. (2004), 'Feasting in Homeric epic', in J. C. Wright (ed.), *The A1ycenaean Feast*, Hesperia, supplement, vol. 73(2), Princeton NJ: American School of Classical Studies in Athens, 181–217.

Shipp, G. P. (1972), *Studies in the Language of Homer*, 2nd edn, Cambridge: Cambridge University Press.

Shipp, G. P. (1978), Νόμος, *Law*, Sydney: Sydney University Press.

Slater, W. J. (ed.) (1969), *Lexicon to Pindar*, Berlin: De Gruyter.

Smyth, H. W. (trans.) (1926), *Aeschylus*, 2 vols, Cambridge, MA: Harvard University Press (Loeb).

Snell, B. ([1946] 1953), 'Pindar's Hymn to Zeus', in Snell (1953), 71–89.

Snell, B. ([1955] 1993), *Lexikon des frühgriechischen Epos*, Göttingen: Vandenhoeck & Ruprecht.

Snell, B. (1953), *The Discovery of the Mind: The Greek Origins of European Thought*, T. R. Rosenmeyer (trans.), Cambridge, MA: Harvard University Press.

Snell, B. (1955), *Pindari carmina cum fragmentis*, Bibliotheca Scriptorum Graecorum et Romanorum Teubneriana, Lipsiae: Teubner.

Snell, B. (1961), *Poetry and Society – The Role of Poetry in Ancient Greece*, Bloomington, IN: Indiana University Press.

Snell, B. (1965), *Heraklit – Fragmente*, München.

Snell, B. (1976), *Die Entdeckung des Geistes. Studien zur Entstehung des Europäischen Denkens bei den Griechen*, Göttingen: Vandenhoeck & Ruprecht.

Snell, B. (1978), *Der Weg zum Denken und zur Wahrheit, Studien zur frühgriechischen Sprache*, Hypomnemata 57, Göttingen: Vandenhoeck & Ruprecht.

Snell, B. (1993), *Lexikon des frühgriechischen Epos*, Göttingen: Vandenhoeck & Ruprecht.

Snodgrass, A. M. (1971), *The Dark Age of Greece. An Archaeological Survey of the Elevetenth to the Eighth Centuries BC*, Edinburgh: Edinburgh University Press.

Snodgrass, A. M. (1980), *Archaic Greece: The Age of Experiment*, London: Dent.

Snyder, J. M. (1989), *The Woman and the Lyre: Women Writers in Classical Greece and Rome*, Carbondale, IL: Southern Illinois University Press.

Solmsen, F. (1949), *Hesiod and Aeschylus*, Ithaca, NY: Cornell University Press.

Solmsen, F. (1990), *Hesiodi Theogonia, Opera et Dies, Scutum*, Oxford: Clarendon Press.

Solmsen, F., R. Merkelbach and L. M. West (1991), *Hesiodi Theogonia, Opera et Dies, Scutum, Fragmenta Selecta*, Oxford: Oxford University Press.

Sommerstein, A. H. (2002), *Greek Drama and Dramatists*, London: Routledge.

Sommerstein, A. H. (2010), 'Orestes' trial and Athenian homicide procedure', in E. M. Harris, D. F. Leão and P. J. Rhodes (eds) (2010), *Law and Drama in Ancient Greece*, London: Bloomsbury.

[Sophocles] (1917), A. C. Pearson (ed.), *The Fragments of Sophocles*, with additional notes from the papers of Sir R. C. Jebb and W. G. Headlam, 3 vols, Cambridge: Cambridge University Press.

[Sophocles] (2003), R. Gibbons and C. Segal (eds and trans), *Sophocles: Antigone*, New York: Oxford University Press.

Sourvinou-Inwood, C. (1988), *Studies in Girls' Transitions – Aspects of the Arkteia and Age Representation in Attic Iconography*, Athens: Kardamitsa.

Sourvinou-Inwood, C. (1989), 'Assumptions and the creation of meaning: reading Sophocles' Antigone', *Journal of Hellenic Studies*, 109: 134–48.

Sourvinou-Inwood, C. (1995), *Reading Greek Death*, Oxford: Oxford University Press.

Sourvinou-Inwood, C. (2003), *Tragedy and Athenian Religion*, Lanham, MD: Lexington Books.

Stanford, W. B. (1967), *The Sound of Greek, Studies in the Greek Theory and Practice of Euphony*, Berkeley/Los Angeles, CA: University of California Press.

Starobinski, J. (1971), *Les Mots Sous les Mots*, Paris: Gallimard.

Starr, C. G. (1977), *The Economic and Social Growth of Early Greece, 800–500 BC*, New York: Oxford University Press.

Stefou, K. C. (2015), 'Νόμος ο πάντων βασιλεύς: Pindar, Callicles and Plato's treatment of Νόμος in the Gorgias', *Akroterion*, 60: 1–11.

Stehle, E. (1997), *Performance and Gender in Ancient Greece: Nondramatic Poetry in its Setting*, Princeton, NJ: Princeton University Press.

Steiner, G. (1984), *Antigones: How the Antigone Legend Has Endured in Western Literature, Art, and Thought*, Oxford/ New York: Clarendon Press.

Stergiopoulou, K. (2014), 'Taking nomos: Carl Schmitt's philology unbound', *October*, 149: 95–122.

Stier, H. E. (1928), 'ΝΟΜΟΣ ΒΑΣΙΛΕΥΣ', *Philologus*, 83: 225–58.

Stimilli, D. (2003), 'Daimon and Nemesis', *RES: Anthropology and Aesthetics*, 44: 99–112.

Stokes, M. C. (1971), *One and Many in Pre-Socratic Philosophy*, Cambridge, MA: Harvard University Press.

Stolfi, E. (2006), *Introduzione allo studio dei diritti greci*, Torino: G. Giappichelli.

Stolfi, E. (2014), 'Dualità nomiche', *Dike*, 17: 101–19.

Strauss, L. (1987), 'On the Minos', in T. L. Pangle (ed.), *The Roots of Political Philosophy: Ten Forgotten Socratic Dialogues*, Ithaca, NY/London: Cornell University Press, 67–79.

Stroh, W. (1976), 'Hesiods Lügende Musen', in H. Görgemanns and E. Schmidt (eds), *Studien Zum Antiken Epos*, Meisenheim am Glan: Anton Hain, 85–112.

Strohm, H. (1970), *Aristoteles, Meteorologie – Über die Welt*, Übersetzt von Hans Strohm, Berlin: Akademie Verlag.

Stroud, R. (1979), *The Axones and Kyrbeis of Drakon and Solon*, Berkeley, CA: University of California Press.

Svarlien, D. A. (1990/1991), *The Odes of Pindar*, in Perseus Project 1.0, New Haven, CT: Yale University Press.

Bibliography

Svarlien, D. A. (1991), *The Odes of Pindar*, in *Perseus Project* 1.0, New Haven, CT: Yale University Press.

Svenbro, J. ([1988] 1993), *Phrasikleia: An Anthropology of Reading in Ancient Greece* (Myth and Poetics), Janet Lloyd (trans.), Ithaca, NY: Cornell University Press.

Svenbro, J. (1976), *La parole et le marbre: Aux origines de la poétique grecque*, Lund: Klassiska Institutionen.

Svenbro, J. (1984), 'La découpe du poème: Notes sur les origines sacri cielles de la poétique grecque', *Poétique*, 58: 215–32.

Swindler, M. H. (1913), *Cretan Elements in the Cults and ritual of Apollo*, dissertation, Bryn Mawr, Pennsylvania.

Symonds, J. A. (1873), *Studies of the Greek Poets*, London: Smith, Elder & Co.

Szegedy-Maszak, A. (1978), 'Legends of the Greek lawgivers', *Greek Roman and Byzantine Studies*, 19: 199–209.

Szondi, P. ([1961] 2002), *An Essay on the Tragic*, P. Fleming (trans.), Stanford, CA: Stanford University Press.

Taddei, A. (2000), 'Introduzione', in L. Gernet (ed.), *Diritto e civiltà in Grecia antica*, Milano: La Nuova Italia, xv–xlii.

Taddei, A. (2001), *Louis Gernet e le techniche del diritto Ateniese – Con il testo delle Études sur la technique du droit athénien à l'époque classique*, Pisa: Giardini.

Tewksbury, I. (2015), 'The feast politic: the εἰλαπίνη in Homeric poetry', *Pithos*, 14: 27–48.

Theiler, W. (1965), 'Νόμος ὁ πάντων βασιλεύς', *Museum Helveticum*, 22: 69–80.

Theunissen, M. (2000), *Pindar: Menschenlos und wende der Zeit*, München: C. H. Beck.

Thom, J. C. (ed.) (2014), *Cosmic Order and Divine Power: Pseudo-Aristotle, on the Cosmos: Introduction, Text, Translation and Interpretative Essays*, Göttingen: Mohr Siebeck.

Thomas, C. G. (1976), 'The nature of Mycenaean kingship', *Studi Micenei ed Egeo-Anatolici*, 17: 93–116.

Thomas, R. (1989), *Oral Tradition and Written Record in Classical Athens*, Cambridge: Cambridge University Press.

Thomas, R. (1992), *Literacy and Orality in Ancient Greece*, Cambridge: Cambridge University Press.

Thomas, R. (1995a), 'The place of the poet in archaic society', in A. Powell (ed.), *The Greek World*, London: Routledge, 104–29.

Thomas, R. (1995b), '"Written in stone?" Liberty, equality, orality and the codification of law', *Bulletin of the Institute of Classical Studies*, 40: 59–74. [Repub. in 1996 as 'Written in stone? Liberty, equality, orality, and the codification of law', in L. Foxhall and A. D. E. Lewis (eds), *Greek Law in its Political Setting: Justifications not Justice*, Oxford: Clarendon Press, 9–32.]

Thomas, R. (2005), 'Writing, law and written law', in M. Gagarin and D. Cohen (eds), *The Cambridge Companion to Ancient Greek Law*, Cambridge: Cambridge University Press, 41–60.

Thomas, Y. (2002), 'La valeur des choses. Le droit romain hors la religion', *Annales, Histoire, Sciences sociales*, 6: 1431–62.

Thomas, Y. (2011), *Les opérations du droit*, Paris: EHESS/Seuil/Gallimard.

Thomas, Y. (2015), *Il valore delle cose*, Macerata: Quodlibet.

Thomsen, A. (2011), *Die Wirkung der Götter*, Berlin: De Gruyter.

Thomson, G. (1946), *Aeschylus and Athens. A Study in the Social Origins of Drama*, London: Lawrence & Wishart.

Thomson, G. (1949), *Studies in Ancient Greek Society. vol. 1: The Prehistoric Aegean*. London: Lawrence & Wishart.

Thucydides (1987), *Thucydides – Peloponnesian War*, C. F. Smith (trans.), 4 vols, Cambridge, MA: Harvard University Press (Loeb).

[Thucydides] (1988), S. H. Jones (ed.), *Thucydidis Historiae*, vols 1–2, Oxford: Oxford University Press.

Thür, G. (1996), 'Oaths and dispute settlements in ancient Greek law', in L. Foxhall and A. D. E. Lewis (eds), *Greek Law in its Political Setting: Justifications not Justice*, Oxford: Clarendon Press, 57–72.

Thür, G. (2003), 'Recht im antiken Griechenland', in U. Manthe (ed.), *Die Rechtskulturen der Antike*, München: Beck, 191–238.

Todd, S. (1992), *The Shape of Athenian Law*, Oxford: Clarendon Press.

Trépanier, S. (2004), *Empedocles. An Interpretation*, London: Routledge.

Treu, M. (1963), 'ΝΟΜΟΣ ΒΑΣΙΛΕΥΣ: Alte und neue Probleme', *Rheinisches museum für philologie*, 106: 193–214.

Treu, M. (1955), *Von Homer zur Lyrik*, Zetemata, 12, München: Beck.

Treu, M. (1959), *Archilochos*, München: Ernst Heimeran Verlag.

Triantaphyllopoulos, J. (1983), 'Cantar le leggi', *Atti dell'Academia Mediterranea delle Scienze Catania*, 1: 27–34.

Tricot, J. (trans.) (1990), *Aristote, Traité du ciel, suivi du traité pseudo-aristotélicien du monde*, Paris: Vrin.

Tsagarakis, O. (1977), *Nature and Background of Major Concepts of Divine Power in Homer*, Amsterdam: Grüner.

Tsagrakis, A. I. (2015), *Religion in the Pre-historic Aegean: The Information from the Aegean Inscriptions/Tablets*, Greek (ed.), Athens: Kardamitsa Institute.

Tsetskhladze, G. R. (ed.) (2006), *Greek Colonisation: An Account of Greek Colonies and Other Settlements Overseas*, vol. 1, Leiden/Boston: Brill.

Tsimbidaros, I. (2011), 'L'harmonie "austère" chez Platon selon Pseudo-Plutarque et Aristide Quintilien: Pratique musicale et pensée philosophique dans l'Antiquité tardive', in M.-H. Delavaud-Roux, *Musiques et danses dans l' Antiquité*, Actes du colloque international de Brest, 29–30 September 2006, Rennes: Université de Bretagne Occidentale, 67–90.

Tsitsibakou-Vasalos, E. (1990), 'Stesichorus' Geryoneis, SLG 15 I–II', *Hellenika*, 41: 7–31.

Tuck, A. (2006), 'Singing the rug: patterned textiles and the origins of Indo-European metrical poetry', *American Journal of Archaeology*, 110: 539–50.

Tuck, A. (2009), 'Stories at the loom: patterned textiles and the recitation of myth in Euripides', *Arethusa*, 42: 151–9.

Turpin, J.-C. (1980), 'L'expression αἰδώς καὶ νέμεσις et les "Actes du langage"', *Revue des Études Grecques*, 93: 442–4, 352–67.

Uchitel, A. (2005), 'Land-tenure in Mycenaean Greece and the Hittite empire: Linear B land surveys from Pylos and middle Hittite land donations', *Journal of the Economic and Social History of the Orient*, 48: 473–86.

Uhlenbrock, J. P. (ed.) (1986), *Herakles: Passage of the Hero through 1000 Years of Classical Art*, New Rochelle, NY: A. D. Caratzas.

Ulf, C. (1990), *Die homerische Gesellschaft*, München: Verlag C. H. Beck.

Ulf, C. (2009), 'The world of Homer and Hesiod', in K. A. Raaflaub and H. van Wees (eds), *A Companion to Archaic Greece*, Malden, MA/Oxford: Wiley Blackwell, 81–99.

Untersteiner, M. (1954), *The Sophists*, K. Freeman (trans.), Oxford: Basil Blackwell.

Usener, H. (1903), 'Dreiheit', *Rheinisches museum für philologie*, 58: 1–47, 161–208, 321–62.

Valentin, P. (1958), 'Héraclite et Clément d'Alexandrie', *Recherches de Science Religieuse*, 46, 1: 27–59.

Vamvouri Ruffy, M. (2004), *La Fabrique du divin: les hymnes de Callimaque à la Lumière des Hymnes Homériques et des Hymnes épigraphiques*, Liège: Centre International d'Étude de la Religion Grecque Antique.

van Compernolle, R. (1976), 'Le tradizioni sulla fondazione e sulla storia arcaica di Locri Epizefiri e la propaganda politica alla fine del V e nel IV secolo av. Cr.', *Annali délia Scuola Normale Superiore di Pisa*, series 3, 3(6): 329–400.

van Compernolle, R. (1981), 'La législation aristocratique de Locres Epizéphyrienne, dite législation de Zaleukos', *L'Antiquité Classique*, 50: 759–69.

van der Ben, N. (ed.) (1975), *The Proem of Empedocles' Peri Physios – Towards a New Edition of All the Fragments – Thirty-One Fragments*, Amsterdam: Grüner.

van Effenterre, H. (1989), 'Droit et prédroit en Grèce depuis le déchiffrement du linéaire B', *Symposion*, 1985, Köln–Wien 1989, 3–6.

van Groningen, B. A. (1955), 'A propos de Terpandre', *Mnemosyne*, 4th Series, 8(3): 177–91.

van Straten, F. (1988), 'The god's portion in Greek sacrificial representation: is the tail doing nicely?', in R. Hägg (ed.), *Early Greek Cult Practice*, Proceedings of the 5th International Symposium, Swedish Institute at Athens, 26–9 June 1986, 51–68.

van Straten, F. (1995), 'Hiera Kala – images of animal sacrifice in archaic and classical Greece', in R. Van den Broek, H. J. W, Drijvers and H. S. Versnel (eds), *Religions in the Graeco-Roman World*, 127, Leiden/New York/Köln: Brill.

van Wees, H. (1995), 'Princes at dinner: social event and social structure in Homer', in J. P. Crielaard (ed.), *Homeric Questions: Essays in Philology, Ancient History and Archaeology*, Including the Papers of a Conference Organised by the

Netherlands Institute at Athens, 15 May 1993, Amsterdam: J. C. Gieben, 147–82.

Veikos, T. V. ([1979] 1985), 'Logos-xynon und die Ordnung der Menschenwelt. Zum Heraklit-Fragment 114', *Epistemonike Epeteris tes Philosophikes Scholes tou Panepistemiou Athinon (EEAth)*, 28: 407–11.

Veikos, T. V. (1988), *The Presocratics*, Athens: I. Zacharopoulos.

Ventris, M. G. F. (1954), 'King Nestor's four-handled cups', *Archaeology*, 7: 15–21.

Ventris, M. G. F. and J. Chadwick (1973), *Documents in Mycenaean Greek*, 2nd edn, Cambridge: Cambridge University Press.

Verdenius, W. J. (1944), 'Aidos bei Homer', *Mnemosyne*, 3(12): 47–60.

Verdenius, W. J. (1966), 'Der Logosbegriff bei Heraklit und Parmenides I', *Phronesis*, 11: 81–98.

Verdenius, W. J. (1967), 'Der Logosbegriff bei Heraklit und Parmenides II', *Phronesis*, 12: 99–117.

Verdenius, W. J. (1971), 'Hesiod, "Theogony" 507–616: some comments on a commentary', *Mnemosyne*, 24: 1–10.

Verdenius, W. J. (1972), 'Notes on the proem of Hesiod's Theogony', *Mnemosyne*, 4(25): 225–60.

Verdenius, W. J. (1983), 'The principles of Greek literary criticism', *Mnemosyne*, 36: 14–59.

Verdenius, W. J. (1985), *A Commentary on Hesiod Works and Days*, Leiden: Brill.

Vergados, A. (2013), 'An unnoticed testimonium to the Hesiodic Melampodia? Psi 14. 1398 and [Hesiod] Melampodia Fr. 276 M-W (= 212 Most)', *Philologus*, 157(1): 5–15.

Vermeule, E. (1979), *Aspects of Death in Early Greek Art and Poetry*, Berkeley, CA: University of California Press.

Vernant, J.-P. (1970), 'Thétis et le poème cosmogonique d'Alcman', Hommages à Marie Delcourt, *Latomus*, 114: 219–33.

Vernant, J.-P. (1981), 'Théorie générale du sacrifice et mise à mort dans la "thysia" grecque', in J. Rudhart and O. Reverdin (eds), *Le sacrifice dans l'Antiquité*, Geneva: Vandoeuvres, 1–21.

Vernant, J.-P. (1989), 'At man's table', in J.-P. Vernant and M. Détienne, *The Cuisine of Sacrifice among the Greeks*, Chicago, IL: University of Chicago Press, 21–86.

Vernant, J.-P. (1991), *Mortals and Immortals: Collected Essays*, F. I. Zeitlin (ed.), Princeton, NJ: Princeton University Press.

Vernant, J.-P. (2006), *Myth and Thought among the Greeks*, J. Lloyd and J. Fort (trans.), New York: Zone Books.

Vernant, J.-P. and M. Détienne (eds) (1989), P. Wissing (trans.), *The Cuisine of Sacrifice among the Greeks*, Chicago, IL: University of Chicago Press.

Vernant, J-P. and P. Vidal-Naquet (1972), *Mythe et tragédie, en Grèce ancienne*, Paris: F. Maspero.

Vernant, J.-P. and P. Vidal Naquet (1988), *Myth and Tragedy in the Ancient Greece*, New York: Zone Books.

Vian, F. (1952), *La Guerre des Géants. Le mythe avant l'époque hellénistique*, Paris: Klincksieck.

Vickers, B. (1973), *Towards Greek Tragedy*, London: Longman.

Vidal-Naquet, P. (1981), 'Land and sacrifice in the Odyssey: A study of religious and mythical meanings', in repr. edn, P. Vidal-Naquet (1986), *The Black Hunter: Forms of Thought and Forms of Society in the Greek World*, A. Szagedy-Mazak (trans.), Baltimore, MD: Johns Hopkins University Press, 15–38.

Vidal-Naquet, P. (1986), *The Black Hunter: Forms of Thought and Forms of Society in the Greek World*, A. Szagedy-Mazak (trans.), Baltimore, MD: Johns Hopkins University Press.

Vincenti, U. (2007), *Diritto senza identità. La crisi delle categorie giuridiche tradizionali*, Laterza: Roma–Bari.

Vischer, W. (1865), 'Zu Sophokles Antigone', *Rheinisches museum für philologie* 20: 44–52.

Vlachos, G. C. (1985), Πολιτικές κοινωνίες στον Όμηρο [Political Societies in Homer], Paize-Apostolopoulou and D. G. Apostolopoulou (trans), Athens.

Vlastos, G. (1953), 'Isonomia', *American Journal of Philology*, 74: 337–66.

Voegelin, E. (1956), *Order and History*, Baton Rouge, LA: Louisiana State University.

Voigt, E. (1971), *Sappho et Alcaeus: fragmenta*, Amsterdam: Athenaeum/Polak & Van Gennep.

Von Erffa, C. E. (1937), 'ΑΙΔΩΣ und verwandte Begriffe in ihrer Entwicklung von Homer bis Demokrit', *Philologus*, supplement, 30(2).

Von Fritz, K. (1943), 'ΝΟΟΣ and noein in the Homeric Poems', *Classical Philology*, 38(2): 79–93.

Von Fritz, K. (1945/1946), '*Nous, Noein*, and their derivatives in pre-Socratic philosophy (excluding Anaxagoras)', *Classical Philology*, 40: 223–42; 41: 12–34.

Von Fritz, K. (1983), 'Zaleukos', *Paulys Realencyclopädie*, 9: A. 2, München: Druckenmüller, 2298–301.

Vos, H. (1956), *Themis*, dissertation, Utrecht.

Wace, A. J. B. and F. H. Stubbings (eds) (1962), *A Companion to Homer*, London: Macmillan.

Wachter, R. (1989), 'Zur Vorgeschichte des griechischen Alphabets', *Kadmos*, 28: 19–78.

Wackernagel, J. (1955), *Kleine Schriften*, 2 vols, Göttingen: Vandenhoeck & Ruprecht.

Walcot, P. (1979), 'Cattle raiding, heroic tradition, and ritual: the Greek evidence', *History of Religions*, 18(4): 326–51.

Wallace, R. W. (1995), 'Speech, song and text, public and private: evolution in communication media and fora in fourth-century Athens', in W. Eder (ed.), *Die athenische Demokratie in 4. Jahrhundert v. Chr: Vollendung oder Verfall einer Verfassungsform?*, Stuttgart: Franz Steiner, 199–224.

Warden, J. (ed.) (1982), *Orpheus: The Metamorphosis of a Myth*, Toronto: University of Toronto Press.

Watkins, C. (ed.) (2000), *The American Heritage Dictionary of Indo-European Roots*, 2nd edn, Boston, MA/New York: Houghton Mifflin.

Weber R. (2014), 'The sonic morality of Mount Olympus: an analysis of the relationship between divine voice and morality in ancient Greek society', *Pithos Journal*, 13: 74–93.

Webster, T. B. L. (1970), *The Greek Chorus*, London: Methuen.

Webster, T. B. L. (1994), 'Personification as a mode of Greek thought', *Journal of the Warburg and Courtauld Institutes*, 17: 10–21.

Węcowski, M. (2002), 'Homer and the origins of the symposium', in F. Montanari (ed.), *Omero: Tremila Anni Dopo*, Rome: Edizioni di Storia e Letteratura, 625–37.

Wegner, M. (1949), *Das Musikleben der Griechen*, Berlin: De Gruyter.

Wehrli, F. R. (1967–9), *Die Schule des Aristoteles – Texte und Kommentare*, Basel: Schwabe.

Weil, H. and T. Reinach (1900), *Plutarque – De la musique. Édition critique et explicative*, Paris: E. Leroux.

Weil, S. (1957), *Intimations of Christianity among the Ancient*

Greeks, E. C. Geissbuhler and P. Kegan (eds and trans), London/New York: Routledge.

Weinstock, H. (1955), *Realer Humanismus*, 2nd edn, Heidelberg: Quelle & Meyer.

Weiss, E. (1923), *Griechisches Privatrecht auf rechtsvergleichender Grundlage I*, Leipzig: Felix Meiner, I, 113–17.

Wersinger, A. G. (2008), *La sphère et l'intervalle. Le schème de l'Harmonie dans la pensée des anciens Grecs d'Homère à Platon*, Grenoble: Éditions Jérôme Millon.

West, M. L. (1965), 'The Dictaean Hymn to the Kouros', *Journal of Hellenic Studies*, 85: 149–59.

West, M. L. (ed.) (1966), *Hesiod, Theogony*, Oxford: Clarendon Press.

West, M. L. (1974), *Studies in Greek Elegy and Iambus*, Berlin/New York: De Gruyter.

West, M. L. (1978), *Hesiod: Works and Days*, Oxford: Oxford University Press.

West, M. L. (1981), 'The singing of Homer and the modes of early Greek music', *Journal of Hellenic Studies*, 101: 113–29.

West, M. L. (1983), *The Orphic Poems*, Oxford: Oxford University Press.

West, M. L. (1985), 'Archilochus: new fragments and readings', *Zeitschrift für Papyrologie und Epigraphik*, 61: 8–13.

West, M. L. (1988), 'The rise of Greek epic', *Journal of Hellenic Studies*, 108: 151–72.

West, M. L. (1989), *Iambi et Elegi Graeci*, 2nd edn, Oxford: Oxford University Press.

West, M. L. (1992), *Ancient Greek Music*, Oxford: Oxford University Press.

West, M. L. (1993), *Greek Lyric Poetry*, Oxford: Oxford University Press.

West, M. L. (1999), 'Sophocles with music? Ptolemaic music fragments and remains of Sophocles, Achilleus', *Zeitschrift für Papyrologie und Epigraphik*, 126: 43–65.

West, S. (1988), 'Books I–IV', in A. Heubeck, S. West and J. B. Hainsworth (eds), *A Commentary on Homer's Odyssey*, vol. 1, 49–245, Oxford: Clarendon Press.

West, S. (1999), 'Sophocles' Antigone and Herodotus Book Three', in J. Griffin (ed.), *Sophocles Revisited: Essays Presented to Sir Hugh Lloyd-Jones*, New York: Oxford University Press, 109–36.

Wheelwright, P. (1964), *Heraclitus*, New York: Atheneum.

White, H. (2001), 'Notes on Pindar', *HABIS*, 32: 31–7.

Whitehead, D. (1977), *The Ideology of the Athenian Metic*, Cambridge: Cambridge University Press.

Whitehorne, J. E. G. (1983), 'The background to Polyneices' disinterment and reburial', *Greece and Rome*, 30(2): 129–42.

Whitley, J. (1991), 'Social diversity in dark age Greece', *Annual of the British School of Athens*, 86: 341–65.

Whitley, J. (1997), 'Cretan laws and Cretan literacy', *American Journal of Archaeology*, 101: 635–61.

Whitman, C. H. (1951), *Sophocles: A Study of Heroic Humanism*, Cambridge, MA: Harvard University Press.

Wilamowitz-Moellendorff, U. von ([1895] 1959), *Euripides: Herakles*, 2 vols, 2nd edn, Berlin: Weidmann, repr. 3 vols, Bad Homburg: Gentner.

Wilamowitz-Moellendorff, U. von (1903), *Timotheos – Die Perser*, Leipzig: Hinrichssche Buchhandlung.

Wilamowitz-Moellendorff, U. von (1921), *Griechische Verskunst*, Berlin: Weidmann.

Wilamowitz-Moellendorff, U. von (1920), *Platon*, vols 1 and 2. Berlin: Weidmannsche Buchhandlung.

Wilamowitz-Moellendorff, U. von (1925), *Reden und Vorträge*, vol. 1, 4th edn, Berlin: Weidmann.

Wilamowitz-Moellendorff, U. von (1931), *Der Glaube der Hellenen*, 1, Berlin: Weidmann.

Wilamowitz-Moellendorff, U. von (1956–9), *Der Glaube der Hellenen*, 2 vols, 3rd edn, Basel: Benno Schwabe.

Wilamowitz-Moellendorff, U. von (1962) *Platon, II: Beilagen und Textkritik*, 3, Berlin: Weidmannsche Verlagsbuchhandlung.

Wiles, D. (1990), 'The Parodos of Euripides' *Helen* (164–90)', *Classical Quarterly* 40(1), New Series: 77–99.

Willi, A. (2014), 'Μέροπες ἄνθρωποι', *Colloquia, Classica et Indogermanica*, VI, *Studies in Memoriam Leonhard G. Herzenberg*, Russian Academy of Sciences, Institute of Linguistic Studies, 51–73.

Wilson, P. (1999), 'The aulos in Athens', in S. Goldhill and R. Osborne (eds), *Performance Culture and Athenian Democracy*, Cambridge: Cambridge University Press, 58–95.

Wilson, P. (2000), *The Athenian Institution of the Khoregia: The Chorus, the City and the Stage*, Cambridge: Cambridge University Press.

Wilson, P. (2003), 'The sound of cultural conflict: Kritias and the culture of mousikē in Athens', in C. Dougherty and L. Kurke (eds), *The Cultures within Ancient Greek Culture. Contact, Conflict, Collaboration*, Cambridge: Cambridge University Press, 181–206.

Wilson, P. (2004), 'Athenian strings', in P. Murray and P. Wilson (eds), *Music and the Muses: The Culture of 'Mousike' in the Classical Athenian City*, Oxford: Oxford University Press, 269–306.

Wilson, P. (2010), 'The man and the music (and the Choregos?)', in O. Taplin and R. Wyles (eds), *The Pronomos Vase and its Context*, Oxford: Oxford University Press, 181–212.

Windekens, A. J. van (1961), 'Réflexions sur le nature et l'origine du dieu Hermès', *Rheinisches Museum für Philologie*, 104: 289–301.

Windekens, A. J. van (1962), 'Sur le nom de la divinité grecque Hermès', *Beiträge zur Namenforschung*, 13: 290–2.

Winnington-Ingram, R. A. (1936), *Mode in Ancient Greek Music*, Cambridge: Cambridge University Press.

Winnington-Ingram R. P. (1980), *Sophocles: An Interpretation*, Cambridge: Cambridge University Press.

Wolf, E. (1950–70), *Griechisches Rechtsdenken*, I. *Vorsokratiker und frühe Dichter*, 4 vols, Frankfurt am Main: Vittorio Klostermann.

Wolf, E. (1955), 'Zur Etymologie von ῥυθμός und seiner Bedeutung in der älteren griechischen Literatur', *Wiener Studien*, 68: 99–119.

Wolff, H. J. (1946), 'The origin of judicial litigation among the Greeks', *Traditio*, 5: 31–87.

Wrede, H. (1986), *Die antike Herme*, Mainz am Rhein: von Zabern.

Wright, J. C. (2004), *The Mycenaean Feast, Hesperia*, 73: 2, Princeton, NJ: American School of Classical Studies at Athens.

Wright, J. C. (2006), 'The formation of the Mycenaean palace', in S. Deger-Jalkotzy and I. S. Lemos (eds), *Ancient Greece: From the Mycenaean Palaces to the Age of Homer*, Edinburgh: Edinburgh University Press, 7–52.

Wright, M. R. (ed.) (1981), *Empedocles: The Extant Fragments*, with introduction, commentary, and concordance, New Haven, CT/London: Yale University Press.

Wright, M. R. (1985), *The Presocratics*, Bristol: Bristol Classical Press.

Xenophon (1923), *Memorabilia, Oeconomicus, Symposium, and Apology*, E. C. Marchant and O. J. Todd (trans.), Cambridge, MA: Harvard University Press (Loeb).

Xenophon (1960), *Hellenica*, C. L. Brownson (trans.), 2 vols, Cambridge, MA: Harvard University Press (Loeb).

Yamagata, N. (1994), *Homeric Morality, Mnemosyne Supplement* 131, Leiden: Brill.

Younger, J. G. (1998), *Music in the Aegean Bronze Age*, Jonsered: Paul Äströms Förlag.

Zacharia, K. (2009), 'Funerary rituals, Aeschylus' Eumenides and Sophocles' Antigone', *Journal of Hellenic Religion*, 3: 53–66.

Zafiri, Y. (2007), 'Chorus and dance in the ancient world', in M. McDonald and J. M. Walton (eds), *The Cambridge Companion to Greek and Roman Theatre*, Cambridge: Cambridge University Press.

Ziegler, N. (2007), *Les Musiciens et la musique d'après les archives royals de Mari*, Paris: Société pour l'Étude du Proche-Orient Ancien.

Zimmermann, B. (1992), *Dithyrambos – Geschichte einer Gattung*, Göttingen: Verlag-Antike.

Zweig, B. (1999), 'Euripides' Helen and Female Rites of Passage', in Mark William Padilla (ed.), *Rites of Passage in Ancient Greece: Literature, Religion, Society*, Lewisburg, PA: Bucknell University Press, 158–82.